ATTENTION AND PERFORMANCE XII
THE PSYCHOLOGY OF READING

Attention and Performance XII
THE PSYCHOLOGY OF READING

edited by

Professor Max Coltheart
Birkbeck College, University of London
London, U.K.

LEA LAWRENCE ERLBAUM ASSOCIATES, PUBLISHERS LEA
Hove and London (UK)   Hillsdale (USA)

Lawrence Erlbaum Associates Ltd., Publishers
27 Palmeira Mansions
Church Road
Hove
East Sussex, BN3 2FA
U.K.

British Library Cataloguing in Publication Data

Attention and performance XII: the psychology
    of reading.
    1. Reading, Psychology of
    I. Coltheart, M.
    428.4′01′9   BF456.R2

    ISBN 0–86377–083–5
    ISBN 0–86377–084–3 Pbk

Typeset by Latimer Trend & Co. Ltd., Plymouth
Printed and bound by A. Wheaton & Co. Ltd., Exeter

Contents

Contributors and Participants

A. D. Baddeley, M.R.C. Applied Psychology Unit, 15 Chaucer Road, Cambridge CB2 2EF, U.K.

P. C. Badgio, Department of Psychology, Institute of Pennsylvania Hospital, 111 North 49th Street, Philadelphia, Pennsylvania 19139, U.S.A.

D. Besner, Department of Psychology, University of Waterloo, Waterloo, Ontario, Canada N2L 3G1

D. Bishop, Department of Psychology, University of Manchester, Manchester M13 9PL, U.K.

M. Black, Department of Phonetics and Linguistics, University College London, Gower Street, London WC1E 6BT, U.K.

P. Brown, Department of Psychology, University of Waterloo, Waterloo, Ontario, Canada N2L 3G1

S. Byng, Department of Psychology, Birkbeck College, University of London, Malet Street, London WC1E 7HX, U.K.

D. Caplan, Department of Neurology, Montreal Neurological Institute, 3801 University, Montreal, P.Q., Canada H3A 2B4

J. Chafetz, Psychology Department, University of Pittsburgh, Pittsburgh, Pennsylvania 15260, U.S.A.

C. Clifton, Department of Psychology, University of Massachusetts, Tobin Hall, Amherst, Massachusetts 01003, U.S.A.

M. Coltheart, Department of Psychology, Birkbeck College, University of London, Malet Street, London WC1E 7HX, U.K.

V. Coltheart, Department of Psychology, City of London Polytechnic, Calcutta House Annexe, Old Castle Street, London E1 7NT, U.K.

M. Daneman, Department of Psychology, University of Toronto, Erindale Campus, Mississauga, Ontario, Canada L5L 1C6

J. Duncan, M.R.C. Applied Psychology Unit, 15 Chaucer Road, Cambridge CB2 2EF, U.K.

J. Dunn, Department of Psychology, University of Western Australia, Nedlands, Perth, Western Australia 6009

L. J. Evett, M.R.C. Applied Psychology Unit, 15 Chaucer Road, Cambridge CB2 2EF, U.K.

F. Ferreira, Department of Psychology, University of Massachusetts, Tobin Hall, Amherst, Massachusetts 01003, U.S.A.

G. Flores d'Arcais, Max-Planck-Institut für Psycholinguistik, Wundtlaan 1, NL—6525 XD, Nijmegen, The Netherlands

K. I. Forster, Department of Psychology, Monash University, Clayton, Victoria, Australia 3168

L. Frazier, Linguistics Department, University of Massachusetts, South College, Amherst, Massachusetts 01003, U.S.A.

L. Henderson, Department of Psychology, Hatfield Polytechnic, P.O. Box 109, Hatfield, Hertfordshire AL10 9AB, U.K.

N. Hildebrandt, Department of Neurology, Montreal Neurological Institute, 3801 University, Montreal, P.Q., Canada H3A 2B4

V. M. Holmes, Department of Psychology, University of Melbourne, Parkville, Victoria, Australia 3052

G. W. Humphreys, Department of Psychology, Birkbeck College, University of London, Malet Street, London WC1E 7HX, U.K.

A. W. Inhoff, Psychology Department, University of New Hampshire, Durham, New Hampshire 03824, U.S.A.

J. Kay, Department of Speech, University of Newcastle-upon-Tyne, School of Education, St. Thomas' Street, Newcastle-upon-Tyne NE1 7RU, U.K.

P. K. Kirsner, Department of Psychology, University of Western Australia, Nedlands, Perth, Western Australia 6009

A. Lévy-Schoen, Groupe Regarde, Laboratoire de Psychologie Experimentale, Universite Rene Descartes, 28 Rue Serpente, 75006 Paris, France

R. S. McCann, Department of Psychology, University of Waterloo, Waterloo, Ontario, Canada N2L 3G1

J. L. McClelland, Department of Psychology, Carnegie-Mellon University, Schenley Park, Pittsburgh, Pennsylvania 15213, U.S.A.

G. W. McConkie, Centre for the Study of Reading, University of Illinois at Champaign-Urbana, 51 Gerty Drive, Champaign, Illinois 61820, U.S.A.

J. E. McDonald, Computing Research Laboratory, New Mexico State University, Las Cruces, New Mexico 88003, U.S.A.

D. C. Mitchell, Department of Psychology, University of Exeter, Washington Singer Laboratories, Exeter, Devon EX4 4QG, U.K.

S. Monsell, Experimental Psychology Department, University of Cambridge, Downing Street, Cambridge CB2 3EF, U.K.

M. Mozer, Institute for Cognitive Science, C-015, University of California, San Diego, La Jolla, California 92093, U.S.A.

R. W. Noel, Computing Research Laboratory, New Mexico State University, Las Cruces, New Mexico 88003, U.S.A.

K. O'Regan, Groupe Regarde, Laboratorie de Psychologie Experimentale, Universite Rene Descartes, 28 Rue Serpente, 75006 Paris, France

xvi   CONTRIBUTORS AND PARTICIPANTS

K. R. Paap, Computing Research Laboratory, New Mexico State University, Las Cruces, New Mexico 88003, U.S.A.

H. Pashler, Department of Psychology, C-009, University of California, San Diego, La Jolla, California 92093, U.S.A.

K. E. Patterson, M.R.C. Applied Psychology Unit, 15 Chaucer Road, Cambridge CB2 2EF, U.K.

A. Pollatsek, Department of Psychology, University of Massachusetts, Tobin Hall, Amherst, Massachusetts 01003, U.S.A.

P. T. Quinlan, Department of Psychology, Birkbeck College, University of London, Malet Street, London WC1E 7HX, U.K.

K. Rayner, Department of Psychology, University of Massachusetts, Tobin Hall, Amherst, Massachusetts 01003, U.S.A.

R. W. Schvaneveldt, Computing Research Laboratory, New Mexico State University, Las Cruces, New Mexico 88003, U.S.A.

M. Seidenberg, Department of Psychology, McGill University, 1205 Dr. Penfield Avenue, Montreal, P.Q., Canada H3A 1B1

P. Standen, Department of Psychology, University of Western Australia, Nedlands, Perth, Western Australia 6009

M. Taft, Department of Psychology, University of New South Wales, Kensington, New South Wales, Australia 2033

T. Tardif, Department of Psychology, University of Toronto, Erindale Campus, Mississauga, Ontario, Canada L5L 1C6

R. Treiman, Department of Psychology, Wayne State University, 71 W. Warren Avenue, Detroit, Michigan 48202, U.S.A.

G. Vallar, Istituto di Clinica Neurologica, Universita di Milano, Via F. Sforza 35, 20122 Milano, Italia

G. Waters, School of Human Communication Disorders, Beatty Hall, McGill University, 1266 Pine Avenue West, Montreal, P.Q., Canada H3G 1A8

A. Weinberg, Linguistics Program, University of Maryland, College Park, Maryland 20742, U.S.A.

B. Wilson, Department of Psychology, Charing Cross Hospital (Fulham), Fulham Palace Road, London W6 8RF, U.K.

D. Zola, Centre for the Study of Reading, University of Illinois at Champaign-Urbana, 51 Gerty Drive, Champaign, Illinois 61820, U.S.A.

PREFACE

The twelfth Attention and Performance meeting took place at Cumberland Lodge, a seventeenth-century mansion ensconced in the tranquillity and solitude of Windsor Great Park, amidst the immemorial elms of rural Berkshire. Croquet on the lawn and dinner in panelled halls provided a remarkable contrast to the jogging and bakeouts enjoyed at Attention and Performance XI, and to the boules and Beaujolais expected of Attention and Performance XIII.

The theme of the meeting was the psychology of reading, and an attempt was made to deal with all of the basic aspects of reading, from visual feature analysis and visual attention through to sentence comprehension and text integration. At the meeting were cognitive psychologists, neuropsychologists, connectionists and linguists. This volume is the result: It is intended as an up-to-date and fully comprehensive review of the subject of reading, approached from a variety of theoretical perspectives.

The meeting itself was vigorous and productive, despite a shadow cast by the absence of Paul Kolers. He had been invited to present a paper on early visual processing and reading, and had accepted this invitation; but illness intervened, and he died before the meeting was held. His energy and his originality were much missed.

Max Coltheart
Organiser, *Attention and Performance XII*

ACKNOWLEDGEMENTS

Financial support was provided by the U.S. Army Research Institute, by the U.S. Office of Naval Research (O.N.R. Contract Number N0001486G0067 to S. Kornblum) and by a grant from the Economic and Social Research Council of Great Britain to M. Coltheart. Even more important was the administrative and organisational assistance provided by Patricia Caple.

PARTICIPANTS AT THE TWELFTH ATTENTION AND PERFORMANCE MEETING, JULY 1986

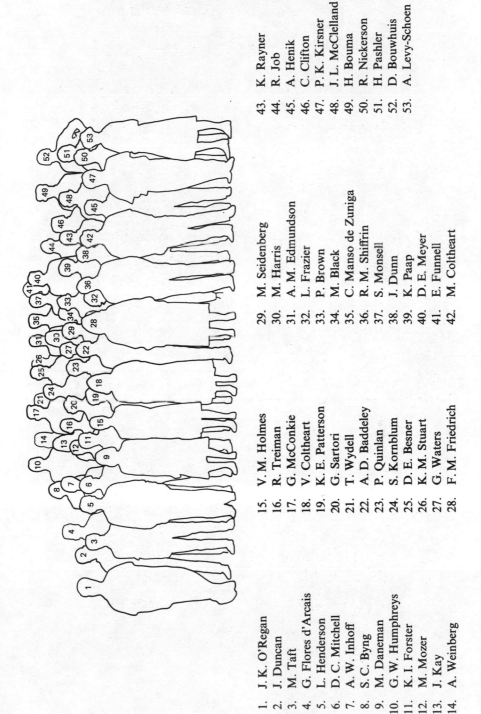

1. J. K. O'Regan
2. J. Duncan
3. M. Taft
4. G. Flores d'Arcais
5. L. Henderson
6. D. C. Mitchell
7. A. W. Inhoff
8. S. C. Byng
9. M. Daneman
10. G. W. Humphreys
11. K. I. Forster
12. M. Mozer
13. J. Kay
14. A. Weinberg

15. V. M. Holmes
16. R. Treiman
17. G. McConkie
18. V. Coltheart
19. K. E. Patterson
20. G. Sartori
21. T. Wydell
22. A. D. Baddeley
23. P. Quinlan
24. S. Kornblum
25. D. E. Besner
26. K. M. Stuart
27. G. Waters
28. F. M. Friedrich

29. M. Seidenberg
30. M. Harris
31. A. M. Edmundson
32. L. Frazier
33. P. Brown
34. M. Black
35. C. Manso de Zuniga
36. R. M. Shiffrin
37. S. Monsell
38. J. Dunn
39. K. Paap
40. D. E. Meyer
41. E. Funnell
42. M. Coltheart

43. K. Rayner
44. R. Job
45. A. Henik
46. C. Clifton
47. P. K. Kirsner
48. J. L. McClelland
49. H. Bouma
50. R. Nickerson
51. H. Pashler
52. D. Bouwhuis
53. A. Levy-Schoen

ASSOCIATION LECTURE

1 The Case for Interactionism in Language Processing

James L. McClelland
Carnegie-Mellon University
Pittsburgh, Pennsylvania, U.S.A.

ABSTRACT

Interactive models of language processing assume that information flows both bottom-up and top-down, so that the representations formed at each level may be influenced by higher as well as lower levels. I describe a framework called the *interactive activation* framework that embeds this key assumption among others, including the assumption that influences from different sources are combined nonlinearly. This nonlinearity means that information that may be decisive under some circumstances may have little or no effect under other conditions. Two attempts to rule out an interactive account in favour of models in which individual components of the language processing system act autonomously are considered in the light of the interactive activation framework. In both cases, the facts are as expected from the principles of interactive activation. In general, existing facts do not rule out an interactive account, but they do not require one either. To demonstrate that more definitive tests of interaction are possible, I describe an experiment that demonstrates a new kind of influence of a higher-level factor (lexical membership) on a lower level of processing (phoneme identification). The experiment illustrates one reason why feedback from higher levels is computationally desirable; it allows lower levels to be tuned by contextual factors so that they can supply more accurate information to higher levels.

INTRODUCTION

When we process language—either in written or in spoken form—we construct representations of what we are processing at many different levels. This process is profoundly affected by contextual information. For example, in reading, we perceive letters better when they occur in words. We recognise words better when they occur in sentences. We interpret the meanings of words in accordance with the contexts in which they occur. We assign grammatical structures to sentences, based on the thematic constraints among the constituents of the sentences. Many authors—Huey (1968), Neisser (1967), and Rumelhart (1977), to name a few—have documented some or all of these points.

Clearly, this use of contextual information is based on what we know about our language and about the world we use language to tell each other about. How does this knowledge enter into language processing? How does it allow contextual factors to influence the course of processing?

In this paper, I will describe a set of theoretical principles about the nature of the mechanisms of language processing that provides one possible set of answers to these questions. These principles combine to form a framework which I will call the *interactive activation* framework. The paper has three main parts. In the first part, I will describe the principles and explore a central reason why they offer an appealing account of the role of knowledge in language processing. In the second part, I will consider two prominent lines of empirical investigation that have been offered as evidence against the view that particular parts of the processing system are influenced by multiple sources of information, as the interactive activation framework assumes. Finally, in the third part, I will discuss one way in which interactive processing might distinguish itself empirically from mechanisms that employ a one-way flow of information.

To summarise the main points of each part:

1.   In the interactive activation framework, the knowledge that guides processing is stored in the connections between units on the same and adjacent levels. The processing units they connect may receive input from a number of different sources. This allows the knowledge that guides processing to be completely local, while at the same time allowing the results of processing at one level to influence processing at other levels, both above and below. Thus, the approach combines a desirable computational characteristic of an encapsulationist position (Fodor, 1983) while retaining the capacity to exploit the benefits of interactive processing.

2.   Two sources of empirical evidence that have been taken as counting against interactionism do not stand up to scrutiny. The first case is the resolution of lexical ambiguity in context. Here I re-examine existing data and compare them with simulation results illustrating general characteristics of interactive activation mechanisms to show that the findings are completely consistent with an interactive position. The second case considered is the role of semantic constraints in the resolution of syntactic ambiguities. Here I review some recent data that demonstrate the importance of semantic factors in phenomena that had been taken as evidence of a syntactic processing strategy that is impervious to semantic influences. In both cases I will argue

that the evidence is just what would be expected from an interactive activation account.

3.   It is an important and challenging task to find experimental tests that can distinguish between an interactive system and one in which information flows only in one direction. Unidirectional and interactionist models can make identical predictions for a large number of experiments, as long as it is assumed that lower levels are free to pass on ambiguities they cannot resolve to higher levels. However, experimental tests can be constructed using higher-level influences to trigger effects assumed to be based on processing at lower levels. I will illustrate this method by describing a recent experiment that uses it to provide evidence of lexical effects on phonetic processing, and I will suggest that this method may also help us to examine higher-level influences on lower levels of processing in other cases.

THE INTERACTIVE ACTIVATION FRAMEWORK

The following principles characterise the interactive activation framework. These principles have emerged from work with the interactive activation model of visual word recognition (McClelland & Rumelhart, 1981; Rumelhart & McClelland, 1982), the TRACE model of speech perception (Elman & McClelland, 1986; McClelland & Elman, 1986), and the programmable blackboard model of reading (McClelland, 1985; 1986). The principles apply, I believe, to the processing of both spoken and written language, as well as to the processing of other kinds of perceptual inputs; however, all the examples I will use here are taken from language processing.

The Processing System is Organised Into Levels.   This principle is shared by virtually all models of language processing. Exactly what the levels are, of course, is far from clear, but this is not our present concern. For present purposes, I will adopt an illustrative set of levels to provide a context in which to discuss the processing interactions that may be involved in reading a sentence. These levels are a visual feature level, a letter level, a word level, a syntactic level, a word-sense level, and a scenario level, on which the representation captures the nonlinguistic state or action described by the sentence being processed. Higher levels are, of course, required for longer passages of text, but the set of levels will provide a sufficient basis for the phenomena we will consider here. For processing speech, we also need a phonetic level and an auditory feature level to provide input to the phonological level.

The Representation Constructed at Each Level is a Pattern of Activation Over an Ensemble of Simple Processing Units.   This assumption is central to the entire interactive activation approach, and strongly differentiates it from other approaches. In this approach, representations are active—they can influence, and be influenced by, representations at other levels of processing. In this paper, I will adopt the formal convenience of assuming that individual processing units stand for individual conceptual objects such as letters, words, phonemes, or syntactic attachments. Thus, a representation of a spoken word at the phonetic level is a pattern of activation over units that stand for phonemes; these units are role-specific, so that the pattern of activation of "cat" is different from the pattern of activation of "tac."

Activation Occurs Through Processing Interactions that are Bi-directional, Both Within Levels and Between Levels. A basic assumption of the framework is that processing interactions are always reciprocal; it is this bi-directional characteristic that makes the system interactive. Bi-directional excitatory interactions between levels allow mutual simultaneous constraint among adjacent levels, and bi-directional inhibitory interactions within a level allow for competition among mutually incompatible interpretations of a portion of an input. The between-level excitatory interactions are captured in these models in two-way excitatory connections between mutually compatible processing units; thus the unit for word-inital /t/ has an excitatory connection to the unit for the word /tac/, and receives an excitatory connection from the unit for the word /tac/.

Between-level Processing Interactions Occur Between Adjacent Levels Only. This assumption is actually rather a vague one, since adjacency itself is a matter of assumption. I mention it because it restricts the *direct* processing interactions to a reasonably small and manageable set, rather than allowing everything to influence everything else directly. One possible set of interactions between levels is sketched in Fig. 1.1. Note that even though some pairs of levels are not directly connected, each level can influence each other level indirectly, via indirect connections.

Between-level Interactions are Excitatory Only; Within-level Interactions are Competitive. A feature of the interactive activation framework that has gradually emerged over the years is the idea that between-level interactions should be excitatory only, so that a pattern of activation on one level will tend to excite compatible patterns at adjacent levels, but will not directly inhibit incompatible patterns. The inhibition of incompatible patterns is assumed to occur via competition among alternative patterns of activation on the same level. This idea is characteristic of assumptions made by Grossberg (1976 and elsewhere), and its utility has become clearer in later versions of interactive activation models (McClelland & Elman, 1986; McClelland, 1985). The principal reason for this assumption is that it allows

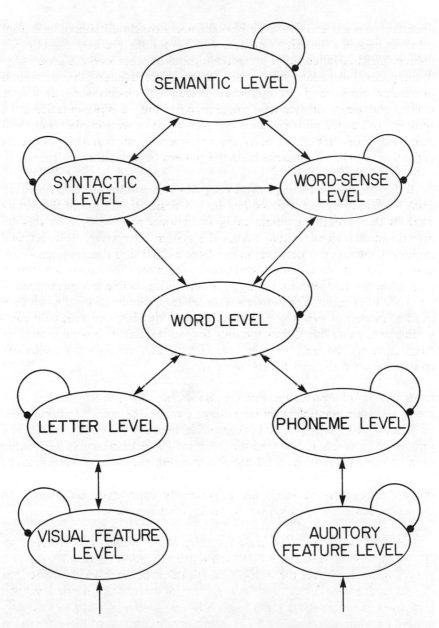

FIG. 1.1.   A set of possible processing levels and connections among these levels. In an interactive activation model, each level would consist of a large number of simple processing units. No claim is made that this is exactly the right set of levels; this set is given for illustrative purposes only. Bi-directional, excitatory connections are represented by double-headed arrows between neighbouring levels. Inhibitory within-level connections are represented by the lines ending in dots that loop back onto each level.

possible alternative representations to accumulate support from a number of sources, then to compete with other alternative possibilities so that the one with the most support can dominate all the others. This allows the network to implement a "best match" strategy of choosing representations; for example, a sequence of phonemes that does not exactly match any particular word will nevertheless activate the closet word. Thus "parageet" for example can result in the recognition of the word "parakeet," even though it does not match parakeet exactly.

Activations and Connections are Continuously Graded. The activation of a representation is a matter of degree, as is the strength of the influence one representation exerts on another. Degree of activation of a unit reflects the strength of the hypothesis that the representational object the unit stands for is present; the strengths of the connections between units reflect the strengths of the contingencies that hold between the representational objects.

The Activation Process is Nonlinear. Each processing unit in an interactive activation network performs a very simple computation. It adds up all of the weighted excitatory influences it receives from other units and subtracts from these the weighted inhibitory influences that it receives from competing units. Then, it updates its activation to reflect this combined (what I will call *net*) input. The activation of the unit is monotonically, but not linearly, related to this sum; at high levels of excitatory input, activation levels off at a maximum value, and with strong inhibitory input, it levels off at a minimum value. Because of these nonlinearities, and because of the competitive interactions among units, inputs that are sometimes crucial for determining the outcome of processing may have little or no effect at other times.[1] The specific details of the nonlinear activation assumptions that I have used are based on, though not identical with, those used by Grossberg (e.g., Grossberg, 1978).

Activation Builds Up and Decays Over Time. It is assumed that processing interactions occur continually, but that the activation process is gradual and incremental, so that it takes time for activation to propagate through the system. New inputs begin to have their effects immediately, but these effects build up over time and then gradually decay away as processing continues.

---

[1] It is worth noting that this nonlinear characteristic is absolutely essential to the operation of the network as a whole; if all units in the system behaved linearly, no purpose would be served by having multiple levels, and none but the most trivial of computational operations could be performed. Furthermore, feedback from higher levels to lower levels can lead to runaway activation in a linear system. For discussion, see Rumelhart, Hinton, & McClelland (1986).

These assumptions are now being applied in the construction of models of higher-level aspects of language processing, such as the assignment of constituents of· sentences to semantic roles and disambiguation of word meaning in context (Cottrell, 1985; Waltz & Pollack, 1985; Kawamoto, Note 4; McClelland & Kawamoto, 1986). At higher levels of processing, I and other researchers have tended to build models that make explicit use of distributed representation, in which a conceptual object is represented by a pattern of activation, rather than a single unit (Hinton, McClelland & Rumelhart, 1986). However, even here it is convenient to speak of whole patterns of activation as though they were separate information-processing constructs, that interact with each other via excitatory and inhibitory contingencies. Indeed the distributed representation can be seen as an implementation of the more abstract, functional description (see Smolensky, 1986 for a discussion of this issue).

Encapsulated Knowledge, Interactive Processing

In his book on modularity, Fodor (1983) explains a virtue of dividing up the knowledge that is used, and encapsulating portions of it in separate modules each dedicated to a specific part of a complex information processing task. Encapsulation of knowledge allows, he notes, for automatised, reflex-like processing in each module, since each module need only consult a finite store of locally-relevant information.

The interactive activation framework adheres to this desirable property. A central feature of the framework is the fact that the knowledge that guides processing is intrinsically local and inaccessible to other portions of the network. To see this, it is useful to focus attention on the connections between some pair of adjacent levels in the system; for example, the connections from the letter level to the word level. These connections are the knowledge that allows the system to form appropriate word level representations from patterns of activation at the letter level. They express contingencies between activations of units at the letter level, and activations of units at the word level. This information is completely encapsulated within this part of the processing mechanism; it is never consulted by any other part of the mechanism. By the same token, this part of the mechanism never consults the knowledge stored in any other part in doing its job, which is simply to supply input to the units at the word level. We have, then, a system in which the knowledge is completely encapsulated.

At the same time, the architecture of the system overcomes what I believe is an unnecessary limitation that Fodor places on modular systems; that is that the output of a module be independent of influences from other sources. Interactive activation provides a framework for processing in which multiple sources of information can influence the construction of representations at each level. This is because each level combines inputs it receives from multiple sources in determining what its pattern of activation shall be. The input a level receives from a particular adjacent level, then, simply constitutes one source of constraint on the construction of a representation that is subject to influence by other sources.

Where Fodor's analysis went astray, I believe, is in assuming that the combined use of constraints from multiple sources requires each module in the system to have access to knowledge of many different types. What the interactive activation framework makes clear is that this is not the case. Each processing level—each set of units—provides a device that performs a very general computation that allows it to combine inputs from a number of sources. This general computational characteristic of interactive activation mechanisms provides a simple way for knowledge at all different levels to exert simultaneous influence on the outcome of processing, without requiring any part of the system to know very much at all.[2]

AN EXAMINATION OF THE EVIDENCE

No-one doubts that the ultimate outcome of processing is sensitive to influences from many levels. The psychological literature is replete with demonstrations of such effects; but many researchers have questioned the view that the influences exerted by higher levels occur through direct influences from higher levels back down into lower levels of processing. There are two poles to this argument. First, the results of some experiments have been taken as evidence against an interactive view, at least with respect to certain aspects of processing. Second, it is often pointed out that results that could be attributable to interactive processing might be explained in other ways; Fodor (1983) makes this point repeatedly.

I will consider these two aspects of the argument against interactionism in turn. First I will consider two cases of experimental findings that have been taken as evidence against interactionism in two specific cases. Here my aim is to show that the experimental facts, when looked at closely, turn out to be perfectly consistent with an interactive activation account. I do not mean to say that they cannot be interpreted without recourse to interaction between levels. Though the phenomena are just what we expect from an interactive

---

[2] I should note that Fodor suggests reasons other than computational efficiency for advocating autonomy of processing. For one thing, he suggests that if modules are autonomous it may be easier for cognitive scientists to analyse exactly what functions each module computes. While this might well be the case, it seems unlikely that the convenience of cognitive scientists entered into the design of our computational machinery; computational considerations seem more likely to have influenced the course of evolution; and my argument is that such considerations favour interactionism.

activation approach, there can be alternative interpretations. In a later section, I will turn specifically to the question of how one might find evidence that more clearly favours an interactive activation view.

The Case Against Interactionism

The two cases I will consider both purport to demonstrate the autonomy of some aspect of processing from higher-level, or contextual influences. One of these cases concerns accessing word meanings. The other concerns the mechanism that determines how constituents should be attached to each other in constructing a representation of the syntactic structure of a sentence.

In examining each of these cases, it will be helpful to have two basic properties of interactive systems in view. The first is that contextual influences often produce what I will call selective, as opposed to predictive, effects. The second is that contextual effects—indeed, the effects of any factor—can be masked by strong effects of other factors. The first fact will be useful when we come to interpret evidence that context appears to exert primarily a selective effect in certain lexical ambiguity resolution experiments; the second will be most relevant when we examine evidence that semantic context effects do not show up in the initial processing of certain grammatical constructions.

To illustrate the first point, let us consider the recognition of an ambiguous phoneme embedded in a context which should favour one interpretation over the other. A simulation illustrating this is shown in Fig. 1.2, using the TRACE model of speech perception (McClelland & Elman, 1986).

To understand the simulation, some facts about the model are necessary. The model consists of units grouped into three processing levels. There is a phonetic feature level, a phoneme level, and a word level. Within each level, there are separate pools of units for each small temporal segment of an utterance. Thus successive phonemes in a word activate phoneme detectors in successive pools of units. It is useful to visualise the feature units as though they are laid out in successive banks from left to right in space, with banks of phoneme units above them and banks of word units above the phoneme units. Each bank of units covers only a small temporal window. Spoken input is swept across this spatial array from left to right, providing input to feature units in successive banks as time progresses. Connections between feature and phoneme units allow active feature units in a particular bank to send excitatory input to units for appropriate phonemes in corresponding banks; phoneme-to-word connections allow phonemes to send excitation to appropriate words in corresponding banks; there are also feedback connections from the word level to the phoneme level and from the phoneme to the feature level. In addition to these excitatory connections, there are also inhibitory connections between units which span overlapping temporal

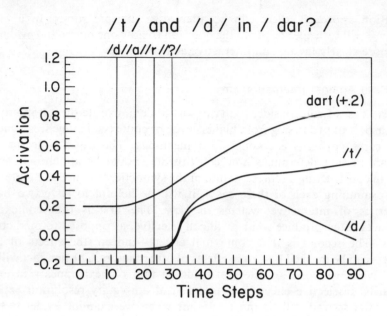

FIG. 1.2.   The time course of activation of units for /d/ and /t/ at the end of the string /dar?/, where the ? stands for a segment ambiguous between /t/ and /d/. The time course of activation of the unit for the word *dart* is also shown.

regions. At the phoneme level, this means that competition occurs only among alternative phonetic interpretations of the same temporal segment of speech.

In our example, we will consider an input that consists of the phonemes /d/, /a/, and /r/, followed by a phonetic segment that is ambiguous between /d/ and /t/. The figure illustrates the build-up of activation for the phoneme units activated by the final ambiguous sound. We can see that, initially, there is a very slight advantage of the /t/ over the /d/. This advantage stays relatively constant for a time, but gradually /t/ begins to dominate /d/ and to push its activation down. While both phonemes are activated initially, only one remains active in the end.

Why is the context effect so small at first? The primary reason has to do with the degree of constraint imposed by the context. Activation of the /t/ over the /d/ results from feedback from the word level, but at the time the /t/ and /d/ are coming in, the relevant word detector (for the word *dart*) is not very active. The reason is simply that there are several other words that are still consistent with the input up to that point. These words are all in competition, so that none are very highly activated. The ambiguous phoneme itself must determine which of these words is really being said, and thereby allow it to dominate the possibilities left open by preceding portions of the input. Only after the ambiguous word strengthens the activation of *dart* over its competitors can *dart* really provide strong support for the /t/ interpretation of the final phoneme.

I want to make it clear that context can and does exert stronger effects than we see here under some circumstances. When, for example, an ambiguous segment comes at the end of a long word that has no remaining competitors a few phonemes before the ambiguous segment is received, we see much stronger context effects in the simulation. These effects are, of course, consistent with the empirical finding that lexical effects in speech processing are larger at later points in words (Marslen-Wilson & Welsh, 1978; Samuel, 1981).

The essential point is that context that is clearly strong enough to exert a potent role in determining the eventual outcome of processing may very well exert its influence primarily by selecting among alternatives as they are becoming activated bottom-up. An initial slight advantage is generally observed for the contextually appropriate alternative, but both appropriate and inappropriate alternatives may receive considerable activation before the resolution of the ambiguity is complete.

Now we consider the second point, namely that effects of context can be blocked if there are other factors that are exerting stronger influences. To demonstrate this, I will show the results of two more simulation runs with the TRACE model, using an unambiguous final /d/ in one case and an unambiguous final /t/ in the other, preceded by the string /dar/. Here context should support the /t/, since *dart* is a word. However, as Fig. 1.3 shows, when the input is unambiguous it produces strong bottom-up support for the phoneme actually presented, and this actually blocks out the effect of context almost completely.

Though there is a slight advantage for the /t/, it is very small and might easily go undetected in an experiment. Certainly, there is no doubt that a /t/ will be heard in one case and a /d/ in the other. The reason is that with strong bottom-up input favouring a particular interpretation, the correct answer is quickly locked into the system and keeps the alternatives from becoming activated, due to competitive inhibition among units standing for alternative interpretations at the same level. The differential feedback support that the /t/ receives does not really become strong enough to influence processing until it is too late.

Again, I want to make clear that the effect of context would be stronger in other cases. When there is a strong expectation before the target occurs, feedback from higher levels can act as a second source of excitation favouring the one alternative; under these conditions, the contextually favoured alternative will have more of an advantage. But in many cases, a context that would be sufficient to disambiguate a borderline stimulus, as we

APPR–B

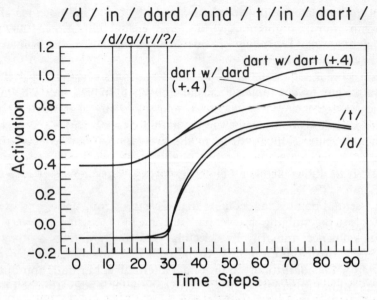

FIG. 1.3.   Time course of activation of detectors for the final /t/ in /dart/ and the final /d/ in /dard/. Also shown is the time course of activation of the detector for the word *dart* in each case.

saw in the previous simulation, will have very little effect when the stimulus is not borderline, as in the present case.

These kinds of effects, where a strong cue overshadows the effects of a weak cue that is known to operate under other circumstances, are absolutely ubiquitous in the literature. They are nicely explained by the interactive activation approach, and by other models such as the Oden-Massaro information integration model (Oden & Massaro, 1978). As just one example, Ganong (1980) found just these kinds of effects in his initial studies of the lexical effect in phoneme identification. He reported that context biased the interpretation of ambiguous sounds at or near the boundary between two phonetic categories, but did not alter the interpretation of unambiguous sounds well within one category or another. One hears the /k/ in (strongly articulated) *kift* correctly, in spite of the unfavourable context. Simulations reported in Elman and McClelland (1986) show that these sorts of effects are expected in the interactive activation framework.

Given these preliminary observations, we are now ready to consider the case against interaction in lexical access and in syntactic analysis. In the first case, the claim has been made that initial access to words occurs autonomously, without regard to context, and that higher levels simply select the appropriate word from those that are made available by the autonomous access mechanism (Tanenhaus, Leiman, & Seidenberg, 1979; Seidenberg, Tanenhaus, Leiman, & Bienkowski, 1982). In the second case, the claim is that the syntactic processing of a sentence is encapsulated, so higher levels of processing only accept or reject possible parses presented to them by the syntactic level. I've chosen to examine these cases for two reasons. First, they are both often cited as evidence of autonomy, and so they are worth considering, in and of themselves. Second, they each illustrate characteristics of the interactive activation framework that ought to be taken into account in attempts to argue against an interactive position.

Word Sense Disambiguation

There are now several studies using a cross-modality priming paradigm to study word sense disambiguation. The first two such studies were those of Tanenhaus et al. (1979) and of Swinney (1979). In these and other studies, the following pattern has been found: Immediately after an ambiguous word, both meanings appear to be activated, even when context is provided which favours one interpretation of the target word over the other. After a delay, the only contextually appropriate meaning appears to remain active.

This pattern of results has been interpreted as favouring a view that I will call the *autonomous lexical access position* (Tanenhaus et al., 1979). According to this position, the process of accessing meanings of words is driven only by the bottom-up processing of the stimulus; context operates only later, to select among the alternatives that are made available by the bottom-up access process.

In this section, I will argue that the results indicate instead a pattern that conforms to what we would expect from an interactive activation model: Initially both meanings appear to be accessed, but—and this is the crucial point—the evidence suggests that the contextually appropriate reading is in fact favoured over the contextually inappropriate reading, even early on in processing.

In documenting this claim, I will focus first on the experiments of Swinney (1979). He presented ambiguous words like "bugs" in contexts which favoured one or the other meaning of this word (insects or snooping devices). The ambiguous word occurred in a spoken passage, and subjects listened to the passages through earphones; at the end of the ambiguous word, they were tested with a visually presented probe word. This word could be related to the contextually appropriate meaning of the ambiguous prime word (*ants*), to the contextually inappropriate meaning (*spy*), or it could be unrelated to the ambiguous word (*sew*). The task was simply to indicate whether the visually presented probe was a word or not. Nonword probes were of course presented on other trials.

The results of Swinney's experiment showed faster lexical decision reaction times to probes related to both meanings of the ambiguous prime word, relative to control. There was a 70msec advantage for the target related to the contextually appropriate meaning of the ambiguous prime, and a 50msec advantage for the target related to the contextually inappropriate meaning of the prime. Both were significantly faster than the responses in the control condition.

In a follow-up study, Swinney replicated his first experiment, and compared the results to the results of a second condition, in which the probe was delayed by three syllables. At 0 delay, the appropriate probe showed 38msec facilitation and the inappropriate probe showed 31msec. After the delay, the appropriate probe showed 47msec and the inappropriate probe was 1msec slower than control. Because the second experiment contains all of the relevant conditions, I have graphed the results in Fig. 1.4.

The basic pattern of results obtained by Swinney was also found by Tanenhaus et al. (1979), hereafter called TLS, and by Seidenberg et al. (1982), hereafter called STLB. In fact, in two conditions of STLB (for noun-noun ambiguities in Experiments 2 and 4) there was a significant selective priming effect at 0 delay. However, in four other conditions over the two experiments, priming of both meanings was found. Looking just at the six different experiments finding priming of both meanings at 0 delay (two of Swinney's, one from TLS, and three from STLB) we find that in five of the six cases, the contextually appropriate target receives stronger priming than the inappropriate one. These findings are summarised in Table 1.1. TLS and STLB also provide confirmation that at a delay, there is strong selection of the contextually appropriate reading; they used a delay of 200msec, by which time the contextually inappropriate probe word showed no residual priming.

While the fact that both meanings are initially primed is consistent with an autonomy position, this result is also completely consistent with an interactive account. Based on our earlier simulation with the ambiguous /d/-/t/ stimulus, this is just what we expect to see. Of course, the consistent slight advantage of contextually appropriate targets at 0 delay is also what we expect on an interactive-activation account. Further support for the idea that there is a context effect for 0-delay probes is provided by some observations of Simpson (1984), regarding another experiment by Onifer and Swinney (1981). He noted that Onifer and Swinney's experiments collected reaction times to probes for each meaning of an ambiguous word, both when the context favoured that meaning and when it favoured the alternative meaning. He then compared lexical decision times when the context was appropriate, against lexical decision times when the context was inappropriate, and found that decision times were consistently faster with appropriate context.[3]

The fact that selection is complete at a longer delay is also fully consistent with the activation-competition processes that are assumed by the interactive activation approach; indeed the simulation shown in Fig. 1.2 is fully consistent with the pattern of results that we see in these experiments.

The initial advantage for contextually appropriate readings is small enough that it does not generally show up as significant. An interactive approach predicts that it should be possible to produce relatively strong contextual effects, even at short delays, when the context exerts relatively strong constraints. The question arises, then: Should we have expected the contexts used in these studies to produce strong effects? In general it is difficult to give a definitive answer to this question, since investigators have not tended to focus specifically on the degree of constraint.[4] The matter certainly deserves further scrutiny. However, there is one experiment that supports the prediction that relatively stronger contextual effects will be found early in processing when relatively strong contexts are used. An experiment by Simpson (1981) bears directly on this point. He selected a group of 60 ambiguous words and identified for each word a dominant and nondominant meaning. He then constructed five context sentences for each word, one that strongly favoured the dominant reading, one that weakly favoured the dominant reading, one that was neutral, one that weakly

---

[3]I should mention two somewhat countervailing caveats concerning the interpretation of data from these experiments. On the one hand, the response to the probe does not occur until several hundred milliseconds after the priming word, even when the probe follows the ambiguous word with 0 delay. Thus there is room for post-access processing of the ambiguous word before the response to the probe is made, even with a 0msec delay; an autonomy position could always take refuge in such a possibility to explain away effects of context at 0 delay. On the other hand, it has been noted that there may be some backward priming effects of the prime on the ambiguous word (Glucksberg, Kreuz, & Rho, 1986); this might have artificially raised the activation of the contextually inappropriate reading at 0 delay (but see Seidenberg et al., 1982).

[4]From an interactive activation point of view, predictability from the preceding context (i.e. *cloze* probability) provides a reasonable operational definition of degree of constraint; from the simulation with the input /dar?/, it was clear that even when there are only three possibilities consistent with the prior context, the context exerts primarily a selective, rather than a predictive effect. In this light, the predominantly selective pattern that is observed in the cross-modal experiments seems consistent with my own best guess about the predictiveness of the contexts used. In Swinney (1979), a single example stimulus is given in which there is a strongly constraining context. However, an examination of the full set of materials used by Onifer and Swinney (1981) indicates that in these later studies, at least, there was a wide range of contextual constraint. For example, consider the context: "The office walls were so thin they could hear the . . ." It seems likely that subjects asked to guess would supply a variety of different continuations, with *ring*, the actual ambiguous word, being only one of many possibilities.

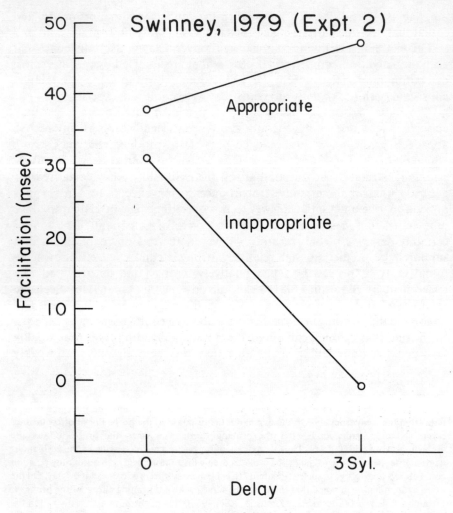

FIG. 1.4.   Interaction of context and delay in the cross-modal priming experiment of Swinney, 1979.

favoured the subordinate reading, and one that strongly favoured the subordinate reading. He presented these sentences to subjects, then followed the final word with a probe related either to the dominant or the subordinate meaning, or with a control, unrelated word. The probe occurred 120msec after the offset of the ambiguous prime word.

I have graphed the facilitation effects Simpson found in Fig. 1.5, as a

TABLE 1.1
Priming Effects of Ambiguous Words in Context, 0 Delay

	Appropriate Meaning	*Inappropriate Meaning*	*A > I?*
TLS 1979	33.5	22	YES
Swinney 1979			
Expt 1	70	50	YES
Expt 2	38	31	YES
STLB 1982			
Expt 3	17.5	13.5	YES
Expt 4			
(noun-verb)	16	28	NO
Expt 5	20	15	YES
MEAN	32.5	26.5	5 out of 6

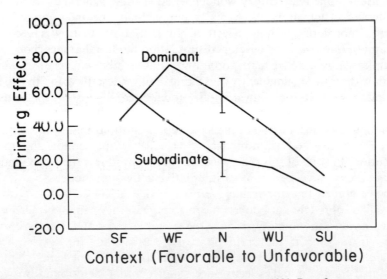

FIG. 1.5.   Effects of dominance and context from Simpson, 1981. Data from two groups of subjects are combined. One group received the strong and neutral contexts, and the other received the weak and neutral contexts. For the neutral conditions, I have connected the points through the mean averaged over the two groups. The horizontals at the top and bottom of the vertical bars represent the values obtained by the strong and weak context groups, respectively.

function of the strength of the context (from strongly favourable to the meaning related to the probe to strongly unfavourable) separately for the dominant and subordinate probes.

As the figure makes plain, there is a strong effect both of dominance and of context, as well as a context by dominance interaction. The interaction is such that when the context is strong, it completely wipes out the effect of dominance. Only when the context is weak or neutral is a strong dominance effect found.

The effects shown in this figure are exactly the kind of effects we would expect to find from an interactive activation model. Each of the two factors manipulated should produce an effect, but only when it is not dominated by the other factor. These kinds of effects are ubiquitous, as I have already noted, and are naturally accounted for by the principles of interactive activation. Unfortunately, there was a delay of 120msec after the ambiguous word in Simpson's experiment before the presentation of the probe; thus there is room to argue that the strong effects of context that he observed were due at least in part to this delay. Thus a definitive test of the predicted immediate context effect with strongly constraining contexts must await further research.

Thus far I have argued from characteristics of interactive activation mechanisms as observed in simulations of lexical effects on phoneme perception. Some readers may wonder whether these general characteristics of interactive activation mechanisms can actually be incorporated in a working model of meaning selection. In fact, both Cottrell (1985) and Kawamoto (Note 4) have developed simulation models that incorporate the principles of interactive activation and that exhibit effects in meaning selection that are analogous to those that I have described for the speech perception simulations. Kawamoto's model used distributed patterns of activation over an ensemble of units to represent the alternative readings of an ambiguous word, instead of the local representations that have been used in the interactive activation models of visual word perception and speech perception. In spite of this difference, his model produces the same kinds of effects that we have seen in other interactive activation models.[5]

I have argued that the results we have reviewed are consistent with the interactive approach, but I do not mean to suggest they cannot be accounted for within an autonomy position. One possible account for early context effects is to suggest that priming can occur within the lexical access mechanism itself. Indeed, Burgess, Seidenberg, and Tanenhaus (Note 1) accounted for the initial, selective access effects that were found in two of

---

[5]I would like to acknowledge here the contributions of Alan Kawamoto's work to this part of this article. His simulations and his review of the literature served as the basis for this discussion of lexical ambiguity resolution.

their experiments in terms of such effects. Intra-lexical priming might also be cited as a possible source of the advantage for contextually appropriate readings in other studies. Unfortunately, the case for this is far from clear at this point. No definitive studies have been done showing that contextual effects only result from intra-lexical factors, controlling for degree of constraint. It would seem that it behoves researchers on both sides of this debate to find ways of separating degree of constraint from intra- vs. inter-level source.

An autonomy account can also be salvaged if it is assumed that the observed priming effects reflect the results of post-access processes. Thus, as I stated at the outset, the finding that there are effects of context on responses to early probes is not compelling evidence against an autonomy account. My purpose has only been to show that the facts that have emerged from these cross-modal priming studies do not speak against an interactive position.

Let me note in closing that there are tests that can be done to test the interactive account. A strong test would be to examine whether context influences the activation of the meanings of an ambiguous word, even under conditions where it is strong enough to allow subjects to guess the identity of the ambiguous word quickly and correctly from the contextual information alone. In such a case interactive activation predicts that the inappropriate meaning will be less active at the earliest point that shows activation for either meaning.

Autonomy of Syntax

Recently, Lynne Frazier and her associates have proposed that syntactic processing is autonomous. In Frazier (Note 3), the suggestion is made that the syntactic processor initially makes decisions in terms of a very general principle known as minimal attachment, and provides a single parse to a "thematic processor" for acceptance or rejection. Here I am not so much concerned with the specific principle of minimal attachment per se, as with the more general claim that initial parsing decisions are unaffected by constraints arising from semantic/thematic considerations.[6] I will consider two experiments that have been taken as evidence for the autonomy position, both reported in Rayner, Carlson, and Frazier (1983). The first shows that plausibility based on knowledge of real-world constraints has little or no effect on the initial processing of reduced relative clauses attached to sentence

---

[6]I do not mean to take a particular stand on the exact characterisation of the higher-level factors that can be brought to bear on syntactic processing; by semantic-thematic constraints (henceforth, simply called *semantic*), I mean to include a range of constraints that arise from our knowledge of the meanings of words and of the ways the entities they refer to might plausibly be interrelated in the situations that we describe in sentences.

intial noun phrases. The second shows a reading-time advantage for sentences containing a prepositional phrase that is minimally attached, compared to matched sentences in which the ultimate interpretation requires nonminimal attachment. I will discuss these in turn, dealing with the first one rather more briefly.

Reduced Relatives

In Rayner et al.'s (1983) first experiment, subjects read reduced relative sentences like the following:

The florist sent the flowers was very pleased.   1a

Such sentences, of course, have been well-studied since the early work of Bever (1970), who used them to support his argument for a particular sentence processing strategy he called the "NVN" strategy. According to the NVN strategy, a sequence that can be interpreted as noun-verb-noun, that is not otherwise marked as subordinate, is taken to specify an actor-action-object sequence. Phrases like "The florist sent the flowers" engage this strategy, and so lead to a garden-path effect, causing the subject to slow down and/or back up when information inconsistent with this effect is encountered.

That this NVN strategy is very potent in English is indicated by the fact that it is strong enough to completely over-ride semantic/thematic constraints. For example, adult English speakers asked to act out the sentence "The pencil kicked the cow" will pick up the pencil and knock over the cow with it, even though pencils are inanimate and therefore cannot ordinarily kick (Bates, McNew, MacWhinney, Devescovi, & Smith, 1982). Apparently, the NVN strategy is strong enough to over-ride semantic constraints in English.

It is important to my argument to note that, in other languages, syntactic constraints need not be so over-riding. For example, in Italian, there is a tendency to use the actor-action-object strategy in interpreting NVN sequences, but this tendency is not over-riding for Italians. Accordingly, Italians interpret analogues of "the pencil kicked the cow" in accordance with semantic constraints, even though they tend to treat the first noun as agent in more neutral sentences, such as "The horse kicked the cow" (Bates et al., 1982).

The point, so far, is that syntactic cues vary in strength from language to language, and there is no universal prepotency of syntax over semantics. It just so happens in English that there is a very strong tendency to treat NVN as actor-agent-object. In English, this particular syntactic cue is strong enough to over-ride semantic constraints such as animacy constraints on the agents of action verbs, as Bates et al. have shown.

In their Experiment 1, Rayner et al. (1983) compare reading times for reduced relative sentences like (1a) in which the NVN = actor-action-object reading of the beginning of the sentence seems very plausible with other sentences in which such a reading seems somewhat less plausible, such as (1b);

The performer sent the flowers was greatly pleased.   1b

Although performers can send flowers, they are less likely to do so than florists. Thus, one might reason, if subjects were able to make use of semantic constraints in on-line syntactic processing decisions, then they should not be as strongly misled in sentences like (1b). However, Rayner et al. found that subjects were slow to process the disambiguating portion of the sentences (in this case, "was greatly pleased"), regardless of the plausibility of the actor-action-object interpretation of the first NVN sequence, indicating that they were led down the garden path in both cases. Similar null effects of animacy of the sentence-initial noun-phrase or of preceding context have been reported by Ferreira and Clifton (1986).

Though the consistent lack of an effect in these cases might seem compelling at first sight, it is important to realise that it does not necessarily mean that syntactic processing decisions are unaffected by plausibility factors in all cases. We have reason to believe from other research that word order is very powerful as a cue in English, and that the NVN sequence is a compelling cue for an agent-action-object interpretation. In contrast, the plausibility manipulation used by Rayner et al. seems rather weak; for example there is no reason to suppose that a performer could not send flowers, say to a rival at the opening of a new show. My argument, quite simply, is that we cannot put weak cues against strong cues and expect that the weak cues will produce strong effects; indeed we have seen how strong cues can completely over-ride weaker ones in one of our initial illustrative simulations. We have independent evidence that demonstrates the potency of the NVN strategy, and so we cannot be surprised to find that weak contextual constraints have no reliable effects. The interactive activation framework makes clear that if we wish to find effects of a particular factor, we must look at situations in which there are no other factors exerting overpowering effects.

Prepositional Phrase Attachment

Just such a situation is provided by PP attachment ambiguities, such as the one that arises in sentences like "The boy hit the girl with the doll." In comprehending such sentences, the reader must decide whether to treat "the doll" as the instrument of hitting, thereby attaching it to the verb phrase; or whether to treat it as an object in the girl's possession, thereby attaching it as constituent of a complex noun-phrase headed by "the girl."

Such decisions are clearly influenced by thematic plausibility constraints. Consider, for example, the following sentences:

The spy saw the cop with binoculars.   2a
The spy saw the cop with a revolver.   2b

In the former sentence, we tend to treat "binoculars" as an instrument; in the latter, we treat "revolver" as a possession of the cop. In general, it appears that the verb and all of the noun phrases influence these decisions. Compare, for example,

The spy shot the cop with binoculars.   3a
The spy shot the cop with a revolver.   3b

and

The woodpecker saw the bird-watcher with binoculars.   4a
The bird-watcher saw the woodpecker with binoculars.   4b

Indeed, Oden (1978) has shown that attachment decisions can be influenced by the identities of the various NPs in the sentence and by preceding context.

No-one doubts the role of these constraints in the ultimate interpretations assigned to sentences. What is at issue is whether such constraints affect the initial attachment decisions subjects make in the course of reading or listening. An interactive account would assume that the initial attachment decision is susceptible to influence from semantic constraints: In view of the fact that both kinds of attachments are encountered frequently, there would be no reason to suppose that there would be a strong syntactic bias in favour of one attachment over the other. Frazier, however, has pointed out that the attachment of the preposition phrase as a constituent of the verb phrase would require the creation of no extra structure, and therefore she has proposed that verb-phrase (VP) attachment is tried first by the syntactic processor, independent of semantic constraints.

The second experiment reported by Rayner et al. (1983) addressed this claim. They presented subjects with sentences like (2a) and (2b), with an extra final clause added, and measured reading time as in their first experiment. They reasoned that, if the syntactic processor initially prefers VP attachments, then reading times should be slower for sentences like (2a), where a VP attachment turns out to be consistent with thematic considerations. The results of the experiment supported this prediction: Reading times were somewhat slower on and after the disambiguating word in the versions of the sentences where the ultimate reading favoured attachment of the prepositional phrase to the preceding noun-phrase (NP).

While the results were consistent with this prediction, it turns out that there is an alternative account. It is possible that the effects observed by Rayner et al. are not due to a syntactic preference for minimal attachment, but to the fact that, in Rayner et al.'s materials, there is a consistent semantic bias in favour of the minimal completion. To show this, Taraban and McClelland (Note 5) asked subjects to read Rayner et al.'s sentences, through the preposition at the beginning of the critical prepositional phrase, and then to generate an expectation for the completion of this phrase. The subject then saw either the VP or the NP completion, and was asked to rate how well the actual completion matched the expectation. Subjects rated the VP completions significantly closer to their expectations, on average, than the NP completions (3.62 vs. 2.90 on a 5-point scale).

To determine whether it was this greater concordance with expectations that was determining the advantage for VP over NP completions, Taraban and McClelland constructed 20 additional sentence pairs that were intended to produce expectations favouring an NP completion. An example is:

I read the article in the . . .   5a

This can be completed with a word like "magazine," in which case the PP is attached to the NP, or with a word like "bathtub," in which case the PP is interpreted by most subjects as being attached to the VP. The completion words used in the two conditions were matched over the set of materials for both length and frequency. As intended, the NP completions of Taraban and McClelland's sentences were rated closer to subjects' expectations than the VP completions (3.90 vs. 2.98).

Once ratings had been collected, both Rayner et al.'s sentences and Taraban and McClelland's new sentences were presented to another group of subjects in a word-by-word reading time task. At the beginning of each trial the subject pressed a button causing the presentation of a row of dashes, blanks, and punctuation marks. Each dash indicated the presence of a letter in the to-be-read sentence, with blanks indicating the spaces between words. The next press of the button caused the first set of blanks to be replaced with the first word of the sentence. Each subsequent press of the button caused the next word to be presented and the preceding word to be replaced with blanks. The last word of the sentence was always the disambiguating word. When the subject pressed the button after reading this word, a question appeared. Subjects were instructed to read the sentences as rapidly as possible consistent with good comprehension, and the answers to the questions were recorded by the experimenter. Accuracy was very high, and did not differ between experimental conditions. In addition to the 29 target sentences, there were 66 filler sentences. Seven of these were used to balance the frequency of NP and VP attachments of sentence final prepositional phrases. The remaining 59 were fillers of many different types included to vary the materials so that subjects would not get into a set of expecting a sentence-final prepositional phrase.

The reading times for the final words of the sentences are shown in Fig. 1.6a, broken down by attachment and source.

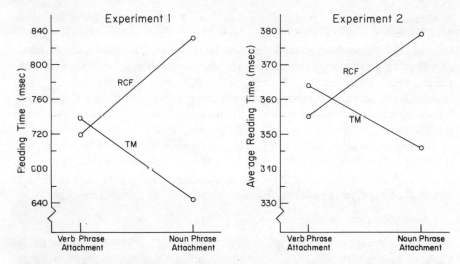

FIG. 1.6.   Opposite effects of attachment on reading time for target words triggering different attachment decisions, for sentences of Rayner et al. (1983) (RCF) and Taraban and McClelland (TM). In the first Experiment, (a), the sentence ended with the target word, and the reading times shown are for this word only. In the second experiment (b), the sentence continued on beyond the target word, and reading times are based on the sum of the time spent reading the target word and the three following words.

Two things are apparent from the results. First, with Rayner et al.'s materials, we were able to replicate their effect showing faster reading times for VP vs. NP attachments. Second, however, we found that with our materials, this effect was reversed, and reading times were actually shorter for NP completions than for VP attachments. There was no main effect of attachment type, but there was a highly reliable interaction of completion type with source (RCF vs. TM). There was also a main effect of source, but this is not interpretable, since Taraban and McClelland's completions were generally shorter and more frequent than those used by Rayner et al.

It has often been suggested that the time spent reading the final word of a sentence reflects extra, integrative processes that do not occur at other points. Thus, the reading times Taraban and McClelland observed in this experiment might reflect such integration effects, and these effects might be masking a real effect of attachment that would appear if it had not been overshadowed by such sentence-final integration effects. To address this problem, Taraban and McClelland extended the sentences. For the Rayner et al. sentences we used continuations they had used, and for our own we constructed completions of the same kind. In all cases, the continuation began with a conjunction that clearly indicated the beginning of a new clause, such as "while" or "because."

Figure 1.6b shows the total reading time for the target word and the following three words, broken down by VP vs. NP attachment and source. Once again there was no main effect of attachment, but there was a strong attachment by source interaction. Finally, Fig. 1.7 shows the difference in reading times between the VP and NP completions of the sentences, on a word-by word basis, starting with the disambiguating word.

The figure indicates that there is no effect of condition on the reading time

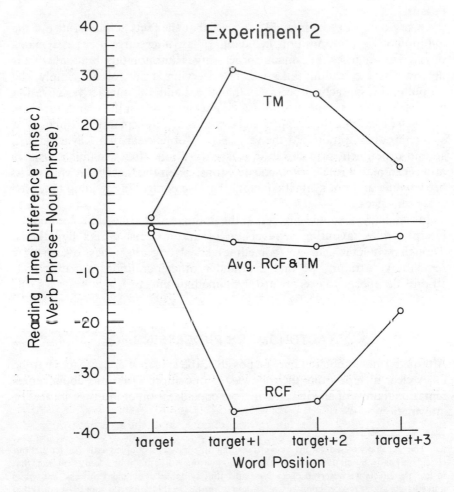

FIG. 1.7.   The time-course of the processing difference between NP and VP attachment versions of the Rayner et al. (RCF) and Taraban and McClelland (TM) sentences. Times shown are reading times for words in the NP-attachment version, minus reading times for words in the VP-attachment version, for the target word and each of the three following words.

for the disambiguating word itself. However, there is an effect in each of the next two words; by the third word after the disambiguation, the difference seems to have disappeared. It would appear from this analysis that processing that occurred on the disambiguating word when it was the last word of the sentence is being spread out over subsequent words in this case. As before, there is no evidence that this extra processing reflects a disruption that occurs with nonminimal completions in general. Rather, it appears that the extra processing occurs for minimal or nonminimal completions, depending on whether the VP or NP completion is closer to the subjects' expectations.

Once again, I do not intend to suggest that the facts actually rule out the autonomous syntax position in favour of an interactive view; it remains possible to suppose that syntactic processing is autonomous, but that what is determining the reading times we are observing is not (or not simply) the output of this syntactic process. On the other hand, the interactive activation approach deserves some credit for giving us guidance in the search for cases in which processing times appear to be dominated by semantic as opposed to syntactic considerations. At the very least it seems clear that Rayner et al.'s second experiment provides little reason to doubt that semantic considerations can play a role in syntactic decisions, given the fact that it appears to be semantic and not syntactic factors that are controlling reading times for these sentences.[7]

In summary, I would suggest that the findings of Rayner et al. need not be interpreted as favouring any version of autonomous syntax hypothesis. Though syntactic cues are sometimes so strong that they overshadow semantic constraints, we find that under other conditions semantic constraints do appear to exert relatively immediate effects.

DISTINGUISHING INTERACTIVE FROM AUTONOMOUS PROCESSING

Although some quibbling may be possible, the evidence appears to me to be fairly clear in supporting the following proposition: Decisions about representational units of all kinds involve the consideration of multiple sources of information.

---

[7]The fact that we used a word-by-word reading time measure, coupled with the fact that our effects only show up on the word *after* the disambiguating word, might be taken as evidence that in fact the effects we observed occur *after* an initial syntactic attachment process that works immediately and is reflected only in eye fixation duration. In this context it should be noted that Rayner et al.'s findings did not show up clearly in fixations on the target word; indeed the statistical evidence for their effect was somewhat weak in their eye-movement data, perhaps because subjects tend to overlap the completion of higher levels of processing with the intake of subsequent words.

However, this can be seen simply as a restatement of some of the basic findings, rather than as a statement about whether the processing system is inherently interactive or not. To see this, I will briefly consider two cases: the lexical effect on phoneme identification (Ganong, 1980) and the role of semantic context in resolving the attachment ambiguities we have been discussing. In both cases, we might account for the results with a purely bottom-up processing system, in which each module operates completely independently of influences from higher levels of processing. Thus in Ganong's case, one may propose that the phoneme level passes to the word level activations indicating which phonemes are consistent with the input and to what extent; and that the word level uses these graded activations, in conjunction with lexical constraints, to determine which word(s) are consistent with the input. Thus if a phoneme ambiguous between /g/ and /k/ is heard, the phoneme level may pass on the ambiguity to the word level. Ganong's finding could simply result from choosing as an overt response the phoneme that is most consistent with the word that the subject has heard. The decision is still based on information from multiple sources, but this integration of information does not occur at the phoneme level of processing within the perceptual system; instead, it occurs in some later decision-making process that can consult the final output of the word level.

In the sentence processing case, the situation is analogous. One could suppose that the syntactic processing mechanisms operate autonomously, passing on to higher levels the output of a preliminary syntactic analysis. In the case of attachment ambiguities such as those considered here, one might assume (contrary to Frazier, but more or less consistent with the recent view of Marcus, Hindle, & Fleck, 1983) that the output reflects the possible attachments that are consistent with the syntax, with each activated to a degree that reflects its relative likelihood based on syntactic considerations. The semantic processor could then make use of this information, in conjunction with semantic constraints, to achieve an interpretation that was jointly constrained by syntactic and semantic factors.

This purely bottom-up story has many of the same implications as an interactive account, since it explains how influences from all levels can have effects on the final outcome of processing. It is certainly consistent with a large number of existing experiments on contextual influences. One might ask, then, whether there is any way of distinguishing this purely bottom-up account from an interactive view.

Fodor (1983) has made one suggestion. He has observed that to counter unidirectional accounts, it is necessary to show "that the information fed back interacts with interlevels of input-processing and not merely the final results of such processing." Thus, for example, if one could show that the results of semantic processing are fed back into the syntactic processor in such a way as to influence subsequent syntactic processing decisions, or that the results of lexical processing are fed back into the phonetic level so as to influence subsequent phonetic processing decisions, then one would have provided evidence that processing is indeed interactive.

To illustrate this approach, I will describe a recent experiment by Elman and McClelland (Note 2). In this experiment, we relied upon the fact that listeners compensate for coarticulatory influences of one speech sound on the acoustic realisation of neighbouring sounds. In the case we exploited, the phonemes /s/ and /S/[8] alter the acoustic realisation of a subsequent /t/ or /k/; listeners compensate for this coarticulation effect by adjusting the perceptual boundary between /t/ and /k/, so that a sound that would be on the boundary in a neutral context tends to be heard as a /k/ when it occurs just after a /s/, but as a /t/ when it occurs after a /S/. We reasoned as follows. First, we assumed that this coarticulatory compensation is an intrinsic characteristic of processing at the phoneme level. Given this, we noted that it should be possible to use lexical constraints to get subjects to interpret a sound halfway between /s/ and /S/ as a /s/ in one context and as a /S/ in another. Now if, as we assumed, this lexical effect operates by feeding back activation to the phoneme level; and if, as we also assumed, interactions at the phoneme level are responsible for the coarticulatory compensation effect, then the lexical effect on the ambiguous /s/-/S/ sound should trigger a coarticulatory compensation effect that influences the phonetic interpretation of an ambiguous /k/-/t/ sound. On the other hand, if Ganong's effect operates only on the final results of phonetic processing, and does not feed back anything to the phonetic level, then we would expect no coarticulatory compensation as a result of the lexical effect.

We therefore took pairs of words (e.g. "tapes/capes") distinguished by initial /t/ vs. /k/ (or /d/ vs. /g/, which exhibit the same effects of preceding /s/ and /S/) and constructed from recorded tokens of these words a set of seven stimuli beginning with sounds varying between /t/ and /k/ in small steps. Each of these stimuli was preceded by one of two context words. In one experiment, one word (e.g. "foolish") actually ended in /S/ and the other (e.g. "Christmas") actually ended in /s/. In another experiment, the same context words were used but the final segments were replaced by an ambiguous sound that was determined in pre-testing to fall halfway between /s/ and /S/, here designated as /?/.

The first experiment simply replicated the coarticulatory influence of /s/ and /S/ on the identification of borderline /t/-/k/ stimuli, as previously described by Mann and Repp (1982); as expected, words ending in /s/ tended to lead to an increased probability of /k/ responses to the subsequent /t/-/k/ stimulus, while the words ending in /S/ tended to lead to an increased probability of /t/ responses.

---

[8] I use /S/ to stand for the "sh" sound in "ship."

The second experiment provided the crucial test for the interaction hypothesis. Here, we found that prior context did indeed trigger coarticulatory compensation for the lexically-determined /s/ or /S/ phoneme; for example, subjects reported /k/ more often after "Christma?" than after "fooli?", just as predicted. The results for several context/target sets involving /t/-/k/ and /d/-/g/ identification are shown in Fig. 1.8.

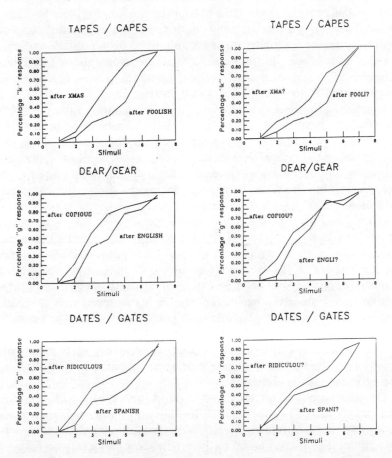

FIG. 1.8. Identification curves for three sets of experimental stimuli used by Elman and McClelland (1986). The left panels show the effects of acoustically distinct "s" and "sh" sounds on /t/-/k/ and /d/-/g/ judgements; the right panels show the effects of acoustically identical (lexically disambiguated) sounds halfway between "s" and "sh" (represented by ?). The label above each panel indicates the words that were used to bracket the ambiguous /t/-/k/ and /d/-/g/ stimuli; the labels associated with each curve indicate the preceding context for the judgement percentages (percentage /g/ or /k/ judgements, depending on the continuum) indicated by the corresponding curve.

The results of this experiment demonstrate that lexical influences on phoneme identification can induce coarticulatory compensation, as predicted from the interaction hypothesis. This is exactly what we would expect if, indeed, feedback from the lexical level actually does influence processing at the phoneme level, rather than simply influencing the interpretation of the outcome of such processing. More importantly, the experiment demonstrates a method that I think holds some considerable promise of providing a way of determining the extent of interaction in perceptual and linguistic processing.

It remains possible to salvage a bottom-up account for these findings, but I do not think this is a very attractive option. To do so, one must suppose that compensation for coarticulation is accomplished by the same "late" mechanism that uses lexical information to make decisions about the identity of phonemes. This seems an unattractive suggestion, because compensation for coarticulation is so often taken as an intrinsic and basic function of the mechanisms of phoneme perception (see, for example, Liberman, Cooper, Shankweiler, & Studdert-Kennedy, 1967). To ascribe this function to some "later" level would be to deprive the machinery of phoneme perception of one of its most crucial roles; or to duplicate needlessly the intricate knowledge of coarticulatory influences that is assumed to be present in the mechanisms of phoneme perception in mechanisms of post-perceptual judgement.

More generally, it would always be possible to say that processing interactions that are assumed to result from intra-level influences were actually occurring at a higher level, and thereby to sidestep any possible applications of Fodor's suggested test. But this step is only palatable, it seems to me, if the higher-level decision can be made using information that would ordinarily be assumed to be available to the higher level. This, it seems quite sensible to suppose that phonetic ambiguity could be passed up to a later stage for resolution at the word level provided the word level does it by using lexical constraints. But if the word must use the very sorts of information usually attributed to the phoneme level, then the entire notion of encapsulation of knowledge is undermined.

This discussion brings up another point, and that is, why bother with feedback? What's the good of it? Why should it matter if higher levels feed back information into lower levels? Why should they not simply resolve the ambiguities that are passed on to them whenever they can, and forget about providing feedback supporting one alternative over the other?

The good of feedback is that it permits processing on lower levels to be guided from above, thereby allowing them to provide higher levels with better information. Our coarticulation study gives one example of this. If higher levels can help lower levels decide on the identity of phonemes that are perceptually indistinct, then lower levels can use this information to adjust for coarticulation better than they could otherwise. Similarly, at the syntactic level, if higher levels can influence the formation of syntactic representations of one constituent, they will allow the syntactic level to be better prepared to provide the best analysis of what will come later on in the sentence. In both cases, this allows the lower level to do a better job in providing information to the higher level.

SUMMARY

In the preceding sections of this paper, I have described a framework for modeling the process of forming representations in processing written and spoken language. I have shown how this framework can help us understand why contextual effects may be obtained under some circumstances and not others, and why it often appears to exert selective, as opposed to predictive, effects.

In the course of making these observations, I have argued that some of the evidence that has been taken in support of the idea that lexical access and syntactic processing are invulnerable to external influences is fully consistent with an interactive account. I do not say that this part of the analysis proves that the autonomy position is wrong, only that several of the reasons that have been given for believing that it is wrong are far from compelling.

Finally, I have indicated that there is hope of finding empirical evidence relevant to distinguishing between interactive and feed-forward accounts of information processing: Such evidence takes the form of demonstrations that higher levels of processing can trigger processes at lower levels, increasing the quality of the results they pass on later to higher levels.

It remains to build explicit models of interactive processing at higher levels. Of course, this is a difficult task for any processing framework; certainly no adequate model of the formation of a representation of the event or scene described by a sentence has been proposed to date. From what we know about the susceptibility of higher levels of language processing to contextual information (cf. Bransford & Johnson, 1973), it seems fairly clear to me that any adequate model will have to incorporate the principles of interactive activation. What is not clear at this point is how these principles will need to be elaborated and supplemented to capture the structural complexities that arise at higher levels. This remains a central issue for future research.

REFERENCES

Bates, E., McNew, S., MacWhinney, B., Devescovi, A., & Smith, S. (1982). Functional constraints on sentence processing: A cross-linguistic study. *Cognition, 11,* 245–299.

Bever, T. G. (1970). The cognitive basis for linguistic structures. In J. R. Hayes (Ed.), *Cognition and the development of language.* New York: Wiley.

Bransford, J. D. & Johnson, M. K. (1973). Considerations of some problems of comprehension. In W. G. Chase (Ed.), *Visual information processing*. New York: Academic Press, 383–438.

Cottrell, G. (1985). *A connectionist approach to word sense disambiguation* (TR-154). Rochester, New York: University of Rochester, Department of Computer Science.

Elman, J. L. & McClelland, J. L. (1986). Exploiting the lawful variability in the speech wave. In J. S. Perkell & D. H. Klatt (Eds.), *Invariance and variability of speech processes*. Hillsdale, N.J.: Lawrence Erlbaum Associates Inc.

Ferreira, F. & Clifton, C. (1986). The independence of syntactic processing. *Journal of Memory and Language, 25*, 348–368.

Fodor, J. A. (1983). *Modularity of mind: An essay on faculty psychology*. Cambridge, Mass.: M.I.T. Press.

Ganong, W. F. (1980). Phonetic categorisation in auditory word perception. *Journal of Experimental Psychology: Human Perception and Performance, 26*, 110–115.

Glucksberg, S., Kreuz, R. J. & Rho, S. H. (1986). Context can constrain lexical access: Implications for models of language comprehension. *Journal of Experimental Psychology: Learning, Memory, and Cognition, 12*, 323–335.

Grossberg, S. (1976). Adaptive pattern classification and universal recoding: Part 1. Parallel development and coding of neural feature detectors. *Biological Cybernetics, 23*, 121–134.

Grossberg, S. (1978). A theory of visual coding, memory, and development. In E. L. J. Leeuwenbert & H. F. J. M. Buffart (Eds.), *Formal theories of visual perception*. New York: Wiley.

Hinton, G. E., McClelland, J. L., & Rumelhart, D. E. (1986). Distributed representations. In D. E. Rumelhart, J. L. McClelland, & the PDP research group (Eds.), *Parallel distributed processing: Explorations in the microstructure of cognition. Vol. I*. Cambridge, Mass.: Bradford Books.

Huey, E. B. (1968). *The psychology and pedagogy of reading*. Cambridge, Mass.: M.I.T. Press. (Reprinted from Macmillian Company, 1908.)

Liberman, A. M., Cooper, F. S., Shankweiler, D., & Studdert-Kennedy, M. (1967). Perception of the speech code. *Psychological Review, 84*, 452–471.

Mann, V. A. & Repp, B. H. (1982). Fricative-stop coarticulation: Acoustic and perceptual evidence. *Journal of the Acoustical Society of America, 71*, 1562–1567.

Marcus, M. P., Hindle, D., & Fleck, M. M. (1983). D-theory: Talking about talking about trees. *Proceedings of the Association for Computational Linguistics*.

Marslen-Wilson, W. D. & Welsh, A. (1978). Processing interactions and lexical access during word recognition in continuous speech. *Cognitive Psychology, 10*, 29–63.

McClelland, J. L. (1985). Putting knowledge in its place: A scheme for programming parallel processing structures on the fly. *Cognitive Science, 9*, 113–146.

McClelland, J. L. (1986). The programmable blackboard model of reading. In J. L. McClelland, D. E. Rumelhart, & the PDP research group (Eds.), *Parallel distributed processing: Explorations in the microstructure of cognition. Vol. II*. Cambridge, Mass.: Bradford Books.

McClelland, J. L. & Elman, J. L. (1986). The TRACE model of speech perception. *Cognitive Psychology, 18*, 1–86.

McClelland, J. L. & Kawamoto, A. H. (1986). Mechanisms of sentence processing: Assigning roles to constituents. In J. L. McClelland, D. E. Rumelhart, & the PDP research group (Eds.), *Parallel distributed processing: Explorations in the microstructure of cognition. Vol. II*. Cambridge, Mass.: Bradford Books.

McClelland, J. L. & Rumelhart, D. E. (1981). An interactive activation model of context effects in letter perception: Part 1. An account of basic findings. *Psychological Review, 88*, 375–407.

Mozer, M. (1987). Early parallel processing in reading: A connectionist approach. In M. Coltheart (Ed.), *Attention and performance XII*. London: Lawrence Erlbaum Associates Ltd.

Neisser, U. (1967). *Cognitive psychology*. New York: Appleton-Century-Crofts.

Oden, G. C. (1978). Semantic constraints and judged preference for interpretations of ambiguous sentences. *Memory and Cognition, 6*, 26–37.

Oden, G. C. & Massaro, D. W. (1978). Integration of featural information in speech perception. *Psychological Review, 85*, 172–191.

Onifer, W. & Swinney, D. A. (1981). Accessing lexical ambiguities during sentence comprehension: Effects of frequency on meaning and contextual bias. *Memory and Cognition, 9*, 225–236.

Rayner, K., Carlson, M., & Frazier, L. (1983). The interaction of syntax and semantics during sentence processing: Eye movements in the analysis of semantically biased sentences. *Journal of Verbal Learning and Verbal Behaviour, 22*, 358–374.

Rumelhart, D. E. (1977). Toward an interactive model of reading. In S. Dornic (Ed.), *Attention and performance VI*. Hillsdale, N.J.: Lawrence Erlbaum Associates Inc.

Rumelhart, D. E., Hinton, G. E., & McClelland, J. L. (1986). A general framework for parallel distributed processing. In D. E. Rumelhart, J. L. McClelland, & the PDP research group (Eds.), *Parallel distributed processing: Explorations in the microstructure of cognition. Vol. 1*. Cambridge, Mass.: Bradford Books.

Rumelhart, D. E. & McClelland, J. L. (1982). An interactive activation model of context effects in letter perception: Part 2. The contextual enhancement effect and some tests and extensions of the model. *Psychological Review, 89*, 60–94.

Samuel, A. G. (1981). Phonemic restoration: Insights from a new methodology. *Journal of Experimental Psychology: General, 110*, 474–494.

Seidenberg, M. S., Tanenhaus, M. J., Leiman, J. M., & Bienkowski, M. (1982). Automatic access of the meanings of ambiguous words in context: Some limitations of knowledge-based processing. *Cognitive Psychology, 14*, 538–559.

Simpson, G. B. (1981). Meaning dominance and semantic context in the processing of lexical ambiguity. *Journal of Verbal Learning and Verbal Behaviour, 20*, 120–136.

Simpson, G. B. (1984). Lexical ambiguity and its role in models of word recognition. *Psychological Bulletin, 96*, 316–340.

Smolensky, P. (1986). Neural and conceptual interpretation of PDP models. In J. L. McClelland, D. E. Rumelhart, & the PDP research group (Eds.), *Parallel distributed processing: Explorations in the microstructure of cognition. Vol. II*. Cambridge, Mass.: Bradford Books.

Swinney, D. A. (1979). Lexical access during sentence comprehension: (Re)consideration of context effects. *Journal of Verbal Learning and Verbal Behaviour, 18*, 645–659.

Tanenhaus, M. K., Leiman, J. M., & Seidenberg, M. S. (1979). Evidence for multiple stages in the processing of ambiguous words in syntactic contexts. *Journal of Verbal Learning and Verbal Behaviour, 18*, 427–440.

Waltz, D. L. & Pollack, J. B. (1985). Massively parallel parsing. *Cognitive Science, 9*, 51–74.

REFERENCE NOTES

1. Burgess, C., Seidenberg, M., & Tanenhaus, M. K. (1986). *Nonword interference and lexical ambiguity resolution*. Paper presented at the Program for the 27th annual meeting of the Psychonomic Society, New Orleans, LA.

2. Elman, J. L. & McClelland, J. L. (1987). *Cognitive penetration of the mechanisms of perception. Compensation for coarticulation of perceptually restored phonemes*. Manuscript submitted for publication.

3. Frazier, L. (1986). *Theories of sentence processing*. Manuscript.

4. Kawamoto, A. H. (1985). *Dynamic processes in the (re)solution of lexical ambiguity.* Unpublished doctoral dissertation, Brown University.
5. Taraban, R. & McClelland, J. L. *The role of semantic constraints in interpreting prepositional phrases.* Manuscript in preparation.

II

EARLY VISUAL PROCESSING AND READING—ATTENTION, MASKING, AND PRIMING

2
Attention and Reading: Wholes and Parts in Shape Recognition —A Tutorial Review

John Duncan
MRC Applied Psychology Unit
Cambridge, U.K.

ABSTRACT

This paper deals with the role of attention in letter and word recognition, and in particular with Treisman's feature integration theory. The key proposal is that serial processing is needed to arrange perceptual parts into wholes. Stimulus sets are developed to deal with the arrangement of strokes in letters, and of letters in words. In tachistoscopic report, there is no general loss of the relative location of stimulus parts. Cross-talk between objects occurs for words but not letters. Visual search using letters can be parallel, at least when nontargets are homogeneous. This applies even when nontarget strokes might be rearranged within the letter to form the target. With words, though, there is no hint of parallel search. Both unattended, peripheral letters and words prime identification of a central stimulus, even when they cannot be recognised. Priming depends mainly on the stimulus parts in a display, not their conjunctions. The results provide several difficulties for feature integration theory, as well as its traditional alternatives. Other proposals are considered briefly.

INTRODUCTION

Even holding our eyes still, we can move attention from one word to another on the page. Theories of attention thus concern selective access of some stimuli, but not others, to a *limited capacity stage* (LCS) in perception; a stage dealing with only one or a few stimuli at once.

One extreme contrast is between *early* and *late* selection theories. The former propose that pattern recognition is the function of LCS (Broadbent, 1971; Neisser, 1967). Without LCS access, simple stimulus characteristics such as location or colour might be functionally available, but details of shape are not. Late selection theories (Deutsch & Deutsch, 1963; Duncan, 1980) propose instead that LCS makes the completed results of pattern recognition available for report. For some purposes, even details of shape and aspects of meaning are available without LCS access.

Recently a third view has emerged, most notably in the feature integration theory of Treisman (Treisman & Gelade, 1980; see also Allport, 1977; Feldman, 1985). It concerns the way that the percept of a whole object is constructed from its parts. Treisman distinguishes two successive perceptual stages; the first parallel across simultaneous stimuli, the second serial (LCS). Processing at the first stage tells which stimulus parts are present in the visual field, but not how they are arranged spatially, or how they are conjoined to form whole objects. The idea has been applied to both letter (Treisman & Gelade, 1980) and word (Treisman & Souther, 1986) perception. For letters, first stage processing might show that the field contains a horizontal line, a vertical line, a closed loop, and a diagonal, but not that these are arranged in the form of a T and a Q. For a display of several words, such processing would leave unspecified which letters or shape features came from which word. Only with LCS access are the different parts of an object synthesised into the correct whole.

In this paper I shall largely be concerned with the application of feature integration theory to letter and word perception, though I shall also have something to say about the extreme positions of early and late selection.

STIMULUS SETS

There has been a good deal of experimental work dealing in some way with the conjunction of stimulus parts in letter and word perception. Relevant are studies of error types in tachistoscopic report, visual search, and priming from unattended stimuli. Some experiments have dealt with the combination of letter strokes to form letters, others with the combination of letters to form words.

The stimulus sets shown in Figs. 2.1 and 2.2 help to organise the issues. Figure 1 shows ten pairs of letter stimuli, two versions (a and b) of each of five display types. (Though some of the stimuli are not real letters, I shall refer to them as such.) Type 1 displays contain a target stimulus, the upright letter L. The remaining types 2 to 5 contain various combinations of nontargets.

In a type 2 display, one letter has the vertical stroke of an L, while the other has the horizontal. If there were some loss of information concerning which stroke came from which letter, the result could be misperception that the target L was present. I call this the *across-object conjunction* display. Type

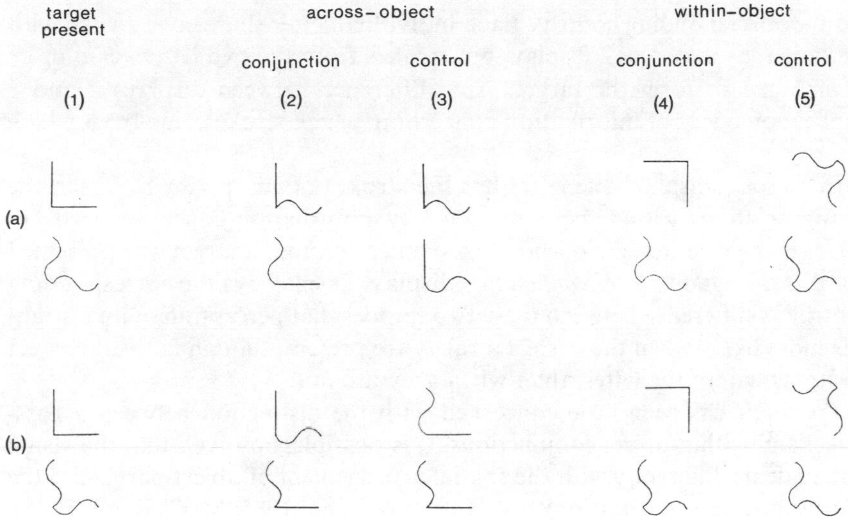

FIG. 2.1. Pairs of letters based on the target L.

	target present	across – object		within – object	
		conjunction	control	conjunction	control
	(1)	(2)	(3)	(4)	(5)
(a)	STAB ICUX	STUX ICAB	STUX STIC	ABST ICUX	ICUX UXIC
(b)	STAB UXIC	STIC UXAB	ICAB UXAB	ABST UXIC	ICUX UXIC

FIG. 2.2. Pairs of letter strings based on the target STAB.

3 is the corresponding control. Each individual letter shares one stroke with the target, as in a type 2 display, but strokes from the two letters cannot be recombined to form the target. Any difference between displays 2 and 3 implies some loss of information concerning which stroke came from which letter.

In a type 4 display, one letter has the strokes of an upright L, but in the wrong positions within the letter. Loss of information concerning within-letter stroke location could lead to misperception that a target was present. I call this the *within-object conjunction* display. Display 5 is the corresponding control. A difference between these two implies that perception of an upright L is more likely when the correct strokes are present, though in the incorrect positions within the letter, than when they are not.

Treisman has been little concerned with the distinction between across-object and within-object conjunctions. It is possible, however, that the visual system deals differently with the spatial arrangement of object parts, and the relative position of whole objects (Hinton & Lang, 1985; McClelland, 1985). Models of word recognition, for example, sometimes assign the letters within a string to perfectly separated "slots," yet suffer cross-talk between simultaneous strings (McClelland, 1985).

Extreme early and late selection theories can also be characterised with respect to displays 1 to 5. If there were no shape information at all without LCS access, then display types 1 to 5 would all be indistinguishable, while if there were information concerning both stroke shape and location, then all would be distinguishable.

Figure 2.2 shows corresponding stimuli for the word target STAB. Loss of information concerning which letters come from which letter string would lead to misperception of the target in a type 2 display, while loss of information concerning where in the string letters were positioned would lead to such misperception in a type 4 display.

These stimulus sets will help to organise the literature on feature conjunction in letter and word perception. I have also used them to carry out comparable studies of: (a) error types in tachistoscopic report; (b) visual search; and (c) priming.

ERRORS IN TACHISTOSCOPIC REPORT

One prediction of feature integration theory concerns what should happen when a person has insufficient time to focus LCS serially on each item of a tachistoscopic display (Treisman & Souther, 1986). Without such serial focusing, there should be uncertainty about how stimulus parts were conjoined in the display. There should be a class of errors termed *illusory conjunctions*: Reports of the correct stimulus parts in the incorrect combinations.

For letters, two studies of across-object conjunctions have given negative results (Butler & Morrison, 1984; Butler, Browse, & Mewhort, Note 1). As long as confusability between individual characters is controlled, there is no evidence that strokes from separate letters recombine to give illusory conjunctions. For within-object conjunctions the case is rather different. Since spatial resolution is not perfect, there must necessarily be cases in which the most common error is a slight misarrangement of strokes actually present. For example, in some fonts the distinction between d and q depends only on whether the loop is towards the bottom or the top of the staff. Arbitrary shortening of the staff will make this distinction arbitrarily difficult. Such an effect has been demonstrated by Chastain (1986).

Different results are obtained with words. Here across-object conjunctions are very common: Errors that are blends of letters actually present in a brief display, but in different words (Allport, 1977; Mozer, 1983). Interestingly, Allport (1977) reported that, when such errors occur, *within-object* location is typically preserved. It is rare, for example, for the last letter of a presented word to appear as the first letter of an error. Though expectations due to chance were not clearly available in this study, the result is important since it is not predicted by feature integration theory. If there has been insufficient time for LCS access, there should be *no* information on the order of a string's letters. Other research suggests that within-string letter location may sometimes be confused in word perception (Johnston & Hale, 1983), though I know of no study comparing such a case (e.g. reporting BCAK as BACK) with the corresponding confusability control (BGHK as BACK).

Feature integration theory also predicts that letters should often be mislocalised in random letter displays. Many studies have confirmed that mislocalisations are common in nonwords, much more common in fact than in words (Estes, 1975; Johnston & Hale, 1983)

Experiments 1 and 2

Two issues are the focus of Experiments 1 and 2. First, under comparable conditions, do letters and words really differ in their production of across-object conjunction errors? Second, can it be confirmed that, when words give such errors, within-string letter location is preserved?

Method.   In Experiment 1, each display consisted of a central digit and a peripheral letter pair, appearing simultaneously. The digit, 16' of arc in height, appeared at fixation. It was either a 1 or a 2. The letters, each 15' × 15', were presented one above the other, separated centre-to-centre by 46'. The pair appeared 54' randomly to left or right of fixation, centred on the horizontal meridian. There were 40 possible letter pairs: the 10 shown in Fig. 2.1, with either member of the pair above, and an equivalent 20 based on the target V rather than L, constructed in exactly the same manner, using strokes of the same length and shape. (To visualise the V stimuli, rotate letters of Fig. 2.1 45° counterclockwise, and close up the angle between strokes to 53°.) The curved lines in Fig. 2.1 are drawn to scale.

On each trial, the subject pressed a foot switch to bring an immediate flash of the stimulus display. The first task was to name aloud the central digit, which was shown for 30msec and not masked. Performance was not scored; this task simply diverted attention from the letters. The second task was to indicate, by pressing one of three keys, whether either target L or V, or no target, had appeared in the periphery. After an exposure duration of 150–180msec, set after the first block of trials to give a probability of target detection between 0.5 and 0.9, the letters were replaced by masks (contour patches similar in size to letters) in the appropriate positions to both sides of fixation. These remained until responses were complete.

Experiment 2 was similar except that the peripheral stimulus was a pair of letter strings (each 16' × 51') like those in Fig. 2.2. Again there were 40 possible pairs, 20 based on the target STAB and an equivalent 20 based on HOPE, formed by replacing every ST with HO and every AB with PE. These materials were chosen so that individual nontarget letters were never confusable with target letters in the same within-string location (based on data in Poulton, 1968). Exposure durations for the letter strings ranged from 200–250msec.

Each of eight subjects served in a single session, with the order of Experiments 1 and 2 counterbalanced. In each experiment there were 5 blocks of 80 trials, the first unscored. Each possible peripheral stimulus appeared twice per block. As in all the present experiments, stimuli were shown on an X–Y display with P24 phosphor.

Results.   The probability of reporting one target (e.g. L) when the display was based on the other (V) was always negligible. Values given are therefore probabilities of reporting the target on which a display was based.

In Experiment 1, the probability of a correct target report (type 1 display, Fig. 2.1) was 0.645. Type 2 and 3 displays gave similar false alarm rates, 0.397 and 0.375 respectively, $F(1,7) = 0.6$. Type 4 and 5 displays gave very much lower rates, 0.049 and 0.047 respectively, again not significantly different, $F(1,7) = 0.1$. The results suggest that individual letters in type 2 and 3 displays were quite confusable with targets, but give no evidence of either across-object or within-object conjunction errors.

In Experiment 2, the probability of correct target report was 0.621. There were many more false alarms with type 2 (0.475) than type 3 (0.275) displays, $F(1,7) = 29.4$, $P < 0.001$. Again type 4 and 5 displays gave very low false alarm rates, 0.012 and 0.004 respectively, not significantly different, $F(1,7) = 1.8$. As suggested by Allport (1977), these results show substantial numbers of across-string conjunction errors, but preservation of within-string letter location.

Discussion.   The results confirm that, while across-object conjunction errors are common for words, they are rare or nonexistent for letters. The explanation may derive from one suggested justification for feature integration theory. In the connectionist perceptual models of Feldman (1985) and others, elementary stimulus features are registered by detectors replicated across all locations in the visual field. Starting from such a scheme, how should complex feature conjunctions be handled? The strategy of connecting a single "conjunction detector" (e.g. for a red circle) to all detectors for the component features (all red detectors and all circle detectors) will not work, since such a detector would be activated even when the components were present at different locations (the cross-talk problem). Yet there are too many complex conjunctions for *their* detectors to be replicated across locations. Feature integration theory offers a solution: A conjunction detector is connected to all detectors for the component features, but inputs are only allowed from one location at a time (serial processing). The present results suggest a compromise: Letter detectors may be replicated across the visual field, avoiding cross-talk even without serial processing; but word detectors may not.

Even for words, however, the results reveal a difficulty for feature integration theory: across-object without within-object conjunction errors. The interesting possibility is that, when cross-talk takes place in word recognition, letters nevertheless are quite accurately tagged for their positions within a string. It is easy to imagine connectionist schemes that would allow this. Note, though, that type 4 displays would only have given false alarms if coding of within-string location had been extremely poor (as predicted by feature integration theory). More work is needed to show exactly how good such coding is under conditions giving across-string cross-talk.

In summary, the results of this section do not suggest a general loss of conjunction information with brief stimulus exposures. Instead they point to a specific problem of cross-talk between letter strings in word recognition.

APPR-C

VISUAL SEARCH

In some visual search tasks, a common experience is that the target "pops out" of the display, nontargets appearing as a blur in the background. The observation suggests that the target draws attention directly to itself; i.e. that nontargets are rejected without gaining access to LCS. Two results support this conclusion. First, in some tasks the time taken to detect a target is almost independent of display size, i.e. the number of nontargets. Second, suppose a subject is asked to decide independently whether targets were present in two separate parts A and B of a brief display. In some tasks, accuracy on part A is much higher when part B contains only nontargets than when it contains a (detected) target (Duncan, 1980; 1985). If attention is drawn to a target in B, the subject is left unsure whether there might also have been one in A.

Visual search results are often taken to suggest either parallel or serial search. It is most unclear, however, that this dichotomy properly describes continuous variations in the effect of display size. Here I shall simply take it that, the smaller the effect, the more efficiently nontargets seem to be rejected without LCS access (Duncan, 1985). As guidelines: In the most efficient cases, effects can be appreciably less than 10msec/item in RT tasks; and in the independent response task, accuracy for part A, given a correct rejection (no target present, no detection response made) for part B, can be as high as accuracy when only part A need be attended.

Previous Findings: Letters

There are many letter search tasks in which the number of nontargets has little if any effect, e.g. search for the target C among nontarget 4s (Egeth, Jonides, & Wall, 1972), or for a tilted T among upright Ts (Beck & Ambler, 1973). This eliminates the extreme early selection view that *no* aspect of stimulus shape can be used (to reject nontargets) without LCS access. There are also, however, tasks in which nontarget rejection is very inefficient, e.g. search for the target R in a display of mixed Ps and Bs (Kleiss & Lane, 1986). Here, late selection theories as they stand (Duncan, 1980) offer no ready explanation.

Feature integration theory predicts that it will be possible to distinguish targets and nontargets without LCS access if the target possesses a unique stroke (e.g. search for R among Ps and Bs). It will not be possible if the target is unique only in its particular *conjunction* of strokes, i.e. if it could be formed by recombining strokes from the nontargets (R among Ps and Qs). That search is indeed more efficient in the former case has been confirmed by Treisman and Gelade (1980) and Duncan (1979). Kleiss and Lane (1986), on the other hand, found very inefficient search in both cases. Indeed, Treisman and Gelade (1980) themselves found by far the most efficient search not simply when the target possessed a unique stroke, but when nontargets were homogeneous (e.g. R among Ps). Many other reported cases of "parallel" search have also used homogeneous nontargets (e.g. Beck & Ambler, 1973; Shiffrin & Gardner, 1972).

This suggests an interesting possibility. If a target is to "pop out" of a display, nontargets must somehow be bundled or grouped together for rejection. This may be easier the more they have in common. Typical conjunction searches then represent an extreme form of nontarget heterogeneity—clearly, the nontargets P and Q each have more in common with the target R than with one another. The difficulty of grouping nontargets together—and the tendency of each to group with the target—may explain the difficulty of these tasks; not that LCS access is needed to establish feature conjunctions.

Several studies (e.g. Beck & Ambler, 1973) have examined within-object conjunctions, using nontargets whose strokes could be rearranged within the letter to form the target (e.g. L among Ts). It has been suggested that the results indicate serial search (Bergen & Julesz, 1983). Most studies, however, have used tasks for which the predictions of a parallel model without capacity limitation are unknown. Humphreys, Riddoch, and Quinlan (1985) found little effect of the number of nontargets (as low as 3msec/item) in search for an inverted T among upright Ts.

Experiments 3, 3a, and 3b investigate: (a) the role of unique target strokes; (b) effects of homogeneity; and (c) within-object conjunctions.

Experiment 3

Method.   Subjects searched letter displays for the target L (two subjects) or V (two subjects). For each subject there were eight tasks, each with a different pair of nontargets, corresponding to (a) and (b) versions of display types 2 to 5 in Fig. 2.1. (For consistency, tasks will be labelled 2a, 2b etc.) For each task there were two forms. In RT forms, displays consisted of 2 or 4 letters like those of Experiment 1, positioned on an imaginary circle of radius 54', centred on fixation. Two-item displays occupied either the 12 and 6 o'clock positions (vertical limb) or 9 and 3 o'clock (horizontal limb). Four-item displays were the union of these two. The target, if present, was randomly placed. Nontargets were chosen randomly and independently. Displays were preceded by a 250msec fixation point, and remained on the screen until response. As quickly as possible, the subject pressed one of two keys to indicate target present (right) or target absent (left). An interval of 750msec preceded onset of the next fixation point.

In independent response forms, a display of four letters was shown on each trial. There were two response keys, one to be pressed for targets detected in the vertical limb, the other for the horizontal. Targets occurred independently in the two limbs, with probability one third each. The trial began when the subject pressed a footswitch. In the *simultaneous* condition, this produced a 400msec fixation point, accompanied for the first 200msec by dots at the centres of the 4 letter locations. The 4-letter display was then presented for a duration of Tmsec (see later), followed at once by a backward mask (4 contour patches like those in Experiment 1) lasting 400msec. The fixation point returned for 1600 + Tmsec, and finally the appearance of an ellipse in the centre of the screen indicated that responses (if any) could be made. One thousand msec later, the screen went blank and the subject was free to initiate the next trial. (Note, however, that to remove time pressure, responses could still be made after the ellipse had vanished.) The *successive* condition was similar except that vertical and horizontal limbs were presented one after the other. At the start of the trial, the 400msec fixation point was accompanied for the first 200msec by only 2 dots, indicating the position of the first limb to be displayed. For two subjects the vertical limb was always first; for the other two, the horizontal. Letters of the first limb were then presented for Tmsec, and masked for 400msec. The fixation point reappeared for a further 400msec, accompanied for 200msec by dots indicating the second limb. Letters of this limb appeared for Tmsec, and in turn were masked for 400msec. An interval of 800msec with only the fixation point present preceded the final appearance of the ellipse indicating that responses could be made.

Each subject served in 10 sessions. Over the first 2, each of the 8 tasks was practised once, with one block of 54 trials for each of the simultaneous and successive conditions of the independent response form, and one block of 40 trials for the RT form. Each of the remaining sessions was devoted to a single task, with task order counterbalanced across subjects. The independent response form was completed first. After 36 trials of practice in each condition, there were 4 experimental blocks, 2 per condition in ABAB or BABA order. Each block had 120 trials, of which the first 12 were discarded. Sixty practice and 120 scored trials of the task's RT form completed the session.

After practice, 2 values of T (exposure duration in independent response forms) were chosen for each subject; one for tasks 2 and 3, the other for tasks 4 and 5. The attempt was to bring probability correct in the successive condition between 0.8 and 0.9. In fact T was always 90msec for tasks 2 and 3, 60–75msec for tasks 4 and 5.

Results.   RT results are presented in the format (h) (i) (s = j), where h and i are mean correct RTs (msec) for two- and four-item displays, and j is the slope of the RT-display size function (msec/item). Individual RTs over 1500msec were excluded from calculations. Values presented are means across a and b versions for each of the tasks 2–5. Since there were no significant slope differences between present and absent responses, values given are means across response type.

Hit and false alarm rates for independent response forms were transformed to the nonparametric sensitivity index A' (Grier, 1971), varying from 0.5 (chance) to 1.0 (perfect). Two scores were always obtained for each limb, one for trials with a concurrent hit (i.e. *on the other limb*, target present and reported), one for trials with a concurrent correct rejection (no target present or reported). In scoring one limb, therefore, trials with an error on the other limb were ignored (Duncan, 1980; 1985). Values presented are means across limbs (horizontal, vertical) and task versions (a, b). The presentation format is (simultaneous = k/l) (successive = m/n), where k,m are scores given a concurrent hit, l,n are scores given a concurrent correct rejection.

RT results were very similar for the across-object conjunction task 2— (512) (594) (s = 41)—and its control task 3—(522) (590) (s = 34). The large effect of display size was significant, $F(1,3) = 30.3$, $P < 0.02$, while the interaction with task was not, $F(1,3) = 0.3$. A' results were also similar for task 2—(simultaneous = 0.80/0.81) (successive = 0.87/0.87)—and task 3— Simultaneous = 0.78/0.82) (successive = 0.89/0.91). The only significant effect was the overall difference between simultaneous and successive conditions, $F(1,3) = 10.0$, $P \simeq 0.05$, showing that both limbs were less accurately perceived when the two were presented together. Since, in the simultaneous condition, there was no effect of concurrent event (hit vs. correct rejection), it does not appear that nontargets could be rejected without LCS access.

In RTs there was a substantial difference between the within-object conjunction task 4—(512) (591) (s = 40)—and its control task 5—(467) (498) (s = 16). There were significant effects of both display size, $F(1,3) = 48.2$, $P < 0.01$, and its interaction with task, $F(1,3) = 10.8$, $P < 0.05$. Note that even for task 5, however, a slope of 16msec/item does not suggest a particularly efficient rejection of nontargets. A' results showed a similar pattern: task 4— (simultaneous = 0.87/0.84) (successive = 0.94/0.93)—harder than task 5— (simultaneous = 0.93/0.93) (successive = 0.97/0.96). The difference between simultaneous and successive conditions was significant, $F(1,3) = 12.1$, $P < 0.05$, as was its interaction with task, $F(1,3) = 13.1$, $P < 0.05$. Again there was no effect of concurrent event, suggesting no rejection of nontargets without LCS access.

In RT forms, error rate was always below 10%, and error data gave no reason to doubt conclusions based on RTs. In independent response forms, the bias parameter B' always lay between 1.0 and 3.0. In these respects results were similar in all the search studies to be reported.

Discussion.   None of the results suggested rejection of nontargets without LCS access. As reported by Kleiss and Lane (1986), search is inefficient with heterogeneous nontargets quite similar to the target.

Two questions may be raised. Although in task 3 the target had a unique stroke, it was unique only in curvature. Would results be different with a stroke unique instead in its position within the letter (c.f. Treisman & Gelade, 1980)? Second, was poor performance in task 4 due only to the presence of a nontarget whose strokes could be rearranged to form the target? Would results be different if *all* nontargets were rotated Ls?

Experiments 3a and 3b

In these experiments the target letter was always L, and only RT forms were used. Figure 2.3 shows nontargets for each of two groups of subjects in Experiment 3a. Each subject had five tasks, two (*heterogeneous*) with a pair of nontargets, three (*homogeneous*) with only one. In the *conjunction* task, strokes from the two different nontargets could combine to form the target,

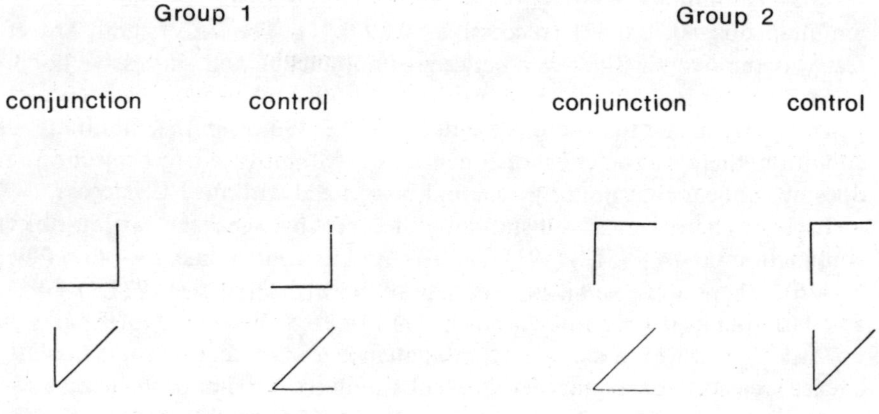

FIG. 2.3.   Nontargets in Experiment 3a.

while in the *control* task, the target had one stroke unique in terms of its position within the letter. The three letters used in homogeneous tasks were the same three used in that subject's conjunction and control tasks. Figure 2.4 shows nontargets for the three heterogeneous tasks of Experiment 3b. In

location and   curvature   location
curvature   alone   alone

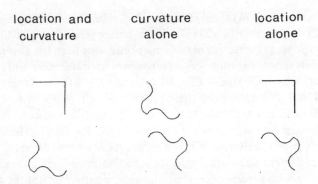

FIG. 2.4.   Nontargets in Experiment 3b.

one of these, one nontarget differed from the target on the basis of within-letter stroke location, the other on the basis of curvature. In the other two, both nontargets differed from the target in the same respect. In total these tasks involved three different nontargets (Fig. 2.4), which were also used in an additional three homogeneous tasks.

Method.   Displays contained 2, 4, or 8 letters, each 15′ × 15′. They were placed on the perimeter of an imaginary circle (radius 54′) centred on fixation, except that, to break up display regularity, each was moved randomly up or down, and randomly left or right, by one half the length of a letter stroke. Ignoring this, there were eight possible letter positions on the perimeter. A randomly-selected arc of adjacent positions was used for two- and four-letter displays. On each trial, the display appeared when a foot switch was pressed, and remained until the response. Between trials there was a blank interval of 750msec.

Experiments 3a and 3b each involved six subjects, each attending for three sessions of about an hour. (In Experiment 3a, three subjects were assigned to group 1 [Fig. 2.3], three to group 2. One subject whose RTs were frequently over 1500msec was replaced.) There were 144 trials per task in the first session, 216 per task in remaining sessions. Task order was counterbalanced across subjects. Scores were based on the last 144 trials per task in the third session.

Results.   In Experiment 3a, homogeneous tasks with arrow nontargets gave (439) (445) (455) (s = 2.7), while rotated L nontargets gave (474) (495) (530) (s = 9.3). There was a significant effect of display size, $F(2,10) = 12.2$, $P < 0.005$, but no interaction with nontarget type, $F(2,10) = 2.6$. The conjunction task gave (474) (520) (608) (s = 22), while the heterogeneous control gave (482) (531) (608) (s = 21). In both heterogeneous tasks the slope for present responses (14msec/item) was markedly less than for absents (29msec/item). Analysis of variance on heterogeneous data gave only significant effects of display size, $F(2,10) = 83.5$, $P < 0.001$, target presence, $F(1,5) = 124.6$, $P < 0.001$, and their interaction, $F(2,10) = 19.6$, $P < 0.001$. A final analysis confirmed that the overall interaction between homogeneity and display size was significant, $F(2,10) = 109.7$, $P < 0.001$. The results show that search is relatively easy when nontargets are homogeneous, even when their strokes might be rearranged within the letter to form a target. Search is much harder with heterogeneous nontargets, whether or not the target has a unique stroke.

In Experiment 3b, homogeneous tasks showed little effect of display size whether the nontarget was a rotated L—(421) (439) (467) (s = 7.4)—a curved L—(439) (458) (473) (s = 5.5)—or both rotated and curved—(401) (410) (413) (s = 1.9). There was a significant effect of display size, $F(2,10) = 36.9$, $P < 0.001$, but no interaction with task, $F(4,20) = 1.9$. In heterogeneous tasks, there was again little effect of display size if both nontargets differed from the target in the same respect, either within-letter stroke location—(426) (453) (470) (s = 6.9)—or curvature—(419) (442) (457) (s = 6.1). As in the main Experiment 3, however, there was a large effect—(465) (507) (579) (s = 18.9)—when one nontarget differed in stroke location, the other in curvature. Analysis of heterogeneous data showed significant effects of both display size, $F(2,10) = 49.7$, $P < 0.001$, and its interaction with task, $F(4,20) = 16.8$, $P < 0.001$. The results confirm that search is easiest when nontargets have a common property distinguishing them from the target.

Discussion.   The results offer little support for feature integration theory, at least if the primitive letter feature is taken to be the stroke. Most important, homogeneous nontargets allow efficient search even if strokes could be rearranged within the letter to form the target. In other work involving search for L among rotated Ls, I have found a slope of only 4.7msec/item. Contrary to the suggestion of Bergen and Julesz (1983), serial processing is not always needed to establish the spatial arrangement of letter strokes. Second, search is much poorer with heterogeneous nontargets, whether or not the target has a unique stroke. More work is needed to establish *when* a unique stroke is helpful.

Another possibility is that the primitive feature is not the stroke but the stroke attribute. An account of at least some results could be given if primitives were *curvature* and *within-letter location*. Poor performance would be expected whenever nontargets contained at least some straight strokes, and at least some in all the target's stroke locations. In this respect the contrasting results of Experiments 1 and 3 are important. According to this revised form of feature integration theory, type 4 is a prototypical conjunction display: one nontarget has strokes matching the target in curvature, the other has strokes matching in location. In Experiment 1 there was no evidence for illusory conjunctions, whereas in Experiment 3, search through type 4 displays was very poor. The contrast suggests an explanation specific to search.

Tentatively, I have suggested that conjunction displays may cause difficulties in search not because the attributes of different nontargets might recombine to form the target, but because there is an extreme form of nontarget heterogeneity—nontargets are each more similar to the target than to one another. The results show that search is very efficient if nontargets are physically identical, and sometimes simply if they have a common property distinguishing them from the target (Experiment 3b). In general it may be that search efficiency increases continuously with increasing nontarget similarity.

Of the theoretical positions outlined earlier, letter search results are most consistent with late selection. If the structure of the task allows nontargets to be bundled together for rejection, efficient search can be based on either stroke shape or within-letter stroke location.

Previous Findings: Words

The few reported studies of word search present a simple picture. Even if target and nontargets share no letters, there is a large effect of display size (Flowers & Lohr, 1985; Karlin & Bower, 1976). Search is even slower when there *are* shared letters, especially if they are in the same positions within the word (Flowers & Lohr, 1985). All results, however, are most consistent with early selection, suggesting that parallel processes cannot distinguish one letter string from another.

Experiment 4

Experiment 4 examined word search under conditions comparable to those of Experiment 3.

Method.   The only change from Experiment 3 was the use of words rather than letters. Targets were STAB (two subjects) and HOPE (two subjects). Nontargets for STAB appear in Fig. 2.2. Those for HOPE were equivalent. In independent response task forms, exposure duration T was set to 60msec for all subjects in tasks 2 and 3, 40–60msec in task 4 and 5.

Results.   In RTs, both tasks 2—(597) (793) (s = 98)—and 3—(525) (617) (s = 46)—showed large effects of display size, $F(1,3) = 16.6$, $P < 0.05$, especially task 2, $F(1,3) = 12.6$, $P < 0.05$ for the interaction. In A', both tasks 2—(simultaneous = 0.67/0.77) (successive = 0.90/0.92)—and 3—(simultaneous = 0.69/0.84) (successive = 0.92/0.93)—showed large differences between simultaneous and successive conditions, $F(1,3) = 135.0$, $P < 0.005$, and, in the simultaneous condition, a large effect of concurrent event, $F(1,3) = 40.4$, $P < 0.01$ for the main effect, $F(1,3) = 15.2$, $P < 0.05$ for the interaction with condition. In short, while simultaneous presentation was always harmful, the lowest accuracy on one limb was associated with hits on the other.

The picture was similar for tasks 4 and 5. In RTs, both tasks 4—(548) (647) (s = 50)—and 5—(478) (536) (s = 29)—showed large effects of display size, $F(1,3) = 9.1$, $P < 0.06$ for the main effect, $F(1,3) = 9.4$, $P < 0.06$ for the interaction with task. In A', both tasks 4—(simultaneous = 0.79/0.88) (successive = 0.96/0.95)—and 5—(simultaneous = 0.83/0.92) (successive = 0.97/0.98)—showed large differences between simultaneous and successive conditions, $F(1,3) = 64.9$, $P < 0.01$, especially task 4, $F(1,3) = 12.6$, $P < 0.05$ for the interaction. Again there was a suggestion that, in the simultaneous condition, performance was worse with a concurrent hit, $F(1,3) = 8.2$, $P < 0.07$ for the main effect of concurrent event, $F(1,3) = 6.8$, $P < 0.1$ for the interaction with condition.

Discussion.   Certainly unique target letters are helpful in word search. Work is also needed on nontarget homogeneity. As they stand, however, the results give no hint of parallel processing even in the easiest cases. It seems likely that, in this respect, word search is very different from letter search.

A possible explanation is suggested by the A' results. Even nontargets make demands on *some* limited capacity system in word processing, since even with a concurrent correct rejection, there is a large difference between simultaneous and successive conditions. Some additional demand, however, is associated with detection of a target. A possible explanation is that two successive limited capacity systems are involved in word recognition. The first deals unselectively with targets and nontargets, while the second takes only targets. I shall return to this possibility later.

PRIMING FROM UNATTENDED STIMULI

What happens when a stimulus is deliberately ignored? One possibility is that access to LCS is denied, i.e. "attention" is withheld. This seems especially likely when a person denies knowledge of stimulus identity.

Attempts to determine the fate of unattended stimuli often rest on some form of priming effect. Priming refers rather loosely to the influence one stimulus (the prime) may have on processing another. Unattended stimuli produce some effects but not others. For example, it can be easier to identify a brief stimulus when another, ignored, stimulus, presented at about the same time, is related in meaning (Allport, 1977; Humphreys, 1981). On the other hand, diverting attention from a printed word substantially reduces the Stroop effect (Kahneman & Henik, 1981). Unattended peripheral words produce little or no bias in the interpretation chosen for a centrally fixated homograph (Inhoff & Rayner, 1980). It is hard to integrate these results. Some differences may be due to altered presentation conditions. Some may concern distinctions between different "priming" effects, since little is known in detail about these influences of one stimulus on another. One may conclude no more than that, under some conditions, there is functional access to the meaning of an unattended stimulus.

Experiments 5 and 6

The strongest evidence that a prime is successfully ignored comes when it cannot be reported. Two points arise. First, the prime should be unreportable because it was ignored, not just because of the exposure conditions (e.g. masking). Second, criteria for what is unreportable vary in strength. Asking subjects about primes at the end of the session (Allport, 1977), or accepting trials on which the subject is unwilling to say what the prime was (Bradshaw, 1974), may strongly be influenced by response bias. The best criterion is probably forced-choice recognition. Experiments 5 and 6 sought to demonstrate priming effects when, through inattention, forced-choice prime recognition was at chance. Under these circumstances, do priming effects depend only on the stimulus parts present in a display, or also on how they are conjoined?

Method.   In Experiment 5, displays contained a central letter L or V, like those used before, and a peripheral pair of priming letters, randomly to left or right, exactly like the letter pairs of Experiment 1. The three letters appeared simultaneously when a foot switch was pressed. A mask in the central position followed after a variable exposure duration, while peripheral masks on both sides always appeared after 72msec. Masks, the same contour patches used before, remained until response. After a blank interval of 2sec, the fixation point appeared for the next trial.

On a random ten elevenths of trials, subjects pressed one of two centrally positioned keys to indicate which letter had been seen in the centre. On the remaining one eleventh of trials, the masking display was accompanied by bars above and below the four peripheral letter positions. The central response was then withheld, and one of two peripherally positioned keys was pressed to indicate whether an L or V had been seen in the periphery. On such trials, the peripheral letter pair was always type 1 (Fig. 2.1); i.e. an L or V was really present. Subjects were asked always to ignore the peripheral letters except when the bars appeared with the masks; then to think back and see whether they had any idea what the peripheral letter could have been. Thus general inattention to primes was accompanied by an occasional forced-choice test of their recognition.

Each of 16 subjects served in a single session. After about 40 practice trials, exposure duration for the central letter was fixed between 24 and 72msec, in an attempt to bring probability correct between 0.75 and 0.90. There were 8 experimental blocks, each containing 8 trials calling for a peripheral response mixed among 80 calling for a central response. Among the former 8 trials, identities of central and peripheral letters were determined randomly. Among the latter 80 trials, each possible combination of central letter and peripheral letter pair (see Experiment 1) occurred once. In a final block of 80 trials, subjects were asked to pay attention to and report only the peripheral stimulus.

Experiment 6 was similar, using the standard set of letter string stimuli based on STAB and HOPE. Exposure duration for the central word varied from 24–48msec.

Results.   For each subject two peripheral report scores were obtained, "unattended" (based on the 64 peripheral report trials of the main experiment) and "attended" (based on the last 64 trials of the final block). Subjects were excluded from further analysis if their number of correct unattended reports lay outside the range 25–39. One subject (number correct = 47) was excluded from Experiment 5, two (number correct = 40 each) from Experiment 6. Among the remainder, mean proportion correct on unattended trials was 0.518 (9/15 subjects above 0.500) in Experiment 5, 0.509 (7/14) in Experiment 6. In each experiment, proportion correct was significantly higher on attended trials, 0.703 (15/15) in Experiment 5, 0.590 (12/14) in Experiment 6. Thus performance was only at chance on unattended trials because stimuli were deliberately ignored.

Error proportions in identifying the central stimulus appear in Table 2.1. In Experiment 5, each target L or V could be accompanied by a prime based on the same letter (congruent) or the alternative (incongruent). Performance was always substantially better with congruent primes, $F(1,15) = 11.5$, $P < 0.005$. In addition there was a significant interaction between congruence and prime type (1 to 5), $F(4,56) = 8.5$, $P < 0.001$. For congruent primes. Newman-Keuls tests showed significant differences ($P < 0.05$) between type 4 primes and each of types 1 and 3. For incongruent primes, types 1 to 3 all differed from types 4 and 5 ($P < 0.005$ in each case). (Note that even type 5 primes contained forms more similar to the congruent than to the incongruent target.) In sum, prime forms resembling the incongruent target were always harmful, especially when both were upright.

TABLE 2.1
Experiments 5 and 6: Error Proportions in Identifying the Central Stimulus

| | | Prime Type | | | |
| | Target Present (1) | Across-object | | Within-object | |
		Conjunction (2)	Control (3)	Conjunction (4)	Control (5)
Letters					
Prime Congruent	0.118	0.134	0.122	0.164	0.151
Prime Incongruent	0.280	0.286	0.286	0.224	0.225
Words					
Prime Congruent	0.146	0.134	0.157	0.161	0.150
Prime Incongruent	0.210	0.212	0.198	0.180	0.136

Experiment 6 again produced a substantial effect of congruence, $F(1,13) = 25.0$, $P < 0.001$. Effects of prime type, $F(4,52) = 3.1$, $P < 0.05$, and the interaction, $F(4,52) = 4.2$, $P < 0.005$, were also significant. Newman-Keuls tests showed no significant differences among congruent primes, but among incongruent primes, type 5 differed from each of the others ($P < 0.05$ or better). In sum, letters in the prime that were incongruent with the target were harmful, while letters that were congruent were no better than neutral controls.

Very similar results were obtained considering only the data for subjects whose unattended peripheral report score was at or below 0.500. The following analysis is also instructive. For each subject, there were 64 central report trials with a type 1 prime, i.e. a prime actually containing the congruent or incongruent target. The probability that the response on these trials (ostensibly a *central* report) would agree with the *peripheral* stimulus (0.599 and 0.534 respectively for letters and words) was actually greater than the probability of a correct response when ostensible report of the peripheral stimulus was required, significantly so for letters, $F(1,15) = 6.9$, $P < 0.02$. (To avoid bias, even subjects excluded from other analyses were included here.) Thus there was more information concerning the peripheral stimulus in central than in peripheral reports.

Discussion.   On the whole, priming in these experiments depended more on the stimulus parts in a display than on their conjunctions. Incongruent strokes (Experiment 5) or letters (Experiment 6) were harmful whether or not they were all contained in the same object (compare primes 1 and 2), and whether or not in total they could combine to form a whole target (compare primes 2 and 3). The one exception is an influence of within-letter stroke location (compare primes 1 and 4).

Such results suggest a lower-level effect than others based on either stimulus meaning (Allport, 1977; Humphreys, 1981) or preserved within-string letter location (Humphreys, Quinlan, & Evett, 1983). As already discussed, we may be dealing here with differences between presentation conditions, and in particular between criteria for unreportability. Alternatively an unattended stimulus may produce multiple priming effects, exerted simultaneously at multiple levels. We need work directly comparing different presentation conditions and different priming effects.

CONCLUSIONS

I have pointed to various difficulties for feature integration theory. When presentation time is short, there is no general loss of information concerning the arrangement of stimulus parts. Instead there is a specific difficulty of cross-talk between letter strings, perhaps preserving within-string letter location. Visual search with letters can be largely parallel, at least when nontargets are homogeneous. This applies even when nontarget strokes might be rearranged within the letter to form a target. Letter search is much less efficient with heterogeneous nontargets, even if the target has a unique stroke. Word search never suggests parallel processing. Less definite conclusions can be drawn for priming, since different priming effects have largely been studied under different conditions. The present work shows that, even when a peripheral stimulus cannot be identified, priming preserves within-letter stroke location.

Early and late selection theories also face difficulties. For example, early selection deals better with word search, while late selection deals better with letter search.

The results suggest we may need a more complex alternative, dealing directly with the differences between letters and words, and with processes that are specific to particular experimental tasks. To speculate: Letter perception may involve only a late limited capacity system, concerning admittance of chosen material to awareness. Prior to this, there may be quite detailed letter "recognition," in that letter identity is functionally available to guide LCS access. In visual search, however, the selection process governing access may be efficient only when nontargets are grouped together by some common property; at least, perhaps, when targets and nontargets are otherwise quite similar. For words, there is preliminary evidence of two successive limited capacity systems. The second may be the late system involved in awareness. The first may be an earlier process dealing serially with letter strings to avoid cross-talk. In this respect, for words (and more complex objects in general?), both feature integration theory and late selection theory may be partly correct.

The priming effects shown here would seem to be very early in such a system, depending as they do on stimulus parts rather than wholes. Of course, other work suggests that there may be other, later effects too (Allport, 1977; Humphreys, 1981).

Such proposals must be considered extremely tentative. What is clear, however, is that something at least this complex is implied by the heterogeneity of the data I have considered.

REFERENCES

Allport, D. A. (1977). On knowing the meaning of words we are unable to report: The effects of visual masking. In S. Dornic (Ed.), *Attention and performance VI*. Hillsdale, N.J.: Lawrence Erlbaum Associates Inc., 505–533.

Beck, J. & Ambler, B. (1973). The effects of concentrated and distributed attention on peripheral acuity. *Perception and Psychophysics, 14*, 225–230.

Bergen, J. R. & Julesz, B. (1983). Parallel versus serial processing in rapid pattern discrimination. *Nature, London, 303*, 696–698.

Bradshaw, J. L. (1974). Peripherally presented and unreported words may bias the perceived meaning of a centrally fixated homograph. *Journal of Experimental Psychology, 103*, 1200–1202.

Broadbent, D. E. (1971). *Decision and stress*. London: Academic Press.

Butler, B. E. & Morrison, I. R. (1984). Do letter features migrate? A note of caution. *Psychological Research, 46*, 223–236.

Chastain, G. (1986). Evidence for feature perturbations from letter misidentifications. *Perception and Psychophysics, 39*, 301–306.

Deutsch, J. A. & Deutsch, D. (1963). Attention: Some theoretical considerations. *Psychological Review, 70*, 80–90.

Duncan, J. (1979). Divided attention: The whole is more than the sum of its parts. *Journal of Experimental Psychology: Human Perception and Performance, 5*, 216–228.

Duncan, J. (1980). The locus of interference in the perception of simultaneous stimuli. *Psychological Review, 87*, 272–300.

Duncan, J. (1985). Visual search and visual attention. In M. I. Posner & O. S. M. Marin (Eds.), *Attention and performance XI*. Hillsdale, N.J.: Lawrence Erlbaum Associates Inc., 85–105.

Egeth, H., Jonides, J., & Wall, S. (1972). Parallel processing of multi-element displays. *Cognitive Psychology, 3*, 674–698.

Estes, W. (1975). The locus of inferential and perceptual processes in letter identification. *Journal of Experimental Psychology: General, 104*, 122–145.

Feldman, J. A. (1985). Four frames suffice: A provisional model of vision and space. *The Behavioural and Brian Sciences, 8*, 265–289.

Flowers, J. H., & Lohr, D. L. (1985). How does familiarity affect visual search for letter strings? *Perception and Psychophysics, 37*, 557–566.

Grier, J. B. (1971). Nonparametric indices for sensitivity and bias: Computing formulas. *Psychological Bulletin, 75*, 424–429.

Hinton, G. E. & Lang, K. J. (1985). Shape recognition and illusory conjunctions. *Proceedings of the Ninth International Joint Conference on Artificial Intelligence*, 252–259.

Humphreys, G. W. (1981). Direct vs. indirect tests of the information available from masked displays: What visual masking does and does not prevent. *British Journal of Psychology, 72*, 322–330.

Humphreys, G. W., Quinlan, P. T., & Evett, L. J. (1983). Automatic orthographic priming: Implications for processing orthography. *The working papers of the London Psycholinguistic Research Group, 5*, 48–55.

Humphreys, G. W., Riddoch, M. J., & Quinlan, P. T. (1985). Interactive processes in perceptual organisation: Evidence from visual agnosia. In M. I. Posner & O. S. M. Marin (Eds.) *Attention and performance XI*. Hillsdale, N. J.: Lawrence Erlbaum Associates Inc., 301–318.

Inhoff, A. W. & Rayner, K. (1980). Parafoveal word perception: A case against semantic preprocessing. *Perception and Psychophysics, 27*, 457–464.

Johnston, J. C. & Hale, B. L. (1983). *Resolving letter-position uncertainty in words* (Technical Memorandum). Murray Hill, N.J.: Bell Laboratories.

Kahneman, D. & Henik, A. (1981). Perceptual organisation and attention. In M. Kubovy & J. R. Pomerantz (Eds.), *Perceptual organisation*. Hillsdale, N. J.: Lawrence Erlbaum Associates Inc., 181–211.

Karlin, M. B. & Bower, G. H. (1976). Semantic category effects in visual word search. *Perception and Psychophysics, 19*, 417–424.

Kleiss, J. A. & Lane, D. M. (1986). Locus and persistence of capacity limitations in visual information processing. *Journal of Experimental Psychology: Human Perception and Performance, 12*, 200–210.

McClelland, J. L. (1985). Putting knowledge in its place: A scheme for programming parallel processing structures on the fly. *Cognitive Science, 9*, 113–146.

Mozer, M. C. (1983). Letter migration in word perception. *Jourr ⸱ of Experimental Psychology: Human Perception and Performance, 9*, 531–546.

Neisser, U. (1967). *Cognitive Psychology*. New York: Appleton-Century-Crofts.

Poulton, E. C. (1968). The measurement of legibility. *Printing Technology, 12*, 2–6.

Shiffrin, R. M. & Gardner, G. T. (1972). Visual processing capacity and attentional control. *Journal of Experimental Psychology, 93*, 72–83.

Treisman, A. M. & Gelade, G. (1980). A feature integration theory of attention. *Cognitive Psychology, 12*, 97–136.

Treisman, A. M. & Souther, J. (1986). Illusory words: The roles of attention and of top-down constraints in conjoining letters to form words. *Journal of Experimental Psychology: Human Perception and Performance, 12*, 3–17.

REFERENCE NOTE

1. Butler, B. E., Browse, R. A., & Mewhort, D. J. K.   (1986, June).   *Do letter features migrate? It depends on the task.* Paper presented at the meeting of the Canadian Psychological Association, Toronto.

3 Attentional Issues in the Identification of Alphanumeric Characters

Harold Pashler
University of California
San Diego, U.S.A.
Peter C. Badgio
The Institute of Pennsylvania Hospital
Pennsylvania, U.S.A.

ABSTRACT

Can alphanumeric characters be identified in parallel, or must they be identified sequentially? Previous experimental work on this issue has typically employed tasks in which subjects attempt to detect pre-specified target characters. Unfortunately, such tasks do not logically require either character identification or accurate conjoining of features. The present experiments used a task designed to force exhaustive identification of digits—naming the highest digit in an array of digits—and also a detection task involving stimuli selected to require accurate feature conjunction. Subjects' accuracy in simultaneous versus rapidly successive presentations of briefly exposed characters was compared. The effects of predictability and order of presentation sequences were also examined. None of these variables produced the effects one would expect if character identification was operating sequentially. We argue that evidence for parallel identification, such as that presented here, does not have particularly direct implications for the issues of capacity limitations, voluntary attentional control, and early versus late selection, although these issues are commonly conflated. The independence of these issues is emphasised by contrasting the present results with a number of earlier findings; the contrast also leads us to a conception of how visual selective attention might operate that is rather different from the traditional early or late selection accounts.

INTRODUCTION

Skilled reading involves co-ordinated and flexible processing of information at a variety of levels, ranging from the early visual system all the way to high-level comprehension processes. It is often useful in attempting to understand very complex mechanisms to start by trying to characterise their basic performance limitations. In this article, we shall consider the limitations on one of the important basic components of reading: identification of letters and digits. The limitations that arise in the visual identification of multiple familiar objects in general has been a focus of research in human information processing since its inception. It is widely believed that simple visual features can be extracted in parallel. It is often hypothesised, however, that processing of familiar stimuli to the point of *identification* requires that some single mechanism—often equated with "attention," or, more recently, "visual attention"—must scan the objects, dealing with them one at a time. Another approach maintains that multiple objects can be identified in parallel (possibly subject to capacity limitations of some kind). This issue has not proven easy to resolve, and strong disagreement persists (see, e.g., Kahneman & Treisman, 1984; Posner, 1982). In the present article, we present new evidence relating to the question of whether identification of alphanumeric characters must proceed serially. Then, in the discussion, it is argued that the parallel/serial issue must be distinguished clearly from some related questions with which it is frequently conflated in theoretical discussions of attention. We argue for the importance of these distinctions on the basis of results from several different experimental tasks we have investigated in the last several years, results which would appear paradoxical if the various questions are tied together as they have been in the traditional approaches.

For the purpose of this discussion, the term *identification* will be used to refer to the mental processes which derive a description of an object as a token of a specific, learned category or type. The context will usually imply what categorisation is intended; thus, to identify a letter implies achieving a description which represents it as an instance of a particular one of the 26 letters of the alphabet.[1] Previous theorising about attentional limits on character identification has mostly been based on results from the visual search task, and strong arguments for parallel identification have been proposed. Some of these results pertain to response times in speeded visual search for characters: Relatively flat slopes in certain experiments, and patterns of facilitation from redundant targets (e.g. Egeth, Jonides, & Wall, 1972; van der Heijden, 1975). Probably the strongest argument in favour of parallel stimulus identification, however, comes from the work of Eriksen and Spencer (1969) and Shiffrin and Gardner (1972), comparing detection accuracy in simultaneously and successively displayed arrays of characters.

In the Shiffrin and Gardner study, subjects made a forced-choice judge-

---

[1]The more common terms "encoding" and "recognition" will be avoided; the former because it has acquired a much broader meaning than that intended here (e.g. in episodic memory research), the latter because it is most commonly used to refer to paradigms requiring the subject to decide if an item was presented before in the experiment.

ment about whether a T or an F was contained in a brief display, consisting of four items, preceded and followed by masks. The stimulus onset asychrony (SOA) between each item and its respective mask was sufficiently short that overall performance was well below ceiling. In the successive displays (Experiment 3), there was a 500msec interval between 2 frames, each containing half of the items in the array. The mask SOA was the same in the successive and simultaneous conditions. The major finding of the study was that accuracy was no better when the four elements were exposed successively rather than simultaneously. In short, while subjects' performance was impaired by the fact that the masks restricted the time available to process each item, it was not affected by whether all of the items had to be processed at the same time. The results speak directly against the involvement of serial visual processes in this task. The reasoning is quite simple: If the items were being scanned serially, then the successive presentation of the displays should have increased the time available for processing each item, improving performance.[2] On the other hand, if the items are processed in independent parallel channels, then the simultaneity of presentation should not affect performance at all.

Eriksen and Spencer (1969) earlier reported essentially the same finding, in studies that limited accuracy by restricting exposure duration, without using masks. The result has now been replicated several times (e.g. Duncan, 1980b) and is frequently cited as the major evidence in favour of parallel character identification (e.g. Posner, 1982). The comparable performance in simultaneous and successive displays argues not only against serial processing, but also against any model suggesting that the efficiency of character identification depends upon a capacity subject to voluntary reallocation (this class of models overlaps the set of parallel models; see, e.g., Rumelhart, 1970). If subjects were capable of reallocating capacity to facilitate processing at desired locations, then they should derive some benefit from the successive presentations. Since the Shiffrin and Gardner work provided 500msec ISIs between the two successive frames, it seems reasonable to assume that there was sufficient time for *any* putative capacity reallocation to occur.

The studies cited above provide evidence for parallel, and possibly capacity-free, stimulus processing in visual search. However, reasonable doubts can be raised as to the nature of the stimulus processing in search tasks, calling into question the standard interpretation of the simultaneous/successive result, and other results suggesting parallel processing in visual

---

[2]This approach makes an assumption: That the masks rapidly terminate the identification process. This does *not* depend upon the claim that the mask operates by interruption rather than integration (Turvey, 1973). Nor does it assume that the mask terminates processing instantaneously. What is assumed is simply that a mask degrades the information available for identification quickly, relative to the rate of any putative serial scanning process.

search. Various authors have pointed out that detecting a target might perfectly well be accomplished with mechanisms quite different from those that would be employed actually to *identify* each element in a display, as that term was defined earlier (e.g. Eriksen & Collins, 1969; Rabbitt, 1978; van der Heijden, 1975). Strictly speaking, the search task requires that target and distractors be discriminated *from each other*, but it doesn't require the system to compute a description of each item *for what it is* (e.g. what letter or digit it is), as required by the term identification. Several writers have suggested that while visual search may proceed in parallel, character identification requires sequential processing. Eriksen and Collins (1969) made the most explicit proposals along these lines. They suggested that while visual search is based upon a parallel "filtering" operation which merely screens out distractors without identifying anything, genuine identification requires sequential scanning at rates an order of magnitude slower than those suggested by slopes observed in visual search tasks. Treisman and Gelade (1980) raised a related but not identical possibility: Many search tasks may require only the detection of a single visual feature present in the target, but absent in the distractors, without requiring accurate conjunction of the features present together in any given location. The concern that identification is being bypassed becomes especially acute with well-practised search tasks, which is where the arguments for parallel search are strongest (Shiffrin, in press). After extensive practice one might reasonably suspect that the system would develop special purpose routines adapted to perform the minimum discriminations necessary to distinguish target from background, without identifying anything (a view advocated by Rabbitt, 1978).

How can one be sure, then, that a subject actually identifies the elements in the display? Tasks requiring report of multiple items can serve this purpose, but they also create decision and memory demands beyond those of the visual search task (cf. Duncan, 1980a); Estes and Taylor (1964) originally introduced the visual search task specifically to minimise these factors. What is needed, then, is a task which has the easy response selection and low memory demands of visual search, while forcing the system actually to identify the stimuli. After investigating a number of possibilities, we found that the task of naming the highest digit in an array of digits seems to meet these specifications. In an earlier article (Pashler & Badgio, 1985), we reported two main findings from experiments involving speeded naming of the highest digit in an array. The first was that the slope relating these RTs to the number of digits in the display was remarkably shallow. The slopes were in the range of 20–40msec/item, which is not much steeper than typical target-absent responses in presence/absence search for a single pre-specified character target. The second observation was that the effect of increasing the number of digits in the display was additive with the effect of visually degrading the digits (the latter accomplished either by reducing display contrast or by superimposing patches of dots over the stimuli). Assuming that these visual degradation effects slow down the identification of the stimuli (Miller, 1979) the data provide a straightforward indication that the stimulus identification is operating in parallel. If it were serial, a multiplicative interaction should have occurred: The effect of degradation should have been added onto the total RT once for each additional element in the display.

This interpretation is intuitively compelling, but it is not invulnerable to alternative accounts (cf. Pashler & Badgio, 1985). In the present experiments, converging evidence for our rejection of serial identification models is sought by using the highest-digit task—to require stimulus identification—and comparing accuracy with simultaneous and successive displays. The principal goal is to test the serial processing hypothesis further, rather than to assess the existence of capacity limits. If digits are processed serially in the highest digit task, this processing must occur at least as fast as one item per 20–40msec, given the slopes just cited. Such a rapid serial process should yield successive advantages with rapid successive presentations, i.e., very short or zero interframe intervals. In employing this form of successive presentations, the present experiments depart from the procedures of Eriksen and Spencer and Shiffrin and Gardner, and therefore do not attempt to address the possibility that capacity reallocation may be feasible on a longer time scale than that permitted by the rapid successive exposures.

EXPERIMENT 1

In the first experiment, subjects reported the identity and location of the highest digit in a square array of four digits, which were flanked by pre- and post-masks to produce an intermediate level of accuracy. The experiment compares accuracy in displays in which all the items are exposed simultaneously with displays in which one diagonal is exposed and, immediately upon its termination, the other diagonal is exposed (in a predictable order).

Method

Subjects.   Twelve undergraduate students participated as subjects in the experiment, in return for payment.

Apparatus and Stimuli.   The stimuli were presented in white on an Amdek Color-I Monitor, controlled by a microcomputer. Subjects' responses were made by pressing keys on the microcomputer keyboard. Each digit measured 0.71 by 0.40cm height and width (0.68 deg by 0.38 deg visual angle, based on a typical viewing distance of 60cm). On each trial, the highest digit was selected at random from the digits three through seven. (The digits eight and nine were omitted, because they are fairly difficult to discriminate in the character set employed). The distractors were chosen randomly (with replacement) from the range zero to one less than the highest on any particular trial. Each pre- and post-mask character consisted of a checkerboard pattern (0.79 by 0.64cm). The display of four characters was arrayed as a square 3.02cm by 3.17cm overall height and width (2.9 by 3.0 deg).

Design. The experiment was divided into 10 blocks of 30 trials (in addition to the practice block described below). The simultaneous vs. successive manipulation was blocked, and blocks of each type alternated.

Procedure. Stimulus timing was controlled with machine language routines that maintained synchrony with the screen refresh cycle. The displays of the critical items were preceded and followed by 500msec exposures of the pre- and post-masks, which also functioned as warning signs. Exposure durations were limited to multiples of 1/60sec. During the practice period (see below), a duration was selected for each subject so as to produce approximately 60% accuracy on the identity judgement in the simultaneous condition. This level of performance is well above chance (5%) but also well below ceiling. For most subjects, the exposure duration was 66.7msec. The entire procedure, including stimulus selection and presentation, was carefully described to each subject. Subjects (run in a lighted room) were instructed to respond as accurately as possible, with no emphasis whatsoever on speed. The subjects made two button push responses, first pressing the digit key corresponding to the identity of the highest digit, then pressing a key corresponding to the location of the highest digit. Four keys on the computer keyboard, arranged roughly in a square, were labelled for this purpose. The interval between the subject's response and the beginning of the next trial was approximately 2.15sec.

The experiment began with a practice block of 50 trials in the simultaneous condition. The practice period included presentations at 83, 67, and 50msec, and the duration used for the rest of the experiment was selected on the basis of performance in practice. Feedback was presented on each trial during the practice portion of the experiment only. The 10 blocks composing the experiment proper were separated by rest periods; the computer displayed for the subject to the overall percent correct on that block, and the subject terminated the rest period when desired.

Results and Discussion

Table 3.1 presents the subjects' performance (by mean proportion), broken down by response category. The primary measure considered here will be the portion of trials on which the identity of the highest digit was reported accurately. The results show a small (2.9%) advantage for the successive condition. There was also disinctly superior performance when the highest digit is in one of the upper two display positions (72.2%) rather than one of the lower positions (51.5%), a result also obtained by Shiffrin and Gardner (1972).

TABLE 3.1
Accuracy in Experiment 1 by Percent

	Condition	
	Successive	*Simultaneous*
Identity & Location Correct	58.0	54.7
Identity Correct, Location Wrong	5.3	5.7
Identity Wrong, Location Correct	8.6	7.5
Identity & Location Wrong	28.0	32.2

To assess the reliability of these effects, each subject's proportion correct for each display position and condition was subjected to an arcsine transformation, to normalise the distributions (Winer, 1962). An analysis of variance was performed on the arcsine transforms. The effect of condition (simultaneous vs. successive) did not reach significance, $F(1,11) = 4.5, 0.05 < P < 0.10$. The effect of position was highly significant, $F(3,33) = 16.2, P < 0.0001$, and the interaction of the two was not significant, $F(3,33) = 1.7, P > 0.15$. An ANOVA on the untransformed proportions produced the same results.

Several other aspects of the data are of interest. When location was reported incorrectly, the conditional probability of correct identity report was 0.15 and 0.16 for simultaneous and successive displays, respectively. These are fairly close to what would be expected by chance if such responses were based upon no identity information whatsoever (0.20). Similarly, the probability of correct location response given incorrect identity report was 0.23 and 0.19 for simultaneous and successive displays, respectively; again, this is reasonably close to the expected value if these responses reflected no location information (25%). Together, the results provide no indication that subjects obtain either location or identity information without obtaining the other form of information in this task.

In this experiment, a relatively small advantage for the successive conditions was observed. The magnitude of this difference is much less than that which would be expected if identification of the digits depended upon a serial attentional scan. If such a scan were involved, the temporal asynchrony of the successive condition should provide major facilitation, since any such scan must be capable of operating at rates from 20–40msec/character, given the data obtained in reaction time versions of the task (Pashler & Badgio, 1985), which used very similar stimuli. The trend toward an advantage for successive displays may well indicate some degree of capacity reallocation, but not the rapid all-or-none form of reallocation hypothesised by the serial model. The strong position effects observed here may be attributable to a bias in the overall allocation of such a capacity. Alternatively, they may reflect nonoptimalities in the later stage(s) of processing concerned with selection of the highest digit. Both of these interpretations are consistent with parallel identification of the digits.

EXPERIMENT 2

The previous experiment found only hints of a small advantage for successive displays in the highest-digit task, arguing against rapid sequential character identification. One possibility worth investigating is that sequential scanning might not operate effectively with the displays of Experiment 1, which would require a shift of attention from one diagonal to the other. Experiment 2, therefore, simply changes the configuration of the displays in a manner that might plausibly facilitate sequential scanning: The characters are arrayed on a line, and in the successive condition they are exposed in pairs from left to right.

Method

Subjects.   Twelve undergraduate students participated as subjects in the experiment, in return for payment.

Apparatus and Stimuli.   The apparatus and stimuli were as in Experiment 1, except for the position and presentation order of the display elements. The four characters were evenly spaced along a row measuring 3.81cm in overall length (3.63 deg). The inter-character distance was 0.74cm (0.71 deg), sufficient to minimise lateral interference (Wolford & Chambers, 1984). The four position response keys were on a line.

Design.   The design followed that of Experiment 1.

Procedure.   The procedure followed Experiment 1, except that in the successive condition, the left two digits were exposed, and then the right two digits, with a zero interstimulus interval.

Results and Discussion

Table 3.2 presents the subjects' performance (by mean proportion) broken down by condition and response category. Overall identity accuracy was 74.8% and 73.2% in the simultaneous and successive conditions, respectively. Positional effects were evident: Overall accuracy in positions 1–4 (numbered left-to-right) was 79.2%, 80.7%, 76.9%, and 59.2%, respectively.

TABLE 3.2
Accuracy in Experiment 2 by Percent

	Condition	
	Successive	Simultaneous
Identity & Location Correct	66.4	66.4
Identity Correct, Location Wrong	6.8	8.4
Identity Wrong, Location Correct	5.5	6.0
Identity & Location Wrong	21.1	19.1

To assess the reliability of these effects, each subject's proportion correct on the identity judgement was computed and subjected to an arcsine transform. The effect of condition (simultaneous vs. successive) was not significant, $F(1,11) = 0.8$, $P > 0.38$. The effect of position was highly significant, $F(3,33) = 11.1$, $P < 0.0001$. The interaction of the two was not significant, $F(3,33) = 0.8$, $P > 0.50$. An ANOVA of the untransformed proportions showed the same results.

The results support those of Experiment 1: The simultaneous condition is now actually superior to the successive condition (but not significantly so). Considering the two results together, it seems likely that any effects of presentation are trivial in magnitude.

EXPERIMENT 3

The previous experiments found minimal or nonexistent advantages for successive over simultaneous displays, running counter to the predictions of serial processing models. One might still suggest, however, that some kind of inflexibility in the sequential scanning process makes it unable to exploit the successive exposures involved in these experiments. The present experiment provides a complementary test of the serial scanning idea, by comparing two different conditions of successive presentation. In some blocks, four digits on a line are exposed successively, one at a time, from left to right. In the other blocks, the order of the exposure varies unpredictably (to the subject) among 12 different irregular sequences. These trials are lacking in both predictability and spatial orderliness, which would surely impair any sequential process. Thus, even if left-to-right successive exposures do not fully exploit a serial scanning mechanism, they should yield performance superior to that obtained with disorderly, unpredictable sequences.

Method

Subjects.   Six undergraduate students participated in three sessions each, in return for payment.

Apparatus and Stimuli.   The apparatus and stimuli were identical to those in Experiment 2.

Design.   Each session included 10 blocks of 36 trials. Half the blocks (presented in alternation) were pure left-to-right blocks (1-2-3-4). The other blocks each included three trials in each of the following twelve orders: 1-2-4-3, 1-3-4-2, 1-4-2-3, 2-1-4-3, 2-3-1-4, 2-4-1-3, 3-1-4-2, 3-2-4-1, 3-4-1-2, 4-1-3-2, 4-2-3-1, 4-3-1-2. These were selected to include every possible combination of positions for the first two items presented, and to minimise the orderliness of the remainder of the sequence.

Procedure.   All displays consisted of a successive presentation, one item at a time, with a zero ISI between items. A plus sign appeared for 500msec in the centre of the screen, and 300msec after its disappearance, the pre-masks appeared. After another 500msec, the successive exposure of the digits commenced. Subjects were advised that in half of the blocks of trials, the items would be presented in a predictable left-to-right order. Each subject served in three sessions. The first session began with a practice block, on the basis of which the exposure duration was set for that and the remaining two sessions.

Results and Discussion

Table 3.3 presents the subjects' performance on the identity judgement (by mean proportion), broken down by response category. The overall perfor-mance was 63.1% and 64.4% in the pure-block and mixed-block conditions, respectively. Accuracy was best for the leftmost item, and poorest for the rightmost item.

TABLE 3.3
Accuracy in Experiment 3 by Percent

	Condition	
	Pure-order Blocks	Mixed-order Blocks
Identity & Location Correct	54.8	56.2
Identity Correct, Location Wrong	8.3	8.2
Identity Wrong, Location Correct	9.3	8.3
Identity & Location Wrong	27.5	26.1

An analysis of variance was performed on the arcsine transforms. The effect of order (pure vs. mixed) was not significant, $F(1,5) = 4.1$, $P > 0.09$, nor was the effect of session, $F(2,10) = 2.1$, $P > 0.15$. The effect of position was significant, $F(3,15) = 7.4$, $P < 0.003$, but the interaction of position by order was not significant, $F(3,15) = 1.1$, $P > 0.35$. No other effects were significant. An ANOVA of the untransformed proportions produced the same results.

The results showed no benefit whatsoever for the predictable exposure condition; in fact, there is a trend toward superior performance in the *unpredictable* order condition. It seems quite implausible that any sequential process would not be impaired when the order of its inputs was completely unspecified, and spatially irregular. This is particularly obvious if the sequential process is equated with movement of the "spotlight" of visual attention, as many have suggested (e.g. Eriksen & Yeh, 1985).

EXPERIMENT 4

The previous experiments have argued against sequential character identification in a task designed to ensure that subjects must actually identify the stimuli. Treisman and Gelade (1980) have argued that evidence for parallel identification in search has arisen in experiments using target/background discriminations that can be based on detection of a single feature.[3] They have

---

[3] Note that the highest digit task might not be immune to this objection, since individual digits might have distinguishing features. Treisman's position does not rule out the possibility that parallel identification might occur in a context where a unique feature-identity mapping existed. Examination of the character set, however, does not naturally suggest any set of features that could uniquely distinguish each of the stimuli.

suggested that different results obtain when the stimuli are chosen so that the target is a conjunction of features present among the distractors. Treisman and Gelade propose that accurate feature conjunction with such stimuli requires sequential scanning of each item with focal attention. The present experiment uses a visual search task involving stimuli which Treisman and Gelade offer as an example of such a configuration: The target E among Fs and Ls, where the E could be created by superimposing the F and the L. One target is always present, and a location judgement is required.[4]

Method

Subjects.   Eighteen undergraduates from the University of California participated as subjects in the experiment, some in return for payment, and some in partial fulfillment of a course requirement.

Apparatus and Stimuli.   The stimuli were presented on Princeton Graphics SR-12 Color Monitors, controlled by IBM PC's equipped with Sigma Color-400 cards for increased resolution. Stimuli were arranged in an approximate square, with outer dimensions 3.0 by 3.9cm (3.4 by 4.5 deg). Each letter measured 0.5cm width by 0.4cm height (0.57 × 0.46 deg). The F and L, superimposed, yielded the E precisely. On each trial, there was a target E present in one of the four positions; the remaining positions were filled with two Fs and one L, or two Ls and one F.

Design.   The experiment was divided into 12 blocks of 40 trials. Half of these blocks consisted of simultaneous presentations, and half consisted of successive presentations. Within each block, 10 trials occurred with a target in each of the 4 positions.

Procedure.   The practice portion consisted of 6 blocks of trials, with decreasing exposure durations. On the basis of performance in practice, an initial duration for the experiment was selected to produce performance as close as possible to 70%. Thereafter, the exposure duration was automatically checked after every pair of blocks, and readjusted if performance deviated far from the desired range; this occurred rarely. The subjects responded only with the location of the target, which was always present in one of the four positions. A central plus sign served as a fixation point; it appeared for 1200msec, and remained up during the pre-mask sequence;

---

[4]According to Treisman and Gelade (1980), location information is always available when features are conjoined by attention; therefore, this measure is appropriate for a test of their hypothesis.

subjects were instructed to keep their eye fixed on it during the entire sequence.

Results and Discussion

The overall accuracy was 70.7% and 69.7% in the simultaneous and successive conditions, respectively, and performance was better in the top two positions than in the bottom positions: 76.6% vs. 63.8%.

An analysis of variance was performed on the arcsine transforms. The effect of condition was not significant, $F(1,17) = 0.35$, $P > 0.50$, but the effect of position was significant, $F(3,51) = 6.2$, $P < 0.001$. The interaction of the two was significant, $F(3,51) = 4.2$, $P < 0.05$. The analysis of untransformed proportions yielded the same results, except that the interaction of condition and position did not reach significance. The cause of this apparent interaction was not clear; the strongest contribution came from superior performance in the lower right-hand element in the successive condition.

This experiment, then, provides evidence against sequential processing with stimuli selected to require accurate feature conjunction, according to Treisman and Gelade (1980). The same target/background combination of letters was employed in a reaction time experiment by Pashler and Badgio (1985), and that evidence also favoured parallel stimulus processing: Visual quality and display size effects were additive. The original evidence which motivated Treisman and Gelade's postulation of serial conjunction search concerned the pattern of RT slopes for positive and negative trials in detecting conjunctions of colour and form in very large displays. Pashler (1987) recently reported a more fine-grained analysis of the slopes in that situation, and found results suggesting that while there is serial checking of clumps of items, there is *not* a serial search of individual items within these clumps.

GENERAL DISCUSSION

The experiments reported here argue that character identification can operate without any need for serial processing. The absence of major advantages for successive presentations, and the lack of an effect of predictability of order in successive displays, would be very difficult to reconcile with a model incorporating rapid sequential scanning as a necessary component of character identification. The present results go beyond previous research in that the tasks were chosen so that they could not be performed by a mechanism which merely "filtered" the stimuli in order to determine if they were targets, or just detected simple features irrespective of their conjunction. These results converge with our earlier findings involving RTs in speeded versions of these same tasks (Pashler & Badgio, 1985). In those studies, the effects of display size and various stimulus degradation factors were found to be additive, arguing directly against sequential operation of the stages affected by degradation.[5]

Together, these results might naturally be interpreted as providing support for late selection theories of attention (e.g. Duncan, 1980b). We believe that such an interpretation would probably be mistaken. Late-selection theories characteristically make a number of assertions which need to be kept quite separate from the parallel identification hypothesis argued for here. In what follows, these assertions are enumerated, and their independence, on logical and empirical grounds, is pointed out.

1. Typically, late selection theories assert not only that identification of familiar stimuli operates in parallel, but also that it operates *without any capacity limitations*. It is well known that parallel processing might co-exist with capacity limitations, i.e., the efficiency with which any stimulus can be processed might be reduced by the number of additional stimuli being processed simultaneously (van der Heijden, 1975; Rumelhart, 1970). As pointed out earlier, the strongest evidence for capacity-free processing is the Shiffrin and Gardner finding of no advantage for successive displays in visual search accuracy even when a 500msec delay was allowed between different frames. More recent results have observed limits on the generality of this finding: Kleiss and Lane (1986) and Foyle and Shiffrin (Shiffrin, in press) found an advantage for successive displays (using long inter-frame intervals) under a number of conditions; notably, decreased target/background discriminability and increased display size.

We have recently replicated this finding, using square displays and a relatively difficult discrimination: T or F among confusable (angular) letter distractors. We compared performance with two intervals between frame onsets (blocked), 117msec and 500msec. No successive advantage was evident at 117msec, but a sizeable advantage appeared at 500msec. If the capacity limitation were a reflection of rapid sequential scanning, the advantage should have emerged at the short SOA, so the results suggest that the limit reflects a "resource" which can only be reallocated rather slowly (a view advocated by Hoffman, 1979).

2. Late selection theories also claim that identification of multiple items occurs *involuntarily*, i.e. that no early "filtering" mechanisms exist which block or attentuate visual information before it reaches the mechanisms

---

[5]Note that none of these studies address the question of whether, once the identities of the digits are computed, the *selection* of the highest operates sequentially or in parallel. Given the relatively shallow slopes in the task, we would tend to doubt that the highest digit is found with the obvious serial algorithm that is characteristically employed in computer sorting programs (cf. Pashler & Badgio, 1985), but our data do not address that issue.

involved in pattern recognition. This point is plainly independent from the parallel/serial and capacity limit questions, although the two are frequently conflated. The findings indicating parallel identification (e.g. the present results, or those of Shiffrin and Gardner) have arisen in tasks in which subjects *deliberately* attempt to "divide their attention" among all the stimuli presented. If they can do this successfully, without sequential scanning, it certainly does not follow that had they wished to ignore other stimuli, they could not have prevented these other stimuli from being identified. This aspect of late selection theory is also empirically dubious: The indirect effects (i.e. Stroop and priming effects) that provide the evidence for processing of unattended stimuli turn out to be modulated by various attentional factors (cf. Francolini & Egeth, 1980; Kahneman & Treisman, 1984). Thus, recent evidence seems congenial to Treisman's original "filter-attenuation" account: The exclusion of unattended stimuli seems to be a graded effect, but one that operates at early levels of processing.

3. The final principal assertion made by late selection theories is the one that gives the theories their name: The view that *selection of a stimulus occurs "late"* in the sequence of processing stages—i.e., after the identification of the stimulus. The kind of situation to which this hypothesis pertains most transparently is one in which multiple stimuli are perceptually available to the subject, and a subset of these stimuli are designated for selection (e.g. for report) on the basis of some attribute which is not correlated with the identity to be reported. For instance, a person might view a display composed of multiple objects, and then try to report the identity of the red object. Logically, the view that parallel identification is possible does not entail the hypothesis that late selection is possible in this sort of situation. It is one thing to have the machinery capable of extracting identities of multiple items in parallel; it is quite another to have the capability of generating a representation of multiple objects which allows the identity of these objects to be fetched using attributes of these objects other than identity as retrieval cues (e.g. colour or location).

Although this hypothesis gives late selection theory its name, very few studies have actually tested it. One fairly straightforward test of the hypothesis was reported by Pashler (1984). Subjects viewed displays of eight letters or digits; a bar probe was presented adjacent to one of the items, requiring a speeded classification response to the identity of the probed item. Two factors were manipulated: the timing of probe and display, and the visual quality of the elements in the display. The crucial prediction tested was the following. When the display is available for preview prior to the appearance of the probe, then according to the late selection hypothesis, the probe triggers the retrieval of the already-computed identity (i.e. automatically computed during the preview). Since the identification of the probed item is complete by the onset of the probe, the visual quality of the probed element should have no effect upon the time required to produce a response. Therefore, preview of the display should eliminate or markedly reduce the effect of visual quality, compared to the condition in which the probe appears before the display. In fact, no reduction was detected in a wide range of experiments of this type, some reported in the article cited and others we have performed more recently. The most straightforward interpretation is that selection is in fact *early* in such tasks—i.e., when the probe appears, subjects proceed to identify the probed element, rather than retrieving an already computed identity.

In summary, we have presented some new empirical evidence for the hypothesis that multiple familiar characters can be identified in parallel. But it was pointed out that traditional late selection theories, to which the idea of parallel identification is most congenial, also make three additional asser- tions. We have suggested not only that these three assertions are logically independent of the parallel identification hypothesis, but also that current evidence suggests these assertions are probably false. This conclusion is admittedly tentative, and there is a clear need for further empirical work examining each of these separate issues. It may also be fruitful, however, to consider possible views of the role of attention in visual information processing which *would* be compatible with the tentative conclusions sug- gested above. A sketch of one such alternative was presented by Pashler and Badgio (1985). This alternative posits the following:

1. Visual attention can optionally be allocated to the *locations* of one or many visual stimuli.

2. Objects in locations that are *not* attended are subject to attenuation early in processing, prior to object identification.

3. All the objects present in locations that *are* attended are identified in parallel.

4. Such parallel identification makes only limited information available "centrally" (i.e., for response selection or conscious awareness); specifically, the *identities* of the attended objects. A concrete metaphor would be that each category of object is represented by a single node, which is activated if there are one or more tokens of the category present in an attended location.

5. The system has an important additional capability; to redirect visual attention to the location where a token of an active identity is present. So, for instance, if three locations containing the letters A, Q, and A are attended simultaneously, then the information made available centrally will simply record the presence of A and Q in the display—this information will not be "tied" to location or other attributes in a way that can be inspected centrally, as late selection theory would have it. If the Q is of "interest," however, the subject can voluntarily narrow attention onto the location of the Q without further inspection of the display; now the As will be attenuated early in

processing. Thus, the connection between identity and location is preserved in an implicit format that allows redirection of visual attention.

6. Finally, it is hypothesised that retrieving any one attribute based on another attribute can only be achieved by narrowing visual attention as described in (5). The only way one attribute of a stimulus (e.g. colour, identity) is tied to another attribute of that stimulus is that detection of an attribute permits narrowing of visual attention onto its location. Once this occurs, the information in the "displayboard" described in (4) will pertain only to the selected object, and other attributes of that object will now be available. Note, however, that nothing can be retrieved from pre-existing representations in this scheme. (Obviously, this account only pertains to rapid attentional selection; presumably longer-term memory representations could be consulted under some conditions, but their capacity may be so restricted that when a stimulus is available, they are not used.)

The account sketched is more complex than the late selection view. However, unlike that view it provides a straightforward account of each of the results discussed here; furthermore, it does not seem unreasonable when considered in light of the apparent functional requirements of the organism. Firstly, it provides an account of why parallel processing should be evident in search tasks and highest-digit tasks such as those reported here: The task requires knowledge of identities present in the display, not retrieval of an identity based upon another attribute. It also explains why a subject required to report an item at a probed location in a display which has been previewed should have to identity the item *after* detecting the probe, despite the preview (Pashler, 1984): Parallel processing of the display during the preview cannot generate a representation which will allow the probe to access the identity directly. It can only produce nonselective (hence irrelevant) identity activation, which can be corrected only by initiating selective processing once the location is known, i.e. by narrowing attention onto the probed location, thereby attenuating unattended locations. The current view also accounts for findings indicating that selection based on nonlocational attributes like colour is mediated by shifts of attention to target location (Nissen, 1985; Snyder, 1972). Finally, it is congenial to findings indicating that unattended items receive little or no processing when they are spatially distant from attended items (Kahneman & Treisman, 1984).

This account may not be the only possible reconciliation of the various empirical constraints discussed; however, it appears to us to be a promising alternative. If correct, it should have strong implications for those engaged in computational modelling of human visual object recognition. The conclusions reached here differ fundamentally from the assumptions adopted in many of these models (e.g. Hinton & Lang, 1984), but they bear some resemblances to the ideas in a computational model of word recognition recently developed by Mozer (this volume). It is certainly to be hoped that a convergence may develop between the constraints on parallel visual processing suggested by experimental studies of human performance, and constraints motivated by computational considerations arising in efforts to construct detailed and neurally plausible models.

ACKNOWLEDGEMENTS

The authors are grateful to Jon Baron, James C. Johnston, and Jack Nachmias for many useful comments on this research; in addition, Manuel Sanches made helpful comments on the manuscript. Address correspondence to the first author at the Dept. of Psychology C-009, University of California, San Diego, La Jolla, CA 92093, U.S.A.

REFERENCES

Duncan, J. (1980a). The demonstration of capacity limitation. *Cognitive Psychology, 12*, 75–96.
Duncan, J. (1980b). The locus of interference in the perception of simultaneous stimuli. *Psychological Review, 87*, 272–300.
Egeth, H., Jondies, J., & Wall, S. (1972). Parallel processing of multi-element displays. *Cognitive Psychology, 3*, 674–698.
Eriksen, C. W. & Collins, J. F. (1969). Visual perception rate under two conditions of search. *Journal of Experimental Psychology, 80*, 489–492.
Eriksen, C. W. & Spencer, T. (1969). Rate of information processing in visual perception: Some results and methodological considerations. *Journal of Experimental Psychology Monograph, 79* (2, Part 2).
Eriksen, C. W. & Yeh, Y.-Y. (1985). Allocation of attention in the visual field. *Journal of Experimental Psychology: Human Perception and Performance, 11*, 583–597.
Estes, W. & Taylor, H. (1964). A detection method and probabilistic models for assessing information processing from brief visual displays. *Proceedings of the National Academy of Science, 52*, 446–454.
Francolini, C. M. & Egeth, H. (1980). On the nonautomaticity of "automatic" activation: Evidence of selective seeing. *Perception and Psychophysics, 27*, 331–342.
Hinton, G. E. & Lang, K. (1984). *Shape recognition and illusory conjunctions.* Technical Report: Carnegie-Mellon University, Dept. of Computer Science.
Hoffman, J. E. (1979). A two-stage model of visual search. *Perception and Psychophysics, 25*, 319–327.
Kahneman, D. & Treisman, A. (1984). Changing views of attention and automaticity. In R. Parasuraman, R. Davies, & J. Beatty (Eds.), *Varieties of attention.* New York: Academic Press, 29–62.
Kleiss, J. A. & Lane, D. M. (1986). Locus of persistence of capacity limitations in visual information processing. *Journal of Experimental Psychology: Human Perception and Performance, 12*, 200–210.
Miller, J. (1979). Cognitive influences on perceptual processing. *Journal of Experimental Psychology: Human Perception and Performance, 8*, 273–296.
Nissen, M. J. (1985). Accessing features and objects: Is location special? In M. Posner & O. S.

M. Marin (Eds.), *Attention and Performance XI*. Hillsdale, N.J.: Lawrence Erlbaum Associates Inc.

Pashler, H. (1984). Evidence against late selection: Stimulus quality effects in previewed displays. *Journal of Experimental Psychology: Huuman Perception and Performance, 10,* 429–448.

Pashler, H. (1987). Detecting conjunctions of colour and form: Reassessing the serial search hypothesis. *Perception and Psychophysics, 41,* 191–201.

Pashler, H. & Badgio, P. (1985). Visual attention and stimulus identification. *Journal of Experimental Psychology: Human Perception and Performance, 11,* 105–121.

Posner, M. (1982). Cumulative development of attention theory. *American Psychologist, 37,* 168–179.

Rabbitt, P. M. A. (1978). Sorting, categorisation, and visual search. In E. C. Carterette & M. P. Friedman (Eds.), *Handbook of perception IX*. London: Academic Press, 85–134.

Rumelhart, D. E. (1970). A multicomponent theory of the perception of briefly exposed visual displays. *Journal of Mathematical Psychology, 7,* 191–216.

Shiffrin, R. (in press). Attention. In R. C. Atkinson, J. Herrnstein, G. Lindzey, & R. D. Luce (Eds.), *Stevens' handbook of experimental psychology*. New York: John Wiley & Sons, Inc.

Shiffrin, R. M. & Gardner, G. T. (1972). Visual processing capacity and attentional control. *Journal of Experimental Psychology, 93,* 72–83.

Snyder, C. R. R. (1972). Selection, inspection, and naming in visual search. *Journal of Experimental Psychology, 98,* 113–118.

Treisman, A. & Gelade, G. (1980). A feature integration theory of attention. *Cognitive Psychology, 12,* 97–136.

Turvey, M. T. (1973). On peripheral and central processes in vision: Inferences from an information-processing analysis of masking with patterned stimuli. *Psychological Review, 80,* 1–52.

van der Heijden, A. H. C. (1975). Some evidence for a limited-capacity parallel self-terminating process in simple visual search tasks. *Acta Psychologica, 39,* 21–41.

Wolford, G. & Chambers, L. (1984). Lateral masking as a function of spacing. *Perception and Psychophysics, 33,* 129–138.

4 Early Parallel Processing in Reading: A Connectionist Approach

Michael C. Mozer
Institute for Cognitive Science
University of California, San Diego
La Jolla, U.S.A.

ABSTRACT

To what extent can information distributed across the visual field be processed in parallel? A connectionist model, capable of recognising multiple words appearing simultaneously on its "retina," is described which addresses this question. The model relies on the notion of a hierarchy of detectors, starting at the lowest level with position-specific primitive-feature detectors, and progressing to a level composed of position-independent "letter cluster" detectors. Intervening levels register successively higher-order features and also collapse over local spatial regions of the level below, resulting in less positional specificity of the detectors. Using an associative learning rule, the model has been taught to recognise a large sample of words in arbitrary retinal locations. Following this training, it is also able to recognise several words simultaneously, although under certain conditions crosstalk among words can become unmanageable. The model includes an attentional mechanism, which can limit crosstalk, and a serial readout mechanism, which is necessary for a word to reach awareness. While exhaustive simulation experiments have yet to be carried out, there are a variety of phenomena, both experimental and anecdotal, that the model appears well-equipped to account for, including: translation and scale invariant recognition, positional uncertainty at the letter and word levels, the recognition of misspelled words, the integration of information across fixations, similarity-based interference effects, and the role of focal attention in localisation.

INTRODUCTION

To what extent can information distributed across the visual field be processed in parallel? As a lower bound, examination of visual cortex reveals the necessary hardware for parallel feature extraction. Many researchers will readily agree that parallel identification of letters is possible (e.g. Duncan, 1980; Schneider & Shiffrin, 1977). As an upper bound, few would argue that meaning can be extracted from an entire sentence in a single glance. Between the letter and sentence levels, however, a host of possibilities remain.

My intuition is that more than one word can be analysed at a time. One source of this intuition is that occasionally, while reading, I am surprised by the appearance of semantically anomalous words. Upon closer examination of the text, I invariably discover that the odd word was actually printed several lines above or below the line being read, or sometimes it never appeared but its components were present on the page. Once, an "applications program" became an "arbitrary program"; the "world's best coffee" in an advertisement became the "world's worst coffee." Perhaps these errors can be accounted for in terms of a failure of serial attentive scanning, but there is a reasonable amount of experimental evidence suggesting that, at very least, irrelevant and unattended words are often processed (Allport, 1977; Bradshaw, 1974; Underwood, 1981; Willows & MacKinnon, 1973). Further, the fact that information appearing in parafoveal vision can facilitate the processing of foveal information appearing shortly thereafter (Rayner, 1975; Rayner, McConkie, & Zola, 1980) seems to imply that, in reading, information is extracted from several regions of the visual field simultaneously.

In this chapter, I present a model of parallel processing in word recognition. In facing the problem of processing several words in distinct locations, the model must deal with a dual problem; that of recognising a single word as being the same, independent of its location (Hebb, 1949; Neisser, 1967). Unfortunately, the dual goals of multiple-word recognition and location-invariant recognition are conflicting. To illustrate this conflict, consider the visual system in terms of its input-output properties. If the system is to process multiple words, its response to simultaneously presented words should be identical to the sum of its responses to each word presented in isolation. That is, the processing of one word should not interact with the processing of another.[1] If the visual system is to achieve this independence, it must operate linearly. Linear systems have the property of superposition, namely that the sum of the responses to several stimuli is equal to the response to the sum of the stimuli.

However, if the system is to achieve a location-invariant response, nonlinearities are required. A location-invariant system that is purely linear cannot detect letter arrangements. For instance, compare the response of such a system to the words ON and NO. Because the system is linear, the response to ON is simply the sum of the responses to O in the first position and

---

[1] At later semantic stages of analysis such interactions are to be expected, but presumably not in a system that is concerned with visual pattern recognition.

N in the second; likewise, NO is the sum of N in the first position and O in the second. Further, because of location invariance, the response to a given letter will be independent of its position; hence the system will respond identically to ON and NO. Thus, the property of superposition will prevent the system from responding to position-dependent interactions within a word.

To summarise, nonlinearities are important for encoding meaningful relations among letters, but when distinct words are to be identified simultaneously, interactions caused by nonlinearities represent only noise. The model to be described gets around the linearity dilemma by having nonlinearities at a local level, to obtain position-dependent interactions among neighbouring letters, but having linearity at a more global level, to obtain superposition of word responses (cf. Cavanaugh, 1984). As simulations of the model will show, this solution turns out to be only approximate. To the degree that it fails, locations of letters are confused, the processing of one word interferes with the processing of others, and, consequently, limits are placed on how much information may pass through the system accurately at any time.

CONNECTIONIST MODELS

Connectionist models are networks of simple neuron-like processing units that operate in parallel. Information processing takes place through interactions among the units, which send excitatory and inhibitory signals to one another. The typical processing unit has many input lines and a single output line. The output of a unit serves as input to other units, or as an output of the model. The output conveys a scalar value, called the *activation level*, which is generally a function of the weighted sum of the inputs. In most cases, the activation level can be thought of as signifying the belief in a particular hypothesis represented by the unit. For instance, in the perceptual domain, the hypotheses concern the presence or absence of visual features.

Models of word recognition have a long-standing connectionist tradition in the work of Morton (1969) and Selfridge (1955). More recently, McClelland and Rumelhart (1981; Rumelhart & McClelland, 1982) have proposed an interactive-activation model that is able to recognise single four-letter words and provides an account of the role of context in letter perception (e.g., McClelland & Johnston, 1977; Reicher, 1969). How might such a model be extended to deal with the simultaneous registration of multiple words? The simplest possibility is to consider constructing several copies of the interactive-activation model, one for each word to be processed. However, this approach requires that all knowledge implicit in the network—the connections that specify how features combine to form letters and letters to form words—must be replicated for each copy of the model. To avoid the knowledge replication problem, McClelland (1985; 1986) has suggested a "connection information distributor" scheme, which allows connection information to be stored centrally and passed to local processing structures; however, duplication of hardware within each processing structure is still necessary. Using this scheme, McClelland has developed a model that is able to process several words simultaneously and exhibits crosstalk when the network is overloaded. The model I will describe shares certain properties with McClelland's—in particular, that parallel processing of multiple words is possible without knowledge replication. A comparison of the two models may be found in Mozer (Note 1).

BLIRNET

The primary component of my model is a network whose purpose is to detect information concerning the identities of words appearing on its "retina," regardless of their locations. This network is called BLIRNET because it Builds Location-Independent Representations of multiple words. BLIRNET is a multilayered hierarchical network, the bottom layer of which serves as input and the top layer as output. Before describing the architecture of BLIRNET, it is useful to consider the representations at the input and output layers.

Input to BLIRNET

The input layer is a retinotopic feature map arranged in a 36 × 6 spatial array, with detectors for 5 feature types at each point in the array. The feature types, inspired by Julesz's (1981) textons, are oriented line segments at 0, 45, 90, and 135 degrees, and line-segment terminator detectors. BLIRNET's simulated retina thus consists of 1080 units that can be activated by the presence of objects in its visual field.

In order to present letters and words, a font was designed in which each letter was encoded as a binary activity pattern in a 3 × 3 retinal region. The letters were upper case, and visually similar letters yielded similar activity patterns. Words were encoded as a sequence of letters placed in immediately adjacent 3 × 3 regions. Figure 4.1 shows the representation of the phrase OUR NATION on BLIRNET's retina.

Output from BLIRNET

Each unit in the output layer of BLIRNET is activated by the presence of a particular sequence of letters in the retina. These units, called *letter-cluster* units, respond to local arrangements of letters but are not sensitive to the larger context or the absolute retinal location of the letters. For example,

```
...........................              ...........................
...........................              ...........................
..::OUR:::NATION::..              ......t.t........t...t.tt.t.....t...
                                          ...........................
...........................              .........t.t...t.t.tt.t.t.t...t.....
```

```
...........................              ...........................
...........................              ...........................
.../.............../........./.........   .....\.....\...\....\\.....
............../...........................    ........\...........\....
....../../................/.........          ...\..\....\.....\....\...
...........................              ...........................
```

```
..|.||.||.|....|.|.....|..|.|.|.|...   ...---..---......-.---------...
...|.||.||......|.||.|.|..|.|.||.|...  ........---...---...........
...|.||.||......|.||.|.|..|.|.||.|...  ...------....---......------...
```

FIG 4.1   The upper-left array shows a sample input to BLIRNET, the phrase OUR NATION. The remaining arrays represent the five retinotopic feature maps. Each character in an array represents the activity of a single unit. A ".” indicates that the unit is off. A "-", "/", "|", "\", or "t" indicates activity of the corresponding unit in the 0, 45, 90, 135 degree, or terminator map, respectively.

there might be a unit that detects the sequence NAT, and it would become activated by words like NATION or DOMINATE in any location, but not by BOTANY or GRANITE. Thus, the only location information retained at the output level consists of the relative positions of letters within a cluster.

I assume that the letter-cluster units respond to letter triples; either a sequence of three adjacent letters, such as NAT, or two adjacent letters and one nearby letter, such as NA_I or N_TI, where the underbar indicates that any letter may appear in the corresponding position. It is not critical that the units represent letter triples; the important property is that each unit encodes that order of information. Presentation of NATION should result in the activation of the following letter-cluster units: **N, **_A, *NA, *_AT, *N_T, NAT, N_ TI, NA_I, ATI, A_IO, AT_O, TIO, T_ON, TI_N, ION, I_N*, IO_*, ON*, O_**, and N**. An asterisk signifies a blank space; double asterisks are used simply to keep all names in the form xxx, xx_x, or x_xx. Note that the first two and last two letters of a word are explicitly encoded as such (here, **N, **_A, O_**, and N**). If a word has more than four letters, however, the positions of the word's inner letters can be determined only by examining the ensemble of letter-cluster activations and "reconstructing" the original arrangement of letters.

While words with fewer than four letters can be packed into a single letter-cluster unit, these words are still represented by the set of all appropriate units. Thus, short words are in principle no different from long words: Each is represented by a *pattern* of activity across the letter-cluster units. Even isolated letters can be represented with triples of the form **x, *x*, and x**. Thus the letter-cluster level of representation can substitute for both the letter and word levels found in many other models (e.g. McClelland & Rumelhart, 1981).

The letter-cluster coding scheme is analogous to Wickelgren's (1969) context-dependent allophone code used to represent the pronunciation of a word. The interesting thing about these schemes is that the unordered set of codes is sufficient (or can be expanded to be made sufficient) to reconstruct the ordered components of the word. Thus, the set of units activated by a word uniquely determines that word.

The letter-cluster coding scheme is interesting in another important respect. It allows for the simultaneous representation of multiple words, up to certain limits on the number of words and the amount of overlap among words. For example, if the letter-cluster units appropriate for the words PINT and TOAD are simultaneously activated, there is sufficient information in the letter-cluster activity pattern to reconstruct the identities of the two words. The problem of reconstruction becomes increasingly difficult with increasing similarity among words. For example, if PINT and HUNT are presented, only three units—*PI, PIN, and PI_T—can help determine which letter follows the P, whereas with PINT and TOAD, units such as P_NT and INT provide supporting evidence. The problem of reconstruction also grows with the number of words, because large sets of words inevitably contain some overlap.

How Many Letter-cluster Units are Necessary?   There are 56,966 possible letter clusters of the form described above. However, not all these clusters are needed. In fact, the 1000 most common letter clusters account for over 50% of all clusters that appear in English words; the top 6000 account for over 95% if word frequency is considered (result based on Kucera & Francis, 1967). Not only can a relatively small number of clusters do a good job of representing English words but, interestingly, the clusters are equally efficient at representing orthographically regular nonwords. Of course, the letter-cluster representation is meaningful only to the degree that it can be used by later stages of processing. I will return to this issue later, but first consider how BLIRNET achieves the desired input-output mapping.

Architecture of BLIRNET

BLIRNET must transform low-level position-specific features into high-level position-invariant features. The architecture to accomplish this transformation is diagrammed in Fig. 4.2. BLIRNET consists of a series of layers, the bottom layer (L_1) being the "retina" described previously and the top layer (L_6) the letter-cluster detectors. Intermediate layers (L_2–L_5) register successively higher-order features with decreasing spatial resolution. Each layer can be thought of as a retinotopic map of certain dimensions, with detectors for a certain number of feature types at each point in the map. L_1 has a 36 × 6 map

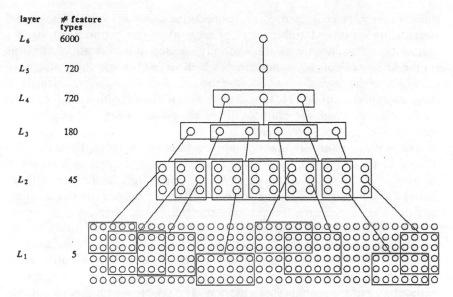

layer	# feature types
L_6	6000
L_5	720
L_4	720
L_3	180
L_2	45
L_1	5

FIG. 4.2.   The architecture of BLIRNET. The network consists of six layers, arranged in retinotopic maps of decreasing dimensions. At each point within a map, indicated by a "O", there is one unit for each feature type. The number of feature types is shown in the column on the left. The receptive field of a unit is depicted by a box around its set of input units. To simplify the sketch, only some connections from L_1 to L_2 have been shown.

with 5 "primitive" feature types. At each successive layer, the map dimensions decrease and the number of feature types increases. L_6 has a 1 × 1 map, meaning that there is no encoding of location, with approximately 6000 feature types—the letter-cluster units.

Figure 4.2 also shows the pattern of connectivity among units. The network is strictly feedforward: Activations flow unidirectionally from the input to the output layer. Each unit in a given position of layer i (L_i) may potentially receive input from all units in a local spatial region of layer i-1 (L_{i-1}). This region is indicated by a rectangular box drawn around the L_{i-1} units and connected to the L_i unit.

The network can be thought of as performing two distinct operations. The L_1–L_5 mapping aims to recode the input into a translation-invariant representation. The L_5–L_6 mapping then recodes this representation into the letter-cluster representation. The distinction between these two parts of the network is reflected in the fact that connection strengths (or *weights*) between units are set differently in each part: in L_1–L_5, weights are prewired and fixed, whereas in L_5–L_6, weights are learned. Learning in L_5–L_6 will be discussed later. In L_1–L_5, however, connections are set such that all weights from L_{i-1} units of feature type x to L_i units of feature type y are identical. Thus, 5 × 45 different weights characterise the connections from L_1 to L_2. The actual weights are either -1 (inhibitory connection), 0 (no connection), or $+1$ (excitatory connection), and are randomly selected under certain constraints on the density of nonzero connections, which serve to ensure that patterns of activity at higher layers do not become too distributed. The overall density of nonzero connections is 0.11. Given this pattern of connectivity, L_2–L_5 units might respond when, for example, there are more tokens of type x within their receptive fields than tokens of type y.

The motivation underlying the mapping from one layer to the next in L_1–L_5 is roughly as follows: If units in L_i encode relations among n-tuples of features in L_{i-1}, spatial resolution in L_i can be cut by a factor of n without losing the information required to reconstruct the relative spatial arrangement of the L_{i-1} features. To demonstrate this point, consider a two-layer network with two spatial positions in the bottom layer (L_b) and one in the top (L_t). In each L_b position are 26 units, one for each letter of the alphabet; in L_t are 26×26 units, one for each pairing of letters. By encoding conjunctions of letters in L_t, information about the ordering of letters is retained even without an explicit spatial representation. The problem with this idea is that for f features at L_b, f^n features are needed at L_t to encode all combinations of size n. This is a problem, however, only if each L_t feature is encoded by a single unit. If each L_t feature is represented as a *distributed* pattern of activity across the L_t units, far fewer L_t units are required (see Hinton, McClelland, & Rumelhart, 1986, for a discussion of the advantages of distributed representations and coarse coding). In practice, I've found that the present architecture requires only on the order of $fn^2 L_t$ units, a significant improvement over f^n.

While the aim of the L_1–L_5 mapping is to construct a translation-invariant representation, the simple rules of connectivity stated above do not permit the network to achieve this goal exactly. What L_1–L_5 actually does is to factor out explicit location information from the input representation. Although the L_5 representation varies as a letter or word is moved across the retina, it does contain translation-invariant *cues*, and the purpose of learning in L_5–L_6 is to discover these cues.

The architecture of L_1–L_5 is in accord with the qualitative neurophysiology and neuroanatomy of the brain (Crick & Asanuma, 1986); it is also quite similar to the architecture of the neocognitron (Fukushima & Miyake, 1982), although the neocognitron was designed primarily for achieving invariance under pattern distortion, not for the recognition of multiple objects. The L_1–L_5 architecture is surely not the only solution to the problem at hand. However, it is known that translation-invariant pattern recognition cannot be realised in a two-layer connectionist network (Minsky & Papert, 1969); thus, all solutions will require multiple layers.

The present architecture has the interesting property that it is not tuned specifically for word recognition; rather, it is a general architecture that can be used for achieving translation-invariant pattern recognition. While it does require the replication of weights across each retinal map, these weights are hardwired and are based on simple rules of connectivity. It is not difficult to imagine genetic instructions to wire cells of one type to cells of another type.

System Dynamics

L_1 units are turned on with an activation level of 1 if the corresponding feature is present on the retina, or 0 otherwise. L_2–L_6 units are set according to the activation rule:

$$o_{fij}^l = s(\sum_x \sum_y \sum_g w_{gf}^l \, o_{gxy}^{l-1}),$$

where o_{fij}^l is the activity level of the layer l unit in location (i, j) of feature type f, and w_{gf}^l is the strength of connection from feature type g in layer l-1 to feature type f in layer l. The function s relates a unit's net input to its activation level:

$$s(x) = \frac{\frac{1}{1 + e^{-k_l x}} - m_l}{M_l - m_l}$$

This is an S-shaped logistic function whose steepness can be adjusted by the constant k_l. Large values of k_l result in highly nonlinear threshold-like behaviour, whereas small values result in nearly linear behaviour. The scaling factors m_l and M_l were selected for each level so that the response of L_2–L_5 units ranged from approximately -1 to 1, and the response of L_6 units from 0 to 1. A large value of k_l was selected for L_2 units, and this value was reduced in each successive layer. This resulted in nonlinearities at lower layers of the network, which are important to encode local relationships among features, and linearity at higher layers, which allows superposition of activations from different words.

During training, when a word was presented on L_1, activations were allowed to flow through BLIRNET to L_6. The L_5 activity pattern was then associated with the word's letter clusters in L_6 by adjusting the weights w_{gf}^6 using the delta rule (Widrow & Hoff, 1960):

$$\Delta w_{gf}^6 = \eta(d_f^6 - o_f^6) o_g^5,$$

where d_f^6 is the desired activation level of letter-cluster unit f, 1 or 0, and η the learning rate, which was fixed at 0.0002. This rule results in increased activity of the appropriate clusters and decreased activity of the inappropriate clusters on future presentations of the word.

SIMULATION EXPERIMENTS

A computer simulation of the model has been implemented and preliminary results are available. Before describing these results, some details of the simulation should be clarified.

Number of Letter-cluster Units

As mentioned previously, 6000 letter clusters do an adequate job of representing English words. However, to keep the simulation manageable, it was necessary to select a subset of these clusters. I settled on using the 600 most frequently occurring clusters in English for L_6. Then 909 words were found that had the property that at least 69% of their clusters were among those in L_6. The words ranged in length from 2 to 10 letters, with a mean of 6.2; the number of letter clusters per word ranged from 6 to 26, with a mean of 15.3.

Training Methodology

During training, words were selected at random from the stimulus set and presented in random locations on L_1. Due to a slight decrease in sensitivity around the edges of L_1, words were not allowed to lie in the top or bottom row or in the three leftmost or rightmost columns. For an n-letter word, these constraints still permitted 62–$6n$ possible locations. There were a total of 22,626 word-location combinations.

On each training trial, a word was presented on L_1, activations were allowed to flow through BLIRNET to L_6, the L_5–L_6 weights were then adjusted, and this procedure was repeated until each of the 909 words had been presented. The iterative weight adjusting procedure is guaranteed to converge eventually on a set of weights that will perform the desired L_5–L_6 mapping, if such a set exists. However, the simulation, with 218,000 L_1–L_5 and 432,000 L_5–L_6 connections, demands considerable computational resources. At the time of this writing, BLIRNET has undergone about 100 passes through the stimulus set and performance continues to improve.

Response to Single Words

Figure 4.3a shows a sample output of the system: the response to BORED in location (17,3). The response to BORED in other locations is quite similar. In Fig. 4.3a, all clusters of *bored* are highly active (the *target activations*, displayed in upper case) as well as a few others (the *spurious activations*, displayed in lower case). As is typically found, spurious activations are of three types: clusters that would be appropriate if: (1) one letter of the word were substituted for another, such as P in position 1 (**P, *PO, *P_R) or L in position 3 (LED, L_D*, LE_*); (2) one or more letters were rearranged or dropped from the word, such as dropping the D would make R_** appropriate; or (3) one or more letters were inserted into the word, such as inserting an N between the E and the D (END, EN_*, ND*).

One measure of BLIRNET's performance is to compare the degree of activation of target and nontarget clusters. Using 5 presentations of each word in random locations, the average activation of target clusters was 0.69, whereas the average activation of nontarget clusters was only 0.01. The summed activity of all target clusters was on average 11.07 per word, compared to only 4.26 for (the nearly 600) nontargets. Further, only 1.4 nontarget activations per word were larger than the average target activation for that word. Admittedly, these statistics do not give the whole story because a few spurious activations might allow an alternative interpretation of the letter-cluster activity pattern.

Has BLIRNET learned to recognise clusters, independent of the string in which they are embedded? That is, is BLIRNET able to generalise from the set of words on which it was trained to novel strings? Figure 4.3b shows the response to one novel string, the pseudoword LING. As with many other examples, BLIRNET produced nearly the appropriate response. Thus, the L_5 activity pattern appears to contain invariant cues for particular letter clusters, and the learning procedure has discovered these cues. Consequently, one should expect BLIRNET to function just as well given a larger stimulus set and a more complete set of letter clusters.

In another series of experiments, BLIRNET was shown four-letter strings containing few familiar clusters, e.g. CTNR. In cases like this, letter-cluster units denoting the starting and ending letters of the string became activated, **C, **_T, N_**, R**, and in this particular example, also *C_N and T_R*, which were existing clusters. Thus, strings of four letters or less with unfamiliar orthographic structure can also be recognised.

Response to Pairs of Words

Figure 4.3c shows the response when two words, ANT and DEN, are simultaneously presented. Although BLIRNET was trained on single words, it is able to process several words simultaneously. I must confess that performance in this example is somewhat better than usual. The problem with multiple words, however, lies not in the structure of the network, but in the nature of the training stimuli. To construct generalised letter-cluster detectors, BLIRNET requires training on each letter cluster in a variety of contexts. The training set used does not provide this variety, and without it, BLIRNET learns only to detect letter clusters *in specific contexts*. Multiple words, which give rise to novel contexts, are thus troublesome. Preliminary experiments have shown that performance on multiple words greatly improves when training includes some multiple-word trials.

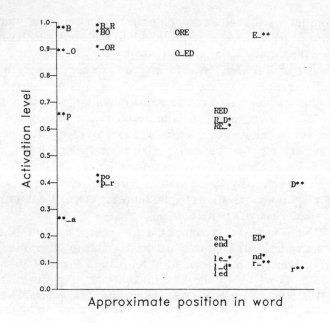

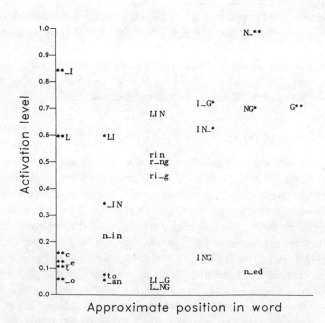

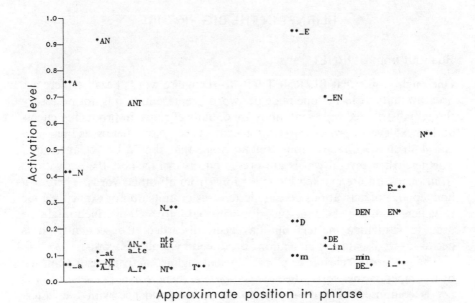

FIG. 4.3.   Letter-cluster activations in response to various inputs. Letter-cluster names printed in upper case indicate target activations; names printed in lower case indicate spurious activations. Spurious activations with activation levels below 0.05 have been omitted. The clusters are spread out along the *x*-axis to represent the approximate positions of the clusters within a word. Note that this dimension is not intrinsic to the letter-cluster representation.
(a) The response to BORED with upper-left corner in location (17,3).
(b) The response to LING in location (13,2).
(c) The response to ANT in location (8,3) and DEN in location (21,3).

Nonetheless, there are limitations, in principle, on the number of simultaneous words that can be processed accurately. As discussed previously, the network contains nonlinearities that cause interactions among simultaneously presented words. One clear case of such interactions can be shown when, for instance, ANT is moved very close to DEN. The words start to run together: the T_EN unit becomes active and T** and **D less so. Reducing nonlinearities will not solve the problem because doing so decreases accuracy of letter localisation within a word and hence increases spurious activations such as **_A or TAN in response to ANT. Thus, the conflicting demands for linear and nonlinear behaviour in the system place bounds on multiple-word performance.

BLIRNET IN THE BIG PICTURE

Readout from BLIRNET

One might argue that BLIRNET fails to recognise words because there are no *word* units. A local "one node per word" representation is not necessary though; distributed representations are equally effective in producing effects at the next level of processing (Hinton et al., 1986). Nonetheless, as Figs. 4.3a and 4.3b show, L_6 activations contain noise that should be "cleaned up." Further, when several words are presented, as in Fig. 4.3c, the activations from one word are masked by activations from all other words. There is a hodgepodge of activations because letter-cluster units do not explicitly code to which word they belong, and all positional information which might be used to straighten matters out has been discarded. Consequently, it is necessary to disentangle activations produced by multiple words.

The process of "cleaning up" and "disentangling" activations is achieved by a competitive network called the *pull-out net* (henceforth, PO net). The PO net is composed of units in one-to-one correspondence with the letter-cluster units. Each letter-cluster unit excites its corresponding unit in the PO net; thus, the pattern of letter-cluster activity is copied to the PO net. Within the PO net, units representing letter clusters that may fit together within a single word (e.g. BOR and ORE) are mutually excitatory, and units representing letter clusters that are inconsistent (e.g. **B and **P) or potentially inconsistent (e.g. BOR and POR) are mutually inhibitory. In addition, "semantic" units that represent higher-order knowledge may come into play to help support sets of units in the PO net that form words. These interactions result in an internally consistent set of letter-cluster activations that represents a single word.[2] By priming semantic or letter-cluster units, pull-out can be biased towards words with distinguishing semantic or orthographic features. (See Mozer, Note 1, for further details.)

If pull-out is successful, all target clusters of the presented word will end up with activation levels of 1.0, all nontarget clusters 0.0. The PO net has been implemented and is functioning in the simulation. Without semantic knowledge, it is capable of cleaning up the output pattern for most words, including pseudowords like LING, and if multiple words are presented, it will generally select out one word. With semantic knowledge, the PO net performs perfectly on words, but has a bias towards turning pseudowords into words.

Pull-out is assumed to be necessary to allow a word to reach awareness, either for report or for further processing. The pull-out stage is capacity

---

[2] The PO net has been designed to select single words; however, it is entirely plausible that over-learned phrases could be pulled out as unitary objects.

limited in that only one item can be pulled out at a time. Note that pull-out implies serial access, not serial identification: All processing for the identification of an item takes place before the pull-out stage. Many late-selection models, which allow a great deal of parallel processing, have similar readout bottlenecks (e.g. Allport, 1977; Duncan, 1980; Johnston & McClelland, 1980; Posner, 1978).

The Role of Focal Attention

If several words are present on BLIRNET 's retina, as would be the case when reading a page of text, the resulting pattern of activation in L_6 may be such a jumble that unambiguous reconstruction of the words is impossible. Even if reconstruction were possible, pull-out must proceed in an orderly fashion—from the left end of a line of text to the right. To control both the amount and sequencing of information passing through the system, a focal attention mechanism is required. The purpose of this mechanism is to aim a "spotlight" at a particular region of L_1, enhancing activations from that region. As these activations propagate through the network, the letter-cluster units appropriate for the attended item(s) will tend to become the most active as well. Consequently, these letter-cluster units will tend to dominate in the PO net competition, causing the attended item to be read out by the PO net. If attention is focused serially, items can be read out in succession. However, if attention is not focused, activations from several items will be equally strong, and random factors will influence which wins the competition. (See Mozer, Note 1, for further details.)

Because the current focus of attention presumably indicates the location from which activations in L_6 are arising, the attentional system can recover the absolute location information that is discarded by BLIRNET.

DATA THAT BLIRNET SHOULD ACCOUNT FOR

There are a variety of phenomena, both experimental and anecdotal, that appear to have natural interpretations in terms of the model. I must express the caveat that exhaustive simulation experiments have yet to be carried out. Thus, the list below serves primarily as a set of predictions that are, in principle, feasible within the framework of the model.

Location- and Scale-invariant Recognition

BLIRNET is able to recognise words regardless of their location on the retina. This location-invariant recognition is achieved in a manner that, unlike some approaches to perception (Hinton, 1981a; 1981b; Palmer, 1984), does not require selection by location as a condition for identification. I also believe that scale invariance can be achieved by adding units in L_2-L_5 with both larger and smaller receptive fields than those of existing units but with identical layer-to-layer connectivity, w_{gf}^l.

Letter Transposition Errors

Even in relatively long presentations of random letter strings, subjects have difficulty localising letters; in particular, adjacent letters are often transposed (Estes, Allmeyer, & Reder, 1976). However, such transposition errors are far less frequent within words (Duncan, this volume; Johnston, Hale, & van Santen, 1983). BLIRNET show positional uncertainty at the letter level due to large receptive fields of L_2-L_5 units and the fact that these units do not encode the relative locations of features within their receptive fields. Indeed, evidence of such uncertainty can readily be found by examination of spurious letter-cluster activations: One common type of spurious activation involves clusters whose letters are present in the display but in a slightly rearranged order. These spurious activations can be suppressed by the PO net if the target activations form a coherent pattern. For example, suppose the word CLAM were presented and, in addition to the appropriate letter-cluster activations, CAL became activated. The activity of CAL is not consistent with the activities of the other units and consequently CAL receives no support in the PO net and is eventually suppressed, whereas units like CLA and LAM provide mutual support. However, if the target is a random-letter string instead of a word or pseudoword, the PO net is less effective in suppressing noise. For example, suppose the CTNR were presented and the appropriate units **C, **_T, N_**, and R** were activated, along with the spurious unit **_C. Because the appropriate clusters cannot provide support for one another (N in position 3 does not imply T in position 2), the PO net has no evidence for determining the true position of C.

Letter Migration Errors

In brief presentations of two-word displays, letters of one word are some-times perceived as belonging to the other word; for instance, when SAND and LANE are presented, subjects might report seeing LAND or SANE instead of SAND (Allport, 1977; McClelland & Mozer, 1986; Mozer, 1983; Shallice & McGill, 1978). BLIRNET can be made to produce these "letter migration" errors: When attention is not focused, letter clusters for both words in the display are activated simultaneously. In addition, there is some spurious activation of clusters sharing letters with either of the presented words (see Fig. 4.3). Clusters sharing letters with *both* of the presented words become particularly active, e.g. S_NE, SA_E, L_ND, and LA_D. These clusters are precisely the ones that belong to the potential migration words. Consequently, the amalgam of letter-cluster activations is consistent not only with the two presented words, but is also reasonably consistent with the two potential migrations, occasionally leading to pull-out of a migration word. See McClelland and Mozer (1986) for a detailed account of migration errors in terms of BLIRNET.

According to this account, joint migrations of several letters may also occur. For instance, BLIRNET on one occasion read PARTING when the display contained PART and SING. Such multi-letter migration errors have been noted by Wilkins (cited in Woodworth, 1938, p. 744), in an experiment where subjects misread phrases like *Psychment Departology* in their more familiar form.

Word Migration Errors

In brief presentations, subjects may identify a word correctly without being able to localise it (Allport, 1977; Mozer, 1983). This corresponds to the subjective experience of glancing at a page of text and seeing a word, but being unsure where the word appeared; or of substituting a word from elsewhere on the page into a line being read. BLIRNET can produce such "word migration" errors because the L_6 activity specifies the identity of a word, but not its location. Unless attention is focused, the spatial source of the L_6 activity may be apprehended incorrectly.

Despite the evidence for word migration errors, Pashler and Badgio (1985; this volume) have argued that the visual system has the capability "to redirect visual attention to the location where a token of an active [letter or digit] identity is present," that is, to recover information about the location of an item given its identity. BLIRNET does not possess this capability because all information about absolute locations has been discarded by the letter-cluster level. BLIRNET thus may have real problems in handling the experimental results discussed by Pashler and Badgio. It remains for simulation experiments to determine whether the attentional mechanism can be guided in the appropriate manner without precise knowledge of item locations or whether the loss of location information in BLIRNET is too severe.

Recognition of Misspelled words

People can identify grossly misspelled words. In fact, it can often be difficult to detect misspellings even after the word is identified, e.g. *execept* or *diminshed*. Models with position-specific letter channels (e.g. McClelland & Rumelhart, 1981) have difficulty accounting for the recognition of misspellings with inserted or deleted letters because such permutations cause misalignment of the letter channels. However, using the PO net, BLIRNET is able to detect a word correctly so long as a reasonable proportion of its clusters are active.

Similarity-based Interference Effects

Many studies have shown that similarity of target and distractor items in a display significantly reduces the accuracy of target identification (Estes, 1982; Gardner, 1973; Krumhansl & Thomas, 1977). Estes concludes that the effect of similarity on discriminability can be attributed to a poorer encoding of target and distractor locations when target and distractors are similar and the target is imperfectly identified. BLIRNET shows similarity effects for exactly this reason. Consider a display similar to that of Estes (1982): Three letters are presented, a target with a distractor on either side. Compare BLIRNET's ability to recognise a target that is visually similar to the distractors, say, I with distractors L and T (LIT), and one that is dissimilar, say, A with L and T (LAT). Certain letter-cluster activations will support the correct responses, e.g. with target I, *LI, **_I, I_**. Other activations support one of the distractors in the centre position, e.g.**_ L, T_**, LL*. These spurious activations will be caused in part by the presence of L and T in the display. Additionally, the target I will add to the spurious activations because of its similarity to the distractors. Simulations of BLIRNET with LIT and LAT have shown that the ratio of activations supporting a distractor in the centre to those supporting the target was 0.80 for LIT but only 0.32 for LAT. Consequently, report of L or T in the centre should be more likely with LIT, and correct report of the target less likely.

At extreme degrees of similarity, namely when display items are identical, BLIRNET shows further interference effects. Because the L_6 representation does not encode location, two isolated tokens of a letter or word, which differ only on their location, cannot be distinguished. Thus, without focused attention and sequential read-out, BLIRNET predicts that detection of repeated tokens should be difficult. This effect is found experimentally (Mozer, Note 1; Santee & Egeth, 1980; Schneider & Shiffrin, 1977, Experiment 3), and could be the source of illusions such as:

PARIS IN THE
THE SPRING

where the repeated word often fails to be noticed.

Integration of Information Across Fixations

Rayner and colleagues (Rayner, 1975; Rayner, McConkie, & Ehrlich, 1978; Rayner et al., 1980) have shown that a word or letter string appearing in parafoveal vision can facilitate the processing of a visually similar word appearing shortly afterwards in the fovea. Thus, information acquired from one region of the visual field can interact with information from another. In BLIRNET, the logical place for such interactions is in L_6, where retinal location has been factored out. If parafoveal cuts produced some activity among the letter-cluster units, this activity would serve to prime the foveally presented word, causing its pull-out to proceed more rapidly.

Early Versus Late Attentional Selection

BLIRNET is in accord with "late selection" theories of attention (e.g. Deutsch & Deutsch, 1963; Norman, 1968; Posner, 1978; Shiffrin & Schneider, 1977) in suggesting that multiple display items can be processed in parallel to a high level of representation, even to the point of making simultaneous contact with semantic knowledge. Selection, which comes about through the action of the PO net, can be based on distinguishing semantic or orthographic features (discussed earlier). BLIRNET may also explain the results of a variety of target detection tasks in which performance is hardly affected by the number of simultaneous nontargets (Duncan, 1980).

In contrast to the supposition of most late selection theories, however, there are costs to processing large number of items in BLIRNET. These costs are of two sorts. First, the processing of an item produces spurious collateral activations that can interfere with the processing of other items. Second, if attention is not focused, information about the location of each item is lost. Reading, as well as many experimental tasks, requires selection by location; word order cannot generally be inferred from an unordered collection of words. These problems suggest the need for sequential processing, which requires the selection of individual items in BLIRNET's retina for analysis. This selection, performed by the attentional mechanism, is much in the spirit of the filtering and attenuation operations of "early selection" theories of attention (Broadbent, 1958; Treisman, 1969). Thus, the model shows characteristics of both early and late selection theories. Pashler and Badgio (1985; this volume) have presented a similar hybrid view of attentional selection.

FUTURE DIRECTIONS

Although this work is at an early stage, BLIRNET shows promise of predicting a variety of results, and it appears that a computational approach can help to clarify issues regarding early processes in reading. For instance, if one believes that a great deal of processing can be performed in parallel, then the relevant issues concern the amount of hardware required. If one believes that parallel processing is limited to early stages of feature extraction, then the issues concern the nature of the processing bottleneck. Quantitative studies of BLIRNET should allow further examination of these and related issues.

ACKNOWLEDGEMENTS

This research was supported by an IBM Graduate Fellowship, a grant from the System Development Foundation, and the Personnel and Training Research Programs, Psychological Sciences Division, Office of Naval Research, Contract No. N00014-85-K-0450, Contract Authority Identification Number, NR 667-548. My thanks to Jay McClelland and Hal Pashler for their thoughtful comments and suggestions.

REFERENCES

Allport, D. A. (1977). On knowing the meaning of words we are unable to report: The effects of visual masking. In S. Dornic (Ed.), *Attention and performance VI*. Hillsdale, N. J.: Lawrence Erlbaum Associates Inc.

Bradshaw, J. L. (1974). Peripherally presented and unreported words may bias the perceived meaning of a centrally fixated homograph. *Journal of Experimental Psychology, 6*, 1200–1202.

Broadbent, D. E. (1958). *Perception and communication*. London: Pergamon.

Cavanaugh, P. (1984). Image transforms in the visual system. In P. Dodwell & T. Caelli (Eds.), *Figural synthesis*. Hillsdale, N. J.: Lawrence Erlbaum Associates Inc., 185–218.

Crick, F. H. C. & Asanuma, C. (1986). Certain aspects of the anatomy and physiology of the cerebral cortex. In J. L. McClelland & D. E. Rumelhart (Eds.), *Parallel distributed processing: Explorations in the microstructure of cognition. Volume II: Psychological and biological models*. Cambridge, Mass.: M.I.T. Press/Bradford Books.

Deutsch, J. A. & Deutsch, D. (1963). Attention: Some theoretical considerations. *Psychological Review, 70*, 80–90.

Duncan, J. (1980). The locus of interference in the perception of simultaneous stimuli. *Psychological Review, 87*, 272–300.

Estes, W. K. (1982). Similarity-related channel interactions in visual processing. *Journal of Experimental Psychology: Human Perception and Performance, 8*, 353–380.

Estes, W. K., Allmeyer, D. H., & Reder, S. M. (1976). Serial position functions for letter identification at brief and extended exposure durations. *Perception and Psychophysics, 19*, 1–15.

Fukushima, K. & Miyake, S. (1982). Neocognitron: A new algorithm for pattern recognition tolerant of deformations and shifts in position. *Pattern Recognition, 15*, 455–469.

Gardner, G. T. (1973). Evidence for independent parallel channels in tachistoscopic perception. *Cognitive Psychology, 4*, 130–155.

Hebb, D. O. (1949). *The organisation of behaviour*. New York: Wiley.

Hinton, G. E. (1981a). A parallel computation that assigns canonical object-based frames of reference. *Proceedings of the Seventh International Joint Conference on Artificial Intelligence*, 683–685.

Hinton, G. E. (1981b). Shape representation in parallel systems. *Proceedings of the Seventh International Joint Conference on Artificial Intelligence*, 1088–1096.

Hinton, G. E., McClelland, J. L., & Rumelhart, D. E. (1986). Distributed representations. In

D. E. Rumelhart & J. L. McClelland (Eds.), *Parallel distributed processing: Explorations in the microstructure of cognition. Volume I: Foundations.* Cambridge, Mass.: M.I.T. Press/ Bradford Books, 77–109.

Johnston, J. C., Hale, B. L., & van Santen, J. P. H. (1983). *Resolving letter position uncertainty in words.* (TM 83–11221–19.) Murray Hill, N.J.: Bell Labs.

Johnston, J. C. & McClelland, J. L. (1980). Experimental tests of a hierarchical model of word identification. *Journal of Verbal Learning and Verbal Behaviour, 19,* 503–524.

Julesz, B. (1981). Textons, the elements of texture perception, and their interactions. *Nature, 290,* 91–97.

Krumhansl, C. L. & Thomas, A. C. (1977). Effect of level of confusability on reporting letters from briefly presented visual displays. *Perception and Psychophysics, 21,* 269–279.

Kucera, H. & Francis, W. N. (1967). *Computational analysis of present-day American English.* Providence, Rhode Island: Brown University Press.

McClelland, J. L. (1985). Putting knowledge in its place: A scheme for programming parallel processing structures on the fly. *Cognitive Science, 9,* 113–146.

McClelland, J. L. (1986). The programmable blackboard model of reading. In J. L. McClelland & D. E. Rumelhart (Eds.), *Parallel distributed processing: Explorations in the microstructure of cognition. Volume II: Psychological and biological models.* Cambridge, Mass.: M.I.T. Press/Bradford Books, 122–169.

McClelland, J. L. & Johnston, J. C. (1977). The role of familiar units in perception of words and nonwords. *Perception and Psychophysics, 22,* 249–261.

McClelland, J. L. & Mozer, M. C. (1986). Perceptual interactions in two-word displays: Familiarity and similarity effects. *Journal of Experimental Psychology: Human Perception and Performance, 12,* 18–35.

McClelland, J. L. & Rumelhart, D. E. (1981). An interactive activation model of context effects in letter perception: Part I. An account of basic findings. *Psychological Review, 88,* 375–407.

Minsky, M. & Papert, S. (1969). *Perceptrons.* Cambridge, Mass.: M.I.T. Press.

Morton, J. (1969). Interaction of information in word recognition. *Psychological Review, 76,* 165–178.

Mozer, M. C. (1983). Letter migration in word perception. *Journal of Experimental Psychology: Human Perception and Performance, 9,* 531–546.

Neisser, U. (1967). *Cognitive psychology.* New York: Appleton-Century-Crofts.

Norman, D. A. (1968). Toward a theory of memory and attention. *Psychological Review, 75,* 522–536.

Palmer, S. E. (1984). The psychology of perceptual organisation: A transformational approach. In A. Rosenfeld & J. Beck (Eds.), *Human and machine vision.* New York: Academic Press.

Pashler, H. & Badgio, P. C. (1985). Visual attention and stimulus identification. *Journal of Experimental Psychology: Human Perception and Performance, 11,* 105–121.

Posner, M. I. (1978). *Chronometric explorations of mind.* Hillsdale, N.J.: Lawrence Erlbaum Associates Inc.

Rayner, K. (1975). Foveal and parafoveal cues in reading. In J. Requin (Ed.), *Attention and performance VII.* Hillsdale, N. J.: Lawrence Erlbaum Associates Inc.

Rayner, K., McConkie, G. W., & Ehrlich, S. (1978). Eye movements and integrating information across fixations. *Journal of Experimental Psychology: Human Perception and Performance, 4,* 529–544.

Rayner, K., McConkie, G. W., & Zola, D. (1980). Integrating information across eye movements. *Cognitive Psychology, 12,* 206–226.

Reicher, G. M. (1969). Perceptual recognition as a function of meaningfulness of stimulus material. *Journal of Experimental Psychology, 81,* 274–280.

Rumelhart, D. E. & McClelland, J. L. (1982). An interactive activation model of context effects in letter perception: Part II. The contextual enhancement effect and some tests and extensions of the model. *Psychological Review, 89,* 60–84.

Santee, J. L. & Egeth, H. E. (1980). Interference in letter identification: A test of feature-specific inhibition. *Perception and Psychophysics, 27,* 321–330.

Schneider, W. & Shiffrin, R. M. (1977). Controlled and automatic human information processing: I. Detection, search and attention. *Psychological Review, 84,* 1–66.

Selfridge, O. G. (1955). Pattern recognition and modern computers. *Proceedings of the Western Joint Computer Conference.* New York: Institute of Electrical and Electronics Engineers.

Shallice, T. & McGill, J. (1978). The origins of mixed errors. In J. Requin (Ed.), *Attention and performance VII.* Hillsdale, N.J.: Lawrence Erlbaum Assocates Inc., 193–208.

Shiffrin, R. M. & Schneider, W. (1977). Controlled and automatic human information processing: II. Perceptual learning, automatic attending, and a general theory. *Psychological Review, 84,* 127–190.

Treisman, A. M. (1969). Strategies and models of selective attention. *Psychological Review, 76,* 282–299.

Underwood, G. E. (1981). Lexical recognition of embedded unattended words: Some implications for reading processes. *Acta Psychologica, 47,* 267–283.

Wickelgren, W. (1969). Context-sensitive coding, associative memory, and serial order in (speech) behaviour. *Psychological Review, 76,* 1–15.

Widrow, G. & Hoff, M. E. (1960). Adaptive switching circuits. *Institute of Radio Engineers, Western Electronic Show and Convention, Convention Record, Part 4,* 96–104.

Willows, D. M. & MacKinnon, G. E. (1973). Selective reading: Attention to the "unattended" lines. *Canadian Journal of Psychology, 27,* 292–304.

Woodworth, R. S. (1938). *Experimental psychology.* New York: Holt.

REFERENCE NOTE

1. Mozer, M. C. (in preparation). *The perception of multiple objects: A parallel, distributed processing aproach.*

5 Orthographic Priming: Qualitative Differences Between Priming from Identified and Unidentified Primes

G. W. Humphreys,
Birkbeck College
London University
London, U.K.

P. T. Quinlan
Birkbeck College
London University
London, U.K.

L. J. Evett
MRC Applied Psychology Unit
Cambridge, U.K.

D. Besner
Department of Psychology
Waterloo University
Ontario, Canada

ABSTRACT

When two letter strings are presented successively for brief durations at the same location, perceptual identification of the second (target) string can be facilitated when it shares letters with the first (prime) string, relative to when the letter strings are unrelated. This "orthographic priming" can occur even when subjects fail to identify the first string.

Two experiments are reported which examine some of the boundary conditions under which orthographic priming occurs. Experiment 1 demonstrates that orthographic priming occurs under conditions where subjects fail to discriminate whether primes are letter strings or rows of Xs, and where subjects fail to report prime letters at a level greater than chance when targets are not presented. It also shows that orthographic priming serves primarily to prevent the prime string from interfering with target identification; an effect which occurs when the strings are unrelated. Experiment 2 involves a contrast between priming effects when primes are masked and not identified (with a short stimulus onset asynchrony [SOA] between the prime and target), and when a long SOA is used and primes can be identified. Orthographic priming occurred only when primes were masked and unidentified.

It is suggested that orthographic priming occurs when primes and targets are not classed as discrete perceptual events. Under this circumstance, there are inhibitory interactions between incompatible strings, and facilitatory interactions when primes activate representations mediating target identification.

Qualitatively different effects arise when primes and targets are identified as separate perceptual events. The implications of these results for interpreting orthographic priming effects are discussed.

INTRODUCTION

Visual word recognition in skilled readers is both fast and relatively effortless (see Humphreys, 1985). These aspects of performance obscure the complexity of the processes involved, and they have led to the invention of devious means of uncovering these processes. One approach has been to study the kinds of information which can be used when words are presented briefly and/or under degraded conditions (e.g. Cattell, 1886; Huey, 1908; Pillsbury, 1897). For instance, presenting words briefly and following their presentation by a pattern mask severely curtails our ability to report them (Michaels & Turvey, 1979; Turvey, 1973). Masking may thus provide a technique for tapping early processes in the time course of word processing.

Most commonly, investigators have studied the processing of words under masking conditions by examining the effects of particular stimulus variables (such as whether a stimulus is a word or a nonword; whether or not it is orthographically regular; etc.) on identification accuracy (e.g. as in studies of the "word-superiority effect"; see Adams, 1979; Johnston & McClelland, 1980; Rumelhart & McClelland, 1982). More recently, investigators have also examined the *indirect* effects of a masked "priming" stimulus on responses to a subsequent target (e.g. Cheeseman & Merikle, 1985; Forster & Davis, 1984; Humphreys, 1981; Marcel, 1980; 1983). Tests of indirect effects offer the intriguing possibility that stimuli which cannot be identified explicitly may nevertheless exert some influence on the processing of subsequent stimuli. Such tests may enable early processes in word recognition to be tapped without contamination by those later processes concerned with response selection and identification (since the masked stimuli are not themselves identified explicitly).

To illustrate this point, consider data reported by Evett and Humphreys (1981). Subjects were presented with a series of four equally brief visual stimuli at the same spatial location (a technique they termed four-field masking). The first and fourth stimuli in the sequence were pattern masks. The second and third stimuli were letter strings (termed the prime and the target respectively). Subjects were asked to identify both letter strings on a trial. Individual thresholds were adjusted until subjects could identify about 40% of the targets correctly; under these conditions primes were typically not reported. Evett and Humphreys found that target identification was facilitated when primes contained many of the same letters in the same positions, relative to when primes and targets were unrelated ("orthographic priming"). This result was not due to simple energy summation between the letters, since primes were in lower case and targets were in upper case, and there was no hint of a correlation between the magnitude of priming and various measures of visual similarity between the stimuli. Evett and Humphreys suggested that target identification was facilitated when primes and targets activated a common orthographic description, so that less target information was then required for an identification response based upon this description. Since primes were not reported, it would appear that the orthographic description mediating priming was not generated intentionally. It follows that investigations of this orthographic priming effect should help elucidate the orthographic description normally mediating early word processing.

However, other interpretations of the orthographic priming effect can be given. When subjects are briefly presented with displays composed of two or more words, identification errors are sometimes made by transposing letters *between* the words (e.g. RUST and VENT into RUNT and VEST; see Allport, 1977; McClelland & Mozer, 1986; Mozer, 1983; Shallice & McGill, 1978; Treisman & Souther, 1986). It could be that, in the four-field masking procedure used by Evett and Humphreys (1981), target identification responses were sometimes based on an amalgamation of letters from primes and targets (i.e. from the intrusion of prime letters into target responses). When primes and targets contain different letters, identification errors would result from such intrusions. When primes and targets contain common letters, intrusion "errors" would sometimes mimic correct target identifications. Target identification would consequently be better when primes and targets contain common letters than when they are unrelated.

In order to judge the relevance of orthographic priming to early processes in visual word recognition, we need to assess whether target identification is genuinely facilitated by an orthographically related prime or whether these effects are simply a by-product of intrusion errors which occur under four-field masking conditions. It would also be helpful to have a better understanding of the conditions under which orthographic priming occurs. Progress could be made by: (1) deriving a better measure of the prime information which subjects can identify explicitly; and (2) clarifying the relationship between priming under masking conditions and those effects which arise when primes are not masked and can be identified. It is possible that priming effects under masking conditions are *qualitatively* different from some of the priming effects which occur when primes are not masked (e.g. Cheeseman & Merikle, 1985; Forster & Davis, 1984; Humphreys, 1985; Marcel, 1980). We would have increased confidence that orthographic priming with masked primes reflects only input processes if we could demonstrate that these effects differ qualitatively from those which obtain with unmasked primes.

The aim of the present paper is therefore threefold:

1. To contrast an orthographic priming account with any intrusion errors that occur under 4-field masking conditions.
2. To generate some on-line measure of the information about primes which subjects can explicitly identify when orthographic priming occurs.
3. To contrast orthographic priming under conditions of masked and unmasked priming.

The first two aims are fulfilled in Experiment 1; the third aim is fulfilled in Experiment 2.

EXPERIMENT 1

Experiment 1 was based on the four-field masking procedure developed by Evett and Humphreys (1981). Various priming conditions were used. In one condition, primes and targets had the same identity (e.g. lost-LOST); this condition yields maximal priming. In the graphemically related condition, primes and targets contained some common letters which fell in the same positions within the letter strings (e.g. lert-LOST); this condition tests for orthographic priming between the stimuli. The effects of orthographic priming were compared with two further baselines. In the unrelated-priming control condition, primes and targets had no common letters (e.g., gerb-LOST). In the neutral-prime control condition, targets were preceded by a row of Xs as a prime (e.g. xxxx-LOST). In the unrelated-prime control condition, any intrusion of prime letters into target responses would produce an incorrect target identification response. The chance level of such intrusion errors may be calculated from the data in the neutral-control condition (since no primes were then presented). The true level of intrusion errors is given by the difference between the levels observed in the unrelated and the neutral-prime control conditions. If genuine orthographic priming does occur, then such priming should either be larger than the intrusion errors observed, or there must be some way of demonstrating that they differ qualitatively.

The conditions outlined do not, on their own, give a direct measure of the prime information that is available for *explicit* identification. Two further steps were taken in order to gain such information. First, a condition was added in which words used as targets in other conditions were presented as primes, and were followed by a row of Xs as a target (e.g., lost-XXXX). Since no target word was present in this condition, it provides the best opportunity for assessing whether subjects can explicitly identify primes, whilst keeping all other conditions in the experiment constant (in effect, trials in the no-target condition served as catch trials). Second, subjects were told that on 3/5 of the trials they would be presented with 2 letter strings, whilst on the other

2/5 of the trials they would be presented with one letter string and a row of Xs. They were asked to discriminate whether two letter strings, or one letter string and one row of Xs, were present on the trial. This enabled us to assess whether subjects could discriminate the visual format of primes (even if primes could not be identified explicitly).

Method

Stimulus presentation and timing were controlled by a PDP 11/10 computer. Displays were point-plotted on an Advance Instrument oscilloscope (05 250), equipped with a P-31 rapid decay phospher (see Evett & Humphreys, 1981, for an illustration of the character set used). Primes and targets were always four characters long; and targets were always in upper case and primes in lower case. Each character covered a visual angle of about 0.5° horizontally by 1° vertically, from the viewing distance of about 50cm. Thus each letter string subtended a horizontal visual angle of about 2°. The pattern mask was constructed out of random letter fragments. It covered the same spatial area as primes and targets and subtended a visual angle of about 3° horizontally by 2° vertically.

There were 150 target words, 75 with frequencies greater than 100 per million in the Kucera and Francis (1967) word count (the high frequency set), and 75 with frequencies less than 10 per million (the low frequency set). The words in each frequency set were divided into 5 groups of 15, matched for frequency. The 5 groups of words appeared in each priming condition by rotating the words across 5 word groups.

There were 5 conditions which were as follows:

1. Primes and targets had the same identity (e.g. lost-LOST).
2. Primes and targets were graphemically related, sharing their end letters (e.g. lert-LOST).
3. Primes and target were unrelated (e.g. gerb-LOST).
3. Targets were preceded by neutral primes (e.g. xxxx-LOST).
5. Primes but no targets were presented (e.g. lost-XXXX).

Each of these conditions was repeated with high and with low frequency targets. As far as possible, all primes in conditions (2) and (3) were nonwords.[1] Subjects were told that they would be presented with displays containing either two letter strings or one letter string and one row of Xs. They were asked to write a one or a two first, to signify whether they thought there were one or two letter strings present. Subjects then had to write down

---

[1] Note that Evett and Humphreys (1981) reported that orthographic priming from nonword primes to word targets was as effective as that from word primes.

any letter strings they thought they saw in the case they thought the letters were presented in. They were allowed to write only single letters, if they were unable to report whole strings. they were also asked to write how confident they were that their identification response was correct. A 7-point scale was used, where 1 = a guess and 7 = very confident.

Prior to the experimental trials, a series of threshold trials was conducted with each subject. During the threshold trials, subjects were presented with a new set of targets preceded by unrelated primes (the unrelated-prime control condition). Threshold trials were run in blocks of eight, and began at durations where targets were relatively easy to identify. The field durations were then reduced until subjects made about 50% correct target identifications in the unrelated-prime condition over 64 trials. After the threshold trials, the experimental trials were conducted using the durations established for each subject. Over subjects, the mean field duration was 41msec, and times ranged between 35 and 50msec.

At the start of each trial, subjects fixated a central dot which fell just below the centre of the letter strings. When fixated, the display was initiated by the subject pressing a button. Trials were self-paced.

There were 15 members of the Birkbeck College subject pool, all with either normal or corrected-to-normal vision. Each took part in a single session lasting about 40 minutes.

Results

Performance was assessed using three measures: correct target identifications; a classification of the errors made to targets; and the confidence with which identification responses were rated.

Target Identification.   Table 5.1 gives the mean percentage correct target identification responses in each condition, along with the percentage of trials in each condition where subjects reported that two letter strings were present.[2] The percentage correct identifications in the no-target condition here indicates the level of whole-string reports of primes.

The identification data were analysed in a mixed design ANOVA, with two within-subjects factors (priming condition and target word frequency), and one between-subjects factor (subject groups).[3] For this analysis, the data from the no-target condition were eliminated, since there were minimal whole-string reports in that condition. There were reliable main effects of

---

[2] For this analysis, only responses which reproduced all the target letters in the correct positions were scored as correct; all other responses (including morphemically related responses) were scored as incorrect.

[3] This procedure enables any finding to be generalised across stimuli.

TABLE 5.1
Table of the Results of Experiment 1

	High Frequency			Low Frequency		
Condition	% Correct	Confidence Rating	% "2" Responses	% Correct	Confidence Rating	% "2" Responses
(a) Same identity (e.g. lost–LOST)	81.77	5.09	41.77	67.12	4.55	42.22
(b) Graphemically related (e.g., lert–LOST)	73.33	4.41	42.67	54.21	4.08	51.56
(c) Unrelated-prime (e.g., gerb–LOST)	57.77	3.77	45.33	44.89	3.26	55.11
(d) Neutral-prime (e.g., XXXX–LOST)	64.01	4.17	43.77	55.99	3.94	43.56
(e) No-target (e.g., lost–XXXX)	1.34	2.14	39.56	0.00	2.11	41.34

NOTE: Showing mean percentage correct target identifications, the mean percentages of trials on which two letter strings were reported as occurring, and the mean confidence rating given for the identification response (rating scale, 1 = guess to 7 = very sure).

both frequency and priming condition [$F(1,10) = 24.65$ and $F(3,30) = 16.13$, both $P < 0.001$]. There was no effect of subject group, and there were no reliable interactions [for the frequency X priming interaction, $F(3,30) = 1.34$, $P < 0.05$].

A Newman-Keuls analysis was conducted to examine the differences between the priming conditions. Target identification was better in the same-identity condition than in all the other conditions ($P < 0.01$ for all comparisons). Performance in the unrelated-prime control condition was also worse than in the graphemically similar and the neutral-prime conditions ($P < 0.01$ and $P < 0.05$ respectively). The graphemically similar and the neutral-prime conditions did not differ.

In the no-target conditions, there were only 3 correct full reports of primes (out of 450 trials). Two of these reports were made by the same subject, and all were of high frequency words. There were no correct reports of primes in the graphemically similar and the unrelated-prime conditions. There were also no reports of lower-case letters.

The data on the percentage of trials on which subjects reported the occurrence of two letter strings were similarly analysed. There was a reliable main effect of target frequency [$F(1,10) = 8.14$, $P < 0.025$]. None of the other main effects, nor the interactions, approached significance. This analysis indicates that subjects were more likely to report the occurrence of two letter strings when the target was of low frequency than when it was of high frequncy. Also, this effect was present across all the priming conditions (i.e. irrespective of whether or not two letter strings were present), suggesting that, at least in part, it reflected subjects' confidence about their responses. Subjects may have been more likely to report the presence of two letter strings when they were unsure about their target identification responses.

Error Analyses.   The full report data from the no-target condition indicate that, even when target letter strings are not present, subjects find it difficult to identify primes in the present conditions. However, it remains possible that single letters from primes were available for report.

To test for the availability of single letters from primes in the no-target condition, the responses in that condition were decomposed to reveal the percentage of trials on which single letters from primes were correctly reported. For this analysis, all correct letter reports were included, irrespective of whether the letters preserved their correct position in the response. The number and percentage of trials on which: (a) at least one; or (b) two or more; prime letters were reported, and their serial positions in primes, are given in Table 5.2.

We need to compare the numbers of prime letters reported in the no-target condition with those expected by chance. Chance report was calculated from the error responses to targets in the neutral-prime condition. For every

TABLE 5.2

The Number and Percentage of Trials on which Prime Letters were Present in Responses in the No-target, Neutral, and Unrelated-prime Conditions in Experiment 1

Condition	Serial Position in Prime			
	1	2	3	4
1. No target (total trials = 450)				
Trials where at least 1 letter reported = 51 (11.3%)				
Trials where 2 or more letters reported = 19 (4.2%)				
Serial positions of letters:	16 (3.6%)	29 (6.4%)	19 (4.2%)	19 (8.4%)
2. Chance prime letter responses in neutral–prime condition (total error trials = 174)				
Trials where at least 1 letter reported = 31 (17.8%)				
Trials where 2 or more letters reported = 2 (1.2%)				
Serial positions of letters:	4 (2.3%)	13 (7.5%)	8 (4.6%)	8 (4.6%)
3. Prime letter responses in the graphemically related condition (total error trials = 164)				
Trials where at least 1 letter reported = 36				
Trials where 2 or more letters reported = 1				
Serial positions of letters:	0	19 (11.59%)	18 (10.98%)	0
4. Prime letter responses in the unrelated–prime condition (total error trials = 214)				
Trials where at least 1 letter reported = 73 (34.1%)				
Trials where 2 or more letters reported = 14 (6.5%)				
Serial positions of letters:	16 (7.5%)	30 (14.0%)	24 (11.2%)	19 (8.4%)

target, a chance intrusion was scored each time a letter in the error response in the neutral condition matched a letter in the prime paired with that target in the unrelated-prime condition, irrespective of the serial positions of the letters (see Table 5.2). For example, a response such as LOSE to the prime-target pairing xxxx-LOST was scored as a chance intrusion, since the prime paired with LOST in the unrelated condition contained the letter "e" (i.e. gerb). An inspection of the data indicates that the report of single letters from primes in the no-target condition was no greater than chance.

Intrusion errors in the graphemically-similar and the unrelated-prime condition were also calculated, ignoring whether the letters maintained or altered their serial positions in the target response.[4] These data are also presented in Table 5.2. The interesting contrast is between the number of intrusion errors in the graphemically similar and the unrelated-prime condi-tions relative to the neutral-prime baseline (the level expected by chance). The percentage of error trials where letters from positions 2 and 3 in the prime were reported was greater in the graphemically-similar condition than in the neutral baseline $[t(14) = 2.13, P < 0.05]$;[5] and, across all letter positions, there were more intrusion errors in the unrelated-prime condition than in the neutral baseline $[t(14) = 3.78, P < 0.01]$. Intrusion rates from the middle letter positions did not differ in the graphemically similar and the unrelated-prime conditons $[t < 1.0]$. Overall, there is a contrast between the reports of prime letters in the no-target condition, which were not greater than chance, and prime letters reported in the graphemically similar and unrelated-prime conditions, which were greater than chance.

The intrusion rates for the middle letter positions do not differ in the graphemically-similar and the unrelated-prime conditions.[6] We can therefore use the rates from the unrelated-prime condition to estimate the contribution of letter intrusions from primes to the increased target identification rates observed in the graphemically-similar condition. First, let us assume that the intrusion rates from positions 1 and 4 in primes will be the same in the graphemically similar and the unrelated-prime conditions.[7] The probability

---

[4]Intrusion errors were not assessed in the same-identity condition because possible intrusion responses could not then be separated from correct target identifications.

[5]In the graphemically similar condition, intrusion errors could only be assessed from positions 2 and 3 because intrusions from positions 1 and 4 could not be separated from correct responses.

[6]In contrast to the present result, subjects make more transposition errors between two simultaneously presented words when the words have more letters in common (see McClelland & Mozer, 1986). This suggests that different processes may be involved when subjects attempt to identify one out of two words presented simultaneously at different spatial locations and when, as here, the words are successively presented at the same location and are perceived as a single event (see Humphreys, Evett & Quinlan, Note 2, for further discussion).

[7]Such an assumption seems reasonable because the observed rates from positions 2 and 3 did not differ.

of an intrusion from letter position 1 in primes, PI(1), was 0.043 (0.075, in the unrelated condition, -0.023, in the neutral condition; see Table 5.2). The probability of an intrusion from letter position 4 in primes, PI(4), was 0.038 (0.084-0.046; see Table 5.2). To produce a correct target identification response, such intrusions would have to combine with the correct identification of target letters in the other letter positions. The probability of particular target letters being identified on error trials can be calculated from the error responses in the neutral condition. The probability that letters from positions 1, 2, and 3 in targets were all identified correctly on error trials, PT(1–3), was 0.2241; the probability that letters from positions 2, 3, and 4 were all identified correctly on such trials, PT(2–4), was 0.0015. The probability of an intrusion error from positions 1 and 4 in primes producing a correct target response, PT(C), is thus given by the joint probability of an intrusion error from position 1 and the correct report of target letters from positions 2, 3, and 4, plus the joint probability of an intrusion error from position 4 and the correct report of target letters from positions 1, 2, and 3 [PI[1] × PT(2–4) + PI(4) × PT(1–3)].[8] Inserting the observed values gives us an estimated target identification increase of 1% [100 (0.043 × 0.0402 + 0.038 × 0.2241)]. In contrast, target identification was an average 12.44% better in the graphemically similar than in the unrelated-prime condition. It could be argued that the probability of intrusion rates from positions 1 and 4 would differ in the graphemically similar and the unrelated conditions because such intrusions, when combined with the appropriate target letters, would only be guaranteed to produce word responses in the graphemically similar condition. However, it makes little difference when the intrusion rates are assessed only from the trials in the unrelated condition where the amalgamation of prime and target letters would produce word responses. For instance, PI(1) is then 0.0402 and PI(4) is 0.089. PT(C) is 0.0215 (0.0402 × 0.0402 + 0.089 × 0.2241), and the estimated increase in target identification is 2.15%. This remains too small to account for the observed target benefit in the graphemically similar condition.

Two further aspects of the intrusion errors in the unrelated-prime condition should be noted. One is that such errors tended to be greater from the central than from the end-letter positions in primes (see Table 5.2). The second is that, when single letters from primes intruded on target responses (on 59 trials), the letters were quite likely to alter their position in the target response (25 position-maintained vs. 34 position-altered trials). In contrast, when there were intrusions of more than one letter, the intruding letters were

---

[8] In calculating PT(C) here, we are using only the single letter intrusion data. There were no instances in the unrelated condition where letters from positions 1 and 4 in primes were jointly transposed, so the contribution of such joint letter transpositions cannot be assessed, and is likely in any case to be minimal.

likely to maintain their positions in the target response. There were 13 trials where 2 prime letters were reported; on 11 of these trials the letters maintained the same specific positions, and on one trial they maintained the same relative positions (dest–LIAR→STAR). There was only one trial where three prime letters were reported, and these letters all maintained their positions (rosh–LICE→POSH). The latter 2 findings have recently been confirmed on a large scale analysis of over 1800 error trials (Humphreys et al., Note 2). These aspects of the intrusion error data contrast with the data on orthographic priming (see below).

Confidence Ratings. The mean confidence rating given to each condition is shown in Table 5.1. The ratings varied both as a function of the priming condition and the target word frequency [$F(4,32) = 165.76$ and $F(1,8) = 21.3$, both $P < 0.001$]. There were no interactions. A Newman-Keuls analysis of the condition effect demonstrated that subjects were least confident in the no-target condition ($P < 0.01$ for all comparisons), followed by the unrelated-prime condition ($P < 0.01$ for all comparisons), the neutral-prime and graphemically related conditions (which did not differ), and the same-identity condition ($P < 0.01$ for all comparisons). These data closely match the target identification results. Subjects were more confident of their responses in the priming conditions where they were most accurate, and they were more confident of their responses to high relative to low frequency words.

The confidence ratings given in the unrelated-prime condition were also broken down according to whether the target on the trial was correctly identified, and, when an error was made, according to whether it was a intrusion error or not. The mean rating given on correct response trials was 4.88, on nonintrusion error trials it was 3.81, and on intrusion error trials it was 3.79. These ratings differed significantly [$F(2,20) = 45.81$, $P < 0.001$]. Ratings on correct trials were higher than on either type of error trial (Newman-Keuls test, $P < 0.01$ for both comparisons), and ratings on the two types of error trials did not differ.

Discussion

Experiment 1 confirms that reliable priming effects can be observed under conditions where subjects have minimal information about prime identities or their visual format. Thus, reliable differences were found between the same identity, the graphemically related and the unrelated-prime conditions, even though subjects failed to discriminate whether primes were letter strings or rows of Xs and even though the report of single letters from primes in the no-target condition was no better than chance. Because the two measures of prime identification used here were mixed with the priming trials, they provide a more accurate test of the information available during the experiment than the pre- or post-experimental tests of prime identification used in other studies of priming under masking conditions (e.g. McCauley, Parmelee, Sperber, & Carr, 1980; Marcel, 1983; see Purcell, Stewart, & Stanovich, 1983).

Experiment 1 also extends previous studies of orthographic priming by including a neutral-prime control. Performance in the neutral condition did not differ from that in the graphemically related condition, and both were better than when primes and targets were unrelated. This suggests that the main effect of orthographic priming is to minimise the interference effect which occurs when the stimuli are unrelated. We must therefore question whether the difference between the graphemically related and the unrelated conditions is due solely to the intrusion of letters from primes into target responses. For instance, intrusions could produce correct target identifications in the graphemically related condition and incorrect identifications (i.e. interference) in the unrelated condition. The error analysis indicated that intrusions did occur in both the graphemically similar and the unrelated conditions. Nevertheless, there are grounds for arguing that such intrusions were not the cause of the difference between the priming conditions. First, the intrusion rates are too small to account for the difference in target identification in the graphemically similar and the unrelated conditions. Second, subjects were relatively unsure of their responses when intrusion errors occurred in the unrelated-prime condition, yet they were relatively confident of their responses in the graphemically related condition. This suggests that the higher accuracy in the related condition reflects something other than intrusion responses. Third, intrusion errors in the unrelated-prime condition tended to be greatest from the middle letter positions, and tended not to preserve the position of the letter. In contrast, orthographic priming is closely tied to letters maintaining the same relative positions in primes and targets, and is greatest when primes and targets have the same end letters (Humphreys et al., Note 2).

We suggest that orthographic priming does occur, and that the effects are not solely a function of intrusion errors between the letter strings. One suggestion is that, when primes and targets are briefly presented at the same spatial location (as in Experiment 1), they compete for perceptual identification (Humphreys, 1985). This competition is lessened when prime information supports target identification. From the present results, it appears that primes support target identification when they share common letters, with the effects being greatest when all the letters are the same. Let us suppose that priming here is mediated by some form of pre-lexical, orthographic representation, in which the relative positions of the letters in the string are coded (Humphreys et al., Note 2). When primes and targets differ, they may compete to establish one representation at this level. Usually the target, by

APPR-E*

virtue of its later presentation, will inhibit the orthographic representation of the prime (cf. Michaels & Turvey, 1979). Thus the prime information inhibited will be that specifying the relative positions of the letters within the string. Competition will be reduced as a function of the orthographic similarity of the stimuli (e.g. in the graphemically related condition), and when primes cannot be adequately represented at an orthographic level (e.g. when they are rows of Xs). Intrusion errors may be a symptom of this competition, in that they may reflect the information available when subjects do not have a distinct orthographic representation of the target. Such information would take the form of single letters not coded for position, and would include prime letters not incorporated into the orthographic representation of the prime. It follows that intrusion errors will not preserve letter locations. The intrusions of two letters from primes into target responses were much less frequent than single letter intrusions, but when they occurred the two letters tended to maintain their relative positions. Such intrusions may occur when the target fails to inhibit the orthographic representation of the prime, so that identification is based upon the orthographic representation of the prime. In suggesting this, we presume that the nature of the intrusion error (e.g. whether or not letters maintain their positions) will be informative about the level of representation at which the letter(s) were last coded correctly. More generally, we suggest that, far from being caused by intrusion errors, orthographic priming tends to reduce such errors by reinforcing the orthographic representation of the target. Furthermore, by maintaining a pre-lexical locus for this effect, we can accommodate its additive relationship with a putatively lexical effect, such as target word frequency.

The lack of prime identification in the no-target condition remains to be explained, given the intrusion errors observed in the unrelated-prime condition. This prime identification failure can be explained in at least two ways. One possibility is that there are strong inhibitory effects of the row of Xs target on prime processing. A second possibility is that, when faced with the problem of establishing an orthographic representation of a possible target in that condition, subjects conclude that they simply missed the target on that trial and fail to use any information which may be available. Whatever the case, the present results indicate that prime information is considerably more difficult to identify explicitly than target information, emphasising that priming in no way reflects the intentional use of prime information.

EXPERIMENT 2

The account of orthographic priming we have proposed holds that priming occurs under conditions where primes and targets compete for identification as a single stimulus event. Priming should therefore differ when primes and targets are perceived as separate stimulus events. This was examined in Experiment 2.

Method

Unless otherwise stated, the method remained the same as in Experiment 1.

There were 24 subjects, all members of the Birkbeck College subject pool, and all with either normal or corrected-to-normal vision. For half the subjects the procedure remained the same as in Experiment 1. For the other subjects a longer SOA was introduced between primes and targets which allowed primes to be identified.

In the long-SOA condition, subjects were presented with the following sequence of stimuli: prime, mask, target, mask. Primes were exposed for a constant duration of 200msec, and the first mask for a constant 100msec. This first mask serves to separate primes perceptually from targets. When the prime is presented for a relatively long duration (as here) and not followed by the mask, primes effect a kind of "perceptual capture" on targets which have the same identity (see Humphreys, 1985; Humphreys, Besner, & Quinlan, Note 1). Individual thresholds were set for the durations of the target and the second mask, so that subjects were able to identify about 50% of the targets in the unrelated-prime control condition, over 64 trials. The mean durations for the target and the second mask was 50msec and there was a range between 40 and 70msec. The durations so established were then used for the experimental trials.

In the short-SOA condition the sequence of fields was the same as in Experiment 1; that is, mask, prime, target, mask. Each field was presented for the same duration. The mean field duration over subjects was 38msec, and there was a range between 30 and 45msec.

There were three priming conditions:

1. Primes and targets had the same identity (e.g. lost-LOST).
2. Primes and targets were graphemically related (e.g. list-LOST).
3. Primes and targets were unrelated (e.g. tame-LOST).

All the primes in the graphemically related and the unrelated conditions were words. Primes in the graphemically related condition shared three of the four target letters, and the position of the letter changed was balanced across the four positions in different prime-target pairs.

In both the short- and long-SOA conditions subjects were told that they would be presented with two words on each trial, and they were asked to write down both words if they could. They were told to write the letters in the case they thought they were presented in.

The same 150 target words were used as in Experiment 1 (75 high and 75 low frequency). For both the SOA conditions these words were rotated across three subject groups so that each target appeared in each condition without being repeated to subjects. In the threshold trials, a new set of low frequncy targets and unrelated primes was used.

Results

The percentage correct target identifications in each condition are shown in Table 5.3.

The data were subject to a mixed design ANOVA with two within-subjects factors (priming condition and target word frequency) and two between-subjects factors (short vs. long SOA and subject groups). There were reliable main effects of priming condition, frequency, and SOA [$F(2,36)=16.15$, $F(1,18)=69.32$ and $F(1,18)=9.81$, $P<0.001$, $P<0.001$ and $P<0.01$ respectively]. The interaction between priming condition and SOA bordered significance [$F(2,36)=2.48$, $0.05<P<0.1$]. None of the other interactions were reliable.

Inspection of the data indicates that, whilst quite strong orthographic priming obtained with the short SOA, there was no orthographic priming with the long SOA. Separate analyses of the effects at each SOA confirms this. At the short SOA, the same-identity condition was better than the graphemically related condition, and the graphemically related condition was in turn better than the unrelated condition (Newman-Keuls analysis, $P<0.01$). At the long SOA, the same-identity condition was facilitated relative to the graphemically related and the unrelated conditions (both $P<0.01$). Graphemically related was no better than graphemically unrelated.

All the primes in the long-SOA condition were correctly reported. None of the primes in the short-SOA condition were correctly reported. There were also no reports of lower-case letters at the short SOA.

Discussion

Experiment 2 demonstrates a qualitative difference between priming at short and long SOAs, with orthographic priming only occurring with short SOAs. The data with short SOAs support those in Experiment 1. Target identification benefited from both graphemic and same-identity priming, relative to when primes were unrelated. The benefits were largest in the same-identity condition, and priming was additive with target word frequency. These findings are entirely consistent with our earlier argument that orthographic priming from masked primes reflects the interaction of primes and targets competing for a single orthographic description. This interaction effectively reduces target identification when the letter strings differ. The data also emphasise that orthographic priming is not caused by the intrusion of letters

TABLE 5.3
Mean Percentage Correct Target Identifications in Each Condition in Experiment 2

| | Masked Prime | | Unmasked Prime | |
Condition	High Frequency	Low Frequency	High Frequency	Low Frequency
Same identity (e.g., Lost–LOST)	71.11	61.39	80.00	72.08
Graphemically related (e.g., list–LOST)	66.67	51.11	66.35	53.33
Unrelated-prime (e.g., tame–LOST)	55.28	35.56	65.83	55.00

from the masked primes. In the graphemically related condition here, primes and targets differed only by one letter, so single letter intrusions should produce the identification of some of these primes in the graphemically similar condition. None were observed.

With the long SOAs, target identification only benefited when primes had the same identity. This failure to find orthographic priming cannot easily be attributed to differences in the overall magnitude of priming at the two SOAs, since such differences were relatively small. Rather, the difference between the effects may be attributed to the lack of competition between primes and targets for an orthographic description when there was a long SOA. At the long SOA there needs to be complete overlap of identity information between primes and targets for target identification to benefit. It appears, then, that the achievement of an episodic representation of the prime changes the nature of the priming effect. One possibility is that partial activation of the representations of stimuli other than the prime is "switched off" (inhibited) once the prime is explicitly identified, so that only identical stimuli will benefit from such pre-activation. Another possibility is that, once explicitly identified, the episodic representation of the prime changes the guessing strategies of subjects to favour only identical stimuli. These possibilities are not mutually exclusive (Humphreys et al., Note 1).

It is also of interest that even with the long SOA in Experiment 2, priming in the same-identity condition was additive with the effects of word frequency (see also Humphreys et al., Note 1, for further confirmation of this result). At present, it remains unclear quite why this result occurred, given previous findings of interactions between frequency and repetition with unmasked primes (see Jacoby & Dallas, 1981; Scarborough, Cortese, & Scarborough, 1977). Further work is currently being undertaken examining this finding.

GENERAL DISCUSSION

The present results demonstrate that:

1. Orthographic priming under four-field masking conditions is not solely due to intrusion errors between primes and targets.
2. Orthographic priming occurs when primes are masked such that subjects do not explicitly identify prime letters when there is no target letter string present.
3. Orthographic priming with unidentified, masked primes differs qualitatively from that found when primes are identified.

With short SOAs between primes and targets, subjects are relatively poor at discriminating both the presence and the visual format of primes (Experiment 1). This suggests that primes and targets are not parsed as discrete perceptual events; consequently, the letter strings may compete for a single identification response. In this case, primes can be thought of as initiating the production of an orthographic description within the word recognition system. In this orthographic description the positions of the letters within the strings are coded. Primes which are orthographically similar to targets will support the orthographic description of the target. Competition between orthographic descriptions will occur with unrelated strings, although the target will receive priority (given its later presentation). The effect of the competition will be to disrupt the orthographic representation of the target. This disruption both decreases target identification and forces performance to be influenced by lower levels of representation, such as those concerned solely with letter identities and not their positions. One consequence would be that target identification would then be vulnerable to the intrusion of prime letters, giving rise to the position-independent intrusion errors observed in Experiment 1. By supporting the target description, orthographic priming helps to reduce such errors. With longer SOAs between primes and targets, primes can be identified. Performance is then no longer influenced by competitive interactions between orthographic representations of the letter strings; rather it appears to be influenced by factors such as the bias produced by an episodic representation of the prime on the identity assigned to the target.

Orthographic priming thus appears to reflect the early processes involved in constructing the orthographic description of a letter string. Forster and his colleagues (Forster, this volume; Forster & Davis, 1984) have recently failed to find orthographic priming from a masked prime on timed lexical decision responses to target words. Various differences between the two procedures could underly this contrast (e.g. in reaction time tasks, targets are usually given long exposures, rather than the short exposures used here), but perhaps the most important difference is the task. Manso de Zúñiga, Quinlan, and

Humphreys (Note 3) have found reliable orthographic priming from masked primes to target words in a naming task where targets received prolonged exposures. It may be that tachistoscopic identification and naming tasks are more sensitive than lexical decision tasks to changes in the state of the orthographic representation of stimuli (perhaps because lexical decisions are made with reference to semantic or familiarity information; see Balota & Chumbley, 1984; Besner, 1983). Whatever the case, the effect of task variables is certainly worthy of further study.

In other studies of orthographic priming under perceptual identification conditions we have found that the effects depend on the letters in primes and targets maintaining the same positions relative to the end letters in the strings (Humphreys et al., Note 2). Orthographic priming is also indifferent to the visual similarity of the letters in primes and targets (see Evett & Humphreys, 1981). It follows that the orthographic description mediating visual word recognition is one in which the identities and positions of the letters are coded in relation to the end letters of the string. This suggestion, for an abstract orthographic description mediating word recognition, converges with work on the effects of peripheral words on eye movements during reading (e.g. Rayner, McConkie, & Ehrlich, 1978) and work on neurological impairments of word recognition (e.g. Saffran, 1980). Orthographic priming may provide a way of examining the characteristics of this description in some detail.

ACKNOWLEDGEMENTS

This work was supported by grants from the ESRC to the first and third authors and from grant #U0051 and A0998 from the Natural Sciences and Engineering Research Council of Canada to the fourth author. We thank Mike Harris for writing the original presentation programs, Clive Frankish for creating the character set, and Chas Manso de Zúñiga for comments.

REFERENCES

Adams, M. J. (1979). Models of word recognition. *Cognitive Psychology, 11*, 133–176.

Allport, D. A. (1977). On knowing the meaning of words we are unable to report: The effects of visual masking. In S. Dornic (Ed.), *Attention and performance VI*. Hillsdale, N.J.: Lawrence Erlbaum Associates Inc., 505–533.

Balota, D. & Chumbley, J. I. (1984). Are lexical decisions a good measure of lexical access? The role of word frequency in the neglected decision stage. *Journal of Experimental Psychology: Human Perception and Performance, 10*, 340–357.

Besner, D. (1983). Basic decoding components in reading: The dissociable feature extraction processes. *Canadian Journal of Psychology, 37*, 429–438.

Cattell, J. M. (1886). The time taken up by cerebral operations. *Mind, 11*, 220–242.

Cheesman, J. & Merikle, P. M. (1985). Word recognition and consciousness. In D. Besner, T. G. Waller, & G. E. MacKinnon (Eds.), *Reading research: Advances in theory and practice. Vol. 5.* New York: Academic Press.

Evett, L. J. & Humphreys, G. W. (1981). The use of abstract graphemic information in lexical access. *Quarterly Journal of Experimental Psychology, 33A*, 325–350.

Forster, K. I. & Davis, C. (1984). Repetition priming and frequency attenuation in lexical access. *Journal of Experimental Psychology: Learning, Memory, and Cognition, 10*, 680–698.

Huey, E. B. (1908). *The psychology and pedagogy of reading*. New York: Macmillan.

Humphreys, G. W. (1981). Direct vs. indirect tests of the information available from masked displays: What visual masking does and does not prevent. *British Journal of Psychology, 72*, 323–330.

Humphreys, G. W. (1985). Attention, automaticity, and autonomy in visual word processing. In D. Besner, T. G. Waller, & G. E. MacKinnon (Eds.), *Reading research: Advances in theory and practice. Vol. 5*. New York: Academic Press.

Jacoby, L. L. & Dallas, M. (1981). On the relationship between autobiographical memory and perceptual learning. *Journal of Experimental Psychology: General, 110*, 306–340.

Johnston, J. C. & McClelland, J. L. (1980). Experimental tests of a hierarchical model of word identification. *Journal of Verbal Learning and Verbal Behaviour, 19*, 503–524.

Kucera, H. & Francis, W. (1967). *Computational analysis of present-day American English*. Providence, R.I.: Brown University Press.

Marcel, A. J. (1980). Conscious and preconscious recognition of polysemous words: Locating the selective effects of prior verbal context. In R. S. Nickerson (Ed.), *Attention and performance VIII*. Hillsdale, N.J.: Lawrence Erlbaum Associates Inc.

Marcel, A. J. (1983). Conscious and unconscious perception: Experiments on visual masking and word recognition. *Cognitive Psychology, 15*, 197–237.

McCauley, C., Parmelee, C. M., Sperber, R. D., & Carr, T. H. (1980). Early extraction of meaning from pictures and its relation to conscious identification. *Journal of Experimental Psychology: Human Perception and Performance, 6*, 265–276.

McClelland, J. L. & Mozer, M. C. (1986). Perceptual interactions in two-word displays: Familiarity and similarity effects. *Journal of Experimental Psychology: Human Perception and Performance, 12*, 18–35.

Michaels, C. F. & Turvey, M. T. (1979). Central sources of visual masking: Indexing structures supporting seeing at a single glance. *Psychological Research, 41*, 1–61.

Mozer, M. C. (1983). Letter migration in word perception. *Journal of Experimental Psychology: Human Perception and Performance, 9*, 531–546.

Pillsbury, W. B. (1897). A study of apprehension. *American Journal of Psychology, 8*, 315–393.

Purcell, D. G., Stewart, A. L., & Stanovich, K. E. (1983). Another look at semantic priming without awareness. *Perception and Psychophysics, 34*, 65–71.

Rayner, K., McConkie, G. W., & Ehrlich, S. (1978). Eye movements and integrating information across fixations. *Journal of Experimental Psychology: Human Perception and Performance, 4*, 529–544.

Rumelhart, D. E. & McClelland, J. L. (1982). An interactive activation model of context effects in letter perception: Part 2. The contextual enhancement effect and some tests and extensions of the model. *Psychological Review, 89*, 60–94.

Saffran, E. (1980). Reading in deep dyslexia is not ideographic. *Neuropsychologia, 18*, 219–223.

Scarborough, D. L., Cortese, C., & Scarborough, H. S. (1977). Frequency and repetition effects in lexical memory. *Journal of Experimental Psychology: Human Perception and Performance, 3*, 1–17.

Shallice, T. & McGill, J. (1978). The origin of mixed errors. In J. Requin (Ed.), *Attention and performance VII*. Hillsdale, N.J.: Lawrence Erlbaum Associates Inc., 193–208.

Treisman, A. & Souther, J. (1986). Illusory words: The roles of attention and of top-down constraints in conjoining letters to form words. *Journal of Experimental Psychology: Human Perception and Performance, 12*, 3–17.

Turvey, M. T. (1973). On peripheral and central processes in vision: Inferences for an information processing analysis of masking with pattern stimuli. *Psychological Review, 80*, 1–52.

REFERENCE NOTES

1. Humphreys, G. W., Besner, D., & Quinlan, P. T. *Event perception and the word repetition effect*. Paper submitted to the Journal of Experimental Psychology: General.
2. Humphreys, G. W., Evett, L. J., & Quinlan, P. T. *The orthographic description in visual word processing*. Paper submitted to Cognitive Psychology.
3. Manso de Zúñiga, C., Quinlan, P. T., & Humphreys, G. W. *Task effects on priming under masking conditions*. Paper in preparation.

6 Form-priming with Masked Primes: The Best Match Hypothesis

Kenneth I. Forster
Monash University
Clayton, Victoria, Australia

ABSTRACT

Priming effects due to similarity of form rather than meaning (i.e. form-priming) are readily demonstrated in a lexical decision task with masked primes that are different by one letter from the target (substitution primes). This effect can be interpreted as an activation process, where activation is induced in the detectors of all words that resemble the stimulus. An alternative account is that form-priming is really a case of identity-priming; X primes Y only if X is taken to be an instance of Y. The strongest version of this account predicts that priming should be restricted to the best match for the prime. Two experimental tests of this hypothesis are reported. Both predictions are falsified. First, it is shown that substitution priming is independent of the lexical status of the prime, i.e., *attitude* and *antitude* prime the target APTITUDE equally well. Priming should not occur in the first instance since APTITUDE could never be the best match for the prime *attitude*. Second, it is shown that the best match hypothesis fails to explain why substitution priming is not obtained for words with a large number of neighbours, since it predicts that priming should be obtained when the number of prime neighbours is kept to a minimum, which was not the case. In a third experiment, it is shown that form-priming does have repetition-like properties, since it persists across an intervening word, which would not be expected in an activation model.

INTRODUCTION

Form-priming occurs when stimulus X (the prime) facilitates perceptual recognition of a subsequently presented word Y (the target), and X and Y have similar but nonidentical forms. For activation models, such as Morton's logogen model (Morton, 1970), or the interactive activation model of McClelland and Rumelhart (1981), form-priming falls out as a natural consequence of the recognition process. These theories propose a bank of word-detectors, each selectively tuned to respond to activation patterns in a bank of letter-detectors coded for position. If the detector for "letter-A-in-first-position" is activated, then the detectors for all words that begin with A are activated, and so forth through each of the letters in the stimulus. Thus, in the process of recognising X, the representation of Y and all other words that resemble X are partially activated. If this partial activation persists until processing of Y begins, then recognition of Y should be facilitated.

However, not all models of word recognition handle form-priming in such a straightforward manner. The most obvious example is the class of models referred to generally as table look-up models. These models associate lexical representations with stimulus tokens by means of a table of correspondences, and recognising a word involves searching through the table until the correct letter-pattern is found. Apart from the possibility that the system somehow "remembers" the search path for X when it encounters Y, there is simply no compelling reason to expect form-priming effects to occur.

Until recently, this seemed to be the correct position to adopt. Although form-priming effects were reported by Hillinger (1980), subsequent investigations provided very little convincing evidence for a genuine form-priming effect (e.g. Bradley, Savage, & Yelland, Note 1; Colombo, 1986). However, for reasons that are not altogether clear, it turns out that the right way to obtain form-priming is to *mask* the prime, so that the subject has little or no awareness of its existence. Under these conditions, extremely robust form-priming effects can be obtained—effects which disappear if the masking is removed (Humphreys, Evett, Quinlan, & Besner, this volume).

The first experiment investigating form-priming with masked primes was carried out by Evett and Humphreys (1981). In their experiment, both the prime and the target were presented very briefly in rapid succession, and both forward and backward masks were used. The prime was always in lower-case letters, while the target was always in upper-case letters. The subject's task was to identify the target. Clear identity-priming and form-priming effects were obtained. That is, recognition of the target TILE was best when it was preceded by *tile* (identity-priming) and worst when it was preceded by a completely different word such as *park* (the control condition), with *file* producing an intermediate result (form-priming).

Forster and Davis (1984) subsequently repeated this experiment using a different paradigm. In their experiment, the prime was masked, but the target was clearly visible, the subject's task being lexical decision on the target. All primes and targets were four-letter words. As in Evett and Humphreys' experiment, primes were in lower-case, and targets in upper-case letters. Forster and Davis were principally concerned with identity-priming, which they interpreted as a short-term repetition effect. A strong effect was detected, which proved to be independent of the frequency of the target.

However, no form-priming effect was observed. Follow-up experiments showed that word-length was a critical variable. Forster, Davis, Schoknecht, and Carter (in press) replicated the null result for short (four-letter) words, but obtained clear form-priming effects for eight-letter words. Thus, although *bamp* did not prime CAMP, *bontrast* did prime CONTRAST.

To explain the identity-priming effect, Forster and Davis (1984) used the analogy of opening and closing files in a disk-operating system. The function of the lexical processor is to locate and "open" the lexical entries corresponding to the input stimulus in order to make the contents of those entries available to higher-order systems, such as syntactic analysis and semantic interpretation. Since these systems may lag behind the lexical processor, lexical entries would have to remain "open" for some limited period of time. So, if the same word is presented twice, its entry may still be in the "open" state on the second presentation. This analysis was based on a table look-up system in which the search is frequency-ordered. Since what is primed is not the method of locating the entry, but the state of the entry when it is eventually accessed, it follows that the frequency effect for primed words and unprimed words should be the same.

But from this perspective, form-priming is a puzzling phenomenon— unless perhaps a mistake is made in consulting the table. For example, if the letter pattern for word Y is very similar to X, then Y might be taken as the correct representation for X. When Y is subsequently presented, there may be some benefit deriving from the apparent repetition of word Y. This effect would give the appearance of being a form-priming effect, but is in reality a special case of repetition priming. So, if *lominant* is taken to be a possible instance of the word *dominant*, the entry for this word would need to be kept open until it was decided whether this analysis was appropriate to the syntactic and semantic features of the context.

For the table look-up approach, form-priming would have to depend on X being misclassified as an instance of Y. This suggests that X and Y would have to be very similar indeed. But for activation theories, there is no such requirement. Theoretically, even a single shared letter might be enough to produce some form-priming. Also, for the partial-activation approach, the outcome of the process of recognising X is irrelevant. Form-priming will occur whether X is correctly or incorrectly recognised. Another difference between these accounts concerns the *range* of the priming effect. In the partial-activation model, *all* words that resemble X to some specified degree should show priming. But in the table look-up model, only *one* word would be primed, namely the word that X was taken to be an instance of.

Deciding which of these theories is correct would seem to be a simple matter. Activation theories would predict a smooth, continuous function relating the amount of priming to the number of overlapping letters, with a wide range of words being primed. The table look-up (TLU) theory predicts a discontinuous function, where priming only occurs when prime and target are very similar. Further, when priming occurs, it should be just as strong as repetition priming (priming with an identical stimulus), and the effect should be limited to just one word. We should also find some indication that the prime was mis-recognised.

Of course, nothing is that simple. TLU models can also predict continuous functions with a wide range if we average over enough subjects and items, since the cutoff point for priming may vary across both sampling domains. This also allows for the possibility that form-priming effects may be weaker than repetition effects, since the probability of X being misclassified as an instance of Y will be less than 1. And it is not necessary for the prime to be mis-recognised, since the error may be discovered and corrected at some later stage.

This somewhat confusing situation sets the stage for a classic confrontation: two theories that are not totally distinct in their predictions, two experimental paradigms that yield slightly different outcomes, and a critical stimulus variable (length) that is probably confounded with at least several other variables. Despite this unpromising state of affairs, we believe that the issue of form-priming plays a key role in pattern-recognition research, since it *directly* implicates the most fundamental properties of the pattern recognition process.

The evidence currently available from the lexical decision task is encouraging for the TLU interpretation in two respects. First, form-priming does appear to demonstrate a certain discontinuity. That is, no priming occurs for short words unless the prime is identical to the target. This creates problems for the partial-activation account, since somehow the activation induced in the target-detector by an overlapping prime must be cancelled. Second, there is at least one situation in which it can be shown that form-priming depends on the outcome of the recognition of the prime. Forster et al. (in press, Experiment 7) were able to show that when the prime and target are related both in form and morphology, the priming effect is just as strong as identity-priming, i.e. *sent-SEND* is equivalent to *send-SEND* (whereas, say, *tent-TEND* produces no priming at all). This clearly implies that priming occurs *after* the prime has been recognised, not during the recognition of the prime.

However, there are also some aspects of the data that clearly favour a partial-activation model. For example, Forster et al. (in press, Experiment 6) obtained evidence of an inhibitory form-priming effect for four-letter targets. Such an effect is difficult to explain by means of the concept of open and closed entries, but may readily be interpreted in an activation model such as that proposed by McClelland and Rumelhart (1981), since this model stresses the importance of lateral inhibition between word-detectors.

In the experiments to be reported here, we take up three further issues. In the first experiment, we consider range effects, and attempt to determine whether a given prime is capable of priming more than one entry at a time, as predicted by a partial-activation account. In the second experiment, we consider further possible reasons why form-priming does not occur for most short words, and in the third experiment, we consider what happens when another word is interpolated between the prime and the target. Once again, the results do not consistently favour one theory or the other, which suggests that radical revisions in both approaches may be required.

EXPERIMENT 1

The Best Match Hypothesis

According to the TLU interpretation discussed earlier, the range of the form-priming effect should be extremely limited. The strongest form of this theory proposes that priming is restricted to just one word, namely the best match for the prime. So, if stimulus X primes word Y, but X and Y are spelled differently, then Y must be the word that most closely resembles X.

This theory can explain the length effects reported by Forster et al. (in press). The critical nonidentical primes in this study were *substitution* primes, formed by changing one of the letters in the target, e.g. *bontrast*. Clearly, a substitution prime will always have a word as a "neighbour," namely the target. This word will be the best match for the prime, provided the prime has no other neighbours (i.e. words spelled the same except for one letter). For long words, this will usually be the case, since long words typically have very few neighbours (Forster et al., in press). But for short words, neighbourhood density is very high (i.e., both the prime and the target are likely to have many neighbours), and hence the target chosen by the experimenter will not necessarily be the best match for the prime.

According to this view, *bontrast* primes CONTRAST because there is no other word that can be formed by changing one letter (the smallest change that we consider). However, *bamp* does not prime CAMP, because there are many other words that can be formed by changing one letter in the prime, e.g. RAMP, DAMP, BUMP. To be more precise, the probability of obtaining priming will be $1/N$ where N is the number of neighbours of the prime. It follows from this account that the way to get form-priming with four-letter targets is to decrease N. This is precisely what Forster et al. (in press) found. Their method was to use four-letter "hermits" such as SOFA as targets, and to construct substitution primes for these words, making sure that the prime did not now resemble a large number of words, e.g. *sefa*. Under these conditions, a priming effect was obtained.

This result provides impressive support for the TLU account. It does not rule out activation accounts, since McClelland and Rumelhart (1981) allow for lateral inhibition between neighbours, and by adjustment of parameters, it may be possible to show that there is a critical value of N such that all partial activation is cancelled if this value is exceeded. At best, the result could be described as challenging for activation models.

A stronger test of the best match hypothesis would be to demonstrate directly that one and only one word is primed by any given prime. Unfortunately, this is not a simple matter, since this word need not be the same word for all subjects, and hence when we average over subjects and items, we obtain an apparent "fan" effect. However, there is a way around this problem. Consider the target IRRITATE. If we use the nonword substitution prime *irrimate*, we should expect some priming, since this prime closely resembles just two words, namely IRRITATE and IRRIGATE, and hence there is a reasonable probability that the target IRRITATE will be the best match for the prime. However, if we use the word *irrigate* as a substitution prime, then there is no way in which IRRITATE could be taken as the best match, since IRRIGATE is a perfect match for the prime. Hence the best match hypothesis predicts no substitution priming at all if the substitution prime is itself a word.

Method

Materials and Design.   The targets consisted of 64 long words (at least 8 letters) that had at least one neighbour (e.g., DENOUNCE, IRRITATE, REPULSION). For each target, four primes were selected: (1) identity (e.g. irritate-IRRITATE); (2) substitution-word (e.g. irrigate-IRRITATE); (3) substitution-nonword, (e.g. irrimate-IRRITATE); (4) control-word (e.g. parallel-IRRITATE). The substitution-word prime was always a word one letter different from the target (i.e. a neighbour of the target). The substitution-nonword prime was also one letter different (the same letter differing as in the previous condition), but was an orthographically legal nonword. The control prime was a randomly selected word of the same length as the target.

In addition, a set of 64 legal nonwords was constructed which matched the words for length. These nonwords again bore no special relation to words, e.g., NOMBRINT, FLIDGENT, TRANNOCK. These were assigned either an identity prime, or a control prime consisting of a completely different nonword of the same length.

Four sets of materials were constructed, so that each target appeared in each condition over all four sets, but only once within any set. Each subject was tested with one of these sets.

Procedure.   Items were presented on a computer-controlled video display in which the timing of the display was synchronised with the video raster. Each stimulus was centred in the viewing screen, and was superimposed on the preceding stimulus. Primes were always presented in lower-case letters, and targets were always in upper-case letters. Each item consisted of three stimuli. The first was a forward mask consisting of a row of 8 hash-marks (duration 500msec). This was immediately followed by the lower-case prime (duration 60msec), which was in turn immediately followed by the upper-case target (duration 500msec). Thus a typical sequence is as follows:

$$
\begin{array}{ll}
\#\#\#\#\#\#\#\# & (500\text{msec}) \\
\text{irrimate} & (60\text{msec}) \\
\text{IRRITATE} & (500\text{msec})
\end{array}
$$

Subjects were asked to make lexical decisions on the item presented in upper-case letters. No mention was made of the number of stimuli that would be presented on each trial. Subjects indicated their decisions by pressing one of two response buttons. Ten practice items were used, and a different pseudo-random ordering of the items was used for each subject. A total of 20 subjects was used, and any subject making more than 20% errors was replaced.

Results

In this, as in all subsequent experiments, error responses were discarded from the analysis, and reaction-times more than two standard deviation units above or below the mean for that subject in all conditions were trimmed to the appropriate cutoff value. The mean lexical decision latencies and error rates in each condition are shown in Table 6.1.

TABLE 6.1
Mean Lexical Decision Times (msec) and Percent Error Rates for Word Targets as a Function of Type of Prime (Experiment 1)

Prime	Example	RT	%Error
Identity	headline-HEADLINE	440	3.7
Substitution-word	deadline-HEADLINE	458	4.7
Substitution-nonword	seadline-HEADLINE	468	6.7
Control	adequate-HEADLINE	496	11.0

The result of the experiment is clear-cut. Far from showing no priming at all, the substitution-word primes produce slightly *stronger* priming than substitution-nonword primes. All three form-related primes produced significantly faster response times than the control condition, $minF'$ $(1,57) = 38.64$, $P < 0.01$ for identity primes, $minF'$ $(1,46) = 13.98$, $P < 0.01$ for the substitution-word primes, and $minF'$ $(1,71) = 12.10$, $P < 0.01$ for the substitution-nonword primes. There was no significant difference between the two substitution primes, $minF'$ (1,56) = 1.10, $P > 0.05$ (neither subject nor item analyses were significant). However, responses in the identity condition were significantly faster than responses in the substitution-word condition, $minF'$ (1,50) = 5.65, $P < 0.05$, and in the substitution-nonword condition, $minF'$ (1,56) = 11.77, $P < 0.05$.

In general, the pattern for errors follows that for reaction times. Significantly fewer errors were made relative to the control condition in the identity and substituted-word cases, but not in the substituted-nonword case. Error rates in the identity condition did not differ from the other two priming conditions.

No priming effects were found for the nonword targets, where identical primes produced a mean reaction time of 519msec, compared with 517msec in the control condition.

Discussion

The results are clearly incompatible with the best match hypothesis, as currently formulated, since a substitution prime that is itself a word produces the same amount of priming as a substitution prime that is not a word.

It might be suggested that this result is not necessarily fatal to the best match hypothesis, since it might be the case that the lexical processor accepts the first entry it finds that reaches some match-criterion, e.g. a certain proportion of matching letters. So, in the case of the item *deadline*-HEADLINE, it might be that in a frequency-ordered search, the entry for the word *headline* is encountered before the entry for *deadline*. Thus, whenever the target has a higher frequency of occurrence than the prime, then a priming effect should occur.

There are several things wrong with this argument. First, it would predict that the word *deadline* could never be perceived, since *headline* would always be accepted as the correct interpretation. So the search must proceed past this initial candidate, no matter how promising it may seem. Second, the relative frequencies of prime and target in this experiment did not systematically favour the prime, but were evenly distributed. Third, the best match hypothesis asserts that the *best* match is located, and this clearly implies an exhaustive search of all potentially relevant entries.

Forster et al. (in press) postulated a multiple-pass search model that could explain how this works. On the first pass, the criterion for a match is set as high as possible. If no matching entry is found, the system reduces the criterion, and sweeps through the lexicon a second time. This has the virtue of explaining why the number of neighbours (N) affects lexical decision times for nonwords, but not words (Coltheart, Davelaar, Jonasson, & Besner, 1977). That is, lexical decision times for the word IRRITATE are not affected by the existence of the word *irrigate*, but decision times for the nonword target IRRIMATE are. In such a system, the lexical decision for IRRITATE is triggered on the first pass when a high match-criterion is used, and hence the existence of a potentially close match for the word *irrigate* is undetected. With a nonword target such as IRRIMATE, the first pass fails to find any matching entry, but on the second pass, with a lower match-criterion, the entries for *irritate* and *irrigate* are both located, giving rise to interference effects in the decision process.

However, this multiple-pass theory also predicts that words could not prime their neighbours, since the search for a word target would never proceed to the second pass. The evidence from the present experiment clearly indicates that this prediction is wrong. Hence we must abandon the notion of a multiple-pass search, and return to a single-pass exhaustive search model with a match-criterion set low enough to detect the presence of *all* entries in which all letters match but one.

It might be puzzling to suggest that the search process is exhaustive, rather than self-terminating, since the presence of a frequency effect in the access process is supposedly produced by a self-terminating search, not an exhaustive search. However, as pointed out by Bradley and Forster (in press), the possibility of lexical ambiguity guarantees that the search must be exhaustive in normal processing situations, since all relevant entries for any target stimulus must be located (the evidence provided by Forster & Bednall, 1976, strongly implies that ambiguous words have more than one entry). This assumption of an exhaustive search does not undermine the explanation of the frequency effect, since the lexical processor may provide output to higher levels as soon as *any* perfect match is located. Thus, the lexical decision may be triggered by the first matching entry that is located, even though other entries may yet be located.

Faced with the evidence from this experiment, we should acknowledge that the partial-activation model provides a far more compelling account of the data. Since priming is assumed to occur during the recognition of the prime, its lexical status must be irrelevant. Hence both *irrigate* and *irrimate* activate the detector for IRRITATE equally well. They also activate the detector for IRRIGATE, but if the target is presented before any competition between IRRIGATE and IRRITATE has developed, we can explain the equivalent priming effects. On the other hand, if competition does begin before target onset, then *irrigate* should be less effective as a prime, since activation in the detector for IRRIGATE should begin to inhibit activation in the detector for IRRITATE. Of course, this flexibility exposes a weakness in the partial-activation approach, since it can predict either that words and nonwords should be just as effective as primes, or that words should be less effective, depending on the precise timing conditions.

To rescue the best match hypothesis, we would have to postulate that "best" really means "better-than-average." Thus, for a stimulus word such as *deadline*, seven out of eight letters matching is clearly exceptional (neighbourhood density is very sparse at these lengths), and hence both the entries for *deadline* and *headline* are opened. Final arbitration between them is left up to a later process that can take additional factors such as context into account.

This seems a sensible arrangement for a system that is designed to recover from misspellings and typographical errors. For example, consider the contrast between the following sentences:

> The car skidded across the road and colladed with a bus.
> The car skidded across the road and colluded with a bus.

In both cases, it seems clear that the intended word *collided* is readily recovered. The fact that the misspelled version in the second example is itself a word seems not to interfere with the recovery process. In each case, we can assume that the lexical processor marks both *colluded* and *collided* as possible interpretations, but once a post-lexical context-checking system considers these alternatives, *colluded* is rejected. Notice also that lexical status *ought* to be irrelevant to such a system, since there is no reason to suppose that the system which produced the input is biased to produce only nonwords as errors.

Hence, when we consider how context might be used to recover from input errors, there is a considerable gain in efficiency if the lexical processor marks *all* "better-than-average" matches as viable candidates, even if one of those candidates is a perfect match for the input. This marking process can then be seen as the basis of the priming effect. This view of lexical access (which resembles the model proposed by Norris, 1986) assumes a bottom-up processing mode, where context plays no role until the lexical processor delivers a list of viable candidates. The important feature of the model is that the lexical processor provides *multiple* outputs for both word and nonword inputs.

EXPERIMENT 2

Priming in High-density Neighbourhoods

The original account offered in Forster et al. (in press) for the absence of substitution priming for short words was that four-letter words have so many neighbours that the best match is unlikely to be the target. Thus, for the item *loke*-LOVE, there are no fewer than 11 neighbours for *loke*, any one of which might be the best match. But if the best match hypothesis is abandoned, this argument collapses, since we now need to assume that multiple entries can be primed, and thus there is no reason why all 11 neighbours of *loke* should not be primed.

But there may still be a reason why no priming occurs in a high-density neighbourhood. Recall that we are dealing with a backup mechanism that can recover optional interpretations if subsequent evidence suggests that the wrong entry has been accessed. If there are only one or two possibilities, then a context-checking mechanism may be able to recover the correct (intended) word with a high degree of certainty. But if there are a large number of equally valued options (the high-density case), context-checking may be virtually useless. In this case, the access system may simply abandon the task of keeping track of optional interpretations once the number of options gets greater than, say, three.

This theory predicts that priming ought to occur for any sample of four-letter targets, provided that the *prime* resembles a small number of words. Similar predictions can be derived from activation models. For example, in the logogen model (Morton, 1970), the assumption is made that the activation produced in any logogen is divided by the total amount of activation produced across all logogens. Hence the amount of activation produced in the target logogen by the prime will be inversely proportional to the number of neighbours of the prime. Similarly, McClelland and Rumelhart's (1981) model might predict that the lateral inhibitory connections between word detectors will damp any activation that is spread widely across a number of detectors.

To test this hypothesis, the sample of four-letter targets that previously showed no substitution priming (Forster et al., in press, Experiment 2) was tested with a new set of substitution primes that varied in the number of neighbours. The expectation is that substitution priming should occur for the low-N primes, and not for the high-N primes.

Method

The targets were the 48 4-letter words originally used in Forster et al. (in press, Experiment 2), for which no substitution priming effects were obtained. The mean number of neighbours for these targets was 9.14. For each target, a low-N nonword substitution prime was constructed, so that N was no larger than 2 (the mean value being 1.38). An N value of 1 means that the target is the only word that is 1 letter different from the prime, while an N of 2 means that there are two words that are 1 letter different from the prime, one of which is the target. For the same target, a high-N nonword substitution prime was selected, where N ranged from 4–7, the mean value being 5.25.

Thus, for the target SICK, the low-N prime was *sicm*, while the high-N prime was *sigk*. Other typical examples are as follows (the target is listed first, followed by the low-N and high-N primes): RIDE: ridx, riqe; HILL: hibl, hilm; WARM: waem, werm; PALE: palb, pahe; SOFT: koft, saft; GOLD: golu, guld.

Unlike the earlier experiment, where the primes were all orthographically legal, the primes in this experiment vary in legality. This is unavoidable for some four-letter words, where all possible legal substitution primes have high-N values. For the low-N condition, there were 14 orthographically illegal primes, while for the high-N condition, there were 5.

Three sets of materials were constructed, so that each target occurred with a low-N substitution prime, a high-N substitution prime, and a control prime, which consisted of a randomly chosen 4-letter word. An additional set of 48 4-letter nonwords was included, which were preceded either by an identity prime, a substitution prime, or a randomly chosen 4-letter nonword.

The method of presentation was the same as in the masked priming condition of Experiment 1, and the task was lexical decision on the target. A total of 18 subjects was used.

Results and Discussion

The mean lexical decision times and error rates for the word targets are shown in Table 6.2. It can be seen that the decision times show no indication that priming is stronger in the low-N condition than in the high-N condition, the difference being 2msec in the wrong direction. Nor is there any clear indication that either condition produces priming (7msec for low-N primes, 9msec for high-N primes), since there was no significant difference between the three conditions, $minF' < 1$. This result corresponds closely to the results of Forster et al. (in press), who found a nonsignificant substitution priming effect of 8msec for the same target items, but with a different set of high-N primes.

Curiously, the error results show a significant reverse priming effect, $minF'$ $(2,90) = 4.23$, $P < 0.05$, with both types of substitution primes produc-

TABLE 6.2
Mean Lexical Decision Times and Error Rates for
Four-letter Word Targets as a Function of the
Number of Neighbours of the Prime (Experiment 2)

Condition	Example	RT	%Error
Low-N	ekin-SKIN	482	13.2
High-N	skun-SKIN	480	10.2
Control	rear-SKIN	489	5.5

ing more errors than the control condition. This result suggests an inhibitory effect of the prime when the target has many neighbours, which is also consistent with the earlier results of Forster et al. (in press, Experiments 2 and 6).

It is perhaps conceivable that priming may have been found if all the low-N primes had been orthographically legal (15 of the 48 low-N primes were not, e.g. *fatp, puxl, gopl*). To test this hypothesis, however, we need a totally new set of word targets for which legal low-N primes can be constructed. We consider it extremely unlikely, however, that legality of the prime has any bearing on the issue, for several reasons. First, 33 of the 48 primes were orthographically legal, so one would still expect to obtain some effect (especially in a subject analysis, which was not the case in this experiment). Second, in several unpublished experiments, we have observed substitution priming with characters such as a blank space, a comma, a digit, or a parenthesis replacing the missing letter in the target (e.g. *unw,nted*-UNWANTED). This insensitivity to "foreign" material placed within a word suggests that the comparison process must consider each constituent letter separately, and hence the presence of an illegal sequence should not preclude detection of a match. Third, if it was the case that the presence of an illegal letter sequence automatically aborted the access process, then it would be difficult to understand why familiar illegal CCC strings such as JFK take longer to reject in a lexical decision task than unfamiliar strings such as KFJ (Novik, 1974).

This experiment suggests, then, that the prime neighbourhood is irrelevant to the amount of priming, which creates problems for all theories of priming, whether of the TLU variety or the activation variety. Logically, the only remaining possibility appears to be that it is the neighbourhood of the *target* that determines whether substitution priming occurs. So, the reason that Forster et al. (in press, Experiment 5) obtained substitution priming for four-letter targets has nothing to do with the fact that *both* the prime and the target had low-N values. Presumably, it would have been sufficient merely to have selected low-N targets.

To explain this effect, it seems that we must propose that a match-criterion is separately defined for each lexical entry, which takes into account the number of neighbours for that word. In detector terminology, we would say that word detectors in high-density neighbourhoods are more narrowly tuned than those in low-density neighbourhoods.

Of course, this proposal does not explain why substitution-priming should be inhibitory with high-N targets, as suggested by the error results in the present experiment, and the results reported in Forster et al. (in press, Experiment 6). Nor have we explained why Evett and Humphreys (1981) did obtain substitution priming for short high-N targets using tachistoscopic identification accuracy, rather than lexical decision. Obviously, there must be something about the conditions of the identification task that enhances form-priming in a high-density neighbourhood, or something about the lexical decision task that suppresses it.

This conclusion is strengthened by the fact that pilot experiments of our own confirm that exactly the same four-letter items show substitution priming with an identification task, but not with a lexical decision task. One possible explanation is that the tachistoscopic effect occurs at a lower (i.e. sublexical) level of analysis. Forster et al. (in press) suggested that unidentified letters in the target might be "copied" across from the prime, producing facilitation when the prime and target are similar. Humphreys et al. (this volume) specifically test for such an effect, and report that although it does occur, it cannot explain the priming effect. They propose that priming occurs when two briefly presented letter strings are treated as a single perceptual event, and compete with each other for a representation. In support of this view, they show that no form-priming effects are obtained when the prime is not masked, and hence is clearly perceived as being a separate event. This contrasts with the present paradigm, where the *target* is not masked, and form-priming effects do occur, provided that low-N targets are used. Clearly, there is much to be discovered about the role of *task* variables, as well as stimulus variables, in determining whether form-priming occurs.

EXPERIMENT 3

So far, the experimental evidence presented here has no direct bearing on the question of whether form-priming can be treated as a type of repetition effect, as the TLU approach suggests. The most promising evidence for this view is the fact that morphological factors play an important role, as shown by the fact that *sent-SEND* is equivalent to *send-SEND* (Forster et al., in press, Experiment 7). This implies that the priming action occurs after the prime has been accessed, which is at least an important prerequisite of the repetition account.

A more direct test is to ask whether form-priming persists across intervening items, i.e., priming at a distance. Forster and Davis (1984) were able to demonstrate that identity priming is capable of exerting an effect across several intervening words, although the effect is considerably diminished if even one word intervenes between the prime and target. However, it is not known whether substitution priming has the same capacity. If it is really a special case of identity-priming, then it should also survive across intervening items.

A partial-activation interpretation suggests the opposite, since persistence of activation across intervening words would add considerable noise to the system, and hence it might be expected that all activation levels are reset to zero when a new word occurs. Even if such activation did persist, it could scarcely exert a very selective effect, since the activation produced by the target and the intervening word would swamp the effects of the prime.

A third possible position proposes that identity priming really consists of two components: a repetition component which persists across intervening items, and a form-priming component which does not. Substitution priming, however, has no repetition component, only the form-priming component. This would explain why identity priming is stronger than substitution priming, and why there is such a marked reduction in identity priming when one word intervenes. This account also predicts no substitution priming across an intervening word.

Method

The targets and primes for this experiment were taken from the eight-letter items in Forster et al. (in press, Experiment 2), where strong substitution priming effects were obtained. These items were presented under the same conditions as previously, except that another randomly chosen eight-letter word was inserted between the prime and the target. This intervening word was presented in lower-case letters for 500msec. Thus a typical sequence was as follows:

Forward mask:	########	(500mscc)
Prime:	bontrast	(60msec)
Intervening:	destroys	(500msec)
Target:	CONTRAST	(500msec)

Three priming conditions were used: identity, substitution, and control. The control prime was a randomly chosen eight-letter word that did not resemble the target. As before, three sets of materials were constructed so that each target was observed in each condition. Nonword items were also constructed in a similar fashion.

The task was lexical decision on the word in upper-case letters. It was stressed to subjects that after the initial sequence of hashes, another lower-case word would appear before the upper-case target appeared. A total of 36 subjects was used.

TABLE 6.3
Mean Lexical Decision Times and Error Rates for Targets Preceded by
Identity and Substitution Primes with One Intervening Word (Experiment 3)

Prime	Example	RT	%Error
Identity	dominant-accident-DOMINANT	527	4.5
Substitution	lominant-mobility-DOMINANT	525	4.3
Control	constant-shutting-DOMINANT	544	6.6

Results and Discussion

Inspection of the mean lexical decision times for the word targets shown in Table 6.3 shows that substitution priming does indeed survive across an intervening item. However there is an additional feature that is entirely unexpected. With an intervening word, substitution priming is no longer weaker than identity priming, but is in fact slightly stronger.

The substitution condition produced faster decision times than the control condition, $minF'$ $(1,68) = 4.77$, $P < 0.05$, while the identity primes produced a strong trend in the same direction, $minF'$ $(1,68) = 3.94$, $P < 0.10$ (both subject and item analyses were significant). Although neither of these effects are large (17msec for identity primes, 19msec for substitution primes), they are of approximately the same magnitude as the remote priming effects reported by Forster and Davis (1984). No other effects were significant, either for decision times or errors.

Once again, we are faced with difficulties wherever we turn for an explanation. The survival of the substitution effect across an intervening word obviously presents difficulties for the activation approach, but not for the TLU approach. However, the fact that the two forms of priming have equivalent effects is embarrassing for the TLU approach. In the original experiment using these items without an intervening word (Forster et al., in press, Experiment 2), the identity priming condition was 26msec faster than the substitution priming condition. The original explanation of this difference was that identity primes had a higher probability of opening the entry for the target. But if this were the case, then substitution primes should have produced a weaker effect than identity primes in the present experiment as well.

If the results can be replicated, a different mechanism will have to be found to explain why identity priming is stronger than substitution priming in the absence of an intervening word. Presumably, we would have to postulate a special priming effect when *successive* inputs are identical. Identity priming and substitution priming share a repetition component (the effect obtained in the present experiment), but the identity condition now has an additional component which does not survive across an intervening word.

GENERAL DISCUSSION

The findings can be summarised as follows:

1. Substitution priming with the lexical decision task is insensitive to the lexical status of the prime. This indicates that priming cannot be restricted to just one entry, namely the entry which matches the input best.

2. Substitution priming in a high-density neighbourhood with the lexical decision task cannot be restored by minimising the number of neighbours of the prime. This indicates that it must be the target-neighbourhood density

that is the controlling variable. If this is high, then there is some evidence that a substitution prime has inhibitory effects.

3. Substitution priming persists across an intervening word (although in a weaker form), which is more compatible with the notion of priming as a repetition effect than a partial activation effect. Further, substitution primes and identity primes have *equivalent* effects under these conditions.

The consequence of the first result for any theory of lexical access that uses TLU mechanisms (i.e. all search theories) is that it can no longer be argued that the lexical processor delivers a single output. Instead, it appears that the lexical processor outputs a *range* of candidates that match the input to varying degrees, as proposed by Norris (1986). This conclusion reduces the distance between activation models and TLU models, since activation models also stress that a given input will excite multiple word-detectors.

The consequence of the second result appears to be that one cannot explain the absence of substitution priming in a high-density neighbourhood in terms of limits placed on the number of entries opened by the prime (in a TLU model), or in terms of competition between the candidates activated by the prime (in an activation model). Instead, it appears that the prime only opens/activates the entries for *some* words, namely those that have few neighbours.

The consequence of the third result is that there must be at least one component of both the identity and substitution priming effects that has the properties of a repetition effect, and which cannot therefore readily be treated in partial-activation terms. However, one must also postulate that the identity effect has an additional component that does not survive across an intervening word, i.e. that depends on the identity of successive inputs.

What this suggests for the TLU approach is that we can no longer think of entries as being either "open" or "closed." Instead, the "open" state must be subdivided into a number of levels. The highest level (call it level 3) is reserved for entries that match the *current* input stimulus perfectly. Level 2 is reserved for neighbours of this stimulus. Finally, level 1 means that an entry is still being considered as a possible interpretation of a *previous* input item. Once the lexical system detects that a new input has occurred, all entries at level 3 or 2 are dropped to level 1. In this way, the system avoids confusion about which entries are viable candidates for the current input item (a problem shared with the activation account). Now, what happens when a target is presented immediately after a masked prime is that the lexical system fails to detect that a new input has occurred, as suggested by Humphreys et al. (this volume). Hence entries opened at level 2 or 3 by the prime remain at that level while the target is being processed. But if another nonmasked word intervenes between the masked prime and the target, these entries are dropped to level 1. Eventually, when the input has been integrated with the context, the entry reverts to the closed state (level 0).

To interpret the results of Experiment 3, all that remains is to postulate that the strength of the priming effect produced by accessing an already-opened entry varies directly with the level. The remote priming effects are level 1 effects, and are the same for both an identity prime and a substitution prime. To take the "colluded" sentence examples discussed earlier, both the entries for *colluded* and *collided* would be kept at level 1 until contextual resolution had selected one or the other interpretation. Evidently, no record is kept of which entry was the best match. However, when the masked prime is immediately adjacent to the prime, entries will be either at level 2 if a substitution prime was used, or level 3 if an identity prime was used. This now provides an account of the fact that identity priming is stronger than substitution priming for adjacent pairs.

Two things should be said about this proposal. First, it is little more than a re-description of the facts (not an entirely trivial achievement in this case). To provide a better explanation, we need to explain why entries change levels in this way, and why the strength of the priming effect varies with the level. Second, this proposal all but obliterates the distinction between the TLU model and an activation model, since entries being opened at different levels are obviously equivalent to word-detectors being in different states of activation. However, some distinctions remain. The TLU model, being a computational system, distinguishes between the levels in a qualitative manner, whereas an activation model distinguishes different activation levels in a purely quantitative fashion. Further, in an activation model, the activation persisting from the prime is indistinguishable from the activation produced by the target. But in the TLU approach, these notions are kept distinct, since the process of locating the entry for the target word is totally unaffected by the state of that entry.

But further problems still remain. There is the question of the possible inhibitory effect of a substitution prime for high-N targets (Experiment 2), and there is the fact that neighbourhood-density effects are not the same for different tasks. One way to begin to make sense of this latter result is to postulate that different tasks may tap the priming process at different stages. Our current working hypothesis is that the prime initially opens a wide range of entries, and that subsequent processing is responsible for "closing down" irrelevant entries. The type of priming effects obtained will then depend on the stage of processing that is being tapped in any particular task. The conditions involved in the tachistoscopic identification task may tap very early stages of processing, where a large number of entries are in an open state. Lexical decision, on the other hand, may tap a very late stage, where only a few entries remain as viable candidates. As an illustration of this process, consider the difficulty that is experienced when one attempts to identify *consciously* the neighbours of words such as *detergent, backward,* and *precious*. Latencies of the order of several seconds (or even tens of seconds in some cases) appear to be involved. Yet these same words act as very powerful primes for their neighbours when masked, as shown by the results of Experiment 1. What this suggests is that the information about who is a neighbour of whom is completely lost by the time the word has been consciously perceived.

This dynamic aspect of priming is well-suited to an activation interpretation, since a feature of these models is the way in which the competitive processes change over time, so that the lexical system gradually narrows in on the correct solution. The clearest evidence for such a process may be the inhibitory effect obtained in Experiment 2 for high-N targets. But note that this approach would still need to explain why priming apparently depends on the neighbourhood of the *target*, rather than the prime. This means either that the letters of the prime do not activate the detectors for words that have many neighbours (which would make it impossible to perceive them), or that activation from the prime only *persists* in the detectors for words that have few neighbours.

Clearly, the priming effect is highly complex, and seems at times to have the properties of both an activation effect and a repetition effect. Perhaps one should not lose sight of the possibility that more than one type of effect is involved; or alternatively, that neither way of looking at the effect is entirely correct.

REFERENCES

Bradley, D. C. & Forster, K. I. (in press). A reader's view of listening. *Cognition*.

Colombo, L. (1986). Activation and inhibition with orthographically similar words. *Journal of Experimental Psychology: Human Perception and Performance, 12*, 226–234.

Coltheart, M., Davelaar, E., Jonasson, J. T., & Besner, D. (1977). Access to the internal lexicon. In S. Dornic (Ed.), *Attention and performance VI*. London: Academic Press.

Evett, L. J. & Humphreys, G. W. (1981). The use of abstract graphemic information in lexical access. *Quarterly Journal of Experimental Psychology, 33*, 325–350.

Forster, K. I. & Bednall, E. S. (1976). Terminating and exhaustive search in lexical access. *Memory and Cognition, 4*, 53–61.

Forster, K. I. & Davis, C. (1984). Repetition priming and frequency attentuation in lexical access. *Journal of Experimental Psychology: Learning, Memory, and Cognition, 10*, 680–698.

Forster, K. I., Davis, C., Schoknecht, C., & Carter, R. (in press). Masked priming with graphemically related forms: Repetition or partial activation? *Quarterly Journal of Experimental Psychology*.

Hillinger, M. L. (1980). Priming effects with phonemically similar words: The encoding-bias hypothesis reconsidered. *Memory and Cognition, 8*, 115–123.

McClelland, J. L. & Rumelhart, D. E. (1981). An interactive activation model of context effects in letter perception: Part 1. An account of basic findings. *Psychological Review, 88*, 375–407.

Morton, J. (1970). A functional model of human memory. In D. A. Norman (Ed.), *Models of human memory*. New York: Academic Press.

Norris, D. (1986). Word recognition: Context effects without priming. *Cognition, 22*, 93–136.

Novik, N. (1974). Parallel processing in a word-nonword classification task. *Journal of Experimental Psychology, 102*, 1015–1020.

REFERENCE NOTE

1.   Bradley, D. C. Savage, G. R., & Yelland, G. W. (1983). *Form-printing or not?* Paper delivered at the Fourth Language and Speech Conference, Monash University.

7 Record-based Word Recognition

Kim Kirsner, John Dunn, and Peter Standen
University of Western Australia
Perth, Australia

ABSTRACT

In this paper we review research that has used transfer effects in repetition priming to examine recognition processes, and describe a theory of word recognition. The main features revealed by the review are as follows: (1) transfer between two words depends on the extent to which they share the same properties; (2) transfer is sensitive to a wide range of properties including surface form, morpho-phonemic similarity, and meaning; and (3) transfer is negatively correlated with attribute memory: Attributes that yield negligible transfer in word recognition (e.g. when FROMAGE is followed by CHEESE) yield reliable discrimination in attribute memory (i.e. people know how each word was presented), and vice versa.

The theory incorporates aspects of the abstract and instance-based approaches. In contrast to the instance-based approach, extensive abstraction is assumed. And, in contrast to the abstract approach, information about low-level properties is not discarded, but makes contact with a detailed record of a particular instance. The theory assumes that: (1) information about surface and structural properties is formed and preserved in an hierarchically organised description of the current stimulus; (2) the description is referred to a qualitatively and quantitatively comparable record for identification; and (3) the structural description of the current stimulus defines an appropriate address in memory.

INTRODUCTION

Two approaches are evident in recent research into word recognition. The first of these involves analytic processes (e.g. Forster, 1976; Morton, 1969; Taft & Forster, 1975). The critical feature in this approach is that the internal referents for each word are *abstractions*. The referents are formed by, and derived from, experience. But the details of that experience are not preserved directly in the recognition system. In the second, or nonanalytic approach, the idea that there is a single abstract referent for each word is discarded, and it is assumed instead that recognition depends on reference to specific *instances* or records (Brooks, in press; Jacoby & Brooks, 1984; Kirsner & Dunn, 1985). In this case, then, each event or act of identification yields a record, and the ensemble of records functions as a recognition resource when new perceptual problems are encountered.

Each of these approaches has some advantages, and some problems. The abstract view provides a direct explanation of the fact that people are able to recognise objects (including words) that are presented in a variety of different ways, both familiar and unfamiliar. It does so by assuming that invariant defining features of a set of instances are abstracted and used in recognition. However, the corollary of this assumption, that information reflecting surface variability is discarded, has not been sustained. Indeed, there is abundant evidence that information about surface form influences recognition and that it is not, therefore, discarded at all (Jacoby & Brooks, 1984; Kirsner & Dunn, 1985; Kolers & Roediger, 1984).

The instance view, on the other hand, provides a direct explanation of surface variability effects. Because each record in memory is a description of an event, information about surface form and context are included as a matter of course, and the observed effects of these variables are to be expected. There is a problem with this approach too, however. The problem concerns contact between descriptions and records. How does a description of an object find the appropriate record in memory? Abstraction plays no part, by definition. And, because the generalised, prototypical object exists only as an epi-phenomenon of the organisation of instances in memeory, it, too, cannot be exploited. Perhaps similarity is the most promising candidate (e.g., Jacoby & Brooks, 1984). But in the absence of analytic processing only the surface characteristics of objects can be considered, and many apparently important characteristics of words cannot therefore be used to reduce entropy.

The account of word recognition introduced here includes elements of both the abstract and the instance-based approaches. However, it is not a "mixed" model in the sense that it depends on representations of both prototypes and instances. The model is described briefly in the next section.

THE ABSTRACT DESCRIPTION: A RECORD OF PROCEEDINGS

Definitions and Terminology

Following Norman and Bobrow (1979), descriptions and records are used with reference to current and past events, respectively. *Descriptions* may be compared with "object files" (Kahneman & Teisman, 1984) and, like object files, they provide a functional location where perceptual information can be stored and organised during interpretation. It is further assumed that the final content of the description is a structured description of the object, and that it includes information about surface form, sub-lexical constituents, and meaning. *Records* are, quite simply, old descriptions, and they do not therefore differ from descriptions in regard to content. As *representation* is used in a more general way, the term *code* is used to refer to the components or elements that constitute a description. It is assumed that codes are formed to preserve, for example, colour, contour, phonemic, graphemic, letter cluster, syllabic, morphemic, and semantic information.

The Role of Abstraction in the Formation of Descriptions and Records

A principal assumption in the present account is that descriptions and records are the products of analytic processes. These analytic processes involve abstraction, the products of these processes are themselves abstractions, and descriptions and records are, therefore, highly articulated structural descriptions of the object. Neither the record nor its progenitor, the description, are unanalysed representations of the stimulus.

Codes: The Product of Sensory Analysis, Parsing, and Re-description

Codes are assumed to be the product of at least three analytic processes; sensory analysis, parsing, and re-description. *Sensory analysis* abstracts information about the physical properties of objects; contour and colour for example. *Parsing* abstracts information about components which function as structural elements by virtue of their correspondence to elements or groups of elements in perceptual memory; morphemes, letter clusters, and graphemes, for example. *Re-description*, which operates on the products of parsing, yields codes in alternative representational media; phonemes given graphemic or letter cluster input, for example.

The Role of Parsing and Re-description in Recognition

Parsing and re-description serve three functions. First, they liberate the perceptual description from the particular constraints imposed by each mode and modality of presentation. Second, by increasing the variety of individual codes in the description they enhance the specificity of the description as a whole, providing a mechanism to compensate for degradation in the signal or the database. Third, they provide the means by which familiar concepts in

APPR-F*

novel formats can be recognised. Thus, when an otherwise familiar word is presented in a novel typefont, parsing and re-description will yield descriptions which correspond to one or more records in all respects except surface form.

Code Displacement: The Corollary of Abstraction

Contrary to accounts that invoke the notion of a prototype, we do not assume that the codes produced by sensory analysis, parsing, and re-description are discarded after they have made their contribution. Instead, it is assumed that these codes are preserved and that, together, they constitute the structural description of the object.

Code Equality and Independence

The codes in the structural description of the object are neither equal nor independent. Where words are concerned, the morphological code (the morpheme, or the BOSS [Taft, 1985] being two obvious candiates) is of paramount importance. If an hierarchical organisation is assumed, the morphological code is at the apex, and the other codes are on the branches. When morphological status has been established, information about the other codes becomes relevant in its own right. Until that point, however, the other codes are only relevant insofar as they contribute to morphological analysis.

Recognition Without Search

The search problem is by-passed in the present account because descriptions and records are structurally equivalent. Similar stimuli will form similar descriptions, and they will therefore make automatic contact with each other's records. Recognition occurs when a familiar combination of codes is re-activated. Thus, there is no search, and there is no search problem. If contact is not made immediately, further parsing and re-description will enhance the description by providing more codes, and the recognition problem can be reviewed. Alternatively, if parsing and re-description have been exhausted, codes can be discarded until the best structural match is found. Presumably, codes that specify surface characteristics will be the first to go.

Similarity

The role of similarity can now be specified with reference to the ensemble of codes that constitute the structural description. Because records preserve detailed information about surface form, structure, and meaning, and recognition depends on re-activation of the overall pattern of activity that constitutes the record, performance will reflect the extent to which the current stimulus description matches that of a recently established record. Although the amount of variance accounted for may, in many cases, be small, the general implication of the model is clear. Performance should be sensitive to variation in each and every stimulus property.

THE RECORD IN WORD RECOGNITION AND ATTRIBUTE MEMORY

In this section we discuss two tasks where performance is consistent with a process of the type described in the preceding section. The first task involves word identification, where people are invited to name words under stimulus-limited conditions. This task is routinely used to investigate lexical processes in reading. The second task involves attribute memory, an explicit memory test. This task is not routinely used to investigate reading. But, because of the procedural disparity between the tasks, it provides an exacting test of the proposition that the record-based model has general implications for perception and memory. The way in which descriptions and records are used to explain performance in these tasks is discussed later.

Repetition Priming and Word Identification

The essence of our account is that word identification is achieved by reference to a record. Similarity is the critical parameter. If the record collection includes an example that is similar to the current stimulus description, identification will be achieved easily and quickly, even under difficult viewing conditions. But if it does not include an appropriate example, a more detailed description of the current stimulus will be required, and performance will be impaired accordingly.

The character of the record collection can be determined by repetition priming. The basic argument is that the magnitude of repetition priming depends on the extent to which the current stimulus description matches a record. Systematic manipulation of the relevant parameters should reveal the precise character of the record.

Consider an experimental example in which subjects are presented with a mixed list of spoken and printed words during the first part of an experiment. The words are presented so that they can be read or heard without difficulty, and the subjects are given no indication that there will be a subsequent test session. During the test session, however, a word identification task is used, and all of the OLD words (words presented during the study phase) are now presented visually at individually tailored threshold values. Assuming that the threshold values have been calculated for NEW words (i.e. for words that were not presented *in any form* during the first part of the experiment), the following patterns can be expected. First, as demanded by the threshold procedure, subjects should be able to identify 50% of NEW words at the threshold value. Second, assuming that the most recent record is used, repetition priming should be observed at its maximum when words are repeated in exactly the same form (i.e. visually in both parts of the experiment). Third, the magnitude of repetition priming in the *transfer* condition (where words were presented auditorily and visually in the first and second parts of the experiment, respectively) should reflect the extent to which the emerging description of the visual test stimulus specifies components that are also present in the most appropriate record; that is, of the visual test word's auditory counterpart from the first part of the experiment.

As both speed and accuracy measures are of interest, a metric-free index of transfer has been adopted. Thus,

$$\text{RELATIVE PRIMING} = (\text{OLD:ALTERNATIVE FORM} - \text{NEW})/ \\ (\text{OLD:SAME FORM} - \text{NEW}) \qquad 1$$

where: (a) the NEW condition comprises visual test words that were not presented during the study phase; (b) the OLD:SAME FORM condition comprises visual test words that were presented in the same form during the study and test phases; (c) the OLD:ALTERNATIVE FORM condition is the transfer condition and comprises visual test words that were presented auditorily during the study phase; and (d) the index can be applied to both speed and accuracy data. With reference to the mixed modality example described above, for example, if the observed values were 50, 60, and 70% correct in the NEW, OLD:ALTERNATIVE FORM, and OLD:SAME FORM conditions, respectively, the RELATIVE PRIMING value would be 0.5.

Figure 7.1 depicts attribute memory (percent correct) as a function of transfer (RELATIVE PRIMING) for four attributes: language, modality, gender and case. The abscissa represents transfer, and indicates the average RELATIVE PRIMING values for four attributes: language, modality, case, and speaker's voice. As shown, the transfer values range from zero, when testing follows prior exposure to translations (e.g. FROMAGE → CHEESE), to unity, when testing follows prior exposure to words in the alternative case (e.g. cheese → CHEESE) or gender (when auditory presentation is used). The observed values for transfer between speech and print, and vice versa, fall midway between these values.

The results shown in Fig. 7.1 represent average values. The RELATIVE PRIMING value shown for each attribute is an average, based on all studies of that type known to the authors. Consideration was restricted to experiments where: (a) the data was obtained under incidental learning condi-

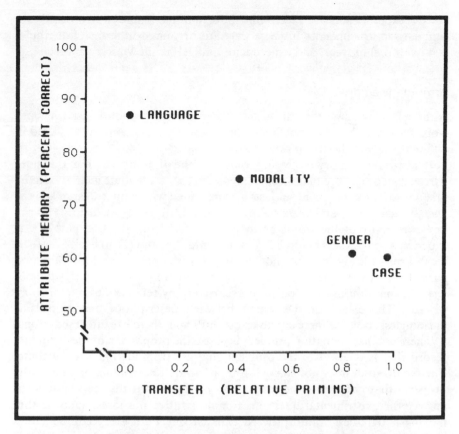

FIG. 7.1.   Attribute memory (percent correct) as a function of transfer (*relative priming*) for averaged data for four attributes; language (morphologically unrelated translations only), modality, gender, and case.

tions—thereby excluding experiments which involved either generation or intentional learning; (b) the study and test phases involved presentation of individual words; and (c) the study and test presentations were "remote," a lag of four items being accepted as the minimum for inclusion.

In addition to word identification (accuracy), the points shown in Fig. 7.1 are based on experiments that used lexical decision (reaction-time) and semantic classification (reaction-time) in the test phase. The assumption is that all of these tasks involve "word recognition," and that they therefore depend on reference to records. That each task also involves unique processes is not in dispute. Essentially the same pattern of transfer effects is also observed for fragment completion (Roediger & Blaxton, in press), although the results from that task are not included in the summary.

The experiments on which this informal meta-analysis is based are summarised in Appendix I, where they are organised in terms of attribute, task, authorship, year, and experiment; and RP is shown in each case.

Attribute Memory

Although we assume that the same source of information is used in both word recognition and attribute memory, that source is sampled and used in different ways in the two tasks.

In attribute memory the basic problem is one of discrimination. Consider a free recall procedure that is sometimes used to test attribute memory. In the first part of the experiment subjects are presented with a mixed list of spoken and printed words and then, to their surprise, they are asked to: (1) write down as many of the words as they can recall from the first part of the experiment, regardless of modality of presentation; and (2) go back over their recall protocols and indicate how each word was presented during the first part of the experiment. Because no test stimuli are presented in this type of test, the question must be resolved exclusively by reference to one or more records. The extent of the match between descriptions and records is meaningless, because there are no test stimuli and, therefore, no descriptions.

There is a discrimination problem because the proportion of the candidate record that is relevant to the problem changes from attribute to attribute. The record itself does not change from attribute to attribute, of course; the property that changes is the proportion of the record that can be used to answer the experimental question. For illustrative purposes, suppose that parsing and re-description proceed exhaustively until every component is represented. The content of a record might then have the following form:

RECORD CONTENT = {(physical case-related codes [e.g. envelope, contour])
(physical case-unrelated codes [e.g. colour, contrast])
(graphemic codes)
(phonemic codes)
(letter cluster codes)
(syllabic codes)
(a morphological code or codes)
(a semantic code or codes) }   2

Now consider the relevance of each code to a question about each attribute. Given a language question, every code except the semantic code is diagnostic. CHEESE and FROMAGE differ in terms of their physical, graphemic, phonemic, letter cluster, syllabic, and morphemic components. Given a modality question, however, several codes now provide no diagnostic information. Even if parsing and re-description are complete, only the physical codes will yield diagnostic information. Finally, for case, only the physical case-related code yields diagnostic information. The other codes are irrelevant, even those that preserve information about other physical properties (e.g. colour). Given one additional assumption, that attribute discriminability is directly related to the proportion of the record that distinguishes the response categories, attribute memory should increase from case to modality to language.

Now consider the ordinate in Fig. 7.1. This axis represents accuracy in attribute memory, and the points are based on inter-experimental averages for each of the four attributes discussed earlier. As shown in that figure, performance ranges from slightly above chance, for case and gender, to over 80% correct for translations. And, as observed for *relative priming*, the modality value falls between these extremes. Consideration was restricted to experiments where: (1) subjects were not instructed to remember the attribute; (2) lists consisted of at least 16 individually presented words; (3) remote study and test phrases were used; and (4) a binary decision was involved (e.g. English or German). The experiments are summarised in Appendix II, where they are organised in terms of attribute, task, authorship, year, and experiment; accuracy values being shown in each instance.

The summary includes data from experiments involving three item presentation procedures. The first of these involves item recall, and was described earlier. The second and third procedures involve item recognition (i.e. OLD or NEW) followed by an attribute decision (e.g. English or German). In the second procedure the test stimuli are presented in one or other of the forms used during the study phase. In the third procedure the test stimuli are presented in a neutral form (e.g. as outline drawings of objects following presentation as English or Italian words; Kirsner & Dunn, 1985). The absolute level of attribute memory varies from method to method, but the relative positions of the attributes are not affected by this variable.

The results summarised in Fig. 7.1 indicate that there is a reciprocal relationship between transfer and attribute memory. Attributes that yield little or no transfer support reliable attribute memory. Attributes that yield extensive transfer between forms do not support reliable attribute memory. More generally, when two events are similar, perception and discrimination are facilitated and impaired, respectively. But when two events are dissimilar, the effects are reversed. The relationship is consistent with the claim that the tasks depend on access to the same source of information, although they use that information in quite different and task-specific ways.

SIMILARITY EFFECTS IN WORD IDENTIFICATION AND ATTRIBUTE MEMORY: SOME EXPERIMENTS WITH LANGUAGE, MORPHOLOGY, MODALITY, AND TYPEFONT

The relationship summarised in Fig. 7.1 involves a series of inter-experimental analyses. This procedure can reveal relationships that do not exist at the level of the single issue experiment. However, it has some limitations, and these need to be specified. One consideration concerns the role of extraneous factors that might influence performance in the task-task space shown in Fig. 7.1. The selection rules were specifically designed to mask such factors and highlight a particular process. However, if the selection rules were modified, other processes would be revealed. A second consideration concerns averaging. The significance of the observed relationship is qualified by the fact that it follows averaging across experiments, subjects, items, and processes (if these fluctuate from trial to trial). The first of these sources of averaging is eliminated in the intra-experimental analyses described below. A third consideration concerns attribute homogeneity. When data from experiments that involve modality manipulations are compared, for example, the product is only interpretable if the *effective* manipulation is the same in each case. Yet there are reasons for suspecting that this assumption is invalid for all of the attributes discussed above. For example, the relationship between spoken and printed forms varies from script to script (e.g. contrast Chinese and Italian) and, in all likelihood, from item to item in the case of a language such as English. Similarly, in the case of language, the relationship between translations such as CHEESE and FROMAGE is quite different from the relationship between cognates such as PUBLICITY and PUBLICIDAD. And in the case of physical attributes such as typefont and voice the relationship is likely to vary from font to font, or even from word to word for one font pair.

The experiments described below were designed to examine the relationship between word recognition and attribute memory at the intra-experimental level, and, more particularly, test some ideas about the content of the record. These goals were achieved by treating selected attributes as variables, and specifying treatment levels for each variable. In general terms, the reciprocal relationship observed at the inter-experimental level is also found at the intra-experimental level. Treatments that increase similarity between word forms increase and decrease transfer and discriminability in attribute memory, respectively. The numbers shown before each experiment in the text correspond to the number in Fig. 7.2.

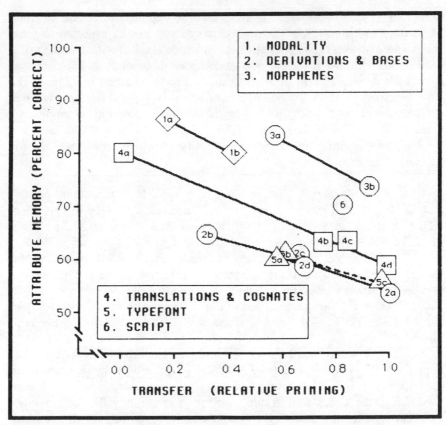

FIG. 7.2.   Attribute memory (percent correct) as a function of transfer (*relative priming*) for six experiments (see labelled sections in text).

Modality

In the account presented here, transfer between spoken and printed words is explained by re-description. Facilitation occurs because the analysis of words presented in one modality yields a representation that can be used later, when the same words are presented in the alternative modality. However, the magnitude of facilitation will reflect the extent to which the two stimuli depend on the same codes.

Consider, for example, the relationship between spoken and printed Chinese words.[1] Assume, first, that the transfer condition involves presentation of spoken words and printed words (i.e. logographs) during the study and test phases, respectively, and, second, that parsing is applied exhaustive-

---

[1] Logographs with phonetic radicals were excluded.

ly in each case. Spoken word analysis can be expected to realise syllabic, phonemic, and tonal codes. Logographic analysis can be expected to yield codes about strokes, groups of strokes, and radicals. But with the exception indicated in footnote 1, the two sets of codes are independent. The components realised by one form of analysis do not have counterparts among the components realised by the other form of analysis. Re-description, even if it occurs, cannot yield codes that will be useful under cross-modal conditions. Thus, there should be less transfer between modalities for Chinese than English, and attribute memory for modality should be more reliable for Chinese than English.

1. Modality Effects: A Comparative Study Involving Chinese and English (Chye, Dunn, & Kirsner, (Note 2)).   Language was a between-subject factor, subjects being tested in English or Chinese (Mandarin). The study phase consisted of a mixed list of spoken and printed Chinese or English words, and the subjects were instructed to match each word with a definition. Lexical decision and attribute memory were tested in the test phase. As expected, Chinese yielded lower RP and higher attribute memory values than English. The results are summarised in Fig. 7.2 where points 1a and 1b depict the Chinese and English results, respectively. The predictions were supported.

Another, logically related example involves English words with typical (e.g. COMIC) and atypical (e.g. ABYSS) grapheme-phoneme conversion (not shown in Fig. 7.2). Because re-description is restricted to pre-lexical processing, the codes that result from re-description will take on quite different functional values in the two cases. When typical words are used, spoken presentation will yield codes that are relevant and useful when a visual test word is presented, but when atypical words are used, spoken presentation will yield codes that are less relevant and, therefore, less useful when a visual test word is presented. In a preliminary study involving transfer from spoken words to printed words, we found that, as predicted, larger RP values are observed for typical words than atypical words; the observed values being 0.67 and 0.37, respectively (Andrews, Dunn, Kirsner, & Standen, Note 1).

Morphology

If it is assumed that the morphological code provides the basic structural description for words, manipulations that reduce the similarity of the relevant code should reduce *relative priming* and increase attribute memory. This was accomplished in Experiment 2 by selecting sets of word pairs where the stem of the derivation and the base form differ systematically in regard to phonemic content and/or stress. In addition, as the words were all studied and tested visually, the presence of word class differences suggests that nonvisual codes are being formed and used, despite the ostensibly visual nature of the experiment. Experiment 3 was the same as Experiment 2 except that the word sets were defined behaviourally, using a variant of Posner's (1969) name match procedure. The study is reported because it emphasises the perceptual character of remote repetition priming and attribute memory.

2. Stress and Phoneme Differences Between Derivations and Base Forms (Downie, Milech, & Kirsner, 1985). Similarity was manipulated in this experiment by selecting derivation-base word pairs where the stems differed in terms of: neither stress nor pronounciation (BANISH-BANISHMENT, 2d in Fig. 7.2); just pronunciation, with a one phoneme difference (RE-PRESS-REPRESSION, 2c); just pronunciation with a two phoneme difference (CONCEIVE-CONCEPTION, 2b); and stress and pronunciation, with one change of each type (VEGETATE-VEGETATION, 2a). The study and test phases in the transfer experiment involved lexical decision and word identification respectively, and parameter estimation by sequential testing was used to determine the threshold for each subject prior to the test phase. The results of this experiment are shown in Fig. 7.2, as points 2a–2d (see this section). If treatment 2a is set aside, the results are consistent with the proposal that relative priming and attribute memory decrease and increase, respectively, as a function of the number of differences between the stem of the derivation and the base form.

3. Behavioural Analysis of Morphological Similarity (Kirsner, Dunn, & Standen, Note 4). Subjects in a preliminary, stimulus selection study were presented with a mixed series of base-derivation and distractor word pairs and instructed to classify each pair with reference to the presence or absence of a common morpheme. Subsequently, the item set was partitioned on the basis of the difference in reaction time between morphological matches (e.g. DERIVATION-DERIVE) and physical matches (DERIVE-DERIVE), the words with large and small differences were assigned to treatments 3a and 3b, respectively, and separate word identification and attribute memory experiments were conducted. The results (see points 3a and 3b in Fig. 7.2) support the similarity hypothesis, and indicate that morphemic transparency in a simultaneous matching task can be used to predict both transfer and attribute memory, further extending the generality of the account.

Morphology and Language

The position of translations in the space defined by transfer and attribute memory (see Fig. 7.1 and Appendix II) is consistent with two interpretations. First, that language per se is the defining feature, and that separate records are automatically established for words from different languages, regardless of morphemic similarity. Second, that morphology alone is critical. Cognates may be used to examine this issue. If records are organised in terms of language, words that are specific to one or other language will depend on distinct records, even when the translations involve the same stem morpheme (e.g. PUBLICIDAD-PUBLICITY). But if morphology is critical, cognates will occupy the same position as derivations (see Experiment 2) in the task-task space defined by transfer and attribute memory.

4. Spanish-English Cognates and Translations (Cristoffanini, Kirsner, & Milech, 1986).   The four word sets used in Experiment 4 consisted of morphologically unrelated translations (e.g. PANADERIA-BAKERY, 4a in Fig. 7.2), cognates with irregular suffix substitution (e.g. CALUMNIA-CALAMITY, 4b), cognates with the regular DAD-TY substitution (e.g. PUBLICIDAD-PUBLICITY, 4c), and cognates with regular CION-TION substitution (e.g. SUCCION-SUCTION, 4d). The study and test phases involved naming (to ensure lingual specificity) and lexical decision, respectively. And the study and test material consisted of mixed language and English lists, respectively. The results are consistent with the proposition that morphology is critical, and they also support the claim that record content systematically influences performance on each task.

Surface Similarity

Whereas the first four experiments included systematic variation in the number of components shared by word forms from different modalities or lexical classes, Experiments 5 and 6 involve variation in surface similarity alone. Experiment 5 used multi-dimensional scaling and behavioural indices to define similarity for pairs of typefonts, the expectation being that transfer and attribute memory would increase and decrease, respectively, as functions of increasing similarity. Experiment 6 involved a more extreme manipulation in which the chosen scripts were totally dissimiliar, even though they are normally used to depict exactly the same spoken words. Given parsing and re-description, the forms used in Experiment 6 can yield identical non-physical codes, and the treatment should therefore occupy a mid-range position in the task-task space (i.e. similar to that occupied by dissimiliar typefont pairs).

5. Typefont (Standen, Kirsner & Dunn, Note 6).   Multi-dimensional scaling and behavioural indices (simultaneous same-different matching) were used to select typefont pairs such that: (a) a standard font was present in each of three pairs of typefonts; and (b) similarity between the standard and the nonstandard fonts increased ordinally from treatment to treatment (5a–5c). Lexical decision was used during the study phase, and the test phase involved word identification (standard font only) or attribute memory. The results are summarised in Fig. 7.2 (points 5a–5c), where it is apparent that transfer and attribute memory are both sensitive to variation in surface similarity.

6. Script (Brown, Sharma, & Kirsner, 1984).   The experimental manipulation involved Hindi and Urdu, language forms where the scripts are totally unrelated (Hindi is written from left-to-right in the Devanagri script whereas Urdu is written from right-to-left in a variant of Arabic) but many of the spoken words are identical. With consideration restricted to words of this type, the outcome (6 in Fig. 7.2) is consistent with the proposition that morpho-phonemic equivalence is sufficient to sustain a mid-range value, even when the surface forms are completely unrelated.

Two qualifications are in order regarding the results summarised in Fig. 7.2. First, the intercept differences between the studies probably reflects the fact that the decision rules and conditionalisation procedures varied from study to study, particularly where attribute memory is concerned. Second, although the reciprocal relationship between transfer and attribute memory is observed consistently, the observed treatment orders do not always follow our pre-experimental expectations (e.g. Experiments 2 and 4). Thus, the tasks provide complementary classifications of the treatments, but our linguistic selection procedures did not correctly predict that classification. Perhaps behavioural as distinct from lingustic criteria should be used to define linguistic treatments in future research.

GENERAL DISCUSSION

The main thrust of the research described in this paper is that word recognition is remarkably sensitive to variation in the similarity of recent events. When word recognition is preceded by prior exposure to an example, speed and accuracy reflect the extent to which that example and the test stimulus share the same properties. The range of properties that influence performance in this way is considerable. As yet, we have found no similarity dimension that does not influence transfer and its correlate, attribute memory.

The general implications of these data are as follows. First, word recognition involves access to an extremely detailed record of one or more instances. Access, in our view, does not involve search in the accepted sense of that term. Rather, the detailed character of the record means that the current stimulus description can "find" the best instance, provided that both it and the record are specified in appropriate and sufficient detail. The address is specified by the particular combination of codes (i.e. pattern of activity) that constitute the record. When the stimulus description re-creates that combination, the record has been "discovered." Recognition efficiency can therefore be expected to reflect both specificity and redundancy, insofar as each of these is present in the description and record, and speed and accuracy should be sensitive to frequency and, presumably, recency.

The second implication concerns the content of the record. This appears to consist of the products of those processes, both sensory and abstract, that were invoked during stimulus recognition. Our provisional list includes morphological (e.g. morpheme or BOSS), sub-morphemic (e.g. graphemes, letter clusters, phonemes, and syllables), and surface (e.g. contour) codes.

The third implication concerns the relative status of each component in the description and, by definition, the record. It is our contention that morphology is critical. If two words do not share the same morphology (as perceived by the listener or reader), the record of one cannot be used to aid recognition of the other. By extension, then, when the words do not share the same morphology, the character of the other codes is irrelevant. But when they do share the same morphology, recognition is facilitated by the extent of correspondence among their "secondary" codes.

The evidence in favour of this proposition is that although the presence of the same morpheme in a study-test pair constitutes a sufficient condition for repetition priming (Stanners, Neiser, Hernon, & Hall, 1979), this is not the case for graphemic information (Murrell & Morton, 1974), phonemic information (Neisser, 1954), or semantic information (Dannenbring & Briand, 1982; Gough, Alford, & Holley-Wilcox, 1981; Henderson, Wallis, & Knight, 1984). Repetition priming experiments using morphemically unrelated translations (see Appendix I), morphologically unrelated spoken and printed forms (Experiment 1, earlier), and synonyms (Roediger & Blaxton, in press) support the same conclusion. Even though the study and test words share some interpretive value, facilitation is not observed.

However, there is evidence that the extent to which study and test stimuli share the same sub- and supra-morphemic components does influence test performance *when the stem morpheme is repeated*. For instance, Experiment 2 included evidence that sub-morphemic variation (between the stems of derived words and their base forms) influences transfer. Similarly, the results of Experiments 5 and 6 support the conclusion that, provided that morphophonemic structure is preserved, variations in surface form do not eliminate transfer. They modify it (Experiment 5), indicating that such information is preserved in the record. But the fact that transfer is observed even when surface form is totally changed (Experiment 6) indicates that surface form occupies a dependent position in the record. And Masson and Freidman (Note 5) have demonstrated that when precisely the same word is used in the study and test phases, the magnitude of repetition priming depends on semantic stability. Thus, when contextual variation ensures that a different interpretation is placed on the word on each occasion (e.g. from savings BANK to river BANK), priming is virtually eliminated.

The fourth implication concerns abstraction. In line with the abstract approach, our account includes the assumption that extensive stimulus analysis occurs, and that the processes concerned define a variety of surface and structural properties. However, instead of assuming that information about these properties is discarded as the prototype is approached, we assume that: (1) information processing is cumulative (i.e. information about the surface and structural properties is preserved); (2) the codes produced by abstraction define the address of the appropriate representation in memory (and are, therefore, instrumental to word recognition); (3) the representation is a complex description of a particular instance, not a prototype; and (4) the structural description of the current stimulus becomes a new record.

Finally, it may be noted that our account differs from instance-based accounts in several ways, just one of which we will discuss here. Although the models developed by Jacoby (1983a; 1983b) and Roediger (Roediger & Blaxton, in press) include reference to specific instances, they emphasise the contrast between data-driven and conceptually-driven processes, positing that the character of specific representations is determined by the balance between these mechanisms. The position advanced here does not falsify the distinction between data- and conceptually-driven processes; however it does highlight several findings that are not readily accommodated by that account. For example, the data-driven account is restricted to explicit stimulus structure. Yet many of the findings reported here show that transfer depends on implicit structure (e.g. Experiments 1 and 6), even under incidental learning conditions. The interaction between word frequency and cross-modal transfer poses another problem for the data-driven approach. According to our interpretation of that account, cross-modal transfer should be higher for high-frequency words than low-frequency words because fewer conceptual resources will be available for low-frequency words. But higher *relative priming* values are invariably obtained for low-frequency words (Kirsner, Milech, & Standen, 1983, Experiments 4, 5, 6, and 7/8), an outcome that is consistent with the proposition that more *abstract* processing is required for low-frequency words.

ACKNOWLEDGEMENTS

The research reported in this paper was supported by a grant from the Australian Research Grants Scheme.

REFERENCES

Bray, N. W. & Batchelder, W. H. (1972). Effects of instructions and retention interval on memory of presentation mode. *Journal of Verbal Learning and Verbal Behaviour. 11*, 367–374.

Brooks, L. (in press). Decentralised control of categorisation: The role of prior processing episodes. In U. Neisser (Ed.), *Categories reconsidered: The ecological and intellectual basis of categories.* Cambridge: Cambridge University Press.

Brown, H. L., Sharma, N. K., & Kirsner, K. (1984). The role of script and phonology in lexical representation. *Quarterly Journal of Experimental Psychology, 36A,* 491–505.

Clarke, R. & Morton, J. (1983). Cross-modality facilitation in tachistoscopic word recognition. *Quarterly Journal of Experimental Psychology, 35A,* 79–96.

Cristoffanini, P. M., Kirsner, K., & Milech, D. (1986). Bilingual lexical representation: The status of Spanish-English cognates. *Quarterly Journal of Experimental Psychology, 38A,* 367–393.

Dannenbring, G. L. & Briand, K. (1982). Semantic priming and the word repetition effect in a lexical decision task. *Canadian Journal of Psychology, 36,* 435–444.

Downie, R., Milech, D., & Kirsner, K. (1985). Unit definition in the mental lexicon. *Australian Journal of Psychology, 37(2),* 141–155.

Forster, K. I. (1976). Accessing the mental lexicon. In R. J. Wales & E. Walker (Eds.), *New approaches to language mechanisms.* Amsterdam: North Holland.

Gough, P. B., Alford, J. A., & Holley-Wilcox, P. (1981). Words and contexts. In O. J. L. Tzeng & H. Singer (Eds.), *Perception of print.* Hillsdale, N.J.: Lawrence Erlbaum Associates Inc.

Henderson, L., Wallis, J., & Knight, D. (1984). Morphemic structure and lexical access. In H. Bouma & D. Bouwhuis (Eds.), *Attention and performance X.* London: Lawrence Erlbaum Associates Ltd.

Hintzman, D. L., Block, R. A., & Inskeep, N. R. (1972). Memory for mode of input. *Journal of Verbal Learning and Verbal Behaviour, 11,* 741–749.

Jackson, A. & Morton, J. (1984). Facilitation in auditory word recognition. *Memory and Cognition, 12(6),* 568–574.

Jacoby, L. L. (1983a). Perceptual enhancement: Persistent effects of an experience. *Journal of Experimental Psychology: Learning, Memory, and Cognition, 9(1),* 21–38.

Jacoby, L. L. (1983b). Remembering the data: Analysing interactive processes in reading. *Journal of Verbal Learning and Verbal Behaviour, 22,* 485–508.

Jacoby, L. L. & Brooks, L. R. (1984). Nonanalytic cognition: Memory, perception, and concept learning. In G. H. Bower (Ed.), *The psychology of learning and motivation: Advances in research and theory, Vol. 18.* New York: Academic Press.

Jacoby, L. L. & Dallas, M. (1981). On the relationship between autobiographical memory and perceptual learning. *Journal of Experimental Psychology, 110,* 306–340.

Kahneman, D. & Treisman, A. (1984). Changing views of attention and automaticity. In R. Parasuraman & D. R. Davies (Eds.), *Varieties of attention.* Orlando: Academic Press.

Kirsner, K., Brown, H. L., Abrol, S., Chaddha, N. N., & Sharma, N. K. (1980). Bilingualism and lexical representation. *Quarterly Journal of Experimental Psychology, 32,* 585–594.

Kirsner, K. & Dunn, J. C. (1985). The perceptual record: A common factor in repetition priming and attribute retention. In M. I. Posner & O. S. M. Marin (Eds.), *Mechanisms of attention: Attention and performance XI.* Hillsdale, N.J.: Lawrence Erlbaum Associates Inc.

Kirsner, K., Milech, D., & Standen, P. (1983). Common and modality-specific units in the metal lexicon. *Memory and Cognition, 11(6),* 621–630.

Kirsner, K. & Smith, M. C. (1974). Modality effects in word identification. *Memory and Cognition, 2,* 637–640.

Kirsner, K., Smith, M. C. Lockhart, R. S., King, M-L., & Jain, M. (1984). The bilingual lexicon: Language-specific units in an integrated network. *Journal of Verbal Learning and Verbal Behaviour, 23,* 519–539.

Kolers, P. A. & Roediger, H. L. (1984). Procedures of mind. *Journal of Verbal Learning and Verbal Behaviour, 23,* 425–449.

Lehman, E. B. (1982). Memory for modality: Evidence for an automatic process. *Memory and Cognition, 10(6),* 554–564.

Light, L. L. & Berger, D. E. (1974). Memory for modality: Within modality discrimination is not automatic. *Journal of Experimental Psychology, 103(5)*, 854–860.

MacLeod, C. M. (1976). Bilingual episodic memory: Acquisition and forgetting. *Journal of Verbal Learning and Verbal Behaviour, 15*, 347–364.

Madigan, S. & Doherty, L. (1972). Retention of item attributes in free recall. *The Bulletin of the Psychonomic Society, 27(4)*, 233–235.

Mandler, G. (1980). Recognising: The judgement of occurrence. *Psychological Review, 87(3)*, 252–271.

Mandler, G., Pearlstone, Z., & Koopmans, H. J. (1969). Effects of organisation and semantic similarity on recall and recognition. *Journal of Verbal Learning and Verbal Behaviour, 8*, 410–423.

Mandler, J. M., Seegmiller, D., & Day, J. (1977). On the coding of spatial information. *Memory and Cognition, 5*, 10–16.

Manelis, L. & Tharp, D. A. (1977). The processing of affixed words. *Memory and Cognition, 5*, 690–695.

Marcel, A. J. (1983). Conscious and unconscious perception: An approach to the relations between phenomenal experience and perceptual processes. *Cognitive Psychology, 15*, 238–300.

Marshall, P. H. & Carareo-Ramos, L. E. (1984). Bilingual frequency encoding. *Journal of Psycholinguistic Research, 13(4)*, 295–306.

Monsell, S. (1985). Repetition and the lexicon. In A. W. Ellis (Ed.), *Progress in the psychology of language, Vol. 1*. London: Lawrence Erlbaum Associates Ltd.

Morton, J. (1969). Interaction of information in word recognition. *Psychological Review, 76*, 165–178.

Morton, J. (1979). Facilitation in word recognition: Experiments causing change in the logogen model. In P. A. Kolers, M. E. Wrolstad, & H. Bouma (Eds.), *Processing of visible language*. New York: Plenum.

Murrell, G. A. & Morton, J. (1974). Word recognition and morphemic structure. *Journal of Experimental Psychology, 102*, 963–968.

Neisser, U. (1954). An experimental distinction between perceptual process and verbal response. *Journal of Experimental Psychology, 47*, 399–402.

Norman, D. A. & Bobrow, D. G. (1979). Descriptions: An intermediate stage in memory retrieval. *Cognitive Psychology, 11*, 107–123.

Posner, M. (1969). Abstraction and the process of recognition. In K. W. Spence & J. T. Spence (Eds.), *The psychology of learning and motivation, Vol. 3*. New York: Academic Press.

Roediger, H. L. & Blaxton, T. A. (in press). Retrieval modes produce dissociations in memory for surface information. In D. S. Gorfein & R. R. Hoffman (Eds.), *Memory and cognitive processes: The Ebbinghaus Centenial Conference*. Hillsdale, N.J.: Lawrence Erlbaum Associates Inc.

Rose, R. G., & Carroll, J. F. (1974). Free recall of a mixed language list. *Bulletin of the Psychonomic Society, 3(4)*, 267–268.

Saegert, J., Hamayan, E., & Ahmar, H. (1975). Memory for language of input in polyglots. *Journal of Experimental Psychology: Human Learning and Memory, 1(5)*, 607–613.

Scarborough, D. L., Cortese, C., & Scarborough, H. S. (1977). Frequency and repetition effects in lexical memory. *Journal of Experimental Psychology: Human Perception and Performance, 3*, 1–17.

Scarborough, D. L., Gerard, L., & Cortese, C. (1984). Independence of lexical access in bilingual word recognition. *Journal of Verbal Learning and Verbal Behaviour, 23*, 84–99.

Siple, P., Fischer, S. D., & Bellugi, U. (1977). Memory for nonsemantic attributes of American sign language signs and English words. *Journal of Verbal Learning and Verbal Behaviour, 16*, 561–574.

Stanners, R. F., Neiser, J. J., Hernon, W. P., & Hall, R. (1979). Memory representation for morphologically related words. *Journal of Verbal Learning and Verbal Behaviour, 18,* 399–412.

Taft, M. (1985). The decoding of words in lexical access: A review of the morphographic approach. In D. Besner, T. G. Walker, & G. E. McKinnon (Eds.), *Reading research: Advances in theory and practice, Vol. V.* New York: Academic Press.

Taft, M. & Forster, K. I. (1975). Lexical storage and retrieval of prefixed words. *Journal of Verbal Learning and Verbal Behaviour, 14,* 638–647.

Winograd, E., Cohen, C., & Barresi, J. (1976). Memory for concrete and abstract words in bilingual speakers. *Memory and Cognition, 4(3),* 323–329.

REFERENCE NOTES

1. Andrews, S., Dunn, J. C., Kirsner, K., & Standen, P. Manuscript in preparation.
2. Teo, Y. C., Dunn, J. C., & Kirsner, K. Manuscript in preparation.
3. Harvey, R. (1981). *The structure of semantic representation in bilinguals.* (Unpublished honours thesis, UWA).
4. Kirsner, K., Dunn, J. C., & Standen, P. Manuscript in preparation.
5. Masson, M. E. J. & Freedman, L. (1985). *Fluency in the identification of repeated words.* Paper presented to the Psychonomic Society, Boston.
6. Standen, P., Kirsner, K., & Dunn, J. C. Manuscript in preparation.

APPENDIX I: WORD RECOGNITION

Translations: Lexical decision: Cristoffanini et al. (1986), E1 = 0.02 (I-E); Kirsner, Brown, Abrol, Chaddha, & Sharma (1980), E1 = −0.20 (HE) & 0.18 (EH); Kirsner, Smith, Lockhart, King, & Jain (1984), E1 = −0.16 (FE) & 0.15 (EF); Scarborough, Gerard & Cortese (1984), E1 = −0.06 (SE). *Semantic classification:* Harvey (Note 3), E1 = −0.04 (IE); Kirsner et al. (1984), E3 = 0.26 (FE) & 0.18 (EF).

Modality: Speech → Print: Lexical decision: Kirsner & Smith (1974), E1 = 0.10; Kirsner et al. (1983), E2 = 0.70 (a), E3 = 0.43; Monsell (1985), E5 = 0.04. *Word identification:* Clarke & Morton (1983), E2 = 0.41, E3 = 0.40 (b); Jacoby & Dallas (1981), E5 = 0.06 (hf) & 0.19 (lf); Kirsner et al. (1983), E1 = 0.56, E4 = 0.49 (hf) & 0.50 (lf), E5 = 0.21 (hf) & 0.72 (lf), E6 = 0.52 (hf) & 0.76 (lf), E7/8 = 0.54 (hf) & 0.69 (lf); Standen, Kirsner & Dunn (Note 6), E1 = 0.53. *Print → Speech: Lexical decision:* Kirsner & Smith (1974), E1 = 0.51; Monsell (1985), E6 = 0.61. *Word identification:* Jackson & Morton (1984), E1 = 0.40; Morton (1979), E4 = 0.22; Standen et al. (Note 6), E1 = 0.56.

Case: Lexical decision: Scarborough, Cortese, & Scarborough (1977), E1 = 0.95 (c). *Word identification:* Standen et al. (Note 6), E2 = 0.98.

Speaker's Voice: Word identification: Jackson & Morton (1984), E1 = 0.85; Standen et al. (Note 6), E3 = 0.82.

APPENDIX II: ATTRIBUTE MEMORY

Translations: Cristoffanini et al. (1986); E2 = 0.80; Kirsner & Dunn (1985), E1 = 0.89; MacLeod (1976), E2 = 0.95; Rose & Carroll (1974), E1 = 0.924; Saegert, Hamayan, & Ahmar (1975), E1 = 0.843 (concrete) & 0.823 (abstract); Winograd, Cohen, & Barresi (1976), E1 = 0.875 (concrete) & 0.750 (abstract).

Modality: Kirsner & Dunn (1985), E1 = 0.74; Lehman (1982), E1 = 0.840, E2 = 0.805. *Speech* → *Print/Speech:* Bray & Batchelder (1972), E1 = 0.825; Hintzman, Block, & Inskeep (1972), E1 = 0.725; Madigan & Doherty (1972), E1 = 0.703; Siple, Fischer, & Bellugi (1977), E2 = 0.676. *Print* → *Print/Speech:* Bray & Batchelder (1972), E1 = 0.740; Hintzman et al. (1972), E1 = 0.760; Madigan & Doherty (1972), E1 = 0.687; Siple et al. (1977), E2 = 0.624.

Case: Brown et al. (1984), E1 = 0.590; Hintzman et al. (1972), E1 = 0.575; Kirsner & Dunn (1985), E1 = 0.63; Light & Berger (1974), E1 = 0.600.

Speaker's Voice: Kirsner & Dunn (1985), E1 = 0.62; Hintzman et al. (1972), E1 = 0.59.

Abbreviations: E = experiment, hf = high frequency, lf = low frequency, i = incidental treatment, IP = in press, IPR = in preparation, EF = English-French, FE = French-English, HE = Hindi-English, EH = English-Hindi, SE = Spanish-English.

Notes:(a) accuracy, (b) lax criterion, (c) approximately.

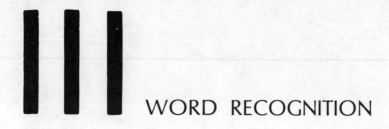

WORD RECOGNITION

8 Word Recognition
A Tutorial Review

Leslie Henderson
Psychology Division
The Hatfield Polytechnic
Hatfield, U.K.

ABSTRACT

Theoretical developments in the study of visual word recognition are surveyed
from three viewpoints; that of Huey, Neisser, and the present day. Early work
tended to treat words as linguistically empty spatial patterns. A major focus of
interest was on the facilitatory effect of stimulus structure on recognition.
Theoretical argument largely rested on the quality of perceptual experience.
Attentional hypotheses played a dominant role in accounts of the limits of
performance and of strategic flexibility. In the 1960s, discovery of the perceptual advantage of unfamiliar but word-like strings heralded more detailed
manipulation of word properties, requiring, in turn, more precision and
differentiation in theoretical accounts. With development of the concept of a
mental lexicon as the interface linking the perceptual to the linguistic domain,
the lexical decision task began its vertiginous climb to prominence. Experimental variables attracted interest as means for diagnosing the nature of lexical
representations and the procedures used for gaining access to them. To this
end, it became increasingly crucial to distinguish between universal and task-
specific effects. As an approach to modelling the traditional boxes and arrows
representation of lexical architecture came to be rivalled by parallel distributed
processing networks.

INTRODUCTION

In the introduction to his classic work, *The psychology and pedagogy of
reading*, Huey (1908) tells a story of the explorer Livingstone exciting wonder
and awe in an African tribe who watched him daily perusing a book that had
survived the rigours of his journey. Eventually the natives, intent on sharing
in the mysteries of reading, captured Livingstone's book and *ate* it. Thus,
perhaps, was born the first information processing model of reading.

From this opening, you will have gathered that I am intent on a broad, historical view. Faced with the appalling task of attempting to embrace all that might be termed *word recognition* within the narrow confines available to me, I am reminded of the plight of the amateur photographer who, attempting to capture in a single frame a vast and complexly wrought edifice, staggers backwards ever farther from the subject, watching with dismay as the essential detail gets fatally compressed in the viewfinder. Anyone walking backwards from the contemporary scene in this way inevitably bumps into Huey. Accordingly, it is with Huey's distillation of 19th-century studies of word perception that I commence. From this culmination of a previous tradition, I turn to the re-emergence of *cognitive psychology*, as it is reflected in Neisser's (1967) book of that title. Many of the shared preoccupations of these two works are neatly expressed in Neisser's chapter heading: *Words as visual patterns*.

Throughout my review of these two landmarks I shall attempt to show how those issues that have persisted have been developed in contemporary work. In a brief, concluding section, I turn my attention to an alternative approach, in which words are treated not as visual objects but as linguistic tokens. Recognition, within this more recent tradition, does not terminate with the formation of a reportable percept. It involves use of the stimulus as an instrument for making available linguistic information.

1908

Cubism, powered flight and the special theory of relativity had just been invented. The discontinuous movement of the eye had been discovered and tachistoscopic glimpses of the written word were everywhere observed. World wars and behaviourism lay ahead. In the laboratory, investigations of reading dynamics were focussed on eye-movements, the eye-voice span and articulatory suppression tasks. Single-frame analyses were concentrated on identification thresholds, especially the amount of material available in full report.

Stimulus Structure

The central phenomenon, indubitably, was the effect on attempted full report of various sorts of structural coherence in the stimulus array. Huey was able to review an abundance of evidence that the amount of material which could be reported from a brief or barely legible display increased substantially when strings of letters were organised into words, or words into phrases.

There was a certain amount of debate about what the significant "units" of perception were. To what extent was word recognition mediated by letter recognition? Could letter-clusters be treated as units? However, these questions were posed at an entirely speculative level and attempts to manipulate stimulus structure experimentally seldom progressed beyond the contrast of words with random letter strings. Concern with linguistic attributes of words was notably absent. The component features that attracted attention were more often ones of spatial configuration such as letter ascenders and descenders. Indeed, Messmer followed Cattell's pioneering study of letter legibility with the first distinctive feature account of letter confusions (Huey, 1908, pp. 90–96).[1]

A remarkable exception to this neglect of linguistic aspects of words is to be found in Huey's own surmise that the greater accuracy in identifying the initial portion of words was due to the tendency of first syllables to carry the primary stress in speech and the fact that the prevalence of suffixation in English results in the "main root" of the word usually residing in the leftward portion. I shall return to such linguistically motivated ideas in my final section.

In Huey's review of the facilitatory consequences of coherent structure in the stimulus array it is possible to discern a number of alternative theoretical accounts. These are itemised in Table 8.1 and we shall consider them in turn.

TABLE 8.1
Some 19th-century Hypotheses About the Source of the Word Apprehension
Effect

1.	Incomplete letter identification supplemented by perceptual inferences based on associative learning.
1a.	Word inferences used to reduce positional uncertainty about letters.
2.	Use of global configuration, e.g. envelope and length, as additional cues to word identity.
3.	Chunking of letter array into higher-level codes to reduce attentional demands of perception.

[1] Since my expository method has been to view the history of ideas about visual word recognition from the standpoints, 60 years apart, of Huey and Neisser, I have not burdened the text with many direct references to primary sources, relying instead on citations from my chosen intermediaries whenever their account will serve. Nevertheless, the early literature repays closer study. Fortunately, the work of Cattell has been collected by Poffenberger (1973). Initial access to the considerable literature in German can be gained through Scheerer's (1981) essay. Retrospective sketches may also be found in Bouwhuis (1979), Geyer (1970), and Henderson (1977).

APPR–G

Fragmentary Sense Data Supplemented by Associative Inference

Toward the end of the 19th century, perceptual theory in general was dominated by the empiricist tradition, stretching back through Helmholtz to the British empiricist philosophers. Broadly speaking this view represented the proximal stimulus as impoverished and ambiguous. These sense data were registered passively and subsequently acted upon by an inferential process which filled in missing data and constructed the stable, continuous, interpreted world of visual experience. The nature of these perceptual inferences was poorly specified but they were held to depend upon past experience of those conjunctions that characterise the structure of the environment. It is this set of general opinions that motivates most of the 19th-century hypotheses concerning the source of contextual facilitation in reading. This thesis, together with its application to the word superiority effect, is particularly clearly illustrated in a passage where Huey likens the superior accuracy of report obtained for linguistically structured stimuli to the filling in and sharpening of detail in the periphery of the visual field (Huey, 1908, p. 63).

In Huey's epistemological vocabulary the words "seeing" and "apperception" were reserved for the uptake of sense-data. "Apprehension" or "assimilation" were the terms applied to the subsequent inferential activity that resulted in perceptual awareness. There is no doubt that he regarded associative inference as contributing to perceptual *experience* rather than merely what could be reported. Indeed, he believed that our hypotheses normally furnish us with the objects of perceptual awareness and only when this constructive process breaks down do we experience the raw feature data (Huey, 1908, p. 43) ". . . in which case the consciousness arises of the *data themselves*, the black-white of the sensations."

If perceptual experience is usually a product of interpretative processes, can we elect to by-pass this stage and gain direct conscious access to a purely stimulus-driven representation? Zeitler, a pupil of Wundt's and perhaps the most important advocate of the inference position besides Huey, argued that (Huey, 1908, p. 83): ". . . ordinarily we cannot distinguish these two processes of apperception and assimilation." However, at sufficiently brief exposures Zeitler believed that readers could be freed from most of the top-down processing and could strain after the sense-data themselves. Huey, himself, was troubled by generalisations about fluent reading that were based upon tachistoscopic presentation and wrote (Huey, 1908, p. 114) of Zeitler's claims as possible ". . . artifacts of the experiments with short exposure and strained attention." In this, he anticipated the opinion of neo-Gibsonian commentators who have asserted that the tachistoscope is a satanic instrument (e.g. Neisser, 1976) and that reading is too unnatural an act to have a place in an ecological account of perception (e.g. Fowler, 1981).

Zeitler shared with Goldscheider and Muller the view that the inferential processes were driven by a description of the image as an incompletely specified array of letters. They agreed on the proposition that the preliminary letter description tended to include letters and letter clusters that were especially distinctive. However, they were divided as to whether this distinctiveness was "optical" (resting on size, shapes, and position in the word) or the very different position that distinctiveness had to do with some linguistic aspect of the word. Goldscheider and Muller differed from Zeitler, for example, in maintaining that it was the phonetic reference of "determining letters" that mediated word recognition.

Zeitler's opinion on the special status of tachistoscopic glimpses was that they afforded a view of the uptake of salient letter information, yielding a skeletal percept without the intervention of the "fleshing out" operations based upon previously experienced conjunctions of letters. This appears to run counter to the widespread modern opinion that contextual effects are *exaggerated* by brief or degraded presentations. However, at least two recent theories attribute special properties to tachistoscopic report. While their assumptions differ considerably, they converge on the prediction that such tasks will be insensitive to word frequency. Besner's account (Besner & Swan, 1982; Besner & McCann, this volume) seems to be closer in spirit to Zeitler's. Besner echoes Allport (1977) in maintaining that visual experience of a stimulus word normally depends on the integration of lexical information with *pictorial* information about the location and appearance of the word. (It is this marriage which allows a lexical output to be *visible*; cf. Neisser's "externally guided thinking"). To the extent that the subject fails to "see" material in the threshold task, this reflects the failure of that integration to take place. Since he holds the integrative process to be frequency sensitive he is able to account for absence of frequency effects in tachistoscopic report.

Paap, Newsome, McDonald, and Schvaneveldt (1982) and Paap, McDonald, Schvaneveldt, and Noel (this volume) assert that it is the coupling of tachistoscopic presentation *with backward masking* that creates a special case.[2] They also assume that partial letter information extracted from the stimulus may be sufficient to activate a lexical entry. In fact the lexicon, in their view, is inherently disposed to react to partial information with an output containing the closest available approximations. (In essence, what Huey called "assimilation" and a version of what I term "inference".) What backward masking prevents, according to Paap et al., is the subsequent (frequency sensitive) process of *verification*, whereby the lexical candidates are evaluated against the stored visual (pictorial?) code.

---

[2] Actually, Paap et al. (1982) vacillate between attribution of a unique role to backward masking in preventing verification and inclusion of any sort of abbreviated presentation in this role.

In both Besner et al.'s and Paap et al.'s theories the conscious recognition experience, on which report is usually predicated, depends upon some sort of matching of a lexical to a visual/pictorial code, although the nature of the matching process and the way that frequency effects enter into it is quite different.

Both theories leave me in some doubt as to the provenance of correct reports in these tachistocopic tasks. If the door is to be entirely barred against frequency effects then correct reports must be based on processes that *precede* the frequency-sensitive matching operation. Since at least some correct reports are based on a visual experience, matching with a pictorial representation cannot be a *necessary* condition for visibility. Furthermore, since at least some correct reports preserve "pictorial" detail, matching cannot be a necessary condition for co-ordinating linguistic and spatial-image representations.

Returning to the "determining letters" theory of Zeitler and Goldscheider and Muller, we find three aspects that are of current interest. First, their views belong to the class of what Neisser (1967) called "fragment" theories. Second, the preliminary fragmentary representation that they posit is expressed in letter units. Finally, the process of word recognition is regarded as being essentially a two-stage affair.

There seems to be a strong correlation between the empiricist position and two-stage theories of perception, although the association is not one of entailment. Scheerer (1981) has drawn attention to the fact that Wundt's conception of the two stages differs from modern interpretations in that for Wundt the first, stimulus-driven cycle is held to be "active"; the subsequent integration of that information with stored knowledge is described as "passive." This seems the converse of the passive-active sequence proposed by contemporary theorists such as Becker (1976), Broadbent and Broadbent (1980), Navon (1977), Neisser (1967), and Treisman and Gelade (1980). In part, this seeming contrast is attributable to vagueness and idiosyncracy in Wundt's use of the terms "active/passive." However, another aspect of the question is that Wundt, like Neisser, appeared to regard the second stage as strategically modifiable. Hence, the unconscious rectification of typographic errors in the percept is attributed to passive "assimilation" of sensory information into associative schemata, but this, Wundt supposes, can be overcome by acts of attention.

An interesting elaboration of the view of word recognition as based upon an incomplete letter code supplemented by inference was sketched by Zeitler. He appears to have been the first commentator to suggest that positional information was highly unstable in briefly inspected letter arrays. He speaks of transpositional oscillation occurring until the letters become "anchored" into the places they are assigned in a word percept (Huey, 1908, p. 87). This view of brief letter arrays as characterised by extreme positional instability has attracted support in recent studies of iconic memory (e.g. Mewhort, Marchetti, Gurnsey, & Campbell, 1984; Coltheart, 1984) and the idea that word context exercises its influence by stabilising position information was explored in detail by Estes (1975).

Two aspects of letter-position information have been of interest to recent students of word recognition: loss of one yields Zeitler's type of error involving transpositions *within* the word; loss of the other yields migration of letters to the same word-position in *another* concurrently displayed word.

A number of studies converge on the idea that subjects are able to use positional information in quite specific ways. Mason (1975) and several others have shown that recognition performance is better for strings that possess higher position-specific letter frequencies. Although it is extremely difficult to disentangle this variable from associated structural properties (see e.g. Henderson, 1982), most of these also involve positional information. Estes (1975) and Johnston (1978) found that positional accuracy of letter report was much higher in words than random strings. It is unlikely that this is the sole basis of the word advantage, however, since Johnston found word superiority even when scoring of full report took no account of position and it seems likely that some loss of positional information is due to the methods used to cue target letters for report.

Estes and Johnston, as well as Duncan (this volume), found very few transpositional errors within familiar words but it seems that such errors can be encountered and Huey (1908, p. 109) discusses a number of naturally occurring transpositions, as more recently does Cowie (1985). Just as the paucity of transpositional errors within words attests to the efficacy of positional analysis, so does the abundance of migration errors that take place between equivalent positions in a pair of words (Allport, 1977; McClelland & Mozer, 1986; Mozer, 1983; Shallice & McGill, 1978; Treisman & Souther, 1986; Woodworth, 1938). Such evidence has led theorists to assume the existence of letter analysis "channels" for each position within the word. This is, for example, a fundamental feature of the design of McClelland and Rumelhart's (1981) interactive model, although various modifications to the model are possible which might loosen the correspondence between position-specific letter (PSL) analysis and word structure. For instance, a PSL analyser might have an additional, weaker, excitatory connection to nodes serving words that contain this particular letter in another position.

There are several difficulties with the strong version of the PSL channels assumption. First, it is inhospitable to transpositions within a word. Second, the evidence that migrations between words respect ordinal position is almost entirely derived from studies of three- or four-letter words with word length (and often CV architecture) fixed. It is difficult to believe that in long words, and perhaps especially in polymorphemic words, precise ordinal position forms the basis for all communication between the letter and word levels. Moreover, Jordan (1986) has reported facilitatory priming between words that share a letter cluster in different positions (e.g. LEMON-MONARCH). An alternative line of thought is to suppose that relative-position information is encoded by activating position-free cluster detectors. This general approach may be particularly attractive in speech processing where word boundaries are often obscure and phonemic segments overlap; thus, such cluster representations have been postulated by Wickelgren (1969) and Marcus (1984) for speech production and perception, respectively. However, more recently a similar idea has been advanced as an account of *letter* migrations (Mozer, this volume; McClelland & Mozer, 1986).

Global, Transletter Features.   In the general realm of object and space perception, the neo-empiricist, inferential account has traditionally been opposed by asserting that higher-order features of the stimulus array are directly available as perceptual primitives. This thesis has been advanced in different ways by the Gestalt psychologists and by J. J. Gibson. Translated into the domain of word recognition, such a hypothesis can be discovered in the 19th-century writings by Cattell (1886) and by Erdmann and Dodge (1898), who maintained that the word advantage resulted from the use of global cues such as word length, and especially, word envelope.

Evaluation of the wholistic position has been bedevilled by a persisting confusion of two quite distinct theses. The first draws attention to the characteristics of perceptual experiences (whether of words or the more usual solid furniture of the world). What is being indicated here is that the typical experiential product of perceptual processing is one in which the various visual properties of the scene, such as the location and the identity of an object, are integrated together into an interpreted composition. This is "wholistic" in the sense that properties which are logically independent and which may have been analysed by separate processing modules are incorpor-ated together in a perceptual description cast in terms of interpreted words or objects. In word recognition, this involves the "marriage" (to use Besner and McCann's word, this volume) of lexical and pictorial information. It actually requires an effort of attention to focus selectively on one of the stimulus properties that has entered this marriage and our ability to do so is severely limited.

The second wholistic thesis involves a much stronger assertion, for it is a claim about process rather than product. It asserts that word identification owes its advantages (e.g. as compared to recognition of unstructured or unfamiliar letter arrays) to the use of wholistic cues, such as length, transletter features, or word envelope shape.

It is important to note that early adherents of letter-mediated theories of word recognition did not deny the first (perceptual product) thesis. Zeitler writes (cited in Huey, 1908, p. 83), for example: "The word-form is indeed apparently assimilated as a whole, *secondarily*; but *primarily*, it is apperceived only in its dominating constituent parts."

Huey (1908, p. 109) is of similar opinion and also reinterprets the fully composed, stable and seamless quality of perceptual experience in terms of the two-stage model:

> ... one is inclined to accept what the experiments of Zeitler, Messmer, and others seem to show, that the first factors of perception in reading are not usually the total form, word-length, etc., but certain striking dominant parts, the appreciation of total word-form coming a little later as the recognition is completed at the suggestion of these dominant cues.

One thing that now seems clear is that the word superiority effect itself does not owe its very existence to use of global shape as a cue. McClelland (1976) and Adams (1979) have shown that the advantage enjoyed by familiar words is undiminished by mutilation of their normal shape. This conclusion requires to be qualified by the fact that in visual comparison experiments mutilation generally reduces the magnitude of the word advantage (e.g. Bruder, 1978). Recently, Besner, Davelaar, Alcott, and Parry (1984) have argued that mutilation only reduced word superiority in tasks where a specific identification response is not required. In latency tasks that do require explicit identification, such as naming, word superiority does not interact with mutilation (Besner, 1983; see also Besner & McCann, this volume).

A possible limitation of all these studies is that they neglect variables that may only manifest themselves when words are read in context. Thus, for example, Broadbent and Broadbent (1981) have argued that global features, extracted from low spatial frequency analyses, may interact with contextual effects. I am tempted, here, to embark on the mischievous argument that the only tasks that rival single-word recognition experiments in artificiality are the typical studies of contextual priming. However, I shall forego that jibe and turn, instead, to studies of continuous reading in which eye-movements are the principal concern. In this sphere, it has been shown that gross information such as word length can be extracted parafoveally from the text ahead and used to determine the next saccadic target. But this stops far short of showing that such global analysis influences *identification* of parafoveal words. Indeed, while there is some dispute on the question, most well-controlled studies seem to establish that such words do not yield up lexical information to the reader. For example, Rayner, McConkie, and Zola (1980) found that a parafoveal word would prime a subsequent foveal target word that shared the same initial letters, whereas under these conditions semantic relatedness had no effect. Furthermore, the orthographic priming effect was undiminished by a change in letter-case from primer to target. A similar priming effect that is indifferent to case change has been reported by Evett and Humphreys (1981) for successive foveal presentations. Such demonstrations seem to converge with the studies employing the Wheeler-Reicher paradigm in showing that global features play little or no role in skilled word recognition and that, to the contrary, word recognition usually depends upon the automatic formation of a preliminary representation specifying abstract letter identities, with some priming interactions mediated by this code.

Before closing this topic it is worth remarking that one single confusion has permeated argument in this area to an extraordinary extent. This is the failure to realise that the features of words that give them their characteristic envelope, the ascenders and descenders, are features of letters that may exercise their influence *at a letter identification stage*. Consider the words *stage* and *shape*. In lower case they possess similar outlines. If we found that under difficult viewing conditions each was a common confusional response when the other had been presented we might be tempted to conclude that this was caused by their shared envelope shape. However, we might equally well interpret such an effect as arising out of the particular confusability at the letter level of *t* and *h* on one hand, and of *g* and *p*, on the other. Bouma (1973) has shown that letters possessing ascenders or descenders tend not only to be confused with others possessing this same feature but that they also tend to be the best-recognised letters in words or random strings, perhaps because this feature is particularly salient and moreover, once detected, it limits the possibilities considerably. These attributes of letter identification would lead one to expect that words with ascenders or descenders are likely to be easier to recognise, *ceteris paribus*, than words lacking these features, and that the omission of letters carrying these features is more likely to be noted (e.g. in proof-reading) than the omission of other letters. Yet Monk and Hulme (1983) appeal to the latter finding as evidence for the efficacy of *word outline* as a recognition cue. Similarly, the letter confusion data suggest that words sharing an envelope pattern are more likely to be mutually confusable than ones which differ in this aspect. Yet Havens and Foot (1963) cite this outcome as evidence favouring a *word envelope* interpretation. Even were one to accept the view that envelope shape is encoded as a primitive feature, it is not necessary to conclude that this feature *is applied directly to the word level* to yield a set of candidate words. The shape information may instead be brought to bear on a preliminary letter analysis, so as to constrain which letter candidates are considered at each position within the word. Posnansky and Rayner's (1977) finding that word recognition is facilitated when the previous stimulus shares the same shape of envelope cannot therefore be said to lend selective support to the view that envelope shape operates at the word level.

Erdmann and Dodge's (1898) original position on global word shape seems to have been less assertive than is usually supposed.[3] They did not deny that preliminary letter identification played a major role in normal viewing conditions, and they suggested that it was their employment of conditions unfavourable to letter discrimination which led to reliance on word shape cues. (Indeed, it seems their experimental conditions were extraordinarily hospitable to a word-level strategy.)

Let us briefly take stock of what we might now safely add to Erdmann and Dodge's speculations. It appears incontrovertible that adequate word recognition is possible under conditions which severely disrupt any transletter and envelope cues. Since (for various reasons which I must pass over) it does not seem plausible to assume that the reader's lexical access in such cases is invariably mediated by translation into a nonvisual (e.g. phonological) code, there is no obvious alternative to the assumption that the surviving competence rests on preliminary letter identification. To be sure, such mutilated script often reduces the fluency of word identification. However, this might simply be due to the impact of the resultant visual strangeness on certain tasks (cf. Besner & McCann, this volume) or to a complication of preliminary letter identification. Our remaining uncertainties are therefore most suitably organised by enquiring whether (and under what circumstances) global features are *ever* employed in direct activation of word entries. So great is the volume of flawed argument in support of the wholistic thesis that many have mistaken its consumption of space for weighty substance, but there is, I suppose, a converse danger of mistakenly assuming that a thesis which attracts such defective support must somehow be inherently unsound. One appealing research strategy is to commence the search for wholistic reading in what we judge to be the most fertile grounds, in hope of being able thereby to isolate its characteristics. We might choose to start with a class of reader such as a certain kind of developmental (e.g. Frith, 1985) or acquired (e.g. Howard, 1986) dyslexic. Alternatively, we might start with special script like the brand name "logo" or lexicalised initials (e.g. *BBC*, Henderson & Chard, 1976).[4] The problem with such points of departure is, of course, how to achieve safe passage back to "normal" reading.[5] This, in turn, obliges us to

---

[3] I am indebted to H. Gunther for drawing my attention to this aspect of the original text. Bouwhuis (1979) also sheds light on the original by observing that the authors based much of their claim on repeated presentations of a small set of words which were over-learned. Since the words seem to have been long and distinctive, it is not surprising that a smattering of features often allowed successful discrimination.

[4] Concerning meaningful initials, I have come to the opinion that the difficulty of recognising e.g. *bbc* has no clear bearing on transletter features. Instead, such examples reflect case-change which has "graphemic" significance for the reader, in the sense that it has the potential to express contrasts (see Henderson, 1985, for elaboration).

[5] The difficulty of generalising to normal, swift reading from very hesitant reading such as that of Howard's (1986) patient is discussed by Besner and Johnston (in press).

confront the issue of what we wish to explain and whether, in particular, it is what processes we are *capable* of employing (the architecture of the possible), or what processes we *typically* employ (the busy ecological slum).

Skill, Chunking and Acts of Attention.   Returning to the ancient accounts of word superiority listed in Table 8.1, we find that hypothesis 3 deals with attention, skill, and chunking. It takes various forms. The general idea is that "acts of attention" are costly for the cognitive system. Where higher-order structure exists in an array of letters the skilled perceiver will be able to achieve a more parsimonious mental description of the stimulus, thus limiting the number of features that require acts of attention. This notion that skill consists in the performer freeing himself from the constraints imposed by attentional limitations by dealing with larger stimulus units is surely one of the most recurrent themes in the study of skilled performance.

For Huey (1908, p. 104) the limitation of attention stems from the fact that: ". . . perceiving is an *act*, a thing that we *do*." He compares (Huey, 1908, p. 105) perceptual acts with motor skills such as skating and executing a tennis serve: "In either case," he writes, "repetition progressively frees the mind from attention to details." The span of apprehension was of such central interest in 19th-century cognitive psychology because it seemed to show (in Huey's words, 1908, p. 69) ". . .that the number of separate recognition acts per moment has rather narrow limits."

In the motor domain, the idea that skill permits the performer to deal with larger units of response is founded on observations such as the fact that, for a skilled driver, gear-change no longer seems to consist of separate actions on the clutch, accelerator, and gearlever, each competing for attention. In the perceptual domain, skill seems to allow the perceiver to package the stimulus into superordinate descriptors. Goldscheider and Muller (Huey, 1908, pp. 75–79) showed that this was as true of the organisation of line segments into geometrical shapes as of the formation of letters into words.

In a loose fashion, Goldscheider and Muller's attempt to bring together, in the same arena, coherence effects in word and in geometric shape arrays foreshadows modern work on object superiority effects (e.g. McClelland, 1978; Pomerantz, Sager, & Stoever, 1977; Williams & Weisstein, 1978; see also Schendel & Shaw, 1976). Just as structure in a letter array allowed the limits of apprehension to be shifted up from the letter to the word level, so structure in an array of line segments allows a more economical stimulus description at the shape level.

Three aspects of Goldscheider and Muller's thinking merit notice. First, they emphasised the strategic flexibility of the reader, who might choose to attend to various levels of description of the stimulus, according to his current purpose. Second, in their discussion of the role of higher-order perceptual schemata they hint at a "perceptual acts" notion, developed much more recently by theorists such as Kolers (e.g. Kolers, 1973; see also Besner & McCann, this volume). In this view, perceptual schemata consist of practised pattern analysing operations (cf. Huey's discussion of the exercise of "apperceptive habits," p. 105). Third, Goldscheider and Muller's treatment of the manner in which these schemata facilitate apprehension of structured stimulus arrays is what we might call, in modern parlance, a "criterion bias" account, in the sense that (Huey, 1908, p. 77): "...this aliveness...for total forms makes us negligent of the details that appear." This notion, that attention to a superordinate level of code occurs at the cost of neglecting detail at the subordinate level, has been pursued recently in the work of Healy (e.g. Healy, 1981), concerned with proof-reading errors as an index of attention to a higher level of code. Gleitman and Jonides (1976) make an analogous claim about the cost of adopting a categorical set in alphanumeric search.

Once again the empiricist position seems to find its most comfortable expression within a two-stage framework. The notion that preliminary letter recognition may take place pre-attentively, which was implicit in Zeitler's two-stage account, was made more explicit by Schumann (1906; see also Huey, 1908, p. 151; Woodworth, 1938, p. 742). He seems to have echoed Goldscheider and Muller's idea that the perceptual advantage enjoyed by words is due to the repackaging of the letter-level information into a higher-order code to prevent information loss during perceptual processing. It is at this latter level that Huey wishes to deny the possibility of "letter-by-letter" reading (that much-misunderstood phrase). A precisely equivalent view of speech has been taken much more recently by Miller (1962), in arguing that phoneme identification cannot be the basis of speech perception since it would entail an implausibly high rate of decision acts. Here, the empiricist distinction between sensation and inference has been fleshed out into the proposition that sensation consists of the passive registration of sense-data, whereas perception is active and judgemental and in consequence constrained by our limited rate of action.

What emerges from all this is the idea of a potential for considerable information loss between the two putative stages of perception, an idea taken up in a different context by Broadbent (1958) and Sperling (1967) in the second flowering of cognitive psychology. For Broadbent, stimulus items that did not receive attention (i.e. selection for the second stage of perceptual processing) merely decayed from sensory storage.

The early students of visual apprehension considered that unreported letters in a tachistoscopic exposure were possibly recognised, but failed to persist in memory until their names could be stated (Huey, 1908, p. 64). In the terms of Sperling's (1967) model this would entail loss in the recognition buffer, while awaiting articulation or transcription into the response made. (Sperling, himself, was indecisive about the source of the limit on amount reportable.)[6]

In early accounts of the role of acts of attention in word recognition there are two quite different underlying assumptions about the source of word superiority which are seldom explicitly distinguished. So far, we have concentrated on the assumption that higher-level codes are subject to less information loss. However, Huey (1908, p. 112) seems to favour an alternative account in terms an intrinsic attentional bias toward the construction of superordinate levels of description: "There is a heirarchy of recognition habits, the exercise of the higher drafting away the consciousness that would otherwise serve for completing the recognition of the particular letters." As we shall see, the implication that the reader can, at least to some extent, choose which level of code to attend to in the second phase of the perceptual cycle is central to Neisser's view, to which we now turn.

1967

Neisser began *Cognitive psychology* with a rejection of the theory of *eidola*. Perception was not based on the assimilation of ghostly replicas of visible objects. Instead (Neisser, 1967, p. 10): "The central assertion is that seeing, hearing and remembering are all acts of *construction* ... The constructive processes are assumed to have two stages, of which the first is fast, crude, wholistic and parallel while the second is deliberate, attentive, detailed and sequential."

In 1967, Neisser regarded the proximal stimulus with the empiricist's typical pessimism. He marvelled (1967, p. 4) that visual cognition can be constucted out of: "as unpromising a beginning as the retinal patterns." His conception of the construction process was motivated in the perceptual domain by the New Look movement in perception, especially Bruner's (1957) theory of "hypothesis testing," and in the domain of memory by Bartlett's (1932) notion of schemata. However, to this Neisser added a newer metaphor, that of the computer's manipulation of information. The label he adopted for the putative second stage of perceptual processing, "analysis by synthesis," reveals his commitment to language perception as the prototypical cognitive activity. Analysis by synthesis had been advanced as a model for the decyphering of speech and handwriting by machine. These are the two

---

[6] Briefly, the problem arises from the nonidentity of the span of full report at brief (say, 50–500msec) exposures and the span of immediate recall with conventional presentation. In Sperling's 1967 model, it seems we should impute the former span to properties of the *recognition buffer* and the latter to the auditory store. An alternative is to assume parallel access from the icon to visual and verbal stores (e.g. Scarborough, 1972).

principal realms in which the stimuli are directly fashioned by the human motor apparatus and where, as a result, the physical form taken by a stimulus item varies according to the constraints imposed by the human production system, so they might be expected to attract "active" theories of perception.

Neisser's chapter on reading begins with the same central preoccupation as the 19th-century cognitive psychologists; the word apprehension effect. The argument does not depart radically from the issues confronted by Huey, 60 years previously, but Neisser's treatment reflects the new, mid-century concern with two apparently continuous aspects of a word's familiarity; frequency of usage and the structural patterning that makes for word-likeness.

The Pseudoword Advantage and Perceptual Units

Zeitler, in the 19th century, had shown that the insertion of vowels into a consonantal string made it easier to report. With the importation of statistical "information theory" measures into the psychology of the 1950s, it became established that briefly displayed letter strings could be more accurately reported, the more their sequential structure approached the transitional probabilities of English. To this, E. J. Gibson and her colleagues added the hypothesis that word position (initial vs. final) was an important source of constraint of the legality of consonant sequences (e.g. Gibson, Pick, Osser, & Hammond, 1962).

This work focussed attention on sub-word, structural regularities and laid the foundations for a vast and inconclusive literature concerning the psychological reality of various measures of orthographic structure (Neisser, 1967, p. 111): "There might be critical features of these strings—and by implication, of words as well—which are 'larger' than individual letters but 'smaller' than the word as a whole."

Two sets of implication stemmed from the work of the Cornell group on orthographic structure. The more general was the notion that the word apprehension effect extended more widely than had been thought. Thus, when the striking Wheeler-Reicher version of the word superiority effect was reported at the end of the 1960s, the way had been paved for Baron and Thurston's (1973) demonstration that much, perhaps all, of the word advantage was shared by orthographically regular pseudowords. This led, in turn, to the empirical question of whether *any* portion of the word superiority effect was peculiar to real words. If so, the theoretical question had to be posed as to whether the word and pseudoword advantages required different explanations.

A more specific influence was exercised by Gibson and her colleagues through their notion that orthographic structure was not merely probabilistic but was instead, in some sense, the product of *rules*. Now, it must be admitted that the discussion of "legal" spelling patterns was extraordinarily vague and seemed to confuse together: (1) phonotactic regularities; (2) orthotactic regularities; (3) spelling-sound mapping regularities; and, perhaps, (4) purely probabilistic tendencies. Nevertheless, however confused its parentage, the notion of legal spelling patterns gave birth to two concepts which came to play major roles in attempts to explain the pseudoword advantage, pronounceability, and letter clusters as perceptual units.

Neisser gave voice to the obvious difficulty that confronts the Gibsonian pronounceability hypothesis when he observed (1967, p. 113): "It makes little sense to say that 'pronounceability confers unity'; a cluster of letters cannot be pronounced until it has been identified." Despite the subsequent ingenious theoretical manoeuvres of Spoehr and Smith (e.g. 1975), the phonological recoding hypothesis has not recovered from its collision with that obstacle. Moreover, it has become clearer how effects that depend on purely orthographic variables may mimic pronounceability effects. For example, McClelland and Rumelhart (1981) have shown that the facilitatory effect of inserting vowels in a consonant string (reported by Zeitler as well as by Spoehr and Smith) can be accounted for in terms of the resultant increase in the number of partially activated units at the word level. These friendly lexical units are activated by virtue of their resemblance to the spelling of the stimulus string and they respond by feeding back activation to their corresponding nodes at the letter level, thus tending to reinforce activation of the orthographic representation of the stimulus. Furthermore, Seidenberg (this volume) discusses an aspect of orthographic patterning which correlates with the boundaries of a unit in the phonological domain, in this case the tendency of syllabic boundaries to be signalled by uncommon letter conjunctions. As Seidenberg acutely remarks, acknowledgement that such orthographic symptoms of phonological structure may influence visual processing does not oblige us to embrace the assumption that these phonological units form an obligatory access code.

Neisser believed that the pseudoword advantage over random strings left no alternative but to postulate letter-cluster detector units. Having invented supraletter units by appeal to logical necessity, Neisser (1967, p. 114) dispatched an individual letter code as incomprehensible: ". . . it is not clear what such an assumption would mean." Now, this is an exceedingly odd position to be taken by one conversant with pandemonium-type models, since such sorting networks positively invite the interpretation of a computational node as a perceptual unit. Thus, we can say of the hierarchical network models of Adams (1979) and McClelland and Rumelhart (1981) that they assume letter-mediated recognition in the *weak sense* that they contain computational nodes that represent letter identities and in the *strong sense* that there are no paths from the input to the word level that do not pass through letter nodes. Neither of these models happens to postulate perceptual units for spelling patterns (letter clusters). However, there is a sense in which bigrams are represented in Adam's model, through the excitatory connections which link letter nodes laterally and which are united to reflect conjoint frequencies of occurrence. This device is used to generate the pseudoword advantage. Both Adams' and McClelland and Rumelhart's models posit feedback from the word to the letter level to account for the real word advantage, but the latter model lacks lateral excitation at the letter level and obtains the pseudoword advantage by the same route as the real word advantage; feedback from the word to letter level. In the pseudoword case, word units are activated that share some letters with the presented pseudoword. Even the McClelland and Rumelhart model may predict bigram frequency effects with certain stimuli; however, these arise due to the tendency for words with high bigram counts to inhabit densely populated orthographic neighbourhoods.

In sum, it is incontrovertible that a computational net with nodes for individual letters and for words and not other intervening level of nodes can supply an account of the pseudoword advantage. Such networks offer us a language for expressing various senses of the term *perceptual unit*. What remains to be seen is whether they capture the more general sense of "perceptual unit" that recurs through Nessier's book, and that is caught up in his central preoccupation with attention as "synthesis," that is, the level of description at which the perceiver decides to construct his percept. Such units are held by Neisser (1967, p. 115) to be ". . . the products of figural synthesis, introspectively available and usually given a verbal label in these experiments."

Attention to the Word as a Whole

How seductive this term "wholistic" seems to be! Neisser's appetite for the epithet is revealed in the index of *Cognitive Psychology*, where entries for "wholistic" processing refer to verbal memory, motion perception, sentence comprehension, word recognition, and several other topics, including "preattentive" processing. This last brings us up against the fact that even in the restricted domain of word recognition he employs the term in two conflicting ways. Both arise out of his central theme, that cognition comprises two phases: the first, parallel and automatic; the second, serial and attentive. (This is Neisser's version of the traditional empiricist's marching tune.) In one usage, "wholistic" is used to characterise the first phase and distinguish it from the second. Here, the term is used roughly as an obscure synonym of "parallel." The second usage has a quite different geometry. It expresses the idea that in word recognition the second phase of cognition consists of branching alternatives, one of which is "wholistic" and the other letter-based (Neisser, 1967, p. 106): "On the one hand, the subject may focus his attention successively on the individual letters . . . on the other hand . . . he may deploy focal attention over the entire word as a Unit."

In the previous subsection we saw how Neisser believed that the perceptual advantage enjoyed by word-like stimuli compelled us to grant the existence of supraletter perceptual units. "Wholism" in his second usage is the abandonment of preliminary letter identification (PLI). He gives three grounds for rejecting PLI supplemented by associative inference as an explanation of word superiority. Introspection, he claims, fails to confirm letter-based analysis as a feature of the word apprehension effect. Schumann (Note 1) had cogently reproached Erdmann and Dodge for such an argument and Huey (1908, p. 151), in a well-known passage, protested that preliminary letter recognition need not be available to introspection: "The automatic functioning of these neural factors and habits, silent but effective workers behind the 'stage-effects' which they arouse in consciousness, is worthy of a greater share of the attention in the discussion concerning how we perceive."

Neisser's second reason echoes Cattell's (1886) claim that word recognition is too fast to be based on preliminary letter identification. Here, Neisser adopts both the fallacies propounded by Cattell, in supposing that letter processing could only be serial and that the time taken to respond to a letter with its name is a reasonable measure of the time taken to activate the mental representations of letters which might mediate word recognition.

Finally, Neisser appeals to findings purporting to demonstrate the reader's use of global, transletter cues.

Despite its conceptual inadequacies, Neisser's attempt to characterise an attentional option in word recognition has some merit. In some ways it anticipates recent experimental demonstrations of apparently strategic phenomena. These include effects of attentional instructions (Johnston & McClelland, 1974), letter spacing (Purcell & Stanovich, 1982) and pre-cuing (Holender, 1986). While Carr, Davidson, and Hawkins (1978) have argued that the word advantage, unlike the pseudoword advantage, is not modified by expectations, segregating words and nonwords in blocks enhances the word advantage in other tasks (e.g. Frederiksen & Kroll, 1976) and it begins to seem likely that the word advantage is only automatic under certain conditons, such as spatial compactness.

Let us suppose that one can, to some extent, elect to see a word as a mere string of letters just as one can choose to see the ambiguous duck/rabbit as a duck. What sort of processing differences might underlie these "seeing as" options? For Neisser (1967, p. 123), seeing a word as a whole must involve fundamentally different sorts of stimulus processing from seeing it as a letter string: "To focus attention on a figure is to devote the lion's share of processing capacity to it, bringing relatively sophisticated analyzers to bear, and thus to construct an appropriate perceptual object."

However, the question of how far down "seeing as" strategies reach and the extent to which they actually reorganise lower-level processes is important and unresolved. Do figure-ground decisions, for instance, influence the extraction of contour information from the grey-level image? Whatever the eventual answer to such questions it seems unlikely to be fruitful to speak of the reorganisation that takes place when, without any shift of gaze, we reinterpret an ambiguous figure as a shift in the focus of analysers.

Neisser complained that taxonomic network models like Pandemonium furnish no account of attentional effects. While this was fair comment on existing models, there is no reason so suppose that their design prohibits such phenomena in principle, and in fact McClelland and Rumelhart (1981) briefly discussed how their model might be supplemented to accommodate such effects as that of adopting a word or letter "set." The parameter on which they focussed for this purpose was the weighting of letter to word inhibition. Consider the following situation. The visual input is of poor quality. In consequence a lot of letter nodes are partially activated. Numerous spurious letters remain in contention since the input is insufficiently precise to exclude them. If the inhibition exercised by a letter node on an incompatible word node (i.e. a word not containing that letter in that position) is set on high gain then word nodes in general will be difficult to activate. Even the veridical word node will receive substantial inhibition from spuriously activated letter nodes. A consequence of this inactivity at the word level is that little feedback is directed from the word level back down to the letter level. For this reason, it is tempting to call this strategy (i.e. high gain on letter-to-word inhibition) *letter oriented*. However, here McClelland and Rumelhart confront us with a paradox, since the main outcome of this strategy applied to their model is usually a depression of the *pseudoword* advantage, whereas performance on words may be largely unaffected. The reasons for this are complicated and have to do with competition between active nodes at the word level.

If the reader adopts a word set by relaxing the amount of letter-to-word inhibition, the consequent overall activation at the word level will be roughly equal for word and pseudoword stimuli, although for a word, relatively more of that activation will be concentrated in the node peculiar to it (thus inhibiting competing neighbouring nodes). Since, however, McClelland and Rumelhart make the far-reaching working assumption that in these tasks *readout is only made from the letter level*, activation of the word nodes can only affect response accuracy via the resultant feedback to the letter level. Hence, even though activation at the word level tends to be focussed on the veridical node when a word is presented, but distributed over a neighbourhood when a pseudoword is presented, after this activation has been fed back down to the letter level it only confers slight advantage on the real word to the extent that less of the feedback is wasted on the irrelevant letter possessed by a lexical neighbour. Whether or not a disposition to entertain word candidates will assist performance may depend upon the precise structure of the orthographic neighbourhood that surrounds the stimulus.

What is interesting in this little illustration is that attention-like effects can be produced which greatly change the distribution of activation across the network and, in particular, the role of different levels of representation in the network, simply by biasing the gain between levels, without any structural reorganisation. A much more radical way to embody attentional bias in the model would be to allow it to influence *readout*. This might enable us to satisfy the intuition that a perceptual set for words consists of using a different level of information to control performance. Note, however, that this still falls far short of Neisser's proposal that a "word strategy" involves employment of a quite different set of visual features (such as transletter cues).

Finally, it is worth remarking that the way in which parallel distributed processing models read out the patterns of activity on which they stabilise, in order to generate task responses, merits closer scrutiny. A central theme in recent work on word recognition is that experimental tasks which were intended merely to tap an aspect of processing seem to invade and pervade the processor, a nasty case of the corkscrew drinking the wine.

Another recent model, that of Paap et al. (1982, see also Paap et al., this volume) permits strategic bias toward the word level of analysis. In this model, both the lexicon and the alphabetum (letter analysis system) can contribute to response decisions. Whether or not a particular word unit is considered as a candidate by the decision machinery depends upon whether its activation exceeds some critical value. It is assumed that this value is under the subject's control and may be biased by expectations of different classes of stimuli. It would also appear that another parameter in their model might be controlled by the subject, himself. This parameter governs the ability of the lexicon to pre-empt letter analysis as input to the decision process. As presently formulated, the lexicon captures the decision if the gross level of lexical activation, totalled across word units, exceeds some critical amount. The notion that this threshold might be subject to strategic bias merits examination.

Much of this model-tuning has been motivated by the desire to accommodate Carr et al.'s (1978) finding that pseudowords, but not words, are more difficult to recognise when they occur unexpectedly. Curiously, no-one seems to have investigated the effect of including pseudoword stimuli on *word* identification. Yet this departure from natural reading material obliges the subject to make much finer discriminations than are normally required, as commentators on the lexical decision task have frequently remarked.

Finally, it is worth recording that the role of attention in word recognition has recently been investigated with renewed vigour; in particular, the thorny questions that surround visual experience have attracted theoretical interest. Much of this has been directed towards the way that separable features are re-assembled as a preliminary to (and perhaps as a necessary condition for) visual experience (e.g. Besner & McCann, this volume; Paap et al., this volume; Prinzmetal & Millis-Wright, 1984; Treisman & Gelade, 1980). As Neisser (1967, p. 301) suggests: "Although the constructive processes themselves never appear in consciousness, their products do."

Word Frequency

The effect of word frequency made its initial impact in the mid-20th century as a methodological complication in word perception experiments (Solomon & Howes, 1951). Early attempts to explain the effect focussed on sophisticated guessing. Neisser's principal interest was to show that the frequency bias influenced what the subject actually saw rather than merely what he reported. This question had been highlighted by Goldiamond and Hawkins' (1958) provocative report of a "frequency effect" when subjects were led to expect a set of stimuli but were instead presented with smudges. Neisser vigorously denied that this demonstration requires a nonperceptual account. Expectations, he emphasised, can affect what we actually experience. Indeed, a recurrent theme in Neisser's book was the continuity of hallucinations with veridical perception. Hallucinations are merely the ultimate in top-down processing.

One qualification of the word-frequency effect engaged Neisser particularly. That was the finding that forced-choice procedures reduce or eliminate the effect of word frequency (e.g. Pierce, 1963). The prevailing account of this had been that the forced-choice set became a substitute for word frequency in governing the subject's expectations and hence his perceptual inferences. Neisser proposed an alternative view in which the embarkation on a forced choice changes the subject's attentional strategy from frequency sensitive "wholistic synthesis" of the word to a letter-by-letter analysis.

The forced-choice procedures that Neisser considered were ones in which the alternatives were known in advance. The subsequent adoption of the word superiority paradigm has provided evidence of performance where the forced-choice *follows* the stimulus, in the form, usually, of a location cue and a pair of letter alternatives at that location. Manelis (1974) showed that this procedure, too, rendered frequency effects undetectable. However, since the same experiments manifest superior performance on words (than on pseudo-words), Neisser's assumption that the procedure inhibits a word-level strategy cannot be maintained, unless we also assume that the word superiority effect and the putative word-level strategy are quite independent.

(Such a dualism is not inconceivable. It might be the case, for instance, that in a letter discrimination task the word superiority effect is the product of an automatic process of lexical consultation which is insensitive to word frequency, whereas tasks in which lexical access is an *explicit objective* show frequency effects.)

However, before pursuing that line of argument it is necessary to dispose of the rather more mundane possibility that the probed letter-alternative procedure is simply not refined enough to detect frequency effects. Gunther, Gfroerer, and Weiss (1984) were emboldened to claim that no forced-choice experiment could be found in the literature which exhibited a reliable frequency effect. However, since the forced-choice procedure can only with difficulty discriminate between the level of performance on common words and pseudowords, this narrow window on lexicality may not permit a view of any frequency effects that obtain. Perhaps we must look beyond the threshold task for other situations in which more substantial lexicality effects obtain that may be frequency insensitive (e.g. McCann & Besner, in press).

RECAPITULATION AND SEQUEL

Orthographic Structure

There is little to be found in Neisser's treatment that cannot be discovered in one of the accounts reviewed by Huey, 60 years previously. Perhaps more importantly, there were surprisingly few new facts available to Neisser that could be used to terminate any of the persisting lines of speculation. For example, progress on the question of whether global features were important in adjudicating between word candidates had to await a shift to a falsificatory mode, as is found in case-mixing disruptions of word shape. One important finding, the pseudoword advantage, might have been used to attack the notion of reliance on global cues. After all, if much of the word superiority effect is shared by unfamiliar but wordlike strings, acquaintance with word envelopes cannot be the *sine qua non* of the effect. However, Gibson and Neisser preferred instead to use the pseudoword effect as a launching pad for the concept of a global letter-cluster detector. Nevertheless, the seeds had been sown of a fresh interest in the psychological reality of various descriptions of the regularities of English orthography. A new generation of computers was set to work tabulating bigram positional frequencies, grapheme-phoneme correspondences, etc. Moreover, despite the inadequacies of Gibson's own attempt to establish a rule-based description of the regularities of English orthography, psychological students of reading were encouraged to consult linguistic descriptions of English spelling. In the fastness of their laboratories they began to interest themselves in the literature on spelling reform. Perhaps most fundamentally, they strove to look beyond the merely statistical descriptions born of "information theory" to an understanding of the way spelling patterns arose out of the tendency of English orthography to reflect various phonological and morphological elements (e.g. Kavanagh & Mattingly, 1972; Massaro, Taylor, Venezky, Jastrzembski, & Lucas, 1980; Venezky, 1970; see also Seidenberg and Taft, this volume).

If the burgeoning interest of experimenters in linguistic properties of words set the present era apart from the tradition culminating in Neisser's book, the predilection for two-stage treatments might seem to reflect a bond, connecting present-day models to the tradition of Huey and Neisser. Despite some superficial similarities such as the serial nature of the hypothetical second stage that is shared by Neisser's, Paap et al.'s, and Treisman's model, I believe that the two-stage formulations differ substantially in form and in motive. The inspiration of 19th-century dichotomous treatments was largely epistemological, partitioning sense-data from inference. Neisser's two stages, on the other hand, were founded in the neo-Broadbentian notion that processing-capacity limitations compelled early *selection* for penetrating analysis. In contrast, Treisman's feature-integration model is motivated by the presumed need to assemble together the outcomes of specialised feature analysis into an integrated object-language description. Neisser's conception of the earlier stage is global whereas Treisman's is analytical. In fact, figure-ground segregation so dominated Neisser's view of the preattentive phase that he neglected to work out its implications for word recognition. Curiously, his other prototypic pre-attentive phenomenon, iconic memory, did not lead him to consider the important possibility of preliminary letter identification that was not accessible to awareness.

The inspiration of the Becker/Paap activation-verification duality seems less immediately obvious but might be sought in the local, technical advantages, in face of additive factor logic, of partitioning the frequency-sensitive process from the context-sensitive one. In this model, the phase-division occurs at quite an advanced stage. Moreover, the seriality of the verification process does not have the *spatial* implications, so evident in Neisser's and Treisman's adoption of the searchlight metaphor of attention.

The Mental Lexicon

Elsewhere (Henderson, 1986), I have suggested that one of the major changes in emphasis that characterises recent work in word recognition is a shift from *words considered as visual patterns* to word recognition as the interface of the perceptual to the linguistic domain. It is a commonplace observation that since the mid-1960s there has been an increasing tendency in studies of word perception to manipulate linguistic variables. Moreover, letter and word search and identification tasks have tended to give way to *transcoding tasks* in which a lexical pathway is assumed at least to be an option (e.g. the naming RT task) or to "deep" classification tasks (e.g. lexical decisions or category verification). In like manner, students of acquired reading and speech disorders abandoned neurology in favour of linguistics and began to erect syndromes upon the foundations of linguistically patterned error co-occurrences. The new diagram makers found that they had more linguistic variables than they had boxes to contain them. Indeed, the word attributes afforded by the language turned out to be inexhaustible. Experimenters chastised themselves with min F, and wept like sanctimonious voluptuaries at the unbearable richness of it all.

Not surprisingly, the aspect of the dictionary metaphor that first attracted the interest of students of word recognition was that of *access*. The question of how we locate desired items in the lexicon with such astonishing speed seems to have impressed investigators of spontaneous speech and of object naming (Cattell, 1886; Oldfield & Wingfield, 1965) more than students of word perception, perhaps because the written or spoken word is assumed to carry in its elementary structure the routine means for searching for its lexical address. It seems to have been the notion of a system of word detectors organised so that the most commonly used were the most readily accessible, which led to explicit importation of the dictionary metaphor into perceptual discussions (Morton, 1964; Oldfield, 1966; Treisman, 1960). There followed a great number of methodological developments which appeared to converge on the event that became known as "lexical access." The lexical decision task rode to prominence astride the assumption that it fulfilled the role of a psycholinguistic microelectrode, enabling the investigator to eavesdrop on the meeting of stimulus with memory. Various priming effects were explained as properties of lexical functioning, but repetition priming was accorded special diagnostic status as a means for distinguishing between different access pathways (e.g. Morton, 1979).

It must be conceded that this entire diagnostic enterprise is currently in a most delicate condition. Word frequency and repetition effects seem to arise from a plurality of sources (see Besner & McCann, this volume; Monsell, this volume). Moreover, it no longer seems safe to defer consideration of what subjects actually do to arrive at a word/nonword decision. The comfortable equation of "word recognition" with "lexical access" has been disturbed by debate as to whether various recognition phenomena occur before, at, or after access (e.g. Forster, this volume). However, the most fundamental challenge has been to the concept of *access* itself. The conception of access as a determinate, instantaneous event seems to be sustained by a spatial metaphor of the lexicon as container, reinforced perhaps by talk of "pre-" and "post-," of "neighbours," and of "unpacking." *Yet, access can only be understood by reference to some particular theoretical model.* It avails us nothing to enquire of, say, the Becker/Paap model whether access takes place in the activation or the verification phase, since the question falsely assumes the existence of some external criterion. *A fortiori*, a discrete access stage is not a useful concept for interpreting interactive models like that of McClelland and Rumelhart, 1981 (see also McClelland, this volume) or distributed processing models like Mozer's (this volume) which attempt to dispense with word nodes.

Successful identification of a word as a visual pattern is not the natural terminus of cognitive activity but a preliminary to morphological, phonological, semantic, and syntactic processing. This realisation led to analyses of the lexical system as a transcoding device which allowed translation at the word (or morpheme) level between the domains of orthography, phonology, and meaning. The flow diagram notation of boxes and arrows was particularly hospitable to such analyses, allowing the codes (boxes) and the transcoding pathways (arrows) to be pictured without the burdensome necessity of specifying precisely what form each coded representation took (e.g. "visual analysis," Morton, 1982) or how the transcoding was accomplished (e.g. how "visual analysis" was used to select a corresponding "visual input logogen").[7] Parallel distributed models presented a different, more microscopic view of the functional architecture of the word recognition system, although it seems unwise to conclude that these approaches differ only in notation and level of description (cf. Broadbent, 1985; Rumelhart & McClelland, 1985).

Word Recognition?

So far we have entertained doubts about almost everything but the label attached to our problem. After all, English orthography appears to deliver up language to the eye in word parcels, so where else should we seek the interface of the perceptual to the lexical? However, it is often argued from a linguistic standpoint that the lexicon should be regarded as the repository of language information *that cannot be derived by rule.* This obliges us to consider that units larger than the word may require lexical representation (e.g. phrasal idioms that cannot be understood straightforwardly from the meanings of their component words). Conversely, some word units may not require explicit representation if their composition is entirely predictable by rule (regular inflections, perhaps some derivational rules).

This latter thought presents us with a radical alternative to the *words as visual patterns* approach, in which it is the characteristics of the underlying

---

[7] Print-to-speech conversion, the most intensively researched transcoding process, is cogently reviewed by Patterson and Coltheart (this volume).

lexical representation that determine the nature and layout of the procedures used to address the lexicon perceptually (Taft & Forster, 1975).[8]

Whether or not this amounts to another story, it will certainly have to be another chapter.

ACKNOWLEDGEMENTS

I am grateful for helpful criticism of an earlier draft by Derek Besner, Hartmut Gunther, and Jay McClelland.

REFERENCES

Adams, M. J. (1979). Models of word recognition. *Cognitive Psychology, 11*, 133–176.

Allport, D. A. (1977). On knowing the meaning of words we are unable to report: The effects of visual masking. In S. Dornic (Ed.), *Attention and performance, VI*. Hillside, N.J.: Lawrence Erlbaum Associates Inc.

Baron, J. & Thurston, I. (1973). An analysis of the word superiority effect. *Cognitive Psychology, 4*, 207–228.

Bartlett, F. C. (1932). *Remembering*. New York: Macmillan.

Becker, C. A. (1976). Allocation of attention during visual word recognition. *Journal of Experimental Psychology: Human Perception and Performance, 2*, 556–566.

Besner, D. (1983). Basic decoding components in reading: Two dissociable feature extraction processes. *Canadian Journal of Psychology, 37*, 429–438.

Besner, D., Davelaar, E., Alcott, D., & Parry, P. (1984). Wholistic reading of alphabetic print: Evidence from the FDM and the FBI. In L. Henderson (Ed.), *Orthographies and reading*. London: Lawrence Erlbaum Associates Ltd., 121–135.

Besner, D. & Johnston, J. C. (in press). Reading and the mental lexicon: On the interaction of visual, orthographic, phonological, and lexical information. In W. Marslen-Wilson (Ed.), *Lexical process and representation*. Cambridge, Mass.: M.I.T. Press.

Besner, D. & Swan, M. (1982). Models of lexical access in visual word recognition. *Quarterly Journal of Experimental Psychology, 34A*, 313–325.

Bouma, H. (1973). Visual interference in the parafoveal recognition of initial and final letters of words. *Visual Research, 13*, 767–782.

Bouwhuis, D. (1979). *Visual recognition of words*. Doctoral dissertation, Katholieke Universiteit te Nijmegen. Eindhoven, The Netherlands: Institute of Perception Research.

Broadbent, D. E. (1958). *Perception and communication*. London: Pergamon Press.

Broadbent, D. E. (1985). A question of levels: Comment on McClelland and Rumelhart. *Journal of Experimental Psychology: General, 14*, 189–192.

Broadbent, D. E. & Broadbent, M. H. P. (1981). Priming and the passive/active model of word recognition. In R. S. Nickerson (Ed.), *Attention and performance, VIII*. Hillside, N.J.: Lawrence Erlbaum Associates Inc., 419–434.

Bruder, G. A. (1978). Role of visual familiarity in the word-superiority effects obtained with the simultaneous-matching task. *Journal of Experimental Psychology: Human Perception and Performance, 4*, 88–100.

---

[8] The decomposition procedure proposed by Taft in this volume (also Taft, 1979) seems not to possess this radical linguistic motivation. See Cutler, Hawkins, and Gilligan (1985) for an argument that the layout of the comprehension processes has influenced the sequencing of morphological information found in words.

Bruner, J. S. (1957). On perceptual readiness. *Psychological Review, 64*, 123–152.

Carr, T. H., Davidson, B. J., & Hawkins, H. L. (1978). Perceptual flexibility in word recognition: Strategies affect orthographic computation but not lexical access. *Journal of Experimental Psychology: Human Perception and Performance, 4*, 674–690.

Cattell, J. M. (1886). The time taken up by cerebral operations. *Mind, 11*, 220–242, 377–392, & 524–538.

Coltheart, M. (1984). Sensory memory: A tutorial review. In H. Bouma & D. G. Bouwhuis (Eds.), *Attention and performance X*. London: Lawrence Erlbaum Associates Ltd.

Cowie, R. (1985). Reading errors as clues to the nature of reading. In A. W. Ellis (Ed.), *Progress in the psychology of language*. London: Lawrence Erlbaum Associates Ltd., 73–107.

Cutler, A., Hawkins, J. A., & Gilligan, G. (1985). The suffixing preference: A processing explanation. *Linguistics, 23*, 723–757.

Erdmann, B. & Dodge, R. (1898). *Psychologische Untersuchungen uber das lesen*. Halle: Niemeyer.

Estes, W. K. (1975). The locus of inferential and perceptual processes in letter identification. *Journal of Experimental Psychology: General, 104*, 122–145.

Evett, L. J. & Humphreys, G. W. (1981). The use of abstract graphemic information in lexical access. *Quarterly Journal of Experimental Psychology, 33A*, 325–350.

Fowler, C. A. (1981). Some aspects of language perception by eye: The beginning reader. In O. J. L. Tzeng & H. Singer (Eds.), *Perception of print: Reading research in experimental psychology*. Hillsdale, N.J.: Lawrence Erlbaum Associates Inc., 171–196.

Frederiksen, J. R. & Kroll, J. F. (1976). Spelling and sound: Approaches to the internal lexicon. *Journal of Experimental Psychology: Human Perception and Performance, 2*, 361–379.

Frith, U. (1985). Beneath the surface of developmental dyslexia. In K. Patterson, J. C. Marshall, & M. Coltheart (Eds.), *Surface dyslexia*. London: Lawrence Erlbaum Associates Ltd., 301–327.

Geyer, J. J. (1970). Models of perceptual processes in reading. In H. Singer & R. B. Ruddell (Eds.), *Theoretical models and processes of reading*. Newark, Del.: International Reading Association, 47–94.

Gibson, E. J., Pick, A. D., Osser, H., & Hammond, M. (1962). The role of grapheme-phoneme correspondence in the perception of words. *American Journal of Psychology, 75*, 554–570.

Gleitman, H. & Jonides, J. (1976). The cost of categorisation in visual search: Incomplete processing of target and field items. *Perception and Psychophysics, 24*, 361–368.

Goldiamond, I. & Hawkins, W. E. (1958). Vexier versuch: The log relationship between word-frequency and recognition obtained in the absence of stimulus words. *Journal of Experimental Psychology, 56*, 457–463.

Gunther, H., Gfroerer, S., & Weiss, L. (1984). Inflection, frequency, and the word superiority effect. *Psychological Research, 46*, 261–281.

Havens, L. L. & Foote, W. E. (1963). The effect of competition on visual duration threshold and its independence of stimulus frequency. *Journal of Experimental Psychology, 65*, 6–11.

Healy, A. F. (1981). The effects of visual similarity on proofreading for misspellings. *Memory and Cognition, 9*, 453–460.

Henderson, L. (1977). Word recognition. In N. S. Sutherland (Ed), *Tutorial essays in psychology*. Hillsdale, N.J.: Lawrence Erlbaum Associates Inc., 35–74.

Henderson, L. (1980). Wholistic models of feature analysis in word recognition: A critical examination. In P. A. Kolers, M. E. Wrolstad, & H. Bouma (Eds.), *Processing of visible language, Vol. 2*. New York: Plenum Press.

Henderson, L. (1982). *Orthography and word recognition in reading*. London: Academic Press.

Henderson, L. (1985). On the use of the term "grapheme." *Language and Cognitive Processes, 1*, 135–148.

Henderson, L. (1986). From morph to morphemei. The psychologist gaily trips where the linguist has trodden. In G. Augst (Ed.), *International research in graphemies and orthography*. Berlin: de Gruyter.

Henderson, L. & Chard, M. J. (1976). On the nature of the facilitation of visual comparisons by lexical membership. *Bulletin of the Psychonomic Society, 7*, 432–434.

Holender, D. (1986). The disruptive effect of precuing of alternatives on the identification of letters in masked words: An attentional explanatory hypothesis. In M. I. Posner & O. S. M. Marin (Eds.), *Attention and performance XI*. Hillsdale, N.J.: Lawrence Erlbaum Associates Inc.

Howard, D. (1986). Reading without letters. In M. Coltheart, G. Sartori, & R. Job (Eds.), *The cognitive neuropsychology of language*. London: Lawrence Erlbaum Associates Ltd., 27–58.

Huey, E. B. (1908). *The psychology and pedagogy of reading*. Reprinted: Cambridge, Mass.: M.I.T. Press, 1968.

Johnston, J. C. (1978). A test of the sophisticated guessing theory of word perception. *Cognitive Psychology, 10*, 123–153.

Johnston, J. C. & McClelland, J. L. (1974). Perception of letters in words: Seek not and ye shall find. *Science, 184*, 1192–1193.

Jordan, T. R. (1986). Testing the Boss hypothesis: Evidence for position–insensitive orthographic priming in the lexical decision task. *Memory and Cognition, 14*, 523–532.

Kavanagh, J. F. & Mattingly, I. G. (1972). *Language by ear and by eye*. Cambridge, Mass.: M.I.T. Press.

Kolers, P. A. (1973). Remembering operations. *Memory and Cognition, 1*, 347–355.

Manelis, L. (1974). The effect of meaningfulness in tachistoscopic word perception. *Perception and Psychophysics, 16*, 182–192.

Marcus, S. M. (1984). Recognising speech: On the mapping from sound to word. In H. Bouma & D. G. Bouwhuis (Eds.), *Attention and performance X*. London: Lawrence Erlbaum Associates Ltd., 151–163.

Mason, M. (1975). Reading ability and letter search time: Effects of orthographic structure defined by single letter positional frequency. *Journal of Experimental Psychology: General, 104*, 146–166.

Massaro, D. W., Taylor, G. A. Venezky, R. L., Jastrzembski, J. E., & Lucas, P. A. (1980). *Letter and word perception*. Amsterdam: North Holland.

McCann, R. S. & Besner, D. (in press). Reading pseudohomophones: Implications of models of pronunciation assembly and the locus of word frequency effects in naming. *Journal of Experimental Psychology: Human Perception and Performance*.

McClelland, J. L. (1976). Preliminary letter recognition in the perception of words and nonwords. *Journal of Experimental Psychology: Human Perception and Performance, 2*, 80–91.

McClelland, J. L. (1977). Letter and configurational information in word identification. *Journal of Verbal Learning and Verbal Behaviour, 16*, 137–150.

McClelland, J. L. (1978). Perception and masking of wholes and parts. *Journal of Experimental Psychology: Human Perception and Performance, 4*, 210–223.

McClelland, J. L. & Mozer, M. C. (1986). Perceptual interactions in two-word displays: Familiarity and similarity effects. *Journal of Experimental Psychology: Human Perception and Performance, 12*, 18–35.

McClelland, J. L. & Rumelhart, D. E. (1981). An interactive activation model of context effects in letter perception: Part 1. An account of basic findings. *Psychological Review, 88*, 375–407.

Mewhort, D. J. K., Marchetti, F. M., Gurnsey, R., & Campbell, A. J. (1984). Information persistence: A dual-buffer model for initial visual processing. In H. Bouma & D. G. Bouwhuis (Eds.), *Attention and performance X*. London: Lawrence Erlbaum Associates Ltd., 287–298.

Miller, G. A. (1962). Decision units in the perception of speech. *IRE Transactions in Information Theory, 8*, 81–83.

Monk, A. F. & Hulme, C. (1983). Errors in proof reading: Evidence for the use of word shape in word recognition. *Memory and Cognition, 11*, 16–23.

Morton, J. (1964). Grammar and computation in language behaviour. *International Audiology, 3*, 216–225.

Morton, J. (1979). Facilitation in word recognition: Experiments causing change in the logogen model. In P. A. Kolers, M. Wrolstad, & H. Bouma (Eds.), *Processing of visible language I*. New York: Plenum.

Morton, J. (1982). Disintegrating the lexicon: An information processing approach. In J. Mehler, E. C. T. Walker, & M. Garrett (Eds.), *Perspectives on mental representation*. Hillsdale, N.J.: Lawrence Erlbaum Associates Inc.

Mozer, M. C. (1983). Letter migration in word perception. *Journal of Experimental Psychology: Human Perception and Performance, 9*, 531–546.

Navon, D. (1977). Forest before trees: The precedence of global features in visual perception. *Cognitive Psychology, 9*, 353–383.

Neisser, U. (1967). *Cognitive psychology*. New York: Appleton-Century-Crofts.

Neisser, U. (1976). *Cognition and reality*. San Francisco: W. H. Freeman.

Oldfield, R. C. (1966). Things, words and the brain. *Quarterly Journal of Experimental Psychology, 18*, 340–353.

Oldfield, R. C. & Wingfield, A. (1965). Response latencies in naming. *Quarterly Journal of Experimental Psychology, 17*, 273–281.

Paap, K. R., Newsome, S. L., McDonald, J. E., & Schvaneveldt, R. W. (1982). An activation-verification model for letter and word recognition. *Psychological Review, 89*, 573–594.

Pierce, J. (1963). Some sources of artifact in studies of the tachistoscopic perception of words. *Journal of Experimental Psychology, 66*, 363–370.

Poffenberger, J. (Ed.) (1973). *James McKeen Cattell*. New York: Basic Books.

Pomerantz, J. R., Sager, L. C., & Stoever, R. J. (1977). Perception of wholes and of their component parts: Some configurational superiority effects. *Journal of Experimental Psychology: Human Perception and Performance, 3*, 422–435.

Posnansky, C. J. & Rayner, K. (1977). Visual-feature and response components in a picture-word interference task with beginning and skilled readers. *Journal of Experimental Child Psychology, 24*, 440–460.

Prinzmetal, W. & Millis-Wright, M. (1984). Cognitive and linguistic factors affect visual feature integration. *Cognitive Psychology 16*, 305–340.

Purcell, D. G. & Stanovich, K. E. (1982). Some boundary conditions for a word superiority effect. *Quarterly Journal of Experimental Psychology, 34A*, 117–134.

Rayner, K. (1984). Visual selection in reading, picture perception and visual search: A tutorial review. In H. Bourma & D. G. Bouwhuis (Eds.), *Attention and performance X*. London: Lawrence Erlbaum Associates Ltd., 67–96.

Rayner, K., McConkie, G. W., & Zola, D. (1980). Integrating information across eye movements. *Cognitive Psychology, 12*, 206–226.

Rumelhart, D. E. & McClelland, J. L. (1985). Levels indeed! A response to Broadbent. *Journal of Experimental Psychology: General, 114*, 193–197.

Scarborough, D. L. (1972). Memory for brief visual displays. *Cognitive Psychology, 3*, 408–429.

Scheerer, E. (1981). Early German approaches to experimental reading research: The contributions of Wilhelm Wundt and Ernst Meumann. *Psychological Research, 43*, 111–130.

Schendel, J. D. & Shaw, P. (1976). A test of the generality of the word-context effect. *Perception and Psychophysics, 19*, 383–393.

Shallice, T. & McGill, J. (1978). The origins of mixed errors. In J. Requin (Ed.), *Attention and performance VII*. Hillsdale, N.J.: Lawrence Erlbaum Associates Inc.

Solomon, R. L. & Howes, D. H. (1951). Word-probability, personal values, and visual duration thresholds. *Psychological Review, 68*, 256–270.

Sperling, G. (1967). Successive approximations to a model of short-term memory. *Acta Psychologica, 27*, 285–292.

Spoehr, K. T. & Smith, E. E. (1975). The role of orthographic and phonotactic rules in perceiving letter patterns. *Journal of Experimental Psychology: Human Perception and Performance, 104*, 21–34.

Taft, M. (1979). Lexical access via an orthographic code: The Basic Orthographic Syllabic Structure (BOSS). *Journal of Verbal Learning and Verbal Behaviour, 18*, 21–39.

Taft, M. & Forster, K. I. (1975). Lexical storage and retrieval of prefixed words. *Journal of Verbal Learning and Verbal Behaviour, 14*, 638–647.

Treisman, A. (1960). Contextual cues in selective listening. *Quarterly Journal of Experimental Psychology, 12*, 242–248.

Treisman, A. & Gelade, G. (1980). A feature integration theory of attention. *Cognitive Psychology, 12*, 97–136.

Treisman, A. & Souther, J. (1986). Illusory words: The rules of attention and of top-down constraints in conjoining letters to form words. *Journal of Experimental Psychology: Human Perception and Performance, 12*, 3–17.

Underwood, G. & Bargh, K. (1982). Word shape, orthographic regularity, and contextual interactions in a reading task. *Cognition, 12*, 197–209.

Venezky, R. L. (1970). *The structure of English orthography*. The Hague: Mouton.

Wickelgren, W. A. (1969). Context-sensitive coding, associative memory, and serial order in (speech) behaviour. *Psychological Review, 76*, 1–15.

Williams, A. & Weisstein, N. (1978). Line segments are perceived better in a coherent context than alone: An object-line effect. *Memory and Cognition, 6*, 85–90.

Woodworth, R. S. (1938). *Experimental psychology*. New York: Holt, Rinehart, & Winston.

Zeitler, J. (1900). Tachistoscopic untersuchungen uber das Lesen. *Philosophische Studien, 16*, 380–463.

REFERENCE NOTE

1. Schumann, F. (1906). *Psychologie des Lesens*. Bericht über den 2e Kongress für Experimental Psychologie in Wurzburg.

9

Word Frequency and Pattern Distortion in Visual Word Identification and Production: An Examination of Four Classes of Models

Derek Besner and Robert S. McCann
University of Waterloo,
Ontario, Canada

ABSTRACT

The joint effects of pattern dIsToRtIoN and word frequency were examined in the context of both lexical decision and speeded naming tasks. Predictions as to how performance would vary as a function of these factors were derived from four classes of visual word identification models: pattern analysing, criterion bias, serial search, and verification. The results were inconsistent with important aspects of all of the models. A framework which takes as its basic premise a distinction between word recognition and word identification is more successful in accounting for these as well as other results. Several distinct loci for word frequency effects in visual word identification, recognition, and production are proposed.

INTRODUCTION

Over the last two-and-a-half decades, considerable interest from an information processing perspective has been directed at the issue of how a reader accesses the mental lexicon from print. In conjunction with an enormous body of literature, there are currently at least half-a-dozen models which concern themselves with various aspects of how words are "recognised." These models are often quite disparate in terms of their structure and processing assumptions, and were frequently designed with particular sets of data from a particular task in mind. It is thus not surprising that the typical publication consists of an experiment or two in which the results are discussed in terms of a favoured model, with little or only passing reference to alternative accounts. While this state of affairs may represent normal science, the result is that it is difficult to get a sense of how the models fare in comparison to one another (but see Norris, 1986 for an exception).

Another cause for concern is that attempts to interpret results have often been cast in terms of a general model, as though such a model would be applicable to all tasks. Consideration of how one or more variables affects performance across different tasks seems likely to provide a more powerful constraint on the range of possible explanations. Such an approach is still the exception rather than the rule.

In the present paper we examine how lexical decision and naming are affected by stimuli whose visual appearance is novel because the letters of the word (or nonword) appear in dIfFeReNt cases, and how such effects are influenced by word frequency. This form of stimulus manipulation is hereafter referred to as pattern distortion. These contrasts are of interest for several reasons.

First, word frequency effects are probably the most powerful and ubiquitous effects in visual word recognition. They are apparent in a variety of tasks (e.g. lexical decision, naming, same-different judgements, tachistoscopic report, semantic categorisation) and they account for a considerable amount of variance in at least some of these tasks (cf. Whaley, 1978). Consequently, all current models of visual word identification offer an account of how word frequency effects arise. The effects on performance of variables such as pattern distortion in combination with a word frequency manipulation thus provides a good basis for between-model comparisons.

Secondly, there are several views concerning how visual information serves visual word identification. One view is that word identification is based upon preliminary *abstract* letter identification (e.g. Allport, 1979; Besner, 1983; Coltheart, 1981; Evett & Humphreys, 1981; McClelland & Mozer, 1986; Paap, Newsome, & Noel, 1984; Rayner, McConkie, & Zola, 1980; Saffran, 1980). On this account, the particular visual form that a letter takes is irrelevant to the process of word identification. A second view is that visual information is important when hypotheses about the stimulus are *verified* against the veridical representation (Becker, 1976; Paap, Newsome, McDonald & Schvaneveldt, 1982). A third view is that the familiarity of the *visual* pattern of the stimulus heavily determines how pattern analysis proceeds (e.g. Kolers, 1985). A consideration of how pattern distortion influences or is influenced by word frequency may offer a basis for discriminating between some of these views, as well as for discriminating between various word identification models.

We chose to contrast lexical decision and naming for two main reasons: (1) these tasks are among the most heavily used tasks in the word perception literature in the past decade or so; and (2) we think they help to illustrate a basic distinction between *recognition* and *identification* that is relevant to the study of word perception (e.g. see Besner, Note 1; 1983; 1984; Besner, Davelaar, Alcott, & Parry, 1984; Besner & Johnston, 1987; see also Balota & Chumbley, 1984).

We turn now to a brief description of the models and the predictions that can be derived from these models. It should be noted that none of these models are formal ones in the sense that predictions can be generated by some algorithm. Consequently, there may be instances in which the reader disagrees with one or more of the predictions which we have made. Nonetheless, we think our approach useful since such disagreements can serve to highlight points where the models are underspecified, and to stimulate consideration of alternative formulations.

THE MODELS

We shall consider four classes of models:

1. Pattern analysing operations (e.g. Kolers, 1985).
2. Criterion bias (e.g. Gordon, 1983; Morton, 1969; 1979; Norris, 1986).
3. Serial search (e.g. Forster, 1976).
4. Verification (e.g. Becker, 1976; 1979; Paap et al., 1982; Paap, McDonald, Schvaneveldt, & Noel, this volume; Schvaneveldt & McDonald, 1981).

Only the essentials of each of the classes of models will be noted, since complete descriptions of each of the models is available in the literature. For each of these models we shall consider four predictions: (a) the effects of pattern distortion in conjunction with word frequency in the context of lexical decision; (b) the effects of pattern distortion in conjunction with word frequency in the context of naming; (c) the effect of pattern distortion on words versus nonwords in lexical decision; and (d) the magnitude of the pattern distortion effect for words in lexical decision versus naming.

1. Pattern Analysing Operations

In this account (e.g. Kolers, 1985; Rudnicky & Kolers, 1984), skilled word identification arises through repeated analyses of stimulus specific visual patterns. Word identification will therefore be impaired when letter size and case are varied within a word as this renders the visual pattern unfamiliar. Consequently, at least initially, word identification will have to fall back upon letter identification. This model holds that when the visual pattern is not distorted, a word frequency effect arises through differential skill associated with these patterns as a function of repetitions. Rendering the visual pattern novel by pattern distortion should eliminate the word frequency effect in both naming and lexical decision (Kolers, Note 3). By similar logic word processing should be more impaired by pattern distortion than should nonword processing, since nonwords can be thought of as very infrequent words in terms of visual pattern analyses. Finally, since there is nothing in Kolers' writings to suggest that the visual pattern analyses underlying lexical decision and naming would be different, our expectation is that the magnitude of the processing time costs associated with pattern distortion will be the same for the words in the two tasks.

2. Criterion Bias

In this content-addressable class of models, word identification is accomplished via a set of word detectors (logogens). There are several variants of this model (Gordon, 1983; McClelland & Rumelhart, 1981; Morton, 1969; Norris, 1986), but the essentials are that for each word a reader knows, there exists a corresponding logogen. A logogen is a simple evidence-collecting device with an adjustable threshold mechanism that is modifiable by experience and/or context. The degree to which the logogen for any word is excited by a letter string is a function of the similarity between the letter string and the logogen. Threshold values of the logogens are assumed to be inversely related to word frequency; less evidence is required to "fire" a logogen corresponding to a high-frequency word than to a low-frequency word. A word is said to have been identified when its logogen has fired.

It is well known that pattern distortion impairs performance in a number of word identification and recognition tasks (see Besner, Davelaar, et al., 1984; Besner & Johnston, 1987; Henderson, 1982 for reviews). This fact is consistent with the view that abstract letter identification underlies word identification if it is assumed that letter identification is more difficult under conditions of pattern distortion (see Besner, 1983; Besner & Johnston, 1987; Paap et al., 1984). If an additive stages model (Sternberg, 1969) is assumed in which abstract letter identification is completed[1] before word identification begins, then a simple set of predictions can be made about the effects of pattern distortion for the criterion bias class of models. Since the output of the abstract letter identification stage carries no information about visual pattern, and is the only basis for word identification, then the time costs of pattern distortion should be additive with word frequency in both lexical decision and naming latency, and should delay word processing in lexical decision to the same extent that it delays word processing in naming. If a "no" decision to nonwords in lexical decision is the result of a variable deadline procedure (cf. Coltheart, Davelaar, Jonasson, & Besner, 1977) then we expect that nonwords will be just as impaired as words by pattern distortion in lexical decision. This follows because the function of the deadline is to maintain a constant average time interval between responses to

---

[1] The discussion section takes up the issue of whether relaxing this assumption by assuming processes in cascade improves any of the models' abilities to handle the data.

words and responses to nonwords such that an acceptable balance between speed and errors is achieved.

3. Serial Search

The main distinction between the criterion bias class of model and the serial search model is that the former are content addressable while in the latter model the correct lexical entry for a stimulus is found through a *serial search* of the internal lexicon (Forster, 1976; Rubenstein, Lewis, & Rubenstein, 1971). High-frequency words are represented towards the top of the list in the lexicon, while low-frequency words occupy lower positions in the list. If the representation which is used to search the lexicon consists of a set of abstract letter identities, and the process of forming this representation[1] is completed prior to initiation of the search process, then the same predictions can be made for the serial search model as for the criterion bias model. There will be main effects of pattern distortion and of word frequency, but no interactions between these factors in either naming or lexical decision. The magnitude of the pattern distortion effect will be the same size in both lexical decision and naming, and will also be the same size for both words and nonwords in lexical decision.

4. Verification

This class of model (Becker, 1976; Paap et al., 1982; Paap et al., this volume; Schvaneveldt & McDonald, 1981) incorporates elements of both criterion bias and serial search models. Hypotheses as to the identity of the presented word are generated by a logogen system. Two key assumptions are that: (a) the logogen system is not a source of word frequency effects; and (b) activation in the logogen system is usually insufficient to specify a single word hypothesis. Instead, the logogen system generates a *set* of candidates whose primitive features are consistent with the presented stimulus. These candidates are then closely examined by retrieving stored, detailed structural descriptions of them, and then comparing these candidates, one at a time, against a veridical representation of the presented stimulus. This serial comparison process is ordered in terms of word frequency. High-frequency candidates are tested before low-frequency candidates; successful matches will therefore be faster for high-frequency words than for low-frequency words.

Compared to the other classes of models, the verification model makes a different set of predictions for how pattern distortion will affect performance, given Becker's assumption as to how the verification process works (Becker, 1976, p. 564). The serial comparison of candidates can be modified (i.e. undergo a transformation of letter case) when there is a mismatch in letter case between a candidate's structural description and the veridical representation of the stimulus. This modification takes time, and occurs for each candidate. Pattern distortion of the veridical stimulus will therefore yield a mismatch for each serial comparison; a successful match will incur extra time costs that are proportional to the candidate's position in the serial comparison process. Since on average there are more unsuccessful matches prior to a successful match for a low-frequency candidate than for a high-frequency candidate, format distortion will delay verification for low-frequency words more than for high-frequency words in both lexical decision and naming. Similarly, nonwords will be more impaired than words by pattern distortion in lexical decision, since a nonword response depends upon the failure to find a match for any of the candidate hypotheses, whereas a word match occurs on average halfway through the verification list. Finally, the delay incurred by pattern distortion should be the same size for words in lexical decision as in naming, because the size of the candidate set is the same.

Summary

Four predictions as to how pattern distortion would affect performance as a function of several other variables were derived for each of four classes of models. The different models make a number of different predictions; these are summarised in Table 9.1.

The Experiments

Subjects.   A total of 128 undergraduates from the University of Waterloo were paid to participate in the experiments. Sixty-four subjects took part in the lexical decision study; the remaining subjects took part in the naming study.

Stimuli.   The stimuli consisted of 4 sets of 30 high-frequency words, 30 low-frequency words and 60 nonwords assigned to groups of 8 subjects on a rotating basis such that, between subjects, all items occurred in both lower case and alternating case. Individual items were seen either in lower case or alternating case within subjects. Each subject saw two of the four sets; half the stimuli in lower case, and half in alternating case, the first letter of all strings always being lower case. The lexical decision task contained 240 stimuli, half words and half nonwords. Half the words were high frequency and half were low frequency. The naming task consisted only of the words used in the lexical decision task. All factors, with the exception of task, were within subjects. All factors were presented to subjects in randomised form; each subject received a unique order of stimuli. The stimulus set can be seen in the Appendix.

TABLE 9.1
Predicted Effects of Format Distortion on Lexical Decision and Naming

Factors	Word Frequency × Format		Lexical Status × Format	Format × Task (Words)
Task	Lexical Decision	Naming	Lexical Decision	Lexical Decision and Naming
Models				
Shape-sensing (Kolers)	HF > LF	HF > LF	W > N	Additive
Content-addressable (Morton; Gordon)	Additive	Additive	Additive	Additive
Serial Search (Forster; Rubenstein)	Additive	Additive	Additive	Additive
Verification (Becker; Paap et al.)	LF > HF	LF > HF	N > W	Additive

NOTE: W – Word; N – Nonword; HF = High Frequency; LF = Low Frequency

Method.   Each task was preceded by a substantial number of practice trials with items which mirrored the conditions to be seen in the experimental trials, but which were only seen in the practice session (see Besner, 1983). In each task, the stimulus was displayed on a CRT slaved to an Apple II + microcomputer, and remained on the screen until the subject responded with a button press in the lexical decision task, or named the stimulus in the naming task. Standard instructions concerning speed and accuracy were given; "try and respond as quickly as you can, but at the same time try not to make too many errors." Responses in the lexical decision task were made with the index fingers of left and right hands resting on response buttons on a small panel placed in front of the subject. Responses in the naming task were recorded via a voice key. An experimenter sitting next to the subject coded whether the naming response was correct, mispronounced, or spoiled due to a cough or premature triggering of the voice key.

Results.   Mean RTs and percentage errors can be seen in Table 9.2. All reported differences are statistically reliable across both subjects and stimuli

($P<0.05$), and are based upon the RT data. Nothing in the error data suggests any obvious speed-error tradeoff which would vitiate the conclusions from the RT analyses. The incidence of spoiled trials in the naming latency task was quite low (2.3% across conditions) and was not a significant source of variance. Spoiled trials, as well as errors, were omitted from analyses of the latency data.

TABLE 9.2

Reaction Time (msec) and Percentage Error Rates as a Function of Format, Stimulus Type, and Task

	LEXICAL DECISION					
	High Frequency		*Low Frequency*		*Nonwords*	
	RT	*%E*	*RT*	*%E*	*RT*	*%E*
Lower Case	510	3.3	582	15.1	646	11.4
Alternated Case	548	9.3	623	20.9	662	11.1
Difference Score	38	6.0	41	5.8	16	–0.3

	NAMING					
	High Frequency			*Low Frequency*		
	RT	*%E*	*Spoiled*	*RT*	*%E*	*Spoiled*
Lower Case	506	0.3	2.0	531	1.7	2.1
Alternated Case	522	1.2	2.6	566	2.7	2.5
Difference Score	16	0.9	0.6	35	1.0	0.4

The results are easily summarised. First, words were more impaired by pattern distortion in the lexical decision task than in naming. As can be seen in Table 9.1, this result is inconsistent with all of the models. Second, pattern distortion impaired words more than nonwords[2] in the lexical decision task. Table 9.1 indicates that this result is inconsistent with all of the models except for the pattern analysing account. Third, low-frequency words were more impaired than high-frequency words by pattern distortion in naming. Table 9.1 indicates that this result is inconsistent with all of the models except the

---

[2]The small effect of pattern distortion upon nonword responses is reliable (see also Besner, 1983). One account of this is that the letter identification process is impaired by pattern distortion (see Paap et al., 1984; Besner, 1983; Besner & Johnston, 1987).

verification class. Finally, word frequency and pattern distortion were additive factors in the context of lexical decision. This result is inconsistent with the verification class and the pattern analysing account.

Discussion

The results of these experiments can be summarised as follows; they were inconsistent with three out of four predictions for each of the four classes of models. It appears from these results that we do not, on the basis of the models discussed here, have an adequate theoretical understanding of why pattern distortion affects words more than nonwords in lexical decision, why pattern distortion affects one task more than the other, or why pattern distortion is additive with word frequency in one task, but interacts with word frequency in another task.

Before assuming that the models we have discussed are inadequate, it is worth considering whether there are assumptions which could be modified so as to improve any of the models' ability to acccommodate the data. An obvious assumption which could plausibly be relaxed concerns the view that letter identification is completed before word identification begins. One could assume instead that letter identification and word identification consist of serially ordered stages of processing that overlap in time as in the cascade model discussed by McClelland (1979) and the interactive activation model described by McClelland and Rumelhart (1981) and Rumelhart and McClelland (1982).

This cascade assumption would appear to have little impact on the pattern analysing or verification accounts. In the former model, no "stages" have ever been described, in the latter, variations in how information is taken up (i.e. how candidates are prepared) would have no impact on how the serial verification process works. The cascade assumption seems to make matters worse for the serial *search* model. If the search starts with an incomplete or impoverished description at the letter level, but this description improves over time and can be utilised as a basis for search later in processing, then we would expect low-frequency words to be *less* impaired by pattern distortion than high-frequency words. This prediction is not confirmed by the data.

On the other hand, this cascade assumption does allow the criterion bias model to account for the interaction between pattern distortion and word frequency observed in the naming latency data. If letter identification and word identification overlap in time, and pattern distortion serves to slow letter identification, then this can be described by the statement that the function relating the accumulation of evidence over time in the word detectors (logogens) is slowed. If word frequency exerts its effects upon a threshold (Morton, 1969), a resting level of activation (McClelland & Rumelhart, 1981), rate of accumulation of evidence over time (e.g. Gordon,

1983), or some plausible combination of these possibilities, then the interaction of pattern distortion and word frequency seen in the naming data follows naturally. This can be seen in Fig. 9.1, where for convenience we have represented word frequency as exerting its effect upon thresholds.

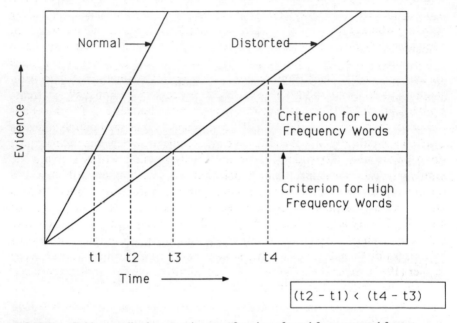

FIG. 9.1.   Evidence collection over time as a function of word frequency and format.

The benefit of adopting the cascade assumption is that the criterion bias model can explain data it previously could not. The cost is that it now cannot account for data it previously explained; namely, the fact that word frequency and pattern distortion are additive factors in the context of lexical decision. If letter identification and word identification are additive stages in which pattern distortion affects the duration of the letter identification process, but not its output, while word frequency affects a word identification stage, then these two factors should have additive effects (cf. Sternberg, 1969). We are very reluctant to accept the purely logical conclusion that letter identification and word identification are overlapping processes in naming, but are additive stages in lexical decision. In addition, there is still the problem of how to account for the fact that words are more impaired by pattern distortion than are nonwords, and the fact that pattern distortion has a larger effect upon words in lexical decision than in naming.

We favour an approach predicated on a distinction between word *recognition* and word *identification* because it appears to be a useful framework within which to consider the present results, as well as other findings (see Besner, Note 1; 1983; 1984; Besner, Davelaar, et al., 1984; Besner and Johnston, 1987). This distinction can be likened to the common experience of recognising a face as familiar (recognition memory) without any idea as to exactly who the person is (identification). Lexical decision can be viewed as a form of recognition memory task which could partially be accomplished by deciding whether the stimulus is sufficiently familiar to be labelled a word. In contrast, it is not possible to name a word by deciding how familiar a stimulus it is. The suggestion is that the process of "lexical decision" includes an assessment of *visual* familiarity which contributes bias to the decision stage. This visual familiarity assessment process is "wholistic"; it treats printed stimuli as visual patterns rather than individual letters. This mechanism is not involved in the word identification process per se; it merely assesses the visual familiarity of a stimulus. Word identification depends in large part upon preliminary letter identification. Visually familiar words activate the familiarity assessment mechanism such that a strong bias towards "yes" in the lexical decision task results. Since pattern distortion renders words visually unfamiliar, the bias contributed to the decision stage now consists of a low familiarity assessment, making it difficult to respond "yes." It follows naturally from this account that words will be more impaired than nonwords by pattern distortion in lexical decision, a result reported here as well as in Besner (1983). Since the naming task does not involve familiarity discrimination, it also follows naturally that words will be less impaired by pattern distortion in naming than in lexical decision, a result also observed here and in Besner (1983).

In summary, these two results can be accommodated within a framework which supposes that lexical access in both lexical decision and naming is subserved by a letter identification process whose rate of processing is slowed by case alternation (Besner, 1983; Besner & Johnston, 1987; Paap et al., 1984). Visual familiarity discrimination, a wholistic appraisal which is affected by case alternation but does not mediate lexical access, contributes to performance in lexical decision but not naming.

A remaining question concerns why pattern distortion and word frequency are additive factors in lexical decision, but interacting ones in naming latency. One would have thought that high-frequency words are the ones with the highest visual familiarity, (Balota & Chumbley, 1984; Besner, Davelaar, et al., 1984) so they are the ones for which pattern distortion should produce the biggest drop in assessed familiarity. However, our theoretical framework includes the assumption that the letter identification process which subserves word identification is slowed by pattern distortion. This process produces an interaction between word frequency and pattern distortion in which low-frequency words are more impaired than high-frequency words. This over-additive pattern is roughly balanced by the under-additive pattern produced by the familiarity assessment. Additivity of pattern distortion and word frequency in lexical decision is due to offsetting trends working in opposite directions. When familiarity assessment plays no role, as in naming, then the over-additive pattern between word frequency and distortion manifests itself, as can be seen in the naming results observed here and in Besner, Davelaar, et al. (1984).

An additional prediction is that if the change in the output of the familiarity assessment mechanism is quite small following an initial sharp drop, then as word frequency decreases further, pattern distortion should start to affect low-frequency words more than high-frequency words. This interaction can occur because the ramp effect (see Fig. 9.1) continues to increase, whereas the bias associated with the output of the familiarity assessment mechanism nears asymptote. Such a function can be seen in Frederiksen's (1978) lexical decision data. When the word frequency range is not too large, there are additive effects of pattern distortion and word frequency; as the effect of word frequency increases, an over-additive interaction between pattern distortion and word frequency emerges.

Another issue concerns the roles of addressed and assembled phonology in naming (see Patterson & Coltheart, this volume). The standard view is that high-frequency words are named only via addressed phonology, but that assembled phonology makes some contribution to the naming of lower-frequency words (cf. Seidenberg, Waters, Barnes, & Tannenhaus, 1984). Pring (1981) found that the pseudohomophone effect in lexical decision (Coltheart et al., 1977) could be eliminated if functional spelling units were violated by pattern distortion, while Besner and Johnston (1987) found that pattern distortion impaired the naming of nonwords more than words. These results suggest that the use of assembled phonology may involve multi-letter sequences which can be treated as single units. If this interpretation is correct, then assembled phonology may make some contribution to the interaction of word frequency and pattern distortion seen in the present naming latency results. We are currently engaged in determining whether the interaction of pattern distortion and word frequency persists in the naming task when all the words are irregular in terms of their spelling-sound correspondences. Pilot data suggest that it does.

SUMMARY

The framework we have proposed is summarised in Fig. 9.2 and consists of three main processing pathways. Word identification proceeds in the main by reference to routes 1 and 2 which rely on preliminary letter identification. Routes 9–10 and 13–10 acknowledge the possibility that multi-letter units

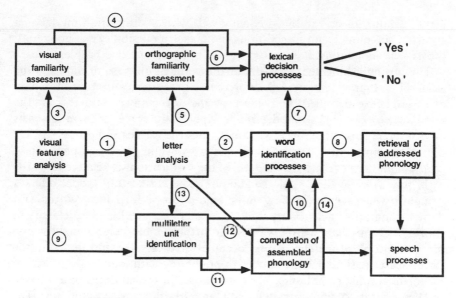

FIG. 9.2.   Processes involved in visual word identification.

may contribute to word identification, although McClelland and Johnston (1977) and Johnston (1978) have failed to find any evidence for this route in the context of tachistoscopic report tasks. Visual familiarity assessment makes a contribution via routes 3 and 4. Routes 5 and 6 exist to acknowledge the suggestion that a familiarity mechanism may also be activated by letter level codes (Balota & Chumbley, 1984). Routes 9, 11, and 12 show the paths for naming letter strings by the assembled route (Brown & Besner, this volume; Patterson, 1982).

Our pro tem summary is that the framework offered here is adequate to account for these and other data (see Besner & Johnston, 1987). The fact that the framework is somewhat complicated seems unavoidable.

CONCLUDING COMMENTS

We conclude by commenting briefly on three issues: (1) alternative models; (2) the word frequency effect as reflecting a unitary phenomenon; and (3) tools for the study of visual word identification.

Alternative Models

A number of the results from the present experiments are clearly inconsistent with all of the models initially discussed. It could be suggested, however, that the framework which proposes a distinction between recognition and identification can be combined equally well with a verification model as a criterion bias model. Our reservations about such a possibility rest upon both theoretical and empirical grounds; we will point to just one problem area.

The distinguishing characteristic of the verification class of model is the assumption that activation in the word detector system cannot result in only one word being identified. Activation specifies too many candidates, and the word detector system cannot determine which is the correct one on the basis of its level of activation; this is what motivates the verification process. If this central asssumption is correct, then words with many orthographic neigh-bours should serve to increase the size of the verification set relative to words with only a few orthographic neighbours. The verification model offers a straightforward account of how this should affect performance. Words with more orthographic neighbours should, on average, take longer to classify in lexical decision than words with fewer orthographic neighbours because more unsuccessful matches would occur prior to a successful match in the former case. A similar logic applies to nonwords with many as opposed to few orthographic neighbours. "No" responses in lexical decision are based on the failure to find a match with any of the word candidates. The verification list will be longer in the case of nonwords with many neighbours, consequently it will delay a "no" response. The data, however, are problem-atic with respect to this view. While it seems to be true that it takes longer to classify nonwords with many neighbours as compared to nonwords with few neighbours, there was, in the same experiment, no evidence that *words* with a large number of neighbours are classified slower than words with fewer neighbours (Coltheart et al., 1977, Experiment 2). A further problem is that when nonwords have many as compared to few neighbours this leads to faster rather than slower *naming* (McCann & Besner, 1987). It seems to us that these results pose some problems for the notion of a verification process as currently motivated and articulated. A related point has been made by Becker (1985, p. 145). There is simply little convincing evidence supporting the firm theoretical distinction made between the primitive features of a stimulus and the relational features of a stimulus.

Do Word Frequency Effects Reflect a Unitary Phenomenon?

The word recognition literature holds, as a basic assumption, the view that all of the word frequency effects that have been observed reflect the action of some unitary mechanism. It may be preferable to avoid the proliferation of mechanisms until absolutely necessary, but Occam's razor cuts both ways. It seems just as sensible to suppose on a priori grounds that word frequency exerts an influence throughout the word recognition system. It would then be just as important to identify those places where word frequency does not influence performance as where it does (e.g. see McCann & Besnet's [in press] claim that the phonological output system is not affected by word frequency). The assumption that the effects of word frequency are distributed throughout the word recognition system also invites comparisons across tasks. Different tasks involve different processing mechanisms; examining patterns of word frequency effects across tasks should be of considerable value in determining which aspects of the word recognition architecture are sensitive to word frequency (McCann & Besner, 1987; McCann, Besner & Davelaar, Note 4).

The present framework, along with other results, suggests that it is time to abandon the assumption that word frequency effects reflect the operation of a unitary mechanism. It is suggested instead that we currently have some basis for supposing at least three loci for word frequency effects. One of these is the visual familiarity assessment mechanism. Other candidates are the thresholds in the word detector system (Morton, 1969), and/or the rate of activation in the word detector system (McClelland & Rumelhart, 1981; but see Humphreys, Besner, & Quinlan, Note 2; McCann & Besner, 1987; McCann et al., Note 4). A final one is the *connections* between an orthograpic input lexicon and a phonological output system (McCann & Besner, 1987). Some resolution is also needed to the dispute which centres on whether the orthographic input lexicon is or is not sensitive to word frequency (Becker, 1976; Forster, 1976; Gordon, 1983; Humphreys et al., Note 2; McCann & Besner, 1987; McCann et al., Note 4; McClelland & Rumelhart, 1981; Morton, 1969; Paap et al., 1982; Paap et al., this volume).

Tools for the Study of Visual Word Identification

What is the appropriate task for the study of visual word recognition? There is no one task which is appropriate for all questions. Moreover, some questions can be addressed in the context of numerous tasks. Our message is that a fruitful approach consists of cross-task comparisons.

ACKNOWLEDGEMENTS

This work was supported by Grants U0051 and A0998 from the Natural Sciences and Engineering Research Council of Canada to Derek Besner. Robert McCann was supported by a postgraduate fellowship from NSERC. We are grateful to Jim Johnston and Max Coltheart for discussion, and to Eileen Davelaar for editorial assistance. Reprint requests to Derek Besner, c/o Psychology Department, University of Waterloo, Waterloo, Ontario, Canada N2L 3G1. Robert McCann is now at Ames Research Center, Moffat Field, California.

REFERENCES

Allport, D. A. (1979). Word recognition in reading: A tutorial review. In P. A. Kolers, H. Bouma, & M. Wrolstad (Eds.), *Processing of visible language, Vol. 1*. New York: Plenum Press.

Balota, D. A. & Chumbley, J. I. (1984). Are lexical decisions a good measure of lexical access? The role of word frequency in the neglected decision stage. *Journal of Experimental Psychology: Human Perception and Performance, 10,* 340–357.

Becker, C. A. (1976). Allocation of attention during visual word recognition. *Journal of Experimental Psychology: Human Perception and Performance, 2,* 556–566.

Becker, C. A. (1979). Semantic context and word frequency effects in visual word recognition. *Journal of Experimental Psychology: Human Perception and Performance, 5,* 252–259.

Becker, C. A. (1985). What do we really know about semantic context effects during reading? In D. Besner, T. G. Waller, & G. E. MacKinnon (Eds.), *Reading research: Advances in theory and practice*. New York: Academic Press.

Besner, D. (1983). Basic decoding components in reading: Two dissociable feature extraction processes. *Canadian Journal of Psychology, 37(3),* 429–438.

Besner, D. (1984). Specialised processors subserving visual word recognition: Evidence of local control. *Canadian Journal of Psychology, 38,* 94–101.

Besner, D., Coltheart, M., & Davelaar, E. (1984). Basic processes in reading: Computation of abstract letter identities. *Canadian Journal of Psychology, 38,* 126–134.

Besner, D., Davelaar, E., Alcott, D., & Parry, P. (1984). Wholistic reading of alphabetic print: Evidence from the FDM and the FBI. In L. Henderson (Ed.), *Orthographies and reading*. Hillsdale, N.J.: Lawrence Erlbaum Associates Inc.

Besner, D. & Johnston, J. C. (1987). Reading and the mental lexicon: On the uptake of visual information. In W. Marslen-Wilson (Ed.), *The lexicon and language processing*. Cambridge: Cambridge University Press.

Coltheart, M. (1981). Disorders of reading and their implications for models of normal reading. *Visible Language, 3,* 245–286.

Coltheart, M., Davelaar, E., Jonasson, J. T., & Besner, D. (1977). Access to the mental lexicon. In S. Dornic (Ed.), *Attention and performance VI*. London: Academic Press.

Evett, L. & Humphreys, G. W. (1981). The use of abstract graphemic information in lexical access. *Quarterly Journal of Experimental Psychology, 33A,* 325–350.

Forster, K. I. (1976). Accessing the mental lexicon. In E. W. Walker & R. J. Wales (Eds.), *New approaches to language mechanisms*. Amsterdam: North Holland Press.

Frederiksen, J. R. (1978). Assessment of perceptual decoding and lexical skills and their relation to reading proficiency. In A. M. Lesgold, J. W. Pellegrino, S. D. Fokkema, & R. Glaser (Eds.), *Cognitive psychology and instruction*. New York: Plenum Press.

Gordon, B. (1983). Lexical access and lexical decision: Mechanisms of frequency sensitivity. *Journal of Verbal Learning and Verbal Behaviour, 22,* 24–44.

Henderson, L. (1982). *Orthography and word recognition in reading*. London and New York: Academic Press.

Johnston, J. C. (1978). A test of the sophisticated guessing theory of word perception. *Cognitive Psychology, 10,* 123–153.

Kolers, P. (1985). Skill in reading and memory. *Canadian Journal of Psychology, 39,* 232–239.

McCann, R. S. & Besner, D. (1987). Reading pseudohomophones: Implications for models of pronunciation assembly and the locus of word frequency effects in naming. *Journal of Experimental Psychology: Human Perception and Performance*.

McClelland, J. L. (1979). On the time relations of mental processes: An examination of systems of processes in cascade. *Psychological Review, 86,* 287–307.

McClelland, J. L. & Johnston, J. C. (1977). The role of familiar units in perception of words and nonwords. *Perception and Psychophysics, 22,* 249–261.

McClelland, J. L. & Mozer, M. (1986). Perceptual interactions in two-word displays: Familiarity and similarity effects. *Journal of Experimental Psychology: Human Perception and Performance, 12,* 18–35.

McClelland, J. L. & Rumelhart, D. E. (1981). An interactive activation model of context effects in letter perception: Part 1. An account of basic findings. *Psychological Review, 88*(5), 375–407.

Morton, J. (1969). Interaction of information in word recognition. *Psychological Review, 76,* 165–178.

Morton, J. (1979). Facilitation in word recognition: Experiments causing change in the logogen model. In P. A. Kolers, M. Wrolstad, & H. Bouma (Eds.), *Processing of visible language I.* New York: Plenum Press.

Norris, D. (1986). Word recognition: Context effects without priming. *Cognition, 22,* 93–136.

Paap, K. R., Newsome, S. L., McDonald, J. E., & Schvaneveldt, R. W. (1982). An activation-verification model for letter and word recognition: The word superiority effect. *Psychological Review, 89*(5), 573–594.

Paap, K. R., Newsome, S. L., & Noel, R. W. (1984). Word shapes in poor shape for the race to the lexicon. *Journal of Experimental Psychology: Human Perception and Performance, 10,* 413–428.

Patterson, K. E. (1982). The relation between reading and phonological coding: Further neuropsychological observations. In A. W. Ellis (Ed.), *Normality and pathology in cognitive function.* London: Academic Press.

Pring, L. (1981). Phonological codes and functional spelling units: Reality and implications. *Perception and Psychophysics, 30,* 573–578.

Rayner, K., McConkie, G. W., & Zola, D. (1980). Integrating information across eye movements. *Cognitive Psychology, 12,* 206–226.

Rubenstein, H., Lewis, S. S., & Rubenstein, M. A. (1971). Evidence for phonemic recoding in visual word recognition. *Journal of Verbal Learning and Verbal Behaviour, 10,* 645 657.

Rudnicky, A. I. & Kolers, P. A. (1984). Size and case of type as stimuli in reading. *Journal of Experimental Psychology: Human Perception and Performance, 3,* 1–17.

Rumelhart, D. E. & McClelland, J. E. (1982). An interactive activation model of context effects in letter perception: Part 2. The contextual enhancement effect and some tests and extensions of the model. *Psychological Review, 89,* 60–94.

Saffran, E. (1980). Reading in deep dyslexia is not ideographic. *Neuropsychologia, 18,* 219–223.

Schvaneveldt, R. W. & McDonald, J. E. (1981). Semantic context and the encoding of words: Evidence for two modes of stimulus analysis. *Journal of Experimental Psychology: Human Perception and Performance, 7,* 673–687.

Seidenberg, M. S., Waters, G. S., Barnes, M. A., & Tannenhaus, M. (1984). When does irregular spelling or pronunciation influence word recognition? *Journal of Verbal Learning and Verbal Behaviour, 23,* 383–404.

Sternberg, S. (1969). The discovery of processing stages: Extension of Donders' method. In W. G. Koster (Ed.), *Attention and performance II.* Amsterdam: North Holland Press.

Whaley, C. P. (1978). Word-nonword classification time. *Journal of Verbal Learning and Verbal Behaviour, 17,* 143–154.

REFERENCE NOTES

1. Besner, D. (1980). *Codes and procedures for accessing the mental lexicon.* Unpublished Ph.D. thesis, University of Reading, England.

2. Humphreys, G. W., Besner, D., & Quinlan, P. T. (1987). Dissociable components of the word repetition effect. *Journal of Experimental Psychology: General* (manuscript under review).

3. Kolers, P. Personal communication.

4. McCann, R. S., Besner, D., & Davelaar, E. (1987). *On the relationship between word frequency and lexical access: None.* Manuscript in preparation.

APPENDIX

Set A

lost	easy	mock	maen	bize	polp
play	ways	crow	clib	sody	beed
road	army	skit	stap	sany	ries
plan	boys	moan	doin	dlay	dyod
rate	blue	bout	dort	stot	bram
town	whom	fake	hirm	foth	gind
love	fall	goat	rame	dast	flin
cost	meet	gore	vack	jall	mest
live	hall	lame	gryl	fent	tost
talk	fine	herb	nour	tuld	rogs
hair	stir	pith	foid	bule	virb
hear	stud	numb	nate	huck	hisp
rest	hilt	fawn	leid	gurm	tarb
cold	malt	lamb	darm	dets	lars
turn	heap	nigh	rolt	labe	durl
form	mink	robe	nime	sush	nilt
help	fade	hind	cace	toet	stup
last	riot	tame	manp	stib	arit
find	mist	crib	dake	hait	blod
deal	flea	bead	piwn	kneb	lask

Set B

near	sure	tick	sode	gola	habe
sort	show	slot	carg	roor	heak
hold	held	bang	hesm	sest	teid
soon	make	sane	sabe	erms	cuve
dead	head	lurk	valk	foed	tuno
else	mind	mame	rost	wued	firl
east	face	lily	bews	bolm	belm
view	read	jogs	enit	foad	lerd
kept	move	hiss	dite	wols	sern
fire	fear	chat	nune	dita	wial
dark	lewd	iced	piut	lene	doch
stop	muck	hive	fook	plam	slak
stay	chew	bump	geep	roal	noak
land	smug	fade	kish	nisp	tiar
home	bard	tilt	nass	feap	hile
part	prim	stew	sayt	pown	zail
list	yoke	vows	dall	doft	loce
year	whim	pots	doog	cerd	yelt
case	wick	nuns	ible	fark	clab
kind	slob	clot	nars	biss	kest

Set C

mean	size	pulp	bost	eaby	moak
club	body	reed	blay	vays	triw
step	many	pies	soad	asmo	sket
main	clay	dyed	glan	loys	boan
born	shot	brim	sate	blut	diut
firm	both	bind	fown	whot	vake
game	past	flip	tove	foll	hoat
lack	call	pest	nost	meit	dure
girl	went	gosh	libe	holl	pame
hour	told	rigs	dalk	jine	merb
paid	bile	verb	mair	srib	bith
note	hack	airs	viar	stid	nume
lead	germ	garb	fest	calt	fawe
farm	nets	jars	vold	nalt	hamb
role	lobe	hurl	nurn	heac	nist
name	sash	wilt	furm	mank	ribe
race	toot	stub	halp	fabe	hond
hand	stab	arid	lasp	glot	jame
take	bait	blob	sind	mirt	crit
down	knob	lass	leal	clea	fead

Set D

side	gone	hare	mear	surt	tish
care	poor	heal	gort	shob	slod
best	test	rein	hald	peld	beng
same	arms	cove	soin	mofe	gine
walk	feed	tune	kead	heod	lcck
rise	wide	fore	elst	sint	mabe
news	bill	helm	nast	nace	kily
unit	food	lard	liew	reat	jols
date	wall	fern	gept	mave	hisk
none	data	dial	jire	fiar	chas
your	lone	dice	cark	liwd	obed
book	plum	slap	atok	meck	bive
deep	roam	sock	stof	chiw	gump
wish	pins	liar	lant	smag	kade
mass	reap	hike	hime	burk	filt
says	gown	pail	nart	srim	staw
ball	loft	lice	bist	hoke	jows
pool	curd	yelp	jiar	thim	bots
able	lark	clan	fise	gick	nens
cars	teas	kegs	dind	slor	clat

10
Frequency and Pronounceability in Visually Presented Naming and Lexical Decision Tasks

Kenneth R. Paap, James E. McDonald, Roger W. Schvaneveldt, and Ronald W. Noel
Computing Research Laboratory
New Mexico State University
Las Cruces, New Mexico

ABSTRACT

An extension to the activation-verification model (Paap, Newsome, McDonald, & Schvaneveldt, 1982) is described that assumes both lexical and non-lexical pathways to pronunciation. The extended model provides an account of pronounceability effects in the lexical decision and naming tasks. The non-lexical pathway is also used to explain why lexical factors, like word frequency, generate smaller effects in naming than in lexical decision. This view is contrasted with Balota and Chumbley's (1984) argument that frequency effects in the lexical decision task overestimate the role of familiarity in word recognition and that naming provides the better baseline. The experiments reported in this paper show that equivalent frequency effects are obtained with both lexical decisions and naming responses when the naming task requires lexical access before the onset of pronunciation.

OVERVIEW OF THE ACTIVATION-VERIFICATION MODEL

For the past several years we have been developing an activation-verification (AV) model for word recognition (McDonald, Note 3; Paap et al., 1982; Paap & Thompson, 1986; Schvaneveldt & McDonald, 1981). Although the current model differs with respect to many details, its principal components are common to earlier versions of the verification model (Becker, 1976; 1980; 1982; 1985; Becker, Schvaneveldt, & Gomez, Note 1).

The AV model consists of encoding, verification, and decision operations. Encoding is the process that leads to the unconscious activation of learned units in memory. The original AV model was concerned with two types of units: whole words stored in a lexicon and individual letters stored in an alphabetum. An array of letter units is assumed for each position in an input string. Activation levels in the letter units are determined by the number of matching and mismatching visual features. Words units are activated to the extent that their constituent letters are activated. The most highly activated lexical entries are placed on a verification list.

Verification follows encoding and usually leads to the conscious recognition of a single lexical entry from the list of candidates. Verification should be viewed as an independent, top-down analysis of the stimulus that is guided by a stored representation of a word. The stored representation of the candidate word, normalised for font, size, etc., is compared to the representation of the input word in the visual store (cf. Fig. 10.1). The verification process is a serial-comparison operation on the set of candidate words generated during encoding. Thus, verification results in a match or mismatch. If the degree of fit between the visual evidence and the candidate word exceeds a decision criterion, then the word is recognised. If the match does not exceed the criterion, then the candidate is rejected and the next candidate verified.

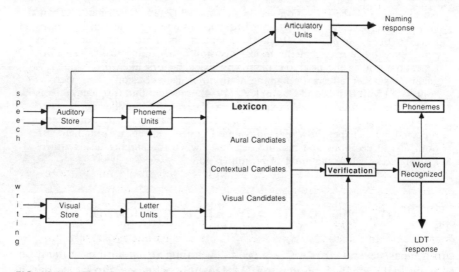

FIG. 10.1.   The expanded activation-verification model.

In McDonald's (Note 3) computer simulation, semantic context affects the definition of the candidate set, whereas word frequency affects the order of verification. A set of contexually supported candidates becomes available early, because context preactivates related words and this enables them to exceed the criterion for becoming candidates with only a minimal amount of sensory support. When this happens verification of the context list will begin before the visual list. If no match is detected among the context-supported candidates, verification proceeds to check the remaining visual candidates in decreasing order of word frequency.

The serial nature of the verification process frequently provokes feelings of uneasiness or worse in audiences. Our computer simulation of verification is strictly serial. Each of the candidates in the context list is checked, one at a time, before candidates from the visual list are considered. This simulation enables us to account for a wide range of phenomena in the lexical decision task, e.g. the effects of frequency, semantic context, and their pattern of additivity and interaction with degradation (McDonald, Note 3). However, the serial assumption is not viewed as sacrosanct and we are currently exploring ways in which verification could accomplish the same goals in a more parallel fashion.

EMPIRICAL JUSTIFICATION FOR THE VERIFICATION STAGE

Patterns of Interaction

The assumption that frequency does not affect the activation process, whereas semantic context does, neatly accounts for the well-established finding that context interacts with the quality of the visual stimulus while frequency and quality are additive (Becker & Killion, 1977; McDonald, Note 3; Meyer, Schvanveldt, & Ruddy, 1975; Stanners, Jastrzembski, & West-brook, 1975). Logogen models that assume that both context and frequency influence activation levels are not consistent with this pattern of interaction and additivity.

In an effort to establish the locus of semantic priming, Meyer et al. (1975) altered the visual quality of target stimuli by superimposing random-dot patterns. The visual degradation produced increased response times for words and nonwords. In addition, priming was greater in the degraded condition. Following Sternberg's additive factors logic, they concluded that degradation and semantic relatedness affects at least one processing stage in common.

Stanners et al. (1975) employed a degradation technique, similar to that of Meyer et al., in an effort to discover the relationship between stimulus quality and word frequency. While both frequency and degradation produced reliable effects on reaction time, these two factors were additive, rather than interactive, in contrast with the effects of context and degradation. Subsequent work by Becker and Killion (1977), in which stimulus intensity was manipulated, supported both the findings of Meyer et al. and those of Stanners et al. It is at this point that logogen models begin to have some difficulty. If both frequency and context influence the activity levels of logogens in the same way, they should produce similar effects. Thus, the need to hypothesise an additional processing stage, such as the verification stage of the AV model.

The general findings reported here have been accepted for some time, at least when the LDT was employed. However, Norris (1984) has reported a significant interaction between frequency and stimulus degradation. He accounted for the discrepancy by arguing that his stimulus intensity manipulation was larger than that reported by Becker and Killion (139msec vs. 46msec) and, thus, that his study was more sensitive to the frequency by stimulus intensity interaction. One should note, however, that this explanation had already been rejected by Becker and Killion on the grounds that they did obtain a significant interaction between semantic priming and stimulus intensity. It seems unlikely that the magnitude of the intensity manipulation was inadequate, given that the main effect of semantic context was no larger than that of frequency.

The logic used by Norris to account for the differences between his results and those of Becker and Killion does not fare well with the earlier work of Stanners et al. These investigators used superimposed random dots and reported a 120msec effect of stimulus degradation. Norris speculated that the different methods of degradation (dots vs. intensity) may have produced qualitatively different effects in the two studies. However, he hedged his bet somewhat by arguing that there was no direct conflict between the two results since the nonsignificant interaction (of only 7msec) obtained by Stanners et al. was in the right direction.

Norris' arguments not withstanding, the preponderance of data attest to a lack of interaction between frequency and stimulus quality using the LDT, just as there have been numerous replications of the context by stimulus quality interaction. In a study in which two versions of the verification model were being compared, McDonald (Note 3) manipulated semantic context, frequency, and stimulus quality in a single study. His results replicated the findings of earlier studies by Meyer et al., Becker and Killion, and Stanners et al. As in the previously reported work, he found a significant context by stimulus quality interaction, but no frequency by stimulus quality interaction, in spite of the fact that the magnitude of the stimulus quality manipulation was quite large (approximately 120msec). The functions for normal and degraded stimuli were perfectly parallel with one another over four levels of frequency using the intensity method of degradation advocated by Norris.

Detection of Related Nonwords

A second major line of evidence that compels us to propose a verification mechanism is the fact that context often enhances the subject's ability to discriminate correct words from misspelled or mispronounced words. In contrast to predictions generated from a basic logogen model that assumes that sensory and contextual evidence feed to the same unit, it is simply *not* the case that top-down processing is likely to make us perceive what we expect to perceive. We have shown in numerous experiments that primes like DOC-TOR do not elevate the error rate to targets like NERSE (McDonald, Note 2; Schvaneveldt & McDonald, 1981; Thompson, Note 5). Many of these experiments have also shown that NERSE is classified as a nonword faster when primed by DOCTOR than when primed by an unrelated word like LION.

This finding also generalises, in a dramatic way, to subjects listening for mispronunciations. Thompson and Paap (Note 6) have reported that highly constraining sentence contexts can improve latencies by 286msec over contexts with virtually no constraint. Mispronunciations are also less likely to be missed if the sentence is highly constraining: 5.5% misses for high constraint compared to 2.9% for little constraint. These results are inconsistent with the view that expectancies lead the listener to recognise words on the basis of less sensory evidence.

GOALS

The purpose of this paper is twofold. First, we would like to extend the original AV model to include aural-based access to the lexicon and a nonlexical pathway for generating the pronunciation of a letter string. This permits an account of how verification models can cope with effects of pronounceability in the lexical decision task (LDT) and the naming task. The LDT requires subjects to determine whether a letter string is a word or a nonword, whereas naming simply requires the subject to pronounce the string. The second part of the paper will examine recent critiques of the LDT, particularly the charge that the LDT grossly overestimates the role of familiarity (frequency) in word recognition.

AURAL FACTORS IN VISUAL PRESENTATION

The insightful analysis by Seidenberg, Waters, Barnes, and Tanenhaus (1984a) shows that the sound of a word has very little influence on lexical decision time when stimuli are presented visually. This is consistent with the AV model's assumption that the primary route from print to the lexicon does not require phonological mediation.

Regularity Effects in the LDT

Many words in English have irregular pronunciations, e.g. PINT. Seidenberg et al.'s experiments support the conclusion that large effects of irregularity probably occur only for low-frequency words, particularly when the regular pronunciation has recently been primed, e.g. by seeing the word HINT somewhat earlier.

The expanded AV model illustrated in Fig. 10.1 shows that activation of the letter units can spread laterally to the phoneme units as well as upwards to the lexicon. It is assumed that letter-to-phoneme connections occur in both single and multiple mappings, e.g. k to /k/ and kn to /n/. Furthermore, interconnections within the grapheme and phoneme levels could insure that orthographic and phonological constraints influenced the final selection of phonology. We agree with Seidenberg et al. that an activation-synthesis process does not obviate the need for grapheme-phoneme-correspondence (GPC) rules, but provides one computational account of them.

The sequence of phonemes, corresponding to the visual letter string, also passes activation to the lexicon. Words with regular pronunciations should activate a word candidate corresponding to the input word. Words with irregular pronunciation will activate the correct word candidate only if there is sufficient acoustic similarity between the synthesised pattern and the correct, but irregular, pronunciation of the input word. That is, if the letters in PINT do not appreciably activate the /aI/ phoneme unit, then the correct pronunciation of PINT will not even become an aural candidate. Indeed, our working hypothesis is that the word-unit criterion for popping an aural candidate is very high and that the aural list will usually consist of only the most likely pronunciation of the string. This corresponds to the subjective impression of a particular pronunciation being heard by the mind's ear.

A small irregularity effect can be predicted as follows. Assume that verification of the aural candidates takes place independent of and in parallel with verification of the visual candidates. Verification of the aural candidates will necessarily begin later than that for visual candidates since their generation requires an additional stage, viz. activation of the phoneme units. Thus, aural candidates should influence lexical decisions only when verification of the visual candidates takes longer than usual.

Since high-frequency words should be at, or near, the top of the visual list, they should be recognised before consideration of the aural candidate and be free of any effects of pronunciation. However, visual analysis of low-frequency words will sometimes be completed at about the same time as the aural analysis. If both the visual and aural candidate have generated a match, then both sources of evidence are compatible with the same "yes" response. This is likely to be the case for low-frequency words with regular pronunciations. However, as suggested above, irregular words will usually fail to generate the correct aural candidate. For example, if PINT is not in the aural list, then the output of aural-based verification (supporting "no") will be conflicting with the visual-based verification (supporting "yes").

The irregularity effect on reaction time occurs reliably only when low-frequency irregular words have recently been primed by regular words with the same spelling pattern. This suggests that aural-based verification usually lags far enough behind visual-based verification to prevent response competition. The priming effect (an earlier occurrence of SAVE making it more difficult to respond yes to HAVE) can be explained by assuming lingering activation on specific letter-to-phoneme pathways. This leads to the quicker nomination of aural candidates and faster completion of aural-based verification.

In order for irregularity to produce an error, the exhaustive search of the aural list (supporting "no") would have to be completed well before the target word was verified on the visual list. This doesn't seem likely and fits with Seidenberg et al.'s report that low-frequency irregular words are not more error prone than low-frequency regular words.

Consistency Effects in LDT

A word with regular pronunciation can have visually similar neighbours with inconsistent pronunciations, e.g. DIVE is regular and rhymes with FIVE and HIVE, but is inconsistent with GIVE. Other regular words, like LUCK, do not have any inconsistent neighbours. In Seidenberg et al.'s LDT experiments, regular words with inconsistent neighbours were *not* responded to slower than those with consistent neighbours. This was true of low- as well as high-frequency words, even if the irregular and inconsistent word (e.g. GIVE) had been presented somewhat before the regular word (e.g. DIVE).

The AV model is consistent with this finding. Recall that low-frequency words with irregular pronunciations sometimes yield somewhat longer lexical decision times, especially when the regular pattern has recently been primed. According to the AV model this occurs because aural and visual-based verification yield competing responses. This can not happen with regular words with inconsistent neighbours, because both the aural and visual candidates should contain the input word. For example, when DIVE is presented the DIVE word-unit will be nominated both visually and aurally since the most likely aural synthesis of DIVE is the true pronunciation. Thus, DIVE will be matched on either or both verification lists.

Regularity and Consistency Effects in Naming

Based on Seidenberg et al.'s investigation it seems reasonable to conclude that, in the naming task, regularity and consistency affect only low-frequency words. Furthermore, consistency effects are reliably produced only when the irregular pronunciation has recently been primed.

The AV account of these effects is a variation of the horse-race model. Pronunciations are computed, in parallel, along the lexical and nonlexical routes. The lexical pathway involves the successive activation of letter units and word units, the verification of a word candidate, the access of the candidate's pronunciation, and a final translation to articulation. The nonlexical pathway involves the successive activation of letter units and phoneme units, and a final translation to articulation. Pronunciations are computed along both pathways. If one wins clearly, that response is governed entirely by that pathway. If two different pronunciations are computed at about the same time, response competition will slow the response. Preference will be given to the lexically derived pronunciation. According to the AV model, high-frequency words should be little influenced by the nonlexical route since their pronunciation should be accessed quickly on the lexical pathway.

Low-frequency irregular words (e.g. PINT) should take longer to pronounce because the nonlexical pathway will frequently produce a competing response corresponding to the regular pronunciation of the letter string. Furthermore, when the stimulus is a low-frequency irregular word, the nonlexical pathway should sometimes generate a pronunciation well in advance of the lexical pathway and result in an error. In fact, this is the only type of word that does produce a high error rate in the naming task (e.g. 9.6%, Seidenberg et al., 1984; Experiment 3).

Regular low-frequency words (e.g. RAVE) with inconsistent neighbours (e.g. HAVE) do not generate more errors than those with consistent neighbours, but they do take longer to name (Seidenberg et al., 1984). The absence of errors follows from the AV model since the nonlexical pathway does not generate an incorrect response that can finish before the pronunciation derived from the lexicon.

However, the AV model does not easily account for Seidenberg et al.'s (1984; Experiment 4) finding that inconsistent neighbours slow the access of the pronunciation of low-frequency regular words. Consider the low-frequency word RAVE. Since its pronunciation is regular, the nonlexical route should generate the correct pronunciation. The correct pronunciation will also become available following lexical access. Yet the existence of the inconsistent neighbour HAVE can slow the naming of RAVE.

It may be tempting to suggest that HAVE somehow interferes with the lexical access of RAVE, but this line of explanation must be resisted, since any explanation that applies to the lexical route in naming should also produce consistency effects in the LDT. As discussed earlier, the consistency effect does not occur in the LDT. By deduction, the consistency effect in the AV model must influence the time it takes to synthesise a pronunciation on the nonlexical route. One possibility is that inconsistency is a mild form of irregularity. For example, _A_E activates the /eI/ phoneme the most, but the /ae/ phoneme is also activated. Resolving the conflict takes more time than for regular consistent words like LUCK that activate only one vowel phoneme. This explanation appears similar to the computational model advocated by Seidenberg et al.

ARGUMENTS AGAINST FREQUENCY IN LEXICAL ACCESS

According to the AV model, frequency plays a large role in word recognition. Frequency information is assumed to be stored in the lexicon and is used to determine the order of verification. High-frequency candidates are verified before those of lower frequency. Thus, the model assumes that frequency is a major determiner of the time it takes to recognise a word.

Most of the evidence in support of the frequency assumption has been gathered from the LDT. Recently, this evidence has been called into question by those who feel that the LDT provides a contaminated estimate of lexical access time. The strongest concerns have been raised by Balota and Chumbley (1984).

Problems of Definition

Before reviewing and addressing their concerns, problems of definition should be considered. Within the framework of the AV model, lexical access is ambiguous and could refer to different stages of information processing. Given visual input, lexical access could refer to the wave of activation within the lexicon generated by the activity of letter units in the alphabetum. The AV model assumes that frequency has no effect on the activation level or threshold for individual word units. Thus, if lexical access is taken to mean the level of activity in word units or the time it takes for word units to reach threshold, then the AV model is in agreement with the position that frequency does not influence lexical access.

Instead of equating lexical access with lexical activation, we shall adopt an alternative definition of lexical access that equates lexical access with recognition, i.e. the process that yields a single interpretation of the stimulus. In the AV model this outcome occurs when the verification process yields a sufficient match between a candidate and the sensory representation of the stimulus. When lexical access is equated with word recognition, then it is clear that the AV model does assume that frequency plays a major role in lexical access.

Balota and Chumbley's Critique

Balota and Chumbley's conclusion, that frequency plays little or no role in word recognition, rests on the assumptions that the large effects of frequency in the LDT are due to post-lexical processes and that a purer measure of lexical access time, naming, shows smaller frequency effects than the LDT. Balota and Chumbley's analysis of the LDT relies heavily on the assumption that an overall evaluation of the familiarity (F) and meaningfulness (M) of a stimulus determines lexical decision time. They suggest that a stimulus quickly generates some particular value on the FM dimension. If the value exceeds a high criterion, it is very likely that the stimulus is a word, and the subject will execute a fast "yes" response. If the value falls short of a low criterion, it is very likely that the stimulus is a nonword, and a fast "no" is executed. For values between the low and high criteria, the response must await the outcome of a slower and more analytic assessment of whether the stimulus is a word or a nonword. According to this model, response time to a specific word is primarily determined by the likelihood of the word generating an FM value greater than the high threshold.

Two sources of overall familiarity are orthographic and phonological structure. Stimuli with regular orthography and phonological translations are assumed to generate higher FM values. We would agree that nonwords with highly irregular orthography can be detected quickly, shortly after an analysis of the identity of the constituent letters. If all or most of the nonwords are highly irregular, then lexical decision can frequently be made on the basis of regularity rather than the completion of the verification operation. This explains why both frequency and semantic-priming effects are reduced when irregular nonwords are used rather than pseudowords (Shulman & Davison, 1977). However, it is quite another matter to assume that regularity contributes to the difference between high- and low-frequency words. Although common words tend to have greater orthographic structure (e.g. summed bigram frequency) than rare words, the low-frequency words are not illegal and it seems less plausible that large frequency effects could be predicted on the basis of small differences in regularity. This does, of course, remain an empirical question and it would be informative to determine if large frequency effects occur when regularity has been equated.

The remaining source of FM evidence is meaningfulness. Balota and Chumbley assume that high-frequency words are more meaningful and that this boosts their value on the FM dimension. Two questions need answers. First, if information about the frequency and meaning of a word is stored with its lexical entry, then why should a lexical decision depend on an evaluation of this information rather than the simple fact that a stored pattern has been matched? (The only answer that occurs to us would be to assume that the decision process has access to the frequency and meaning information, but not to the fact that recognition has occurred. The answer does not strike with a lot of force).

The second question focusses on meaning. Consider, for the moment, that "word" responses cannot be issued simply because there is a match between input and stored representation and that a fast "word" decision requires some criterial amount of accessed meaning. What kind of meaning? The most frequent 200 words in the English language are dominated by preposition, pronouns, auxiliary verbs, and comparative adjectives. In terms of imagery, concreteness, or the number of semantic primitives these words are paupers and should not generate high-powered values of meaningfulness.

Error rates are also likely to cause problems for the Balota and Chumbley model of the LDT. They assume that both frequency and contextual priming increase FM values. This means that nonwords that are visually similar to either high-frequency words or semantically related words should be very susceptible to false "yes" responses. There is no evidence to support this prediction and some that is contradictory.

Frederiksen and Kroll (1976) formed nonwords by replacing 1 letter of words selected from 4 frequency classes ranging from 1 or fewer occurrences per million to more than 30 per million. For example, PORSON was formed from the high-frequency word PERSON, while TUNGO was formed from the low-frequency word TANGO. If the nonwords formed from high-frequency words generate higher values on the FM dimension than those based on low-frequency words, then the high-frequency nonwords should exceed the low criteria more often, require more analytic checking, and produce slower response times. The high-frequency nonwords might also exceed the high criteria leading to a fast, but incorrect, "yes" response. However, in Frederiksen and Kroll's data the nonwords formed from high-frequency words are neither more error prone nor slower than those formed from lower-frequency words.

In summary, reasonable concerns can be raised about the alternative model offered by Balota and Chumbley. Are the differences in regularity between high- and low-frequency words sufficient to account for large frequency effects? Are high-frequency words more meaningful than low-frequency words? If yes, why should the decision wait for an evaluation of meaningfulness when the perceptual system has already matched a stored representation? Finally, how can this model account for the fact that primed nonwords (e.g. DOCTOR-NERSE) are responded to quickly and accurately?

WHICH TASK IS MORE CONTAMINATED?

If Balota & Chumbley's model of the LDT is correct, then the obtained frequency effects provide a grossly inflated estimate of the influence of frequency on lexical access time. Accordingly, the magnitude of the frequency effect should be significantly greater in the LDT than in a task that provides a cleaner measure of lexical access time. It has been argued that the naming task does provide a better measure and that naming can be used as a baseline for measuring the contamination of post-lexical processing in the LDT (Balota & Chumbley, 1984; Lorch, Balota, & Stamm, 1986; Seidenberg, Waters, Sanders, & Langer, 1984b).

It is true that the magnitude of the frequency effect is greater in the LDT than in naming (Balota & Chumbley, 1984; Forster & Chambers, 1973; Frederiksen & Kroll, 1976; Hudson & Bergman, 1985; Seidenberg et al., 1984b). However, we will eventually argue that the LDT remains the best paradigm for studying word recognition. Before doing so, we concede that the LDT is not lily-white. The choice of nonword foils is very important. For example, lexical decisions will be governed by a nonlexical discrimination if the nonwords are highly irregular.

The choice of words is also important. Many subjects will be somewhat uncertain about the spelling of low-frequency words with very unusual orthography (e.g. YACHT). These words are likely to be subject to a spelling check that is not normally used. In Seidenberg et al.'s (1984a) Experiment 4 there is a relatively huge effect of frequency for "strange" words that have both irregular orthography and pronunciation. This large frequency effect is probably exaggerated since the less familiar "strange" words (e.g. AISLE) require a spelling check, whereas the familiar ones (e.g. SCHOOL) do not. The term "strange" is probably a misnomer for the high-frequency words with irregular orthography and pronunciations. Within the framework of the AV model their spelling and visual form is well learned and provides a good match to correctly spelled input.

In summary, we suggest that differences in lexical decision time provide good indices of factors important to word recognition, if the nonword foils require the decision to be based on completion of the verification process (i.e. word recognition) and if low-frequency words with irregular orthography and pronunciations are avoided.

PROBLEMS WITH THE NAMING TASK

Nonlexical Derivations

For several reasons we feel that the naming task is a very poor choice as a substitute task for investigating word recognition. The primary problem is that pronunciations can be derived without lexical access via a grapheme-phoneme translation. If a naming response is viewed as a horse-race between the output of the lexicon and the recoding of graphemes to phonemes, then lexical factors like word frequency should be reduced in proportion to the likelihood that the nonlexical route wins the race.

It is important to note that this account of why the frequency effect shrinks in the naming task does not require a completely reliable nonlexical route to the pronunciation of a letter string. The voice-key can be activated by a translation of the first segment of the stimulus. For example, the initial /s/ sound of SORT can be initiated before recognition of the word and the complete articulatory specification of the rest of the syllable. We need not assume that a complete and correct pronunciation has been assembled on the nonlexical route before the onset of naming.

This position is in agreement with the conclusion that Frederiksen and Kroll (1976, p. 368) arrived at on the basis of an analysis of orthographic factors in the naming of nonwords: "... we are led to conclude that a translation of the initial consonant cluster precedes articulation, while phonological translation of the right-hand portion of the array takes place only after articulation has been initiated."

Differences Across Languages

Our account of the naming task relies heavily on the assumption that the nonlexical route wins a fair proportion of the races, particularly against low-frequency words. In contrast, Balota and Chumbley, in advocating the naming task as a better tool for studying lexical access, must rely on the assumption that the lexical route usually wins.

A recent report by Frost, Katz, and Bentin (in press) shows that the relative contributions of the lexical versus the nonlexical route to pronunciation depends upon the simplicity and veridicality of a language's GPC rules. When GPC rules are simple (Serbo-Croatian), subjects will usually rely on the nonlexical route and naming time will be relatively insensitive to lexical factors: word vs. nonword, frequency, and semantic priming. When GPC rules are complex or absent (Hebrew), subjects will usually look up the pronunciation of a word following its recognition and naming time will be more affected by the lexical factors. A language with intermediate complexity (English) yields intermediate sensitivity to lexical factors. The results are certainly consistent with the view that naming in English is significantly influenced by both routes.

In summary, it can reasonably be argued that the naming task will underestimate the involvement of any lexical factor, like frequency, to the extent that the onset of naming is controlled by a nonlexical route that recodes graphemes into phonemes. Furthermore, as described in the following subsections, the naming task is susceptible to its own set of post-lexical factors.

Production Effects

The naming task does not provide a simple tool for studying word recognition since recognition effects must be teased apart from production effects. Balota and Chumbley (1985) have attempted to do this by having subjects wait for a cue before starting to name the word. If the cue is delayed past the point of recognition, then any remaining frequency effects could be attributed to production rather than recognition.

When Theios and Muise (1977) completely controlled for production factors by having subjects pronounce a large set of homophones (e.g. break-brake) in a standard naming task, the frequency effect was only 11msec. These results suggest that whatever frequency effects that are obtained in the naming task are highly contaminated by production effects.

The effect of frequency on production can be viewed from at least two perspectives. If the question is how good is the naming task as a tool for studying word recognition, then the answer is; not very good. True lexical effects can be severely reduced by lost races to the nonlexical route. The residual lexical effects are then camouflaged by production effects. Another view focusses on the issue of whether or not skilled word recognition is affected by frequency. If one is predisposed to answer no, then production can be used to explain away the substantial frequency effects that sometimes occur in the naming task, just as Balota and Chumbley's dual criteria model can be used to dismiss the large effect found in the LDT.

Competition from Aural Pathways

The series of experiments by Seidenberg et al. show that the naming task is more sensitive than the LDT to regularity and consistency. The extended AV model discussed earlier suggests that most of these effects are due to competing responses from alternate routes and not to the primary route for visual word recognition. Nowhere is this clearer than in the homograph condition tested in Experiment 1 (Seidenberg et al., 1984a). Homographs like TEAR and WIND generated much longer naming times (+76msec) than their matched controls, but showed no effect in the LDT (−7msec). Apparently, homographs often generate competing responses that must be resolved before naming can begin. However, since both pronunciations correspond to words, the different pronunciations both map onto the same "yes" response in the LDT.

These observations make it difficult to understand why Balota and his colleagues (e.g. Lorch et al., 1986, p. 96) should conclude that in the naming task "there is no decision process to bias" and that naming "minimises post-lexical processing relative to the lexical decison task."

FREQUENCY EFFECTS IN WORD RECOGNITION: OTHER PARADIGMS

Balota and Chumbley claim that the frequency effect in the LDT is inflated by post-lexical processes and that skilled word recognition takes place without reference to frequency information. We claim that the frequency effect in the naming task is deflated by the nonlexical route and that word recognition is significantly influenced by frequency information during the verification operation. Evidence from other paradigms would be helpful.

Many investigators have reported word frequency effects for tachistoscopic word recognition. Whole report, however, is undeniably susceptible to post-recognition guessing effects. Furthermore, when guessing is controlled, as in the Reicher (1969) paradigm for studying the word-superiority effect, no frequency effect is observed (Paap & Newsome, 1980; Paap et al., 1982). This outcome is consistent with the AV model because backward masking prevents verification, but it is otherwise uninformative with respect to the current question.

Balota and Chumbley (1984) report a minimal effect of word frequency in a category verification task. Subjects were instructed to decide as quickly as possible whether each exemplar was a member of the designated category. Since the task certainly requires lexical access, a failure to find large frequency effects could be used to argue that word recognition does not usually rely on frequency information.

Alternatively, it can be argued that the category-verification task does not require the strict verification process that usually leads to word recognition. That is, in strict verification the AV model assumes that the list of context candidates are verified first and, failing to find a match, the list of sensory candidates is then examined by order of frequency. However, it is logically possible to perform the category-verification task by examining only the context list. If a match is found the subject will correctly respond "yes"; if no match is found the response is "no." This strategy would fail only for atypical exemplars that are not included on the context list.

Paap and Thompson (1986) have referred to this type of task-specific strategy as risky verification in an analysis of the aural-sentence condition of Thompson's (Note 5) dissertation. Although additional work is needed in order to understand when readers or listeners will adopt the risky verification strategy, it appears to require fairly strong context and is elusive in the sense that changes in modality or task (e.g. from lexical decision to listening for mispronunciations) may shift the strategy from risky to strict verification.

Fixation durations during reading could provide more compelling evidence for frequency effects in word recognition. Balota and Chumbley (1984) correctly point out that earlier eye movement data was ambiguous at best. For example, Kliegl, Olson, and Davidson (1982; 1983) found that word frequency accounted for only 1%–3% of the variance when other confounding variables such as word length were partialled out. However, more recently Inhoff and Rayner (1986) have systematically manipulated frequency while controlling for word length and predictability. In a normal reading condition where a full line of text was always available, gaze durations were significantly longer (37.5msec) for low-frequency words.

LEXICALLY CONTROLLED NAMING

If our rejoinder to Balota and Chumbley's criticism of verification models and the LDT is correct, then naming and LDT should yield comparable and significant effects of frequency and semantic priming whenever pronunciations are generated from the lexical route.

It is possible that global context effects may influence the degree to which the nonlexical route is used in the naming task. The magnitude of semantic priming is usually smaller in naming than in the LDT (Lorch et al., 1986; Seidenberg, Waters, Sanders, & Langer, 1984). However, an earlier comparison of the two tasks reported by Meyer et al. (1975) yielded a 48msec priming effect that did not interact with task.

An intriguing difference between these experiments was that Meyer et al. presented nonword as well as word primes, and required an overt lexical decision to the prime before the target was presented for pronunciation. Thus, each naming target was immediately preceded by a string that had to be processed through the lexicon in order to determine the correct response. If reliance on lexical processing carried through to the target, then pronunciation would always be generated from lexical look-up and comparable word-frequency effects would be expected.

In order to gather further evidence that naming and the LDT will yield equivalent frequency effects when naming is predicated on lexical access, we sought to devise a new task. The new task is called the affixed-naming task. Monosyllabic words like LIFE are presented with either a prefix (e.g. NEVLIFE) or a suffix (e.g. LIFEGER). The subject's task is to find the word and to pronounce just the word (e.g. LIFE) as quickly as possible. At reasonable levels of accuracy it is clear that naming must follow recognition in this task.

The task was designed to eliminate those aspects of the LDT that Balota and Chumbley hypothesised to be the cause of inflated frequency effects. The response is not binary and frequency is not correlated with the correct articulatory response, i.e. a post-lexical assessment of familiarity or meaningfulness can not be used to trigger one particular fast response.

Sharp arbiters of this controversy will already have spotted the fact that the affixed-naming task contains embedded lexical decisions. That is, subjects must parse the string and select either the beginning or end as the most promising choice for the hidden word. If the first segment turns out to be a nonword, then a second lexical decision must be made with respect to the remaining segment. It may even be necessary to reparse the string at a new boundary and execute additional lexical decisions. Thus, Balota and Chumbley could account for inflated word-frequency effects in this task if familiarity could be used to guide the parsing. For this reason, care was also taken to remove any possible advantage of the high-frequency words with respect to figure-ground contrast. The affixes were chosen by selecting either the first or second syllable from the 400 most common words in the Kucera & Francis (1967) word count, e.g. the prefix NEV was selected from the occurrence of NEVER. Thus prefixed words look like the beginning of a familiar word and suffixed words appear to have the ending of a familiar word. Thus, if any differences exist, it should be the high-frequency words that are more difficult to discriminate from their background.

Finally, the orthographic and phonological structure of the high- and low-frequency words were carefully matched. For each high-frequency word (e.g. LIFE), a low-frequency comparison word was selected (e.g. LIME) that: (1) had the same length; (2) began with the same two letters; (3) began with the same two phonemes; and (4) had the same pattern of consonants and vowels at the end. Most of the pairs had regular pronunciations. If one member of the pair was an exception word, so was the other.

Experiment 1

The purpose of the first experiment was to show that we could replicate the usual pattern of frequency effects with the set of high-and low-frequency words to be used in the affixed naming task to follow. One group of subjects participated in a normal naming task, the other in an LDT.

Method

Materials.   Twenty monosyllabic high-frequency words were drawn from the 200 most frequent words in the Kucera and Francis (1967) word count. Their frequency ranged from 325 to 4369, with a median of 663. Each of the high-frequency words was paired with a monosyllabic low-frequency word of the same length that began with the same two letters and phonemes, and that terminated with a similar consonant-vowel pattern. The low-frequency words ranged from 0 to 34 with a median frequency of 5.

Apparatus.   The stimuli were displayed and timing operations controlled by a Terak 8510 microcomputer. All verbal responses were recorded with a Teak C-1 cassette recorder and onsets were detected with a modified Lafayette 6602A voice-key.

Procedure.   In the naming task each trial was initiated with a 50msec warning tone. The word appeared 500msec after the onset of the tone. The display was turned off as soon as the voice-key detected the onset of the naming. The word was redisplayed after a 400msec delay. When the word reappeared, subjects were required to press a right-hand key if their verbal response was correct and a left-hand key if anything went wrong, e.g. they mispronounced the word or accidently triggered the voice-key with a cough,

APPR-I

etc. A tape-recording of the experimental session was used to confirm the correct responses. Although subjects did fail to identify some of their mispronunciations, both measures of accuracy always yielded the same pattern of results. Forty practice trials were followed by 40 experimental trials.

The timing of events was the same in the LDT as in naming. In order to reduce some of the response differences between tasks, the LDT required subjects to say "yes" to words and "no" to nonwords. There were an equal number of words and nonwords. The nonwords were pseudowords formed by changing one letter of a base word. Eight practice trials were followed by 2 blocks of 40 experimental trials. In both tasks subjects were instructed to go as fast as they could without making errors.

Design.   A group of ten subjects participated in each task. Half of the ten subjects in each group were drawn from the introductory psychology pool at New Mexico State University, while the remaining subjects were faculty and graduate students who were naive to the hypothesis under investigation. The same set of high- and low-frequency words was used in both tasks.

Results and Discussion

Errors.   Subjects followed instructions and maintained low error rates in both tasks. Based on the subject's post-trial validation response, "something went wrong" on 1.5% of the naming trials and 4.0% of the LDT word trials. In both tasks more errors occurred in response to low-frequency words than high-frequency words.

Response Times.   Median response times for correct responses to the high-frequency and low-frequency words were computed for each subject. These medians were submitted to a subjects analysis, treating task as a between-subject variable and frequency as a within-subjects variable. Median times for each item were also computed by considering the set of correct responses across the ten subjects in each task. These medians were submitted to an item analysis.

Mean response times (based on the subject analysis) and error rates for the two tasks are shown at the top of Table 10.1. The frequency effect is 99msec in the LDT and only 31msec in the naming task. Both the subject and item analysis yielded significant main effects of task and frequency. More important for present purposes is that both analyses yielded a significant task by frequency interaction, $F(1,18) = 10.03$, $P < 0.05$ by subjects and $F(1,38) = 8.12$, $P < 0.05$ by items.

Thus, we have replicated with our materials the typical finding that the frequency effect is smaller in naming than in the LDT.

TABLE 10.1
Mean Response Times (msec) and Errors for the Three Tasks

Task	High Frequency	Low Frequency	Difference
LDT	700 (2.5)%	799 (5.5%)	+99 (+3.0)
Naming	495 (0.5%)	526 (2.5%)	+31 (+2.0)
Affixed-naming	789 (1.4%)	896 (4.1%)	+107 (+2.7)

Experiment 2

Experiment 2 used the same set of high- and low-frequency words in an affixed-naming task. As described earlier, large frequency effects are predicted for both prefixed and suffixed words.

Method

Affix Materials.   Ten prefixes and 10 suffixes were obtained by selecting either the first or second syllable of the 2-syllable words included among the 400 most common words in the Kucera and Francis count. A syllable was discarded as a possible affix if it was a word (e.g. UP or WARD of UPWARD) a common prefix (e.g. PRE), or a common suffix (e.g. ING). Words and affixes were paired together, with the restriction that the fusion of words and affixes could not form a new word across the old syllabic boundary (e.g. HOSE + TER forms SET in the middle).

Of the two words in each frequency class, one had three letters, two had five letters, and the remainder consisted of four letters. The length of the prefix or suffix was selected so that all strings were seven letters long.

In order to counterbalance the camouflaging properties of particular affixes, four sets of materials were prepared. Set A was generated first. Half of the words in each frequency class were randomly assigned to the prefix condition and the remaining to the suffix. In Set B, affixes were exchanged between the high- and low-frequency words of each pair, e.g. NEVLIFE and TAKLIME from set A, became TAKLIFE and NEVLIME in set B. Sets C and D ensured that each word was tested with both a prefix and a suffix: For example, the prefixed NEVLIFE in Set A appeared with a suffix in Set C, LIFEBER.

Procedure.   Other than a change in instructions, the procedure was identical to that used for naming in Experiment 1. Subjects were instructed to find the word, ignore the meaningless affix, and pronounce only the word. The word alone reappeared 400msec after the onset of the verbal response and the subjects were asked to confirm with an appropriate key press whether their response was correct or if something had gone wrong.

Design. There were eight subjects in each of the four groups. About half the subjects were graduate students or faculty, and the remaining subjects were recruited from the introductory psychology subject pool. For each group, word frequency and affix type were factorially combined to form four conditions. Each subject was presented, in random order, ten words from each condition.

Results and Discussion

Errors. The error rate was a very low 2.7%. Errors were as likely to occur on prefixed words as on suffixed words, but there was a significant main effect of frequency, $F(1,31) = 8.76$, $P < 0.05$, with low-frequency words (4.1%) more error prone than high-frequency words (1.4%).

Response Times. Since the purpose of the four stimulus sets was to counterbalance the effects of specific affixes, all analyses were collapsed across sets. The four conditions formed by the combination of two frequency levels and two affix types were analysed both by subjects and by items. In the subject analysis, medians for each condition were based on the ten observations for each word in a condition. In the item analysis, medians for each condition were based on the 16 subjects that saw a particular word as either prefixed or suffixed.

There were large main effects of both frequency (107msec) and affix type (107msec) that were significant both by items; $F(1,38) = 9.90$, $P < 0.05$ for frequency, $F(1,38) = 8.42$, $P < 0.05$ for affix type; and by subjects $F(1,31) = 23.25$, $P < 0.01$, $F(1,31) = 50.89$, $P < 0.01$. The frequency by affix type interaction was not significant in either analysis. Thus, although words with prefixes took longer to name, the magnitude of the frequency effect for prefixed and suffixed words did not differ significantly. On this basis, the data from both affix types were combined to perform the analyses reported below.

Comparisons Between Experiments

The purpose of this pair of experiments was to test the prediction that naming would produce frequency effects equivalent to those obtained in the LDT, if naming was contingent upon lexical access. It was argued that lexical access is often bypassed during the standard naming task, but that pronunciation would be contingent upon lexical access in the affixed naming task.

Means for the three tasks are shown in Table 10.1. The essence of the predictions described here can be captured with the three planned orthogonal contrasts described next.

The data from both experiments can more readily be combined in an item analysis than a subject analysis because all subjects were presented with the same 40 items, but there were more subjects in affixed-naming (32) than LDT or naming (10). The first contrast tests the prediction that the mean of the combined frequency effect in LDT and affixed-naming is greater than the mean frequency effect obtained in normal naming. This contrast was significant, $F(1,114) = 6.76$, $P < 0.05$. The second contrast tests the prediction that frequency effects in affixed naming was significantly greater than in the traditional naming task. This contrast was also significant, $F(1,114) = 6.30$, $P < 0.05$. The final contrast tests whether affixed naming and the LDT produce equivalent frequency effects. The nonsignificant contrast is consistent with this hypothesis, $F(1,114) > 0.10$. A similar analysis by subjects, where the problem of unequal n was handled by the method of proportionate cell frequencies, yielded the same pattern of results.

Recall that each of the 20 high-frequency words was carefully matched on a number of variables to one of the low-frequency words. In a final analysis, we computed the proportion of trials on which the high-frequency member of each pair yielded faster response times than its low-frequency mate. This proportion was exactly 64% for all three tasks! Within the framework of the expanded AV model discussed earlier, this would suggest that the presence of the nonlexical route in the simple naming task frequently leads to faster responses for most low-frequency words. This generates considerable saving when measured in msec and accounts for the smaller frequency effects reported here and elsewhere. However, the reduction in time is not likely to be great enough to make these normally slow words faster than the best high-frequency words. This would account for why the proportion of high-frequency winners remains the same across tasks.

Taken together, the results of these experiments strongly support the view that the magnitude of the frequency effect obtained in the standard naming task severely underestimates the role of frequency in word recognition. We continue to believe that the speed of the verification process is highly influenced by frequency information.

REFERENCES

Balota, D. A. & Chumbley, J. I. (1984). Are lexical decisions a good measure of lexical access? The role of word frequency in the neglected decision stage. *Journal of Experimental Psychology: Human Perception and Performance, 10*, 340–357.

Balota, D. A. & Chumbley, J. I. (1985). The locus of word-frequency effects in the pronunciation task: Lexical access and/or production frequency? *Journal of Verbal Learning and Verbal Behaviour, 24*, 89–106.

Becker, C. A. (1976). Allocation of attention during visual word recognition. *Journal of Experimental Psychology: Human Perception and Performance, 2,* 556–566.

Becker, C. A. (1980). Semantic context effects in visual word recognition. *Memory and Cognition, 8,* 493–512.

Becker, C. A. (1982). The development of semantic context effects: Two processes or two strategies? *Reading Research Quarterly, 17,* 482–502.

Becker, C. A. (1985). What do we really know about semantic context effects during reading? *Reading Research: Advances in Theory and Practice, 5,* 125–166.

Becker, C. A. & Killion, T. H. (1977). Interaction of visual and cognitive effects in word recognition. *Journal of Experimental Psychology: Human Perception and Performance, 3,* 389–401.

Forster, K. I., & Chambers, S. M. (1973). Lexical access and naming time. *Journal of Verbal Learning and Verbal Behaviour, 12, 627–635.*

Frederiksen, J. R. & Kroll, J. F. (1976). Spelling and sound: Approaches to the internal lexicon. *Journal of Experimental Psychology: Human Perception and Performance, 2,* 361–379.

Frost, R., Katz, L., & Bentin, S. (in press). Strategies for visual word recognition and orthographical depth: A multi-lingual comparison. *Journal of Experimental Psychology: Human Perception and Performance.*

Hudson, P. T. & Bergman, M. W. (1985). Lexical knowledge in word recognition: Word length and word frequency in naming and lexical decision tasks. *Journal of Memory and Language, 24,* 46–58.

Inhoff, A. W. & Rayner, K. (1986). Parafoveal word processing during eye fixations in reading: Effects of word frequency. *Perception and Psychophysics, 40*(6), 431–439.

Kliegl, R., Olson, R. K., & Davidson, B. J. (1982). Regression analyses as a tool for studying reading processes: Comment on Just and Carpenter's eye fixation theory. *Memory and Cognition, 10,* 287–296.

Kliegl, R., Olson, R. K., & Davidson, B. J. (1983). On problems of unconfounding perceptual and language processes. In K. Rayner (Ed.), *Eye movements in reading: Perceptual and language processes.* New York: Academic Press, 333–343.

Kucera, H. & Francis, W. N. (1967). *Computational analysis of present day American English.* Providence, Rhode Island: Brown University Press.

Lorch, R. F., Balota, D. A., & Stamm, E. G. (1986). Locus of inhibition effects in the priming of lexical decisions: Pre- or postlexical access? *Memory and Cognition, 14,* 95–103.

Meyer, D. E., Schvaneveldt, R. W., & Ruddy, M. (1975). Loci of contextual effects in visual word recognition. In P. M. A. Rabbitt & S. Dornic (Eds.), *Attention and performance V.* New York: Academic Press.

Norris, D. (1984). The effects of frequency, repetition, and stimulus quality in visual word recognition. *The Quarterly Journal of Experimental Psychology, 36A,* 507–515.

Paap, K. R. & Newsome, S. L. (1980). A perceptual-confusion account of the WSE in the target search paradigm. *Perception and Psychophysics, 27,* 444–456.

Paap, K. R., Newsome, S. L., McDonald, J. E., and Schvaneveldt, R. W. (1982). An activation-verification model for letter and word recognition: The word-superiority effect. *Psychological Review, 89* (5), 573–594.

Reicher, G. M. (1969). Perceptual recognition as a function of meaningfulness of stimulus material. *Journal of Experimental Psychology, 81,* 275–280.

Schvaneveldt, R. W. & McDonald, J. E. (1981). Semantic context and the encoding of words: Evidence for two models of stimulus analysis. *Journal of Experimental Psychology: Human Perception and Performance, 7,* 673–687.

Seidenberg, M. S., Waters, G. S., Barnes, M. A., & Tanenhaus, M. K. (1984a). When does irregular spelling or pronunciation influence word recognition? *Journal of Verbal Learning and Verbal Behaviour, 23,* 383–404.

Seidenberg, M. S., Waters, G. S., Sanders, M., & Langer, P. (1984b). Pre- and postlexical loci of contextual effects on word recognition. *Memory and Cognition, 12*, 315–328.

Shulman, H. G. & Davidson, T. C. B. (1977). Control properties of semantic coding in a lexical decision task. *Journal of Verbal Learning and Verbal Behaviour, 16*, 91–98.

Stanners, R. F., Jastrzembski, J. E., & Westbrook, A. (1975). Frequency and visual quality in a word-nonword classification task. *Journal of Verbal Learning and Verbal Behaviour, 14*, 259–264.

Theios, J. & Muise, J. G. (1977). The word identification process in reading. In N. J. Castellan, D. B. Pisoni, & G. R. Potts (Eds.), *Cognitive theory. Vol. 2*. Hillsdale, N.J.: Lawrence Erlbaum Associates Inc., 289–327.

REFERENCE NOTES

1. Becker, C. A., Schvaneveldt, R. W., & Gomez, L. (1973). *Semantic, graphemic, and phonetic factors in word recognition*. Paper presented at the meeting of the Psychonomic Society, St. Louis.

2. McDonald, J. E. (1977). *Strategy in a lexical decision task*. Unpublished master's thesis, New Mexico State University.

3. McDonald, J. E. (1981). *An information processing analysis of word recognition*. Unpublished doctoral dissertation, New Mexico State University.

4. Paap, K. R. & Thompson, J. S. (1986). *Verification under seige. How is it holding up?* Paper presented at the Eleventh Annual Interdisciplinary Conference, Whistler, British Columbia.

5. Thompson, J. S. (1986). *Context effects in reading and listening: Are they the same?* Unpublished doctoral dissertation, New Mexico State University.

6. Thompson, J. S. and Paap, K. R. (1983). *Activation-verification in detecting mispronunciations*. Meeting of the Psychonomic Society, San Diego, California, November.

11 Sublexical Structures in Visual Word Recognition: Access Units or Orthographic Redundancy?

Mark S. Seidenberg
McGill University
Montreal, Quebec, Canada

ABSTRACT

Several theories assume that words are parsed into sublexical structures such as syllables, morphemes, or BOSSes as part of the recognition process. Empirical evidence for each of these units has been inconsistent; moreover, the notion that such units function as "access" codes is problematic in light of the properties of English orthography. An alternative view is that the effects of such units derive from orthographic redundancy. The present studies used feature integration errors to examine the perceptual groupings of letters in visual word recognition. Experiment 1 showed that syllables rather than BOSSes influenced feature integration errors. Experiment 2 showed that such errors occur when syllables are marked by low-frequency bigrams. Experiment 3 showed that orthographically similar pairs such as NAIVE and WAIVE act alike with respect to feature integration errors. The results suggest that recovering structures such as syllables or BOSSes is not a necessary stage in processing. To the extent that such units emerge, it is because they consist of spelling patterns that are salient in terms of orthographic redundancy. The results are discussed in terms of connectionist models in which there are no parsing mechanisms or access units.

INTRODUCTION

There have been several proposals that complex words are *parsed* or *decomposed* into sublexical units as part of the recognition process. These sublexical units (sometimes termed access units; Taft, 1985) are then used to search lexical memory until an entry is found that corresponds to the input string. Examples of this approach include the Spoehr and Smith (1973) model, in which the access units were assumed to be syllables and the parsing heuristics were based on iterative application of Hansen and Rodgers' (1968) syllabification rules; Taft's (1979a) prefix stripping model, in which the access unit is the stem of a prefixed word, and the parsing heuristics simply strip prefixes to yield stems; and Taft's (1979b) BOSS model, in which the access unit ("BOSS") is defined as "the first part of the stem morpheme of a word, up to and including all consonants following the first vowel, but without creating an illegal consonant cluster in its final position" (Taft, this volume). Examples include LANT in LANTERN and RHUB in RHUBARB.

Within this framework, two issues have arisen. First, what are the sublexical units that mediate lexical access? Pretheoretically it appears that words contain several potential subunits—syllables, morphemes, BOSSes—and it seems unlikely that all would be tried in parallel. Empirical studies have focused on determining which of these is actually used. A second, closely related question concerns the processes by which the relevant units are recovered; here research has focused on identifying parsing heuristics that will yield correct decomposition given the vagaries of written English.

Extensive research has failed to converge on the identity of a unique access unit. Although space limitations preclude a thorough review of this literature, it can be summarised by saying that there is both positive and negative evidence for several different units. For example, Jared and Seidenberg (Note 1) review the experiments on the role of syllables; these studies have yielded remarkably inconsistent results. Similarly, Taft (1979b) provided evidence implicating the BOSS unit, while Lima and Pollatsek (1983) found evidence against the BOSS in one study and for both syllables and BOSSes in another. The latter finding is particularly distressing to the word parsing approach, because it implies that there is no single "access unit." Much of the evidence for morphological units in recognition derives from studies using the repetition priming methodology, which has yielded results of a similar character (see Monsell, 1985; Henderson, 1982; Seidenberg, in press). Other problems with the parsing approach centre on the parsing heuristics themselves; see, for example, the Coltheart (1978) and Henderson (1982) discussions of the Spoehr and Smith model.

Analogous problems have arisen in connection with the role of phonological codes in visual word recognition. The dual-route model (Coltheart, 1978; Forster & Chambers, 1973; Meyer, Schvaneveldt, & Ruddy, 1975) assumes that most words in English can be recognised on the basis of phonological information; spelling-sound correspondence rules are applied to input strings to yield a phonological representation which functions as the access code. The irregularities in the spelling-sound correspondence of English, illustrated by minimal pairs such as GAVE-HAVE, PAID-SAID, and LEAF-DEAF, dictate that even a felicitous set of rules will generate incorrect phonological codes for some words. Thus, a backup mechanism is required for cases where the rules fail; the "direct" visual pathway.

The similarities to word parsing should be clear: Parsing heuristics take the place of spelling-sound rules, and sublexical units such as syllables or morphemes take the place of phonological codes. As in the case of spelling-sound rules, even a felicitous set of parsing heuristics will fail in a large number of cases, owing to the fact that, like phonology, syllabic and morphological structures are not consistently coded in the orthography. The inconsistencies among syllables are illustrated by minimal pairs such as WAIVE-NAIVE, BAKED-NAKED, and PROVED-PROVEN. The analogous morphological problem is illustrated by prefixed-pseudoprefixed pairs such as REWRITE-REVEAL, DECODE-DELIVER, and DISLIKE-DISPLAY, and compound-pseudocompound pairs such as MANHOLE-MANDATE and SWEETSHOP-SWEETBREAD. As in the dual-route model, there will have to be a backup mechanism to handle the irregular cases (possibly direct access again). The only other alternative is to allow the parsing mechanism to iterate through the rules repeatedly, testing alternative parses until the correct one is selected (as both Spoehr & Smith and Taft have considered). The question which arises is why the processor would bother with this trial-and-error method. Each word can be discriminated from every other word simply on the basis of its component letters. The overhead associated with parsing—which is considerable if reiteration is required—calls into question whether this process would provide any net benefit over simple pattern matching. Other questions concerning this alternative are addressed by Henderson (1982).

The problem in all of these domains lies in the assumption that readers attempt to recover phonological, syllabic, or morphological access codes by applying rules. In all three cases it has been difficult to identify the "correct" set of rules. In all cases, the rules will often fail, requiring backup mechanisms that introduce a high degree of redundancy into the processing system. In all cases there have to be complicated assumptions about the interactions between the two recognition processes which have yet to be worked out. These problems derive from properties of English orthography; phonemes, morphemes, and syllables are represented simultaneously and no one of these types of information can be independently characterised by a set of mapping rules. This makes it difficult to ensure that the processor will recover the correct access code (Seidenberg, in press).

In a writing system such as that for English, then, the notion of an access code is problematical. What would be lost by abandoning this notion entirely? In effect, that is what recent connectionist or parallel processing models of lexical processing do (Kawamoto, Note 3; McClelland & Rumelhart, 1981; Seidenberg & McClelland, Note 4). In these models, there are no levels of representation corresponding to syllables or morphemes.[1] The

---

[1]The levels aren't there because the models were not intended to apply to complex words. The claim is that this is not a bug; it's a feature.

lexicon embodies the reader's knowledge of the spelling and pronounciation of words, and similarities among words in terms of orthographic and phonological overlap. A word is recognised when the information extracted from the signal, together with the reader's knowledge of the structure of the lexicon, isolates a unique candidate from a range of possibilities. Seidenberg (1985; in press) argues that an approach along these lines will give a unified account of several different aspects of phonology and reading. The conceptual similarities between the problems of recovering phonological information on the one hand, and syllabic and morphological information on the other, suggest that it might be useful to think of the latter in terms of this process as well.

An alternative approach might be developed by considering properties of words that parsing models have tended to ignore. Syllables, for example, are usually defined in terms of rules governing the combination of consonants and vowels (*types* of letters). In the Spoehr and Smith models, for example, letters must be classified as consonants or vowels because the syllabification rules take CV strings into syllables; they do not operate directly on the letter strings themselves. However, the distributional properties of letter patterns in the lexicon (its redundancy) ensure that syllables will tend to be marked by particular letter *tokens*. As Adams (1981) noted, syllable boundaries are often flanked by letter patterns with relatively low transition frequencies. In words such as ANVIL or VODKA, for example, the syllable boundary bisects the lowest frequency bigram in the word. If one plots the frequencies of the component bigrams, the syllable boundary is marked by a dip or trough. These examples are by no means idiosyncractic, as seen by considering some additional cases. Taft (1979b) and Lima and Pollatsek (1983) report experiments on lexical decomposition which employed a total of 93 bisyllabic words. The positional bigram frequencies (Solso & Juel, 1981) for the bigram preceding the syllable boundary, the bigram straddling the syllable boundary, and the bigram following the syllable boundary, averaged across all 93 items, exhibit the trough pattern (the mean frequencies are 790, 559, and 857, respectively). The 80 most frequent bisyllabic words in Kucera and Francis (1967) also exhibit this pattern. Of course, many items deviate from this pattern; nonetheless it represents a general tendency. The trough pattern, then, is a consequence of orthographic redundancy, reflecting the fact that the letters within a syllable co-occur more often than the letters that mark syllable boundaries. This is largely a consequence of the fact that written English is a cipher for speech and there are more constraints on the phonemes that can occur within syllables than between (Seidenberg, in press). The trough pattern represents one consequence of orthographic redundancy; many others could be identified (see Adams, 1981).[2]

---

[2]This discussion of orthographic redundancy and syllabic structure owes a great deal to Adams (1981).

If the processing system were able to exploit orthographic redundancy, sublexical units such as syllables would influence recognition without parsing or decomposition. Models such as Adams (1979), McClelland and Rumelhart (1981), and Kawamoto (1986) appear to have the potential to make use of this information. Orthographic redundancy reflects facts about the distribution of letters in the lexicon; this information is implicitly coded in the connection structure of the lexical networks in these models. In the McClelland and Rumelhart (1981) model, what are termed "neighbour-hood" effects are effects of orthographic redundancy mediated by word-letter interconnections. An interesting hypothesis is that sublexical units are an emergent property of the parallel activation process leading to recognition. According to this view, sublexical units reflect coalitions of letters that have been mutually reinforced during the parallel activation process. Given the facts about the distribution of letter patterns in the lexicon, the parallel activation process will, in general, isolate sublexical coalitions that correspond to such higher-level units. However, it does so merely by exploiting this distributional information; neither syllabic nor morphemic units are directly represented, and there are no parsing routines dedicated to recovering them. This system will not have to retreat to a separate backup mechanism in irregular cases. In a parsing system, these cases are devastating because the primary recognition mechanism requires the recovery of the appropriate access units. In the present account, there are no "access units"; there is simply activation of component letters. Syllabic or morphological irregularities might slow recognition, but would not pose a special problem.

The following experiments were designed to obtain additional empirical evidence bearing on this account. Given the inconsistent results of previous studies, the basic goal was to gain evidence concerning the type(s) of sublexical units that emerge in word recognition and the conditions under which they emerge. A second goal was to explore a new method of investigating effects of sublexical structure. Each of the methods used in previous research has serious limitations. Subjects' strategies for performing lexical decisions are greatly affected by the composition of the stimuli in an experiment (Shulman, Hornak, & Sanders, 1978; Waters & Seidenberg, 1985). Naming latencies may not be sensitive to sublexical structures if subjects begin to initiate their responses before they have completed processing of a word (Henderson, 1985); furthermore they may be affected by factors related to articulation rather than lexical access (Balota & Chumbley, 1985; Landauer & Streeter, 1973). Marking syllable structures through case alternations (e.g., CONtent vs. CONTent) and other manipulations of stimulus characteristics may induce subjects to use units that would otherwise be ignored. Hence it would be useful to have a better method of assessing on-line effects of sublexical structure.

OVERVIEW OF METHODOLOGY

The experiments employed a methodology introduced by Prinzmetal and Millis-Wright (1984; also Prinzmetal, Treiman, & Rho, 1986) which uses feature integration errors (Treisman & Schmidt, 1982) to diagnose perceptual groupings of letters. Treisman and Schmidt tachistoscopically presented stimuli consisting of numbers and letters drawn in different colours. In a variety of tasks, subjects reported incorrect conjunctions of alphanumeric characters and colours at rates greater than expected by chance. Prinzmetal and Millis-Wright (1984) showed that structural properties of letter strings influenced the pattern of feature integration errors. For example, there were more erroneous conjunctions in words and psuedowords than in random letter strings.

Prinzmetal et al. (1986) extended this methodology to examine effects of syllabic structure. Consider a word such as ANVIL printed in two colours, *AN*vil.[3] The word is displayed tachistoscopically for a duration that produces about 10% errors over trials. The subject's task is to report the colour of a target letter, e.g., V. Prinzmetal et al. reasoned that, if subjects recover syllabic units during recognition, they should not tend to respond erroneously with the colour of N, since N and V are in different syllables. That is, the syllable boundary should act as a barrier to feature integration errors. In contrast, if the display were *ANV*il, subjects might tend to report that V was actually the colour of *il*, because VIL forms a syllable. Errors of the first sort, which "crossed" the syllable boundary, will be termed "violation" errors; errors of the second type, which respected the syllable boundary, will be termed "preservation" errors. If syllables influence the pattern of feature integration errors, there should be more preservation errors than violation errors. Prinzmetal et al. (1986) reported five experiments, four of which yielded this pattern, and concluded that syllables are perceptual units in reading. These studies are discussed in greater detail below.

EXPERIMENT 1

The first experiment examined two potential subunits; syllables and BOSSes. Although syllables are familiar units, their theoretical status is unclear (cf. Kahn, Note 2); there are clear cases that all theories of syllable structure treat alike and unclear cases where they differ. For example, what is the syllabic structure of CAMEL? According to Hoard's (1971) syllabification rules, which maximise intrasyllabic consonant strings surrounding a stressed vowel, it is CAM/EL (this is also how it is treated in dictionaries). According to a "maximal syllable onset" principle, proposed frequently in the linguistics

---

[3] Here and in the remainder of this paper different colours will be represented by different cases. In the experiments, all letters were presented in upper case.

literature (see, e.g., Hansen & Rodgers, 1968; Selkirk, 1980), it is CA/MEL. According to Kahn (Note 2), the M in CAMEL belongs to both syllables. As an alternative to syllables, Taft (1979b) proposed the BOSS (Basic Orthographic Syllabic Structure). Taft was not responding to the fact that syllables are hard to define. Rather, his goal was to define an access code that would be identical for morphologically related words. The syllabification of FASTER, for example, is fas/ter; morphologically, however, it is fast/er. If the access code were the syllable, the recognition process would differ for FAST and FASTER; however, the Taft and Forster (1976) model suggests that morphologically related items are recognised by accessing a common entry in the lexicon. This could be accomplished if the BOSS were the access unit.

As noted earlier, existing evidence concerning both syllables and BOSSes is inconsistent. The feature integration error methodology provides a simple way to contrast these units. Consider the stimulus conditions in Table 11.1. In words where the BOSS is simply one letter longer than the initial syllable, an error that preserves one unit violates the other. When errors are defined in terms of syllable boundaries, the predictions are as follows: If syllables are recovered during prelexical processing, preservation errors should outnumber violation errors; if BOSSes are recovered, violations should outnumber preservations. Experiment 1 examined these alternatives.

TABLE 11.1
Stimulus Conditions, Experiment 1

Display	Target	Type of Error	
		Syllable	BOSS
BURden	D	Violation	Preservation
BURDen	D	Preservation	Violation
PASture	T	Violation	Preservation
PASTure	T	Preservation	Violation

NOTE: Words were presented in upper-case letters in two colours. In all tables, different cases indicate different colours. Violation errors cross the boundary between units; preservation errors occur within the unit.

Method

The experiment was run in two parts. The stimuli in Experiment 1a were 34 words, a random subset of the items from the Taft (1979b) and Lima and Pollatsek (1983) materials. As noted above, these words exhibit the trough pattern. These bisyllabic words were presented in the conditions given in Table 11.1. Because each word was, in effect, tested against itself, the BOSS unit in each word was necessarily one letter longer than the syllable. Experiment 1b was run in order to address this potential confound. The stimuli in Experiment 1b were 15 pairs of words (also from the Taft and Lima & Pollatsek materials); pairs were matched so that the BOSS of one was equal in length to the syllable of the other. In PASTURE, for example, the BOSS is PAST; it was matched with THUNDER, in which the initial syllable, THUN, is also four letters long.

In both experiments, each word was presented in two display conditions. In Experiment 1a, the 34 words × 2 display conditions per item yielded 68 test trials, plus 8 catch trials. Order of stimulus presentation and assignment of colours per trial were randomised for each block of 76 stimuli. Four blocks were presented per subject (N = 13). In Experiment 1b, the 30 words × 2 display conditions per items yielded 60 trials, plus 8 catch trials. Randomisation was as in Experiment 1a. Each subject (N = 12) was presented with 3 blocks.

The procedure closely followed Prinzmetal et al.'s (1986). Each stimulus word was displayed tachistoscopically in two colours, followed by a high-contrast mask. The subject's task was to identify the colour of a target letter designated on each trial. On catch trials, the target letter did not occur in the string. Display durations were set for each subject to produce approximately 10% errors. Errors of the following types could occur: (1) misses (subject incorrectly reports that target letter did not occur in stimulus); (2) false alarms (subject responds with a colour on a catch trial or responds with a colour that was not in the display); (3) feature integration errors (subject responds with the colour of a different letter in the display).

The rates of (1) and (2) errors were very low and these errors were randomly distributed across display conditions in all experiments. Only the last type of error is of theoretical interest; it includes the preservation and violation errors. In the presentation of the results, preservation and violation are defined with respect to the syllable boundary.

Stimuli were presented in large upper-case letters on a Commodore colour monitor controlled by an Apple IIe computer. Stimulus colours were red, blue, green, and white. Each trial began with the presentation of a target letter in the centre of the monitor. After 1.5sec, the target was replaced by a solid white rectangle that covered most of the screen. The stimulus word was then presented for a brief duration in one of the four corners of the screen in order to prevent subjects from focusing on one or two letter positions. It was then replaced again with the white masking rectangle. The subject then indicated by pressing one of five response keys either: (1) the colour of the target letter; or (2) the absence of the target letter from the display (catch trials).

Display durations were calibrated in terms of the number of 16.67msec refresh cycles. These durations were set for each subject during 3 blocks of 30 practice trials. The experimenter adjusted the number of cycles until the subject was making approximately 10% errors overall. Display durations were modified between test blocks to keep the error rate at this level. This procedure was used in all experiments described herein. The mean exposure duration per subject across experiments was 11 refresh cycles (about 183msec), with a range of 7–15 cycles.

Results and Discussion

The overall error rate was 11.2%. Subjects incorrectly reported that a target letter was not present in the stimulus on 0.7% of trials, responded with a colour when the target was not actually present on 0.3% of trials, and responded with a colour that was not in the display on 0.3% of trials. Preservation or violation errors occurred on 11.5% of the trials when the target letter was actually present. Table 11.2 presents the proportions of preservation and violation errors in both versions of the experiment. These proportions represent the number of errors of each type out of the number of trials on which such an error could occur. For both sets of stimuli, there were more preservation errors than violations, indicating that syllabic boundaries affected feature integration errors more than BOSS boundaries. Because of the difference in the number of trials per condition in the two versions, the data were analysed separately. For Experiment 1a, the difference between preservation and violation errors was significant, $t(12) = 2.23$ by subjects and $t(33) = 2.91$ by items, both $P < 0.05$. The same outcome held for Experiment 1b, $t(11) = 4.88$ by subjects and $t(29) = 4.18$ by items, both $P < 0.01$.

TABLE 11.2
Mean Percent Errors, Experiment 1

	Violation	Preservation
Experiment 1a	8.0	14.1
Experiment 1b	7.5	17.0

NOTE: Errors are defined in terms of syllables.

The results suggest that syllables rather than BOSSes were utilised during the recognition of these words. The reason why the present results are inconsistent with Taft's (1979b) is unclear, since the stimuli in this experiment were a subset of those he used. Taken with the results of Lima and Pollatsek (1983), which included the same stimuli, it appears that the BOSS is not perceptually salient.

This conclusion is not altered by the results of three additional studies Taft (this volume) interprets as providing further evidence for the BOSS. In each of these studies, three potential units were contrasted: the initial syllable, the BOSS, and the BOSS plus one letter. In the word THUNDER, for example, the units are THUN, THUND, and THUNDE, respectively. The stimuli were presented in ways that emphasised these units. For example, each unit was used as a prime prior to presentation of the complete word. The logic of the experiments was that if the display emphasised a unit that was relevant to processing, responses would be facilitated. The results of the experiments are mixed. In all experiments, the BOSS conditions yielded faster responses than the syllable conditions. As Taft noted, this comparison is confounded with length. In order to conclude that the BOSS is salient, it would also have to differ from the still longer BOSS + 1. However, in none of the experiments is there a reliable difference between BOSS and BOSS + 1. Taft's comparisons involve a complex confounding of length, type of unit, and orthographic redundancy, making if difficult to interpret the results.

EXPERIMENT 2

The second experiment examined the conditions under which syllabic effects emerge. Prinzmetal et al.'s (1986) first three experiments showed that orthotactically marked syllable boundaries affect feature integration errors. The stimuli were words such as ABHOR and ANVIL, in which the bigrams straddling the syllable boundaries (BH, NV) always appear in different syllables in multisyllabic words. That is, there is an orthotactic constraint in written English that dictates that these letters cannot appear within a syllable in a word with two or more syllables. Their fifth experiment showed that syllable boundaries that coincide with morphological boundaries (e.g. LETUP, TODAY) also affect colour errors. Their fourth experiment examined words in which the syllable boundary was marked in neither of these ways (e.g. CAMEL, SALAD). Prinzmetal et al. considered these syllables to be phonologically defined. Because the syllable boundaries in these words failed to affect colour errors, they concluded that syllables are only used when they are orthotactically or morphologically marked. These results present a problem for simple word parsing schemes that search for syllables defined in terms of CV structures (e.g. Smith & Spoehr, 1974), because they do not consider orthotactic or morphological factors.

There may be another explanation for Prinzmetal et al.'s (1986) failure to obtain syllabic effects in this experiment, however. The items in the experiments that yielded syllabic effects exhibited the trough pattern around the syllable boundary. The stimuli in the experiment that failed to yield a syllabic effect did not. The latter included 5-letter words with the syllable boundary either after letter 2 (e.g. LA/PEL, "2/3 " items) or after letter 3 (e.g., CAM/

EL, "3/2" items). There were 12 words of each type. Mean positional bigram frequencies were calculated (from Solso & Juel, 1981) for the bigrams preceding, straddling, and following the syllable boundary. For the 2/3 words, the mean bigram frequencies were 815 (preceding), 352 (straddling), and 348 (following); for 3/2 words, they were 797, 684, and 685, respectively. Hence, the results are consistent with the generalisation that the frequencies of the letter patterns determine "syllabic" effects; neither orthotactic nor morphological factors need to be invoked. This generalisation is consistent with the results of Experiment 1, in which the stimuli also exhibited the trough pattern around the syllable boundary.[4]

These observations led to Experiment 2, a replication of Prinzmetal et al.'s Experiment 4 with some modifications. As in their experiment, the stimuli were bisyllabic words with "phonologically" defined syllables. The syllable boundary did not correspond to a morpheme boundary and the bigrams straddling the syllable boundary were not of the orthotactically constrained type. The stimuli had the same CV structure as their words. However, in contrast to their materials, all of the items exhibit the trough pattern. Twelve of these words were taken from Prinzmetal et al.'s stimuli, and 12 new items were added. If these items exhibited syllabic effects, it would indicate that the failure to obtain these effects in Prinzmetal et al.'s experiment was not due to the fact that their syllables lacked orthotactic or morphological cues; rather it was because they were not marked by the transition frequencies of the component letters.

Method

The stimuli were 24 bisyllabic 5-letter words, 12 with the dictionary-defined syllable boundary after letter 2 (e.g. LAPEL), and 12 with the boundary after letter 3 (e.g. SONIC). All words had the structure CVCVC; hence none of the bigrams straddling the syllable boundary were of the graphotactically constrained type. All words exhibited the trough pattern around their respective syllable boundaries.

The procedure closely followed that in Experiment 1. Each stimulus word was displayed tachistoscopically in two colours (Table 11.3). The subject's task was to identify the colour of a target letter designated on each trial. The target letter was always the third in the five-letter string. On catch trials, the target letter did not occur in the string. Display durations were again set for each subject to produce approximately 10% errors.

The 24 items × 4 display conditions per item yielded 96 test trials, plus 8 catch trials. The order of stimulus presentation and the assignment of specific

---

[4]It is interesting to note that many of the stimuli in Prinzmetal et al.'s experiment were items, such as CAMEL, for which the syllabic structure is theoretically unclear.

TABLE 11.3
Stimulus Conditions, Experiment 2

Display	Target	Type of Error
*LA*pel	P	Violation
*LA*Pel	P	Preservation
*VIG*or	G	Violation
*VI*gor	G	Preservation

colours were randomised for each block of 104 stimuli. Four blocks were presented per subject (N = 18). Stimulus presentation was as in Experiment 1.

Results and Discussion

The overall error rate was 10.9%. Subjects incorrectly reported that a target letter was not present in the stimulus on 0.9% of trials, responded with a colour when the target was not actually present on 0.3% of trials, and responded with a colour that was not in the display on 0.8% of trials. Preservation or violation errors occurred on 9.6% of the trials when the target letter was actually present. Table 11.4 presents the distribution of these errors by stimulus condition. The results indicate that subjects made more preservation errors than violation for both 2/3 and 3/2 words. This difference was significant, $F(1,34) = 18.29$ by subjects $P < 0.05$, and approached significance by items, and $F(1,94) = 3.11$ by items, $0.05 < P < 0.10$. The effect of word type and the interaction were not significant in either analysis. Syllabic effects appeared slightly larger for the 3/2 items than for the 2/3 items, which Prinzmetal et al. (1986) also observed.

The results indicate that the presence of neither an orthotactically constrained bigram nor a morpheme boundary is necessary in order to produce

TABLE 11.4
Mean Percent Errors, Experiment 2

Display Type	Error Type	Percent Errors
3/2 Words		
*VIG*or	Violation	7.9
*VI*gor	Preservation	12.8
2/3 Words		
*LA*pel	Violation	7.4
*LA*Pel	Preservation	10.2

syllabic effects on illusory feature conjunctions. Moreover, the stimuli in the present study and in Prinzmetal et al.'s were similar in terms of CV structure, and hence would be treated similarly by syllabification rules. However, the stimuli in the present experiment were marked by the trough pattern, while Prinzmetal et al.'s were not. Hence it appears that presence of these orthographic cues is necessary in order to produce syllabic effects.

There is another piece of evidence consistent with this conclusion. Prinzmetal et al. failed to obtain a syllabic effect in one other condition. Their fifth experiment included nonwords such as XETUH derived from words such as LETUP. Although the words showed the pattern of errors associated with syllabification, the nonwords did not. As in this example, the nonwords were created by replacing the first and last letters of the word stimuli with letters that created very low-frequency bigrams. The effect of this manipulation is to eliminate the trough pattern, consistent with the failure to obtain an effect of syllabic structure. The result indicates that it is not simply the presence of a lower frequency bigram at the syllable boundary that is critical; rather, it is the frequencies of the series of bigrams which create the trough pattern.

EXPERIMENT 3

The third experiment examined pairs such as NAIVE and WAIVE, which are orthographically similar but differ in terms of syllables. If feature integration errors are influenced by syllabic structure, the two types of words should differ, with only the bisyllabic items producing more preservation errors than violation. If the errors merely reflect the grouping of sublexical coalitions of letters, the two types should act alike.

Method

The stimuli were 15 pairs like NAIVE/WAIVE. Other examples include CREATED/PLEATED, NAKED/BAKED, FLUID/FRUIT, and PROVEN/PROVED. Pairs were matched in length (4–8 letters) and the letters that differed did not adjoin the syllable boundary. The display conditions were analogous to those in Experiment 1. Each word contained two colours; the target letter was the item before or after the syllable boundary (or the same letter in a nonsyllabified word). Violation errors occurred when subjects incorrectly responded with the colour of a letter in the adjoining syllable (or the comparable letter in a nonsyllabified word); preservation errors occurred when they incorrectly responded with the colour of the other letters in the target's syllable (or the comparable letter in a nonsyllabified word). An example of the stimulus conditions follows: display = NA*ive*; target = I; error = violation; display = NAI*ve*; target = I; error = preservation; display = WA*ive*; target = I; error = "violation"; display = WAI*ve*; target = I, error = "preservation". The 30 items × 2 display conditions per item yielded 60 test trials, plus 12 catch trials. The order of stimulus presentation and the assignment of specific colours were randomised for each block of 72 stimuli. Six blocks were presented per subject (N = 31). Display durations were set as in the previous experiment.

Results and Discussion

The overall error rate was 10.3%. Subjects incorrectly reported that a target letter was not present in the stimulus on 0.4% of trials, responded with a colour when the target was not actually present on 0.2% of trials, and responded with a colour that was not in the display on 0.5% of trials. Preservation or violation errors occured on 11.0% of the trials when the target letter was actually present.

Results are presented in Table 11.5. The two types of words produced similar results even though only one type contained a syllable boundary. The pattern of results, more preservation errors than violation, is similar to that in the previous experiments. The main effect of type of error was significant by subjects, $F(1,30) = 13.92$, $P < 0.01$, and approached significance by items, $F(1,28) = 2.65$, $0.05 < P < 0.10$. The main effect of word type and the interaction were not significant in either analysis. A difference score (violation errors-preservation errors) was calculated for each word, and the correlation between the two types of words on this measure was 0.68 ($P < 0.05$). Hence the pairs of words tended to act alike with respect to the pattern of errors.

The primary result of this experiment is that words that are orthographically matched acted similarly in regard to perceptual grouping of letters. Hence it was the orthographic properties of the words, rather than their

TABLE 11.5
Mean Percent Errors, Experiment 3

Display	Error Type	Percent Errors
Bisyllabic Words		
*NA*ive	Violation	10.2
*NAI*ve	Preservation	13.0
Monosyllabic Words		
*WA*ive	"Violation"	8.8
*WAI*ve	"Preservation"	12.2

syllabic structure, that affected subject errors. A second finding is that there were more preservation errors than violation errors. These effects were smaller than in previous experiments and they were significant by subjects but not by items. The absence of a significant effect by items indicates that only some words produced more violation errors. These errors did not depend on whether the stimuli actually contained a syllable boundary or not.

GENERAL DISCUSSION

The results of these experiments, taken with Prinzmetal et al.'s, are consistent with the hypothesis that perceptual groupings of letters in visual word recognition are due to orthographic redundancy. Several considerations point to this conclusion. The trough pattern is the modal profile for bisyllabic words. The experiments which yielded syllabic effects (Prinzmetal et al.'s; our Experiment 1) used stimuli that fit this profile. The experiment that failed to obtain syllabic effects (their Experiment 4) used stimuli that did not fit this modal pattern. When that experiment was replicated using syllables with the same CV structure as in the earlier experiment, but exhibiting the trough pattern, syllabic effects were obtained (our Experiment 2). Finally, words that are similar in terms of orthography act alike with respect to feature integration errors, despite differences in number of syllables (our Experiment 3).

All of these results point to a theory in which the emergence of sublexical units in early decoding depends on the orthographic properties of words. The results are not easy to reconcile with the view that multisyllabic words are recognised by recovering their underlying syllabic structure, which provides an access unit used to search lexical memory. It appears that some words are correctly syllabified; others are syllabified incorrectly (our Experiment 3) or not syllabified at all (Prinzmetal et al.'s Experiment 4). Hence, recovering the correct syllabic structure cannot be a necessary stage in lexical access. The results are more consistent with a theory in which coalitions of letters emerge to the extent that they are marked in the orthography. These coalitions typically correspond to units such as syllables; however, nonsyllabic units that exhibit the right kind of orthographic structure will sometimes emerge and syllables will not emerge when spelling patterns have the properties of monosyllables. These graded effects of sublexical organisation obtain because the coalitions are simply a secondary consequence of parallel activation processes. The system exploits orthographic redundancy because it is encoded in the connection structure of the lexicon but is not obliged to recover the correct syllabification.

I have focused on syllables in this paper, but it should be clear that the same principles may account for the effects of other structures such as morphemes or subsyllabic onset/rime units (Treiman, this volume). Consider a morphologically based parsing strategy such as prefix stripping. Prefixes tend to be highly salient in terms of orthographic redundancy; they are very high-frequency spelling patterns that recur in many words. The bigrams within a prefix will be higher, on average, than the bigrams straddling the boundary between prefix and stem. Hence, prefixes should tend to act as processing units because of their orthographic properties, not because they are morphemes. Similarly, the onset and rime units derive from properties of speech (i.e. closing and opening gestures of the vocal tract). These properties will tend to be reflected in an alphabetic orthography. Clearly, the view I have proposed suggests that it should be possible to derive the effects of these units from strictly orthographic factors. This view would be shown to be incorrect if it were the case that, unlike syllables, other units affect processing whether they are marked by orthographic redundancy or not.

The main limitation of the account I have offered is that there is no specification of exactly which aspects of orthographic redundancy are relevant to processing. The reason for this is obvious: Orthographic redundancy reflects a complex set of facts about the distribution of letter patterns in the lexicon; measures such as bigram frequency, the frequency of a series of bigrams, or positional letter frequency capture very little of this structure. This is perhaps a case in which computational modelling provides a useful alternative to traditional experimental approaches. Instead of deriving statistics that summarise aspects of orthographic redundancy, we can simulate the structure of the lexicon itself. J. L. McClelland and I have recently developed a connectionist model of visual word recognition (Seidenberg & McClelland, Note 4). The model consists of a network of units that encode facts about orthographic redundancy and orthographic-phonological correspondences. This information is carried by the weights on the connections between units. Weights are set during a learning phase in which the model is effectively discovering the structure of the lexicon based on experience. It would be difficult to characterise this connection structure in terms of measures analogous to bigram frequences. However, what the model provides instead is very detailed information concerning the *effects* of this structure; specifically, one can derive measures concerning the relative activation of individual letters and letter patterns. My hope is that this measure will prove to be related to empirical phenomena of the sort considered in the experiments detailed in this chapter.

Exploration of the model is only in its initial stages. However, a number of suggestive results have already been obtained. The model was developed in order to account for facts about the role of orthographic redundancy and orthographic-phonological correspondences in the processing of monosyllabic words, which it does quite well. However, these factors also account for effects of syllabic structure on tasks such as lexical decision, naming, and colour identification. The model takes letter strings as inputs and yields two types of output: A pattern of activation across the phonological output nodes (a phonological code) and a recreation of the input letter string across the orthographic nodes (an orthographic code). In general, naming responses depend on the former, lexical decisions on the latter. The model was tested on the stimuli from Experiment 3. The WAIVE and NAIVE types of words produced similar orthographic output. However, when naming was simulated, the two conditions differed. The bisyllabic words are more difficult to pronounce, because they contain two vowels, and vowels are a source of ambiguity in terms of orthographic-phonological correspondences. Jared and Seidenberg (Note 1) provide behavioural evidence consistent with the model. Lexical decision latencies for these types of words do not differ. Thus, lexical decisions are based on the results of orthographic processing; because the words are similar in terms of orthographic redundancy, they yield similar decision latencies. However, the two types of words produce different results on naming, with the bisyllabic words yielding longer latencies.

The model was also tested on pairs such as BLEACH-BLAZER. Like the WAIVE-NAIVE pairs, the BLEACH-BLAZER pairs differ in terms of orthographic-phonological correspondences; the bisyllabic items contain two vowels, each of which can be pronounced several ways, while the monosyllabic words only have one. Hence, when naming is simulated, the BLAZER-types of words are more difficult to pronounce than the BLEACH-types. In contrast to the WAIVE-NAIVE items, however, the words also differ in terms of orthographic redundancy. BLEACH, for example, contains higher-frequency spelling patterns and has more neighbours (Glushko, 1979) than BLAZER. Hence, the BLAZER types produce poorer orthographic output than the BLEACH types. Consistent with these outcomes, Jared and Seidenberg (Note 1) found that for human subjects, the BLAZER type of words produce longer latencies than the BLEACH type on both naming and lexical decision.

In sum, the effects of syllabic structure on recognition are simulated by a model which only encodes facts about orthographic redundancy and orthographic-phonological regularities. Syllables are not directly represented and there is no parsing mechanism. Because the model encodes orthographic redundancy directly, it provides an alternative to summary statistics such as bigram frequencies. Hence it may provide the basis for a more subtle account of the effects of word structure on processing.

ACKNOWLEDGEMENTS

I would like to thank William Prinzmetal who generously provided the software used to run these experiments. The assistance of Tina Hausen and Alison Phinney is also gratefully acknowledged. This research was supported by grants from the Natural Science and Engineering Council of Canada (A7924), the Quebec Ministry of Education (FCAR EQ-2074), and National Institute of Child Health and Human Development (HD-18944). A list of the stimuli used in these experiments is available from the author.

REFERENCES

Adams, M. (1979). Models of word recognition. *Cognitive Psychology, 11*, 133–176.

Adams, M. (1981). What good is orthographic redundancy? In H. Singer & O. J. L. Tzeng (Eds.), *Perception of print*. Hillside, N.J.: Lawrence Erlbaum Associates Inc.

Balota, D. A. & Chumbley, J. I. (1985). The locus of the word frequency effect in the pronunciation task: Lexical access and/or production? *Journal of Memory and Language, 24*, 89–106.

Coltheart, M. (1978). Lexical access in simple reading tasks. In G. Underwood (Ed.), *Strategies of information processing*. New York: Academic Press.

Forster, K. I. & Chambers, S. (1973). Lexical access and naming time. *Journal of Verbal Learning and Verbal Behaviour, 12*, 627–635.

Glushki, R. J. (1979). The organisation and activation of orthographic knowledge in reading aloud. *Journal of Experimental Psychology: Human Perception and Performance, 5*, 674–691.

Hansen, D. & Rodgers, T. S. (1968). An exploration of psycholinguistic units in initial reading. In K. S. Goodman (Ed.), *The psycholinguistic nature of the reading process*. Detroit: Wayne State University Press.

Henderson, L. (1982). *Orthography and word recognition in reading*. London: Academic Press.

Henderson, L. (1985). Issues in the modelling of pronunciation assembly in normal reading. In K. Patterson, M. Coltheart, & J. C. Marshall (Eds.), *Surface dyslexia*. London: Lawrence Erlbaum Associates Ltd.

Hoard, J. (1971). Aspiration, tenseness, and syllabification in English. *Language, 47*, 133–140.

Kucera, H. & Francis, W. N. (1967). *Computational analysis of present-day American English*. Providence, Rhode Island: Brown University Press.

Landauer, T. & Streeter, L. (1973). Structural differences between common and rare words: Failure of equivalence assumptions for theories of word recognition. *Journal of Verbal Learning and Verbal Behaviour, 12*, 119–131.

Lima, S. & Pollatsek, A. (1983). Lexical access via an orthographic code? The Basic Orthographic Syllabic Structure (BOSS) reconsidered. *Journal of Verbal Learning and Verbal Behaviour, 22*, 310–332.

McClelland, J. L. & Rumelhart, D. M. (1981). An interactive-activation model of context effects in letter perception. *Psychological Review, 88*, 375–407.

Meyer, D., Schvaneveldt, R., & Ruddy, M. (1975). Functions of graphemic and phonemic codes in visual word recognition. *Memory and Cognition, 2*, 309–321.

Monsell, S. (1985). Repetition and the lexicon. In A. W. Ellis (Ed.), *Progress in the psychology of language, Vol. 2*. London: Lawrence Erlbaum Associates Ltd.

Prinzmetal, W. & Millis-Wright, M. (1984). Cognitive and linguistic factors affect visual feature integration. *Cognitive Psychology, 16*, 305–340.

Prinzmetal, W., Treiman, R., & Rho, S. H. (1986). How to see a reading unit. *Journal of Memory and Language,25*, 461–475.

Seidenberg, M. S. (1985). The time course of information activation and utilisation in visual word recognition. In D. Besner, T. Waller, & G. E. MacKinnon (Eds.), *Reading research: Advances in theory and practice. Vol. 5.* New York: Academic Press.

Seidenberg, M. S. (in press). Reading complex words. In G. Carlson & M. K. Tanenhaus (Eds.), *Lexical processing and linguistic theory.* Cambridge: Cambridge University Press.

Selkirk, L. (1980). *On prosodic structure and its relation to syntactic structure.* Bloomington, Indiana: Indiana University Linguistics Club.

Shulman, H., Hornak, R., & Sanders, E. (1978). The effects of graphemic, phonemic, and semantic relationships on access to lexical structures. *Memory and Cognition, 6,* 115–123.

Smith, E. E. & Spoehr, K. T. (1974). The perception of printed English: A theoretical perspective. In B. H. Kantowitz (Ed.), *Human information processing: Tutorials in performance and cognition.* Potomac, Maryland: Lawrence Erlbaum Associates Inc.

Solso, R. L. & Juel, C. L. (1981). Position frequency and versatility of bigrams for two-through nine-letter English words. *Behaviour Research Methods and Instrumentation, 12,* 297–343.

Spoehr, K. T. & Smith, E. E. (1973). The role of syllables in perceptual processing. *Cognitive Psychology, 5,* 71–89.

Taft, M. (1979a). Recognition of affixed words and the word frequency effect. *Memory and Cognition, 7,* 263–272.

Taft, M. (1979b). Lexical access via an orthographic code: The Basic Orthographic Syllabic Structure (BOSS). *Journal of Verbal Learning and Verbal Behaviour, 18,* 21–39.

Taft, M. (1985). The decoding of words in lexical access: A review of the morphographic approach. In D. Besner, T. G. Waller, & G. E. MacKinnon (Eds.), *Reading research: Advances in theory and practice. Vol. 5.* New York: Academic Press.

Taft, M. & Forster, K. I. (1976). Lexical storage and retrieval of polymorphemic and polysyllabic words. *Journal of Verbal Learning and Verbal Behaviour, 15,* 607–620.

Treisman, A. & Schmidt, H. (1982). Illusory conjunctions in the perception of objects. *Cognitive Psychology, 14,* 107–141.

Waters, G. S. & Seidenberg, M. S. (1985). Spelling-sound effects in reading: Time course and decision criteria. *Memory and Cognition, 13,* 557–572.

REFERENCE NOTES

1 Jared, D. & Seidenberg, M. S. (1986). The emergence of syllabic structure in visual word recognition. Manuscript submitted for publication.

2. Kahn, D. (1976). *Syllable-based generalisations in English phonology.* Unpublished University of Massachusetts Ph.D. thesis.

3. Kawamoto, A. (1986). *Interactive processes in the resolution of lexical ambiguity.* Manuscript submitted for publication.

4. Seidenberg, M. S. & McClelland, J. L. (1987). *A distributed, developmental model of visual word recognition.* Unpublished manuscript.

12

Morphographic Processing: The BOSS Re-emerges

Marcus Taft
University of New South Wales
Kensington, N.S.W., Australia

ABSTRACT

The series of experiments reported in this paper examines the status of the Basic Orthographic Syllabic Structure (BOSS) in word recognition. The BOSS is the first syllable of a word defined in morphological and orthographic terms. The first three experiments use three different experimental paradigms to demonstrate that a word divided after its BOSS is faster to process than one divided after its phonological first syllable. Doubts about the definition of the BOSS led to Experiment 4 which examined whether the transitional probability of a medial consonant cluster influenced which consonants were included in the BOSS. However, no significant effect of bigram frequency was observed. The final experiment demonstrated that nonwords which are one letter different to a word take longer to classify as nonwords than those with the same BOSS but which are more than one letter different to a word (e.g., MOBOT versus MOBUS). This result proved to be a problem for the strongest characterisation of the BOSS in the word recognition process, but not an insurmountable one.

INTRODUCTION

Several years ago, I published a paper which put forward the view that a lexical entry is accessed in visual word recognition when the first part of the presented word is found to match with an equivalent mental representation of that word (Taft, 1979; and see Taft, 1985). In particular, I have defined the important first part of the word as being the orthographically and morphologically defined first syllable of the word, terming this the Basic Orthographic Syllabic Structure (or BOSS). The BOSS is the first part of the stem morpheme of a word, up to and including all consonants following the first vowel, but without creating an illegal consonant cluster in its final position.

An illegal final consonant cluster is one that cannot terminate a word (e.g., BL, TR, YC). Thus the BOSS of LANTERN is LANT, the BOSS of CONCENTRATE is CENT, the BOSS of BOYCOTT is BOY, and the BOSS of SPADE is SPAD. (The rationale for this definition is given in Taft, 1979.) Since the BOSS is defined both orthographically and morphologically, I have termed it a morphographic unit.

The way I characterised the word recognition process was to say that there is a specific listing of BOSSes that is separate from the full lexical information found in the lexicon proper. Lexical access takes place via this listing of BOSSes. The locating of an appropriate BOSS makes available the full information about the word in the lexicon. This is depicted in Fig. 12.1. As can be seen from the figure, words which are morphologically related like FINAL, FINISH, etc., are listed together in some way within the lexicon proper. While this is not an essential requirement of the model, the possibility that the lexicon is sensitive to such morphological relationships is an interesting one to speculate on.

The evidence that supports the notion of the BOSS is of two types. First, it has been demonstrated (Luszcz, Bungey, & Geffen, 1984; Taft, 1979; Taft, 1986; Taft & Forster, 1976) that nonwords which are BOSSes of real words (e.g. the TRAUM of TRAUMA or the SPAD of SPADE) take longer to classify as nonwords than nonwords which are the first part of words but are not their BOSSes (e.g. the SCOUN of SCOUNDREL, or the BLEN of BLEND). Similarly, nonwords that begin with real words and nonwords that begin with BOSSes take equally longer to classify as nonwords than nonwords that do not (e.g. LENDY and MURDY versus MALDY; cf. Manelis & Tharp, 1977). The interpretation of these results is that the nonword decision has been interrupted by the accessing of an inappropriate lexical entry via the BOSS.

The second type of evidence comes from experiments where stimulus words are presented with a division occurring after their BOSS or elsewhere in the word. In my 1979 paper, I reported two experiments demonstrating that words divided after their BOSS (e.g. LANT/ERN) were faster to be recognised than words divided after their phonological first syllable (e.g. LAN/TERN). This suggested that the BOSS division coincided more closely to the representation of the word in the lexicon than did the syllable division. Subsequent work by Lima and Pollatsek (1983), however, failed to replicate this finding, though they also failed to replicate their own results in the same paper, thus somewhat weakening their argument. Nonetheless, it was certainly apparent that evidence for the BOSS was not easy to come by using this division technique.

My interest in pursuing the BOSS via the word division method was recently revived, however, when Sanchez-Casas, Bradley, & Garcia-Albea (Note 1) reported at a conference that they were consistently finding that a

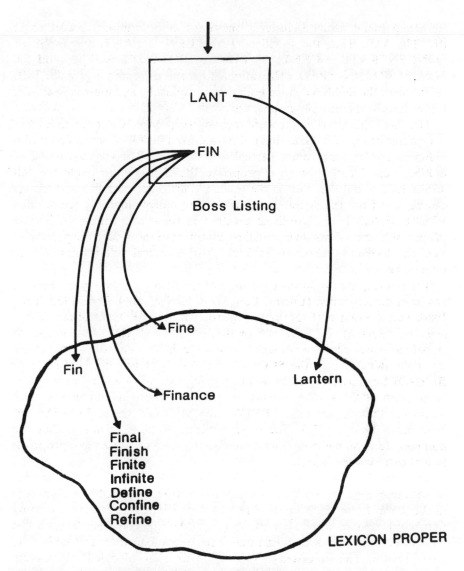

FIG. 12.1.   Model of lexical access according to Taft (1979).

BOSS division facilitated response times relative to other divisions. Division of the word was achieved by presenting part of the word for a brief period before the whole word appeared. (Lima and Pollatesk had also used this temporal priming technique.) Most of the BOSS divisions used by Sanchez-Casas et al. were also phonological syllable divisions. However, in one experiment this was not the case and yet an advantage for the BOSS was still maintained. Spurred on by this result, and also the seeming sensitivity of the temporal priming task to word structure effects, I ran a set of new experiments examining the BOSS via word division.

One concern about any experiment that compares BOSSes and phonological syllables as primes is that the BOSS contains more letters than the phonological syllable and therefore potentially conveys more information about the word. The following 3 experiments used the same set of 39 words selected specifically to avoid such problems (see Appendix). The items were chosen such that the phonological first syllable was the beginning of as many words as was the BOSS, usually only one word.[1] For example, there are no words other than THUNDER that begin with THUN and there are no words other than RHUBARB that begin with RHU. Therefore, if THUND primes THUNDER more than THUN does or RHUB primes RHUBARB more than RHU does, it should not be because the former unit is more informative about what the word is than the latter unit. However, in case the absolute number of letters in the prime is important despite this (e.g. because redundancy might be useful), a third type of prime was used, namely, the BOSS plus one letter. If THUNDE primes THUNDER more than THUND does, then it cannot be argued that there is anything special about the BOSS, but rather that the number of letters in the prime is what determines the amount of priming.

Three different techniques were used to compare phonological syllable (PS) divisions, BOSS divisions, and BOSS + 1 divisions.

EXPERIMENT 1

Method

This experiment employed the temporal priming technique of Sanchez-Casas et al. and Lima and Pollatsek. The prime appeared for 200msec before the whole word was presented, and subjects were required to decide by button press whether the complete item was a word or not. To make this task meaningful, there were 36 nonword items randomly mixed together with the word items. Three groups of eight subjects undertook the experiment such that each of the three types of prime was presented for each word across the three groups, but any single subject saw only one type of prime for each word. All subjects received 13 items in each of the 3 conditions.

---

[1] There were inadvertently three cases where the phonological first syllable defined more words than the BOSS (the LEC of LECTURE also begins LECHER, the MYS of MYSTERY begins MYSELF, and the PLAU of PLAUSIBLE begins PLAUDIT). These words did not appear to be treated differently to the other items in any of the three experiments.

Results and Discussion

The mean reaction time for correct responses to words primed by their BOSS was significantly shorter than for words primed by their PS: 603msec v. 648msec, $F_1(1,21)=5.951$, $P<0.05$, $F_2(1,38)=8.837$, $P<0.01$. The mean reaction time for words primed by their BOSS + 1 fell in between the other two conditions with a mean of 615msec, and was not significantly different from either. The percentage error rates for the three conditions were 4.2%, 2.7%, and 3.1% for the PS, BOSS, and BOSS + 1 conditions respectively.

This experiment therefore provides evidence for saying that the BOSS is somehow represented in the lexical representation of a word. Even though the phonological first syllable was equally as predictive of the whole word as was the BOSS, it nevertheless was not as effective as a unit of preview. This cannot be explained simply because the BOSS has one more letter than the PS, since the BOSS + 1 provided no greater priming than the BOSS, and if anything showed less priming.

EXPERIMENT 2

Method

The same 39 words were presented for subjects to identify. There were no nonwords in the experiment. The words were degraded in such a way that word recognition was made difficult while the three different types of word division (PS, BOSS, and BOSS + 1) could be imposed. This was achieved by presenting in rapid alternation the first part of the word followed by hatching marks and the remaining part of the word preceded by hatching marks. For example, in the BOSS condition, subjects saw THUND## followed by #####ER in rapid succession, while in the PS condition, subjects saw THUN### followed by ####DER. Each presentation lasted 50msec with 20 alternations of each presentation per word. Subjects responded by saying the word as soon as they recognised it, with the latency being measured from the first presentation to the onset of the vocal response. Thirty subjects were assigned to one of three groups in the same way as in Experiment 1. None of the subjects had participated in the first experiment.

Results and Discussion

As in the first experiment, the BOSS division words were identified more quickly than the PS division words;[2] 965msec vs. 1015msec, $F_1(1,27)=5.454$,

---

[2]Two items were removed from the analysis owing to excessive error rates. SMOULDER was mostly read as SHOULDER, and subjects were quite erratic in their pronunciation of GEYSER.

$P < 0.05$, $F_2(1,36) = 6.833$, $P < 0.02$. The BOSS + 1 items behaved like the BOSS items with a mean reaction time of 964msec, which was significantly different from the reaction time to PS items, $F_1(1,27) = 8.122$, $P < 0.01$, $F_2(1,36) = 5.089$, $P < 0.05$. (The percentage errors rates were 1.2%, 1.6%, and 1.5% for the PS, BOSS, and BOSS + 1 conditions respectively.) Therefore the same conclusion is drawn from Experiment 2 as was drawn from Experiment 1, using a very different experimental paradigm.

EXPERIMENT 3

If access is gained to a lexical entry via the BOSS of a word, then subjects should be able reconstruct a word from its BOSS more readily than from its phonological first syllable. This was examined in the third experiment.

Method

Subjects were presented with word fragments that were either a PS (e.g. THUN), a BOSS (e.g. THUND), or a BOSS + 1 (e.g. THUNDE). These were randomly mixed with 36 fragments that did not begin a word (e.g. FEG, STEMB, MIRKE). The subjects were required to decide whether each presented letter string was the beginning of an English word or not, and to record their response via a button press. Again 30 new subjects were randomly assigned to each of 3 groups in the same way as in the first 2 experiments.

Results and Discussion

As predicted, the BOSS fragments were recognised as being the first part of a word more rapidly than were the PS fragments; 967msec vs. 1030msec, $F_1(1,27) = 8.756$, $P < 0.01$, $F_2(1,39) = 4.807$, $P < 0.05$. The BOSS + 1 fragments, as in Experiment 1, fell in between the other two conditions with a mean of 989msec, and did not significantly differ from either. (The percentage error rates were 6.3%, 4.8%, and 5.0% for the PS, BOSS, and BOSS + 1 conditions respectively.) This result is therefore consistent with those obtained in the first two experiments. It appears that the BOSS is indeed an important unit within a word as far as lexical access goes.

It is interesting to note, however, that according to the characterisation depicted in Fig. 12.1, subjects should essentially be unable to say that a PS like THUN is the beginning of a word, since THUNDER is not accessible via this unit. Although there were more mistakes made with PS fragments than BOSS fragments, there was not a significant difference.

To handle this result it can be proposed that the word completion task is performed on a phonological basis as well as on a visual basis. For example, the letter string THUN may be converted by grapheme-phoneme conversion into /θʌn/ and then access attempted via the speech system, after visual access fails to locate an entry for THUN. Recently, I have presented evidence which suggests that lexical entries are accessible via units smaller than the BOSS when the material is in a spoken form (Taft, 1986). For example, whereas the visually presented letter string BLEN (from BLEND) was no slower to classify as a nonword than BLET, the spoken utterance /blɛn/ was slower than /blɛt/. That is, BLEN did not access the lexical entry for BLEND, whereas /blɛn/ did. Given the apparently greater flexibility of the auditory access system compared to the visual access system, it seems likely that subjects would make use of the former when the task requires word restorations that cannot be made via the latter.

Having demonstrated that the BOSS has a status in lexical access that other units within the word do not have, I would like to consider two further important issues. The first is the adequacy of the definition of the BOSS and the second is the adequacy of the characterisation of the lexicon as depicted in Fig. 12.1.

ADEQUACY OF DEFINITION

Part of the definition of the BOSS states that consonants are included in the BOSS unless they create an illegal letter combination. For example, the BOSS of TABLE is TAB rather than TABL because BL is illegal at the end of a word. There are, however, problems associated with this definition. For example, the BOSS of NAVY and NAVAL is taken to be NAV, yet no normal English words end in V and therefore final V should not be allowed in a BOSS. One might then argue that convention requires a silent E after a final V and this is ignored when determining the BOSS. However, the same could be said of the BL of TABLE, so why not allow a BOSS to end in BL?

In addition to this problem of inconsistency, there is also the problem that readers are expected to know what are and are not permissible consonant clusters in English when determining the access unit for any word. Since it is not at all obvious that readers do have this knowledge about consonant legality, I entertained the possibility that the consonants that are included in the BOSS are determined on a probabilistic basis. In particular, if two consonants rarely occur together in English, like the W and T of PEWTER, then perhaps they are unlikely to be included together in the BOSS. That is, perhaps the BOSS of PEWTER is taken to be PEW rather than PEWT, such that PEWTER should be easier to recognise if divided after the W than after the T. This possibility was tested in the next experiment.

EXPERIMENT 4

Method

The temporal priming technique of Experiment 1 was employed in this experiment. BOSS priming was compared to PS priming for two types of words which were matched for frequency of occurrence according to Carroll, Davies, and Richman (1971). Words had a medial consonant pair of either low transitional probability (e.g. PEWTER, GARBAGE, FRENZY) or high transitional probability (e.g. BANDIT, CACTUS, BOULDER) as determined from the norms of Mayzner and Tresselt (1965). There were 28 words of each type (see Appendix).

Subjects were randomly assigned to 2 groups, with 12 in each group. Each word was presented in the experiment with both a BOSS division and a PS division, though no single subject saw the same word with both divisions.

TABLE 12.1

Mean Reaction Times in Msec and Error Rates for Experiment 4

	PS Prime		BOSS Prime	
Low Transitional Probability				
Example	PEW	PEWTER	PEWT	PEWTER
RT		757		703
% Error		4.5		4.2
High Transitional Probability				
Example	BAN	BANDIT	BAND	BANDIT
RT		746		726
% Error		2.7		3.6

Results and Discussion

The mean reaction times for the items of Experiment 4 are presented in Table 12.1. Across transitional probability conditions the BOSS primes led to faster responses than the PS primes (as was also found in Experiment 1), $F_1(1,22) = 18.800$, $P < 0.001$, $F_2(1,54) = 8.454$, $P < 0.01$. There were no other significant effects. Note that, if anything, the size of the BOSS effect was larger for the low transitional probability words than the high transitional probability words.

Clearly, it is not the probability of co-occurrence that determines how many consonants are included in the BOSS. If it were, then the words with a low transitional probability consonant cluster would have shown weaker

BOSS priming relative to PS priming than the words with a high transitional probability consonant cluster. If anything, the opposite was true. This trend can be explained by saying that two consonants that frequently combine together (e.g. ND) are readily linked together even when they have been physically separated. Therefore, there is not a great difference between presenting the word with a division between the two consonants and after the two consonants. On the other hand, when there is only a weak link between two consonants (e.g., WT) then this link is greatly disrupted when the two consonants are physically separated, thus disrupting access to the BOSS.

The idea that letters with a high frequency of co-occurrence might be more strongly linked than those with a low frequency of co-occurrence suggests a model of word recognition where information about the strength of linkage between letters is somehow represented in the access system. Seidenberg (this volume) subscribes to such a model, where the activation level of sublexical units is reinforced by the activation of words that contain those units. In Seidenberg's connectionist model, all effects of internal word structure on word recognition are explained in terms of the frequency of such sublexical units. However, the pattern of data observed in Experiment 4 is difficult to reconcile with this account. Facilitation of word recognition performance was greater with the larger sublexical unit of preview (i.e. BOSS versus PS) regardless of bigram frequency. It seems that the BOSS is an important sublexical unit that needs to be incorporated into the connectionist model, although it needs to be determined why Seidenberg failed to find evidence for the BOSS while I continue to succeed in this regard. Presumably the answer lies in the different methodology employed, but just what the important difference might be remains to be established.

Experiment 4, then, points again to the relevance of the BOSS in lexical access, but fails to elucidate what the best way of defining the BOSS might be. Perhaps the correct way to view the BOSS is as a "folk morpheme," that is, it is part of a word that appears to be a stem morpheme even though it may not be. For example, PEWT might be considered to be the BOSS of PEWTER because ER seems to form a single unit, thus leaving PEWT as the "stem". Similarly, the BOSS of TABLE would be taken to be TAB, since LE forms a single unit. In most cases this pseudostem will be the BOSS as previously defined, but it need not always be so. For example, the BOSS of MAINTAIN may be more commonly thought of as MAIN rather than MAINT since TAIN seems to form a unit (cf. RETAIN and CONTAIN). Similarly, it is possible that some people may think of the BARB of RHUBARB as being a unit, thus isolating RHU as the BOSS for those people. By defining the BOSS in this way, one can never be absolutely sure what the appropriate BOSS is for any particular word, for any particular person. However, the fact that words divided on the basis of the original BOSS definition were found to be recognised more quickly than words divided on the basis of their phonological syllabic structure suggests that the original BOSS definition provides a reasonable working approximation to what the BOSS actually is.

It should be noted that questions regarding the definition of the BOSS are relevant only to the issue of BOSS storage. The issue of BOSS retrieval is not affected by the definition question. BOSS retrieval is achieved via a left-to-right parsing technique (Taft, 1979), that will locate the BOSS no matter how it is defined. That is, if MAINTAIN is represented by MAINT in the BOSS listing then this entry will be located after MA, MAI and MAIN are found to be inappropriate and a match is attempted for the next largest unit, namely MAINT. On the other hand, if MAINTAIN is represented by MAIN then this will be located after MA and MAI have failed to find an appropriate match. So, whatever it is that is stored can always be retrieved.

Finally, we turn to the question of the best characterisation of the BOSS within a model of lexical access.

ADEQUACY OF THE STRONG MODEL

The model put forward in 1979, as depicted in Fig. 12.1, is the strongest model possible. Here, the primacy of the BOSS in lexical access is captured by giving each BOSS a lexical listing that is independent of the lexical representation that describes the complete word. The BOSS is therefore the code through which access to the complete word is made possible. Since the BOSS is the only means of getting to the lexical entry when a word is visually presented, the model would need to be reappraised if it were demonstrated that a letter string can access a lexical entry when the BOSS is not intact. Chambers (1979) performed experiments that appeared to demonstrate exactly this.

Chambers' study examined the interference to nonword classification responses brought about by the similarity of the nonword to a word. The finding of particular concern was that when a nonword was created by changing one consonant of a five-letter word by substitution, it made no difference whether that substitution was made in the first position (e.g. LOTOR from MOTOR), middle position (e.g. FIBAL from FINAL) or final position (e.g. MUSIT from MUSIC). All showed as much interference as each other relative to a nonword that was more than one letter different to a word (e.g. TOSOL or GIMAL).[3] According to the strong BOSS account,

---

[3]In fact, Chambers concludes that the letter substitution items showed no interference relative to the control nonwords. This was because her *minF'* analysis was not significant. However, if one adopts a less stringent criterion for significance (as I have here), namely a significant F_1 and F_2, then Chambers' data can be seen as being supportive of an interference effect.

only the final letter substitution nonwords should have produced interference, since the BOSS of the similar word is disrupted in the case of the first position and middle position substitution nonwords. That is, the FIB of FIBAL should not gain access to the lexical entry for FINAL since access should only be achieved via FIN, whereas the MUS of MUSIT should be able to access MUSIC.

However, it happens that Chambers' items were such that most of the first position and middle position nonwords began with the BOSS of a word other than the word to which it was one letter different. For example, although FIB is not the BOSS of FINAL, it is the BOSS of FIBRE. None of the control nonwords (like TOSOL and GIMAL) began with real BOSSes. Therefore it is possible that the interference observed by Chambers came from this source. This possibility was tested in Experiment 5.

EXPERIMENT 5

This experiment tested whether one still observes interference effects for first position and middle position substitutions when the control items have the same BOSSes as the experimental items. For example, MOBOT (from ROBOT) was compared to MOBUS, and DUSIC (from MUSIC) was compared to DUSAL.

Method

Nonwords were created from 20 5-letter words with a CVCVC structure (see Appendix). Pairs of items were constructed such that an experimental item was one letter different to a word while its matched control had the same BOSS but was more than one letter different to a word. The experimental items either had their substitution in the first position (e.g. MOBOT, DUSIC) or in the middle position (e.g. RODOT, MULIC). Each of the 24 subjects saw 10 items in each condition and only ever saw 1 member of each experimental-control item pair, and also only ever saw 1 experimental item based on the same word. So, one group of subjects saw MOBOT, DUSAL, MULIC, and RODUS (the control item matched with RODOT), while the other saw DUSIC, MOBUS, RODOT, and MULAN (the control item matched with MULIC). There were 40 words randomly interspersed among the nonword items, and the task was to decide whether the letter string was a word or not.

Results and Discussion

The first position substitution nonwords (e.g. MOBOT) showed significant interference relative to the control nonwords (e.g. MOBUS): 860msec vs.

824msec, $F_1(1,22) = 7.820$, $P < 0.02$, $F_2(1,19) = 4.582$, $P < 0.05$. Percentage error rates were 4.2% and 1.5%. An RT difference was also found between the middle position substitution nonwords (e.g. RODOT) and their control nonwords (e.g. RODUS), though the effect was not quite significant on the analysis of item means: 854msec vs. 813msec, $F_1(1,22) = 6.122$, $P < 0.05$, $F_2(1,19) = 3.286$, $0.05 < P < 0.1$. Percentage error rates were 3.8% and 2.3%.

It appears, therefore, that a nonword that is one letter different from a word is able to access that word (and thus produce interference) even when the BOSS of that word has been disrupted. Such a conclusion is problematical for the strong account of BOSS representation, since one should only be able to access a word through a representation of its BOSS. In order for the strong account to explain this result, it must become more flexible and allow approximate sensory-to-lexical matches to be made. So, MOBOT accesses ROBOT because MOB is sufficiently similar to ROB for it to access the BOSS listing for ROB.

One can think of this in terms of an activation model like the logogen account of Morton (e.g. 1969; 1980). When MOBOT is presented, all entries in the BOSS listing (or BOSS input logogen system) that have features in common with MOB are activated. These include MOB itself, as well as ROB, SOB, MOT, MOL, and so on. Sufficient activation of an entry in the BOSS listing will lead to an examination of the associated entries found in the lexicon proper. These are then checked back against the original stimulus; the closer the match, the greater the inclination to accept the entry as being correct. Since the entry ROBOT (activated by MOB) is closer to the stimulus MOBOT than to the stimulus MOBUS, the former stimulus will be more difficult to classify as a nonword than the latter.

Similarly, if one were to compare responses to a nonword with an intact BOSS, like MUSAL, with a control nonword like DUSAL, the former should take longer than the latter. This is because MUSAL is more similar to an accessed entry (namely MUSIC) than is DUSAL (ignoring the word DUCAL which would be in the lexicon of very few people). In addition, one could make the assumption that the greater the activation in the BOSS listing, the greater the likelihood of proceeding to the top-down verification stage, and that therefore DUSAL does not always access the lexical entry for MUSIC whereas MUSAL always does.

It turns out, then, that the results obtained by Chambers (1979), and confirmed by Experiment 5 here, do not eliminate the strong account of lexical access where there is a special listing of BOSSes, though one needs to add the requirement of approximate access to BOSS representations. However, the data are more readily accounted for by a weaker version of BOSS representation where there is no special BOSS listing. According to this weaker version, the sensory-to-lexical match is made on the basis of the whole word but with more weight being given to the BOSS. Thus, any part of a word can activate the lexical entry for that word to some extent (e.g. the BOT of ROBOT), but it is the BOSS that provides the most activation. Therefore, presentation of the BOSS prior to the whole word will facilitate recognition more so than prior presentation of any other parts of the word.

While the weaker model has an advantage over the stronger model in its flexibility, it loses the economy of collapsing lexical entries on the basis of structural similarity. For example, while the related words FINISH and FINAL can be accessed via the same representation in the strong model, they must be seen as independent lexical entries in the weaker model. It is not entirely the case, though, that the weaker model overlooks the structural relationships that occur between words. When the word FINISH is presented, all words that include FIN as their BOSS will be activated since the major activation comes from the BOSS. Therefore, the lexical entry for FINAL will be activated to some degree when the word FINISH is presented. However, it is not readily apparent what advantage it is to the recognition system for this to happen, since any unrelated word beginning with FIN will also be activated (e.g. FINANCE, FINE, and FIN). Indeed, it is not readily apparent in the weaker model why the BOSS should be given more weight than any other part of the word at all. There is no advantage to the system for any particular component of the word always to have priority over any other component of the word, since all of the letters of the word are always available for inclusion in the sensory-to-lexical match. Therefore, before the stronger model is replaced by the weaker model, the basis for the weaker model must be justified.

SUMMARY AND CONCLUSION

The first three experiments have demonstrated that there is something special about the first orthographic syllable of a word, the BOSS, in that it seems to have a primary role in word recognition. Problems in the definition of the BOSS have not, however, been elucidated by the fourth experiment. It has been suggested that the BOSS might best be conceived as being the part of a word that the reader treats as being the stem of the word, even if it is not linguistically a genuine morpheme.

Finally, consideration has been given to the issue of whether the primacy of the BOSS should be captured by a special listing of BOSSes in the lexicon or by extra weight being given to the BOSS in a sensory-to-lexical match based on the whole word. The latter is favoured for its flexibility, particularly in the light of the fifth experiment which demonstrated the need for flexibility. However, the former, stronger model has not been discarded as a possibility, since flexibility could be added into it, and, in addition, the weaker model failed to provide any reason for the BOSS being given more weight than any other part of the word. Therefore, the best way to characterise the BOSS in the word recognition process is still an open question. However, what seems clear, at least from the experiments reported here, is that the BOSS does have a special status in the word recognition process.

REFERENCES

Carroll, J. B., Davies, P., & Richman, B. (1971). *The American heritage word frequency book*. Boston: Houghton-Mifflin.

Chambers, S. M. (1979). Letter and order information in lexical access. *Journal of Verbal Learning and Verbal Behaviour, 18*, 225–241.

Lima, S. D. & Pollatsek, A. (1983). Lexical access via an orthographic code? The Basic Orthographic Syllabic Structure (BOSS) reconsidered. *Journal of Verbal Learning and Verbal Behaviour, 22*, 310–332.

Luszcz, M. A., Bungey, J., & Geffen, G. (1984). Orthographic-morphemic factors in reading: A developmental study. *Australian Journal of Psychology, 36*, 355–365.

Manelis, L. & Tharp, D. A. (1977). The processing of affixed words. *Memory and Cognition, 4*, 53–61.

Mayzner, M. S. & Tresselt, M. E. (1965). Tables of single-letter and digram frequency counts for various word-length and letter-position combinations. *Psychonomic Monograph Supplements, 1*, 13–32.

Morton, J. (1969). Interaction of information in word recognition. *Psychological Review, 76*, 165–178.

Morton, J. (1980). The logogen model and orthographic structure. In U. Frith (Ed.), *Cognitive processes in spelling*. London: Academic Press.

Taft, M. (1979). Lexical access via an orthographic code: The Basic Orthographic Syllabic Structure (BOSS). *Journal of Verbal Learning and Verbal Behaviour, 18*, 21–39.

Taft, M. (1985). The decoding of words in lexical access: A review of the morphographic approach. In D. Besner, T. G. Waller, & G. E. MacKinnon (Eds.), *Reading research: Advances in theory and practice. Vol. V*. Orlando, Fla: Academic Press.

Taft, M. (1986). Lexical access codes in visual and auditory word recognition. *Language and Cognitive Processes, 1*, 49–60.

Taft, M. & Forster, K. I. (1976). Lexical storage and retrieval of polymorphemic and polysyllabic words. *Journal of Verbal Learning and Verbal Behaviour, 15*, 607–620.

REFERENCE NOTE

1. Sanchez-Casas, R., Bradley, D. & Garcia-Albea, J. (1984). *Syllabification, stress, and segmentation in lexical access*. Paper presented at the 11th Experimental Psychology Conference, Deakin University, Geelong, Victoria, Australia, May.

APPENDIX

1. The following list shows the 39 words used in Experiments 1, 2, and 3, with their BOSS indicated by a slash.

THUND/ER, RHUB/ARB, DWIND/LE, POULT/RY, SYST/EM, DRAST/IC, FRUST/ RATE, GHAST/LY, JASM/INE, LECT/URE, PLAUS/IBLE, SLAUGHT/ER, BOLST/ER, CLUST/ER, XYL/OPHONE, BOIST/EROUS, CEIL/ING, CRYST/AL, FLUCT/UATE, GEST/URE, GLIST/EN, JUXT/APOSE, NIMB/LE, PLECT/RUM, CIRC/LE, SPLEND/ID, MYST/ERY, CLOIST/ER, SQUAND/ER, SMOULD/ER, CIST/ERN, CYMB/AL, FUNCT/ION, GEYS/ER, THIMB/LE, TUNGST/EN, NUIS/ANCE, TUIT/ION, RHEUM/ ATISM

2. The following list shows the items used in Experiment 4, namely the 28 words with a low transitional probability medial consonant pair (LTP) and the 28 words with a high transitional probability medial consonant pair (HTP). The words are presented in LTP/HTP pairs matched on word frequency. BOSSes are indicated by slashes.

SUBT/LE, EARN/EST; ALB/UM, ANT/ICS; ULC/ER, VAND/AL; FALC/ON, BAND/IT; CHIMN/EY, CACT/US; ANV/IL, ANT/IQUE; ENV/Y, DENT/AL; FRENZ/Y, BOULD/ ER; CARB/ON, JOURN/EY; TURB/INE, PARD/ON; GARB/AGE, EMP/IRE; CARP/ET, STURD/Y; PURP/LE, CAST/LE; COSM/IC, DICT/ATE; PRETZ/EL, TEND/ON; PEWT/ ER, VIRT/UAL; POWD/ER, ACT/UAL; DAWD/LE, MART/YR; CALC/IUM, MURD/ ER; VULG/AR, CORT/EX; BANJ/O, DELT/A; BARB/ER, HOST/ILE; JASM/INE, GAST/ RIC; BAWD/Y, HURT/LE; HARP/OON, NOST/RILS; ALG/AE, KERN/EL; BALC/ONY, LAUND/RY; HARB/OUR, PAST/URE.

3. The following list shows the 80 nonwords used in Experiment 5. The items are presented in quadruplets in the following order: letter substitution in the initial position, control nonword, letter substitution in the middle position, control nonword.

MOBOT, MOBUS, RODOT, RODUS; DUSIC, DUSAL, MULIC, MULAN; NULIP, NULUS, TUSIP, TUSAR; RISON, RISAR, BILON, BILAR; MIGAR, MIGIP, CINAR, CINIP; PADAR, PADON, RAVAR, RAVAD; HIVAL, HIVAR, RISAL, RISIC; KUNAR, KUNON, LUBAR, LUBON; DORON, DORAR, MODON, MODOT; BOMAD, BOMIN, NOBAD, NOBUS; DIRUS, DIRAD, VILUS, VILON; FUTOR, FUTAN, TUGOR, TUGAL; FEDAL, FEDAC, SERAN, SERAR; VILAC, VILEL, LINAC, LINAZ; GOTEL, GOTOT, HOGEL, HOGOR; ROCUS, ROCON, FODUS, FODAR; WITAL, WITOR, VIBAL, VIBAC; SYLON, SYLAL, NYBON, NYBAL; LAJOR, LAJAZ, MACOR, MACEL; ROPAZ, ROPOR, TONAZ, TONON.

13

Are There Onset- and Rime-like Units in Printed Words?

Rebecca Treiman
Wayne State University
Detroit, Michigan, U.S.A.
Jill Chafetz
University of Pittsburgh
Pittsburgh, Pennsylvania, U.S.A.

ABSTRACT

An important question for theories of word recognition concerns the nature of orthographic units in printed words and the extent to which these units mirror the phonological units of spoken words. A common assumption is that spoken words are strings of syllables, which in turn are strings of phonemes. This assumption leads to the view that monosyllabic printed words are parsed into units that correspond to phonemes. However, recent work suggests that spoken syllables have a hierarchical rather than a linear internal structure. The syllable consists of an *onset* (initial consonant or cluster) plus a *rime* (vowel and any following consonants). These units are in turn composed of phonemes. Based on this view, we hypothesise that printed words include units that correspond to onsets and units that correspond to rimes. Support for this hypothesis was provided in three experiments. In Experiments 1 and 2, which used an anagrams task, subjects found a word like TWIST more easily when it was divided into TW and IST than when it was divided into TWI and ST. For words with three-consonant initial clusters, like SPREE, a SPR EE division was easier than a SP REE division (Experiment 2). Experiment 3 used a lexical decision task, finding that stimuli with slashes after the initial consonant letters (e.g. CR//ISP) yielded faster response times than stimuli with slashes after the vowel (e.g. CRI//SP). These results support the notion of orthographic units that correspond to the onset and rime units of spoken syllables.

INTRODUCTION

Since the written form of a language represents its spoken form, we might expect the units of the written language to correspond in some way to the units of the spoken language. In particular, the structure of the written word may reflect the phonological structure of the spoken word. Readers may parse written words into orthographic units that correspond to the phonological units of the spoken language. It is often assumed that spoken words are strings of syllables, which in turn are strings of phonemes. If this assumption is correct, then written words should be parsed into units that correspond to syllables and units that correspond to phonemes. For example, the word CONTAIN may be parsed into the letter groups CON and TAIN since each of these groups corresponds to a syllable (e.g. Spoehr & Smith, 1973). Syllable units themselves may be divided into letters and groups of letters that correspond to phonemes. For example, Coltheart (1978), following Venezky (1970), proposes that readers parse a syllable like SHIP into three units—SH, I, and P. The letters S and H are treated as a group because they together correspond to the phoneme /š /.[1] In Coltheart's view, the word SLIP is parsed into S, L, I, and P; SL is not an orthographic unit since the letters S and L each correspond to a phoneme.

The idea that monosyllabic written words are parsed into strings of units that correspond to phonemes is based on the assumption that monosyllabic spoken words are strings of phonemes. If there are no levels of phonological structure intermediate between the syllable and the phoneme, there is no reason for printed words to show intermediate-sized units. However, recent work in linguistics and psycholinguistics suggests that syllables are *not* simply strings of phonemes. Rather, there seems to be at least one level of phonological structure intermediate between the syllable and the phoneme, the level of *onset* and *rime*. The onset of a syllable is its initial consonant or consonant cluster. In English, an onset can contain up to three phonemes. For example, /sɪp/ has the onset /s/, /slɪp/ has the onset /sl/, and /strɪp/ has the onset /str/. The rime is the vowel and any following consonants. The syllables /sɪp/, /slɪp/, and /strɪp/ all have the rime /ɪp/; the syllable /si/ has the rime /i/. Syllables do not necessarily contain an onset (as in the syllable /ɪt/), but the rime is obligatory. Thus, syllables are seen to have an hierarchical internal structure: They are composed of onsets and rimes, which in turn are composed of smaller units. Evidence for the onset/rime division comes from linguistic constraints on the distributions of phonemes within syllables (e.g. Selkirk, 1982), speech errors (e.g. MacKay, 1972), errors in short-term memory for spoken syllables (e.g. Treiman & Danis, in press), and experiments in which subjects manipulate spoken syllables in various ways (e.g., Treiman, 1983; 1986). (For a review of this evidence, see Treiman, in press.) As an example, Treiman (1986) found that subjects prefer to keep onsets and rimes intact; they find novel word games that respect these units easier to

---

[1] Key to notation: /š/ as in *sh*ip, /ɪ/ as in sh*i*p, /i/ as in sh*e*.

learn than those that do not. These results held for words and nonwords and for onsets containing one, two, and three consonants.

If spoken words contain an initial consonantal portion or onset followed by a remainder or rime, written words may contain parallel units. For example, SLIP may have the unit SL, which corresponds to the onset, and IP, which corresponds to the rime. These units in turn consist of units that correspond to phonemes, namely S, L, I, and P. As another example, CONTAIN has the syllable units CON and TAIN, the onset and rime units C, ON, T, and AIN, and the phoneme units C, O, N, T, AI, and N. Our proposal, then, is that written words have several levels of structure. They not only contain units that correspond to syllables and units that correspond to phonemes, but they also contain units that correspond to onsets and rimes.

Patterson and Morton (1985) and Kay and Bishop (this volume) have also postulated orthographic units that correspond to the rimes of spoken syllables. They have called these units *bodies*. According to Patterson and Morton (1985), translation from orthography to phonology involves both letters and letter groups that correspond to phonemes (e.g. S, SH) and vowel plus final consonant sequences (e.g. IP, AIN).

The hypothesis that written syllables contain units that correspond to onsets and units that correspond to rimes makes different predictions from the hypothesis that written syllables contain only phoneme-sized units. In the former view, a word like SLIP contains the multi-letter units SL and IP in addition to the single-letter units S, L, I, and P. In the latter view, a word like SLIP contains only units that correspond to single phonemes (i.e. S, L, I, P). To distinguish between these two hypotheses, Experiment 1 used an anagrams task. In this task, subjects see a string of four groups of letters on a single line—for example, FL OST ANK TR. They judge whether two of the fragments can combine to yield a real word. In the example, FL and ANK form the word FLANK. The word is broken into a portion that corresponds to the onset (FL) and a portion that corresponds to the rime (ANK). On another trial, subjects see the string FLA ST NK TRO. Here, the word is broken after the vowel—a division that does not correspond to the onset/rime boundary. If written words contain onset- and rime-like units, the FL/ANK division should be more natural than the FLA/NK division; subjects should more easily locate the word when it is presented in the former manner. On the other hand, of monosyllabic words contain only units that correspond to phonemes, there is no reason why the FL/ANK division should be easier than the FLA/NK division. In this view, the written word FLANK contains no multi-letter units since each letter stands for a separate phoneme.

EXPERIMENT 1

Method

Stimuli.   Each subject received 216 test trials. A trial consisted of four groups of two or three upper-case letters each, ten letters in all. The letter groups were arranged on a single line with two blank spaces between each of the groups. On *positive* trials, two of the groups of letters could combine to form a real word. On *negative* trials, none of the letter groups could combine to form a real word. There were 144 positive trials and 72 negative trials.

To construct the positive trials, we chose 72 5-letter words. All the words had two consonant letters followed by a vowel followed by two consonants. Phonemically, they were CCVCCs.[2] Examples are FLANK and TWIST. The words were chosen so that neither the initial CC, the final VCC, the initial CCV, or the final CC were themselves real words. The average frequency of the words in the Kučera and Francis (1967) corpus was 20 (range 1–221). The words were divided into 3 sets of 24 such that the sets had approximately the same mean frequency. Each set was further divided into two subsets, A and B. Again, the frequencies of the subsets were were closely equated.

In addition, 288 nonwords were chosen. Like the words, these were spelled with two consonant letters followed by a vowel letter and two consonant letters. They were pronounced as CCVCCs. Examples are PROMP and TROST.

Six different lists of positive trials were arranged. Each list included 12 types of positive trials, which differed in break point, spacing, and order. Break point refers to the way in which the word was divided. On 2/3 trials, the word was divided between the second and third letters, corresponding to the onset/rime division of the spoken word. Thus, FLANK was divided into FL and ANK. On 3/4 trials, the word was divided between the third and fourth letters (e.g. FLA NK). Each word occurred twice per list, once with a 2/3 break and once with a 3/4 break. The positive trials also varied in spacing; that is, whether the fragments that made up the word were one position apart, two positions apart, or three positions apart. In each list, one set of words occurred with each spacing. The assignment of word sets to spacing conditions was counterbalanced across the six lists of positive trials. In each spacing condition, each of the possible combinations of positions was equally frequent. For example, in the one-apart condition the word fragments were placed an equal number of times at positions 1 and 2, 2 and 3, and 3 and 4. Order refers to whether the two fragments that formed a word were arranged in forward order (i.e. the initial CC before the final VCC or the initial CCV before the final CC) or in backward order. The stimuli in subset

---

[2]There was one word that was phonemically CCVC; DRAWN.

A or a given set always occurred in forward order and the stimuli in subset B always occurred in backward order. The two fragments that made up a word occupied two positions in each positive trial; in the other two positions were two fragments of a nonword. The nonword was always divided at the same point (2/3 or 3/4) as the real word. The fragments of the nonword were in forward order for half the trials of each type and in backward order for the remaining trials. The nonword was chosen so that a real word could not be formed by combining a fragment of the nonword and a fragment of the word. Table 13.1 shows sample positive trials of each of the 12 types. Each subject received one list of positive trials.

A single list of 72 negative trials was used for all subjects. These trials were similar to the postive trials but contained no real words. Sample negative trials are shown in Table 13.1. In addition to the test trials, there were 48 practice trials.

Apparatus.   The experiment was run on an Apple II+ computer equipped with a Digitry CTS system that controlled the presentation of the stimuli and the timing of responses. A response box with two buttons labelled "yes" and "no" was used. Subjects' oral responses were tape-recorded.

Procedure.   Each subject was given written instructions explaining the task. The experimenter went over the instructions with the subject. The subject was told to press "no" if no word was present on a trial. If a word was present, the subject was to press "yes" and say the word aloud. The subject then went through the practice stimuli with the experimenter present. One subject had to repeat the practice list before the experimenter was satisfied that he understood the task. Each subject then received 216 test trials

TABLE 13.1
Sample Stimuli for Experiment 1

	2/3 Break	*3/4 Break*
Positive Trials		
One-apart, Forward	SK UNK PR OMP	SKU NK PRO MP
One-apart, Backward	EFT IST TW PL	FT ST TWI PLE
Two-apart, Forward	FL OST ANK TR	FLA ST NK TRO
Two-apart, Backward	PR IBS UNT CR	PRU BS NT CRI
Three-apart, Forward	BL ULK SP OND	BLO LK SPU ND
Three-apart, Backward	ENT OFS SL SP	NT FS SLO SPE
Negative Trials	IPS BR ORD SP	
	CRA LK ST STO	

consisting of 1 list of 144 positive trials intermixed with the 72 negative trials. The order of the test trials was randomly chosen for each subjects.

Subjects.   The subjects were 24 Indiana University students. All subjects in this and subsequent experiments were native speakers of English. Six subjects received each list of positive trials. For half the subjects the right hand was used for "yes" responses and the left hand was used for "no" responses; for the other half the assignment was reversed.

Scoring.   Using the tape-recording of each subject's "yes" answers, the experimenter noted any incorrect "yes" responses; that is, trials on which a subject pressed the "yes" button on a positive trial but said an incorrect word. These mistaken responses (which were less than 1% of all responses) were eliminated from the analyses.

Results

Table 13.2 shows the mean response times for correct responses for each of the 12 types of positive trials and for the negative trials. Also shown are the mean error rates for each trial type.

The response times for correct responses on positive trials were subjected to an analysis of variance for a two (break point) by three (spacing) by two (order) repeated measures design. The main effect of break point was highly significant: $F(1,23) = 82.63$, $P < 0.001$. As the table shows, 3/4 divisions took longer than 2/3 divisions at all spacings for both forward and backward orders. All 24 subjects showed longer response times on 3/4 divisions than on 2/3s. Break point also interacted with order: $F(1,23) = 8.00$, $P < 0.01$. The decrement on 3/4 divisions relative to 2/3 divisions was greater when the words were in backward order than when they were in forward order. The interaction between break point and spacing was not significant: $F(2,46) = 3.14$, $P > 0.05$. In addition, there was a main effect of spacing: $F(2,46) = 9.70$, $P < 0.001$. Words tended to be found more quickly when the fragments were one position apart than when they were two or three positions apart. The main effect of order was not significant: $F(1,23) = 3.92$, $P > 0.05$. Spacing and order did interact significantly: $F(2,46) = 13.55$, $P < 0.001$. There was a strong advantage for the forward order over the backward order when the the word fragments were one position apart, but no such advantage when the fragments were two or three positions apart.

Errors were analysed in the same way as response times. The analysis of the errors again showed a main effect of break point: $F(1,23) = 8.40$, $P < 0.01$. More errors were made when the word was divided at the 3/4 boundary than at the 2/3 boundary. Break point did not interact with any other variable. There was no main effect of spacing: $F(2,46) = 2.74$, $P > 0.05$. However, there

TABLE 13.2
Mean Response Times for Correct Responses and Mean Error Rates
Averaged Across Subjects, Experiment 1

	Mean RT (sec) for Correct Responses	Mean Error Rate (%)
Positive Trials		
One-apart, Forward		
2/3 Break	3.99	12.8
3/4 Break	4.55	12.5
One-apart, Backward		
2/3 Break	4.68	8.3
3/4 Break	6.37	12.2
Two-apart, Forward		
2/3 Break	5.16	16.0
3/4 Break	5.73	22.6
Two-apart, Backward		
2/3 Break	4.28	11.4
3/4 Break	5.63	11.4
Three-apart, Forward		
2/3 Break	5.38	17.3
3/4 Break	5.85	22.6
Three-apart, Backward		
2/3 Break	4.94	5.3
3/4 Break	5.69	10.4
Negative Trials	9.31	3.5

was a main effect of order: $F(1,23) = 23.41$, $P < 0.001$, such that *more* errors were made when the words were in forward order than in backward order. Also, spacing and order interacted: $F(2,46) = 5.33$, $P < 0.01$. The decrement on forward order relative to backward order was largest for words whose parts were three positions apart.

The effect of break point is clear and consistent. Subjects found words more rapidly when they were divided into an initial CC and a final VCC (the 2/3 break) than when they were divided into an initial CCV and a final CC (the 3/4 break). There were fewer errors in the former case than in the latter. The spacing of the word fragments influenced response times, words being found more quickly when the fragments were close together. Spacing had no significant effect on errors. With regard to the factor of order, there appeared to be a trade-off between speed and accuracy. In terms of response times, there was an advantage to the forward order over the backward order when the fragments were one position apart. However, the error rate was higher when the fragments were in the forward order.

The data for positive trials were also analysed across stimuli. We averaged the results for the four subjects who received each list of positive trials and then averaged the results for each word over the six lists. The superiority of 2/3 divisions over 3/4 divisions held in t tests across stimuli for both reaction times ($t[71] = 6.38$, $P < 0.001$, one tailed) and errors ($t[71] = 3.71$, $P < 0.001$, one tailed).

The means in Table 13.2 show that negative trials took longer than positive trials and led to fewer errors. Since the factors of break point, spacing, and order were not systematically varied in the negative trials, performance on these trials was not analysed further.

Discussion

Subjects found a word like FLANK more readily when the word was divided between the initial consonant cluster and the vowel (FL ANK) than when it was divided after the vowel (FLA NK). The *spoken* forms of the words used in this experiment have a boundary between the initial consonant cluster and the remainder; that is, between the onset and the rime. Apparently, the corresponding point in the *printed* word is a natural boundary in the anagrams task. It is conceivable, however, that a division between the second and third letters of a word is easy for some reason that is unrelated to the phonological structure of the word. If so, we should find the same results for words like SPREE as for words like SPILL. If, on the other hand, the phonological structure of the stimulus is crucial, stimuli like SPREE and stimuli like SPILL should behave differently. For stimuli like SPREE, 3/4 divisions should be easier than 2/3 divisions. This is because a division between the third and fourth letters corresponds to a division between the initial consonant cluster or onset and the rime. For stimuli like SPILL, on the other hand, 2/3 divisions should be easier than 3/4 divisions, as found in Experiment 1. Experiment 2 compared performance on stimuli with two-consonant and three-consonant initial clusters. Our hypothesis predicts an interaction between stimulus type—two-consonant initial cluster vs. three-consonant initial cluster—and break point—after the second letter vs. after the third letter.

EXPERIMENT 2

Method

Stimuli.   Each subject received 160 test trials. As in Experiment 1, a trial consisted of four groups of two or three letters each. There were 80 positive trials and 80 negative trials.

The positive trials were based on 20 words spelled with 2-consonant initial clusters (CC words) and 20 words spelled with 3-consonant initial clusters (CCC words). All the words had five letters. The CC words had two consonant letters followed by a vowel followed by two consonants. The consonant letters corresponded to one phoneme (e.g. the SH and LL in SHALL) or two phonemes (e.g. the SC and NT in SCANT). The CCC words were spelled with three consonant letters followed by two vowels (e.g. SPREE) or with three consonant letters followed by a vowel and a consonant (e.g. SPRIG). The three-consonant initial clusters corresponded to three phonemes (e.g. SPR) or two phonemes (e.g. SHR). The words had an average frequency in the Kučera and Francis (1967) corpus of 69 (range 0–782); the CC and CCC words did not differ significantly in frequency.

The negative trials were based on 40 nonwords, half spelled with 2-consonant intial clusters (CC nonwords) and half spelled with 3-consonant initial clusters (CCC nonwords). The nonwords used the same initial clusters as the words. An additional 80 nonwords served as fillers in the positive and negative trials.

Because of the small number of English words with three-consonant initial clusters, it was not possible to ensure that the fragments of each word were nonwords. The final 3-letter fragment (e.g. the RIG of SPRIG) was a word for 16 of the 20 CCC words, while none of the other fragments were words. To ensure that any obtained differences between the CCC and CC words did not reflect a difference in the number of real word fragments, the CC words were chosen such that 16 of the final 3-letter fragments were words. Also, the nonwords on which the negative trials were based were chosen such that the last three letters formed a real word the same number of times.

Two lists of trials, each with 40 positive trials and 40 negative trials, were arranged. For half the stimuli of each type, the stimulus was divided between the second and third letters (a 2/3 break) in List A and between the third and fourth letters (a 3/4 break) in List B. The assignment was reversed for the remaining stimuli. The spacing of the two stimulus fragments and whether the fragments were presented in forward or backward order was randomly chosen for each stimulus. The same spacing and order were used for a given stimulus in both lists. Two fragments of a filler nonword completed each trial. The filler nonword was always divided at the same point as the real word, and the same filler was used with each stimulus in List A and List B. For each stimulus, we randomly chose whether the fragments of the filler nonword appeared in forward or backward order. No real word could be formed by combining the fragments of the filler with the other fragments. Sample positive and negative trials are shown in Table 13.3.

A list of 32 practice trials was also constructed. Since most of the five-letter English words with CCC initial clusters were used in the test stimuli, sufficient words of this type did not remain for the practice stimuli. Therefore, six-letter stimuli with initial CCC and CC clusters (e.g. STRICT,

TABLE 13.3
Sample Stimuli for Experiment 2

	2/3 Break	3/4 Break
Positive Trials		
CC	ILL TH ORF SP	LL THO RF SPI
CCC	RAY TH REB SP	AY THR EB SPR
Negative Trials		
CC	TH OBS OLD ST	THO BS LD STO
CCC	RAB ST SC RIG	AB STR SCR IG

STARCH) were used. The practice trials were in other respects similar to the test trials.

Apparatus.   The apparatus was the same as that of Experiment 1.

Procedure.   The procedure was like that of Experiment 1. Subjects received the practice trials first, followed by the two lists of test trials. A short break was given between the two test lists.

Subjects.   The subjects were 24 Wayne State University students. The order of Lists A and B was counterbalanced across subjects, as was the asignment of hands to "yes" and "no" responses. Two additional subjects were run but were replaced due to very poor performance. These subjects responded "no" on 50% or more of the positive trials. (No subject in Experiment 1 performed at such a low level.)

Scoring.   The scoring was the same as in Experiment 1.

Results

Table 13.4 shows the mean response times for correct responses and the mean error rates for each trial type, averaged across subjects. The data were analysed using both subjects and stimuli as the unit of analysis.

The response time data will be considered first. Both analyses showed a significant interaction between stimulus type (CC or CCC) and break point (2/3 or 3/4): $F(1,23) = 21.28$ across subjects; $F(1,76) = 35.44$ across stimuli; $P < 0.001$ for both tests. Planned comparisons showed that for CC stimuli, 2/3 breaks produced significantly faster responses than 3/4 breaks: across subjects $t(23) = 5.87$; across stimuli $t(39) = 5.24$; $P < 0.001$, one tailed, for both analyses. For CCC stimuli, the planned comparisons showed the

TABLE 13.4
Mean Response Times for Correct Responses and Mean Error Rates
Averaged Across Subjects, Experiment 2

	Mean RT (sec) for Correct Responses	Mean Error Rate (%)
Positive Trials		
CC		
2/3 Break	3.42	14.0
3/4 Break	3.90	17.1
CCC		
2/3 Break	4.02	19.4
3/4 Break	3.72	17.1
Negative Trials		
CC		
2/3 Break	6.97	7.5
3/4 Break	7.66	7.7
CCC		
2/3 Break	7.20	4.8
3/4 Break	6.90	4.4

opposite pattern: 3/4 breaks were significantly faster than 2/3 breaks: across subjects $t(23) = 2.49$, $P < 0.02$, one tailed; across stimuli $t(39) = 2.98$, $P < 0.005$, one tailed. The only other effect to be significant in both the analysis by subjects and the analysis by stimuli was the main effect of trial type (positive or negative). Subjects responded faster on trials that contained words than on trials that did not: $F(1,23) = 101.04$ across subjects; $F(1,76) = 343.50$ across stimuli; $P < 0.001$ for both.

Two effects were significant in the analysis by subjects but not in the analysis by stimuli. The first was the main effect of break point: $F(1,23) = 6.98$, $P < 0.05$ across subjects; $F(1,76) = 2.61$, $P > 0.10$ across stimuli. The trend was for 2/3 breaks to produce faster responses than 3/4 breaks. This trend could reflect the fact that many of the fragments on 2/3 trials were themselves real words, while none of the fragments on 3/4 trials were words. Also, the analysis by subjects showed an interaction between stimulus type (CC or CCC) and trial type (positive or negative): $F(1,23) = 11.47$, $P < 0.005$. The reaction time advantage on positive trials relative to negative trials appeared to be greater for CC stimuli than for CCC stimuli. However, this interaction was not significant in the anslysis by stimuli: $F(1,76) = 1.10$, $P > 0.25$.

The analyses of the error data revealed a main effect of trial type, negative trials producing fewer errors than positive trials: $F(1,23) = 33.67$ across subjects; $F(1,76) = 19.85$ across stimuli; $P < 0.001$ for both. The interaction between stimulus type and break point was significant in the analysis across stimuli: $F(1,76) = 5.32$, $P < 0.05$; but did not reach significance in the analysis across subjects: $F(1,23) = 3.28$, $P > 0.05$. The trend was for 2/3 breaks to produce fewer errors than 3/4 breaks for CC stimuli: across subjects $t(34) = 1.47$, $P > 0.05$; across stimuli $t(39) = 1.92$, $P < 0.05$; both tests one tailed. For CCC stimuli, the apparent advantage for 3/4 breaks was not significant either across subjects: $t(23) = 1.01$; or across stimuli: $t(39) = 1.27$. Finally, the analysis across subjects found an interaction between stimulus type and trial type: $F(1,23) = 4.34$, $P < 0.05$. The error advantage on negative trials relative to positive trials appeared to be greater for CCC stimuli than for CC stimuli. However, this interaction was not significant in the analysis across stimuli: $F(1,76) = 1.05$, $P > 0.30$.

To summarise, Experiment 2 had two main results. First, there was a crossover interaction between break point and stimulus type. For CC stimuli, 2/3 breaks were significantly faster than 3/4 breaks and also seemed to cause fewer errors. For CCC stimuli, on the other hand, 3/4 breaks were significantly faster than 2/3 breaks. Second, negative trials produced slower response times but fewer errors than positive trials.

Discussion

The most important result of Experiment 2 was the interaction between break point and stimulus type. As in Experiment 1, words with two-consonant initial clusters were found more easily when divided after the second letter (e.g. SP ILL) than when divided after the third letter (e.g. SPI LL). With nonwords, as well, decisions were faster given CC and VCC fragments than CCV and CC fragments. A different pattern occurred for stimuli with three-consonant initial clusters. These stimuli showed an advantage for breaks after the third letter (e.g. SPR EE) as compared to breaks after the second letter (e.g. SP REE). The different results for stimuli with two-consonant and three-consonant initial clusters allow us to rule out the hypothesis that divisions between the second and third letters of a five-letter stimulus are always easier than divisions between the third and fourth letters. Rather, the structure of the stimulus determines which division is easier. Subjects perform best in the anagrams task when the units of the printed stimuli mirror the onset and rime units of the corresponding spoken stimuli.

Experiment 3 asked whether the findings in the anagrams task generalise to another task, lexical decision. Do stimuli with slashes between the initial consonant cluster and the remainder (e.g. CR//ISP; TH//ING) have an advantage over stimuli with slashes after the vowel (e.g. CRI//SP; THI// NG)?

EXPERIMENT 3

Method

Stimuli. Words and nonwords spelled with two consonant letters followed by a vowel followed by two consonants were used. In the five-phoneme condition, the consonant clusters stood for two-phoneme sequences, so the pronunciations of the stimuli contained five phonemes. In the three-phoneme condition, each consonant cluster stood for a single phoneme and so the stimuli had three phonemes in their pronunciations. There were 24 words and 24 nonwords in the 5-phoneme condition. Because of the small number of suitable English words, only 12 words and 12 nonwords were used in the 3-phoneme condition. The words in the 2 conditions had an average frequency in the Kučera and Francis (1967) corpus of 245 (range 0–3560). Although the words in the three-phoneme condition tended to be more frequent than the words in the five-phoneme condition, the difference was not significant. The stimuli were presented in upper-case letters. They had two slashes between the second and third letters (a 2/3 break) or two slashes between the third and fourth letters (a 3/4 break). Examples are shown in Table 13.5. For each condition, there were eight additional practice stimuli.

TABLE 13.5
Sample Stimuli for Experiment 3

	2/3 Break	3/4 Break
5-phoneme Condition		
Words	CR//ISP	CRI//SP
Nonwords	FL//UNT	FLU//NT
3-phoneme Condition		
Words	TH//ING	THI//NG
Nonwords	WH//ECK	WHE//CK

Apparatus and Procedure. The experiment was run on an Apple 2+ computer. Subjects were told to ignore the slashes and to press the "yes" button if the letters formed a word and "no" if they did not. The order of the test trials was randomly chosen for each subject. The assignment of hands to "yes" and "no" responses was counterbalanced across subjects.

Subjects. Thirty-four Indiana University students participated in each condition. One subject in the three-phoneme condition responded "no" to all but two stimuli and was replaced with another subject.

Results

Table 13.6 shows the mean response times for correct responses and the mean error rates for stimuli of each type. The response times were analysed using a two (break point) by two (lexical status) by two (number of phonemes) design. The main effect of break point was significant: $F(1,66) = 7.19$, $P < 0.01$; 2/3 breaks produced faster responses than 3/4 breaks. There was also a main effect of lexical status: $F(1,66) = 30.00$, $P < 0.001$. "Yes" responses were faster than "no" responses. No other main effects or interactions approached significance. A t test across stimuli confirmed that 2/3 breaks produced faster responses than 3/4 breaks: $t(71) = 2.32$, $P < 0.02$, one tailed.

TABLE 13.6
Mean Response Times for Correct Responses and Mean Error Rates
Averaged Across Subjects, Experiment 3

	Mean RT (sec) for Correct Responses	Mean Error Rate (%)
5-phoneme Condition		
Words		
2/3 Break	0.849	4.4
3/4 Break	0.892	4.2
Nonwords		
2/3 Break	1.126	5.4
3/4 Break	1.132	5.4
3-phoneme Condition		
Words		
2/3 Break	0.745	13.5
3/4 Break	0.802	14.9
Nonwords		
2/3 Break	0.951	12.0
3/4 Break	0.976	11.3

The only significant effect in the error data was the main effect of number of phonemes: $F(1,66) = 12.57$, $P < 0.001$. There was a higher error rate in the three-phoneme condition than in the five-phoneme condition.

Discussion

The main result of Experiment 3 is that subjects were faster to make lexical decisions for CCVCCs with two slashes after the initial consonant letters than those with two slashes after the vowel. The superiority of 2/3 divisions over 3/4 divisions, previously observed for CCVCCs in the anagrams task of Experiments 1 and 2, appears to generalise to the lexical decision task. Experiment 3 found an advantage for breaks after the initial consonant letters whether these letters corresponded to a single phoneme, as in THING, or two phonemes, as in CRISP. These results suggest that it is not only sequences of letters that represent a single phoneme that are unitised. Letter sequences that correspond to a higher level linguistic unit—an onset or a rime—also seem to be cohesive.

GENERAL DISCUSSION

We have asked whether printed words contain units that are intermediate in size between those that correspond to syllables and those that correspond to phonemes. Given that *spoken* words have at least one level of structure between the syllable and the phoneme—the level of onset and rime—do *printed* words also have such structure? Our results suggest that they do. Subjects performed best in an anagrams task and a lexical decision task when stimuli were divided into letter groups that corresponded to onsets and rimes; groups like syllable-initial TW and syllable-final IST or syllable-initial SPR and syllable-final EE. Orthographic units of this kind seem to be more natural than orthographic units like TWI and ST or SP and REE. The results of Experiments 2 and 3 suggest that nonwords, too, are most easily processed when broken down into units that correspond to onsets and rimes.

Further research is needed to determine whether the present results extend to other reading-related tasks. Some such evidence has recently been found by Taft (Note 1), who ran an experiment in which pairs of nonwords were presented in rapid alternation. Each nonword was presented 20 times for 30msec each time. Subjects were told that the two-letter strings that were being presented in this manner were actually two words, and were asked to identify the words. An example of a nonword pair is BLASS and GROCK. If subjects were analysing these stimuli into onset- and rime-like units, they should report seeing BLOCK and GRASS. On the other hand, if subjects analysed the nonwords into an initial CCV and a final CC, they should report BLACK and GROSS. Another group of subjects saw the pair BLOSS and GRACK. According to the onset/rime hypothesis, these subjects should be more likely to report BLACK and GROSS than BLOCK and GRASS. The results were consistent with the onset/rime hypothesis. Subjects were significantly more likely to report a word like BLOCK given BLASS and GROCK than given BLOSS and GRACK.

We suspect that onset- and rime-like units may be involved in the translation of printed letter strings into phonological representations as well as in visual word recognition. With regard to phonological processes, standard dual process models (e.g. Coltheart, 1978) postulate two methods by which a printed stimulus can be pronounced. The first process involves word-specific knowledge: The pronunciation of the whole stimulus is retrieved from memory. The second process involves spelling-sound rules: The stimulus is first parsed into letters or letter groups that correspond to phonemes; then, spelling-sound rules assign a phoneme to each of the units. Both word-specific knowledge and spelling-sound rules may be involved in the pronunciation of real words, but nonwords must be pronounced via spelling-sound rules. Dual process models, in their strong form, make two major assumptions. First, spelling-sound rules are abstract rules that do not refer to the pronunciations of specific known words. The pronunciation of nonwords is not influenced by knowledge of how particular real words are pronounced. Second, spelling-sound conversion operates only at the level of phonemes. That is, rules are of the form B→/b/ or SH→/š/.

Our results suggest that the second assumption of standard dual process models may be incorrect. Although letters and letter groups that correspond to phonemes may be units at some level, these do not seem to be the *only* units. Letter groups that correspond to onsets and letter groups that correspond to rimes also behave as units. Such letter groups sometimes stand for a single phoneme (e.g. the M and E of ME), and in this case are indistinguishable from phoneme-based units. Often, however, onset and rime groups represent more than one phoneme (e.g. the SL and IP of SLIP).

One alternative to standard dual process models (e.g. Glushko, 1979; Kay & Marcel, 1981) is that the pronunciations of *both* words and nonwords are derived by activating and synthesising the pronunciations of specific known words. Analogy theorists reject the first assumption of standard dual process theory—the assumption that nonwords are pronounced via abstract rules without reference to the pronunciations of specific known words. A critical question for analogy theories concerns the nature of the set of words that is activated upon presentation of a stimulus. For example, GAID might activate words with initial GAI (e.g. GAIN), final AID (e.g. SAID), initial G and final D (e.g. GOOD), and so on. Are words of all types activated equally, or do some possible analogies influence pronunciation more than others? Work within the analogy framework has not addressed this important question systematically, although a priority for vowel plus final consonant units has often been assumed (e.g. Glushko, 1979).

Another alternative to standard dual process theories has been suggested by other researchers (e.g. Baron, 1979; Patterson & Morton, 1985; Shallice, Warrington, & McCarthy, 1983). Their view, which we will call modified dual process theory, rejects the second postulate of the standard theory. Instead of assuming that rules operate only at the level of phonemes, these researchers claim that rules also operate with larger units; units that correspond to more than a single phoneme. An important question for modified dual process theories concerns the types of large-unit rules that are used. Rules are often assumed to operate on vowel plus final consonant segments, but this assumption has rarely been put to empirical test. While recent evidence indicates that initial consonant plus vowel segments may be used in some cases (see Kay, 1985), we would suggest that rules based on vowel plus final consonant segments are more typical.

There has been much debate between proponents of dual process theories (standard or modified) and proponents of analogy theories (e.g. Humphreys & Evett, 1985). We have suggested that both types of theories need to be fleshed out by specifying the units into which written words are parsed. Unless this can be done, the theories are insufficiently constrained and it is difficult to test them experimentally. Once modified dual process theories and analogy theories have been specified further, we suspect—along with Patterson and V. Coltheart (this volume)—that the differences between them will be less consequential than they have appeared.

Going beyond the debate between dual process theories and analogy theories, our results support the general view that the structure of printed English reflects in some detail the phonological structure of spoken English. Spoken words have several levels of structure, including syllables, onsets and rimes, and phonemes. Written words, it appears, have corresponding units.

ACKNOWLEDGEMENTS

This research was supported by NSF Grant BNS 81–09892 and NICHD Grant HD18387 and 20276. Assistance was provided by Cathy Beiser, Peggy Ericson, Bea Gattuso, Shellie Haut-Rogers, Erica Motley, and Martha Powell. Thanks to Max Coltheart, Derek Besner, and another reviewer for their comments.

REFERENCES

Baron, J. (1979). Orthographic and word-specific mechanisms in children's reading of words. *Child Development, 50*, 60–72.

Coltheart, M. (1978). Lexical access in simple reading tasks. In G. Underwood (Ed.), *Strategies of information processing*. London: Academic Press.

Glushko, R. J. (1979). The organisation and activation of orthographic knowledge in reading aloud. *Journal of Experimental Psychology: Human Perception and Performance, 5*, 674–691.

Humphreys, G. W. & Evett, L. J. (1985). Are there independent lexical and nonlexical routes in word processing? An evaluation of the dual-route model of reading. *Behavioural and Brain Sciences, 8*, 689–740.

Kay, J. (1985). Mechanisms of oral reading: A critical appraisal of cognitive models. In A. W. Ellis (Ed.), *Progress in the psychology of language, vol. 2*. London: Lawrence Erlbaum Associates Ltd.

Kay, J. & Marcel, A. (1981). One process, not two, in reading aloud: Lexical analogies do the work of nonlexical rules. *Quarterly Journal of Experimental Psychology, 33A*, 397–413.

Kučera, H. & Francis, W. N. (1967). *Computational analysis of present-day American English.* Providence, Rhode Island: Brown University Press.

MacKay, D. G. (1972). The structure of words and syllables: Evidence from errors in speech. *Cognitive Psychology, 3,* 210–227.

Patterson, K. & Morton, J. (1985). From orthography to phonology: An attempt at an old interpretation. In K. Patterson, J. C. Marshall, & M. Coltheart (Eds.), *Surface dyslexia.* London: Lawrence Erlbaum Associates Ltd.

Selkirk, E. O. (1982). The syllable. In H. Van der Hulst & N. Smith (Eds.), *The structure of phonological representations, Part II.* Dordrecht, Holland: Foris.

Shallice, T., Warrington, E. K. & McCarthy, R. (1983). Reading without semantics. *Quarterly Journal of Experimental Psychology, 35A,* 111–138.

Spoehr, K. T. & Smith, E. E. (1973). The role of syllables in perceptual processing. *Cognitive Psychology, 5,* 71–89.

Treiman, R. (1983). The structure of spoken syllables: Evidence from novel word games. *Cognition, 15,* 49–74.

Treiman, R. (1986). The division between onsets and rimes in English syllables. *Journal of Memory and Language, 25,* 476–491.

Treiman, R. (in press). The internal structure of the syllable. In G. Carlson & M. Tannenhaus (Eds.), *Linguistic structure in language processing.* Dordrecht, Holland: D. Reidel.

Treiman, R. & Danis, C. (in press). Short-term memory errors for spoken syllables are affected by the linguistic structure of the syllables. *Journal of Experimental Psychology: Learning, Memory, and Cognition.*

Venezky, R. L. (1970). *The structure of English orthography.* The Hague: Mouton.

REFERENCE NOTE

1. Taft, M. Personal communication.

14

Nonvisual Orthographic Processing and the Orthographic Input Lexicon

Stephen Monsell
Department of Experimental Psychology
University of Cambridge
Cambridge, U.K.

ABSTRACT

Reading requires access to word-specific knowledge about spelling patterns—an "orthographic lexicon." This paper reports on an attempt to explore the question of whether the orthographic lexicon (or lexica) used during reading is (or are) also accessed during the performance of skills that depend on orthographic knowledge but need not involve visual input. The tasks examined are: (1) writing a defined or spoken word; and (2) identifying a word spelled out letter-by-letter.

The methodology is based on long-term repetition priming. It is first argued that, under *some* conditions, the facilitation of visual recognition by a prior visual encounter with the word can be interpreted as reflecting a persistent change in the accessibility of that word's representation in a lexicon. Given such conditions, one can compare to this visual→visual priming effect the effect produced by a prior nonvisual task requiring access to the word's orthography. If the nonvisual task fails to prime later visual identification, this suggests it does not result in access to the same lexicon. If priming occurs, this is compatible either with the hypothesis that both tasks access the same orthographic lexicon, or with a hypothesis of separate lexica so linked that activation of a word's representation in one can activate its representation in another. The latter hypothesis allows the possibility that there will be conditions under which priming does not occur.

Three experiments on writing are described. In one (already reported elsewhere), writing a word blind in response to a (visual) definition failed to prime a later visual lexical decision. But in two others, writing a spoken word blind while matching it to a (visual) definition did prime later visual lexical decision or semantic categorisation. In combination these conflicting outcomes are, prima facie, compatible only with the hypothesis of separate but linked lexica. However, other aspects of the data suggest that only the first experiment fully met the criteria for a priming effect associated solely with lexical identification.

A final experiment shows that naming an item spelled letter-by-letter primed later visual lexical decision for words (but not for nonwords), suggesting that this task does activate the lexicon used for reading.

INTRODUCTION

To read text it is necessary to access orthographic knowledge—knowledge about the spelling patterns of our language. Some of this knowledge concerns submorphemic correspondences between spelling and sound (see papers on "phonological processes" in this volume). But readers of scripts in which a high proportion of words cannot be pronounced by rule, such as English, must somehow also store a large number of word-specific spelling patterns. Hence the concept of an *orthographic input lexicon*. Once the concept has been admitted, there is no reason to deny that this lexicon must represent the spelling pattern of all adequately familiar words, regardless of whether their pronunciations can or cannot be derived from sublexical spelling→sound correspondences. Otherwise, we would be forced to make the implausible assumption that the mechanism responsible for learning spelling patterns performs a test of orthographic regularity before the learning process is enabled.

Elsewhere in this volume, there are papers addressing the nature of the orthographic lexicon used in reading, the nature of the process of lexical access, and the relative contribution of a "direct" lexical route and a sublexical "phonological assembly" route to the pronunciation and/or identification of printed words. This paper addresses a different question: To what extent is the orthographic lexicon used in reading a mechanism (or a component of a mechanism[1]) *specific to the processing of visual input*? There are skills other than reading that rely on access to orthographic knowledge: Two in particular will be examined in this paper. The first is writing; the second is our ability to identify words when they are spelled aloud—"letter-by-letter identification."

Hence the main theme of this paper is whether word-specific orthographic knowledge is represented in the head just once in a general-purpose lexicon, or is replicated in more than one use-specific lexica. I introduce the theme by noting two opposed a priori principles (or prejudices) with which one might approach this issue.

---

[1] In only 5000 years or so of literacy, man cannot have evolved brain mechanisms specialised for identifying letter strings per se. Hence our ability to identify orthographic patterns must be parasitic on our ability to identify complex and abstractly specified patterns in general. The question remains: Is this ability embodied in a mechanism specific to the processing of these patterns as visuo-spatial *input*?

Representational Parsimony.   Word-specific spelling-patterns are, in an obvious sense, *the same* for reading, writing (typing, spelling), and letter-by-letter word identification. To some it seems unparsimonious to suppose that this knowledge is replicated, and must be separately acquired, in functionally distinct subsystems (cf. Allport & Funnell, 1981).

Procedural Parsimony.   Spelling patterns are not merely *represented* in the head; they must be *represented-for-use*. Information processing seems to be accomplished in the brain largely by specialised processing modules: Each performs a certain kind of transformation upon its input, and has encapsulated within it the knowledge it needs to do so, organised in a manner appropriate for that transformation. It may well be computationally more straightforward to organise knowledge of orthographic patterns in one way for mapping visual input onto them, and in a quite different way for generating them from meaning. An analogy. Consider the standard organisation of a French–English dictionary: The same word↔word correspondences are duplicated in the French→English section and the English→French section. Why the duplication? In order to provide simple addressing procedures for *access* to the information for each direction of translation.

The representational parsimony principle reflects what may be called a "declarative" view of the lexicon; it assumes that word-form knowledge can readily be represented in a *use-independent* way. The alternative is a "procedural" view, in that word-form knowledge is embodied (only?) within specialised transcoding procedures. The contrast between the two raises a question which should briefly be acknowledged before we proceed. I have referred to the necessity for assuming that we use in reading *an* orthographic lexicon. But is one enough, even for reading? "Boxes-and-arrows" diagrams of the functional anatomy of the lexicon, especially those expressed within the British "logogen" tradition, tend to contain a box labelled something like "visual input logogens" (Patterson & Shewell, 1986) or "orthographic (lexical) codes" (Funnell & Allport, 1987). Visual input is mapped both to meaning and to pronunciation via this one box. How does such a diagram deal with neuropsychological evidence for a double disssociation between access to meaning and access to pronunciation from printed words (see Coltheart, 1985, for review)? The patients must be interpreted as having disconnections between the box containing spelling patterns (represented in function-neutral—i.e. "declarative"—manner) and meaning representations on the one hand, or phonological representations on the other; i.e. word-form representations are preserved, but one of two access pathways *from* them is impaired. In the alternative, "procedural" idiom, we would be said to possess two (distinct) transcoding procedures, one for converting spelling patterns to pronunciation and one for mapping spelling patterns onto meaning. These procedures appear to be anatomically dissociable. *Each* procedure independently incorporates lexical knowledge in transcoding-specific form: That is, we have *two* orthographic lexica for reading. However, while these alternative conceptions may influence the framing of theoretical possibilities (cf. discussion in Monsell, 1987), it is not yet clear (at least to me) whether these two conceptions of lexical knowledge can have distinguishable empirical consequences.

These subtleties aside, the question to be asked is: Do nonvisual tasks making use of word-specific orthographic knowledge involve access to the orthographic lexicon (or lexica) used for reading? (To avoid the awkward singular/plural hedge I shall henceforth refer to this lexicon—or these lexica—as "the OL(R).") How can the question be asked empirically? We need a measure that will tell us whether a word's "entry" in the OL(R) is accessed as a consequence of processing that word in the nonvisual task under consideration. The basic test used in the present experiments is: Does processing the word in a nonvisual, but orthographic, task facilitate a later test of visual identification for that word? I now review the rationale for this test.

REPETITION PRIMING

Various tasks requiring identification of a *visual* word—namely, lexical decision (LD) time (Scarborough, Cortese, & Scarborough, 1977), naming time (Scarborough et al., 1977), syntactic or semantic categorisation time (Monsell, 1985) and tachistoscopic report accuracy (Clarke & Morton, 1983; Jacoby, 1983)—show facilitation from a prior *visual* encounter with the same word, even though repetitions are unexpected and occur after a lag of tens of minutes occupied by the processing of hundreds of other words. The mechanism of this long-term priming effect is a matter of controversy. Whatever the detailed mechanisms of lexical access, we can distinguish four logically necessary steps in producing an observable response to a visual word via the OL(R) (see Fig. 14.1):

1. Formation of a pre-lexical orthographic description of the input sufficiently abstract that the same word written in different typefaces, scripts, and—probably—cases is reduced to an equivalent description.
2. Finding the best match between this (temporary) description of the input and those (permanently) stored in the OL(R).
3. Retrieving the associated attributes (phonological, semantic, syntactic) required by the task.
4. Mapping the retrieved attributes to the overt response specified by the task set: which button to press, what to say, etc.

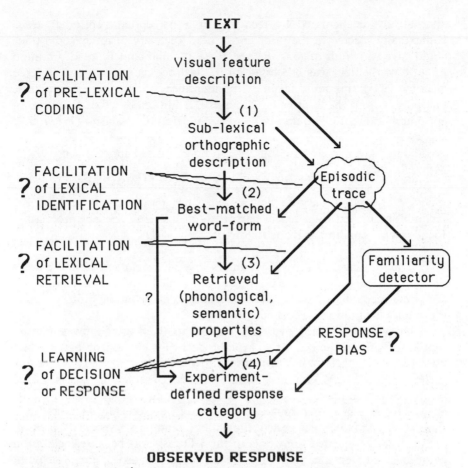

FIG. 14.1. Possible loci of repetition priming effects with respect to a lexical processing pathway.

(Logically speaking, the lexical decision task could skip the third step. However, semantic properties of a word [James, 1975] and its semantic congruence with sentential context [Forster, 1981] both influence LD time, suggesting that the duration of step 4 may be *influenced* by step 3, whether step 3 is or is not a precursor of step 4.)

Suppose that we observe—as many have—that visual LD time is facilitated by a previous visual encounter with the word in the lexical decision task. Such a priming effect could be associated with any of the four processing steps (or more than one). Moreover, there is debate about whether the effect (at whatever level it operates) derives from a persisting but noncontext-preserving "ahistoric" change of state in lexical pathways, or, alternatively, is mediated by recovery of a perceptual "episodic" trace contextually specific to the prior encounter. Recovery of an episodic trace could have two kinds of consequence. First, it could contribute information about how the item was processed on the last occasion it was encountered (Jacoby, 1983); this could facilitate the identification, retrieval, or response mapping steps I have already discussed. Additionally, the detection of episodic "familiarity" could, as Feustel, Shiffrin, and Salasoo (1983) have suggested, bias a lexical decision towards the response: "word." These possibilities are depicted in Fig. 14.1 (and discussed more extensively in Monsell, 1985).

My strategy has been to try to find conditions which—at least some-times—allow me to argue that at least the major component of the facilitation enjoyed by a repeated word is at a *lexical* level of processing. Ideally, these conditions are as follows:

1. The priming and probe encounters involve *unrelated tasks*. It cannot then easily be argued that the priming effect is due to the subject *learning* on the prime encounter what *decision or response* to make on the probe task; i.e. it excludes facilitation associated with step 4.[2]

2. Nonwords repeated over lags similar to the words show either no significant priming effect, or a rapidly decaying effect, while the effect observed for words is stable. Such a result would appear to rule out a purely prelexical locus (step 1) for any facilitation effect observed for words. Either result would also make it hard to argue that the repetition effect for words derives from a bias to respond "word" to an episodically familiar item. Feustel et al. (1983) suggested that the (commonly observed) lack of facilitation for repeated nonwords in the LD task was because facilitation enjoyed by any repeated item (from repetition of nonlexical components of processing) was, for a repeated nonword, cancelled out by the bias against responding "nonword" to an episodically familiar stimulus. But it is implausible that so nice a balance of independent after-effects would apply over a wide range of lags. Moreover, episodic familiarity decays, and repetition priming attributable to a response bias caused by episodic "fami-liarity" should decay symmetrically: A decreasing inhibitory effect for nonwords should be matched by a decreasing facilitatory effect for words, regardless of whether additional facilitatory effects of repetition are super-imposed upon the bias.

Next, there is evidence to suggest that repetition priming of lexical decision is not due purely to repeated retrieval of the same attributes (i.e. step 3):

---

[2]One should not neglect the possibility that Task A provides opportunity and incentive for *incidental* learning of the decision or response appropriate to Task B.

1. Several authors have reported failure to obtain long-lasting priming of visual LD in bilinguals from a prior encounter with a noncognate word of the same meaning in the other language (e.g. Kirsner, Smith, Lockhart, King, & Jain, 1984). This is contrary to what one might expect if the facilitation derived from the act of retrieving/activating a specific word-sense per se.

2. Lexical decision is facilitated by prior visual encounter with the word either in a "semantic" task, or by prior naming. In the latter case, there is as much facilitation as from a prior lexical decision (Monsell and Banich, Note 1, Experiment 1).

Both findings suggest that (under these restricted conditions) the effect of repetition on lexical decision time is associated with *lexical identification*, i.e. the process of matching to or accessing the word-form representation, rather than the retrieval of some specific set of attributes. In contrast, the "deeper" tasks of semantic and syntactic categorisation may involve a task-specific component. Monsell (1985, Experiment 4) compared long-lag repetition priming across and within orthogonal syntactic (adjective/noun) and semantic (nice/nasty) classification tasks. The repetition effect observed was substantially, though not completely, task-specific, though it was not clear whether this task-specificity was due to repeated retrieval of the same subset of attributes or to learning of a particular decision. A further indication of the task-specificity of repetition priming of semantic categorisation will be provided by Experiment 2 in the present paper.

What about the "ahistoric" vs. "episodic" nature of the LD repetition effect? If it can be demonstrated that, under the conditions used, the effect on LD has a *lexical* locus (steps 2 or 3), with some evidence favouring lexical identification (step 2), then we can go ahead and use it as a measure of whether access to the OL(R) has occurred. We do not need to resolve the thorny issue of whether the effect is mediated by a contextually nonspecific after-effect, or by recovery of an episodic trace. It does not matter whether finding the best match in the OL(R) is facilitated by something like a change in the sensitivity of a "logogen" or "word detector," or by recovery of an "episodic trace" that somehow tells you which word this is (rather than what to do about it) (Jacoby, 1983).

Thus, the basic research strategy is to determine whether visual lexical decision time is primed by a prior encounter with the word in the nonvisual task under consideration. If the nonvisual encounter produces substantial priming (assessed in comparison to a suitable visual priming task) it can be argued that the nonvisual task has *resulted in* access to the OL(R). It cannot yet be concluded that the nonvisual task *requires* access to the OL(R). One possibility for distinguishing "resulted in" from "requires" would be to determine whether the priming effect can somehow be blocked under some conditions, while it occurs under others.

PRIMING OF READING BY WRITING?

When we write, we visually monitor the output, partly for visual guidance of the hand and partly to check the orthographic output. Normally, therefore, writing involves reading. To exclude this relatively uninteresting route for activation of the OL(R), subjects in the present experiments were required to write "blind"—that is, with their hand and the paper upon which they wrote concealed from view.

There are three broad classes of theory about the relationship between the orthographic lexica used in reading and writing:

1. *"Independent lexica" theories*: These assume separate pathways: (a) from visual analysis to meaning and/or pronunciation; and (b) from meaning and/or pronunciation to graphemic output, each pathway having its own "lexicon" (e.g. Ellis, 1982; Patterson & Shewell, 1986). The two pathways are linked via meaning, and also via sublexical connections from input to output, to enable letter-by-letter copying and tracing. On such an account, there is no reason to expect writing a word blind to prime later visual identification (assuming that priming is localised in access to the OL(R)).

2. *"Common lexicon" theories*: These assume a single lexicon of ortho-graphic word-forms accessed both for identification of those word-forms and for generation of them (e.g. Allport & Funnell, 1981; Coltheart & Funnell, 1987). If access to a particular word-form facilitates later access to that *same* word-form, then writing a word ought *always* to prime later identification of it.

3. *"Separate-but-linked lexica" theories*: These supplement an independent lexica model with a sublexical pathway from graphemic output to graphemic input. (The one "lexical anatomy" paper I know of that actually depicts such a loop—albeit with no explicit justification—is that of Newcombe and Marshall, 1980). This output→input loop may be seen as the orthographic analogue to, and might serve functions similar to those suggested for, a "sub-vocal" or "phonological" output→input loop (see Monsell, 1987, for discussion). These functions include: efference copy (to ready perceptual systems for, or stabilise them against, the sensory consequences of motor output); internal spelling checks (of to-be-written output against OL(R) word-forms); and rehearsal and manipulation of an orthographic "image". Indeed, this loop might be but one aspect of a general imagery system or "visuo-spatial sketch-pad" (Baddeley & Lieberman, 1980; Kosslyn, 1980). According to this class of theory, generating an orthographic word-form in the output pathway *can* prime later visual identification through activating the OL(R) in the pathway via the output→input loop. But this priming may not be obligatory. That is, activation via the output→input loop may be *optional* or *blockable* (depending on its default state). Thus it seems possible in principle to distinguish the three models.

Before we attempt to do so, I need to take issue with Allport and Funnell's (1981) claim that priming of visual recognition by writing is not *necessarily* predicted by a common lexicon model. They suggest that priming of lexical identification may be located in the pathways of "access" from case-independent visual letter units to word-units, and that different pathways are activated for access *from* the same word-units to graphemic output units. However, what this means seems to depend on how "word-units" are construed. If as logogens (as in Allport & Funnell, 1981), then this is really a two-lexicon model, since orthographic lexical knowledge is represented twice, in two independent sets of connections which can be activated separately: those from visual letter units onto logogens, and those from logogens onto graphemic output units. On the other hand, consider the common lexicon view expressed within a parallel distributed processing (PDP) framework of the kind favoured by Allport (1985) and Funnell and Allport (1987). There is a common domain of orthographic (O) feature elements. There exists a matrix of interconnections from visual (V) to O elements, another matrix from O to graphemic output (G) elements, one from O to semantic (S) elements, and another from S to O elements. There is also a matrix of auto-associative interconnections among the orthographic feature elements: These can be visualised as a set of overlapping "cats' cradles," each of which represents an orthographic word form. Translated into this idiom, the Allport and Funnell (1981) argument now plays as follows. Priming of word identification reflects a change in the weights of the V→O connections, not the O↔O interconnections. It therefore does not influence the spread of activation via the S→O→G pathway during word production. But this seems problematic for two reasons. First, nonword repetition should produce a priming effect (whether positive or negative) as robust as that for words, because nonwords as well as words will activate, and thus change the weights of, V→O connections. Second, and especially in the light of the explicit treatment of repetition effects within the PDP framework by McClelland and Rumelhart (1985), the idea that the auto-associative O↔O connections should be immune to having their strengths changed by experience of orthographic input, while the strengths of V→ O connections are modified, seems unreasonable: Such a system would not *learn* word-forms!

The Monsell and Banich (M&B) Experiment

I first tried the proposed test in collaboration with Marie Banich, in an experiment I will refer to as "the M&B experiment" (Monsell & Banich, Note 1, Experiment 2). After some practice blocks, subjects received 6 blocks, each consisting of 20 priming trials followed by 48 visual lexical decision trials.

The priming trials were of four kinds, all of which occurred, in a random sequence, in each block. All involved display of a sentence with a missing word, such as "Swan Lake is a famous ———," or "A rolling stone gathers no ———."

1. On a SEE trial, one second after the sentence appeared, a word was displayed below it (in upper case), and the subject pressed a key to indicate whether the word fitted into the frame. (Only words which did fit were later used as probe items.)
2. On a HEAR trial, one second after the sentence appeared, the subject heard a word and pressed a key to indicate whether it fitted the frame.
3. On a WRITE trial, the subject wrote the missing word blind (in upper case). The sentences had been pretested to ensure a near 100% success rate.
4. On a SAY trial, the subject spoke the missing word.

Immediately after the priming trials, 48 visual (lower-case) items were presented for lexical decision in a random sequence. The words included eight new items and four from each priming condition, half repeated across a lag of at least three minutes, half over a shorter lag. (Items were rotated around conditions over subjects.) In order to avoid the confounding of repetition and lexical status, nonwords were also repeated, some within sequences of lexical decisions, some across adjacent blocks, and some from the practice blocks. The results for words are depicted in Fig. 14.2a. Only the SEE priming condition resulted in significant facilitation of visual LD time. Hearing or saying the word had no detectable effect. This reinforces the presupposition that the effect observed for SEEN words is indeed associated with an *orthographic* mechanism isolated from phonological processing. Secondly, words previously written blind were responded to an insignificant 5msec faster than novel words. Even if taken seriously this effect is only 18% of the priming effect observed for SEEN words. This would appear to be prima facie evidence against the common lexicon class of models.

The nonword data in Fig. 14.2b support the claim that this is an after-effect located at a strictly lexical level of processing. Repetition of nonwords had no significant effect overall, nor was this absence of effect modulated by repetition lag. Also, the priming observed for words did not decrease with lag. (Nor did it matter whether the subject lacked [during the first experimental block] or possessed [during the remaining blocks] grounds for expecting that items might be repeated, so the effect is not a product of actively expecting repetitions.)

The lack of priming of visual LD by writing blind is compatible both with independent lexica and with separate-but-linked lexica. In terms of the latter, it might be hypothesised that, although there exists a sublexical output→

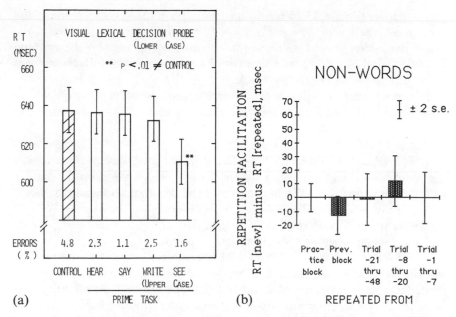

FIG. 14.2.   Lexical decision data from the Monsell and Banich (Note 1) experiment. (a) Word trials: Mean correct RT and error rate. (b) Nonword trials. Mean facilitation due to repetition at various lags (i.e. mean correct RT for a given lag subtracted from mean correct RT for comparable unrepeated items). (Standard errors over subjects.)

input loop for activating the OL(R) by writing, activation via this route was in this experiment discouraged or somehow blocked. Indeed there was a plausible source of such inhibition: the continued display, while the subject wrote the target word, of the sentence frame used to evoke the target.

Experiment 1

My next experiment was intended first to replicate this failure of blind writing to prime reading, and secondly to determine whether this lack of effect depended, as I have just suggested, on the concurrent processing of text other than the target word. Subjects were now required to write a heard or seen word blind, either with or without concurrent display of a definition to which they had to compare the word.

The 24 subjects first experienced 4 blocks of priming trials. Each block involved a different writing condition, the order of blocks being counter-balanced by means of a Latin square. In each block, 24 words were primed. (That these words would later be repeated was carefully concealed from the subjects.) The subject was then given 3 practice blocks of 41 visual lexical

APPR–K*

decision trials containing no repetitions. Finally, in the "probe" phase of the experiment, there were 6 more blocks of LD trials. In each half of the probe phase there were presented 12 words encountered in each of the priming conditions and 24 new words, along with 24 new nonwords and 24 nonwords repeated from the LD practice blocks.

In every priming condition, the subject wrote a word blind as quickly as possible while deciding whether it matched a definition. The four conditions were:

1. HEAR & WRITE (+ TEXT). The subject heard the experimenter say the word, and then 0.5sec after its onset saw the definition on the screen, where it remained while the subject wrote the word and decided whether it matched the definition. This condition was intended to be like the WRITE condition in the M&B experiment, in that the subject was required to write one word while other words were visually present.

2. HEAR & WRITE (+ SPEECH). The subject heard the experimenter say the word and then the definition. While writing the word, the subject fixated a cross in the centre of an otherwise blank screen. This condition was intended to test whether priming of reading by writing had been suppressed in M&B's experiment by the concurrent presence of other textual input.

3. SEE & WRITE (+ SPEECH). The word to be written was displayed for 1.2sec. Coincident with its onset, the subject heard the definition read aloud. This condition, which must activate the OL(R), and in which priming is therefore expected, was intended as one benchmark against which to compare any priming in the first two conditions.

4. SEE & WRITE (+ TEXT). The word to be written and the definition were displayed at the same time, one above the other. After 1.2sec the word was removed from the display while the definition remained. This condition was intended as a second benchmark, to allow for the possibility that concurrent display of text might "dilute" any priming effect of seeing the target word.

The timing of auditory events, although approximate,[3] was adequate to ensure that the definition was being presented while the subject was writing or just about to write. The definitions were such as to make the decision straightforward, but false definitions were constructed to force attention to the whole definition. (E.g. CHOIR—"a band of trained singers and acrobats.") When the subject had finished writing the word, he marked a tick or a cross to indicate whether the word did or did not match the definition. The writing and decision were to be accomplished as quickly as possible. Subjects

---

[3]The experimenter timed the onset of his speech with the aid of a pair of beeps from the computer used to display the visual material and record responses.

printed each word in upper-case letters on a small square of paper. After writing, they used their other hand to move the top sheet of paper to a collection box where it could be seen by the experimenter. A barrier prevented the subject from seeing the papers or their writing hand at any time. On the LD trials, the subject saw a vertical fixation arrow, which was followed after a half a second by the letter string displayed above it in lower case, with the left-most letter aligned with the arrow; the subject then responded with a key press.

The vocabulary included 144 words, between 1 and 15 per million in frequency (according to Kucera & Francis, 1967). To enable the same words to be used in Experiment 2, these were concrete nouns: a set of 72 "animate" nouns (person or animal names) and a set of 72 "inanimate" concrete nouns, matched in frequency. A high proportion of the words involved sound-spelling correspondences sufficiently unpredictable that a purely nonlexical spelling strategy would have been error-prone. Each set of 72 comprised 24 4-letter monosyllabic words, 24 5-letter words, and 24 6-letter disyllabic words, each divided into 6 groups matched for frequency and rotated around the conditions over the 24 subjects so that every combination of item assignment and order of priming conditions occured just once. For each word a true and a false definition of between 6 and 11 words (35 to 55 characters) was written. Half the words were primed with true and half with false definitions. The vocabulary also included 96 phonologically and orthographically legal nonwords matched to the words in length, and rotated around repetition conditions.

Results and Discussion.   LD to a primed word was no quicker when the word had matched the definition on the priming encounter than when it had not (547 vs. 544msec; $F = 1.2$), nor did this interact with priming condition. Figure 14.3a shows the LD data averaged over this variable, but separately for the two halves of the probe phase of the experiment. (Repetition in the second rather than the first half implies a somewhat longer lag.) There was a significant priming effect for both correct RT: $P < 0.01$, $F(4,80) = 4.0$; and error rate: $P < 0.05$, $F(4,80) = 3.5$. The priming effect was stable: It did not interact with half, nor with the order of priming conditions. A test of pairwise differences showed that only two prime conditions, HEAR & WRITE (+ TEXT) and SEE & WRITE (+ TEXT), were significantly faster than the control condition.

By itself, this outcome would be perfectly compatible with a common lexicon theory: Blind writing primed later visual LD. But the outcome is also completely at variance with that of the M&B experiment. They found no priming from their WRITE condition, while the most similar condition in the present experiment, namely HEAR & WRITE + TEXT, produced the largest priming effect! In fact, the amount of priming in the present experiment

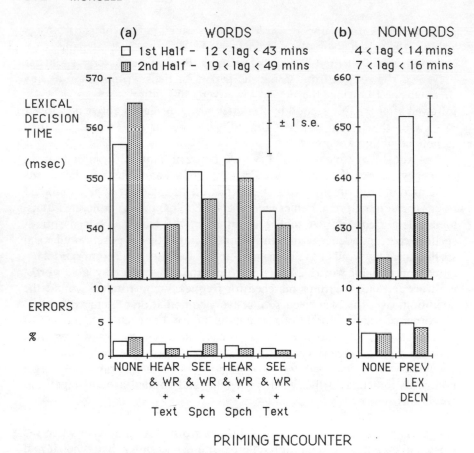

FIG. 14.3.   Mean correct lexical decision time and error rates for Experiment 1.

appears to depend not so much on whether the subject saw or heard the critical word as on whether the subject saw or heard the definition. If they heard the definition, even the effect of seeing the target word was relatively weak. It seems that, crudely speaking, the more "attention" was diverted to process *speech*, the less priming of the OL(R) occurred. However, that will not resolve the conflict between the HEAR & WRITE conditions of the present study and the WRITE condition of M&B's study, since the latter involved no speech. Apart from the possibility that one or the other result is a statistical fluke, there seem to be two possible explanations:

1. A "separate-but-linked lexica" theory is correct, and there exists a route via which writing *can* activate the OL(R)—but it does not *automatically* do so. Under the conditions of Experiment 1 this route was activated;

under the conditions of the M&B experiment it was not. Why? Perhaps because the present experiment imposed a much heavier processing load during the priming condition (in that subjects had simultaneously to write to dictation and process a definition). This might have induced subjects to try to exploit the temporary storage capacity provided by the sublexical output →input loop. Further research is obviously needed to explore this and other possibilities.

2. Unlike the M&B experiment, Experiment 1 picked up something other than a pure lexical identification facilitation effect. Here the nonword data are relevant. As Fig. 14.3b shows, in the present experiment there was a systematic effect of repeating nonwords. LD was significantly *slower*—by 12.2msec—for repeated nonwords than for new nonwords ($P < 0.001$). This effect was somewhat weaker at the longer lag, but not significantly so ($F < 1$). An inhibitory effect of repetition for nonwords suggests the presence of a response bias due to episodic "familiarity," as suggested by Feustel et al. (1983). However, it seems unlikely that the whole of the repetition effect for words can be attributed to this response bias. The word effect was larger than the nonword effect and, if anything, increased with lag; the repetition lags for words were substantially longer; the words were, unlike the nonwords, repeated across tasks.

It is an unfortunate property of the lexical decision task that being "familiar" is correlated with belonging to one response category. For this reason I conducted a very similar experiment using semantic categorisation as the probe task instead of lexical decision. Regrettably, the result merely contributes additional puzzlement, and I will describe the experiment, briefly, more because of what it says about repetition priming than for its contribution towards resolving the main issue.

Experiment 2

The priming phase of the experiment was (apart from minor details of timing) the same as that of Experiment 1, save for one condition. The SEE & WRITE (+TEXT) condition was replaced by one identical to the HEAR & WRITE (+SPEECH) condition, with the additional feature that, after writing, the subject took the piece of paper from under the barrier and looked briefly at what was written on it. (The idea was that the effect of looking at one's own writing might be a better benchmark than looking at print for assessing the effects of writing blind.) There then followed 2 practice blocks (with no repetitions) and 6 probe blocks of 25 semantic categorisation trials. The repetition of words in the probe blocks followed the design of Experiment 1. The subject pressed one key if the word was an *animate* noun—i.e. described a person or animal—and another if it described an *inanimate* thing.

The same words and definitions were used as in Experiment 1. (Data for a few words which proved problematic with respect to this categorisation—e.g. GERM, CLAM, HIVE—were excluded from the analysis.)

Results and Discussion.   Average correct reaction time (error rate) in this task was 626msec (1.7%) for "animate," and 675msec (1.4%) for "inanimate" words, as compared to 552msec (1.6%) for lexical decisions to the same words in Experiment 1. There was significant priming (i.e. a comparison of 4 types of priming encounter and the control yielded a significant main effect, $P < 0.05$, $F(4,80) = 3.1$). However, as Fig. 14.4 shows, the amount of facilitation depended both on response category and on whether the word matched the definition on the prime trial. A by-subjects ANOVA on the facilitation effects (mean difference between each primed condition and the appropriate control) yielded significant effects of response category: $P < 0.05$, $F(1,20) = 6.1$; match/mismatch x type of priming encounter: $P < 0.05$, $F(3,60) = 3.6$; and the three-way interaction of these: $P < 0.05$, $F(3,60) = 3.3$.

The most striking observation is that clear facilitation was observed only for the "animate" response category. But it is implausible that "inanimate" decisions were made by default: The distributions of mean RTs for animate and inanimate words show considerable overlap. Two interpretations seem possible:

1. There was, superimposed on a rather small (but universal) priming effect, a subtle response bias, such that detection of "familiar" biased towards the response "matches the animate category." For the inanimate category this bias cancelled out the advantage due to the facilitation of lexical identification by priming.

2. The priming effect observed in this task cannot be associated with lexical identification (step 2 in Fig. 14.1). Instead the priming effect is located at a later stage: retrieval of the appropriate attributes (steps 3 or 4 in Fig. 14.1). Why should such priming occur only for animate words? Definitions of the animate words, both true and false, tended to be of the form "CAMEL— a desert *animal* with [one or two humps/a large body and wings]." The priming trials could thus have served to reinforce the knowledge that these words were members of the (natural) categories "animal" or "person." In contrast, the inanimate words' definitions were not such as to train the subject explicitly in the membership of the arbitrary and negative category "inanimate thing" or "not a person or animal." However, granting this account, why should the semantic categorisation task not *also* enjoy the benefits of priming of lexical identification enjoyed by lexical decision and naming? The "procedural" view of lexical representation I sketched earlier hypothesised distinct lexical pathways for orthography→pronunciation, and for orthography→meaning transcoding. Could priming of "lexical identifi-

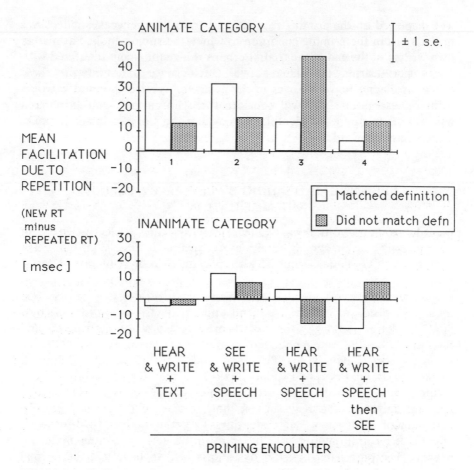

FIG. 14.4.   Facilitation of semantic categorisation time resulting from the four types of priming encounter in Experiment 2.

cation" be restricted to the orthography→pronunciation pathway? If it is, then it should not influence a task performed using only the orthography →meaning pathway. It is plausible that animate/inanimate classification is such a task, while naming and lexical decision depend (at least in part) on the orthography→pronunciation procedure.

Interesting though such speculations may be to repetition priming buffs, they provide no further enlightenment on the reading/writing question. There were not clear differences between the two conditions in which the subject wrote the word without seeing it, whether with text (9.4msec priming effect overall) or without (13.7msec), and the condition in which the word was displayed on the priming trial (18.2). Strangely, the weakest effect was obtained from the priming condition in which the subject looked at his/her own writing at the end of the trial. (Perhaps this requirement interfered with the category-learning postulated above?) But since we cannot interpret these effects as diagnostic of changes in the accessibility of orthographic word-form representations, we will consider them no further, and turn from writing to letter-by-letter identification, where the story so far is, happily, more straightforward.

PRIMING OF READING BY LETTER-BY-LETTER IDENTIFICATION?

Identification of a word from a sequence of letter-names is clearly dependent on the skills of literacy. Its main use in everyday life is probably the encryption of communications between parents of not-yet-literate children. But this tells us little about how it is accomplished. Theoretical speculation about this skill seems to have been restricted to discussions of acquired dyslexia. Indeed, some dyslexic patients appear able to read words *only* by a "letter-by-letter" strategy—the "word-form dyslexics" of Warrington and Shallice (1980), the "letter-by-letter" readers of Patterson and Kay (1982).

One theory, favoured by Patterson and Kay (1982) and Coltheart, Masterson, Byng, Prior, and Riddoch (1983), is that letter-by-letter identification is accomplished via the orthographic input lexicon used for normal reading. Patterson and Kay suggest that, instead of the normal parallel matching of a string of letter identities to orthographic word-forms in OL(R), letter information can be transmitted serially to the matching process. The pure letter-by-letter dyslexic is held to have lost the normal process of parallel access, but retains the serial access process; hence the appearance of strong word-length effects in such a patient. Coltheart et al. (1983) observed that typical "surface dyslexic" errors occur in patients not only when they read, but also when words are spelled out to them; this suggests a common mechanism.

An alternative theory, first proposed by Warrington and Shallice (1980) and more explicitly stated by Shallice and McCarthy (1985), says that letter-by-letter reading is not accomplished via the OL(R) but is instead parasitic upon a separate "spelling" system (presumably that normally used for writing, typing, etc.). They propose that one can assemble a list of letter names in (phonological) short-term memory, and then, via a somewhat mysterious process called "reverse spelling," match it to an entry in the "spelling system" and retrieve its name. Word-form dyslexics have an impairment of the OL (R) or access to it, and must thus resort to "reverse spelling."

The repetition priming methodology outlined here would appear to offer a straightforward, although asymmetric, test between these two theories. If letter-by-letter identification is accomplished by access to entries in the OL(R), albeit by a slow serial strategy, then later visual LD should be primed. But if letter-by-letter identification of a word is *not* accomplished via the OL(R), then it would be possible to observe no priming of later visual LD for the intact word-form.

The experiment also manipulated the number of letters per word, motivated by the following conjecture. One might activate the OL(R) from discrete letter-identities by constructing an orthographic "image" whose contents then activate (in parallel) matching lexical word-forms. But it is universally agreed that the representational capacity of the image "buffer" (Kosslyn, 1980), the "schematic short-term visual memory" (Phillips, 1974) or the "visuo-spatial sketch-pad" (Baddeley & Lieberman, 1980) is severely limited. However, there appears to be little information available to specify this capacity in terms of letter forms. Posner and Taylor (1969) found that the advantage of physically over nominally identical stimuli found in same-different comparisons of single characters applied only to the first two or three characters of multi-character arrays. It might be inferred that only a very limited number of distinct letter forms can be represented simultaneously, and this would be compatible with the lack of visual confusion errors in visual memory span tasks (Conrad, 1964).

Experiment 3

The design was similar to the previous experiments. Thirty subjects experienced 3 priming conditions, in each of which 48 items (half words, half nonwords) were primed. The priming conditions, whose order was counterbalanced, were:

1. V-WORD. The subject named a word or nonword displayed in upper case in the centre of the screen (for 200msec).
2. V-SPELL. A fixation asterisk and then the letters of the word were displayed one-by-one in the centre of the screen at a rate of one per 1.2sec (200msec on, 1000msec off). Immediately following offset of the final letter a 50msec beep cued the subject to name the item as quickly as possible.
3. A-SPELL. Just like the V-spell condition except that instead of the subject seeing the letters, the experimenter read them aloud to the subject, who was blindfolded (to minimise distracting visual input).

Subjects were led to believe that naming RT was the focus of the experiment.

However, after the 3 priming conditions, the subject received instructions for and then performed 2 practice blocks (30 trials each) and 6 probe blocks (40 trials each) of visual lexical decision trials. The 240 items presented for lexical decision in the probe blocks comprised in equal proportion 6-letter words, 3-letter words, 6-letter nonwords, and 3-letter nonwords. All were monosyllabic. The words were nonhomophonic nouns or verbs. The 3- and 6-letter words had a similar distribution of frequencies, ranging from 1–10 per million (Kucera & Francis, 1967), and of concrete and abstract items. The nonwords were orthographically and phonologically legal and included no pseudohomophones. Each group of 60 items was divided into 5 matched sets of 12. One set was assigned to each priming condition and two used as non-repeated controls (distributed evenly over the six priming blocks). These assignments were rotated over the five subjects assigned to each order of priming conditions, so that each item served equally in every condition.

Results.   Mean correct RT and error rates for the lexical decision trials are shown in Fig. 14.5. Consider first the word data. There was a significant effect of priming condition both on mean correct RT: $P < 0.001$, $F(3,72) = 15.5$, by subjects; $P < 0.001$, $F(3,354) = 23.1$, by words; and on error rates: $P < 0.001$, $F(3,72) = 12.0$, by subjects; $P < 0.001$, $F(3,354) = 12.9$, by words. Pairwise comparisons (based on the by-subjects analysis) indicated that performance on words primed in each of the naming tasks was significantly faster ($P < 0.01$) and more accurate ($P < 0.05$) than nonrepeated control words. The only other significant ($P < 0.05$) pairwise difference was between the RTs for the V-WORD and A-SPELL conditions.

Hence the main outcome is clear: Both letter-by-letter identification tasks produced substantial and significant priming of visual LD, though the RT effect was weaker than that obtained from naming the intact word. The after-effect was stable, in that the effect of prime condition did not interact with the order of prime conditions ($F < 1$). Error rates were quite high, but partitioning the data into those derived from words more and less error-prone than the median indicates that the RT effects were just as strong for words on which errors were almost never made.

The repetition effect appears roughly twice as large for the longer words. This interaction falls just short of significance: $F(3,72) = 2.7$. It is nevertheless sufficient to refute the prediction from my "imagery conjecture"—that letter-by-letter priming would be less effective for long words.

Does the repetition effect observed for words meet my criteria for *lexical identification* priming? No significant effects of priming were obtained for nonwords: $F(3,72) = 1.8$. Nevertheless, a small inhibitory priming effect can be discerned in the mean data (see Fig. 14.5). This might be taken to support the influence of a "familiarity bias" as suggested by Feustel et al. (1983). However, since the effect is small, a response bias could account for, at best, a minor component of the facilitation observed for words. Moreover, the inhibitory priming of nonwords was largely limited to short items, whereas the facilitatory effect observed for words was much stronger for the longer words.

Discussion. My conclusion is therefore that letter-by-letter identification of words *does* activate the orthographic lexicon normally used for reading. Further, either this activation does not require simultaneous "imaging" of the whole letter string, or six letters is well within the capacity of this system. We do not then need to resort to Shallice and McCarthy's "reverse spelling" process to account for letter-by-letter reading in normal people, nor, possibly, in letter-by-letter dyslexic readers.

Two caveats. First, it remains possible that letter-by-letter identification does not *require*, but only *results in*, activation of the OL(R). Presumably such epiphenomenal activation would be assumed to occur via an output→

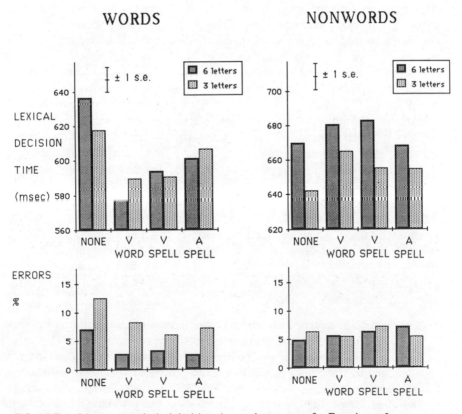

FIG. 14.5.   Mean correct lexical decision time and error rates for Experiment 3.

input loop of the kind posited by the separate-but-linked lexica model. This interpretation would leave us dependent on the mysterious "reverse spelling" process, but it cannot be refuted without further data.

Secondly, subjects in the letter-by-letter conditions may well have used a sublexical phonological assembly strategy to pronounce the words, in addition to trying to "see the item in the mind's eye." A few "regularisation" errors were observed for words. My assumption, that it is "inner seeing" rather than "inner hearing or pronouncing" that causes the priming of visual LD, depends upon the finding in the M&B experiment (see also Monsell, 1985, Experiment 1; Clarke & Morton, 1983) that visual identification is not primed by previous auditory or articulatory processing of the word in a different task. Ideally, Experiment 3 should be repeated with an additional priming condition in which the subject hears the whole word.

CONCLUSIONS

This paper is a progress report on a line of research in which I attempt to exploit a particular technique—repetition priming—to ask whether and how mechanisms used to access word-specific orthographic knowledge in reading are involved in the performance of other "orthographic" tasks. Data from the M&B experiment (in which the attribution of priming to the process of lexical identification seems most secure) suggest that it is *possible* to write a word without activating the orthographic lexicon used in reading. The priming of reading by writing observed in Experiments 1 and 2 could be due to the (optional) exercise of a sublexical output→input loop, and/or reflect other types of repetition priming. Experiment 3 indicates that identifying a word from its spelling activates the OL(R), but whether this is *necessary* for performance of the task I cannot yet say.

Firmer conclusions would at present be premature. This is in part because we do not yet possess adequate understanding of or control over the priming phenomena upon which the method rests. Is this line of research, then, a bramble-infested cul-de-sac from which a prudent explorer should retreat? One would do so with relief if superior pathways to the truth were clearly in prospect. Other lines of attack on the relation between reading and writing currently being explored include:

The search for neuropsychological associations or dissociations between reading and writing impairments (Coltheart & Funnell, 1987).

Investigation of whether words consistently misspelled by a person are judged by them to be misspelled when presented visually (Campbell, in press).

Investigation of whether reading can be shown to provide an independent check of spelling (cf. Tenney, 1980).

Use of dual tasks, along the lines developed by Shallice, McLeod, and Lewis (1985) for the domain of speech: Can one read and write different words at the same time, as separate lexica might allow?

I have no space to review these other approaches here, but I hope it will not be interpreted as a slur on the considerable ingenuity and rigour of my fellow explorers if I remark that at present the brambles seem equally dense elsewhere in this thicket!

ACKNOWLEDGEMENTS

This research is supported by a project grant from the Science and Engineering Research Council. Experiments 1 and 2 were conducted with the able assistance of Michael Doyle. Experiment 3 was run as an undergraduate research project by Vivienne Fowler and Pam Sherwin, to whom I am grateful for agreeing to my description of it here. I thank Max Coltheart, Elaine Funnell, and an anonymous reviewer for their comments on a draft.

REFERENCES

Allport, D. A. & Funnell, E. (1981). Components of the mental lexicon. *Philosophical Transactions of the Royal Society of London, B295*, 397–410.

Allport, D. A. (1985). Distributed memory, modular subsystems, and dysphasia. In S. Newman & R. Epstein (Eds.), *Current perspectives in dysphasia*. Edinburgh: Churchill Livingstone.

Baddeley, A. D. & Lieberman, K. (1980). Spatial working memory. In R. S. Nickerson (Ed.), *Attention and performance VIII*. Hillsdale, N.J.: Lawrence Erlbaum Associates Inc.

Campbell, R. (in press). One or two lexicons for reading and writing words; can misspellings shed any light? *Cognitive Neuropsychology*.

Clarke, R. & Morton, J. (1983). Cross-modality facilitation in tachistoscopic word recognition. *Quarterly Journal of Experimental Psychology, 35A*, 79–96.

Coltheart, M. (1985). Cognitive neuropsychology and the study of reading. In M. I. Posner & O. S. M. Marin (Eds.), *Attention and performance XI*. Hillsdale, N.J.: Lawrence Erlbaum Associates Inc.

Coltheart, M., Masterson, J., Byng, S., Prior, M., & Riddoch, J. (1983). Surface dyslexia. *Quarterly Journal of Experimental Psychology, 35A*, 469–495.

Coltheart, M. & Funnell, E. (1987). Reading and writing: One lexicon or two? In D. A. Allport, D. G. Mackay, W. Prinz, & E. Scheerer (Eds.), *Language perception and production: Relationships among listening, speaking, reading, and writing*. London: Academic Press.

Conrad, R. (1964). Acoustic confusions in immediate memory. *British Journal of Psychology, 55*, 75–84.

Ellis, A. W. (1982). Spelling and writing (and reading and speaking). In A. W. Ellis (Ed.), *Normality and pathology in cognitive functions*. London: Academic Press.

Feustel, T. C., Shiffrin, R. M., & Salasoo, A. (1983). Episodic and lexical contributions to the repetition effect in word identification. *Journal of Experimental Psychology: General, 112*, 309–346.

Forster, K. I. (1981). Priming and the effects of sentence and lexical contexts on naming time: Evidence for autonomous lexical processing. *Quaterly Journal of Experimental Psychology, 33A*, 465–495.

Funnell, E. & Allport, D. A. (1987). Nonlinguistic cognition and word meanings: Neuropsychological exploration of common mechanisms. In D. A. Allport, D. G. Mackay, W. Prinz, & E. Scheerer (Eds.), *Language perception and production: Relationships among listening, speaking, reading, and writing*. London: Academic Press.

Jacoby, L. L. (1983). Perceptual enhancement: Persistent effects of an experience. *Journal of Experimental Psychology: Learning, Memory, and Cognition, 9*, 21–38.

James, C. T. (1975). The role of semantic information in lexical decisions. *Journal of Experimental Psychology: Human Perception and Performance, 1*, 130–136.

Kirsner, K., Smith, M. C., Lockhart, R. S., King, M. C., & Jain, M. (1984). The bilingual lexicon: Language-specific units in an integrated network. *Journal of Verbal Learning and Verbal Behaviour, 23*, 519–539.

Kosslyn, S. (1980). *Image and mind*. Cambridge, Mass.: Harvard University Press.

Kucera, H. & Francis, W. N. (1967). *Computational analysis of present-day American English*. Providence, R.I.: Brown University Press.

McClelland, J. L. & Rumelhart, D. E. (1985). Distributed memory and the representation of general and specific information. *Journal of Experimental Psychology: General, 114*, 159–188.

Monsell, S. (1985). Repetition and the lexicon. In A. W. Ellis (Ed.), *Progress in the psychology of language, Vol. 2*. London: Lawrence Erlbaum Associates Ltd.

Monsell, S. (1987). On the relation between lexical input and output pathways for speech. In D. A. Allport, D. G. Mackay, W. Prinz, & E. Scheerer (Eds.), *Language perception and production: Relationships among listening, speaking, reading, and writing*. London: Academic Press.

Newcombe, F. & Marshall, J. C. (1980). Transcoding and lexical stabilisation in deep dyslexia. In M. Coltheart, K. Patterson, & J. C. Marshall (Eds.), *Deep dyslexia*. London: Routledge & Kegan Paul.

Patterson, K. E. & Kay, J. (1982). Letter-by-letter reading: Psychological descriptions of a neurological syndrome. *Quarterly Journal of Experimental Psychology, 34A*, 411–441.

Patterson, K. E. & Shewell, C. (1986). Speak and spell: Dissociations and word-class effects. In M. Coltheart, R. Job, & G. Sartori (Eds.), *Cognitive neuropsychology of language*. London: Lawrence Erlbaum Associates Ltd.

Phillips, W. A. (1974). On the distinction between sensory storage and short-term visual memory. *Perception and Psychophysics, 16*, 283–290.

Posner, M. I. & Taylor, R. L. (1969). Subtractive method applied to separation of visual and name components of multi-letter arrays. *Acta Psychologica, 30*, 104–114.

Scarborough, D. L., Cortese, C., & Scarborough, H. S. (1977). Frequency and repetition effects in lexical memory. *Journal of Experimental Psychology: Human Perception and Performance, 3*, 1–17.

Shallice, T. & McCarthy, R. (1985). Phonological reading: From patterns of impairment to possible procedures. In K. E. Patterson, J. C. Marshall, & M. Coltheart (Eds.), *Surface dyslexia*. London: Lawrence Erlbaum Associates Ltd.

Shallice, T., McLeod, P., & Lewis, K. (1985). Isolating cognitive modules with the dual-task paradigm: Are speech perception and production separate processes? *Quarterly Journal of Experimental Psychology, 37A*, 507–532.

Tenney, Y. J. (1980). Visual factors in spelling. In U. Frith (Ed.), *Cognitive factors in spelling.* London: Academic Press.

Warrington, E. K. & Shallice, T. (1980). Word-form dyslexia. *Brain, 103*, 99–112.

REFERENCE NOTE

1. Monsell, S. & Banich, M. T. (in preparation). *Repetition priming across modalities and the functional anatomy of the lexion.*

IV EYE MOVEMENTS AND READING

15 Eye Movements in Reading
A Tutorial Review

Keith Rayner and Alexander Pollatsek
University of Massachusetts
Amherst, Massachusetts, U.S.A.

ABSTRACT

A large body of research dealing with eye movements in reading is reviewed. The introduction contains a brief historical review of eye movement research followed by a brief discussion of the basic characteristics of eye movements in reading. The remainder of the review is in two main sections. In the first, the focus is on what is known about the role of eye movements in reading (i.e. the role of eye movements in the intake of visual information from the printed page). In the second, the focus is on the use of eye movements to understand the underlying cognitive processes in reading. We argue that understanding eye movements in reading requires an understanding of cognitive processing in reading and vice versa and that there has been significant recent progress in both these areas. We also compare eye movements as a measure of on-line processes in reading to other popular techniques.

INTRODUCTION

The study of reading by experimental psychologists has a rich tradition dating back to work reported by Huey (1908). It is interesting to note that following his introductory chapter, Huey's second and third chapters were entitled *The work of the eye in reading* and *The extent of reading matter perceived during a reading pause*, respectively. The next two chapters likewise appeal on numerous occasions to eye-movement data to adjudicate between alternative positions concerning word recognition processes. Experimental work reported by Dearborn, Dodge, Javal, Huey, and their contemporaries formed the basis for much of what we know about the basic characteristics of eye movements during reading. It is a tribute to these early researchers that their findings, often obtained with what now seem to be relatively crude and cumbersome types of apparatus and recording techniques, have held up when replicated with far more sophisticated equipment.

Following the seminal work by Huey and his contemporaries, eye movements in reading were intensively studied by Buswell, Tinker, and others. While a great deal of information was gathered about eye movements during this period, in retrospect the work does not seem as informative about basic processes in reading as does the earlier work. Undoubtedly, the fact that Buswell and Tinker worked during the peak of the behaviourist era in experimental psychology contributes to this feeling. Tinker's (1958) final review in the *Psychological Bulletin* ends on the rather pessimistic note that almost everything that could be learned about reading from eye movements (given the state of technology at the time) had been discovered. Perhaps that opinion was widely held, because between the late 1950s and the mid-1970s little research on eye movements and reading was undertaken.

Since the mid-1970s, however, we have been in the middle of a third era of eye-movement research in which a great deal more has been learned about reading from eye-movement data (Rayner, 1978a). This resurgence has been partly due to improvements in eye-movement recording systems, which have allowed measurements to be more accurate and more easily obtained. Perhaps more importantly, it has been due to the interfacing of computers with eye-movement recording systems. This combination has allowed large amounts of data to be collected and analysed and has also allowed for innovative techniques such as having the visual display contingent on the position of the eyes. In addition, the development of more detailed theories of language processing has allowed psychologists to use eye-movement records for a critical examination of the cognitive processes underlying reading.

In this resurgence of interest in eye movements in reading, there have been two somewhat different foci. The first has been in using the task of reading as a means to study the role of eye movements in visual cognition. It is widely believed that a major reason for eye movements in general is to bring new areas of the visual field into the fovea, where the ability to process detail is more acute. Since fairly continual eye movements are necessary in reading to bring new words in or near the fovea, reading may be an ideal situation in which to study basic processes of oculomotor control in vision. On the other hand, it may be the case that reading may be special and the way eye movements are controlled in reading does not generalise to other situations in visual cognition. The second focus has been in using eye movements to reveal important aspects of the process of reading. Many current researchers have hoped that the movement of the eyes would serve as an ideally unobtrusive measure of ongoing cognitive processes in reading and other visual tasks—a window to the mind. Although some research has focused on eye movements per se while other research has focused on eye movements as a tool for understanding reading, most researchers have been interested in both since you clearly can't understand one without the other.

In this review we will first discuss (rather cursorily) some of the basic characteristics of eye movements in reading. We will then discuss a number of issues about eye movements that are endemic to understanding what the eyes do in reading. Finally, we will focus on issues related to what eye movements can reveal about the processing of language.

BASIC CHARACTERISTICS OF EYE MOVEMENTS IN READING

Most of the basic facts about eye movements during reading have been known since Huey's time. When we read, our subjective impression is that our eyes move smoothly across the page. However, this is an illusion, since we actually make a series of rapid eye movements called *saccades*, separated by fixational pauses that last about 200–250msec each. Virtually all new information is extracted from the text during these fixational pauses (Wolverton & Zola, 1983). The function of the saccade is to move the eyes rapidly from one position to another, with the average saccade length being about 7–9 character positions, or a bit over one word. We will use character spaces as the metric for saccades since the number of characters traversed by saccades is relatively invariant when the same text is read at different distances, even though the character spaces subtend markedly different visual angles (Morrison, 1983; Morrison & Rayner, 1981; O'Regan, 1983; O'Regan, Levy-Schoen, & Jacobs, 1983). (However, fixation time increases somewhat when the visual angle subtended by a letter is appreciably smaller than in normal reading.)

It is obvious that the primary function of a saccade is to bring a new region of text into foveal vision for detailed analysis, since reading on the basis of only parafoveal and peripheral information is difficult to impossible (Rayner & Bertera, 1979). While a majority of the words in a text are fixated during reading, many words are skipped so that foveal processing of each word is not necessary. For example, Carpenter and Just (1983) reported that when their subjects read technical material, they fixated on 83% of the content words and 38% of the function words. In addition, word length influences the probability that a word is skipped (see Table 1). Readers do not relentlessly go forward, however, and about 10–15% of the saccades in normal reading are *regressions*. It is generally believed that the two most common reasons for regressions are either that the reader has not understood some part of the text or that a saccade was a bit longer than intended and the reader has to make a corrective movement.

While we have cited averages of fixation durations and saccade lengths,

TABLE 15.1

Frequency of Fixating on a Word and Probability of Fixating on a Word as a Function of Word Length

	Number of Characters in Word														
	1	*2*	*3*	*4*	*5*	*6*	*7*	*8*	*9*	*10*	*11*	*12*	*Sp^a2*	*Sp^b*	*$Punc^c$*
Frequency of Fixating the Word	0.081	0.233	0.341	0.505	0.642	0.846	0.963	0.997	1.073	1.167	1.259	1.424	0.144	0.156	0.053
Probability of Fixating the Word	0.077	0.201	0.318	0.480	0.588	0.724	0.792	0.817	0.851	0.922	0.920	0.973	0.120	0.140	0.053

[a]Spaces between words
[b]Spaces between sentences
[c]Punctuation marks

SOURCE: Data are taken from Rayner and McConkie (1976).

the variability of both measures is of greater interest (see Fig. 15.1). For an individual reader, fixation durations typically range from under 100msec to well over 500msec, while saccades typically vary from 1 letter position to 15 letter positions. The average fixation duration, average saccade length, and frequency of regressions not only vary from reader to reader, but vary with text difficulty; more difficult text leads to longer fixations, shorter saccades, and more regressions. A point of crucial importance for our present purposes is that the variability in these measures is not only useful as a global index of the difficulty of the text or the skill of the reader; it can also be used to study moment-to-moment cognitive processes "on-line." There is, of course, a purely motoric component to this variability as well. For example, even when spatial and temporal uncertainty about where and when to move are eliminated, there is still variability in the latency of eye movements (Arnold & Tinker, 1939; Rayner, Slowiaczek, Clifton, & Bertera, 1983; Salthouse & Ellis, 1980). Similarly, there is variability in where the eye lands even when a fixed target is given (Coeffe & O'Regan, 1987). While this "noise" of motoric variability makes it more difficult to interpret the cognitive "signal" in the eye-movement record, the discussion below will make clear that the signal is there and that great strides have been made in understanding reading and the cognitive control of eye movements. We first turn to work that has as its focus the acquisition of visual information during reading and the role of eye movements in that skilled perceptual act.

EYE MOVEMENTS AND THE ACQUISITION OF VISUAL INFORMATION IN READING

In this part of the review, we will discuss three basic issues: (1) the size of the perceptual span; (2) how information is integrated across saccades; and (3) the control of eye movements in reading. While the research touches on linguistic issues, chiefly lexical access, the primary focus is on the acquisition of visual information.

Perceptual Span

How much useful information do we obtain from the text during each fixational pause of the eyes? While many different types of techniques have been used to estimate the size of the effective field of view or the *perceptual span* in reading, most have severe limitations and will not be discussed here (see Rayner, 1975; 1978a; 1984 for detailed discussion). Instead, we will focus on the "moving window" technique developed by McConkie and Rayner (1975), which provides the most definitive information about the size of the perceptual span.

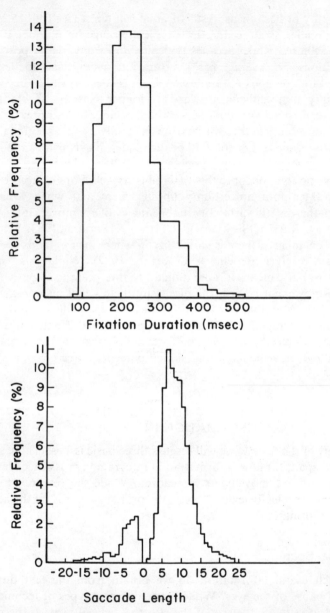

FIG. 15.1.   Frequency distribution of fixation duration (upper graph) and saccade length
(lower graph) for college-age readers reading easy text. Return sweeps of the eye have been
excluded from the saccade length distribution as have regressions back to earlier lines. Short
fixations following return sweeps and fixations under 75msec have been excluded.

The moving window technique utilises on-line eye-movement recording systems to record subjects' eye movements in order to present text on a computer-controlled visual display contingent upon where the reader is fixating. In particular, characteristics of the text are mutilated except for an experimenter-defined *window region* around the reader's point of fixation. Wherever the reader looks, the original text is visible, while outside of the window area the text is mutilated in some way. Readers are free to move their eyes whenever and wherever they wish, but the amount of useful information that is available on each fixation is controlled by the experimenter. Each time the reader moves his or her eyes, a new region of text is exposed while the region previously fixated is mutilated. In some experiments using this technique the text is mutilated outside of the window only on selected fixations. For example, in the *boundary technique* developed by Rayner (1975), a single critical word in a sentence or paragraph is altered. When the reader's saccade crosses over a prespecified boundary location in the text before the critical word location, the altered word is restored. Alternatively, in a technique developed by McConkie and Zola (1979), a single critical word in a given target location alternates back and forth with each saccade between two different words. Finally, in a variation of the boundary technique introduced by McConkie and Hogaboam (1985), the text is masked (or simply removed) following a given saccade and the reader must report the last word that was read. The results of studies using these various techniques have been very consistent. Figure 15.2 shows examples of these techniques.

A large number of studies (DenBuurman, Boersma, & Gerrissen, 1981; Ikeda & Saida, 1978; McConkie & Rayner, 1975; Pollatsek, Rayner, & Balota, 1986; Rayner, 1986; Rayner & Bertera, 1979; Rayner, Inhoff, Morrison, Slowiaczek, & Bertera, 1981; Rayner, Well, Pollatsek, & Bertera, 1982) have been consistent in indicating that the size of the perceptual span is relatively small. Research suggests that the perceptual span extends from the beginning of the currently fixated word but no more than 3–4 letters to the left of fixation (McConkie & Rayner, 1976; Rayner, Well, & Pollatsek, 1980; Underwood & McConkie, 1985) to about 15 letter positions to the right of fixation (DenBuurman et al., 1981; McConkie & Rayner, 1975; Rayner, 1986; Rayner & Bertera, 1979; Rayner et al., 1981). Thus, the perceptual span is asymmetric to the right for readers of English. However, for readers of right-to-left orthographies like Hebrew, the perceptual span is asymmetric to the left of fixation (Pollatsek, Bolozky, Well, & Rayner, 1981). Research on children has found that one year of reading instruction results in an asymmetric perceptual span for beginning readers (Rayner, 1986). The perceptual span was, however, about 25% smaller for beginning readers than for adults.

While the results of various studies seem to be consistent with respect to the size of the perceptual span, there are some slight differences evident in the

APPR-L

```
The fluent processing of words during silent reading        Normal text
```

```
XXXXXXXXXXprocessing ofXXXXXXXXXXXXXXXXXXXXXXXXXXXXXXX
              .
XXXXXXXXXXXXXXXssing of wordXXXXXXXXXXXXXXXXXXXXXXXXX
                       .
```
13-character
window (spaces
filled)

```
XXX XXXXXX processing of XXXXX XXXXXX XXXXXX XXXXXXX
              .
XXX XXXXXX XXXXXssing of wordX XXXXXX XXXXXX XXXXXXX
                   .
```
13-character
window (spaces
preserved)

```
XXX XXXXXX processing of XXXXX XXXXXX XXXXXX XXXXXXX
              .
XXX XXXXXX XXXXXXXXXX of words XXXXXX XXXXXX XXXXXXX
                   .
```
2-word
window

```
The fluent processing of green during silent reading       Boundary
                   .                                       technique
1he fluent processing of words during silent reading
```

FIG. 15.2.   Examples of techniques used to study the perceptual span. The top example shows a normal segment of text. The second and third examples show 2 fixations using the moving window paradigm: The window size is 15 letter spaces. The fourth example is a moving window with the window defined by number of words visible instead of number of letters visible. In the boundary technique example, during the reader's saccade, the target word (*words*) replaces the initially presented stimulus (*green*). In the variation used by McConkie and Hogaboam, as soon as the reader's saccade leaves the word *processing*, the entire line of text is masked and the reader is asked to report the last word read.

research concerning the types of information obtained within the field of effective vision. Although results of a number of studies (Ikeda & Saida, 1978; McConkie & Rayner, 1975; Rayner, 1986) indicate that word length information is acquired further to the right of fixation (out to about 15 letter positions) than is letter information, the estimates of how far from fixation letter information is obtained vary somewhat. To some extent, the differing estimates are probably related to the fact that there is some variability in how much letter information is processed per fixation (Rayner, 1984; 1986). However, the different estimates obtained appear also to be due to different measures being used to assess the region of letter processing. Using a window technique in which letters beyond the window were mutilated on selected fixations, Underwood and McConkie (1985) found that erroneous letters lying eight or more letter positions to the right of fixation had no significant effect on either the current fixation duration, the ensuing saccade length, or the subsequent fixation duration. When Pollatsek et al., (1986) used the boundary technique, they found that the first fixation duration on the target word was unaffected when the erroneous letters were more than eight letter positions from fixation. However, the *gaze duration* (the total fixation time on a word before another word is fixated) on the target word was influenced by letters at least nine characters from fixation. Thus, we see that the particular measure one uses as a dependent variable can influence the conclusions reached.

Is the size of the perceptual span for letters better thought of in terms of the number of letters or the number of words? The answer appears to differ to the left and right of fixation. Rayner, Well, et al. (1980) demonstrated that the left boundary of the perceptual span was primarily defined by the beginning of the fixated word, although it never appeared to extend more than four letters to the left of fixation. In contrast, Rayner et al. (1982) found that the right boundary of the perceptual span was primarily defined in terms of number of letters. When they compared reading performance when the window was defined in terms of number of letters available to the right of fixation with reading performance when the window was defined by the number of words to the right of fixation, there was no difference between "word window" conditions and "letter window" conditions when they were roughly equivalent in average size. More importantly, detailed analyses of the data revealed that performance in the word window conditions (in which word integrity was maintained) could be predicted very accurately from knowing the number of letters available on each fixation, while performance in the letter window conditions could not be predicted from knowing the number of words available on each fixation. Since the acquisition of letters is thus not tied to words being intact, these results suggest that readers acquire partial word information from parafoveal vision.

Further evidence that readers utilise partial word information from parafoveal vision comes from another study reported by Rayner et al. (1982). They asked readers to read text when: (1) only the word fixated was available and all other letters to the right of fixation were replaced by another letter (a *one-word window*); (2) the word fixated and the word to the right of fixation were available and all other letters were replaced by another letter (a *two-word window*); or (3) the word fixated was available and partial information about the word to the right of fixation was available. In the third condition, either one, two, or three letters of the word to the right of fixation were available on each fixation. When the first three letters of the word to the right of fixation were available and the remainder of the letters were replaced by visually similar letters, reading rate was not much different from when the entire word to the right was available. Experiments reported by Lima and Inhoff (1985) and Lima (1987), examining fixation time on a target word, also found that the amount of time that a reader looked at the word decreased when the first three letters of the word were available on the prior fixation (in comparison to a condition in which the first three letters were not available on the prior fixation).

While a number of other experiments (Inhoff & Rayner, 1986; Pollatsek et al., 1986; Rayner, 1975) are consistent with the conclusion that partial word information is obtained parafoveally, McConkie, Zola, Blanchard, and Wolverton (1982) reported an experiment which led them to conclude that information used to identify a word is obtained only on the fixation on which the word is completely identified. That is, a word can either be identified parafoveally or foveally, but partial word information is not obtained. In their experiment, the letters in a target word location alternated with each eye movement so that, for example, *bears* changed to *peaks* after a saccade and then back to *bears* after the following eye movement. The fixation duration on the target word was 10msec longer in the alternating condition than in a control condition in which the letters in the target location did not alternate back and forth (a nonsignificant difference). After reading each sentence, subjects were required to make forced choices indicating which words they identified as they read. Subjects generally indicated that they had read only one of the target words and they did not perceive words such as *beaks* which were combinations of the beginning letters of the target word (when it was parafoveally available) with other letters following the saccade. On the basis of a failure to find such "illusory conjunctions" of letters and a lack of significant interference due to changing letters, McConkie et al. (1982) concluded that partial word information is not obtained parafoveally.

However, more recently Balota, Pollatsek, and Rayner (1985) reported a similar experiment which provides evidence for partial word information being obtained parafoveally. They used the boundary technique described earlier and initially presented visually similar or dissimilar nonwords which changed to the target word when the reader's saccade crossed the boundary. Balota et al. found that the duration of the first fixation on the target word was 14msec shorter when the initially presented stimulus was visually similar than when it was dissimilar to the target word (a significant difference). However, when gaze duration was examined, the difference between visually similar and dissimilar conditions was much greater (32msec). Since several experiments have found significant effects of partial word information (Balota et al., 1985; Lima, 1987; Lima & Inhoff, 1985; Rayner, 1975; Rayner et al., 1982), we can conclude that the use of partial word information is likely to be a general phenomenon and that the failure of McConkie et al. to find significant effects from changing letters may be due to insufficient power in their experiment. On the other hand, their finding that subjects do not combine letters viewed on the two fixations is important, since it indicates that the visual information in all letter positions of fixated words is at least examined unless the word was completely identified in the parafovea.

In concluding this section, we would like to make three points about letter processing within the perceptual span region. The first is that it is probably appropriate to think about different types of processing spans. While letters are processed in the area 3–4 letter spaces to the left of fixation to 6–10 (or perhaps even more on some fixations) letter spaces to the right of fixation, the letters processed on any given fixation are not necessarily used for word identification processes on that fixation. We concluded earlier that to the right of fixation the perceptual span region is not tied to words and that partial word information is obtained. From these two conclusions, it follows that there may well be different perceptual spans: (1) the *total perceptual span*, which is the total region from which useful information is acquired; (2) the *letter identification span*, which is the region from which letter information is obtained; and (3) the *word identification span*, which is the region from which information is used on the current fixation for word identification processes. From the data that we have reviewed, it appears that the total perceptual span may be larger than the letter identification span, which in turn may be larger than the word identification span.

The second point is that all three of these types of spans should be thought of as being somewhat variable. That is, the techniques that have been used to estimate these spans yield a *maximum* span estimate rather than an absolute value (Well, 1983). Furthermore, there is evidence to suggest that these regions of processing vary as a function of orthography (see Ikeda & Saida, 1978; Osaka, 1987; Pollatsck ct al., 1981) and, more importantly, as a function of the difficulty of the text (Balota et al., 1985; Rayner, 1986) or reading conditions (Inhoff, Pollatsek, Posner, & Rayner, Note 2). There may also be differences due to reading ability. While Rayner (1986) found that the total span for beginning readers was a bit smaller than for skilled readers, Underwood and Zola (1986) found no difference in the size of the letter identification span between good and poor readers in the fifth grade.

The third point is that within the word identification span, letter processing seems to involve parallel, rather than serial, processes. A number of recent experiments (Blanchard, McConkie, Zola, & Wolverton, 1984; Inhoff et al., Note 2; Slowiaczek & Rayner, in press) have failed to find evidence for a rapid left-to-right serial scan of letters in the centre of fixation, leading to the conclusion that letter processing in the word identification span occurs via parallel processes.

In summary, research on the perceptual span has been consistent in indicating that the total perceptual span region is rather small (extending no more than 15 letter spaces to the right of fixation) and asymmetric (extending much further to the right of fixation than to the left). Word length information is certainly acquired out to 15 letter positions to the right of fixation and is useful in determining where to look next (McConkie & Rayner, 1975; Pollatsek & Rayner, 1982; Rayner et al., 1981). A bit more controversial are issues related to: (1) how far from fixation letter information is obtained; and (2) the extent to which partial word information is acquired parafovcally. We have suggested that the conclusions one reaches on these latter two issues may be related to the dependent variable examined. We move now to a discussion of parafoveal processing and the integration of information across saccades.

Parafoveal Processing and Integration of Information Across Saccades

In the prior section, we argued that word information acquired parafoveally is used in reading. Obviously, one way in which parafoveal word information can be used in reading is that on some fixations, the fixated word and the word to the right of fixation are both identified. In such cases, the word to the right of fixation would generally be skipped over by the ensuing saccade (Ehrlich & Rayner, 1981; Balota et al., 1985; O'Regan, 1979). A second way in which parafoveal information can be used is that partial information acquired about the parafoveal word on fixation n could be integrated with information about that same word (now in foveal vision) following the saccade on fixation $n+1$.

Word length may influence how parafoveal information is used. That is, enough parafoveal letter information may often be extracted from short words so that they can be skipped, whereas parafoveal letter information extracted from longer words may rarely allow full identification of them but facilitate subsequent foveal processing. A recent experiment by Blanchard, Pollatsek, and Rayner (Note 1) documents this pattern. A parafoveal preview enabled readers to skip short words (1–3 letters) significantly more of the time, whereas it had a negligible effect on how often long words (6–10 letters) were skipped. On the other hand, a parafoveal preview significantly shortened the gaze durations on the long words, but had a much smaller effect on the gaze durations on the short words.

We will return to word skipping in the next section on eye control. Our present focus will be the extraction of partial information. The extraction of useful partial information from the parafovea implies that it must be integrated in some way with the foveal information from the subsequent fixation. The type of information that survives the saccade between fixations and is subsequently integrated may provide an important tool for understanding which codes are important in lexical access as well as for understanding skilled reading. In particular, it seems important to know whether the codes being extracted from words in the parafovea and later used are visual features, sound codes, morphemes, abstract (case- and font-independent) letters, or something else.

Important data on this question have been obtained both from reading (with fixation time on a target word as the primary dependent variable) and from a timed word naming task. In the naming task (introduced by Rayner, 1978b), subjects fixate on a cross and a word or letter string is presented parafoveally. When the subject makes an eye movement to the parafoveal stimulus, it is replaced by a word which the subject must name as rapidly as possible. Integration is assessed by examining the effect of the parafoveal letters on naming time. While these naming time studies (Balota & Rayner, 1983; McClelland & O'Regan, 1981; Rayner, McConkie, & Ehrlich, 1978; Rayner, McConkie, & Zola, 1980) have been very influential in our thinking on the type of parafoveal information integrated across eye movements, we will focus on the studies in which text was read. However, virtually identical conclusions have emerged from the two paradigms.

The evidence against the use of visual codes in integration across saccades is quite strong. Both reading and naming times for words are unaffected when the case changes (e.g. cHaNgE to ChAnGe) from fixation to fixation (McConkie & Zola, 1979; Rayner, McConkie, et al., 1980). If visual codes were important in integration of information, then the change of features between lower- and upper-case letters should have disrupted reading and word identification. There is also evidence against sound codes, since the amount of facilitation from the beginning of a parafoveal preview word depends on whether the beginning letters are the same rather than whether the beginning phoneme is the same (Rayner, McConkie, et al., 1980).

Another candidate for a code conveying partial information is the morpheme. One morpheme that could be extracted from the beginning of a word is a prefix. To test whether prefixes are encoded as a unit in the parafovea, Lima (1987) inserted words that had true prefixes (e.g. *revive*) and words that were "pseudoprefixed" (e.g. *rescue*) in the same place in a sentence. If extracting morphemes were a significant part of the benefit of parafoveal preview, then one should observe a larger parafoveal preview benefit (i.e. difference in performance between when a parafoveal preview of the target word was present from when the preview was absent) for the prefixed words. In fact, there was equal benefit in the two cases, suggesting that prefixes are not active units in integration across saccades. A second morpheme that could plausibly be extracted from the parafovea is the first part of a compound word. Inhoff (this volume) compared the preview benefit from seeing the first morpheme of a compound word such as *cow-* in *cowboy* with that from seeing the first part of a "pseudocompound" word such as *car-* in *carpet*. The advantage was greater for the true compound than the pseudocompound, suggesting that the initial segment of a compound word may be an active unit in integration across saccades.

A related candidate for a unit is the semantic feature. It has been hypothesised that an unidentified parafoveal word is semantically pre-processed (presumably some semantic features extracted) which aids later identification of the word (Underwood, 1980; 1981). Results from word identification paradigms which looked for "subliminal" identification of meaning from parafoveal words are mixed (Bradshaw, 1974; Inhoff, 1982; Inhoff & Rayner, 1980). Moreover, in the studies that obtained positive results, the effects were small and there were possible methodological problems. A direct test of the semantic preprocessing hypothesis in reading was carried out by Rayner, Balota, & Pollatsek (1986) using the boundary technique described earlier. Each sentence contained a single target word (e.g. *tune*), with the parafoveal preview either visually similar (*turc*), semanti-cally similar (*song*), or unrelated (*door*). (The semantically similar pairs were shown to produce the standard priming effect in a separate naming experi-ment.) Gaze durations on the target word were appreciably shorter when the preview was visually similar to the target word, but there was no difference between the semantically similar and unrelated conditions. Thus, semantic preprocessing or extraction of semantic features is not a viable explanation for the parafoveal preview benefit in reading.

In summary, the experiments to date indicate that words and abstract letters (Coltheart, 1981; Rayner, McConkie et al., 1980) are likely to be active units in integration across saccades in reading or word identification, while sound codes and letter features are not. The only evidence of "deeper" subword units being active in integration is that the first morpheme of a compound word (a word itself) appears to be a unit.

It is also of interest whether the extraction and integration of parafoveal information can be influenced by higher-order information such as lexical or sentential constraint. To answer the first question, Lima and Inhoff (1985) presented sentences in which one of two words appeared in a target location (e.g. "The weary *dwarf*. . . ." or "The weary *clown* . . . ."). The target words *dwarf* and *clown* were selected to have equal frequency in the language and be equally predictable in the context, but the initial letters *dwa* are shared by few words in the lexicon while *clo* are shared by many. Since prior studies had demonstrated that seeing the first three letters of the parafoveal word produced large benefit, Lima and Inhoff reasoned that if lexical constraint were a potent variable in parafoveal processing, then the preview benefit for *dwarf* should be greater than that for *clown*. In fact, there was equal preview benefit in the two cases, indicating that lexical constraint does not operate on parafoveal information. They did find, however, that the fixation time on *clown* was actually less than that for *dwarf* (regradless of whether there was a preview or not), indicating that the frequency of the word-initial letter sequence influences the time taken to process a word foveally.

The effect of sentential constraint on parafoveal processing was examined by Balota et al. (1985). They varied both the predictability of a target word and the availability of parafoveal information using the boundary technique. Two findings of interest emerged. First, they replicated earlier findings that a predictable target word is more likely to be skipped than an unpredictable one (Ehrlich & Rayner, 1981; O'Regan, 1979), indicating that sentential constraint, unlike lexical constraint, does appear to influence the usefulness of parafoveal information. Of greater interest are those occasions when the target word was not skipped. The gaze duration on the target word was shorter when the word was more predictable (cf. McConkie et al., 1982), but more importantly, the benefit of a parafoveal preview was greater when the target word was more predictable, indicating that (in some sense) extraction of parafoveal information is more efficient when guided by sentential context. Additional analyses indicated that more letters were extracted from the parafovea when context was high. Both of these findings (especially the latter) run counter to a modular view of lexical access in which variables such as predictability do not affect lexical access and are consistent with more interactive views (e.g. Paap, Newsome, McDonald, & Schvaneveldt, 1982; Rumelhart & McClelland, 1982).

In sum, the evidence to date points to the conclusion that words, letters, and some morphemes are being extracted from parafoveal vision and that sentential context can affect the amount of useful information that is extracted from the parafovea. A word of caution is in order: In the Balota et al. experiment, the "constrained" words were highly predictable from the prior sentence context. We suspect that only such extreme forms of constraint would measurably alter how visual information is extracted during reading.

Control of Eye Movements in Reading

One factor that dampened interest in eye movements as a tool to study reading was the belief that eye movements were unrelated to the details of ongoing cognitive processes. However, over the last ten years abundant evidence has accumulated indicating that both fixation time and saccade length are related to aspects of the text currently fixated. These data have led some researchers to posit the opposite extreme from the position that there is no relation between eye movements and cognitive processes. According to the *immediacy hypothesis* (Just & Carpenter, 1980), all cognitive processes needed to understand a word are completed before the eye moves on. As we shall see, the situation is unfortunately more complex than that: While some cognitions about a fixated word are reflected immediately on that fixation, the effects of others are less immediate. Such a finding implies that one will have to understand the details of how the eyes are controlled in reading in order to use eye movements to study cognitive processes.

The earliest unambiguous demonstration that events on a fixation can affect the length of the next saccade and/or the duration of the current fixation was provided by Rayner and Pollatsek (1981). They varied physical aspects of the text randomly from fixation to fixation and showed that the behaviour of the eyes mirrored what was seen on that fixation. In one experiment, the size of the window of normal text was randomly varied from fixation to fixation and saccade length was shown to vary accordingly. In another experiment, the foveal text was delayed after the onset of a fixation (with the delay time varying randomly from fixation to fixation) and fixation durations varied accordingly (see also Morrison, 1984). In addition, the manipulations appeared to affect saccade length and fixation duration independently, so that there is reason to believe that the decisions of *where* to move the eyes and *when* to move the eyes can be made independently (Rayner & McConkie, 1976).

The decision on where to move the eye depends on several factors. As indicated above, an important influence is the amount of useful information to the right of fixation. The Balota et al. (1985) experiment discussed earlier demonstrated that letter information to the right was important in determining whether a word was skipped. However, word boundary information (primarily conveyed by spaces) influences the size of the saccade as well. The importance of word boundary information is suggested by the fact that the saccade is influenced by both the length of the fixated word and the length of the word to the right of the fixated word (O'Regan, 1979; 1980; 1981; Rayner, 1979). Such a relationship, however, could also be a result of the linguistic characteristics of the words (e.g. short words have a higher frequency in the language). To examine the independent effect of word boundary information, text has been presented in which all the letters to the right of the window boundary were replaced by *x*s but the spaces were preserved. This condition has been compared to one in which the spaces were also replaced by *x*s (McConkie & Rayner, 1975; Rayner, 1986). While the mean saccade length decreased somewhat when the letter information to the right of fixation was removed, it decreased far more when word length information was removed as well. In addition, Pollatsek and Rayner (1982) showed that saccade length decreased markedly when the spaces between words were filled in, even when the letters were left intact. These experiments suggest that letter information may be of little value in guiding the eye if word boundary information is not present.

The decision to regress (move the eyes backward) is partly due to higher-level decisions. For example, Frazier and Rayner (1982) demonstrated that when readers encountered a word indicating that their prior interpretation of the sentence was in error (this will be discussed in more detail later), they often made a regression as soon as they encountered the disambiguating information. There is also evidence that contextual variables influence whether the reader refixates a word. Balota et al. (1985) showed that readers were less likely to refixate a word that was more predictable in the sentence context. In addition, our prior discussion of word skipping implies that context influences whether the word to the right of fixation is skipped.

Thus, both textural variables and word boundary information appear to influence where the eye will move. The textual variables appear to influence the decision of whether to make the next fixation on the current word, the next word, further on, or move back. While word length information plays at least as important a part in where the eye moves to, we are less certain exactly what role it plays.

The previous discussion of textual variables suggests that the readers have at least some control of which word they move to. Are they also in control of where they move to on a word? The evidence indicates that they are. Although there is variability in where the eye lands on a word, for the most part, readers fixate near the middle of words (McConkie & Zola, 1984; O'Regan, 1981; Rayner, 1979). Rayner (1979) termed this place where the reader tends to fixate—about halfway between the beginning and middle of the word—the *preferred viewing location* on a word. The position of the preferred viewing location makes sense, since it is well known that the beginning of a word is more informative than the end. More recently, O'Regan (1981; O'Regan & Levy-Schoen, this volume; O'Regan, Levy-Schoen, Pynte, & Brugaillere, 1984) has made a distinction between the preferred viewing location and the *convenient viewing location*, which is the ideal fixation point on a word in order to identify the word. According to O'Regan and Levy-Schoen (this volume), the convenient viewing location is a bit to the right of the preferred viewing location (see their chapter in this volume for a discussion of this issue). In any event, the data do clearly show that there is a strong tendency for readers to fixate near the middle of words. Evidence that word boundary information helps to guide the eye toward the preferred viewing location comes from conditions in which there was no parafoveal letter information (Morris, Note 3). When the space indicating the location of the end of word $n+1$ was visible in the parafovea, the subsequent first fixation on that word was closer to the preferred viewing location than when the parafoveal preview didn't contain that space information.

The amount of time a word is fixated appears to be influenced largely by the characteristics of that word. For example, word frequency is known to affect fixation time on a word (Just & Carpenter, 1980; Rayner, 1977). While infrequent words are generally longer than frequent words, Inhoff and

Rayner (1986) and Rayner and Duffy (1986) have shown that the first fixation on low-frequency words was longer than for high-frequency words, even when the length of the word was controlled for. In addition, several studies (Inhoff & Rayner, 1986; Lima, 1987; Pollatsek et al., 1986) have shown that first fixations on a word are shorter when the letter information was available in the parafovea on the prior fixation than when it was not. Both of these results suggest that the speed of identifying the fixated word influences the length of a fixation. In addition, fixations are longer when the subsequent word is skipped than when it is not (Hogaboam, 1983; Pollatsek et al., 1986), indicating that the decision to move the eye is sometimes delayed in order to complete lexical access of the subsequent word. The circumstances under which contextual variables influence the first fixation duration on a word may be limited. Inhoff (1984) found that word frequency affected the first fixation on a word, whereas the degree to which the word made sense in the sentence context only affected the gaze duration (which primarily reflects the first fixation duration and the probability of refixating a word). Similarly, whereas Balota et al. (1985) obtained a large predictability effect on gaze duration, they failed to find an effect of predictability on the duration of the first fixation on the target word. However, Ehrlich and Rayner (1981) and Zola (1984) both found that the first fixation duration on a word was shorter when it was highly predictable from sentence context. This suggests that the first fixation duration on a word may be affected by how well the word fits in a sentence context only in the case when the context makes the word extremely predictable.

To summarise, there is now clear evidence that the decisions of where and when to move the eyes are affected by characteristics of the text processed. The decision where to move the eyes is affected by the letters in the words around fixation and word length information, while the duration of a fixation appears to be influenced primarily by the letters in the words around fixation; Rayner and Pollatsek (1981) found that if all letters of the fixated word were visible, eliminating word boundaries in the parafovea had little effect on fixation duration. In addition, both variables are influenced by sentential context, as we will discuss later in some detail.

What Goes on During a Fixation in Reading?

From the discussion, it should be clear that we are far from having a definitive model for the sequence of events on a fixation. However, the available data allow us to make some educated guesses, which we would like to present. The data above demonstrate that the frequency of the fixated word in the language affects the length of time it is fixated. Thus, some cognitive event indexed by word frequency is signalling the eyes to move on at least some fixations. There are three plausible candidates for such an event. The first is lexical access of the fixated word. The second is some event prior to lexical access. One possibility is that a sequence of letters activates a "neighbourhood" of lexical entries (Paap et al., 1982; Rumelhart & McClelland, 1982), and that the triggering event for an eye movement is when the total excitation from all activated entries in the lexicon exceeds some threshold. Such an event may predict that successful lexical access is likely to occur within a few milliseconds. The third type of triggering event would be a process "deeper" than lexical access, such as integrating the fixated word into the ongoing sentence or story structure.

At present, we have little to decide among these alternatives. Since lexical access is the simplest conceptually, we will assume that it is the process indexed by word frequency. If lexical access of the fixated word is the triggering stimulus for the ensuing eye movement, the following sequence of operations must occur within the time of that fixation: (1) the visual information passes from the eye to the brain; (2) lexical access is accomplished; (3) a signal (program) is sent out to move the eye on the basis of lexical access (e.g. move the eye to the next unidentified word); (4) the program for the eye movement is executed. (We will refer to control of an eye movement that terminates a fixation by information encoded on that fixation as *direct control*.) One reason for some researchers being reluctant to believe that direct control can be important in a normal fixation of around 200–250msec is that they believe that the sum of stages 1, 3, and 4 takes about 175msec, which would presumably not leave sufficient time to do significant cognitive processing on the currently fixated word. One basis for the 175msec estimate of the sum of stages 1, 3, and 4 is the latency of simple eye movements to prespecified locations (Rayner, Slowiaczek et al., 1983; Salthouse & Ellis, 1980).

The earlier Rayner and Pollatsek (1981) data demonstrated that direct control is possible. Moreover, we believe that it is plausible that direct control is a regular event in normal reading. First, it is not improbable that lexical access can occur in something like 50–75msec after the message enters the brain (i.e. 225–250msec of a reading fixation minus 175msec of a simple eye-movement latency). For example, Rayner et al. (1981) demonstrated that reading rates and comprehension were approximately normal even if the entire line of text was masked 50msec after the beginning of each fixation. While this might merely mean that the visual stimulus can be deposited into a mask-impervious buffer within 50msec of arriving in the brain, it is also consistent with stage 2 taking about 50msec. Moreover, it may be that lexical access does not have to be quite that rapid to have an effect.

An extremely elegant technique for determining the time course of events during a fixation has been developed by McConkie and co-workers (e.g. McConkie, Underwood, Zola, & Wolverton, 1985; McConkie & Zola, this volume). Their basic procedure is to manipulate a visual event at some point during a fixation and determine when the eye-movement system "notices" the event. When the conditional probability of moving the eye in some time window is affected by whether a prior visual event has occurred or not, they conclude that the eye movement system has "noticed" the event in that time window. For example, McConkie et al. (1985) changed the text in two different ways 100msec after the fixation began. They discovered that the histograms of first fixation duration from these conditions were significantly different from each other at about 200msec, indicating that the type of text change was influencing eye behaviour only 100msec later. Thus, it appears that the sum of stages 1, 3, and 4 may take as little as 100msec, and if so, stage 2 could last as long as 125–150msec and still exercise direct control. (We should point out that 100msec is an estimate of the *minimum* time for stages 1 + 3 + 4 rather than the *mean* time.)

A mechanism facilitating direct control is preview information from the parafovea, which should speed lexical access considerably. In fact, Inhoff and Rayner (1986) found no effect of word frequency on the duration of the first fixation on a word when there was no parafoveal preview. Thus, lexical access may be fast enough to influence the decision *when* to move the eye only when there is a parafoveal preview. However, in the same experiment, it was found that word frequency affected the probability that a second fixation would be made on a word even when there was no parafoveal preview. Thus, it appears that the decision to refixate the word (a decision *where* to move the eye) can be made later in the fixation.

The fact that word frequency did not affect the first fixation duration on a word when there was no parafoveal preview indicates that, in this condition, the decision of when to move the eye was not influenced by lexical access. It is possible that, in normal reading, the decision when to move the eye is not always made on the basis of direct control either. One striking piece of evidence against direct control on all fixations is that fixations of 50–100msec sometimes occur in normal reading. One possibility for nondirect control is that there is a completely automatic process that sends the eye forward (perhaps at the conclusion of a preset deadline) if lexical access (or some other signalling process) does not occur. Another is that some eye movements are preprogrammed on prior fixations.

Morrison (1984) provided evidence for such preprogramming using a paradigm in which a foveal region of the text was delayed a variable amount of time after the eye began a fixation. (A mask appeared in the foveal region followed by the text.) He replicated Rayner and Pollatsek's (1981) finding that some "anticipation" eye movements were made before the text actually appeared, and were thus not made on the basis of processing the foveal word. Only anticipation eye movements that were greater than 150msec reflected the size of the foveal mask, indicating that the mask information took 150msec to have an effect on the eye movement system. He argued that, since the shorter anticipation eye movements were thus not due to avoiding the mask, they were most plausibly the result of a command to move the eyes that had been made on the prior fixation. On the basis of these and other data, he proposed a model in which eye movements can be programmed in parallel. His model assumes that each word in the text is processed in sequence and, as each is processed, an internal attention mechanism turns to the following word. This attention mechanism also triggers an instruction to execute an eye movement to that word. However, if a second attention shift occurs within a certain "time-window" of the first, the first eye-movement instruction may be cancelled and only the second one executed (cf. Becker & Jurgens, 1979).

Morrison's model has certain attractive properties. First, it can explain why words are skipped. If the word to the right of fixation is processed quickly, then the second attention shift will cancel the first eye-movement instruction and the eye will move directly to the second word from fixation. The same mechanism also explains why fixations are longer when the succeeding word is skipped. In addition, it can explain very short fixations. If a second attention shift occurs in a fixation, but not quickly enough after the first attention shift, the first eye-movement instruction will not be cancelled but a second will be programmed as well. Thus two eye movements will be programmed on fixation n: the one terminating fixation n and the one terminating fixation $n + 1$. If the second saccade programmed on fixation n was programmed sufficiently early in the fixation, then its execution could occur within about 50msec after the beginning of fixation $n + 1$. These preprogrammed saccades need not be so short, however, if they are programmed on the basis of visual information extracted relatively late on fixation n. Blanchard et al. (1984) provided evidence from experiments in which the text changes in the middle of a fixation that visual information can be extracted throughout the fixation, and thus that such late information extraction is plausible.

This model clearly can not be complete, since it does not explain why the reader would ever fixate a word more than once or why regressions would ever occur. It thus appears that some additional mechanism is needed, one that can be interposed relatively late in a fixation to cancel the forward saccade and/or alter the decision of where the eye is to move: i.e. remain on the current word or move back. Perhaps "higher-order" cognitive operations such as text comprehension express themselves only through this additional mechanism. The model is also vague about how the landing location on a word is selected. The Rayner and Pollatsek (1981) and Pollatsek and Rayner (1982) experiments discussed earlier suggest that word boundary information is processed early in the fixation and that a separate mechanism decides on a suitable landing place on the word to the right of fixation early in the fixation.

Such an expanded version of Morrison's model raises the possibility that all eye movements in reading (even those after 50–100msec fixations) are under cognitive (though not necessarily direct) control. However, it is clear that the relationship between the pattern of eye movements and the underlying cognitive operations, given such a model, would be far from simple. If there are, in addition, eye movements that are not under any cognitive control, the relationship would be still more complex. With this cautionary note, we turn to a discussion of how eye movements can help to elucidate cognitive processes in reading, beginning with a brief discussion of what measures various researchers have used.

EYE MOVEMENTS IN READING

The above discussion suggests that employing eye movements to study cognitive processes in reading is not easy. The ensuing discussion hopefully will suggest that it is not only possible but valuable. The first question to be raised is how one summarises the eye-movement record to understand cognitive processing. If a larger linguistic unit such as a sentence or phrase is selected as the unit of analysis, then the total fixation time on that larger unit is invariably used as the primary measure of interest. When a finer analysis is being performed—with the word the unit of analysis—the appropriate measure to use has been the subject of some controversy. If readers always made one fixation on each word, then there would be little problem. However, as we have seen, words are sometimes fixated more than once and words are sometimes skipped.

The problem of multiple fixations on words has led to different solutions. For example, some researchers appear to use the first fixation duration on a word as the measure of lexical access (e.g. Inhoff, 1984; McConkie et al., 1982). While the reasons are not always explicit, the assumption appears to be that what goes on beyond the first fixation reflects higher-order processing (Inhoff, 1984) or is noise. However, the opposite assumption appears to have been made by O'Regan (see O'Regan et al., 1984), who believes that refixations are often caused by originally landing in a "bad" place on a word and moving to a more informative spot. His evidence (from experiments with words in isolation; O'Regan et al., 1984) is that readers refixate words when they land in a bad spot (such as the end of the word) and further that processing of the word is distributed over two or more fixations in those cases.

O'Regan's position seems to suggest that: (1) most refixations on words should take the eye to the middle of the word; and (2) that second fixations on a word should be longer than first fixations (since less information would be obtained when the eye is in a bad place). We examined all words of four to ten letters on which ten readers made two fixations. For the vast majority (87%) of cases, an initial fixation on a word was followed by a rightward movement within the word. By far the most frequent pattern was to fixate near the beginning of the word followed by a fixation near the end of the word. The first fixation was longer than the second 48% of the time, with the means being 166msec for the first fixation and 163msec for the second fixation. Thus, we suspect that most refixations on words are made for reasons other than that the reader was initially in a bad position on the word.

Clearly the argument about which measure is best to use as an index of processing time partly depends on what you are interested in measuring. Inhoff (1984) thought that the duration of the first fixation on a word and the gaze duration (the total fixation time on a word prior to the eye moving to another word) reflected different processes. In his data, both first-fixation duration and gaze duration were affected by word frequency, but only gaze duration was affected by the predictability of the word in the context. He thus posited that first-fixation duration was the measure of lexical access whereas gaze duration reflected text integration processes as well. However, much of the data we have discussed suggest that this distinction does not hold up in general and that the difference is more quantitative. The data are consistent with the model that the decision to refixate can be made later in a fixation than the decision when to move the eye; if a cognitive operation is really fast, it will affect the first-fixation duration, while if it is a bit slower, it may still affect gaze duration.

Assuming the gaze versus first-fixation duration problem were solved, there is still a problem in trying to assess the average time spent in processing a word (whether up to the point of lexical access or beyond). The problem is that words are processed when they are not fixated. This is most clearly demonstrated by word skipping, where all the processing of a word occurs when it is not fixated. One solution to the skipping problem was suggested by Carpenter and Just (1983), who used *conditionalised gaze duration*, the mean gaze duration given that the word had been fixated for at least 50msec. The problem with this measure is that it ignores the time spent on a word processing words to the right (shown most clearly by the fact that fixations are longer when the word to the right is skipped). Perhaps this measure would be better if conditionalised on not skipping either the word being fixated or the following word. A second solution is the *read to the right of gaze* (RRG) algorithm (Blanchard, 1985; Hogaboam & McConkie, 1981). The RRG measure sums fixations on words receiving more than one fixation; when words are skipped, the fixation time is equally distributed between the last word fixated and the word that was skipped. The equal division of processing time between the two words is clearly arbitrary, but may be a reasonable zero-order approximation to the truth.

Both methods assume, however, that (except for skipping) a word is processed only when it is fixated. As we have argued earlier, however, partial parafoveal information from a word is extracted on many fixations that facilitate identification of a word on a later fixation. The time spent extracting this information should be added to the fixation time on the word and should be subtracted from the time spent on the prior word. All the above assumes, of course, that words are processed in series. If certain processes overlap, then the calculations of processing times would be even more complex. In addition, such measures assume that processing of a word is completed by the time the eye moves. To the extent that processing a word "spills over" onto subsequent fixations, these measures will also be in error.

It thus appears that any single measure of "processing time per word" will be a pale reflection of the reality of cognitive processing. Therefore, we feel that the strategy of analysing large amounts of text using a single measure of processing is likely to be of limited value in measuring "on-line" processing. Such a strategy was adopted by Just and Carpenter (1980) when they applied multiple regression techniques to analyse eye movements over large amounts of text. Their procedure has been criticised by a number of researchers (Fisher & Shebilske, 1985; Hogaboam & McConkie, 1981; Kliegl, Olson, & Davidson, 1982). We will not repeat these criticisms here, but simply comment that many of the criticisms follow because any such procedure must make unjustifiable simplifying assumptions about the relationship between the measure being used and cognitive processing during reading.

An alternative strategy that many researchers have adopted is to select target locations in the text for careful analysis (usually on the basis of some theoretical consideration) employing many different measures: e.g., first-fixation duration, gaze duration, probability of fixating a target word, number of fixations on the target word, how long the saccade off the target word is, and "spillover" effects such as the fixation time on the next word. From the total pattern of such measures, it is possible to draw some reasonable inferences about how text is processed in the target region. If there are enough interesting target word situations, one can start to build a general theory of reading.

Lexical Access and Context

We have documented above that the frequency of a word influences the fixation time on a word. We have also documented that words that are predictable from prior context receive shorter fixations than words that are not predictable (Balota et al., 1985; Ehrlich & Rayner, 1981; Inhoff, 1984; Zola, 1984) and that the predictable ones are more likely to be skipped over (Balota et al., 1985; Ehrlich & Rayner, 1981). There are two likely causes for such effects: (1) the lexical entries of more frequent and/or more predictable words could be accessed more quickly than less frequent and/or less predictable words; (2) frequent and/or predictable words could be integrated into the discourse structure or mental text representation more easily than less frequent and/or less predictable words. The Balota et al. finding that parafoveal visual information is used more effectively when the word is predictable argues that predictability is affecting lexical access (although it could be affecting later stages as well). Since most studies on context in reading have not manipulated the visual information available, it is difficult to determine whether the effects observed reflect lexical access, some later text integration stage, or both. Hence, in the discussion to follow, we will primarily distinguish between whether the effect is *immediate* (reflected in the fixation time on the target word) or *delayed*. We will assume that the decision to move off a word indicates that some process at least as deep as lexical access has been completed (which we will term *word identification*) so that delayed effects should reflect stages subsequent to lexical access. We turn to a discussion of several factors that would plausibly affect word identification.

One question is whether all context effects can be reduced to the predictability of the target word from the prior text. Another possible mechanism for facilitation of the processing of words is "priming" (Meyer & Schvaneveldt, 1971). Priming effects were recently demonstrated in reading (Carroll & Slowiaczek, 1986). A target word such as *sparrow* or *vulture* was preceded in a sentence either by the category name *bird* or a neutral word *thing* and gaze durations on the target word were shorter when the category prime appeared earlier. Interestingly, even though the low-typicality targets were fixated longer than the high-typicality targets, there was a priming effect even when the exemplar *vulture* was low typicality (and hence quite unpredictable). Therefore the priming effect observed was unlikely to be merely a predictability effect. While lexical priming may explain some part of the predictability effect, it is unlikely to be the whole story (e.g. skipping predictable function words). Thus, there appear to be at least two separate mechanisms by which context affects the ease of identifying words in reading.

A second question of interest is the role of lexical ambiguity in reading. Rayner and Duffy (1986) examined gaze durations on two classes of lexically ambiguous words: those whose two meanings were approximately equally dominant and those in which one of the two meanings was highly dominant. The preceding context was neutral with respect to the intended meaning of the polysemous word. The ambiguous words with a dominant meaning were processed as quickly as roughly synonomous unambiguous control words. However, when the two meanings were equally dominant, gaze durations were longer on the ambiguous words than the unambiguous control word. Thus, it appears that both meanings of the equally dominant ambiguous words were accessed, whereas only the highly dominant meaning of the other ambiguous words was. This conclusion is strengthened by the finding that, when the rest of the sentence was consistent with the less dominant meaning of the word, readers spent more time with the remainder of the sentence than when the two meanings were equally dominant.

A second study by Rayner and Duffy (1987) attempted to decide whether the lengthened fixation time for the equally dominant ambiguous words was due to increased time for lexical access or to post-lexical processes. On the latter view, both meanings are accessed in parallel and then some sort of selection process takes place. Rayner and Duffy found that when the prior context made one of the meanings more plausible than the other, the gaze durations on the equally dominant ambiguous words and the control words did not differ. Thus, the lengthened times on the ambiguous words in the first study appear to be due to post-lexical selection processes that were made unnecessary by the disambiguating prior context. The pattern of data for equally dominant meanings thus indicate that both meanings are accessed in parallel, regardless of the prior context, a conclusion consistent with other work on lexical ambiguity (Seidenberg, Tanenhaus, Leiman, & Bienkowski, 1982; Swinney, 1979). We do not know, however, in the case of one meaning dominating, whether the less dominant meaning is never accessed or accessed and quickly lost.

Another interesting question is the effect of the distance between a target word and some preceding context. Variations in fixation times on target words have been obtained as a function of the distance between the target word and the prior mention of either the exact word (Schustack, Ehrlich, & Rayner, in press) or a related referent (Ehrlich & Rayner, 1983). Carroll and Slowiaczek (1986) showed that such distance effects may not merely be measured in number of words between two words. They found that priming occurred when the prime and target were in the same clause but not when they were in different clauses, even though the distance between prime and target (in number of words) was matched in the two cases. While these distance effects are consistent with the hypothesis that the prior mention of a related word makes lexical access easier when that prior word is closer, they are also consistent with the hypothesis that subjects have to search longer through memory to fit the word into some sort of discourse structure when the prior word is more distant. As indicated above, in an eye movement experiment, Schustack et al. found that fixation time on a target word varied as a function of how far it was from a previous referent. However, in a different experiment involving the same materials, Schustack et al. found that the time to name the target word was not affected by its distance from the prior referent. If naming is taken as a "pure" measure of lexical access, this result argues that the distance effects on fixation times in reading are likely to index post-lexical processes. We will return to this issue later when we discuss effects more clearly related to antecedent search.

Do Eye Movements Reveal Syntactic Parsing Strategies?

One of the earliest studies using eye-movement data to study reading in the third era of eye-movement research examined parsing strategies (Mehler, Bever, & Carey, 1967). Although there is some reason to question the results of that study (see Frazier, 1983; O'Regan, Note 5; Rayner, 1978a), a large number of recent studies have also utilised eye-movement data to investigate on-line parsing strategies. In these studies, eye movements are of interest in that they provide a moment-to-moment record of the readers' attempts to deal with syntactic information in understanding sentences. The primary technique that has been used involves asking subjects to read sentences containing temporary structural ambiguities and examining the eye-movement records to see how readers coped with the ambiguity, and how they recovered from misanalysis when they were "led down the garden path."

Since most of these studies are described elsewhere in this volume by Frazier, the details of the experiments will not be discussed here. Suffice it to say that these studies (see Carroll & Slowiaczek, 1987; Ferreira & Clifton, 1986; Frazier & Rayner, 1982; in press; Holmes & O'Regan, 1981; Kennedy & Murray, 1984; Rayner, Carlson, & Frazier, 1983; Rayner & Frazier, in press) show quite clearly that using eye-movement data is very informative with respect to understanding parsing strategies. Basically, the results of the studies show that readers are generally committed to a single interpretation of an ambiguous string of words, since when the disambiguating information is inconsistent with the interpretation assigned there is considerable disruption. The most important factor in such studies is that the investigator has a clear theoretical position from which to predict how readers will respond to various types of syntactic ambiguity and disambiguation. Frazier and Rayner (1982) found that when readers reached the disambiguating information they either: (1) fixated for a very long time and then proceeded to read quite normally; (2) made a regression back to the ambiguous material; or (3) were very disrupted in their reading (as evidenced by very long fixations and short saccades) and after they had finished the sentence started over again. In the first case, readers apparently were able to reanalyse the sentence in their minds without looking back. In the second case, reanalysing the sentence involved looking back to the ambiguous material and re-reading it. In the third case, it appears that sometimes readers did not understand the sentence and had to re-read it in order to make sense of it.

Questions concerning syntactic parsing are very important and eye-movement recording gives the experimenter an opportunity to examine on-line processes concerning the types of strategies used and the decisions made. Results of experiments using eye-movement data have proved to be very informative in comparison to other types of tasks that have been used. They have also resulted in systematic answers to questions about the strategies that readers use (see Frazier, this volume). Finally, eye-movement data as an on-line measure have been very useful in enlightening us concerning the extent to which the language processing system in reading is divided into modules that consist of separate subsystems (see Carroll & Slowiaczek, 1987; Ferreira & Clifton, 1986; Rayner, Carlson, et al., 1983).

Are Higher-Order Processes Reflected in Eye Movements?

As we mentioned earlier, Just and Carpenter (1980) argued that all processes associated with comprehending a given word are completed while that word is fixated (the immediacy hypothesis). Carpenter and Just (1983) qualified this by noting that in some cases the complete representation of a word cannot be computed until more information is available; when a reader encounters the adjective *large* he or she will not really completely understand the word until the next word is processed (for example, *insect* vs. *house*). According to their analysis, however, all processes that can be completed while a word is fixated are completed. Implicit in Just and Carpenter's position is the idea that higher-order semantic processes, as well as lexical access processes, should be reflected in fixation times. In addition, their technique of choice, multiple regression, assumes that the various factors that influence fixation times produce additive effects. This would be true, in general, only if the various cognitive processes in reading were serial.

There is evidence against the immediacy hypothesis, since a number of studies (some discussed previously) have demonstrated that processing can spill over onto the subsequent fixation or fixations (Balota et al., 1985; Ehrlich & Rayner, 1983; McConkie et al., 1985; Rayner & Duffy, 1986; Rayner & Pollatsek, 1981). In addition, there are possible reasons to suspect the assumption that visual processing of text and higher-order comprehension processes are serial. For example, if certain visual processes involved in lexical access were automatic and relatively modular they would occur in parallel with higher-order processes. Under such conditions, the time taken in higher-order processing would be difficult to recover from the eye-movement record, both because it would be spread across several fixations and because it would go on, at least to some extent, in parallel with lexical access. In fact, in Just and Carpenter's (1980) multiple regression analysis, higher-order factors accounted for only a small percentage of the variance of fixation times. However, we feel that the eye-movement record can illuminate understanding of higher-order processes in some cases if a suitably sensitive experiment is employed. Several examples follow.

One such higher-order process is deciding which prior noun is the referrent of a pronoun. Ehrlich and Rayner (1983; see also Vonk, 1984) varied the distance between the mention of the referent and the initial mention of the pronoun. Analyses of fixation times in the region of the pronoun provided information concerning when the referent assignment was completed. They found that when the distance between antecedent and target was close, antecedent search was completed on the fixation on which the target was fixated (see also Just & Carpenter, 1978); when the distance between the two increased, however, there was a tendency for the antecedent search process to spill over and produce larger fixations on the word following the target word. Unfortunately, the data from some recent studies suggest that reliable fixation time effects in the region of a pronoun may be difficult to obtain (Blanchard, in press; Carroll & Slowiaczek, 1987). It is not clear why there are discrepancies between the studies. One problem is a lack of power, as the pronoun itself tends not to be fixated. A second is that the relevant measure of distance may be in terms of some "deep-structure" of the text rather than the number of intervening words between the pronoun and antecedent (see Clifton & Ferreira, this volume).

A second type of higher-order process in reading is making inferences, or adding a proposition not contained explicitly in the text. Many researchers have assumed that inferences during reading are made on-line (i.e. as soon as the information allowing them to be drawn is encountered) and are stored in memory together with the explicit information of the text. The evidence for on-line inference is weak, however, since the data used to demonstrate it are open to the alternative explanation that the inference is made only when the inference is probed for. Since so many investigators assume that on-line inferences are important to reading comprehension, it is important to demonstrate their existence empirically. A recent study (O'Brien, Shank, Myers, & Rayner, Note 4) has demonstrated that fixation times on a specific target word (for example, *knife*) were faster when *knife* was mentioned previously than when a more general word (*weapon*) was mentioned previously. However, if *weapon* was mentioned together with attributes that would lead the reader to infer that it was a knife, then fixation times were the same as when *knife* was explicitly mentioned, suggesting that subjects had stored equivalent representations of "knife" in the two cases, and thus that they had made an inference prior to fixating the target word.

Finally, a number of studies have investigated whether there are clausal and sentence "wrap-up" effects, that is, extra time spent at the ends of clauses and sentences. Unfortunately there has been inconsistency in the results, with some studies finding such effects (Carrithers & Bever, 1984; Just & Carpenter, 1980) and others not (Blanchard, 1985; Kliegl et al., 1982). This inconsistency may be due to the fact that most of the studies used a multiple regression analysis (where position in the clause or sentence is entered as a possible predictor variable) which is probably insensitive to subtle effects. In a recent study in our lab, clause and sentence boundaries were varied experimentally so that the same lexical items appeared either in the middle of a clause or sentence or at the end of the syntactic constituent. For example, short passages were prepared so that the same phrase was in the middle of a sentence in one case, but ended the sentence in the other case. The results of the experiments showed quite clearly that gaze durations were longer on the last critical word in the phrase when it ended the sentence than when it was in the middle of the sentence. Similar effects were obtained for clauses.

CONCLUSIONS

The third era of research in reading (the mid-1970s to the present) has yielded many interesting findings which have been reviewed in this chapter. As we noted at the outset, some researchers have been interested in studying eye movements because they are interested in the properties of the eye movements per se, while others have studied eye movements to reveal important aspects of language processing. Results of studies that we have reviewed in this chapter have revealed that it is difficult to study one without the other. However, much has been learned, and the strategy of using eye movements to study the reading process appears to be paying great dividends.

Since a great deal has been learned recently (and in the first era of eye-movement research) about reading from eye movements, it is somewhat strange that some have levied some rather strong criticisms of eye-movement data (see Aaronson, 1984; Aaronson & Ferres, 1986; Haberlandt & Graesser, 1985; Ward & Juola, 1982). It appears to us that such criticisms are primarily offered as a justification for using some on-line substitute for eye movements. The two most common substitutes are: subject-paced word-by-word reading, in which subjects push a button to have the next word appear in the fovea; and *rapid serial visual presentation* (RSVP), in which the words of the text appear rapidly in sequence (at a fixed rate) in the same physical location.

The two major problems with both word-by-word techniques are: (1) they generally do not allow the reader to have a parafoveal preview of an upcoming word; and (2) they do not allow the reader to regress back to material that they did not understand or misanalysed. Sequential paradigms which attempt to compensate for these problems by presenting more than one word at a time end up losing the power of associating the resulting reaction time with the processing of a specific word. There are other problems as well. In the subject-paced tasks, reading is generally slowed down appreciably. On the other hand, while RSVP reading can occur at least as rapidly as normal reading with good comprehension (at least for sentences), it appears to place heavy attentional demands on the reader. In addition, since performance is assessed by a memory test, the RSVP task loses a lot of power in assessing moment-to-moment processing. Thus, if one wants to understand natural silent reading, there is no substitute for the natural reading situation that one has when eye movements are monitored; all other experimental situations are different enough that inferences from them to natural reading are hazardous.

Many researchers interested in studying reading seem committed to the standard methodologies of cognitive psychology (e.g. the self-paced reading paradigm is a complex manual reaction time technique and the RSVP paradigm is a complex tachistoscopic technique). It is not clear whether they favour such methods because they think they allow more experimental control or because reaction time experiments are easier to do. Clearly, one has to sacrifice quite a bit of ecological validity to gain control and much of that control may be illusory. In the self-paced reading method, for example, one probably has less of an idea of why the finger moved than why the eye moves in normal reading. Although the standard laboratory tasks, such as lexical decision or naming, clearly allow more control than monitoring eye movements in reading, it is by no means clear that this control allows better measurement of basic cognitive processes. For example, measures of lexical access time derived from these tasks (e.g. lexical decision time or naming time) have many of the same interpretative problems as the attempts to infer lexical access time from eye fixation times. However, judicious use of such techniques in combination with eye-movement measurements in reading may add to our knowledge about reading if there is converging evidence that the technique is getting at many of the same processes as normal reading and yet there is enough control that something more can be learned. Some studies of this type have begun to appear in recent years (see Balota & Rayner, 1983; O'Brien et al., Note 4; Rayner, McConkie et al., 1980; Schustack, Ehrlich, & Rayner, in press), and more will probably appear in the future.

ACKNOWLEDGEMENTS

Preparation of this paper was supported by grants BNS85-10177 and BNS86-09336 from the National Science Foundation. We thank Charles Clifton, Lyn Frazier, Kevin O'Regan, and Mark Seidenberg for their comments on an earlier version.

REFERENCES

Aaronson, D. (1984). Computer methods and ecological validity in reading research. *Behavior Research Methods and Instrumentation, 16*, 102–108.

Aaronson, D. & Ferres, S. (1986). Reading strategies for children and adults: A quantitative model. *Psychological Review, 93*, 89–112.

Arnold, D. & Tinker, M. A. (1939). The fixation pause of the eyes. *Journal of Experimental Psychology, 25*, 271–280.

Balota, D. A., Pollatsek, A., & Rayner, K. (1985). The interaction of contextual constraints and parafoveal visual information in reading. *Cognitive Psychology, 17*, 364–390.

Balota, D. A. & Rayner, K. (1983). Parafoveal visual information and semantic contextual constraints. *Journal of Experimental Psychology: Human Perception and Performance, 5,* 726–738.

Becker, W. & Jurgens, R. (1979). An analysis of the saccadic system by means of double-step stimuli. *Vision Research, 19,* 967–983.

Blanchard, H. E.. (1985). A comparison of some processing time measures based on eye movements. *Acta Psychologica, 58,* 1–15.

Blanchard, H. E. (in press). Pronoun processing during fixations: Effects on the time course of information utilization. *Bulletin of the Psychonomic Society.*

Blanchard, H. E., McConkie, G. W., Zola, D., & Wolverton, G. S. (1984). The time course of visual information utilization during fixations in reading. *Journal of Experimental Psychology: Human Perception and Performance, 10,* 75–89.

Bradshaw, J. L. (1974). Peripherally presented and unreported words may bias the meaning of a centrally fixated homograph. *Journal of Experimental Psychology, 103,* 1200–1202.

Carpenter, P. A. & Just, M. (1983). What your eyes do while your mind is reading. In K. Rayner (Ed.), *Eye movements in reading: Perceptual and language processes.* New York: Academic Press.

Carrithers, C. & Bever, T. G. (1984). Eye-movement patterns confirm theories of language comprehension. *Cognitive Science, 8,* 157–172.

Carroll, P. & Slowiaczek, M. L. (1986). Constraints on semantic priming in reading: A fixation time analysis. *Memory & Cognition, 14,* 509–522.

Carroll, P. & Slowiaczek, M. L. (1987). Modes and modules: Multiple pathways to the language processor. In J. Garfield (Ed.), *Modularity in knowledge representation and natural language processing.* Cambridge, Mass.: M.I.T. Press.

Coeffe, C. & O'Regan, J. K. (1987). Reducing the influence of nontarget stimuli on saccade accuracy: Predictability and latency effects. *Vision Research, 27,* 227–240.

Coltheart, M. (1981). Disorders of reading and their implications for models of normal reading. *Visible Language, 15,* 245–286.

DenBuurman, R., Boersma, T., & Gerrissen, J. F. (1981). Eye movements and the perceptual span in reading. *Reading Research Quarterly, 16,* 227–235.

Ehrlich, S. F. & Rayner, K. (1981). Contextual effects on word perception and eye movements during reading. *Journal of Verbal Learning and Verbal Behavior, 20,* 641–655.

Ehrlich, K. & Rayner, K. (1983). Pronoun assignment and semantic integration during reading: Eye movements and immediacy of processing. *Journal of Verbal Learning and Verbal Behavior, 22,* 75–87.

Ferreira, F. & Clifton, C. (1986). The independence of syntactic processing. *Journal of Memory and Language, 25,* 348–368.

Fisher, D. F. & Shebilske, W. L. (1985). There is more that meets the eye than the eyemind assumption. In R. Groner, G. W. McConkie, & C. Menz (Eds.), *Eye movements and human information processing.* Amsterdam: North-Holland.

Frazier, L. (1983). Processing sentence structure. In K. Rayner (Ed.), *Eye movements in reading: Perceptual and language processes.* New York: Academic Press.

Frazier, L. & Rayner, K. (1982). Making and correcting errors during sentence comprehension: Eye movements in the analysis of structurally ambiguous sentences. *Cognitive Psychology, 14,* 178–210.

Frazier, L. & Rayner, K. (in press). Resolution of syntactic category ambiguities: Eye movements in parsing lexically ambiguous sentences. *Journal of Memory and Language.*

Haberlandt, K. F. & Graesser, A. C. (1985). Component processes in text comprehension and some of their interactions. *Journal of Experimental Psychology: General, 114,* 357–374.

Hogaboam, T. W. (1983). Reading patterns in eye-movement data. In K. Rayner (Ed.), *Eye movements in reading: Perceptual and language processes.* New York: Academic Press.

Hogaboam, T. W. & McConkie, G. W. (1981). The rocky road from eye fixations to comprehension. (Tech. Rep. No. 207). Champaign, Illinois: University of Illinois, Center for the Study of Reading.

Holmes, V. M. & O'Regan, J. K. (1981). Eye fixation patterns during the reading of relative-clause sentences. *Journal of Verbal Learning and Verbal Behavior, 20,* 417–430.

Huey, E. B. (1908). *The psychology and pedagogy of reading.* New York: Macmillan.

Ikeda, M. & Saida, S. (1978). Span of recognition in reading. *Vision Research, 18,* 83–88.

Inhoff, A. W. (1982). Parafoveal word perception: A further case against semantic preprocessing. *Journal of Experimental Psychology: Human Perception and Performance, 8,* 137–145.

Inhoff, A. W. (1984). Two stages of word processing during eye fixations in the reading of prose. *Journal of Verbal Learning and Verbal Behavior, 23,* 612–624.

Inhoff, A. W. & Rayner, K. (1980). Parafoveal word perception: A case against semantic preprocessing. *Perception & Psychophysics, 27,* 457–464.

Inhoff, A. W. & Rayner, K. (1986). Parafoveal word processing during eye fixations in reading: Effects of word frequency. *Perception & Psychophysics, 40,* 431–439.

Just, M. A. & Carpenter, P. A. (1978). Inference processes during reading: Reflections from eye fixations. In J. W. Senders, D. F. Fisher, & R. A. Monty (Eds.), *Eye movements and the higher psychological functions.* Hillsdale, N.J.: Lawrence Erlbaum Associates Inc.

Just, M. A. & Carpenter, P. A. (1980). A theory of reading: From eye fixations to comprehension. *Psychological Review, 87,* 329–354.

Kennedy, A. & Murray, W. S. (1984). Inspection times for words in syntactically ambiguous sentences under three presentation conditions. *Journal of Experimental Psychology: Human Perception and Performance, 10,* 833–849.

Kliegl, R., Olson, R. K., & Davidson, B. J. (1982). Regression analyses as a tool for studying reading processes: Comment on Just and Carpenter's eye fixation theory. *Memory & Cognition, 10,* 287–295.

Lima, S. D. (1987). Morphological analysis in sentence reading. *Journal of Memory and Language, 26,* 84–99.

Lima, S. D. & Inhoff, A. W. (1985). Lexical access during eye fixations in reading: Effects of word-initial letter sequence. *Journal of Experimental Psychology: Human Perception and Performance, 11,* 272–285.

McClelland, J. L. & O'Regan, J. K. (1981). Expectations increase the benefit derived from parafoveal visual information in reading words aloud. *Journal of Experimental Psychology: Human Perception and Performance, 7,* 634–644.

McConkie, G. W. & Hogaboam, T. W. (1985). Eye position and word identification in reading. In R. Groner, G. W. McConkie, & C. Menz (Eds.), *Eye movements and human information processing.* Amsterdam: North-Holland Press.

McConkie, G. W. & Rayner, K. (1975). The span of the effective stimulus during a fixation in reading. *Perception & Psychophysics, 17,* 578–586.

McConkie, G. W. & Rayner, K. (1976). Asymmetry of the perceptual span in reading. *Bulletin of the Psychonomic Society, 8,* 365–368.

McConkie, G. W., Underwood, N. R., Zola, D. & Wolverton, G. S. (1985). Some temporal characteristics of processing during reading. *Journal of Experimental Psychology: Human Perception and Performance, 11,* 168–186.

McConkie, G. W. & Zola, D. (1979). Is visual information integrated across successive fixations in reading? *Perception & Psychophysics, 25,* 221–224.

McConkie, G. W. & Zola, D. (1984). Eye movement control during reading: The effects of word units. In W. Prinz & A. F. Sanders (Eds.), *Cognition and motor processes.* Berlin: Springer-Verlag.

McConkie, G. W., Zola, D., Blanchard, H. E., & Wolverton, G. S. (1982). Perceiving words during reading: Lack of facilitation from prior peripheral exposure. *Perception & Psychophysics, 32,* 271–281.

Mehler, J., Bever, T. G., & Carey, P. (1967). What we look at when we read. *Perception and Psychophysics*, 2, 213–218.

Meyer, D. E. & Schvaneveldt, R. W. (1971). Facilitation in recognizing pairs of words: Evidence of a dependence between retrieval operations. *Journal of Experimental Psychology*, 90, 227–234.

Morrison, R. E. (1983). Retinal image size and the perceptual span in reading. In K. Rayner (Ed.), *Eye movements in reading: Perceptual and language processes*. New York: Academic Press.

Morrison, R. E. (1984). Manipulation of stimulus onset delay in reading: Evidence for parallel programming of saccades. *Journal of Experimental Psychology: Human Perception and Performance*, 10, 667–682.

Morrison, R. E. & Rayner, K. (1981). Saccade size in reading depends upon character spaces and not visual angle. *Perception & Psychophysics*, 30, 395–396.

O'Regan, J. K. (1979). Eye guidance in reading: Evidence for the linguistic control hypothesis. *Perception & Psychophysics*, 25, 501–509.

O'Regan, J. K. (1980). The control of saccade size and fixation duration in reading: The limits of linguistic control. *Perception & Psychophysics*, 28, 112–117.

O'Regan, J. K. (1981). The convenient viewing position hypothesis. In D. F. Fisher, R. A. Monty, & J. W. Senders (Eds.), *Eye movements: Cognition and visual perception*. Hillsdale, N.J.: Lawrence Erlbaum Associates Inc.

O'Regan, J. K. (1983). Elementary perceptual and eye-movement control processes in reading. In K. Rayner (Ed.), *Eye movements in reading: Perceptual and language processes*. New York: Academic Press.

O'Regan, J. K., Levy-Schoen, A., & Jacobs, A. M. (1983). The effect of visibility on eye-movement parameters in reading. *Perception & Psychophysics*, 34, 457–464.

O'Regan, J. K., Levy-Schoen, A., Pynte, J., & Brugaillere, B. (1984). Convenient fixation location within isolated words of different length and structures. *Journal of Experimental Psychology: Human Perception and Performance*, 10, 250–257.

Osaka, N. (1987). Effect of peripheral visual field size upon eye movements during Japanese text processing. In J. K. O'Regan & A. Levy-Schoen (Eds.), *Eye movements: From physiology to cognition*. Amsterdam: Elsevier Science Publishers.

Paap, K. R., Newsome, S. L., McDonald, J. E., & Schvaneveldt, R. W. (1982). An activation-verification model for letter and word recognition: The word superiority effect. *Psychological Review*, 89, 573–594.

Pollatsek, A., Bolozky, S., Well, A. D., & Rayner, K. (1981). Asymmetries in the perceptual span for Israeli readers. *Brain and Language*, 14, 174–180.

Pollatsek, A. & Rayner, K. (1982). Eye movement control in reading: The role of word boundaries. *Journal of Experimental Psychology: Human Perception and Performance*, 8, 817–833.

Pollatsek, A., Rayner, K., & Balota, D. A. (1986). Inferences about eye movement control from the perceptual span in reading. *Perception & Psychophysics*, 40, 123–130.

Rayner, K. (1975). The perceptual span and peripheral cues in reading. *Cognitive Psychology*, 7, 65–81.

Rayner, K. (1977). Visual attention in reading: Eye movements reflect cognitive processes. *Memory & Cognition*, 4, 443–448.

Rayner, K. (1978a). Eye movements in reading and information processing. *Psychological Bulletin*, 85, 618–660.

Rayner, K. (1978b). Foveal and parafoveal cues in reading. In J. Requin (Ed.), *Attention and performance VII*. Hillsdale, N.J.: Lawrence Erlbaum Associates Inc.

Rayner, K. (1979). Eye guidance in reading: Fixation locations within words. *Perception*, 8, 21–30.

Rayner, K. (1984). Visual selection in reading, picture perception, and visual search: A tutorial review. In H. Bouma & D. Bouwhuis (Eds.), *Attention and performance X*. Hillsdale, N.J.: Lawrence Erlbaum Associates Inc.

Rayner, K. (1986). Eye movements and the perceptual span in beginning and skilled readers. *Journal of Experimental Child Psychology, 41*, 211–236.

Rayner, K., Balota, D. A., & Pollatsek, A. (1986). Against parafoveal semantic preprocessing during eye fixations in reading. *Canadian Journal of Psychology, 40*, 473–483.

Rayner, K. & Bertera, J. H. (1979). Reading without a fovea. *Science, 206*, 468–469.

Rayner, K., Carlson, M., & Frazier, L. (1983). The interaction of syntax and semantics during sentence processing: Eye movements in the analysis of semantically biased sentences. *Journal of Verbal Learning and Verbal Behavior, 22*, 358–374.

Rayner, K. & Duffy, S. A. (1986). Lexical complexity and fixation times in reading: Effects of word frequency, verb complexity, and lexical ambiguity. *Memory and Cognition, 14*, 191–201

Rayner, K. & Duffy, S. A. (1987). Eye movements and lexical ambiguity. In J. K. O'Regan & A. Levy-Schoen (Eds.), *Eye movements: From physiology to cognition*. Amsterdam: Elsevier Science Publishers.

Rayner, K. & Frazier, L. (in press). Parsing temporarily ambiguous compliments. *Quarterly Journal of Experimental Psychology*.

Rayner, K., Inhoff, A. W., Morrison, R., Slowiaczek, M. L., & Bertera, J. H. (1981). Masking of foveal and parafoveal vision during eye fixations in reading. *Journal of Experimental Psychology: Human Perception and Performance, 7*, 167–179.

Rayner, K. & McConkie, G. W. (1976). What guides a reader's eye movements. *Vision Research, 16*, 829–837.

Rayner, K., McConkie, G. W., & Ehrlich, S. F. (1978). Eye movements and integrating information across fixations. *Journal of Experimental Psychology: Human Perception and Performance, 4*, 529–544.

Rayner, K., McConkie, G. W., & Zola, D. (1980). Integrating information across eye movements. *Cognitive Psychology, 12*, 206–226.

Rayner, K. & Pollatsek, A. (1981). Eye movement control during reading: Evidence for direct control. *Quarterly Journal of Experimental Psychology, 33A*, 351–373.

Rayner, K., Slowiaczek, M. L., Clifton, C., & Bertera, J. H. (1983). Latency of sequential eye movements: Implications for reading. *Journal of Experimental Psychology: Human Perception and Performance, 9*, 912–922.

Rayner, K., Well, A. D., & Pollatsek, A. (1980). Asymmetry of the effective visual field in reading. *Perception & Psychophysics, 27*, 537–544.

Rayner, K., Well, A. D., Pollatsek, A., & Bertera, J. H. (1982). The availability of useful information to the right of fixation in reading. *Perception & Psychophysics, 31*, 537–550.

Rumelhart, D. E. & McClelland, J. L. (1982). An interactive activation model of context effects in letter perception: Part 2. *Psychological Review, 89*, 60–94.

Salthouse, T. A. & Ellis, C. L. (1980). Determinants of eye fixation duration. *American Journal of Psychology, 93*, 207–234.

Schustack, M. W., Ehrlich, S. F., & Rayner, K. (in press). The complexity of contextual facilitation in reading: Local and global influences. *Journal of Memory and Language*.

Seidenberg, M. S., Tanenhaus, M. K., Leiman, J. M., & Bienkowski, M. (1982). Automatic access of the meanings of ambiguous words in context: Some limitations of knowledge-based processing. *Cognitive Psychology, 14*, 489–537.

Slowiaczek, M. L. & Rayner, K. (in press). Sequential masking during eye fixations in reading. *Bulletin of the Psychonomic Society*.

Swinney, D. A. (1979). Lexical access during sentence comprehension: (Re)consideration of context effects. *Journal of Verbal Learning and Verbal Behavior, 18*, 645–659.

Tinker, M. (1958). Recent studies of eye movements in reading. *Psychological Bulletin, 55,* 215–231.

Underwood, G. (1980). Attention and nonselective lexical access of ambiguous words. *Canadian Journal of Psychology, 34,* 72–76.

Underwood, G. (1981). Lexical recognition of embedded unattended words: Some implications for the reading process. *Acta Psychologica, 34,* 267–283.

Underwood, N. R. & McConkie, G. W. (1985). Perceptual span for letter distinctions during reading. *Reading Research Quarterly, 20,* 153–162.

Underwood, N. R. & Zola, D. (1986). The span of letter recognition of good and poor readers. *Reading Research Quarterly, 21,* 6–19.

Vonk, W. (1984). Eye movements during comprehension of pronouns. In A. G. Gale & F. Johnson (Eds.), *Theoretical and applied aspects of eye movement research.* Amsterdam: North-Holland, 203–212.

Ward, N. J. & Juola, J. F. (1982). Reading with and without eye movements: Reply to Just, Carpenter, and Woolley. *Journal of Experimental Psychology: General, 111,* 239–241.

Well, A. D. (1983). Perceptual factors in reading. In K. Rayner (Ed.), *Eye movements in reading: Perceptual and language processes.* New York: Academic Press.

Wolverton, G. S. & Zola, D. (1983). The temporal characteristics of visual information extraction during reading. In K. Rayner (Ed.), *Eye movements in reading: Perceptual and language processes.* New York: Academic Press.

Zola, D. (1984). Redundancy and word perception during reading. *Perception & Psychophysics, 36,* 277–284.

REFERENCE NOTES

1. Blanchard, H. E., Pollatsek, A., & Rayner, K. (1987). *The influence of parafoveal information on eye movement behavior in reading.* Manuscript in preparation.

2. Inhoff, A. W., Pollatsek, A., Posner, M. I., & Rayner, K. (1987). *Covert attention and eye movements during reading.* Manuscript in preparation.

3. Morris, R. K. (1987). *Continuous processing of word boundary information during eye fixations in reading.* Unpublished Masters thesis, University of Massachusetts.

4. O'Brien, E. J., Shank, D. M., Myers, J. L., & Rayner, K. (1987). *Elaborative inferences during reading: Do they occur on-line?* Submitted for publication.

5. O'Regan, J. K. (1975). *Structural and contextual constraints on eye movements in reading.* Unpublished doctoral dissertation, University of Cambridge, England.

16

Eye-movement Strategy and Tactics in Word Recognition and Reading

J. Kevin O'Regan and Ariane Lévy-Schoen
Groupe Regard, Laboratoire de Psychologie Expérimentale
Université René Descartes, CNRS, EHESS, EPHE
Paris, France

ABSTRACT

There is a position in each word, the "convenient viewing position," where the eye should first fixate in order for the word to be recognised most quickly. For every letter of deviation from this "ideal" initial fixation position, there is a penalty of about 20msec in recognition time.

This phenomenon, as well as the detailed underlying eye-movement behaviour that generates it, can be explained satisfactorily in terms of the combined action of three types of factors: sensory (acuity, lateral masking), lexical (word structure), and oculomotor. It seems that the time loss arising when the eye initially fixates in an "inconvenient" position arises predominantly, not from increased fixation durations, but from a higher probability of making additional fixations in the word. When the initial fixation is near the convenient viewing position, only a single fixation need be made. This fixation will be of comparatively long duration, and its duration may be affected by linguistic variables. When the initial fixation is far from the convenient viewing position: two fixations are made in a word; processing is distributed over both; each of these is of short duration; and their summed duration is about 75msec longer than if a single fixation had been made. In the two-fixation case the duration of the first of the two fixations is determined mainly by oculomotor and not by lexical processing.

INTRODUCTION

If you fixate a word under normal reading conditions, the letter being directly fixated benefits from the eye's maximum resolution, which is about $\frac{1}{2}$ minute arc. But the letters on each side of the centrally fixated letter are seen with only $\frac{2}{3}$ min arc of resolution, and at the third letter from the fixation point, resolution is at 1 min arc, that is, twice its central value (Anstis, 1974; Jacobs,

1979). In addition to these acuity limitations, strong lateral interactions between parafoveal letters (both at the sensory and featural levels) further degrade visibility.

Yet under normal conditions we do not have the subjective impression of seeing bits of words, but rather, whole words. This impression is partly the result of the fact that, though we are unaware of it, the eye can move around within the word if more detail about certain of its parts is needed. In addition, the fact that the letters viewed must form a known word, and the fact that this word must fit into the given linguistic context, may in many cases make extra eye fixations unnecessary.

These remarks suggest that word perception in reading is governed by three kinds of constraints: sensory constraints (acuity and lateral masking), oculomotor constraints, and processing constraints (lexical and linguistic). What are their relative roles? In answering this question a particular experimental paradigm has proved helpful. This consists of artificially imposing the position where the eye initially fixates in a word, and measuring the subject's oculomotor behaviour and the time it takes him or her to recognise the word. As appears from the studies to be considered here, sensory and oculomotor constraints are more important than expected.

IMPOSING INITIAL FIXATION LOCATION

In all the experiments to be discussed, each trial starts with the subject fixating a fixation mark on a computer screen. When the computer detects accurate fixation on the mark, a group of words appears at the fixated position. The test word is the first of the group, and it is located at the position occupied by the fixation mark, with the remaining words on the right.

The variable manipulated in these experiments is the position the eye is initially fixating at the moment the test word appears. Thus, the test word may appear laterally displaced to the right or to the left relative to the fixation mark in such a way that, on appearance, the eye is fixating its first, second, third, etc. or last letter. The eye is then free to move around in the test word before going on to the next word, and it may make one or more fixations before doing so. The subject reads the group of words and then makes a decision, indicated by a button press. We need to prevent interference between processing of the test word and the remaining words; while the subject's eye is on the test word, the other words in the phrase are masked out by being spattered with random dots. As soon as the subject's eye leaves the test word the fog of dots lifts from the other words and definitively descends upon the test word (thereby preventing further processing of it). We have used two types of task: a semantic decision, and a simple word-comparison task.

THE CONVENIENT VIEWING POSITION EFFECT

Figure 16.1 (replotted from Experiment 2 of O'Regan, Lévy-Schoen, Pynte, & Brugaillère, 1984) shows the observed gaze durations on the test word: that is, the total time spent by the eye on the word before going on to the next word. They show that the position where the eye has been forced to start in the word is critical in determining the total time spent on it. There is a "convenient viewing position," near the centre or (for long words) slightly left of centre, where the eye should start in the word for recognition to be most rapid. Notice that the penalty for not starting at the convenient viewing position is rather large: about 20msec per letter of deviation. In O'Regan et al. (1984) the effect of the eye's initial position was highly significant except

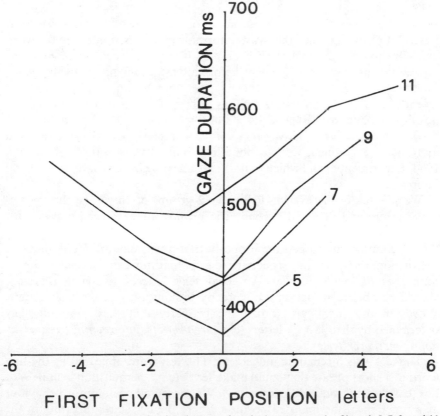

FIG. 16.1.   Total time spent fixating (i.e. gaze duration) on test words of length 5, 7, 9, and 11 letters as a function of the position, relative to word middle, that the eye was fixating at the moment the word appeared ("first fixation position"). Each data point is the mean over 12 subjects and 20 test words. Data replotted from O'Regan et al. (1984, Experiment 2).

APPR-M

for five-letter words, and more recent work has shown significant effects even for five-letter words (cf. Fig. 16.8). The convenient viewing position effect has also been observed by other authors both for isolated words (Underwood, Hyönä, & Niemi, 1987) and in normal reading (Blanchard & McConkie, personal communication). The effect is probably caused by the way sensory, oculomotor, and lexical constraints interact. It provides a useful tool for studying the relative roles played by these different kinds of constraints. In the following we will first discuss the influence of lexical processes in determining the effect. Further analyses will then be done which reveal the importance of oculomotor constraints.

LEXICAL INFLUENCES IN THE CONVENIENT VIEWING POSITION EFFECT

What determines the exact location of the convenient viewing position? Lexical processing and the way information is distributed in a word undoubtedly play a role. For example, if certain word parts must be processed before others (e.g. stems before affixes), it might be advantageous for the eye to start by fixating those parts. With Virginia Holmes we have recently been doing some work on how affixes affect the convenient viewing position (Holmes & O'Regan, 1987), but the results are not clear cut, and we need to do more work. However, some very interesting data came out of a more naive experiment we had done in a limited version (O'Regan et al., 1984, Experiment 3) and which (with V. Holmes) we have now replicated and improved.

We selected in the French dictionary 2 groups of 10 words, the "begin-ning" group and the "end" group. The groups were matched pairwise for length (10–12 letters) and for frequency (mean: 3.5 per million). Each word in the "beginning" group had the property that it was uniquely determined in the dictionary by its first six letters (e.g. *perquisition, attroupement, arres-tation, auxiliaire, hirondelle*). An ideal lexical access machine therefore should be able to recognise the word by looking only at these six letters. Words in the "end" group had the property that they were uniquely determined by their last six letters (e.g. *circonspecte, interrogatif, transversal, approfondi, architecte*).

The task was a semantic judgement: The test word appeared as the first word of a short phrase that could make sense (e.g. "perquisition brutale") or not (e.g. "gymnastique de la solidité"). We measured oculomotor behaviour as a function of the imposed position where the eye started fixating in the word, using the same paradigm as described earlier.

In the hypothetical case that lexical access can make use of word-end constraints as effectively as word-beginning constraints, the convenient viewing position for the "beginning" words should be near the beginning, and for the "end" words should be near the end of the word. In reality, lexical access presumably cannot make equally good use of word-end constraints. Nevertheless, since information content was shifted rightward in the "end" words, we expected at least some rightward shift of the convenient viewing position.

Figure 16.2 shows the gaze durations as a function of position initially fixated in the word. The typical U-shaped convenient viewing position curves are found again. For the "beginning" words, the convenient viewing position is near the fourth letter. The "end" words have a less well-defined convenient viewing position, but it is clear that, as expected, this is shifted rightwards to a larger zone somewhere near the middle of the words.

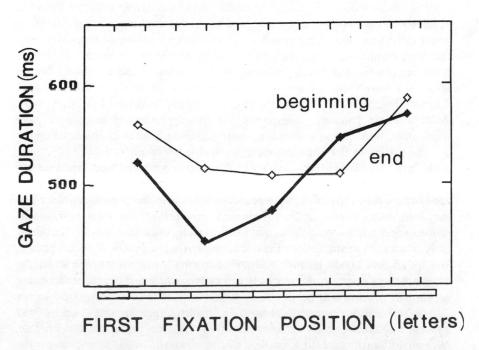

FIG. 16.2.   Total time spent fixating (gaze duration) on test words matched for length and frequency, uniquely determined by their first six letters ("beginning") or last six letters ("end"), as a function of the position the eye was fixating at the moment the word appeared ("first fixation position"). Each data point is the mean over 50 subjects reading 2 words. Ten words contributed to each graph (latin square design). Data from O'Regan and Holmes (in preparation).

CAUSE OF THE EFFECT OF POSITION: MORE FIXATIONS OR LONGER FIXATION DURATIONS?

The fact that we have been able to change the convenient viewing position by changing the informational structure of a word confirms that the convenient viewing position phenomenon is sensitive to lexical processing constraints. But a closer look at the fine details of eye-movement behaviour will also show the importance of visual and oculomotor constraints. For this we will return to the data of O'Regan et al. (1984), which will be subjected to new analyses.

We will begin by considering the question: When the eye fixates in an "inconvenient" position, where does the extra time taken to recognise the word come from: Does it come from making more fixations, or fixations of longer duration?

Figure 16.3a shows the probability of making a single fixation in the word as a function of the position initially fixated. When the initial position fixated is at the convenient viewing position, the probability of making a single fixation in the word is high. As the initial fixation position deviates from the convenient viewing position, the probability of making a single fixation drops, and that of making two fixations (middle graph) and three fixations (bottom graph) increases. An analysis of variance on the mean number of fixations made as a function of the initial position fixated shows highly significant effects of position for each word length: 5 letters: $F(2,18) = 20.53$; 7 letters: $F(3,24) = 30.79$; 9 letters: $F(4,20) = 20.69$; 11 letters: $F(5,30) = 21.54$. All $P \ll 0.005$. Thus one component of the position dependence of gaze durations comes from the fact that more fixations tend to be made when the eye starts further from the convenient viewing position.

Figure 16.4 provides the answer to the question of whether durations are affected by the position initially fixated. The figure shows the different recognition times required in the separate cases when recognition occurs in a single fixation, in two, and in three fixations. (Note that data points near word ends are missing in the single fixation case, since this occurs frequently only when the eye starts near the convenient viewing position.) As expected, the data show that the more fixations that are made in scanning the word, the longer the eye stays on the word. When only a single fixation is made in the word, its duration will be of about 400msec (this is long compared to the 250msec durations generally found in reading, presumably because the present word recognition situation involves no preceding linguistic context). When two fixations occur (middle set of curves), the total time spent on the word is around 475msec. This is 75msec longer than the single fixation case, suggesting about 75msec penalty when processing is distributed over two fixations. This 75msec perhaps partly corresponds to the slowing of lexical processing owing to the necessity of simultaneously planning saccade execution. Perhaps collecting information in a distributed way is also less

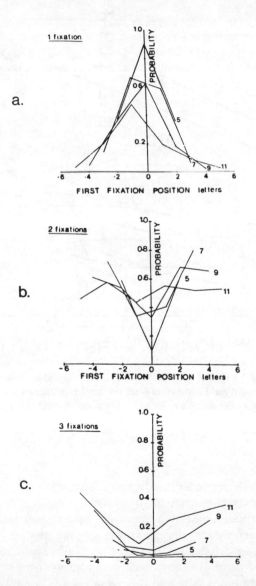

FIG. 16.3.   Analysis of data of O'Reagan et al. (1984, Experiment 2) showing the probability of making 1, 2, or 3 fixations in words of length 5, 7, 9, and 11 letters, as a function of the position, relative to the middle of the word, the eye was first fixating in the word when it appeared.

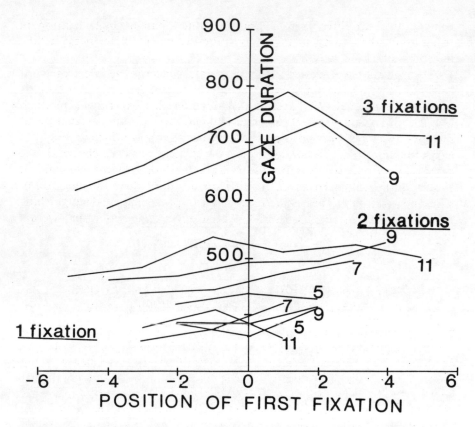

FIG. 16.4.   Data of O'Regan et al. (1984, Experiment 2) analysed to show separately the total time spent fixating the test word in the cases when the word was scanned in exactly one fixation, exactly two fixations, and exactly three fixations. Data are shown only when a given strategy occurred more than 10% of the time (data points are missing in the one-fixation and three-fixation cases). The abscissa is the position the eye was fixating in the word when it appeared.

efficient than collecting it in a single fixation. The penalty for three fixations is about 200msec above the single fixation case.

Note the essential point that the two- and three-fixation curves are virtually flat: Given that a particular strategy (one, two, or three fixations) has been chosen, we can deduce the time that will be spent on the word. The position initially fixated does not affect the duration of the strategy. Because of insufficient data in the one- and three-fixation cases, analyses of variance could only be performed on the two-fixation data. For these, there is no significant position effect: 5 letters: $F(2,18)=0.11$; 7 letters: $F(3,24)=2.4$; 9 letters: $F(4,20)=2.1$; 11 letters: $F(5,30)=1.86$; all $P>0.10$.

To summarise the answer to the question of what takes more time when the eye fixates in the "wrong" place: It is purely the increased probability of using a two- or three-fixation strategy rather than a single fixation in recognising the word, and not position-dependent differences in the durations of each strategy.

A further noteworthy aspect of these data concerns the effect of word length. In the present experiment, the effect of word length is confounded with word frequency. We have recently done another experiment in which frequency was controlled (O'Regan & Holmes, in preparation). Analysis of the one-, two-, and three-fixation strategies shows that word length does not affect the duration of the strategy, once the strategy has been chosen: If the word is scanned in two fixations, the time taken will be the same independent of the word's length. However, word frequency does affect the duration of scanning strategies. These differences appear promising in distinguishing lexical from sensory components of eye-movement behaviour, and we are investigating them further.

DISTRIBUTED PROCESSING: FIXATION LOCATIONS IN THE TWO-FIXATION STRATEGY

It seems that if the eye starts near the convenient viewing position, only a single fixation need be made in the word. All the processing of the word can be done at that fixation. But if the eye starts far from the convenient viewing position, then only part of the processing can be done at the initially fixated position, and processing must be distributed over the word in two (and sometimes three) fixations. What is particularly interesting is the fact (shown by the flatness of the curves in Fig. 16.4) that when processing is distributed over several fixations, there appears to be no effect of the order in which the word parts are scanned: Scanning from right to left appears to be as efficient as scanning from left to right. (It might be argued that the reason gaze durations in the two-fixation case are independent of order of scanning is that when scanning order causes difficulty, a third fixation is made, and no effect is seen in the two-fixation times. But then the probability of making three fixations should be larger when the eye starts at the end of the word than when it starts at the beginning of the word; yet this is not the case—cf. Fig. 16.3, bottom graph).

We shall now look more closely at what happens in the case when processing is distributed over two fixations in the word. The first question is, where does the eye go in the word after leaving the first fixation position? There are two possibilities. One possibility is based on the idea that processing of the word might only begin once the eye arrives near the convenient viewing position. We would then expect the eye always to saccade to this position when it starts too far away from it. The alternative is that, instead, processing could be spatially distributed over the word: Some use could be made of partial processing done in a not very informative region, and the eye could jump beyond the convenient viewing position and go further into the territory remaining to be processed. For example, if the eye's first fixation was near the beginning of the word, then on the second fixation, rather than jumping to the convenient viewing position, the eye could overshoot this and land somewhat nearer the end of the word.

Figure 16.5 gives histograms of the eye's second fixation position as a function of the position initially fixated. When the eye starts very near the beginning or very near the end of the word, the second fixation leads to a position on the other side of the word, slightly beyond the middle. When the initial fixation position is further into the word, the second fixation position moves further beyond the middle. When the initial fixation position is near the middle of the word, the eye may move right or left (there is little data here because generally the eye will only make a single fixation!).

The data are more consistent with the idea that processing is spatially

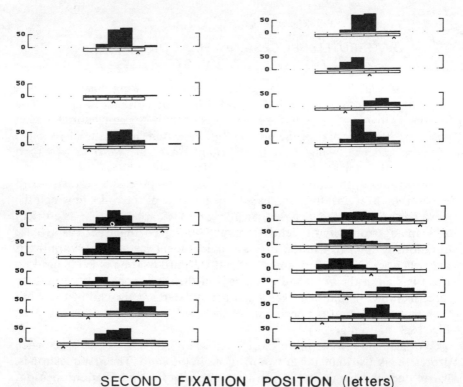

SECOND FIXATION POSITION (letters)

FIG. 16.5.   Analysis of the subset of the data of O'Regan et al. (1984, Experiment 2) when exactly two fixations were made: Histograms (unnormalised) showing the positions in the word where the second fixation occurred in the word, plotted as a function of the first-fixation positions (shown by arrows under each graph). The four panels are for 5, 7, 9, and 11-letter words.

distributed over the word. When two fixations are made, the eye does not always jump to the same place near the convenient viewing position, but seems to spread its scanning in a fairly even way over the word.

DISTRIBUTED PROCESSING: FIXATION DURATIONS IN THE TWO-FIXATION STRATEGY

The pattern emerging suggests that: (1) if the eye starts fixating a word near the convenient viewing position, only a single fixation need be made in the word, and all the processing of the word will be done there; and (2) if the eye starts further away from the convenient viewing position, it will do whatever processing is possible where it starts, and then jump to the other side of the word to do whatever processing remains to be done. If this is true, we expect the following: If the first fixation is far from the convenient viewing position, since little processing of the word can be done there, its duration should be short. The eye should move quickly to the other side of the word where the major part of processing can be done: The second fixation should thus be of long duration. A different pattern is expected if the first fixation occurs closer to the convenient viewing position: This time most processing can be done on the first fixation, which should be long, and only little remains to be done on the second fixation, which should be short. In order to represent graphically this expected trade-off between first and second fixation durations in the two fixation case, Fig. 16.6 plots the first fixation duration as a function of where this occurred in the word. Above each first fixation point is plotted the duration of the corresponding second fixation (even though it occurred elsewhere in the word).

The expected trade-off is found, strikingly verifying the idea of distributed processing. The analyses of variance confirm highly significant effects of position both on first and on second fixation durations for all word lengths except 5 letters: 5 letters: first fixation $F(2,18) = 1.19$; second fixation $F(2,18) = 1.24$; both n.s.; 7 letters: first fixation $F(3,24) = 9.75$, $P < 0.005$; second fixation $F(3,24) = 27.74$, $P \ll 0.0005$; 9 letters: first fixation $F(4,20) = 15.63$, $P \ll 0.0005$, second fixation $F(4,20) = 15.2$, $P \ll 0.0005$; 11 letters: first fixation $F(5,30) = 15.46$, $P \ll 0.0005$, second fixation $F(5,30) = 10.45$, $P \ll 0.0005$.

LEXICAL PROCESSING DOES NOT DETERMINE FIRST-FIXATION DURATIONS

Unfortunately further work shows the present interpretation to be only partly correct. It is indeed true that when two fixations are made, processing is distributed over the word, and that what is not done on the first fixation is

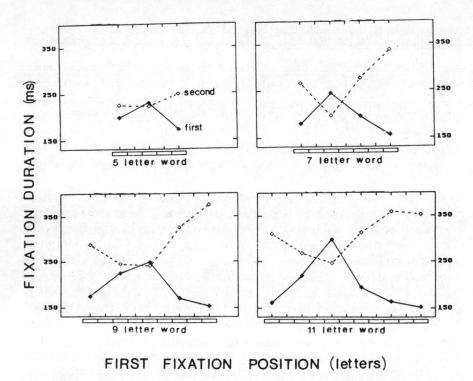

FIRST FIXATION POSITION (letters)

FIG. 16.6.   Subset of the data of O'Regan et al. (1984, Experiment 2) when exactly two fixations were made: Individual fixation durations, as a function of the position where the first fixation occurred, that is, where the eye was fixating at the moment the word appeared. Note that the second-fixation durations (dotted lines) are plotted at the abscissa positions where the corresponding first fixation (solid lines) occurred. In this way, the total time spent on the word can be read off by summing data points aligned vertically at a given abscissa value.

done on the second. However, the processing involved is not just lexical processing, but also oculomotor processing. In particular, the hump in the first-fixation duration curve is caused by oculomotor and not by lexical processing. The dip in the second-fixation duration curve is determined partly by oculomotor processing, and partly by lexical processing.

We will consider in detail the arguments showing that the hump in the first-fixation duration curve is caused by oculomotor and not lexical processing. A first argument is theoretical (cf. also McConkie, Underwood, Zola, & Wolverton, 1985; Rayner, Slowiaczek, Clifton, & Bertera, 1983): Research on the oculomotor system suggests that the fastest reaction time the eye can display (simple stimulus, predictable moment and location of appearance) is of the order of 150msec (though for correction saccades, which are a special case, means are closer to 100msec). Since this is the duration of the first fixations observed when the eye started fixating near the beginning or end of a word, we can assume that no lexical processing of the word is attempted in that case. Now consider the case when the eye starts fixating a little closer to the centre of the word. In that case we observe slightly longer first-fixation durations, let us say 10msec longer. Can this 10msec correspond to 10msec of lexical processing being done? Surely not, since 10msec seems to be too short an increment over the elementary oculomotor reaction time, because during this time the following things must be done: (1) decide to do some lexical processing rather than move immediately; (2) do that processing; (3) decide that not very much processing can be done; and (4) trigger a saccade. Thus the fact that the first-fixation duration curve increases *gradually* rather than abruptly by a large increment from the base value of 150msec argues against the idea that this increase is due to lexical processing. (Analysis of the histograms of fixation durations also show no bimodality.)

Several sources of experimental evidence further confirm that the hump in the first-fixation duration curves are not related to lexical processing. Consider again the experiment mentioned earlier in which the position of "information" in a word was manipulated. We saw that the convenient viewing position shifted to the right when the useful information was at the right-hand end of the word. If we look at cases where two fixations occur in a word, we again find the mirror-image curves for first- and second-fixation durations (Fig. 16.7). But if the duration of first fixations reflected the amount of processing being done during these fixations, we would expect the "beginning" words to have their peak of processing in first-fixation duration near the beginnings, whereas the "end" words should display a first-fixation duration peak further to the right. However, the curves for first-fixation durations are identical. Differences between the two types of words only appear in the second-fixation durations.

A similar argument comes from another experiment we have done recently in collaboration with Virginia Holmes. In this, words of high (115 per million) and low (2.2 per million) frequency were used in the same experimental paradigm as before. As before we find the typical U-shaped convenient viewing position curves (Fig. 16.8) and, as expected, the low-frequency words take longer overall than the high-frequency words. Such differences are processing differences, and should be reflected in first-fixation durations, particularly when most of the processing is done on the first fixation. However, again, in the cases where exactly two fixations occur, there is no difference in the first-fixation durations, only in the second-fixation durations (Fig. 16.9).

A final line of evidence comes from other experiments we have done using stimuli consisting of a string of xs. The subject's eye starts at a position somewhere in the string, and the task is to saccade to the middle of the string

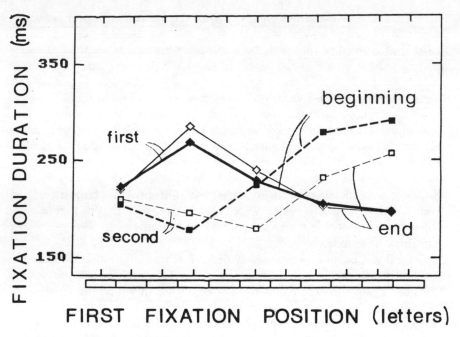

FIG. 16.7.   Subset of the data of O'Regan and Holmes (in preparation) when exactly two fixations are made: First- (solid lines) and second- (dotted lines) fixation durations for words of type "beginning" and "end." Data are plotted as in Fig. 16.6.

(which may or may not be marked), where a target letter will appear. No processing of the target letter is possible before the eye gets to the target, because the target only appears when the eye lands at the middle of the string. Yet there is still a maximum in the first-fixation duration curve at the points corresponding to the case when the eye starts off near the target position.

The conclusion seems compelling: The shape of the first-fixation duration curve seems unrelated to processing. We are currently investigating a number of possible explanations: it might be difficult for the eye to make small saccades; there might be an oculomotor dead zone where the impetus to make a saccade is weak; there might be more difficulty making a saccade away from a point if the distribution of luminance is symmetrical about the point. Pilot experiments suggest that none of these factors are important. Two other factors we are now investigating appear to bear more promise: the ease with which the location of the saccade target can be determined, and the ability of using contour information to determine the eye's proximity to the desired position.

In any event, we are now convinced that the factors affecting first-fixation

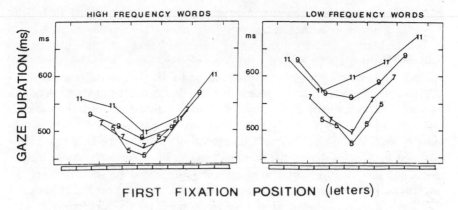

FIG. 16.8.   Total gaze durations for high-frequency and low-frequency words as a function of position initially fixated in the word. Data from O'Regan and Holmes (in preparation). The different curves correspond to words of length 5, 7, 9, and 11 letters.

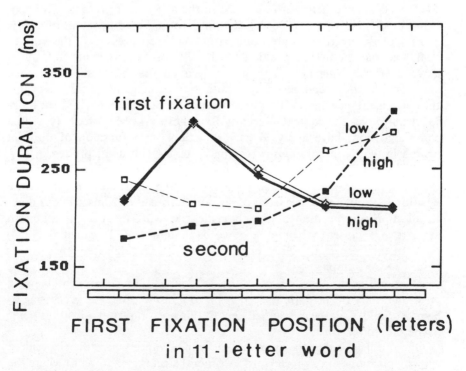

FIG. 16.9.   Subset of the data for high- and low-frequency words (cf. Fig. 16.8) for which exactly two fixations occurred: first- and second-fixation durations. The data are plotted as in Fig. 16.6. Only data for 11-letter words are shown.

duration, in the case when two fixations occur, are not related to lexical processing but to visuomotor control.

What about the second fixation? Is this also being determined by some oculomotor process? Certainly not completely, since we observed that second-fixation durations were sensitive to lexical frequency and informational structure. However, some recent work also shows the existence of an oculomotor component determining second-fixation durations. This seems to come from the fact that the saccade following the second fixation will usually lead to the next word. This saccade can therefore be prepared in advance, as early as during the *first* fixation. As this fixation becomes longer (for whatever reason), correspondingly less time need be spent in saccade programming on the second fixation, and this second fixation will be shorter. We have not yet quantified the relative sizes of the oculomotor and processing components contributing to the second-fixation duration.

READING

The effects studied here were observed in the absence of preceding context. What modifications are to be expected in a normal reading situation?

First of all, preceding context and parafoveal preprocessing of the word to be fixated may modify the position which it is most "convenient" to fixate in a word. These same factors may also weaken the requirement to make additional fixations and generally facilitate processing. We therefore expect the convenient viewing position phenomenon to be weakened, and the more so, the stronger the context. Recently Blanchard and McConkie, (personal communication) have analysed gaze durations as a function of position fixated in words in continuous reading of texts. The data, plotted in Fig. 16.10 (top graph), show an evident convenient viewing position effect, and as expected, it is weaker: The penalty for not fixating at the convenient viewing position is about 9msec per letter of deviation instead of 20msec in our data. In addition, the position of the convenient viewing position in the word appears to be closer to the middle of words than in the O'Regan et al. (1984) data: In this respect the data resemble our data for high-frequency words (Fig. 16.8, left graph).

A second point to consider is the following: Our convenient viewing position is only the position the eye *ought* to go to in order for processing to be most rapid. Can the eye actually get to this position from a fixation point in the preceding word?

One problem is that the eye can't know in advance where the convenient viewing position is in a given word. A general strategy of going to where the convenient viewing position is *expected* to be is the only possibility. Several authors have observed that the eye's "preferred viewing position," that is, the position the eye tends to saccade to on entering a new word, is somewhere left

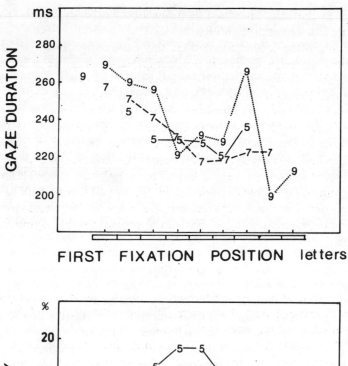

FIRST   FIXATION   POSITION   letters

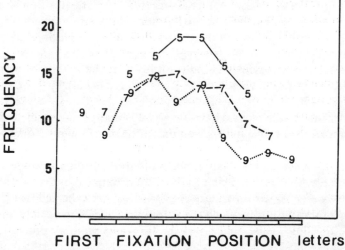

FIRST   FIXATION   POSITION   letters

FIG. 16.10.   Graphs plotted from data on continuous reading of texts, provided by Blanchard and McConkie (personal communication). The top graph gives the total gaze duration on words of length 5, 7, and 9 letters as a function of the first position the eye fixated in the word. The first point of the graph for each word length is not connected to the other points because it corresponds to a fixation occurring in the space preceding the word. For word lengths 5, 7, and 9, the data are derived from 2578, 1642, and 623 fixations, respectively. The last 3 data points for the 9-letter case oscillate because of lack of data. The lower graph gives histograms of the positions where the first fixations fell, expressed as a percentage of the total number falling on the word or in the preceding space.

of centre of a word for long words (Coëffé, 1985; Dunn-Rankin, 1978; Rayner, 1979). The bottom graph in Fig. 16.10 plots the preferred landing positions observed in the data Blanchard and McConkie provided us. These data also confirm that the most probable landing position is at the third letter for seven-letter words and between the third and fifth letters for nine-letter words. Why is the preferred viewing position not at the middle of words, where Blanchard and McConkie (top graph) observed the gaze duration to be shortest (i.e. the convenient viewing position)? Surely if the eye generally saccades to a position left of the convenient viewing position, reading efficiency will be hampered, since additional fixations will tend to be made.

A possible explanation of why the preferred viewing position is not at the convenient viewing position is that the eye cannot go exactly where it wants, for oculomotor reasons. There is a body of data in the oculomotor literature that shows that when the eye saccades to a target in the visual field, the saccade is strongly deviated away from the target by the presence of nontarget elements (Findlay, 1982). In a recent experiment (Coëffé & O'Regan, 1987), we looked at the eye's ability to saccade to a particular place marked by crosses in a string of nine letters (Fig. 16.11, upper picture). When the target position is near the beginning or end of the string, the eye is incapable of accurately landing on the target: Its landing position is deviated away from the target by the other string elements. Our data show that for a target position at the middle of the string, the landing position is between the third and fourth letters. This is consistent with Blanchard and McConkie's finding that the convenient viewing position is at the middle of words, but that the actual position where the eye tends to land is near the third or fourth letter.

Another interesting fact we have observed is that the accuracy with which the eye can attain a target depends on the duration of the preceding fixation. Figure 16.11 (lower picture) summarises the data for a condition in which the time the eye spends on the fixation mark before saccading into the stimulus was artificially lengthened. This was done by training subjects to make their saccade only after the fixation mark extinguished. We expected that the effect of this extra delay (during which the stimulus is visible in peripheral vision) would be to allow visual analysis of the target location to proceed further than usual before saccade triggering. As expected we observed that accuracy improved.

CONCLUSION: EYE MOVEMENTS AS MEASURES OF PROCESSING IN READING?

We propose the following tentative suggestion as to how eye movements are controlled from moment-to-moment in word recognition and reading.

Because saccade programming takes times of the same order as lexical

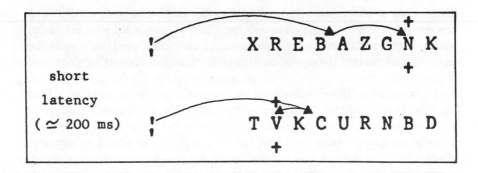

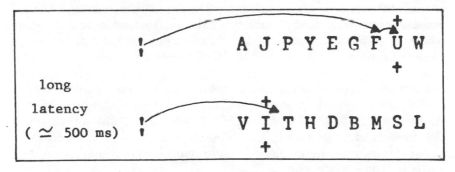

FIG. 16.11.   Typical data from Coëffé and O'Regan (1987) showing the positions where the eye lands in a nine-letter string when aiming for the positions indicated by crosses.

processing itself, it would be inefficient always to wait for lexical processing before moving the eye. Readers will therefore (unconsciously) adopt a general eye-movement strategy which can operate purely on the basis of rapidly available low-level information (like word boundaries), and which does not require access to the mental lexicon. This strategy makes use of the fact that the convenient viewing position in words tends to be somewhere near their middles (of course the strategy breaks down for exceptional words where this is not the case). The strategy says: "If the eye is near the middle of a word, program a saccade to the next word. If the eye is not near the middle, make an additional fixation in the word, and then go to the next word." (We presently have no suggestion about groups of short words.) How precisely the eye must be fixated near the word middle for a single fixation to occur is a parameter of the global oculomotor strategy which is set in advance as a function of the desired reading speed.

At the same time as this strategy operates, lexical and sentence processing proceed. These provide local tactics that can modulate the general oculomotor strategy from moment to moment by delaying (or possibly accelerating) the occurrence of a saccade. But any such modulation must wait for lexical and semantic processing to occur, and so can only affect the later stages; that is, only the second fixations or the long first fixations of within-word scanning.

The essence of this description, namely that reading consists of a basic oculomotor strategy modulated in a delayed fashion by linguistic processing, is not new, and has been suggested by most authors before. What is new is the attempt to quantify precisely the influences of sensory and oculomotor constraints, thereby opening for the future the possibility of calculating, by subtraction, the effects due to lexical and linguistic processing. Among the sensory and oculomotor effects we have observed are: the existence of a convenient viewing position itself (although this is determined also by lexical processing constraints); the inability of the eye to land accurately at an aimed-for position; the dependence of this aiming accuracy on preceding fixation duration; the fact that when two fixations are made in a word, the first-fixation duration is determined essentially by an as yet unknown visuomotor process, and that the second-fixation duration depends on the oculomotor preparation period that has been possible during the first fixation; and the fact that when two fixations are made, possibly because of the necessity of programming an additional saccade, there is a penalty of about 75 msec in total gaze duration as compared with the time taken when a single fixation is made.

In any case, the work we have presented shows the importance of sensory and oculomotor factors in determining eye-movement behaviour in word recognition and reading. It appears that before interpreting a given aspect of eye movements as a measure of processing, it is necessary to check whether this aspect is not also being influenced by sensory or oculomotor factors.

REFERENCES

Anstis, S. M. (1974). A chart illustrating variations in acuity with retinal position. *Vision Research, 14,* 589–592.

Coëffé, C. (1985). La visée du regard sur un mot isolé. *L'Année Psychologique, 85,* 169–184.

Coëffé, C. & O'Regan, J. K. (1987). Reducing the influence of nontarget stimuli on saccade accuracy: Predictability and latency effects. *Vision Research, 27,* 227–240.

Dunn-Rankin, P. (1978). The visual characteristics of words. *Scientific American, 238,* 1, 122–130.

Findlay, J. M. (1982). Global visual processing for saccadic eye movements. *Vision Research, 22,* 1033–1045.

Holmes, V. M. & O'Regan, J. K. (1987). Decomposing French words. In J. K. O'Regan & A. Lévy-Schoen (eds.), *Eye movements: From physiology to cognition.* Amsterdam: North-Holland, pp. 459–466.

Jacobs, R. J. (1979). Visual resolution and contour interaction in the fovea and periphery. *Vision Research, 19*, 1187–1196.

McConkie, G. W., Underwood, N. R., Zola, C., & Wolverton, G. S. (1985). Some temporal characteristics of processing during reading. *Journal of Experimental Psychology: Human Perception and Performance, 11*, 168–186.

O'Regan, J. K., Lévy-Schoen, A., Pynte, J., & Brugaillère, B. (1984). Convenient fixation location within isolated words of different length and structure. *Journal of Experimental Psychology: Human Perception and Performance, 10*, 2, 250–257.

Rayner, K. (1979). Eye guidance in reading: Fixation locations within words. *Perception, 8*, 21–30.

Rayner, K., Slowiaczek, M. L., Clifton, C., Jr., & Bertera, J. H. (1983). Latency of sequential eye movements: Implications for reading. *Journal of Experimental Psychology: Human Perception and Performance, 9*, 912–922.

Underwood, G., Hyönä, J., & Niemi, P. (1987). Scanning patterns on individual words during the comprehension of sentences. In J. K. O'Regan & A. Lévy-Schoen (Eds.), *Eye movements: From physiology to cognition*. Amsterdam: North-Holland, pp. 467–477.

17 Visual Attention During Eye Fixations While Reading

George W. McConkie and David Zola
Center for the Study of Reading
University of Illinois at Urbana-Champaign
Champaign, Illinois, U.S.A.

ABSTRACT

An eye fixation in reading is the period of time during which the visual system is exposed to the text stimulus array. This paper discusses issues concerning the nature of visual attention as it occurs during these fixations, including: (1) what is attended; (2) the time of attending; and (3) the basis for selecting a location to attend on a new fixation. An integrative overview of visual attention during fixations in reading is suggested.

INTRODUCTION

Reading, like most other on-going visual tasks, is carried out by making a series of eye fixations, each of which exposes the processing system to a large and complex stimulus array, retino-topically displaced from the last and with the highest visual resolution at a slightly different stimulus region. During reading, these displaced views of the text occur four times per second, on the average. Thus, about every quarter of a second the reader selects from the stimulus array the information that is needed to further an understanding of the text. The goal of this paper is to raise and discuss several issues concerning selective attention during reading: what is attended, when it is attended, and what is the basis on which words are selected during each new eye fixation. The paper deals primarily with research from our own laboratory, assuming the tutorial paper (Rayner & Pollatsek, this volume) to be more comprehensive.

Recent literature on vision takes the position that early visual processing yields a representation of the stimulus array that is divided into regions specified by boundaries of various types (Pinker, 1984). These regions are then organised hierarchically into objects, probably through an interaction of top-down and bottom-up influences (Duncan, 1984). Attentional selectivity has often been conceptualised as being spatially defined, as though an attentional spotlight were illuminating a stimulus region for further consideration (Eriksen & Yeh, 1985). However, Duncan (1984) has suggested that at least under certain circumstances attention appears to be more object-based. For example, attention can be focused on either of two patterns occupying the same physical region, to the exclusion of the other (Rock & Gutman, 1981). If this object-based representation is hierarchical, as Duncan suggests, then attention can be given to larger, higher-level objects (e.g. a person) or to smaller, lower-level objects (e.g. the person's nose), with corresponding differences in the detail that is considered.

While the stimulus array that is typically present during reading may seem complex when compared to many of the stimuli used in research on perceptual processing, it is simple in comparison with most stimulus arrays in the real world. The reading stimulus can be conceived as a four-level object hierarchy, completely represented in two-dimensional space. At one level, letters are usually spatially isolated, continuous objects in English text and most other written languages. At a second level, words consist of letter groups separated spatially from other words. At a third level, text lines are rows of words. At the fourth level, a page consists of blocks of lines. Other levels can also occur, such as blocks of lines that constitute a paragraph, depending on the spatial layout of the text. Without such problems as three-dimensionality, overlapping objects, and shadows, early visual processes should be able to provide an object-based representation directly without assistance from top-down processes.

Recent research on local vs. global processing of object hierarchies having two levels of objects suggests that both the size of the objects and the nature of the task determine the level that will be attended (Ward, 1982). In reading from a page of text, both of these influences probably favour attention to objects at the word level. Their size (typically 1–2deg of visual angle) is closer to that preferred by the attentional system than are letters (typically $\frac{1}{4}-\frac{1}{6}$ deg) or lines (5–20deg depending on the text format and distance from the eyes). Also, words are the smallest units of the object-hierarchy that map onto meaning-bearing language units.

Another characteristic of the text stimulus array that is likely to influence attentional selectivity is the fact that objects at each level are relatively homogeneous in size and shape. Furthermore, the variance that exists is not strongly correlated with the relative importance of the objects for the task of reading, though short words are more likely to be function words. Thus, the stimulus array itself provides little basis for directing attention to one object rather than another. However, since language is sequential in nature, the reading task imposes strong constraints (with some flexibility permitted) on the sequence with which the stimulus objects are to be attended.

VISUAL ATTENTION DURING READING:
THEORETICAL APPROACHES

Current literature provides us with four ways of thinking about attentional selectivity during reading. These are referred to as spotlight theory, location-based object selection theory, content-based theory, and state-based theory.

Spotlight theory assumes that a spatially defined region of the stimulus array is given priority, and that this region can vary in size, shape and retinotopic location. Furthermore, the level of detail available for further processing varies inversely with the size of the region attended (Eriksen & Yeh, 1985).

The remaining three theoretical approaches all assume that attentional selection is defined in terms of objects in the stimulus array. Such object selection requires that early visual processing yield an object-based representation of the visual array, such as that described earlier, enabling these entities to be available for attentional selection (Pinker, 1984). However, the actual selection could occur on any of three bases. An object could be selected because of its spatial location (viz. location-based object selection theory), because of its content in relation to the task (viz. content-based theory), or because of its state in relation to the states of other objects competing for attention (viz. state-based theory).

A location-based object selection theory requires a location-indexed representation of objects, plus a set of rules for selecting among them. In reading, this might be handled by an algorithm that selects next the word-object to the right of the last-attended object, and, when there is no such object, selects the left-most word of the next line. In addition, information about recently attended words would be indexed to their spatial location, providing a basis for selecting previously attended words when the basic algorithm is over-ridden by the language processing system's need for information from an earlier part of the text. This conceptualisation is similar to a proposal made by Levy-Schoen (1981).

A pure content-based object selection theory that does not use location information can be derived from Rumelhart's (1977) interactive theory of reading. During each eye fixation, any word lying within the retinal region within which identification is possible is entered onto the message centre and routines or productions sensitive to these words are triggered by their presence. This registration leads to the arousal of lexical information for each such word. However, the higher-level routines or productions that create the coherent meaning representation of the text are only affected by information from those words matching their triggering requirements. Thus, if the state of the system is such that it is ready to respond to an animate noun, then words of other types (such as articles and verbs), though present in the message centre, will have no effect on comprehension other than possible arousal effects on related words. In this type of theory, attention requires no decision-maker, but rather it results naturally from having a system that can only be affected by information having certain momentarily specified characteristics. A pure content-based object selection system, then, provides a mechanism for selecting among available objects without reference to their spatial location. Of course, the acuity characteristics of the visual system place limits on the spatial region within which objects of different types are available during an eye fixation, particularly for word objects in reading.

An example of a state-based object selection theory would be one in which each object has an activation level which determines, in competition with other objects, its likelihood of being attended (Ullman, 1984). For example, suppose that attending to a word inhibits the attraction of that word, thus reducing its ability to attract attention in the future. Furthermore, if words that are more visually distinct (that is, that lie in or near the fovea) have greater attraction, then a theory of this type would account for the reader's tendency to progress sequentially along the line from word to word once the first word of a line of text has been attended. As with a content-based theory, selecting an object is accomplished without a high-level decision-maker. However, such a theory would have to be supplemented to account for the reader's ability to: (1) proceed from the end of one line to the beginning of the next; (2) track a single line rather than being drawn to words on the line above or below that may be closer to the eyes' current location; and (3) direct attention back to earlier parts of a sentence when language processing difficulties are encountered.

Obviously, these four types of theories are not completely independent nor mutually exclusive. A final description of visual attention during reading may have characteristics of more than one. We turn now to two fundamental issues raised by these theories: whether attention selects by region or by object during reading, and whether attentional selection is based on spatial location.

REGION-BASED VERSUS OBJECT-BASED ATTENTION

In order to identify what is being attended at one time as opposed to another we have used research techniques involving eye-movement-contingent display control (McConkie, Zola, Wolverton, & Burns, 1978). This involves sampling eye position during reading at a high rate (i.e. 1000 samples per second) and then changing the text display at selected times in response to events of the eye-movement pattern. In the studies to be described here, college students read text that was presented one line at a time on a cathode-ray tube (CRT). They were able to call up the next line at any time by pushing a hand-held button. This setting allows subjects to read long passages even though only one line is present at any moment. Text lines were up to 73 characters in length, displayed in upper and lower case, with 4 characters subtending 1deg of visual angle. The text line was refreshed over 300 times per second, making it possible to change it within a 3msec period.

Previous studies have found that readers distinguish among letters within a relatively small region, extending not more than four character positions to the left of the directly fixated letter, nor more than seven or eight to the right (Underwood & McConkie, 1985). We conducted the following study to determine more precisely the relative likelihood of incorporating letters lying at different distances to the left and right of the directly fixated letter into their reading, and to determine whether attention is being given to spatially defined regions or to word objects.

Pairs of words were identified that differ in only a single letter position, such as the words *leaks* and *leans*. These words are called the critical words and the letter distinguishing them is referred to as the critical letter. Contexts were written into which either member of a pair would fit appropriately, such as *John does not store his tools in the shed any more because it {leaks|leans} so much*. These contexts ranged from one to three sentences in length, and are referred to as passages. Critical words were three, five, or seven letters in length, and critical letters occurred equally at each possible letter position except for the third and fifth positions in seven-letter words.

Thirty-two subjects each read 312 of these passages as their eye movements were being monitored, half in the experimental condition and half in the control. In the experimental condition, during each saccadic eye movement in a region near the critical word the critical letter was changed. Thus, the critical word was different on each successive eye fixation, alternating between the two members of a pair. In the control condition, no such changes occurred.

After reading each passage, a series of four words was presented on the screen, one at a time. This presentation included the two critical words, and two additional words that also differed from each other by a single letter. Of these additional words, both, one, or neither might have appeared in the passage. When each word appeared, the subject indicated whether or not it had been in the passage just read by pressing one of two buttons.

An analysis of responses to test words after reading passages presented in the control condition indicated that the subjects responded with 88% accuracy on critical words. Thus, subjects were able to do the task with considerable, but not perfect, accuracy. In a series of analyses of the eye-movement data from the experimental condition, evidence was sought to indicate that reading was being disrupted by the changing letter. The only place where such evidence could be found was in cases where subjects reread the section of text containing the critical word. Since the frequency of these rereadings was similar in the experimental and control conditions (22% and 20% of all passages), they were not being induced by the letter changes. Excluding these rereadings, the mean duration of the fixation on or immediately to the left of the critical letter was 255msec in the experimental group and 253msec in the control group. The mean duration of the next fixation was 254msec and 253msec. The means of the fixation durations of all fixations lying within 5 letter positions to left and right of the critical letter were 255msec and 253msec. None of these pairs differed significantly. Lengths of saccades and frequencies of regressions also showed no differences between conditions. These results are consistent with the hypothesis that a reader attends to a given letter position during only one eye fixation, unless that section of text is reread.

Our next analysis was designed to indicate where the eye is centred when a given letter is attended. An index, called the letter perception index (LPI), was computed for each character position to the left and right of the critical letters in the study, indicating the relative frequency with which the critical letter was attended during fixations centred at that location. The LPI was computed in the following manner. First, for each subject, passages presented in the experimental condition were identified on which that subject selected one, and only one, of the two critical words on the word test. Second, in data from reading these passages, all eye fixations were identified that lay between ten character positions to the left of the critical letter and five character positions to the right, and that were part of the initial reading of the text (i.e. no fixation had previously been located farther to the right on that line). Third, these fixations were grouped according to their location with respect to the location of the critical letter. For example, all fixations on which the eyes were centred two letter positions to the left of the critical letter were put into one group and all fixations on which the eyes were centred directly on the critical letter were put into another. Fourth, for each of the fixations in a group, we determined whether the word present on the screen during that fixation was or was not the word that the subject selected on the word test. If it was not, we made the assumption that this was not a fixation on which that letter position was attended. Finally, an LPI was calculated for each such group of fixations (i.e. for each letter position in the region around the critical letter) by calculating the proportion of those fixations on which the word present in the text was the same as the word later selected on the word test.

Figure 17.1 presents the LPI for each letter position around the critical letter. The resulting curve indicates the relative frequency of attending the critical letter during fixations lying different distances to the left and right of

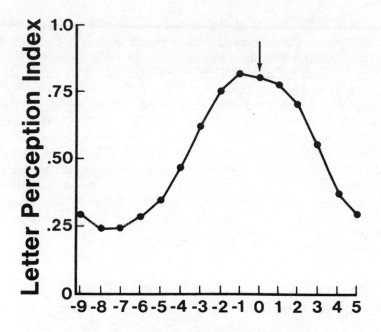

**Letter Positions in Text
With Respect to Changing Letter**

FIG. 17.1.   Letter perception distribution curve for combined data. The X-axis represents the location of eye fixations on the line of text with respect to the critical letter. Negative values indicate character positions to the left; and positive values, positions to the right of the critical letter. The Y-axis indicates the proportion of fixations at each location on which the word displayed during that fixation was the one the subject later reported as having read. The arrow indicates the data point for fixations centred directly on the critical letter.

it, given the assumption that a letter is attended during a single fixation. From another perspective, the curve indicates the relative likelihood of attending to letters lying at different distances to left and right of the directly fixated letter during a fixation. This type of curve is referred to as a letter perception distribution curve. This curve has characteristics similar to results from earlier studies using different methods to estimate the size of the perceptual span during eye fixations in reading (McConkie, 1983). The distribution is offset to the right, indicating a tendency to attend further to the right than to the left (Rayner, Well, & Pollatsek, 1980). It is in agreement with current estimates that during reading, letters are discriminated up to about four character positions to the left of the fixated letter, and about six–eight to the right (Underwood & McConkie, 1985; Rayner, 1984). However, the letter perception distribution curve also indicates that within this region there are large differences in the likelihood of attending letters at different locations. Thus, previous estimates of the size and location of the perceptual span during fixations in reading indicate a region within which letters are sometimes attended but do not specify the region that is actually attended during each, or perhaps any, fixation.

We next investigated whether the region within which a letter is attended varies as a function of the length of the word it is in, or the serial position it occupies in the word. To do this, separate letter perception distribution curves were prepared for critical words of different lengths, with critical letters at different positions. Three curves are shown in Fig. 17.2a; those for the first, third, and fifth letters in five-letter words. In this figure, LPIs for fixations centred on a letter in the critical word are indicated by open figures, and LPIs for fixations centred directly on the critical letter are indicated by an arrow.

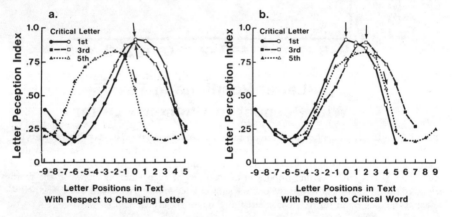

FIG. 17.2.   Letter perception distribution curves for passages on which the critical word was five letters in length. Separate curves are presented for passages in which the critical letter was the first, third, or fifth letter in the word. Data points for fixations centred on letters in the word are indicated by open figures. Arrows indicate data points for fixations centred directly on a critical letter. Figure 17.2a presents these curves aligned with respect to the location of the critical letter (data points indicated by arrows are aligned vertically). Figure 17.2b presents the same curves aligned with respect to the location of the initial letter in the word (data points indicated by open figures are aligned vertically).

While the three curves in Fig. 17.2a are quite similar in shape, they are displaced along the X-axis. This means that the likelihood of attending a letter that lies a certain distance from the currently fixated letter differs considerably for different letter positions in a word. However, there are two striking characteristics of these curves. First, on perceptual grounds we might have expected the initial letter of a word to be picked up when the eyes are furthest to the left of it, since that letter suffers less from lateral inhibition than do internal letters (Bouma, 1978). However, this is not the case; the curve for the middle letter actually lies further to the left than that for the initial letter. Second, a letter is not always most frequently identified when it lies at the centre of the fovea, where visual resolution is best. For example, when the critical letter is the last letter of a word, it is more likely to be attended when the eyes are centred to the left of it than when they are directly on it. Both of these patterns are even more pronounced in data for seven-letter words, not shown here. These observations lead to the conclusion that the acquisition and use of letters during reading reflects strong attentional influences, rather than simply principles of visual discriminability.

A better understanding of what is taking place is gained by examining Fig. 17.2b. This figure presents the same letter perception distribution curves as does Fig. 17.2a, but the curves have been shifted to align the LPIs with respect to letter positions in the word, rather than with respect to their distance from the critical letter location (that is, the open figures are vertically aligned, rather than the arrows). This transformation brings the curves together, a fact that serves as evidence that the readers were attending to the text in word units rather than in some other type of region. When a well-known word in this length range is attended, apparently all letter positions of that word are attended during a single fixation, regardless of their distance from where the eyes are centred. Of course, it is possible that more than one word may be attended during a fixation, and that longer or less well-known words may be picked up piecemeal over multiple fixations. These possibilities need further study.

Word-level objects also appear to be the basis for selecting locations to move the eyes to. Fixations are more frequent at the centres of words than at their ends (McConkie & Zola, 1984; Rayner, 1979). We have found this to be the case even for long saccades of 15 character positions.

ALTERNATIVES TO LOCATION-INDEXED ATTENTION

Given that text is attended in word units during skilled reading, both for identification and eye-guidance purposes, we turn next to the question of whether or not these words are selected on the basis of their spatial location. The two alternatives to location-based selection described earlier are selection based on content, and selection based on some state indicator.

Considering first the possibility of strict content-based selection, our evidence is in the form of an "arm-chair" experiment. The following is a two-sentence passage which, after the first three words, has pairs of words, one above the other, at each word position. Only one member of each pair is appropriate to the context, and reading the passage involves selecting the appropriate word at each location. If a strict content-based selection theory were accurate, the reader should be able to read this passage as smoothly as if there were a single word at each location, since inappropriate words would never become involved in the language processing.

Once upon a blanch there   was I king   can   but in   I fixing
            time   image see a before who   lived ox   a castle

in England. He was I lye   medical   king.
sin bought.   Id cry   a very   generous spit.

While it is possible to read a passage in this format, and in fact with practice one can read such a passage orally quite smoothly, in our experience this is accomplished by rapidly considering and selecting between the alternatives, rather than only the appropriate word at each location controlling the processing. Furthermore, rewriting the passage with the correct word always as the bottom (or top) member of each pair makes the passage seem much easier to read. This does not argue that content has no role in the selection process, but does imply that it is not the sole determiner of what is selected for further consideration. Selecting the correct word when it is signalled by location, in addition to content, makes reading much easier than selecting on the basis of content alone.

The potential of a state-based object selection theory for accounting for visual attention during reading can only be assessed by working out examples of such a theory. However, such a theory must account for the reader's ability to proceed successfully along one line of text on a page, move from the end of one line to the beginning of the next, and regress to previously attended word-objects when difficulty is encountered during reading. Each of these seems to require a location-indexed representation of the text for maintaining the current state of word-objects, as Ullman (1984) has proposed.

From these considerations, we argue that the selection of word-objects for processing during reading is accomplished at least partly, and probably primarily, on the basis of their location. We know of no non-location-based alternative that can account for basic facts of reading.

THE TIME OF ATTENDING

Our discussion of attention has implied the existence of two sets of processes in perception. First, there are massively parallel visual processes that represent the full and complex detail that is available from the stimulus array, and that parse this array into an object hierarchy. Second, there are higher levels of cognition that deal only with selected subsets of the information aroused by the stimulus array. We assume that the first of these is initiated on each eye fixation as soon as the eyes settle into their new location. The time at which information necessary for reading becomes available at the cortex has been estimated to be about 60msec after the beginning of a fixation (Russo, 1978). Sequential characteristics of the letters in words can affect processing within another 60msec (McConkie, Underwood, Zola, & Wolverton, 1985). The question to be addressed here concerns the time during the fixation at which the higher processes make their selection. Is this selection made as soon as information becomes available or at some later time?

This issue was addressed in a study using materials like those described earlier, in which changing a single letter in a critical word creates a new word that is still appropriate in its context (Blanchard, McConkie, Zola, & Wolverton, 1984). In this study, however, the change was made partway through each fixation. Thus, the word that was present early in the fixation was different from the word that was present at the same location later in the fixation. In order to hide the local movement associated with changing a single letter during a fixation, the entire line of text was masked for 30msec at some time during each eye fixation with a row of Xs. In the experimental condition, when the text returned following the mask, the critical word had been changed. The original word then returned during the following saccade. This created a situation in which one word (e.g. leaks) was present at the critical word location during the first part of every eye fixation, and another word (e.g. leans) was present during the latter part. After reading each passage, subjects were again presented with four words, one at a time, including the two critical words, and asked to indicate for each whether they had seen it in the text as they read. Our interest was in learning whether subjects would consistently report seeing the word that was present early in the fixation.

In the study, the mask occurred either 50, 80, or 120msec following the onset of each eye fixation. A control condition was included in which the mask occurred but the word did not change.

In the experimental conditions, 65% of the time subjects indicated having seen only one of the two critical words. In practically all the remaining instances they indicated having seen both. There was a striking phenomenological difference between these two outcomes: In the first, there was no awareness that another word had ever been present, and in the latter, both words were clearly identified. All subjects had both types of experience. In addition, in cases where only one word was reported, the eye-movement patterns were no different from those for the control condition, whereas when two words were seen, a sizeable increase in fixation time on the critical word was observed. In those cases in which single word was perceived, it was the word that was present early in the fixation on 45% of the trials, and the later word on 55%. Thus, words present early in the fixation were not more likely to be perceived. The data also indicated that the longer a word was displayed the more likely that it would be selected by the subject.

If we again make the strong assumption that unreported words were not attended, these results suggest that there is not a standard time during each fixation at which attentional selection occurs. Rather, we proposed a *variable utilisation time hypothesis*, with higher-level processes selecting information to support the reading at the time it is needed, and with this time varying from fixation to fixation. While in discrete word identification tasks the visually provided information may be utilised as soon as it is available (McClelland & Rumelhart, 1981), in an ongoing task such as reading, the time of selection is probably determined to a greater extent by activities at the higher processing levels.

THE CONTENT OF ATTENDED UNITS

Given the assumption of two sets of processes involved in perception, one massively parallel and one highly selective, the question to be addressed next concerns the level of representation to which the first of these sets of processes takes the information. In essence, what is the nature of the visually provided database from which selection can occur? This, of course, determines what the second set of processes receive when information is selected or attended.

Recent literature on priming argues that the presence of meaningful visual shapes on the retina has the ability to arouse lexical classification and interpretation automatically, with activation then spreading to semantically related cognitive units (Marcel, 1983). Thus, though the objects of attention may be spatially indexed, in fact each such index could point to a host of already aroused information concerning the corresponding object.

The question for theories of reading is whether the attentional processes select word-objects to enable lexical access to occur, to whether lexical access occurs automatically for all visually resolvable words prior to their being attended. The studies we have conducted in which words are changed between and within eye fixations lead us to believe that if parallel lexical arousal of all resolvable words does occur on each fixation, it must not play an important role in reading. If this type of parallel arousal were important to reading, then we would expect to see either of two types of effects in our studies. On the one hand, having two words aroused and associated with the same physical location might create interference in reading. On the other hand, having some other word previously aroused rather than the one attended might be expected to reduce the facilitation that such arousal is expected to produce. Either of these possibilities would be expected to produce effects on the eye-movement pattern. The lack of such effects when a word is changing from fixation to fixation, and when a word is being changed within a fixation, fails to support either of these expectations. That being the case, we are left with two choices. We can adopt the working assumption that during ongoing skilled reading, the first level of processing does not involve lexical access or semantic arousal (Holender, 1986). Rather, these and higher processes occur only for words that are attentionally selected. Or alternatively, we can assume that lexical arousal occurs for all visually resolvable words but that this plays no significant role in the ongoing reading process. Only the contents of a word location at the time it is selected and incorporated into the flow of reading has any influence. To resolve this issue, research is needed that explores the fate of unattended words during reading.

PLACE-KEEPING DURING READING

Earlier in this paper, we concluded that the selection of word-objects to attend is based at least partly on their location. For spatial location to be used for this purpose, there must be some means of place-keeping. Each new fixation presents the visual system with a large array of word-objects. How does the system decide which of these words to attend? One approach is always to attend to the word or words that lie at a certain retinal location. The fact that the region within which words are identified during fixations is small makes this approach plausible. However, results presented earlier indicate that words located at different retinal positions differ in their likelihood of being perceived during a fixation, and that this selectivity is so great that even words directly fixated are not always attended. Thus, it does not seem to be the case that retinal location alone is the sole determiner of whether a word will be attended.

A second approach to selecting word-objects during a fixation would involve keeping an enduring spatio-topic map of all or part of the stimulus page that survives saccades, and using that map as the basis for attentional selection (Ullman, 1984). This could be done in either of two ways. First, the system could maintain a global representation of the stimulus array and add to it the array that results from each new fixation. This has been referred to as an *integrative visual buffer* (Rayner, 1975). Reading could then be based on accumulated information in this representation, rather than on the spatially displaced images encountered from fixation to fixation, thus providing a stable base for making decisions on where to attend next. Alternatively, a map of the locations of higher-level objects could be maintained across eye fixations, without maintaining detailed information about the objects themselves. In either case, it is necessary to justify the input spatially from each new eye fixation with the enduring representation. This could be done either by using information about how far the eyes were moved, or by matching certain characteristics of the new stimulus array with those of the enduring representation (Cumming, 1978).

We have conducted a series of studies to try to understand the characteristics of such a representation. In one study, subjects read text printed in aLtErNaTiNg CaSe, with every other letter capitalised (McConkie & Zola, 1979). During selected saccades the case of every letter was changed. We assumed that if the shapes of letters and words were being integrated from fixation to fixation, then this type of stimulus manipulation would be disruptive to perceptual processing. No detectable disruption occurred, and the subjects showed no awareness of the change. The same result was obtained in a word-naming study (Rayner, McConkie, & Zola, 1980). These findings argue against the integration of word and letter shapes across saccades.

Studies described earlier indicate that words can be changed from fixation to fixation without disturbing reading, and at times can even be changed within a fixation if a brief mask is used. This argues against integrating full letter and word information in a spatial representation. On the other hand, current evidence for a "peripheral preview" effect suggests that some information is obtained about the word or words that will be attended on the following fixation (see Rayner & Pollatsek, this volume).

A study was conducted in which we   spaced the   words of   the text   unevenly, alternating   between one   and three   spaces in this manner. During selected saccades, the spatial arrangement was changed, with every triple space being replaced by a single space, and every single space replaced by three spaces. Although this changed the spatial arrangement of the words, and the exact spatial location of half the words, it was not detected by the readers, nor did it appear to disrupt their reading. In a related study, during a saccade in the middle of the line of text, ten letters were deleted from either the left or right end of the line, and were then restored during the following saccade. Thus, the line was shortened for a single fixation. This manipulation was occasionally noticed by some of the subjects, but it did not seem to affect their eye-movement patterns.

While there is obviously much work to be done on this issue, results to date suggest that there is no large-scale integration of images from one fixation to the next during reading. Furthermore, if a map to locations of objects is maintained across fixations, it probably represents relative locations rather than absolute spatio-topic co-ordinates.

Finally, the existence of a peripheral preview effect suggests a third possibility for the spatial basis of attentional selection. It may be that local information is acquired about upcoming words during one fixation that then assists in localising the word or words to be attended during the next fixation. This could involve the use of low spatial frequency information since it has two desirable properties: first, it is available from peripheral areas on each fixation where the upcoming word typically lies, and second, it becomes available from central retinal areas early in the fixation, enabling its use in early selectional decisions. With this third alternative, there is no need for an enduring map or spatial representation of the stimulus array. Instead, the spatial decision of what object to attend next is made during the prior fixation when the full stimulus array is present. The only information that must then be maintained across the saccade is that which enables the reader to pick out the selected object from objects lying in the foveal or near-foveal area on the next fixation.

OVERVIEW

On the basis of current research on vision and visual attention, and of studies of perception during reading conducted in our laboratory, we suggest the following view of visual attention during skilled reading. Early in each eye fixation the visual system provides a representation of the full page of text as currently present, organised as a spatially indexed object hierarchy. Typically, attention is given to objects at the word level both for identification and for the direction of eye movements. There may be three cases in which attention is given to objects at other levels in the hierarchy. On the initial fixation on a page, orientation may require attending at the page level. During initial or final fixations on a line, line-level objects may be attended as the reader orients to the following line. And when a word is not readily identifed, attention to objects at the letter level may be necessary.

Words are selected to further the reading only if they lie within a rather small region, extending about four letter positions to the left of the letter on which the eyes are centred, and about eight letters to the right. Within this region, the likelihood of a word being attended varies with its location. The relative likelihood of attending words at different locations is given by letter perception distribution curves, an example of which is presented in this paper. However, within this region, the acquisition of information from letters and words is determined by attentional selectivity rather than by perceptual variables. Even the directly fixated letter can have no influence on reading if the word containing it is not attended during that fixation.

The time during the fixation when a word is attended varies and is probably determined by the needs of the language processing taking place.

Spatial locations of words are important in their selection. However, there does not seem to be a full integration of visual representations of the text across fixations, nor a precise spatial map of the locations of objects in the array that survives saccades. Rather, there may be an index to the relative locations of objects, or the perceptual system may only maintain information about certain identifying characteristics of the word to be attended next, allowing it to be picked out from words lying in the foveal or near-foveal region on the next fixation.

A basic unanswered question concerns whether attending to a word enables the arousal of its lexical information, or whether this arousal occurs automatically for all visually resolvable words during a fixation and attending a word simply enables the use of that information in the ongoing reading. The fact that words in the text can be changed between and within fixations with so little impact on the ongoing processing leads us to favour the first of these alternatives. Research on the effects of words that are not attended during fixations in reading is needed to provide a final answer to this question.

Finally, it is important to note that most of this description has come from research and theory appearing within the last ten years. This fact indicates that rapid progress is currently being made in understanding the perceptual aspects of reading.

ACKNOWLEDGEMENTS

The research reported in this paper was supported by Grant MH32884 from the National Institute of Mental Health, Grant HD18116 from the National Institute of Child Health and Human Behaviour, and Contract NIE-C-400-76-0116 from the National Institute of Education to the Center for the Study of Reading. The authors express their thanks to Gary Wolverton who developed the computer system that made this research possible, and to Harry Blanchard, who was intimately involved in much of the data collection and analysis. Communications concerning this paper may be directed to either author at the Center for the Study of Reading, 51 Gerty Drive, Champaign, IL 61820 U.S.A.

REFERENCES

Blanchard, H. E., McConkie, G. W., Zola, D., & Wolverton, G. S. (1984). The time course of visual information utilization during fixations in reading. *Journal of Experimental Psychology: Human Perception and Performance, 10*, (1), 75–89.

Bouma, H. (1978). Visual search and reading: Eye movements and functional visual field: A tutorial review. In J. Requin (Ed.), *Attention and performance VII*. Hillsdale, N.J.: Lawrence Erlbaum Associates Inc., pp. 115–147.

Cumming, G. D. (1978). Eye movements and visual perception. In E. C. Carterette & M. P. Friedman (Eds.), *Handbook of perception*. New York: Academic Press, 221–255.

Duncan, J. (1984). Selective attention and the organisation of visual information. *Journal of Experimental Psychology: General, 113*, 501–517.

Eriksen, C. W. & Yeh, Y. Y. (1985). Allocation of attention in the visual field. *Journal of Experimental Psychology: Human Perception and Performance, 11*, 583–597.

Holender, D. (1986). Semantic activation without conscious identification in dichotic listening, parafoveal vision, and visual masking: A survey and appraisal. *Behavioural and Brain Sciences, 9*, 1–22.

Levy-Schoen, A. (1981). Flexible and/or rigid control of oculomotor scanning behaviour. In D. F. Fisher, R. A. Monty, & J. W. Senders (Eds.), *Eye movements: Cognition and visual perception.* Hillsdale, N.J.: Lawrence Erlbaum Associates Inc., 299–314.

Marcel, A. J. (1983). Conscious and unconscious perception: Experiments on visual masking and word recognition. *Cognitive Psychology, 15,* 197–237.

McClelland, J. L. & Rumelhart, D. E. (1981). An interactive activation model of context effects in letter perception: Part 1. An account of basic findings. *Psychological Review, 88,* 375–407.

McConkie, G. W. (1983). Eye movements and perception during reading. In K. Rayner (Ed.), *Eye movements in reading: Perceptual and language processes.* New York: Academic Press, 65–96.

McConkie, G. W., Underwood, N. R., Zola, D., & Wolverton, G. S. (1985). Some temporal characteristics of processing during reading. *Journal of Experimental Psychology: Human Perception and Performance, 11,* 168–186.

McConkie, G. W. & Zola, D. (1979). Is visual information integrated across successive fixations in reading? *Perception and Psychophysics, 25,* 221–224.

McConkie, G. W. & Zola, D. (1984). Eye-movement control during reading: The effects of word units. In W. Prinz & A. F. Sanders (Eds.), *Cognition and motor processes.* Berlin: Springer-Verlag, pp. 63–74.

McConkie, G. W., Zola, D., Wolverton, G. S., & Burns, D. D. (1978). Eye movement contingent display control in studying reading. *Behaviour Research Methods and Instrumentation, 10,* 154–166.

Pinker, S. (1984). Visual cognition: An introduction. *Cognition, 18,* 1–63.

Rayner, K. (1975). The perceptual span and peripheral cues in reading. *Cognitive Psychology, 7,* 65–81.

Rayner, K. (1979). Eye guidance in reading: Fixation locations within words. *Perception, 8,* 21–30.

Rayner, K. (1984). Visual selection in reading, picture perception, and visual search. In H. Bouma & D. G. Bouwhuis (Eds.), *Attention and performance X.* Hillsdale, N.J.: Lawrence Erlbaum Associates Inc., 67–96.

Rayner, K., McConkie, G. W., & Zola, D. (1980). Integrating information across eye movements. *Cognitive Psychology, 12,* 206–226.

Rayner, K., Well, A. D., & Pollatsek, A. (1980). Asymmetry of the effective visual field in reading. *Perception and Psychophysics, 27,* 537–544.

Rock, I. & Gutman, D. (1981). The effect of inattention on form perception. *Journal of Experimental Psychology: Human Perception and Performance, 7,* 275–285.

Rumelhart, D. E. (1977). Toward an interactive model of reading. In S. Dornic (Ed.), *Attention and performance VI.* Hillsdale, N.J.: Lawrence Erlbaum Associates Inc., pp. 573–603.

Russo, J. E. (1978). Adaptation of cognitive processes to the eye-movement system. In J. W. Senders, D. F. Fisher, & R. A. Monty (Eds.), *Eye movements and the higher psychological functions.* Hillsdale, N.J.: Lawrence Erlbaum Associates Inc., 89–112.

Ullman, S. (1984). Visual routines. *Cognition, 18,* 97–159.

Underwood, N. R. & McConkie, G. W. (1985). Perceptual span for letter distinctions during reading. *Reading Research Quarterly, 20,* 153–162.

Ward, L. M. (1982). Determinants of attention to local and global features of visual forms. *Journal of Experimental Psychology: Human Perception and Performance, 8,* 562–581.

18 Parafoveal Word Perception During Eye Fixations in Reading: Effects of Visual Salience and Word Structure

Albrecht Werner Inhoff
Department of Psychology
University of New Hampshire
Durham, New Hampshire, U.S.A.

ABSTRACT

Eye fixations on six-letter target words were measured to determine effects of perceptual salience and of word structure on parafoveal word processing. Two types of target words were used; compound words (e.g. *cowboy*), which were composed of two morphological subunits (*cow* and *boy*), and pseudocompound words (e.g. *carpet*) which could not be separated into two three-letter morphological constituents (*car* and *pet*). Sentences containing the target words were read in a standard left-to-right direction or in a reversed right-to-left direction and readers either obtained a parafoveal preview of the word initial trigram or of the word final trigram prior to fixation. The results showed significant parafoveal preview benefits when the word initial trigram of a compound word was provided; no significant preview benefit was obtained, however, when the word initial trigram of a pseudocompound word was available prior to fixation. The results support a morphologically defined lexical access code. Specifically, parafoveal previews of a word may be used to initiate the lexical access of a word; lexical access may be completed after the word is being fixated.

INTRODUCTION

A fluent reader obtains visual information from the fixated (foveal) word and from the word that is to be fixated next (in the following I will refer to this word as the *parafoveal* word). When parafoveal word information is withheld, reading rate decreases sharply (McConkie & Rayner, 1975; Rayner & Bertera, 1979; Rayner, Inhoff, Morrison, Slowiaczek, & Bertera, 1981; Rayner, Well, Pollatsek, & Bertera, 1982). For example, Rayner et al. (1982) showed that reading rate was slowed by approximately one third when only the fixated word was available during each fixation: When additional parafoveal word information was provided, consisting of the initial three letters of the parafoveal word, reading rate increased substantially and was similar to the reading rate under unrestricted viewing conditions. Why do substantial preview benefits accrue when the initial letters of the parafoveal word are viewed prior to the fixation of the word? In the following, two hypotheses will be tested, the *visual salience* hypothesis and the *lexical structure* hypothesis.

The word initial letters of a parafoveal word are projected on a retinal position that is relatively close to the fovea; the degree of visual acuity at this retinal position may be sufficient to identify word initial letters correctly. The word final letters of the parafoveal word are projected somewhat farther into the parafovea, where the decreased visual acuity may no longer afford an accurate identification of the word's final letters. The benefit derived from the preview of the word initial letters of the parafoveal word may thus be a function of the visibility of the letters of the parafoveal word. In the following, this possibility will be referred to as the visual salience hypothesis.

Another possibility that may account for the parafoveal preview benefit is that word initial letters are of particular importance in lexical access. It has been found that word recognition is hurt more by disruption of word initial letters than by disruption of word final letters (Bruner & O'Dowd, 1958; Oleron & Danset, 1963; Pillsbury, 1897). Delaying the presentation of an initial segment of a word is more detrimental to word recognition than is delaying the presentation of a word final segment (Lima & Pollatsek, 1983; Mewhort & Beal, 1977). Recent models of lexical access have proposed that the mental lexicon is contacted on the basis of word initial letter information alone (Marslen-Wilson & Welsh, 1978; Taft, 1979; Taft & Forster, 1976). In fluent reading, information concerning lexical subunits may be obtained from the parafoveal word and could be used to initiate lexical access. Lexical access may then be completed during the following fixation. In the following, this possibility will be referred to as the lexical structure hypothesis.

One version of the lexical structure hypothesis, which maintains that lexical access is based on the initial letter sequence of a word, was tested by Lima and Inhoff (1985). In the experiment, subjects were instructed to read sentences of the type (1) and (2) while eye movements were monitored.

The weary *dwarf* hated his job.   1
The weary *clown* hated his job.   2

Each sentence contained a target word (in italic) in which the initial letters were either shared with a relatively small number of words in the mental lexicon (sentence 1), or shared with a relatively large number of words (sentence 2). If lexical access is based on word initial letter sequences, then word initial letters of parafoveal words of type (1) are more informative than previews of word initial letters of words of type (2) because they permit the reader to narrow the set of potential word candidates to a relatively large degree. Consequently, if a parafoveal preview is used to initiate lexical access, previews of words of type (1) should be more beneficial than previews of words of type (2). The results of the experiment did not support this prediction. Equivalent amounts of preview benefit were obtained from words of type (1) and type (2).

The results of Lima and Inhoff (1985) reject one specific version of the lexical structure hypothesis. The results do not, however, rule out alternative versions of the hypothesis that account for the preview benefit. Words of type (1) (e.g. *dwarf*) and (2) (e.g. *clown*) were matched on the number of syllables and morphemes. The finding that equivalent amounts of preview benefits were obtained from both types of words could thus indicate that the word initial syllable or morpheme was coded prior to the fixation of these words. Using a lexical decision task and foveal word presentations, Taft (1979; Taft & Forster, 1976) found evidence that lexical access occurs via the word initial syllable which is orthographically defined; using the same task, Lima and Pollatsek (1983) found evidence that lexical access occurs via the word initial morpheme.

The goal of the present experiment was to determine whether the visual salience hypothesis, one of the two versions of the lexical structure hypothesis, or some combination of the visual salience and lexical structure hypotheses, can account for the parafoveal preview benefit. One version of the lexical structure hypothesis states that the word initial syllable of the parafoveal word is the word access code; another version states that the word initial morpheme is the access code.

In the experiment subjects read sentences of the forms (3) to (6) while their eye movements were monitored.

The tired *cowboy* pursued the cattle.	3
cattle. the pursued *cowboy* tired The	4
The expensive *carpet* was finally sold.	5
sold. finally was *carpet* expensive The	6

Each sentence contained a six-letter target word (in italic) and was either read in a standard left-to-right direction (3 and 5) or in a reversed right-to-left direction (4 and 6). Orthogonal to reading direction, each sentence was presented in one of four viewing conditions. In a *one-word* window condition, the fixated word, including text that had already been read, was displayed during each fixation; however, no preview of the word that was to be fixated next was provided. In a *two-word* window condition, the fixated word plus a parafoveal preview of the to-be-fixated word was provided during each fixation. In two *partial preview* conditions, the fixated word plus a preview of either the word initial three letters or of the word final three letters of the

APPR–N*

parafoveal word were provided during each fixation. If visual salience was the only critical factor in the preview benefit derived from the parafoveal word, then preview benefits should be obtained primarily from word initial letters when reading in a standard left-to-right direction: When reading in a reversed right-to-left direction, preview benefits should be obtained primarily from word final letters (the term *word initial letters* refers to the first letters of a word, and the term *word final letters* refers to the last letters of a word, regardless of reading direction).

Target words in sentences of type (3) and (4) were *compound words*, each of which consisted of two three-letter words; e.g. the word *cowboy* consists of the morphemes *cow* and *boy*. Targets in sentences of type (5) and (6) were *pseudocompound* words which cannot be decomposed morphologically into constituent words; e.g. *carpet* does not consist of the morphemes *car* and *pet*. If morphological subunits are used to initiate lexical access and the partial preview of a compound word consists of the word's lexical access code, then parafoveal preview benefits should be obtained for compound words. Partial previews of pseudocompound words, in contrast, should not lead to substantial preview benefits since the parafoveal preview will garden-path the reader. For example, the preview of *car* in the parafovea should only access words which are morphologically related to *car*, such as *carpool* or *carwash*; a morphologically unrelated word such as *carpet* should, however, not be facilitated. If word initial phonological subunits were used to access a word in the internal lexicon, then preview benefits should be obtained from compound and pseudocompound words. For example, the word initial syllable of both *cowboy* and *carpet* consists of the word's initial three-letter sequence.

First-fixation durations and gaze durations on the target were measured. First fixations, which consisted of the initial fixation placed on a target word, were of primary interest since they have been shown to be sensitive to the initial processing of a word (Inhoff, 1984; 1985; Lima & Inhoff, 1985). Gaze durations, consisting of the cumulated viewing time on a target prior to the saccade leaving the target, were of secondary interest. Gaze durations, which include refixations of the word, are likely to emphasise post-lexical processing operations (Inhoff, 1984; 1985; Just & Carpenter, 1980).

METHOD

Subjects

Sixteen students at the University of Massachusetts were paid to participate in the experiment. All subjects had normal vision and were able to read without the aid of corrective lenses.

Materials

The material consisted of 64 sentences each containing a 6-letter compound word, and 64 sentences each containing a 6-letter pseudocompound word; 64 filler sentences were interspersed between sentences containing sentences with compound and pseudocompound target words. All sentences were simple declaratives in which the target word never occupied the sentence initial or sentence final positions. Care was taken to make the preceding sentence context relatively neutral with respect to the target. A sample of the sentences containing compound, pseudocompound, and filler words is shown in Table 18.1. The complete set of compound and pseudocompound words is listed in the Appendix.

TABLE 18.1
Sample Sentences with Compound, Pseudocompound, and Filler Words Used in the Experiment

Compound Targets (lin italics)
1. An iron *teapot* was steaming on the stove.
2. The tired *cowboy* sat on his horse.
3. Her old *toybox* was filled with games.
4. The athlete *outran* the whole competition.
5. The damaged *hatbox* was under her seat.

Pseudocompound Targets (in italics)
1. The huge *budget* could not be approved.
2. He was a living *legend* known by all.
3. She took one *tablet* several times a day.
4. They had tried to *manage* several hotels.
5. Too much *hatred* remains between nations.

Sentences with Filler Words
1. The damaged mirror was for sale.
2. The sumptuous picnic was well attended.
3. A dark shadow revealed his hiding place.
4. His unfailing intent was to succeed.
5. He liked to doodle during phone calls.

All compound words consisted of two three-letter component words. All but two compound words were "right-headed" (Selkirk, 1982); that is, the head morpheme consisted of the word final morpheme. For example, the lexical head of *cowboy* is *boy*, its nonhead is *cow*. All pseudocompound words could be divided into two three-letter words, comprising the initial and final three letters of the word. Both trigram sequences constituted a legal word, but were not morphemes of the pseudocompound word. For example, the pseudocompound *carpet* can be divided into the two three-letter words *car* and *pet*, neither of which is a morpheme of *carpet*. In all but four instances, the word initial trigram of the pseudocompound word also corresponded to the word initial syllable. Because of the limited number of six-letter compound and pseudocompound words the two groups of words could not be matched on word frequency. The average word frequencies of compound and pseudocompound words were 7 and 23 per million (Kučera & Francis, 1967), respectively. The average word frequency of the heads and nonheads of compound words was 429 and 414 per million, respectively.

Design

Two lists of sentences were constructed, each containing 32 sentences with compound targets, 32 sentences with pseudocompound targets, and 32 filler sentences. Each list was segmented into four blocks of sentences, each of which contained one fourth of the three types of sentences. Each block of sentences was displayed in one of four different viewing condition: a one-word window, a two-word window, a one-word plus word initial three-letter preview, and a one-word plus word final three-letter preview conditions. In all viewing conditions, readers viewed the currently fixated word plus text that had already been read. In the one-word window condition no preview of the to-be-fixated (parafoveal) word was available during each fixation, in the two-word condition a preview of the complete parafoveal word was available, and in the two partial preview conditions either the word initial three letters or word final three letters of the parafoveal word were provided during each fixation. The sequence of viewing conditions in each list of sentences was counterbalanced across four successive subjects. One list was read in a standard left-to-right direction, the second list was read in a reversed right-to-left direction. Half of the subjects read the first list in a left-to-right direction and the second list in a right-to-left direction; the order was reversed for the remaining subjects.

Two different types of parafoveal mutilation were used to determine effects of mutilation outside the experimentally defined window on fixation durations. For half of the subjects, all letters outside the experimentally defined window were replaced with *X*s; for the remaining subjects, all letters outside the window were replaced with dissimilar letters, e.g. an ascending letter (b) was replaced with a descending letter (q), and a letter with round features (c) was replaced with a letter with sharp features (z). Interword spaces between words were maintained outside the window in all cases.

Since compound and pseudocompound words could not be matched on word frequency, separate analyses of variance (ANOVAs) were run on the two sets of words. In each ANOVA, reading direction (left-to-right vs. right-to-left) and window size (one word, two word, one word plus word initial letters, and one word plus word terminal letters) were within-subjects

variables; type of mutilation outside the experimentally determined window
(Xs vs. dissimilar letters) was a between-subjects variable.

Apparatus

In the experiment, the subject's eyes were 46cm from a Hewlett Packard
1300A cathode-ray tube (CRT) that was used to present the sentences. The
CRT has a P-31 phosphor with the characteristic that removing a character
results in a drop to 1% of maximum brightness within 0.25msec. Three
character spaces of text equalled 1deg of visual angle. The sentences were
presented in lower case except for the first letter of the sentence. Luminance
was adjusted to comfortable viewing level; display intensity was occasionally
reduced during the study as the reader became more adapted to the dark.

Eye-movement recording was accomplished with a Stanford Research
Institute Dual Purkinje Eye Tracker. The eye tracker has a resolution of
10min of arc and output is linear over the visual angle subtended by each
sentence. The eye tracker and CRT were interfaced with a Hewlett Packard
2100A computer which controlled the experiment. The signal from the eye
tracker was sampled every msec by the computer. Each 4msec of eye tracker
output was compared to the output of the prior 4msec to determine whether
the eye was fixated or in motion. A saccade was deemed to have started if two
successive fixations were more than half a character space apart. Testing of
the display changes indicated that the changes associated with the completion of an eye movement were completed within 5msec.

Procedure

Subjects were tested individually. When a subject arrived, a bite bar was
prepared that served to eliminate head movements during the experiment
Each subject received detailed instruction about the experimental procedure
and was familiarised with the equipment. A calibration of the system began
each session.

After calibration, three crosses were displayed at the left, centre, and right
of the screen. The subject's focal point was marked by a fourth cross that
moved in synchrony with the reader's eyes. When the fourth cross superimposed itself over the three marked positions, as the subject sequentially
fixated each position, the calibration was considered successful and the first
of eight practice sentences which began the session was displayed. Each
sentence was read in the following manner: A fixation marker was displayed
at the left and right side of the CRT; in the left-to-right reading condition,
subjects were instructed to fixate on the left marker, in the right-to-left
reading condition, subjects were instructed to fixate the right marker. This
position coincided with the display of the first word of a sentence on the line

of text. After fixation of the respective fixation marker, the experimenter displayed one sentence. After reading the sentence, the subject pressed a button which replaced the sentence with the fixation markers. The subject was instructed to read each sentence for comprehension so that he/she would be able to paraphrase its content. Occasionally, readers were asked to repeat or paraphrase a sentence immediately after reading it. All subjects were able to report the sentence easily.

Scoring

A target was considered fixated when a reader's point of fixation fell on one of its constituent letters or the blank space immediately preceding or following it. Trials in which the eye tracker lost track were excluded from analyses. This accounted for approximately 1% of the trials. Approximately 4% of the trials were lost due to equipment malfunction and 1% of the trials were excluded because of eye blinks.

RESULTS AND DISCUSSION

First-fixation Duration

Analyses of variance (ANOVAs) performed on first-fixation durations on compound and pseudocompound words showed significant main effects of parafoveal mutilation, reading direction, and parafoveal window. First fixations on compound and pseudocompound words were 29msec and 31msec shorter when letters outside the window were replaced with dissimilar letters, than when letters outside the window were replaced with uninformative Xs: $F(1,14) = 10.32$, $P < 0.01$ and $F(1,14) = 7.85$, $P < 0.01$, respectively. The presence of Xs outside the window appears to have created a less familiar visual display which may have increased average first fixations on target words.

Effects of reading direction and window size, which did not interact with parafoveal mutilation, are shown in Table 18.2.

Reading in the familiar left-to-right direction resulted in shorter first fixations than reading in the reversed right-to-left direction. The difference amounted to 30msec when compound words were fixated: $F(1,14) = 17.00$, $P < 0.01$; and to 31msec when pseudocompound words were fixated: $F(1,14) = 23.63$, $P < 0.01$. Both reading directions showed substantial parafoveal preview benefits for the two sets of words when first fixations in the one-word window condition were compared with first fixations in the two-word window condition. Overall, the main effect of parafoveal window was significant in the analysis of compound words: $F(3,42) = 7.31$, $P < 0.01$; and

TABLE 18.2
First-fixation Durations and Gaze Durations (in Parentheses)

| | Compounds | | | Pseudocompounds | |
| | Reading Direction | | | | Reading Direction | |
Preview	L–R	R–L	Preview	L–R	R–L
xxxxxx	287 (353)	316 (411)	xxxxxx	276 (348)	299 (365)
xxxcup	279 (354)	310 (400)	xxxpet	267 (340)	299 (373)
teaxxx	271 (326)	291 (373)	carxxx	266 (327)	296 (346)
teacup	251 (295)	292 (337)	carpet	236 (268)	274 (327)
Mean	272 (332)	302 (380)		261 (321)	292 (353)

NOTE: Results for compound and pseudocompound words as a function of parafoveal preview condition and reading direction (L-R corresponds to left-to-right and R-L corresponds to right-to-left). Preview examples shown depict the parafoveal mutilation condition in which letters outside the experimentally defined window were replaced with Xs. Results are collapsed across mutilation conditions.

pseudocompound words: $F(3,42) = 6.25$, $P < 0.01$. A more detailed account of the window effects is now provided within the context of the visual salience and lexical structure hypotheses.

The *visual salience hypothesis* predicts that the usefulness of a parafoveal preview should be influenced by the proximity of the preview to the current fixation. Specifically, a preview of letters immediately adjacent to the fixated word (proximal preview) should yield larger preview benefits than a preview of letters which are nonadjacent to the fixated word (distal preview). This should be reflected in shorter first fixations on parafoveal words with proximal previews than with distal previews. The first-fixation data on compound and pseudocompound words do not support this prediction. Preview of the proximal trigram (i.e. the word initial trigram when reading from left-to-right and the word final trigram when reading from right-to-left) resulted in average first fixations of 290msec on compound words and of 282msec on pseudocompound words. Preview of the distal trigram (i.e. the word final trigram when reading from left-to-right and the word initial trigram when reading from right-to-left) resulted in first fixations of 285msec on compound words and of 281msec on pseudocompound words. Since the effects of proximity were negligible (3msec) and opposite to the predicted direction, the visual salience hypothesis cannot account for parafoveal preview effects.

The *lexical structure hypothesis* predicts that the preview of a specific sub-word unit which consists of the word access code should be more useful than preview of one which does not. Two possible candidates were of primary interest: the word initial syllable and morphologically defined sub-word units. If the word initial syllable was the access code, then a preview of the word initial trigram of compound and pseudocompound words should be useful. If, however, the access code was a morpheme, then a preview of a word initial or word final trigram should be useful only if compound words are parafoveally available, but not if pseudocompound words are available.

Using the one-word window condition as a baseline, the analysis of compound words revealed a preview benefit of 21msec when the word initial trigram, which constituted the word initial syllable and morpheme, was available prior to the first fixation on the word. Simple comparisons showed that this difference was significant: $F(1,14) = 15.04$, $P < 0.01$. Preview of the word final trigram, which constituted the morphological head of the compound word, reduced average first fixations on compound words by 6msec; this difference was not significant: $F < 1$. The cumulated benefits from previews of word initial and word final trigrams (27msec) were nearly identical to the preview benefit in the two-word window condition (29msec), when the complete six-letter word was parafoveally available prior to fixation. This suggests that morphologically defined three-letter previews left parafoveal word processing relatively intact.

Again, using the one-word window condition as a baseline, the analysis of pseudocompound words showed a preview benefit of only 7msec when the word initial trigram, which constituted the word initial syllable but not the word initial morpheme, was available prior to the first fixation on the word. This difference was not significant: $F < 1$. The benefit from a preview of the word final trigram amounted to 5msec, which was also not significant: $F < 1$. The failure to obtain a reliable preview benefit when the word initial trigram coincided with the word initial syllable argues against the use of the word initial syllable as word access code. A disruption of parafoveal word processing is also evident when parafoveal previews of the two partial preview conditions are compared with the two-word window condition. The cumulated preview benefit from word initial and word final trigrams amounted to 13msec, which is substantially smaller than the 27msec preview benefit from the complete 6-letter pseudocompound word.

On the one hand, the pattern of window effects is consistent with one version of the lexical structure hypothesis which assumes that the lexical access code is the word initial morpheme. On the other hand, the data are inconsistent with two alternative versions of the lexical structure hypothesis. They argue against the possibility that the access code consists of the word initial syllable and against the possibility that the lexical access code of a compound word is the word's lexical head. When parafoveal previews consisted of the word initial syllable, preview benefits from the word initial trigram were small and failed to reach significance. Similarly, when previews consisted of the lexical head of compound words, preview benefits were not significant. For all but two of the compound words, the lexical head was the distal part of the parafoveal word in the standard left-to-right reading condition and the proximal part in the reversed right-to-left reading condition. If the access code consisted of the lexical head of the compound word, a significant interaction of reading direction and partial parafoveal preview should have been obtained; this interaction did not occur: $F < 1$.

Gaze Durations

Gaze durations, which include intraword refixations of targets, are also shown in Table 18.2. The probabilities of refixating compound and pseudo-compound words were 0.30 and 0.29 respectively with no parafoveal preview, 0.31 and 0.22 with a preview of the word initial trigram, 0.29 and 0.22 with a preview of the word final trigram, and 0.21 and 0.20 when the complete target was parafoveally available prior to fixation. As in the first-fixation durations, gazes were shorter when letters outside the window were replaced with dissimilar letters than when they were replaced with Xs: $F(1,14) = 7.85$, $P < 0.025$ for compound words; $F(1,14) = 2.47$, $P < 0.15$ for pseudocompound words. Furthermore, gazes were 48msec shorter on compound words and 35msec shorter on pseudocompound words when reading proceeded in the standard left-to-right direction than when it proceeded in the reversed right-to-left direction: $F(1,14) = 9.63$, $P < 0.01$, and $F(1,14) = 23.63$, $P < 0.01$, respectively. The effects of parafoveal window were also significant: $F(3,42) = 7.46$, $P < 0.01$ for compound words; $F(3,42) = 6.25$, $P < 0.01$ for pseudocompound words.

The data of the window conditions are, again, inconsistent with the visual salience hypothesis. Gazes on compound and pseudocompound words were 363msec and 350msec respectively when the proximal trigram of the target was parafoveally available and 364msec and 346msec respectively when the distal trigram was available. Consequently, proximity did not affect gaze durations in the present experiment. As in the first-fixation data, a parafoveal preview of the word initial morpheme was useful. Preview of the word initial trigram of compound words decreased gazes by 33msec when compared to the one-word window condition: $F(1,14) = 3.08$, $P < 0.09$. The corresponding preview benefit from the word initial trigram of pseudocompound words was much smaller (5msec) and nonsignificant: $F < 1$. Benefits associated with a preview of the word final trigram were nonsignificant, regardless of whether a compound word (5msec benefit) or pseudocompound word (0msec benefit) was fixated: both $F < 1$.

GENERAL DISCUSSION

The experiment reported here was designed to determine the mechanism underlying one essential component skill of fluent reading: the effective use of parafoveally obtained word information. Two main hypotheses, the *visual salience hypothesis* and the *word structure hypothesis* were tested. The visual salience hypothesis suggests that the magnitude of the parafoveal preview benefit is a function of the visibility of the parafoveal letter string. As the letters of the parafoveal word are projected farther into the parafovea, less useful information should be acquired. The analysis of first fixations and of gaze durations on compound words disconfirms this hypothesis. Substantially larger preview benefits were obtained from a word initial trigram than from a word final trigram, regardless of proximity to the fixated word.

The word structure hypothesis suggests that a specific type of information is sought from the parafoveal word which is used to make contact with a representation of that word in the mental lexicon. The contacted representation could then be elaborated during the following fixation. The finding that the word initial letter trigram of compound words lead to substantial parafoveal preview benefits in the first fixation durations supports this hypothesis. In addition, the pattern of first-fixation durations on compound words leads to the rejection of three interesting versions of the lexical structure hypothesis.

The data do not support the logical possibility that the lexical head of compound words (Selkirk, 1982) is used as word access code; they agree with prior findings which attribute this role to the word initial morpheme (Lima & Pollatsek, 1983; Taft & Forster, 1976). The preview benefits obtained from the word initial trigram, which generally consisted of lexical nonheads, and of word final trigrams, which generally consisted of lexical heads, were 21msec and 7msec, respectively. A possible role for the lexical head could be post-access integration. Specifically, the lexical head may assist in establishing anaphoric reference. For example, in the sentence *the tired cowboy sat on his horse*, only the lexical head or the complete compound can be used as the anaphoric referent for the sentence ending *sat on his horse*. However, the present data do not support this possibility, since first fixations and gaze duration show the identical pattern of effects.

The second possible access code that can be rejected by the first-fixation durations on compound words is the orthographically defined Basic Orthographic Syllabic Structure (BOSS) (Taft, 1979). The BOSS is defined, in essence, by word initial letters including all consonants that follow the first vowel. The BOSS can be defined orthographically (the term oBOSS is used by Lima and Pollatsek to refer to this definition), in which case the word initial trigram of compound words may not coincide with the boundaries of the oBOSS. The oBOSS of *cowboy* is, for example, *cowb*, not *cow*. An inspection of the stimuli revealed that the oBOSS consisted of more letters than the word initial trigram in 62 of the 64 words. If the access code consisted of the oBOSS, preview of the word initial trigram would not have been sufficient for lexical access in the experiment and no significant preview benefit should have emerged.

Finally, some researchers have argued that parafoveal previews are only effective when the complete parafoveal word has been identified (McConkie, Zola, Blanchard, & Wolverton, 1982; Monk, 1985). Although the largest parafoveal preview benefits were obtained when the complete parafoveal word was available prior to fixation, a significant preview benefit also accrued when a sub-word unit of a compound word was available prior to fixation. This demonstrates that effective parafoveal information can be obtained from sub-word units.

First-fixation durations on pseudocompound words, which did not show significant preview benefits from word initial trigrams, argue against additional versions of the lexical structure hypotheses. Specifically, the data argue against the possibility that useful parafoveal information is obtained from individual letters (or graphemes) and from word initial syllables. A differential weighting of letters (or graphemes), in which word initial letters are weighted more than final letters, could account for the larger preview benefits from word initial letters when the first-fixation durations on compound words are considered. However, if differentially weighted letters were the source of the parafoveal preview effect, similar effects should have emerged in the first fixations on pseudocompound words. It could be possible, however, that the word initial morpheme of a compound word (e.g. *cow*) has a higher word frequency count than the word initial "pseudomorpheme" of a pseudocompound word (e.g. *car*). The results could then simply replicate earlier findings which show larger parafoveal preview benefits for high-frequency words than for low-frequency words (Inhoff & Rayner, 1986). A comparison of the word frequencies of word initial morphemes of compound words and of word initial pseudomorphemes of pseudocompound words does not support this possibility. The average word frequency of word initial morphemes was 414, the corresponding frequency of word initial "pseudo-morphemes" was 1066 per million.

Finally, first fixations on pseudocompound words stand in empirical disagreement with the version of the lexical structure hypothesis which asserts that the word initial syllable is the access code. In nearly all cases, pseudocompound words afforded the reader a preview of the complete word initial syllable; yet, no significant preview benefits accrued.

Two views remain plausible. The access code could consist of the *word initial morpheme*, in which case, the word initial trigram of compound words but not of pseudocompound words corresponds to the access code. Alternatively, the access code could consist of the *mBOSS* (as defined by Lima &

Pollatsek, 1983). The mBOSS is a BOSS unit which does not transcend a morphological boundary; the mBOSSes of *cowboy* and *carpet* are, for example, *cow* and *carp*. For 48 out of the 64 pseudocompound words, the word initial letter trigram contained fewer letters than the mBOSS, so its preview may not have been sufficient to access the correct lexical entry.

If the word access code consisted of the word initial morpheme or mBOSS, it would be reasonable to predict that the parafoveal preview of a pseudomorpheme will garden-path the reader. For example, the parafoveal preview of *car* should access words which are morphologically related to *car*; seeing instead the unrelated word *carpet* after the word is being fixated might actually interfere with the access of *carpet*. An inspection of the pattern of refixations suggests, however, that a misleading parafoveal access code will not garden-path the reader. When previews of the word initial trigram were provided, refixations of compound words were actually somewhat more likely than refixations of pseudocompound words. Furthermore, preview of the word initial trigram of pseudocompound words did not increase first fixations as compared to the one-word window condition. It is possible that entry in the mental access file is relatively cost-free. It is also possible that an incorrectly activated access code may have resulted in some inhibition; this may have been masked by a facilitation that occurred because some letters were identified parafoveally.

The two remaining versions of the lexical structure hypothesis can be tested experimentally. For example, if the mBOSS view was correct, significant preview benefits should be obtained when the mBOSS of a pseudocompound word is parafoveally available. If the morphological access view is correct, only a preview of the complete pseudocompound word should lead to a preview benefit.

ACKNOWLEDGEMENTS

I would like to thank Cynthia Connine, John Limber, Ken Forster, and an anonymous reviewer for their helpful comments on an earlier draft of this paper. I would also like to thank Keith Rayner for the use of his laboratory at the University of Massachusetts.

REFERENCES

Bruner, J. S. & O'Dowd, D. (1958). A note on the informativeness of parts of words. *Language and Speech*, *1*, 98–101.

Inhoff, A. W. (1984). Two stages of word processing during eye fixations in the reading of prose. *Journal of Verbal Learning and Verbal Behavior*, *23*, 612–624.

Inhoff, A. W. (1985). The effect of activity on lexical retrieval and postlexical processing during eye fixations in reading. *Journal of Psycholinguistic Research*, *14*, 45–56.

Inhoff, A. W. & Rayner, K. (1986). Parafoveal word processing during eye fixations in reading: Effects of word frequency. *Perception and Psychophysics, 40*, 431–439.

Just, M. A. & Carpenter, P. A. (1980). A theory of reading: From eye fixations to comprehension. *Psychological Review, 87*, 329–354.

Kučera, H. & Francis, W. N. (1967). *Computational analysis of present day American English.* Providence, Rhode Island: Brown University Press.

Lima, S. D. & Inhoff, A. W. (1985). Lexical access during eye fixations in reading: Effects of word initial letter sequence. *Journal of Experimental Psychology: Human Perception and Performance, 11*, 272–285.

Lima, S. D. & Pollatsek, A. (1983). Lexical access via an orthographic code? The basic orthographic syllabic structure (BOSS) reconsidered. *Journal of Verbal Learning and Verbal Behavior, 22*, 310–332.

Marslen-Wilson, W. D. & Welsh, A. (1978). Processing interactions and lexical access during word recognition in continuous speech. *Cognitive Psychology, 10*, 29–63.

McConkie, G. W. & Rayner, K. (1975). The span of the effective stimulus during a fixation in reading. *Perception and Psychophysics, 17*, 578–587.

McConkie, G. W., Zola, D., Blanchard, H. E., & Wolverton, G. S. (1982). Perceiving words during reading: Lack of facilitation from prior peripheral exposure. *Perception and Psychophysics, 32*, 272–281.

Mewhort, D. J. & Beal, A. L. (1977). Mechanisms of word identification. *Journal of Experimental Psychology: Human Perception and Performance, 3*, 629–640.

Monk, A. F. (1985). Theoretical note: Co-ordinate systems in visual word recognition. *The Quarterly Journal of Experimental Psychology, 37A*, 613–625.

Oleron, P. & Danset, A. (1963). Donnees sur l'apprehension des mots [Data on the understanding of words]. *Psychologie Française, 8*, 28–35.

Pillsbury, W. B. (1897). A study of apperception. *American Journal of Psychology, 8*, 315–393.

Rayner, K. & Bertera, J. H. (1979). Reading without a fovea. *Science, 206*, 468–470.

Rayner, K. & Duffy, S. (1986). Lexical processing during eye fixations in reading. *Memory and Cognition, 14*, 191–201.

Rayner, K., Inhoff, A. W., Morrison, R. E., Slowiaczek, M. I., & Bertera, J. H. (1981). Masking of foveal and parafoveal vision during eye fixations in reading. *Journal of Experimental Psychology: Human Perception and Performance, 7*, 167–181.

Rayner, K., McConkie, G. W., & Zola, D. (1980). Integrating information across eye movements. *Cognitive Psychology, 12*, 206–226.

Rayner, K., Well, A. D., Pollatsek, A., & Bertera, J. H. (1982). The availability of useful information to the right of fixation in reading. *Perception and Psychophysics, 31*, 537–550.

Selkirk, L. (1982). *The syntax of words.* Cambridge, Mass.: M.I.T. Press.

Taft, M. (1979). Lexical access via an orthographic code: The basic orthographic syllabic structure (BOSS). *Journal of Verbal Learning and Verbal Behavior, 18*, 21–39.

Taft, M. & Forster, K. I. (1976). Lexical storage and retrieval of polymorphemic and polysyllabic words. *Journal of Verbal Learning and Verbal Behavior, 15*, 607–620.

APPENDIX

List of compound words used in the experiment:

waylay/ layout/ madman/ offset/ popgun/ suntan/ sunset/ tiptoe/ ragtag/ bedpan/ hotbed/ eyelet/ oddjob/ outsit/ outran/ heyday/ hogtie/ busboy/ output/ boxcar/ eyelid/ cobweb/ lapdog/ icecap/ flyway/ outwit/ anyone/ earwax/ runway/ hatbox/ payday/ lawman/ icebox/ teacup/ jetset/ toybox/ armpit/ teapot/ jetlag/ ragtag/ outrun/ cowboy/ catnip/ madcap/ outset/ outlaw/

outlet/ outfit/ airgun/ gunman/ peanut/ mudpie/ hitman/ seaman/ airbag/ paycut/ outcry/
cabman/ midday/ sunday/ bowman/ midway/ barman/ tomcat

List of pseudocompound words (a dash is inserted between the word initial and word final
trigram; this dash was not present when the word were presented in the experiment) used in the
experiment:
car-pet/ sup-ply/ dam-pen/ bud-get/ car-rot/ dam-age/ car-ton/ cot-ton/ sat-urn/ pep-per/ hum-
bug/ ant-hem/ par-son/ leg-end/ sup-per/ bet-ray/ sea-son/ sew-age/ par-rot/ nap-kin/ pup-pet/
pal-ace/ kid-nap/ for-ego/ mar-gin/ for-get/ per-use/ ass-ail/ win-try/ bat-her/ cop-per/ war-den/
pan-try/ err-and/ for-mat/ tar-get/ ten-ant/ ham-let/ can-did/ ham-per/ rot-ate/ has-ten/ bar-red/
par-don/ for-age/ for-bid/ fix-ate/ man-age/ tab-let/ cut-let/ off-ice/ off-end/ but-ton/ not-ice/
may-hem/ per-son/ kit-ten/ sat-ire/ pal-ate/ fat-her/ fin-ale/ hat-red

V

PHONOLOGICAL PROCESSING
AND READING

19

Phonological Processes in Reading
A Tutorial Review

Karalyn Patterson
MRC Applied Psychology Unit
Cambridge, U.K.
Veronika Coltheart
City of London Polytechnic
London, U.K.

ABSTRACT

This paper will attempt to provide a review, as simple and straightforward as possible given their complexities, of current conceptions about phonological processes in reading. Not surprisingly, the review will be organised around the twin questions of how orthography is translated to phonology when people read aloud and whether orthography is translated to phonology when people read silently.

Consideration of alternative theoretical conceptions, especially with respect to the first of these issues, will concentrate mainly on areas of agreement between them. It appears (see various commentaries on Humphreys & Evett, 1985) that what were once considered genuinely contrasting, opposing views ("dual-routine" and "analogy" models) are becoming difficult to distinguish. A character in a novel by Elizabeth Jane Howard comments that when his servant went into a bulk, the champagne and the bathwater became precisely the same uninviting temperature. Without specifying which (of analogy and dual-routine models) is the champagne and which the bathwater, the review will suggest that the temperatures of these two approaches are indeed now rather similar.

Perhaps as a natural reaction against early beliefs in essential phonological mediation of written-word recognition, *all* phonological processes appear to be persona non grata in much recent thinking about reading. But we suggest that whilst it may be appropriate to dismiss phonological coding as a *basis* for word recognition in reading, phonological representations for recognised words may be activated automatically, even in silent fluent reading.

INTRODUCTION

This review of phonological processes in reading will be organised into two sections and a postcript. In the first section (From Print to Sound: How?), we examine phenomena in the pronunciation of single printed words and nonwords for clues to the procedures involved. In the second (The Sounds of Silence), we assess evidence for phonological processes in silent text reading. In the postcript (From Print to Sound: Why?), we briefly consider some notions about why phonological codes may be computed in reading.

In casting our net, we will pick up the occasional observation either on children who are still acquiring the ability to read or on adults who have lost some aspect of this ability as a result of neurological injury; but the review will mainly involve data from normal, competent, adult readers.

FROM PRINT TO SOUND: HOW?

The year 1987 is an unpropitious time to be reviewing the mechanisms of translation from print to sound. First of all, a number of major articles and chapters providing precisely this service have just been published (e.g. Carr & Pollatsek, 1985; Henderson, 1985a; Humphreys & Evett, 1985; Kay, 1985; in press; Patterson & Morton, 1985; Seidenberg, 1985b). Secondly, there is the bathwater/champagne problem referred to in the abstract of our paper. It would be inaccurate to claim that various theories of the translation process have reached a genuine consensus; on the other hand, as theorists have begun to appreciate the range and complexity of the phenomena to be accounted for and have responded with increased complexity in their accounts, the differences between these accounts begin to look somewhat inconsequential. This point is made by at least seven of the commentaries on Humphreys and Evett (1985) in *Behavioural and Brain Sciences*.

The two "camps" which were thought to oppose one another are of course the "dual-routine" and "analogy" approaches; given the extensive airing that these models have had recently, they need not be described here. It does, however, seem appropriate to review the reasons for increasing proximity between the two approaches. There are two issues here: (1) whether the two types of models were ever as different as one thought them to be; and (2) what changes or concessions each has recently made, resulting in genuinely decreased differences.

Our reason for claiming that the conflict was *always* more apparent than real is that most analogy models happen also to be dual-process models. Both approaches typically entail the assumption that print-to-sound translation procedures for a new word or nonword differ from those for a known word. This point is made by: (1) Baron (1985), who comments that the existence of separate mechanisms for familiar and unfamiliar words is not challenged by the analogy theorists Humphreys and Evett (1985); and also (2) Pollatsek (1985), who notes that the separate mechanisms may not be so obvious in analogy theories because their proponents do not assign the two mechanisms to separate boxes. To use Pollatsek's example of the operation of these separate mechanisms, if we ask you to pronounce ONE, you will readily say /wʌn/ ("won") but if we ask you to pronounce ONE by rule, you will almost as readily say /oɯn/("own").

We hasten to acknowledge that this example by no means demonstrates the use of abstract rules[1] to achieve your second pronunciation. Analogy theories certainly and genuinely differ from standard (and modified) dual-routine models in their account of the procedure which yields "own" for ONE. As Humphreys and Evett emphasise, this difference centres mainly on the issue of whether separate sources of knowledge (lexical representations and mapping rules which are nonlexical, at least in the sense that they can be applied without reference to specific lexical instances) underlie the two mechanisms. Our current point is simply that the majority of theories about translation from print to sound, even those in which new words are pronounced by reference to known words, incorporate two different translation mechanisms. In one procedure, sometimes called *addressed* phonology (Patterson, 1982), the phonological representation for a printed word can be looked up or addressed as a stored entity corresponding to the whole letter string. In the other procedure, *assembled* phonology, the phonological code must be cobbled together or assembled from phonological translations of orthographic sub-components of the letter string.[2]. A printed nonword like DAKE with no whole-string representation could only be pronounced by assembling a phonological code; a word with a typical spelling-to-sound relationship like LAKE could be pronounced by either addressed or assem-

---

[1] In a short diversion here, we note that theorists proposing nonlexical "abstract rules" for translation must sometimes have been inexplicit, or even misleading, about what such rules might consist of. This realisation is forced on us by the surprising form of Glushko's (1981) attempt to test the existence or use of such rules. He found (to, we are confident, no-one's consternation) that pronunciation could not be primed by prior processing of a word sharing the same abstract rule of the sort that "the final e in a VCe sequence is silent and lengthens the vowel." We concur with Henderson's (1985b) assessment: As a test of pronunciation assignment by rule, Glushko's study is irrelevant. Probably writers using the term "abstract rule" are to blame; but they surely never meant anything like Glushko's interpretation. The rule part of the term was meant in the sense of a mapping rule or a production rule: That is, when the system is confronted with a particular condition (for example, the graphemic letter sequence SH), it should respond in a particular way (i.e. provide the phonological equivalent /ʃ/. The abstract part of the term was meant in the sense of an abstraction from specific instances: That is, in order to map or translate from SH to /ʃ/, the system need not consult those lexical representations (like the words *shout* or *hush*) from which this mapping rule was originally abstracted.

[2] The only sense in which we feel mildly dissatisfied with these terms is that, as Marcel (1980; Note 6) argues, phonological representations for known words may not be stored as fully assembled units. The main evidence favouring this view comes from the speech errors of normal people. If this is a more accurate characterisation, then of course what we are calling "addressed" phonology (for known words) will also require some assembly procedures. But as these are likely to be less complex than the procedures demanded by a completely unfamiliar string, the distinction still seems an appropriate one.

bled phonology; a word with an unusual spelling-sound correspondence like PINT could also be assigned a pronunciation by either procedure but would be vulnerable to an incorrect *assembled* pronunciation by recourse either to lexical analogy words like MINT and HINT or to a grapheme-phoneme translation "rule" like I + consonant(s) → short vowel.

Before we continue our review of specific notions regarding the operation of addressed and assembled phonological routines, it may be worth emphasising a more general point which is sometimes misunderstood. The proposal that there are two procedures by which a reader can obtain a phonological representation for a printed word is *not* a theory about a role for phonology in word recognition. Many discussions of dual-routine models have assumed that addressed and assembled phonology represent two routines for word recognition or comprehension (see for example Treiman & Hirsh-Pasek, 1985; Waters & Seidenberg, 1985). But they do not: These routines are conceived as procedures for obtaining a phonological code; to what subsequent use (if any) that code might be put is an entirely separate question. It is hardly surprising that this point might be the source of some confusion. Many earlier accounts of reading entertained the notion of necessary phonological mediation in written-word recognition (see Coltheart, 1980, for a list of quotations to this effect), and of course the phonological procedure thought to perform this mediating role was assembled phonology—since assembled phonology can precede word recognition but addressed phonology can only follow it. We will return later in this chapter to the issue of whether and how phonological codes, assembled or addressed, may contribute to processes of work identification, word comprehension, or text comprehension in reading. But we want it to be entirely plain that when we speak of phonological processes in reading, we refer to the procedures by which a reader translates a printed letter string into a phonological representation, and nothing else.

Thus far, apart from an anecdote about two different possible pronunciations for a word like ONE, we have offered no evidence to support the proposal that there are two phonological routines. For people who, quite reasonably, prefer to base such theoretical distinctions on quantitative experimental data rather than anecdotes, we suggest that separate mechanisms for addressed and assembled phonology may be indicated by the following fact: Pronunciation latencies are substantially and reliably faster to words than to nonwords. This must be one of the most replicable phenomena in an area notoriously short on replicability, and occurs not only in a phonologically "deep" orthography like English but also in a phonologically "shallow" orthography like Serbo-Croatian (Katz & Feldman, 1983; Seidenberg & Vidanovic, Note 8) or Japanese kana (Besner & Hildebrandt, 1987; Coltheart & Wydell, Note 1). Now of course, words differ from nonwords in both orthographic and phonological familiarity as well as in the putative procedures for translating from one code to the other; therefore this latency advantage for pronouncing words need not exclusively reflect the separate translation mechanisms. But we would argue that it primarily does so, for two reasons.

Firstly, the word advantage in pronunciation latency is large even when the actual spoken response to the words and nonwords is identical. McCann & Besner (in press) provide data for words and nonword pseudohomophones which are, phonologically speaking, the exact equivalent of the words. Mean pronunciation latency to the set of 80 words (e.g. PROVE) was substantially less than that for the pseudohomophones (e.g. PRUVE). Phonological familiarity does speed pronunciation, since McCann and Besner's subjects were significantly faster at naming pseudohomophones than "ordinary" nonwords. But this phonological familiarity obviously cannot explain the massive word advantage.

Secondly, whilst it is clearly not possible to equate words and nonwords for whole-string orthographic familiarity, one can reduce the unfamiliarity of the nonwords by using common spelling patterns matched across words and nonwords. However, such a manipulation leaves intact a large and reliable RT advantage for regular, consistent words (like PINK) over matched nonwords (e.g. BINK) (Glushko, 1979; Stanhope & Parkin, 1987).

In summary, although words may have permanently stored orthographic and phonological codes which make them familiar and therefore easier to handle than nonwords, it seems that the robust word advantage in oral reading cannot be explained entirely by the existence of these stored representations. We conclude that the word advantage in pronunciation latency is attributable primarily to the fact that a familiar printed word can retrieve its phonological form directly and as a whole, whereas phonology for a nonword requires retrieval of an assembly of subword segments.

Our claims so far are: (1) that there is both quantitative and qualitative evidence favouring at least partially different procedures underlying addressed (word-level) and assembled (subword-level) phonology; (2) that since claim (1) is undisputed by many models postulating a lexical analogy procedure for assembling phonology, such models never were quite as radical a departure from "classical" dual-routine models as one might have supposed.

We turn now to the second, more substantial section in From Print to Sound: How?: A summary of recent revisions or refinements within both classes of model which have brought their temperatures even more into line. Although a plausible structure for this section would be to deal with each class of model in turn, we choose instead to organise our discussion around a set of issues. Needless to say, one could select different issues and/or characterise differently those that we have selected. What follows is just one of many potential patterns into which the data have temporarily settled.

Speed of Processing

Historically speaking, speed of processing is associated with traditional dual-routine models (e.g. Coltheart, 1978) by virtue of their "horse-race" formulation (see Henderson, 1982 for a review of this topic). Recent attention to this issue, on the other hand, is attributable to the "time course model" of Seidenberg and his colleagues (e.g. Seidenberg, 1985a; 1985b; 1985c; Seidenberg, Waters, Barnes, & Tanenhaus, 1984) who are strongly critical of dual-routine models (see for example Seidenberg, 1985a). Be that as it may, virtually every theory now seems to acknowledge that a major determinant of one class of phonological effects in reading tasks—effects concerning the predictability of spelling-to-sound relationships—is speed of processing.

The substance of the issue appears almost trivially simple. As we have seen in the previous section, assembling a phonological code for a printed letter string is a relatively slow procedure. In consequence, the effects of assembled phonology (mainly a difference between "regular" and "exception" words) will only be observed when processing is slow. According to Seidenberg, the actual reason for the slowness of processing may be rather inconsequential. For example, it may be due to the nature of the task (e.g. pronunciation vs. lexical decision), the difficulty of the task (e.g. hard vs. easy lexical decision), or the nature of the stimuli (e.g. nonwords vs. words, or low-frequency vs. high-frequency words). The scenario is as follows: As soon as a printed letter string is encountered, all sorts of procedures commence, including those intended to produce both an addressed and an assembled phonological code. If the configuration of task, stimulus, and subject are such that the necessary processing can be completed before the assembled phonological code becomes available, then phonological effects (such as latency or accuracy differences between regular and exception words) are unlikely to be observed. Regarding this scenario, it seems genuinely irrelevant whether the procedure for assembling phonology relies on mapping rules or on segmented lexical representations.

This deceptively simple point about speed of processing sorts out a number of phenomena. For example, it accounts for the interaction between word frequency and regularity of spelling-to-sound correspondences in word pronunciation data (Seidenberg et al., 1984). One or more aspects of the procedures required to pronounce a familiar word, perhaps most plausibly the process of addressing the word's phonology from its lexical orthographic representation (McCann & Besner, 1987), are slower for low-frequency than for commonly encountered words. Thus it is only on these slower, low-frequency words that assembled phonology will have any influence. We need not rehearse all of the phenomena to which a similar analysis applies, as most of them are suggested by our list (in the previous paragraph) of potential reasons for slow processing, and all of these are described in more detail by

Seidenberg (1985b; see also Waters & Seidenberg, 1985). We will just make three further points.

Firstly, there might be some small danger associated with such a principle if it is used post hoc: That is, whenever phonological effects are observed, we conclude that processing must have been slow enough to permit these effects and, after the fact, we go looking for the source of difficulty that engendered the slowness of processing. It would be prudent to keep this danger in mind; but it seems unlikely to be a genuine problem if speed of processing accounts for a range of phenomena.

Secondly, we suggest that the compatibility of this notion with models postulating a nonlexical routine for assembled phonology vitiates one major criticism of these models by analogy theorists. As both Humphreys & Evett (1985) and Seidenberg (1985a; 1985b) comment, one of the unsatisfying features of first-generation dual-routine models was the assumption of strategic control over the operation of the nonlexical phonological routine. This assumption was thought necessary to account for certain apparently capricious phenomena, such as reliable regularity effects in pronunciation but not lexical decision (Parkin, McMullen, & Graystone, 1986; Seidenberg et al., 1984), or the dependence of a nonword pseudohomophone effect in lexical decision on the presence of homophones amongst the *word* stimuli (Dennis, Besner, & Davelaar, 1985). Perhaps, given the speed-of-processing principle, this assumption can be abandoned. It will not be missed, since a more plausible assumption is that all manner of cognitive analyses of any stimulus input are initiated relatively automatically (Henderson, 1985a; Seidenberg, 1985a; 1985b; and others).

Finally, we wish to call attention to an intriguing extension of the speed-of-processing logic by Rosson (1985), whose conception of assembled phonology includes *both* a rule-based and a lexical analogy procedure. She suggests that pronunciation assembly by rule will typically be faster than by analogy; as a consequence, so long as the spelling-to-sound relationship of the word or nonword in question is characterised by strong, unambiguous rules, the slower, analogy-based procedure will not be completed in time to produce any observable lexical neighbourhood effects. Rosson's (1985) data, consisting of pronunciation latencies for words and nonwords constructed to vary in strength of both rule and lexical information, are compatible with this notion (see Kay & Bishop, this volume for further discussion of this point).

Translation Units for Assembling Phonology

A simplified characterisation of the two classes of model (prior to their recent refinements) with respect to this issue would be: nonlexical mapping rule = small units, lexical analogy = large units (Henderson, 1985a). Things are now different. The variety of segment most favoured in analogy accounts, namely the medial vowel (or vowel cluster) plus terminal consonant (or consonant cluster) of a monosyllabic word, is now represented in the nonlexical routine of revised dual-routine accounts (see for example Patterson & Morton, 1985, who refer to this segment as the "body" of a monosyllable; it is also often called the "rime," see Treiman & Chafetz, this volume). Likewise, the variety of segment most favoured in early nonlexical accounts, namely the letter or letter cluster corresponding to a single phoneme, is now more emphasised in analogical accounts of assembled phonology. Because the idea that orthographic and phonological lexical representations are either segmentable or stored in segmented format is an extendable principle, small-level units (individual graphemes and phonemes) always were available in analogy accounts of assembled phonology (see for example Marcel, 1980); but the emphasis tended to be on units as marginally subword as possible, in particular (as noted above) the "body" of a monosyllable (e.g. Glushko, 1979).

What has caused each camp to become more broad-minded concerning sizes of translation unit? Nothing very esoteric: Simply data produced by camp A (or B) which cannot be explained with sole reference to camp B's (or A's) preferred size of unit. A nonlexical routine is required to include bodies by virtue of numerous demonstrations that a nonword (e.g. FOTH) with a body that is pronounced in several different ways in words (MOTH vs. BOTH) is sometimes assigned the irregular pronunciation.[3] This is especially true if an irregular word exemplar sharing the same body has just been encountered (e.g. Kay & Marcel, 1981) but it does occur even in unprimed nonword pronunciation (Glushko, 1970; Kay, Note 4). An analogy procedure is required to attend to small units by virtue of two sorts of observations. Firstly, even for a nonword like JOOK, where a perfectly good and predominantly irregular body-level analogy exists (e.g. 10/11 monosyllabic words ending -OOK are pronounced irregularly as in BOOK), the majority of subjects assign a regular pronunciation to the nonword (Kelliher, Note 5; Patterson & Morton, 1985; but see Kay, 1985). Secondly, as emphasised by a number of writers (e.g. Carr & Pollatsek, 1985; Coltheart, 1981; Henderson, 1985a), readers easily assign pronunciations to nonwords (like JOOV or KWIJ) which have no lexical friends at the body level, or indeed at virtually any level larger than single graphemes and phonemes.

We have commented thus far only on these two units for translating from print to sound, because these are (not surprisingly, given the nature of the two theories) the levels at which most of the experimental evidence has been directed. It should be noted, however, that some of Kay's recent work (Kay,

---

[3] It has not escaped our notice that this demonstration in fact forced two major alterations to dual-routine models. That is, the nonlexical routine now had to represent not just larger translation units but also multiple correspondences. We shall come onto this point shortly.

1985; in press) demonstrates a role for the front-end counterpart of a monosyllable's body (i.e. the initial consonant plus medial vowel). In fact, as Henderson (1985a, p. 495) eclectically concludes ". . . the recent accumulation of evidence points incontrovertibly to a broad range of size." It remains to be seen whether both nonlexical routine and analogy models are in fact headed for something more like the multiple levels model of Shallice and his colleagues (Shallice & McCarthy, 1985; Shallice, Warrington, & McCarthy, 1983).

Regularity or Consistency?

For any given size of translation unit, one needs now to consider what aspect of a letter string's print-to-sound relationship is influential. Traditionally, of course, the relevant variable was regularity, and this was a dichotomous variable: A word either conformed to the most predictable correspondences between spelling and sound, in which case it was regular, or it did not, in which case it was irregular. Then along came Glushko (1979) with his bombshell of a suggestion: not regularity but consistency. What had not seemed to occur to people prior to Glushko was that, if two words (like MOTH and BOTH) have the same orthographic body but different pronunciations, then whilst one of them can be regular, neither of them can be consistent. Therefore regular words, previously considered immune to any harm from the procedure of assembled phonology, suddenly became vulnerable if they were regular inconsistent words and the relevant dimension was consistency. Of course, only an analogy theory could give a sensible account of such a phenomenon. By a traditional dual-routine account, if the nonlexical routine for assembled phonology managed to make itself heard, it should provide the same, regular pronunciation as the correct lexical phonology. Therefore Glushko's apparent demonstration of slowed pronunciation latencies to regular, inconsistent words was, as Parkin (1985) has aptly commented, perhaps *the* unequivocal case for analogy theory and against (at least traditional versions of) a nonlexical routine for assembled phonology.

As every science knows, however, theories are not so easily demolished. The size and the generality of the consistency effect have gradually been whittled down by various investigations subsequent to Glushko's. Consistency is indeed the relevant variable where nonwords are concerned; but then, it could hardly have been regularity because there can be no such thing as an irregular nonword. A word is irregular only by virtue of the fact that its unique, correct pronunciation deviates from the norm, and nonwords (as Forster, 1985, has recently emphasised) do not have unique, correct pronunciations. So, consistency for nonwords; but where words are concerned, it now looks once again as if regularity is the prominent variable.

APPR–O

First, Seidenberg et al. (1984) showed that consistency effects occurred only for low-frequency words; but that is all right and indeed is compatible with Seidenberg's time course model and the importance of speed of processing. Then, Parkin (1985) re-analysed Glushko's (1979) data and found slowed pronunciation latencies only for those regular, inconsistent words whose bodies are genuinely "ambiguous" with respect to pronunciation. That is, the alternative, irregular pronunciation(s) of the orthographic body must be reasonably common (as in the case, for example, with bodies like -EAD or -OVE); where a body (like -INT) has a single heretic word (PINT), no inconsistency effects are found for the regular words (e.g. MINT). Further support for this limiting factor (phrased in slightly different terms) can be found in the chapter by Kay and Bishop in this book: their Table 20.4 (p. 460) shows a latency disadvantage for low-frequency regular inconsistent words only when these have very few (or no) "friends" (words with the same pronunciation) amongst the set of words sharing that orthographic body. Once again, then, a regular inconsistent item like CRUSH (which has BRUSH, HUSH, THRUSH, etc. to support it) is not affected by the inconsistent neighbour PUSH). Only a regular word like BOUGH, with almost no mates to share both orthography and phonology, is subject to a penalty in pronunciation time. Finally, at least some experiments (Seidenberg et al., 1984, Experiment 2; Stanhope & Parkin, 1987) have found that pronunciation of an inconsistent regular word like BEAD is only slower when an irregular neighbour (e.g. HEAD) has previously been encountered in the list. This reduces the generality of the effect still further: As a number of investigators have recently commented (e.g. Forster, 1985; Henderson, 1985a; 1985b; Parkin, 1985), pronunciation effects produced by priming may be theoretically informative; but if we want to know what determines the assignment of phonology to a familiar or unfamiliar word under normal circumstances, then these priming studies are of limited significance.

In summary, regularity effects (i.e. slower latencies to pronounce words with an irregular spelling-to-sound relationship) are larger, more reliable and more general than consistency effects (i.e. slower latencies to pronounce regular inconsistent words). It should be pointed out, however, that while proponents of a rule-governed routine for assembled phonology may celebrate the re-emergence of their favoured variable, regularity, they have had to relinquish the dichotomy. There is now considerable evidence, both from normal (e.g. Parkin, 1984) and neurologically impaired (e.g. Shallice et al., 1983) readers, that we must distinguish between mildly irregular and more grossly irregular words. This seems to be the case even if one parcels out the separate dimension of *orthographic* irregularity (that is, words such as YACHT which, in addition to an atypical spelling-to-sound correspondence, have a strange spelling pattern). We now know from experiments by both Seidenberg and Parkin that orthographic strangeness has an effect on pronunciation latency, over and above spelling-to-sound irregularity. The two dimensions have been confounded in many experiments, and very irregular spelling-to-sound word samples tend to be more contaminated by this orthographic dimension than are mildly irregular spelling-to-sound items. Nonetheless, a simple, dichotomised classification of words as regular or exceptional in their spelling-to-sound relationship is no longer tenable. Very irregular words (like PINT; no other word with this spelling has a similar pronunciation) and mildly irregular words (like HEAD; EA is more typically pronounced /iː/, but many -EAD words are pronounced like HEAD) behave differently (Parkin, 1984).

Multiplicity of Correspondences

The behaviour of mildly irregular words (like HEAD) and in particular that of nonwords sharing these ambiguous bodies (like YEAD) force the following further revision to models in which print is translated to sound by rule: These rules must be probabilistic rather than deterministic (Coltheart, 1985; Patterson & Morton, 1985; see also Brown & Besner, this volume). In other words, -EAD must be translatable as both /iːd/ and /ed/. One-to-several (rather than one-to-one) mapping rules are of course a nuisance: How is the system to decide between the several options? This nuisance does not, however, discriminate between rule-based and analogy models. There are regular analogies (BEAD) and irregular analogies (HEAD) and even several lexical exemplars which are in themselves ambiguous (READ and LEAD); how is the system to decide between the options? In other words, while rule-based models have had to make substantial concessions on the topics of both size of translation unit and multiplicity of translation options, neither of these issues currently offers much basis for choice between the two approaches.

As a single departure, in this first part of the chapter, from data on isolated words/nonwords, we note the clever demonstration by Campbell and Besner (1981) of another aspect of multiplicity of correspondences. In oral reading of sentences containing some nonwords, assignment of a voiced or an unvoiced pronunciation to the initial TH- in a nonword like THAP is significantly influenced by its position in the sentence. The large cohort of TH-initial function words in English (THIS, THAT, THE, THOSE, etc.) all have a voiced pronunciation; and subjects' (presumably tacit) knowledge of this fact biases them towards a voiced pronunciation for a TH-nonword occupying a function word position.

Interaction of Addressed and Assembled Phonology

Thus far, we have said almost nothing about addressed phonology, i.e. translation from a word's lexical orthographic representation to its whole-word lexical phonological representation, except to comment that it is typically faster than assembled phonology. But now, for the final issue in our section on From Print to Sound: How?, we must consider this procedure at least briefly so that we can discuss the interaction of the two phonological procedures. There is little in the way of theoretical dispute regarding addressed phonology; but then perhaps there is not much here about which to dispute. Theories certainly differ widely in their conceptions of the procedure that precedes addressed phonology, orthographic word recognition; but that is the problem of a different section of this book, and is only relevant here in one sense that we shall mention but not explore.

When a letter string (word or nonword) is being analysed, to what extent do lexical representations of other, orthographically similar words respond? Since highly activated orthographic neighbours may address *their* phonological representations, this is of course a potential source of alternative phonological segments which might bias or conflict with phonological translation of the target string. We have already noted that such a phenomenon is essentially irrelevant to high-frequency words for which word-specific phonology will be retrieved too promptly for anything else to have an influence. But a lower-frequency word with phonologically discrepant orthographic neighbours does seem to suffer delay in retrieval of its own correct phonological representation (see Kay & Bishop, this volume), suggesting activity within this neighbourhood. Furthermore, there are substantial consistency effects for nonwords; and whilst it is possible to interpret these in terms of variable mapping rules between sub-word orthographic and phonological units, a more natural account may reside in activation of orthographically similar lexical representations. Kay (Note 4) and Kay and Marcel (1981) have demonstrated strong bias effects in nonword pronunciation induced by inclusion of a real word inside a nonword. For example, the body -OST has a "regular" pronunciation (as in COST) and an "irregular" pronunciation (as in POST); the nonword NOST, containing the word NO, is more likely to be assigned the irregular of these two alternative pronunciations than is the nonword VOST. Kay (in press) also suggests that initial segments of nonwords which are not whole morphemes but which occur in many words will bias choice of pronunciation to the nonword in a manner suggesting lexical activation of words in the orthographic neighbourhood. For further discussion of this issue, we refer the reader to Kay (in press), and also to a shorter but pertinent discussion by Rosson (1985).

The claim regarding addressed phonology is that a familiar printed word makes contact with a representation in an orthographic (input) lexicon which directly addresses a corresponding representation in a phonological (output) lexicon. The efficiency of this addressing procedure appears to be a monotonic function of word frequency (e.g. Bub, Cancelliere, & Kertesz, 1985; McCann & Besner, 1987; Seidenberg et al., 1984). Also, this addressed phonology probably characterises skilled reading in any language, whatever the nature of the relationship between orthography and phonology. Although our review is very much biased towards evidence from English, it is worth a reminder that languages whose orthographies *could* support error-free pronunciation on the basis of assembled phonology have also (where tested) provided evidence for addressed phonology. This arrives in the familiar form of a significant advantage in pronunciation latency for words over nonwords, which has been demonstrated for Japanese kana (Besner & Hildebrandt, 1987; Coltheart & Wydell, Note 1) and for Serbo-Croatian (Katz & Feldman, 1983; Seidenberg & Vidanovic, Note 8; see also Besner, in press).

Now, the conception of many theories seems to be that procedures for translating orthography to phonology at word and sub-word levels both commence as soon as possible for a printed letter string. For a parallel distributed processing model, like that developed over some years by McClelland and Rumelhart (e.g. 1985) and applied to word pronunciation by Sejnowski and Rosenberg (Note 9) and by Seidenberg (see e.g. 1985b), it is rather meaningless to ask how and where the two translation processes interact: They do so continuously and bi-directionally. On the other hand, this is a meaningful question both for analogy theories not tied to a distributed processing framework and for dual-routine models with a rule-based procedure for assembling phonology.

Since virtually all dual-routine models deal with regularity effects by assuming that assembled phonology can interfere with addressed phonology, it was always clear that dual-routine models had to include a mechanism for the interaction of the two routines. One solution (offered by Morton, 1985; Norris, 1985; Underwood, 1985; and others) is to locate this interaction at a "late" stage, after both phonological codes have been fully achieved; in Morton's logogen model (see for example Morton, 1969; 1980; Morton & Patterson, 1980; Patterson & Morton, 1985), this stage would correspond to the response buffer, where phonological codes are converted to articulatory codes. Recent evidence may require some alteration to this solution: Since pronunciation is significantly quicker to nonword pseudohomophones than to "ordinary" nonwords (McCann & Besner, 1987), an alternative or additional locus for the interaction of the two routines may be the phonological lexicon. This could occur either by direct contact between the phonological assembly routine and the phonological lexicon or by a mechanism of feedback from the response buffer to the phonological lexicon. Although McCann & Besner's result may be a compelling demonstration of the need for one of these altered assumptions, this requirement was in fact entailed by a previously known phenomenon. As noted by various people (e.g. Humphreys & Evett, 1985; Henderson, 1985b; Underwood, 1985), since regularity effects turn up primarily (though not exclusively) on latency rather than accuracy of pronunciation, dual-routine models always had to include the notion of a "lexical check," Interrogating the phonological lexicon with an assembled phonological code, either directly or via the response buffer, would constitute such a check.

It turns out that, as well as being demanded by the data, contact between the two phonological routines is attractive for another reason. Recently, and rather frequently, the following idea has been cropping up: Assembled phonology, which (in English) is capable of interfering with or delaying production of the uniquely correct phonological code for a word, may provide much more benefit than cost (Brown & Besner, this volume; Carr & Pollatsek, 1985; Norris & Brown, 1985; McCann & Besner, 1987; also Brown, 1987, whose model allows *only* benefit, no cost). In all of these views, the nature of the benefit is more efficient access to phonology for a printed word than would be possible on the basis of lexical addressing alone. The precise mechanism for this benefit differs amongst the various views. In some (e.g. Norris & Brown; see also Henderson, 1982), it derives from the competitive quality of the two procedures; whenever the routine for assembly works relatively quickly, which will tend to be the case for low-frequency words, it will offer an early phonological code which, though not entirely trustworthy, will be correct for the many regular spelling-to-sound words in English. In other models (e.g. Carr & Pollatsek; Brown & Besner), the routine for sub-word phonology works rather differently, producing quick translation not of an entire letter string but of those individual letters and letter combinations, primarily consonants, which do have highly predictable spelling-to-sound correspondences in English. In Carr and Pollatsek's (1985) description, these "islands of reliability" from assembled phonology can combine with lexical knowledge, reinforcing rather than racing with it. Brown and Besner's somewhat similar conception, in which sub-word phonological translation provides a frame with which to search the phonological lexicon, is fully outlined elsewhere in this book.

We have said virtually nothing about the interaction between the two phonological routines in analogy theory. This is mainly because, with both addressed and assembled phonology referring to the "same" phonological representations (albeit as whole words in one case and subword segments in the other), analogy models could give a readier account of the interaction than was convenient in at least first-generation dual-routine models. Now that revised (or better specified) dual-routine models propose direct or indirect contact between an assembled phonological code and the phonological lexicon, this issue (like all of the five that we have reviewed) seems to leave rather little discrepancy between the two approaches.

In summary of this first part of our review, it no longer seems appropriate to characterise the relationship between analogy and rule-based accounts of phonological translation as one of opposition. Furthermore, whilst bath-water and champagne each becomes less appetising when taking on the other's temperature, these theories of phonological coding are more palatable as a result of their increased proximity. As with many areas in cognitive psychology, increased sophistication seems largely to involve recognition of the multiplicity of processing procedures. Emphasis on particular procedures, or rather (assuming that many or most of these processes are initiated automatically), emphasis on attention to the outcome of particular procedures will be a function of the task being performed.

It is relatively easy, by manipulations of task and/or stimuli, to obtain results that seem closer to the spirit of one or other account (see for example Rosson, 1985). It is far less easy to find or even to imagine a result that is frankly incompatible with either account. For people (unlike Perfetti, 1985 or Seidenberg, 1985a) who find neuropsychological data persuasive, such a result might come in the form of a neuropsychological dissociation, namely the hypothetical patient outlined by Shallice and McCarthy (1985). If we observed a neurological patient (a normal, competent reader prior to cerebral insult) who correctly read aloud nonwords and words regular in spelling-to-sound correspondences and who produced plausible regularised pronunciations for virtually all exception words, this might be taken as a demonstration of an intact routine for translation by mapping rules but no available whole-word lexical representations upon which to base pronunciations by analogy. The patient reported by Bub et al. (1985), the closest to this pattern yet described, gave enough correct pronunciations of high-frequency irregular words (though fewer for lower-frequency words) to violate the pattern. Whether a patient fitting this description is possible *in principle* remains an issue of dispute between the two theories.

THE SOUNDS OF SILENCE

The suggestion from the first part of this review is that, using both of two procedures, one based on words and the other based on sub-word segments, the reader automatically translates printed words into a phonological representation. The data used to arrive at this conclusion were obtained almost entirely from experiments in which subjects are asked to read aloud sets of individual words and/or nonwords. Under such circumstances, one can scarcely ask whether or why the reader is translating from orthography to phonology. But most reading is silent rather than oral, and of text rather than individual words; hence we must ask whether the conclusion stated above applies to normal reading for meaning.

In order to discuss phonological processes during silent reading, one must consider not only whether phonological codes (addressed or assembled) are obtained but how such codes may enter into processes of reading comprehension. We emphasised earlier that phonological processing and its possible uses are independent issues; but of course once the task under consideration is silent reading comprehension rather than reading aloud, one can only determine that phonological processing is occurring if it influences comprehension. Before we review experimental evidence for phonological processing in silent reading, therefore, we offer a brief discussion of the possible "fate" of an addressed or assembled phonological code.

The majority of current views about reading, based on both normal and neurologically impaired individuals, assume that word recognition and comprehension are separate processes (see for example Morton, 1969). In other words, there is a stage or procedure at which a printed word is recognised or categorised as a token of its type (often called the visual or orthographic input logogen or lexicon); the code or address obtained at this stage then permits retrieval of information from the semantic system, yielding comprehension of the word. Furthermore, quite separate from the system for orthographic word recognition, there is assumed to be a parallel component (the auditory or phonological lexicon or logogen system) for recognising spoken words.

Assembled phonology involves translation between orthographic and phonological units that: (1) are smaller than whole words; and (2) are not specific to any one lexical item but rather occur in many words. In principle, such an assembled phonological code could play a role in recognition of a printed word by making contact with a phonological or auditory lexicon. This is presumably the procedure that a subject uses to make a positive response when asked whether the printed nonword PHOCKS *sounds like* a real word (see Besner, Davies, & Daniels, 1981, for data from this kind of phonological lexical decision experiment). If such a procedure works for PHOCKS, it could of course work for FOX. Indeed, this is the procedure, often called phonological "coding" or "re-coding," which was considered by many early theories to be the basis for phonologically mediated recognition of written words. However, as reviewed by Coltheart (1980) and others, many lines of evidence make it implausible that this could be the primary basis for word recognition in reading: The predominant source of information in written-word recognition is undoubtedly orthographic information. But of course the fact that skilled readers can recognise printed words without reference to phonology does not mean that they always and exclusively do so. The possibility remains that an assembled phonological code might contribute, at least on occasion, to word recognition in normal reading. Evidence to this effect, which we shall assess in a moment, might come in one of two forms: (1) an influence, in reading comprehension, of the spelling-to-sound regularity of the word(s) in a sentence; or (2) misrecognition (indexed by false positive errors) of a nonword pseudohomophone as its word counterpart.

What about addressed phonology? Since, unlike assembled phonology, this procedure involves retrieval of the whole lexical phonological representation specific to the word in question, then the letter string must already have been identified or categorised as an instance of that word. So addressed phonology cannot enter the process of word *recognition*; but as word *comprehension* is thought to occur separately from and subsequently to word recognition, an addressed phonological code could access the semantic system and in this way contribute to a reader's comprehension of the printed word. If lexical phonology does combine with (or on occasion perhaps even dominate) orthographic information in leading the reader to the meaning of a word, then one would expect to observe occasional confusions between word homophones in reading comprehension. We turn now to a review of the evidence for these phonological effects in silent reading.

The history of this line of research begins with Baron (1973), who asked subjects to read short phrases and judge whether each phrase made sense. Some of the incorrect phrases included a homophonic word that made the sentence sound correct, e.g. *tie the not*. Although subjects were not slower to reject such sound-correct sentences than sentences which both looked and sounded wrong, they did make significantly more false-positive errors on the sound-correct sentences. This result implies that competent readers at least sometimes translate orthographic to phonological representations when comprehending printed sentences.

Four subsequent studies (Doctor, 1978; Doctor & Coltheart, 1980; Treiman, Freyd, & Baron, 1983; and Coltheart, Laxon, Rickard, & Elton, Note 2) have used more or less the same paradigm as Baron's but with greater sophistication than the original, in two senses. Firstly, since Baron's (1973) stimulus materials neither included any nonword homophones nor specifically manipulated the regularity of spelling-to-sound correspondences in the word homophones, his study permits no inferences about contributions of addressed and assembled phonology to the effect. These later studies do. Secondly, over the time frame in question, investigators using words as stimulus materials have increasingly discovered (often to their anguish; Cutler, 1981) how much care is needed in constructing and matching stimulus materials in order to rule out alternative interpretations. With regard to homophone effects in reading, for example, one must ensure that incorrect homophonic and nonhomophonic alternatives have equal orthographic similarity to the words in question (e.g. Martin, 1982). The studies subsequent to Baron's, especially Treiman et al. (1983) and Coltheart et al. (Note 2), have applied these more stringent criteria in the selection of stimulus items. Some of these experiments have been directed to questions of phonological translation in the reading of children at several levels of

APPR-O*

chronological and/or reading age; regrettably, we do not have space to deal with the developmental aspects of this issue.

Viewed collectively, the adult studies consistently show significantly higher error rates on all-word incorrect sentences which sound right (e.g. *He bought a pear of gloves*) than on matched all-word sentences which are phonologically as well as orthographically wrong (e.g. *He bought a peer of gloves*). This result obtains whether the incorrect homophone is characterised by regular or irregular spelling-to-sound correspondences, indicating that it is an *addressed* phonological code that is affecting comprehension. Across the various experiments (which cannot, obviously, be compared directly due to differences in procedure, materials, etc.), error rates to sentences with homophones tend to be in the range 10–25%. In other words, when orthographic and phonological codes yield different "answers," orthography is still more likely to determine the decision. But these substantial and replicable homophone effects do imply that in silent reading, a recognised word typically retrieves its phonological representation, even if the phonology (when misleading) does not always lead the reader astray. The same conclusion, from a slightly different variation on the Baron paradigm, applies to the results of Black, Coltheart and Byng (this volume).

In one study (Treiman et al., 1983), in addition to the error effect, there were also significantly slowed latencies to reject the all-word sound-correct sentences. It is not entirely clear what predictions one wants to make about errors vs. reaction times. Strict orthographic checking of the incorrect word yielding an acceptable phonological representation perhaps should produce augmented latencies but no error effect. Some of the data in Black et al. (this volume) are germane to the question of error vs. latency results of phonological coding.

Results from three other paradigms reinforce the conclusion that lexical phonological codes are retrieved and may influence comprehension during silent reading.

1. In a silent reading task involving single words rather than text, Van Orden (in press) asked subjects to judge whether target words belonged to specified semantic categories. Homophones of genuine category members (e.g. Is this a type of food? MEET; Is this a flower? ROWS) engendered significantly higher false positive rates than nonhomophones with equivalent orthographic similarity to a correct instance (e.g. Is this a type of food? MELT).

2. Davidson (1986) gave subjects short passages of text presented one word at a time at a 300msec rate, followed by a prose retention test. During text presentation, periodically an underlined word (or nonword) appeared which required a lexical decision; a decision word could be related to the preceding text in one of several ways. Homophones of a text word, the only

crucial condition for our purpose, received significantly faster lexical decisions than control words, suggesting activation of phonological representations for the words in the text.

3.   Daneman and Carpenter (1983) investigated readers' ability to recover from an inconsistency in text, using two types of ambiguous words: homonyms (words with a single pronunciation but two meanings, e.g. BANK, BAT) and homographs (words where each of two meanings is associated with a different pronunciation, e.g. ROW, LEAD). Inconsistency was introduced by contextual priming of one meaning which had to be revised in the light of subsequent information implicating the other meaning (e.g. . . . he looked among his baseball equipment. He found a large brown bat that was flying . . .). Phonological processes are implicated by the finding that subsequent recall of the correct interpretation was significantly greater for homonyms than for homographs.

This evidence all suggests that in normal silent reading, having recognised words in text on the basis of orthographic information, skilled readers use the output of this orthographic recognition system not only to address the semantic system but also to address a lexical phonological representation, which itself can provide input to the semantic system.

What about evidence for assembled phonology in silent reading tasks? As indicated earlier, experiments using meaningfulness judgements on sentences with homophones can be designed to include nonword as well as word homophones (e.g. *The tode swam in the pond*). Coltheart et al. (Note 2) found a significantly higher error rate to the sound-correct sentences with pseudo-homophones than to sentences with control nonwords. Unlike beginning readers, adult readers are always very unlikely to accept sentences containing nonwords, whether the nonwords are appropriate pseudohomophones or not: The false positive rates for these two conditions in the experiment by Coltheart et al. were 4% and 1%, respectively. Nonetheless, nonwords which sound appropriate occasionally slip through the net whilst phonologically irrelevant nonwords virtually never do; this result implicates assembled as well as addressed phonological processes.

It is perhaps worth noting that, under different experimental conditions, Humphreys, Evett, and Taylor (1982) found a significant influence of word but not nonword homophones. Given a tachistoscopic two-word sequence preceded and followed by a pattern mask, subjects were almost never aware of the first ("prime") word but were significantly facilitated in their report of the second (target) word when the prime was a homophone of the target. As in the sentence experiments discussed earlier, this homophone effect applied both to regular and exception words, and was obtained in a design with careful matching of experimental and control items to rule out an orthographic basis for the homophone effect. Humphreys et al. did not, however, obtain significant facilitation of report when the prime was a nonword pseudohomophone of the target word. Their interpretation, that automatic phonological priming occurs only as a result of whole-word lexical phonology, may of course apply primarily to conditions of masked brief exposures. In other words, whilst these data add to the generality of a claim for automatic addressed phonology, they do not rule out the operation of assembled phonology under different circumstances.

Further observations compatible with the occurrence of assembled phonology come from sentence reading experiments employing a contrast between regular and exception words. Treiman et al. (1983), in sentence-meaningfulness judgements, obtained higher false positive rates to incorrect sentences with an exception word that would sound right if given a regularised pronunciation (e.g. The *are* is quite polluted) than to sentences with an incorrect regular word (e.g. Who *air* all these people?). And Waters, Seidenberg, and Bruck (1984), in sentence completion judgements, found a higher rate of miss errors on two-sentence frames with an irregular completion word (e.g. The glass fell on the floor. I hope it did not . . . *break*) than to comparable sentences where the completion word had a regular spelling-to-sound relationship. The example that we have presented (which is the only complete sentence pair offered in the Waters et al. paper) comes from the set of high-frequency irregular words, for which in fact there was a numerically (but not significantly) higher error rate. The statistically reliable difference between regular and exception words was confined to low-frequency items. Both the Treiman et al. and the Waters et al. studies suggest that in sentence processing, adult readers engage in assembled phonology and, at least for lower-frequency words, may be influenced by this assembled phonological code.

FROM PRINT TO SOUND: WHY?

In the first section of this review, we concluded that adult readers have two procedures for (or at least two levels of) translation from print to sound. In the second section, we concluded that translation from print to sound, particularly at the whole-word, addressed phonological level, occurs not only when it must (i.e. in oral reading) but probably also in silent reading for meaning. In this brief postcript, we consider the question of what utility there might be for these sounds of silence.

Our first point is one to which we have alluded earlier: It is perfectly legitimate to look for the uses of a particular kind of cognitive processing; but the conclusion that such processing occurs does not depend upon our finding uses for it. Analysis of any stimulus event (in this case a printed message) along its various dimensions (orthographic, phonological, semantic, syntactic, pragmatic, whatever) may be initiated immediately and automatically. This might appear a profligate expenditure of resources, but it would probably be more costly still to be deciding continually which analyses are appropriate for the situation at hand. Whether the reader subsequently attends to the results of analyses in these various domains is of course another question, and probably depends on the specific task being performed. It is often claimed that the subjective experience of "hearing" an inner voice while reading is more common or more obvious when reading a scientific article (for example) than when reading a light novel. To the extent that such introspective data have serious implications for processing theories, this phenomenon could mean that readers translate from print to sound only when the reading task is difficult. The automaticity principle, however, would suggest that the difference between easy and difficult reading conditions is not in whether we compute phonological representations, but in whether we attend to them.

Automaticity aside, "Why?" is still a meaningful question. It appears that assembled phonology has a measurable but very minor influence on word recognition and comprehension, and that addressed phonology makes a more substantial but still inessential contribution to word comprehension. But even if orthographic information constitutes a wholly adequate basis for processing of individual words in text, comprehension is of course more than the sum of individual words. And so we come at last to the notion that phonological representations may assist text comprehension by virtue of their compatibility with short-term memory. It is generally accepted that a phonological or speech-based code is particularly stable or retrievable, especially with respect to the order of a set of elements like the words of a sentence (e.g. Baddeley, Vallar, & Wilson, this volume; Saffran, in press; see also Shankweiler & Crain, 1986). The value of a temporary record in phonological form to aid comprehension of connected language is certainly a plausible idea with regard to speech comprehension, where the message is "in front of" the listener (so to speak) for only a brief moment. Why should it also apply to reading comprehension, where readers can typically look at the message for as long as they like? Our tentative answer to this comes in two parts. The first is that, when people learn to read, they have well-established procedures for comprehending and producing speech. It would seem inefficient, not to say perverse, if the reading skills to be acquired failed to make use of the sophisticated and elaborate language "equipment" already available. The second point is that, as argued compellingly by Barnard (1985), different cognitive subsystems or domains operate on different time bases. In the process of translating from one code domain to another, temporal incompatibility will necessitate buffered processing. The processes of extracting structure and meaning from a heard message should, under normal conditions, be compatible with the rate at which speech arrives. If the speech input is either very fast or very complicated, parsing procedures may lag behind, thus requiring a phonological copy of the input to which post-"real-time" reference can be made (see also Martin, Note 7; Shallice, 1979; Wanner & Maratsos, 1978).

Since information in reading arrives in a totally different format with a totally different time base, Barnard's (1985) principle suggests that, if this visual information is to make use of the established procedures for speech comprehension, it will need to be re-coded and copied into a phonological buffer. Barnard in fact takes this line a step further, arguing that certain linguistic procedures such as appreciating the significance of word order, of function words, and of bound morphemes cannot be handled from a purely visual domain and will require access to phonological representations. We find this notion an appealing one, given the very common association in neurological patients between phonological deficits and problems with just these aspects (i.e. word order and grammatical morphemes) in both speech and reading comprehension (see for example Saffran, 1982). This specific issue aside, however, the more general point is that maintenance of information in a phonological form may provide an efficient interface between orthographic input and procedures designed for speech comprehension.

We are well aware of the minefield lying in wait for anyone postulating a necessary relationship between phonological processes and language comprehension. Some of the mines take the form of complexities regarding the precise nature of these phonological processes. One must distinguish between phonological representations for individual words and phonologically coded memory for strings of items (e.g. Campbell & Butterworth, 1985; Vallar & Baddeley, 1984) and also between phonological and articulatory codes (e.g. Baddeley & Lewis, 1981; Besner & Davelaar, 1982; Besner et al., 1981); some models incorporate separate input and output stores or buffers (see Baddeley, 1986, for discussion); and many models distinguish between input and output phonological lexicons (e.g. Morton, 1979; Morton & Patterson, 1980) whilst others do not (e.g. Allport & Funnell, 1981); and so on. Thus anyone daring to state that phonology is implicated in comprehension must be prepared to offer very detailed proposals about what sort of phonology or speech-related code is meant.

Another set of mines is to be found in the precise nature of the comprehension task. A strong hypothesis obviously predicts that any person with impaired phonological skills ought to have impaired comprehension; but since comprehension of simple sentences may be intact whilst comprehension of more complex sentences is impaired (Vallar & Baddeley, 1984; Martin, Note 7), a failure to find comprehension impairments in a phonologically impaired patient is always open to the question of whether the material was complex enough or was complex on the appropriate dimension (e.g. syntactic intricacy vs. number of propositions; see Waters, Caplan, & Hildebrandt, this volume).

A further problem concerns the distinction between developmental and acquired deficits. We have not forgotten the intriguing case of RE (Butterworth, Campbell & Howard, 1986; Campbell & Butterworth, 1985) who has unimpaired whole-word addressed phonology but significantly impaired phonological skills at levels both below (assembled phonology, phonological segmentation) and above (phonological short-term memory) the single word. The fact that her speech and reading comprehension appear to be intact might seem sufficient grounds to reject a vital role for phonological STM in comprehension; but since the hypothesis does or at least may concern the way in which people normally accomplish these skills, the fact that RE is a developmental case may be essential here. She is also unusually clever, and could have learned alternative strategies for language skills which, in the normal listener and reader, do indeed rely on phonological processes. Therefore, more crucial evidence may be whether acquired phonological deficits, in adults who learned to understand spoken and written language in the absence of such deficits, ever co-exist with entirely normal comprehension. So far as we know, they do not. (See Baddeley, Vallar, & Wilson, this volume, for further discussion).

To conclude, we have reviewed evidence to suggest that there are two different phonological procedures in reading, addressed and assembled phonology. We've argued that both of these procedures are automatically invoked, not only for reading aloud but also during silent reading of text. These phonological procedures (especially assembled phonology) are probably of minor importance with respect to recognition and comprehension of individual written words. Nonetheless, to the extent that complex linguistic procedures in reading are parasitic upon the speech comprehension system, phonological processing (particularly addressed phonology) may be a significant component of fluent silent reading.

REFERENCES

Allport, D. A. & Funnell, E. (1981). Components of the mental lexicon. *Philosophical Transactions of the Royal Society (London), B295*, 397–410.

Baddeley, A. D. (1986). *Working memory*. Oxford: Oxford University Press.

Baddeley, A. D. & Lewis, V. (1981). Inner active processes in reading: The inner voice, the inner ear and the inner eye. In A. M. Lesgold & C. Perfetti (Eds.), *Interactive processes in reading*. Hillsdale, N.J.: Lawrence Erlbaum Associates Inc.

Barnard, P. (1985). Interacting cognitive subsystems: A psycholinguistic approach to short-term memory. In A. W. Ellis (Ed.), *Progress in the psychology of language, Vol. 2*. London: Lawrence Erlbaum Associates Ltd.

Baron, J. (1973). Phonemic stage not necessary for reading. *Quarterly Journal of Experimental Psychology, 25*, 241–246.

Baron, J. (1985). Back to basics. *The Behavioural and Brain Sciences, 8*, 706.

Besner, D. (In press). On the relationship between orthographies and phonologies in visual word recognition. In A. Allport, D. MacKay, W. Prinz, & E. Scheerer (Eds.), *Language perception and production*. London: Academic Press.

Besner, D. & Davelaar, E. (1982). Basic processes in reading: Two phonological codes. *Canadian Journal of Psychology, 36*, 701–711.

Besner, D., Davies, J., & Daniels, S. (1981). Reading for meaning: The effects of concurrent articulation. *Quarterly Journal of Experimental Psychology, 33A*, 415–438.

Besner, D. & Hildebrandt, N. (1987). Orthographic and phonological codes in the oral reading of Japanese kana. *Journal of Experimental Psychology: Learning, Memory and Cognition, 13*, 335–343.

Brown, G. (1987). Resolving inconsistency: A computational model of word naming. *Journal of Memory and Language, 26*, 1–23.

Bub, D., Cancelliere, A., & Kertesz, A. (1985). Whole-word and analytic translation of spelling to sound in a nonsemantic reader. In K. E. Patterson, J. C. Marshall, & M. Coltheart (Eds.), *Surface dyslexia: Neuropsychological and cognitive studies of phonological reading*. London: Lawrence Erlbaum Associates Ltd.

Butterworth, B., Campbell, R., & Howard, D. (1986). The uses of short-term memory: A case study. *Quarterly Journal of Experimental Psychology, 38A*, 705–737.

Campbell, R. & Besner, D. (1981). This and thap—constraints on the pronunciation of new, written words. *Quarterly Journal of Experimental Psychology, 33A*, 375–396.

Campbell, R. & Butterworth, B. (1985). Phonological dyslexia and dysgraphia in a highly literate subject: A developmental case with associated deficits of phonemic processing and awareness. *Quarterly Journal of Experimental Psychology, 37A*, 435–475.

Carr, T. H. & Pollatsek, A. (1985). Recognising printed words: A look at current models. In D. Besner, T. G. Waller, & G. E. MacKinnon (Eds.), *Reading research Vol. 5*. Orlando: Academic Press.

Coltheart, M. (1978). Lexical access in simple reading tasks. In G. Underwood (Ed.), *Strategies of information processing*. London: Academic Press.

Coltheart, M. (1980). Reading, phonological recoding, and deep dyslexia. In M. Coltheart, K. Patterson, & J. C. Marshall (Eds.), *Deep dyslexia*. London: Routledge & Kegan Paul.

Coltheart, M. (1981). Disorders of reading and their implications for models of normal reading. *Visible Language, 15*, 245–286.

Coltheart, M. (1982). Psycholinguistic analysis of the acquired dyslexias. *Philosophical Transactions of the Royal Society, B298*, 151–164.

Coltheart, M. (1985). Cognitive neuropsychology and the study of reading. In M. I. Posner & O. S. M. Marin (Eds.), *Attention and performance XI*. Hillsdale, N.J.: Lawrence Erlbaum Associates Inc.

Cutler, A. (1981). Making up materials is a confounded nuisance, or: Will we be able to run any psycholinguistic experiments at all in 1990? *Cognition, 10*, 65–70.

Daneman, M. & Carpenter, P. A. (1983). Individual differences in integrating information between and within sentences. *Journal of Experimental Psychology: Learning, Memory and Cognition, 9*, 561–584.

Davidson, B. J. (1986). Activation of semantic and phonological codes during reading. *Journal of Experimental Psychology: Learning, Memory and Cognition, 12*, 201–207.

Dennis, I., Besner, D., & Davelaar, E. (1985). Phonology in visual word recognition: Their is more two this than meats the I. In D. Besner, T. G. Waller, & G. E. MacKinnon (Eds.), *Reading research Vol. 5*. Orlando: Academic Press.

Doctor, E. A. & Coltheart (1980). Children's use of phonological encoding when reading for meaning. *Memory and Cognition, 8*, 195–209.

Forster, K. I. (1985). The mechanisms of naming. *The Behavioural and Brain Sciences, 8*, 711–712.

Glushko, R. J. (1979). The organisation and activation of orthographic knowledge in reading aloud. *Journal of Experimental Psychology: Human Perception and Performance, 5*, 674–691.

Glushko, J. (1981). Principles for pronouncing print: The psychology of phonography. In

A. M. Lesgold & C. A. Perfetti (Eds.), *Interactive process in reading.* Hillside, N.J.: Lawrence Erlbaum Associates Inc.

Henderson, L. (1982). *Orthography and word recognition in reading.* London: Academic Press.

Henderson, L. (1985a). Issues in the modelling of pronunciation assembly in normal reading. In K. E. Patterson, J. C. Marshall, & M. Coltheart (Eds.), *Surface dyslexia.* London: Lawrence Erlbaum Associates Ltd.

Henderson, L. (1985b). Oral reading: Duel but not rout. *The Behavioural and Brain Sciences, 8,* 713–714.

Humphreys, G. W. & Evett, L. J. (1985). Are there independent lexical and nonlexical routes in word processing? An evaluation of the dual-route theory of reading. *The Behavioural and Brain Sciences, 8,* 689–740.

Humphreys, G. W., Evett, L. J., & Taylor, D. E. (1982). Automatic phonological priming in visual word recognition. *Memory and Cognition, 10,* 576–590.

Katz, L. & Feldman, L. B. (1983). Relation between pronunciation and recognition of printed words in deep and shallow orthographies. *Journal of Experimental Psychology: Learning, Memory and Cognition, 9,* 157–166.

Kay, J. (1985). Mechanisms of oral reading: A critical appraisal of cognitive models. In A. W. Ellis (Ed.), *Progress in the psychology of language, Vol. 2.* London: Lawrence Erlbaum Associates Ltd.

Kay, J. (in press). Phonological codes in reading: Assignment of sub-word phonology. In A. Allport, D. MacKay, W. Prinz, & E. Scheerer (Eds.), *Language perception and production.* London: Academic Press.

Kay, J. & Marcel, T. (1981). One process, not two, in reading aloud: Lexical analogies do the work of nonlexical rules. *Quarterly Journal of Experimental Psychology, 33A,* 397–413.

Marcel, T. (1980). Surface dyslexia and beginning reading: A revised hypothesis of the pronunciation of print and its impairments. In M. Coltheart, K. Patterson, & J. C. Marshall (Eds.), *Deep dyslexia.* London: Routledge & Kegan Paul.

Martin, R. C. (1982). The pseudohomophone effect: The role of visual similarity in nonword decisions. *Quarterly Journal of Experimental Psychology, 34A,* 395–409.

McCann, R. S. & Besner, D. (1987). Reading pseudohomophones: Implications for models of pronunciation assembly and the locus of word frequency effects in naming. *Journal of Experimental Psychology: Human Perception and Performance, 13,* 14–24.

McClelland, J. L. & Rumelhart, D. E,. (1985). Distributed memory and the representation of general and specific information. *Journal of Experimental Psychology: General, 114,* 159–188.

Morton, J. (1969). The interaction of information in word recognition. *Psychological Review, 76,* 165–178.

Morton, J. (1979). Facilitation in word recognition: Experiments causing change in the logogen model. In P. A. Kolers, M. E. Wrolstad, & H. Bouma (Eds.), *Processing of visible language, Vol. 1.* New York: Plenum.

Morton, J. (1980). The logogen model and orthographic structure. In U. Frith (Ed.), *Cognitive processes in spelling.* London: Academic Press.

Morton, J. (1985). Criticising dual-route theory: Missing the point. *The Behavioural and Brain Sciences, 8,* 718.

Morton, J. & Patterson, K. (1980). A new attempt at an interpretation, or, an attempt at a new interpretation. In M. Coltheart, K. Patterson, & J. C. Marshall (Eds.), *Deep dyslexia.* London: Routledge & Kegan Paul.

Norris, D. (1985). So the "strong" theory loses; but are there any winners? *The Behavioural and Brain Sciences, 8,* 718–719.

Norris, D. & Brown, G. (1985). Race models and analogy theories: A dead heat? A reply to Seidenberg. *Cognition, 20,* 155–168.

Parkin, A. J. (1984). Redefining the regularity effect. *Memory and Cognition, 12*, 287–292.

Parkin, A. J. (1985). Dual-route theory and the consistency effect. *The Behavioural and Brain Sciences, 8*, 720–721.

Parkin, A. J., McMullen, M., & Graystone, D. (1986). Spelling-to-sound irregularity affects pronunciation latency but not lexical decision. *Psychological Research, 48*, 87–92.

Patterson, K. E. (1982). The relation between reading and phonological coding: Further neuropsychological observations. In A. W. Ellis (Ed.), *Normality and pathology in cognitive functions.* London: Academic Press.

Patterson, K. & Morton, J. (1985). From orthography to phonology: An attempt at an old interpretation. In K. Patterson, J. C. Marshall, & M. Coltheart (Eds.), *Surface dyslexia: Neuropsychological and cognitive studies of phonological reading.* London: Lawrence Erlbaum Associates Ltd.

Perfetti, C. A. (1985). Some reasons to save the grapheme and the phoneme. *The Behavioural and Brain Sciences, 8*, 721–722.

Pollatsek, A. (1985). Only the simplest dual-route theories are unreasonable. *The Behavioural and Brain Sciences, 8*, 722–723.

Rosson, M. B. (1985). The interaction of pronunciation rules and lexical representations in reading aloud. *Memory and Cognition, 13*, 90–99.

Saffran, E. M. (1982). Neuropsychological approaches to the study of language. *British Journal of Psychology, 73*, 317–337.

Saffran, E. M. (in press). Short-term memory impairment and language processing. In A. Caramazza (Ed.), *Advances in cognitive neuropsychology and neurolinguistics* Hillsdale, N. J.: Lawrence Erlbaum Associates Inc.

Seidenberg, M. S. (1985a). Explanatory adequacy and models of word recognition. *The Behavioural and Brain Sciences, 8*, 724–726.

Seidenberg, M. S. (1985b). The time course of information activation and utilisation in visual word recognition. In D. Besner, T. G. Waller, & G. E. MacKinnon (Eds.), *Reading research Vol. 5*, Orlando: Academic Press.

Seidenberg, M. S. (1985c). The time-course of phonological code activation in two writing systems. *Cognition, 19*, 1–30.

Seidenberg, M. S., Waters, G. S., Barnes, M. A., & Tanenhaus, M. K. (1984). When does irregular spelling or pronunciation influence word recognition? *Journal of Verbal Learning and Verbal Behaviour, 23*, 383–404.

Shallice, T. (1979). Neuropsychological research and the fractionation of memory systems. In L. G. Nilsson (Ed.), *Perspectives in memory research.* Hillsdale, N.J.: Lawrence Erlbaum Associates Inc.

Shallice, T. & McCarthy, R. (1985). Phonological reading: From patterns of impairment to possible procedures. In K. Patterson, J. C. Marshall & M. Coltheart (Eds.), *Surface dyslexia: Neuropsychological and cognitive studies of phonological reading.* London: Lawrence Erlbaum Associates Ltd.

Shallice, T., Warrington, E. K., & McCarthy, R. (1983). Reading without semantics. *Quarterly Journal of Experimental Psychology, 35A*, 111–138.

Shankweiler, D. & Crain, S. (1986). Language mechanisms and reading disorder: A modular approach. *Cognition, 24*, 139–168.

Stanhope, N., & Parkin, A. J. (1987). Further explorations of the consistency effect in word and nonword pronunciation. *Memory and Cognition, 15*, 169–179.

Treiman, R., Freyd, J., & Baron, J. (1983). Phonological recoding and use of spelling-sound rules in reading of sentences. *Journal of Verbal Learning and Verbal Behaviour, 22*, 682–700.

Treiman, R. & Hirsh-Pasek, K. (1985). Are there qualitative differences in reading behaviour between dyslexics and normal readers? *Memory and Cognition, 13*, 357–364.

Underwood, G. (1985). Interactive processes in word recognition. *The Behavioural and Brain Sciences, 8*, 727–728.

Vallar, G. & Baddeley, A. D. (1984). Phonological short-term store, phonological processing and sentence comprehension: A neuropsychological case study. *Cognitive Neuropsychology, 1*, 121–142.

Van Orden, G. C. (in press). A ROWS is a ROSE: Spelling, sound and reading. *Memory and Cognition, 15*.

Wanner, E. & Maratsos, M. (1978). An ATN approach to comprehension. In M. Halle, J. Bresnan, & G. A. Miller (Eds.), *Linguistic theory and psychological reality*. Cambridge, Mass.: M.I.T. Press.

Waters, G. S. & Seidenberg, M. S. (1985). Spelling-sound effects in reading: Time-course and decision criteria. *Memory and Cognition, 13*, 557–572.

Waters, G. S., Seidenberg, M. S., & Bruck, M. (1984). Children's and adults' use of spelling-sound information in three reading tasks. *Memory and Cognition, 12*, 293–305.

REFERENCE NOTES

1. Coltheart, M. & Wydell. T. (1987). *Japanese reading*. Submitted for publication.
2. Coltheart, V., Laxon, V., Rickard, M., & Elton, C. (1986). *Phonological recording in reading for meaning by adults and children*. Paper presented to the Experimental Psychology Society, Padova, Italy; April 1986.
3. Doctor, E. (1978). *Studies of reading comprehension in children and adults*. Unpublished PhD thesis, Birbeck College, University of London.
4. Kay, J. (1982). Psychological mechanisms of oral reading of single words. Unpublished PhD thesis, University of Cambridge.
5. Kelliher, S. (1983). *Orthographic rules in relation to print-to-pronunciation in oral reading*. Unpublished BSc project dissertation, Psychology Division, The Hatfield Polytechnic.
6. Marcel, T. Personal communication.
7. Martin, R. C. (1985). *The relationship between short-term memory and sentence comprehension deficits in agrammatic and conduction aphasics*. Paper presented to the Academy of Aphasia, Pittsburgh, October, 1985.
8. Seidenberg, M. S. & Vidanovic, S. (1985). *Word recognition in Serbo-Croatian and English: Do they differ?* Paper presented to the Psychonomic Society meeting, Boston, November 1985.
9. Sejnowski, T. J. & Rosenberg, C. R. (1986). NETtalk: A parallel network that learns to read aloud. *The Johns Hopkins University Electrical Engineering and Computer Science Technical Report, JHU/EECS—86/01*.

20 Anatomical Differences Between Nose, Palm, and Foot, or, the Body in Question: Further Dissection of the Processes of Sub-lexical Spelling-sound Translation

Janice Kay
Department of Speech
Newcastle University
Newcastle-upon-Tyne, U.K.

Dorothy Bishop
Department of Psychology
Manchester University
Manchester, U.K.

ABSTRACT

We report two experiments which were designed to explore further the factors which underpin regularity and consistency effects in speeded word naming. Our results suggest that the *body* of a monosyllabic word, its vowel and terminal consonant(s), has more influence than the vowel alone in determining pronunciation latency. The concept of *strength* of correspondence between the body unit and the way it is pronounced in words (e.g. *have, cave, save, rave*, etc.) is examined. It is suggested that a *weak* pronunciation of the body (one which is dominated by a pronunciation which is more common in word neighbours) results in a reaction-time cost to low-frequency words. Inconsistent regular words and exception words with weak bodies are penalised to the same extent. Consistency effects are explained in terms of number of neighbours (strength of body correspondence) and competition between neighbours. A model of assignment of sub-lexical phonology is outlined.

INTRODUCTION

In tasks of speeded word naming, it appears that we can use information not only about the spelling and pronunciation of the words as wholes, but also about their sub-lexical components. Over the past few years, argument has focused on the *size* of sub-lexical units that are available. It has long been claimed, for example, that the influence of rule-governed *grapheme-phoneme correspondences* (GPCs) can be traced in naming words. For present purposes, graphemes can be regarded as orthographic units which correspond with single sounds or phonemes (e.g. $d+r+ea+m$ in *dream*). The most popular pronunciation of each unit is conventionally referred to as its *regular* form (e.g. Coltheart, 1978; Wijk, 1966). Thus, *ea* can be pronounced as /i/, /ei/ and /ɛ/, but, according to a type count of all words containing this unit, /i/ is the commonest sound. It has often been recorded that words like *dream* with regular, rule-governed correspondences are pronounced significantly faster and with fewer errors than rule-breaking, *exception* words like *great* (e.g. Baron & Strawson, 1976; Gough & Cosky, 1977; Stanovich & Bauer, 1978).

Glushko (1979) claimed, however, that this reaction-time cost was due not to the influence of graphemes and phonemes, but to larger multi-letter spelling patterns such as *-eam* and *-eat*. In line with Patterson and Morton (1985), we are going to refer to this type of segment as the *body* of the word. In support of his claim, Glushko showed that words like *treat*, which, though regular, have conflicting pronunciations of the body when visually similar words are taken into account (e.g. *great*), take longer to pronounce than words like *dream* (which have regular GPCs *and* consistent pronunciations of the body cluster), and take just as long to pronounce as exception words. Following Glushko's findings, much experimental work has been taken up in trying to discover the form in which these larger-sized units are represented (e.g. Kay & Marcel, 1981; Rosson, 1985). Two broad classes of model have been proposed. One is the *dual-route model*, in which sub-lexical components such as the body are represented as rule-governed information which is separate from lexical knowledge about whole words (e.g. Patterson & Morton, 1985). The second is the *lexical analogy model* in which sub-lexical information is not found in a separate store, but is computed directly from lexical information supplied by visually similar words (e.g. Henderson, 1982; Marcel, 1980).

Glushko's (1979) findings have recently been called into question, however. It seems that a role for grapheme-phoneme correspondences in translating print into pronunciation cannot be discounted. As several researchers have recently pointed out (cf. Humphreys & Evett, 1985, p. 733) nonwords like *joov* and *kwub* are readily pronounceable yet they are made up of large-sized segments (e.g. *joo-* and *-oov*) that are not found in word exemplars. Our ability to decide rapidly upon pronunciations for such letter strings must be based upon some form of GPC knowledge. Moreover, Rosson (1985) has provided data which suggest that this sort of knowledge can be used in speeded *word* naming. Rosson demonstrated that words which occur infrequently in the language and which are therefore low in *lexical frequency* do not suffer a significant reaction-time penalty compared with words of high frequency, as long as they are made up of *strong* grapheme-phoneme correspondence rules (*strength* is defined according to the number of words exemplifying a rule and is, as we have seen, the measure of a word's regularity). A penalty only occurs if low-frequency words have *weak* rules. In contrast, high-frequency words with weak rules are named as fast as high-frequency, strong-rule words. This latter finding appears to complement earlier work by Seidenberg, Waters, Barnes, and Tanenhaus (1984) which suggests that effects of consistency of pronunciation of body segments observed by Glushko do not occur in high-frequency words and are only observed for words of low frequency.

EXPERIMENT 1

Our first experiment was designed to re-examine the part played by the body segment in word naming: A leading role according to Glushko's (1979) findings, a mere member of a supporting cast if one extrapolates from the work of Seidenberg et al. (1984) and Rosson (1985). We decided to vary systematically the strength of correspondence ("strong" or "weak") of *both* the body segment and (vowel) GPCs. Strength of correspondence was again defined according to the number of word exemplars of a particular unit. On their own, Glushko's findings suggest that as long as the body of a word has a pronunciation which is strongly represented in words, the word should suffer no reaction-time cost if its vowel (GPC) pronunciation happens to be weak. By the same token, Rosson's findings suggest that a strong vowel pronunciation should protect against a weak, less common pronunciation of a body. Taken together, these findings would seem to imply that words with weak pronunciations of body *and* grapheme-phoneme correspondences should take longer to pronounce than in cases in which just the body segment is weak (with strong GPCs), or just the GPC component is weak (with a strong body).

Method

Subjects

Sixteen people, undergraduate and post-graduate students at Newcastle University, took part in the experiment. All had normal or corrected-to-normal vision. All were native speakers of English, and, in addition, spoke with received pronunciation (RP) or near-RP accents.

Materials

Words used in this and the second experiment were selected with the aid of a software program written by one of us (DB). The program allowed us to generate all exemplars from a 6190-word corpus (taken from the frequency-ordered list from the Francis and Kučera, 1982, norms) which contain each of the simple stressed vowels (e.g. *a* in *can* and *a-e* in *cane*) and vowel digraphs (e.g. *ai* in *pain*, *ea* in *head*). In this way we were able to make a count of each type of pronunciation of these units. We included only monosyllabic words in our count. The program also enabled us to generate word exemplars with different body types (terminal vowel and consonant clusters such as *-ead* in *head* and *-eat* in *sweat*).

We used the type counts to select words which fall into each of the four following categories.

1.   Weak GPC/Weak Body.   In which the pronunciation of both the vowel and the body is not the most common (e.g. *ea* and *eat* in *sweat* are more usually pronounced as /i/ and /it/). The majority of words in this condition have unique pronunciations of the body segment but vary in the number of neighbours with alternative pronunciations (e.g. *aunt* vies with only *taunt*, *haunt* and possibly *vaunt*, whereas *pint* is greatly outnumbered: *mint*, *hint*, *print*, *tint*, etc.).

2.   Strong GPC/Weak Body.   In which the pronunciation of the vowel is the most common, but that of the body segment is not the most common (e.g. *plough* contains the most popular pronunciation of the vowel *ou* according to our counts, whereas *ough* is pronounced variously as /ʌf/ in *tough* and *rough*, /u/ in *through*, /oʊ/ in *dough* and *though*, etc.). Words in this condition sometimes had unique pronunciations of their body segment (e.g. *bomb*, *foul*), but sometimes shared this type of pronunciation with other words (e.g. *ear*→/iə/ occurs in *spear*, *ear*, and *near*, but is matched by an alternative pronunciation in *bear*, *pear*, *wear*, etc.).

3.   Weak GPC/Strong Body.   In which the body segment represents the most common pronunciation of that segment, but the vowel segment alone is not the most frequent (e.g. *grind* has the more frequent pronunciation of the segment *ind*, whereas *i* followed by a consonant or consonants is usually pronounced /ɪ/). Body segments that were represented in the words had pronunciations that were dominant in visually similar words and, in the main, had no, or only one, opposing neighbour.

4.   Strong GPC/Strong Body.   In which the pronunciation of both the vowel and the body is the most common (e.g. *ea* and *eak* in *streak* both represent the most frequent pronunciations of these units).

Words chosen from each of the four categories were matched as closely as possible for number of letters and phonemes, Kučera-Francis (Kucera & Francis, 1967) frequency, and positional digram frequency (Mayzner & Tresselt, 1965). Matching was carried out across individual words in each of the categories. Group means and median summed positional digram frequencies are shown in Table 20.1.

TABLE 20.1
Statistical Analysis of Experimental Stimuli Used in Experiment 1

	Strong GPC Strong Body	Strong GPC Weak Body	Weak GPC Strong Body	Weak GPC Weak Body
Mean Letter Length	4.57	4.64	4.64	4.64
Mean Phoneme Length	3.50	3.57	3.43	3.50
Mean K-F[a] Frequency	20.60	21.93	22.43	22.28
Median Summed Positional Digram Frequency	153.00	167.20	153.00	130.50

[a]Kučera and Francis (1967) norms.

Selection focused on words that are low in lexical frequency, since Seidenberg et al. (1984) have reported that consistency effects appear in words in this frequency band, rather than in high-frequency words. An attempt was also made to choose words with similar orthographic and phonological structure, so that a word beginning with a consonant cluster was matched with others of the same structure in the other three conditions. These criteria for inclusion in the stimulus set limited the choice of words to 14 in each category.

Words that fall into any of these four categories can be regarded as *inconsistent*, since at least one of their elements can be pronounced in a way that conflicts with other constituent units. A further 56 words were selected which had *consistent* pronunciations of their body segments and the most frequent pronunciation of the vowel. This subset was matched as closely as possible with the critical set on the relevant dimensions. All of the words used in the experiment were monosyllabic. None of the body segments was repeated in the stimulus lists.

Design and Procedure

Two different orders of presentation were prepared. In each one, words from all categories were mixed in random order, but words with either orthographically similar vowels (e.g. *bread* and *streak*) or vowels that had the same sound (e.g. *clerk* and *vase*) were always separated by at least nine other words. Eight subjects were given one order of presentation, the remaining eight were given the other. Eighteen words were appended to the beginning of each list and served as practice. The word lists were presented to individual subjects using an Apple IIe microcomputer. Reaction times to name each word were collected using an Apple Clock Card and with the aid of a microphone used as a voice key. On each trial, subjects first saw a central fixation field, followed after a short delay by a stimulus word. The word stayed on until it was pronounced. The screen then went blank for two seconds and the sequence recycled automatically. Subjects sat in a dimly-lit room to view the stimuli. They were told that their reaction times to name individual words were being measured and that they were to pronounce each word as quickly but as accurately as they could. Pronunciation errors were noted at the time by an experimenter, but recordings of each session were made as a back-up.

Results

Errors of pronunciation were discarded from reaction-time analyses. Pronunciation latencies that were more than or less than 2.5 standard deviations from a subject's grand mean were replaced by those values. Mean pronunciation latencies for each of the four conditions after these preparations had been carried out are shown in Table 20.2. Numbers of errors are also given in parentheses. Mean latencies for each word in each condition are given in the Appendix.

Two two-way analyses of variance (by subjects and by items) were carried out on the data, with GPC strength and body strength serving as separate within-subjects (-items) factors. The "by subjects" analysis showed a significant main effect of strength of pronunciation of the body ($F = 31.59$; $df = 1$,

TABLE 20.2
Mean Pronunciation Latencies and Number of Errors for Words in
Each Condition

	Strong Body		Weak Body	
	RT (msec)	*NE*	*RT (msec)*	*NE*
Strong GPC	493	1	506	1
Weak GPC	479	5	511	27

15; $P < 0.001$), but *no* main effect of strength of grapheme-phoneme correspondence ($F = 1.20$; df = 1,15). The analysis also indicated a smaller but significant interaction between effects of body and GPC components ($F = 8.53$; df = 1,15; $P < 0.05$).

On the basis of the findings of Seidenberg et al. (1984) and Rosson (1985), we expected to observe an interaction between effects of body and GPC components such that words with weak representations of both components would take longer to pronounce than words in which just one component is weak (or, indeed, in which both components are strong). Our analyses of main effects indicate that, overall, words with weak bodies took longer to name than words with strong bodies (509msec vs. 486msec respectively). However, examination of subjects' means in Table 20.2 suggests that, for words with weak bodies, there was no extra reaction-time cost when GPCs were also weak. A test of simple main effects comparing weak-body, strong-GPC words with weak-body, weak-GPC words confirms this suspicion ($F = 0.56$; df = 1,15). It appears that the interaction between the two sizes of unit has come about because of an effect of grapheme-phoneme correspondences on words with strong bodies. The effect is paradoxical: Strong-body words with *weak* GPCs were named *faster* than those with strong GPCs ($F = 5.29$; df = 1,15; $P < 0.05$).

The main effect of strength of pronunciation of the body observed in the "by subjects" analysis was also significant "by items" ($F = 9.68$; df = 1,13; $P < 0.01$). The effect of GPC strength again failed to reach significance ($F = 0.19$; df = 1,13), but in this analysis there was no significant interaction ($F = 2.11$; df = 1,13).

As Table 20.2 shows, far more errors were made in pronouncing words with weak body and GPCs like *breast* and *vase* than were made in other conditions. It is therefore possible that, in these cases, subjects were prepared to sacrifice accuracy in favour of speed of response and that fewer errors would have resulted in slower reaction times. Closer examination revealed, however, that 18/27 mispronunciations occurred on just 2 words in the weak-GPC, weak-body condition: *clerk* (pronounced as /klɜk/ ["clurk"] rather than British English /klɑk/ ["clark"]) and *plait* (pronounced as /pleit/ ["plate"] rather than /plæt/ ["plat"]). Reaction times for these words, along with those for matched words in each of the other three conditions, were excluded from item means. With these exclusions, item means were then reanalysed. The main effect of strength of pronunciation of the body was still significant ($F = 8.04$; df = 1,11; $P < 0.01$), and we feel confident in rejecting a speed-accuracy trade-off as an explanation for a failure to find differences in naming latency between weak-GPC, weak-body and strong-GPC, weak-body words.

Discussion

The results of this experiment suggest that *bodies* have a substantial part to play in speeded word naming. To pick up the anatomical analogy from the title of our paper, words like *beard* and *breast* with weak pronunciations of the body were pronounced significantly more slowly than those with strong pronunciations of this segment (*nose* and *palm*), *regardless of strength of vowel correspondence*. No extra reaction-time cost accrued if words had weak vowel correspondences in addition to a weak body. Although the reader should need no prompting, we should perhaps point out that our findings cut across and contradict what is predicted by standard definitions of regularity. Indeed, we have shown that certain exception words (i.e. with weak GPCs but strong bodies) were pronounced *faster* than regular words.

These results are broadly in accord with Glushko's (1979) original findings, and those of Seidenberg et al. (1984), which show that low-frequency regular-inconsistent words (equivalent, in the main, to our strong-GPC, weak-body words) take longer to name than low-frequency regular-consistent (strong-GPC, strong-body) words. Glushko also reported that exception words (weak-GPC, weak-body) took no longer to name than regular-inconsistent words, a finding which we have also observed.[1] However, our data would appear to contradict Rosson's recent findings. Her work suggests that strong GPC rules *can* substantially facilitate naming time of low-frequency words. What might be the reason for the discrepancy between the two studies? There are some differences in how word materials were selected: Strength of grapheme-phoneme correspondences was calculated differently, for example.

Rosson categorised a word as having strong or weak rules according to "the log frequency of its weakest rule." As in our experiment, frequency was based on a type count of all words containing a particular correspondence, but whereas we simply calculated the frequency of vowel correspondence (assuming that to represent the weakest rule), Rosson took all GPCs in a word into account. Unlike our words, however, the majority of vowels in her experimental set had few alternative correspondences (e.g. *filth*, *copse*) and it was possible for consonants to embody the weakest rule (e.g. *th*→/θ/).

---

[1]Although Seidenberg et al. (1984) did not include exception words in their search for consistency effects with low-frequency regular-consistent, and regular-inconsistent words (Experiment 4), results of their earlier experiments show that regular-inconsistent words *were* named faster than exception words (when orthographically similar spelling patterns were not repeated within lists). We should, however, point out that our set of strong-body, strong-GPC words, which we have called regular-consistent for present purposes, have (with one exception) an alternative pronunciation of the body (albeit much weaker in terms of representation in word neighbours). Such words *are*, therefore, in strict terms, inconsistent. On the basis of our results, we would expect to find reaction-time differences between low-frequency regular-inconsistent and exception words *if* the former were strong bodied and the latter weak bodied.

Another difference, and one which we consider to be more important, is that Rosson selected words with "unique cores (spellings following the initial consonant)." In many cases this meant that the words had *no* word neighbours with the same body. We speculate, quite simply, that knowledge of GPCs may have been brought into play with low-frequency words because phonological information from body segments was unavailable. One problem for our interpretation is that Rosson reports that low-frequency words with strong rules were pronounced almost as fast as high-frequency words. This finding suggests that GPC information *can* be mobilised as quickly as that from larger segments (up to the level of the word), so why did strong GPC words with weak bodies suffer a reaction-time penalty in our experiment? We will not challenge Rosson's main claim that strong letter-sound rules can significantly speed the pronunciation of low-frequency words. However, it is possible that when orthographic and phonological information from higher-order units (words, syllables, bodies) is also available, it can take priority over that from grapheme-phoneme correspondences. We shall return to this suggestion concerning the priority-ordering of lexical and sub-lexical components in the General Discussion.

EXPERIMENT 2

The work on sub-lexical translation that we have so far discussed has rested on one important assumption: That the *strength* of a particular correspondence is a function of *the number of words in which it appears regardless of the frequency of usage of individual words*. Type frequency is a general principle which has driven the notion of rule assignment in linguistics: Regularity is governed by the number of instances of a particular feature (cf. Hockett, 1958, p. 280). It has also been used by psychologists to determine regularity of grapheme-phoneme correspondences (e.g. Coltheart, 1978). We do not wish to argue that sub-lexical correspondences are necessarily stored as rules; we simply want to claim that type frequency may underpin assignment of sub-lexical phonological units.

In previous work, one of us (with A. J. Marcel) has claimed that type frequency (rather than frequency of individual word tokens) influences the pronunciation of inconsistent nonwords (Kay & Marcel, 1981; Kay, 1985; 1987). Thus, most words ending in -*ave* rhyme with /eiv/; *have* is an exception. It is also a very common word, but, nonetheless, the nonword *tave* was generally pronounced as /teiv/ by our subjects. In Experiment 1, we showed that words with strong bodies were named significantly faster than words with weak bodies, where strength was based on type frequency counts. The words in this experiment were all low in lexical frequency, however, and we wanted to see whether there would still be an effect of type frequency with high-frequency words.

Clearly, our suggestion is that type frequency is used as a basis for distinguishing between alternative pronunciations of a particular sub-lexical unit: The pronunciation /aind/ rather than /ind/ may be selected for the segment -*ind* because almost all words with this ending are pronounced in this way. In Experiment 1, "strong bodies" were those that were superior in numbers to their counterparts according to our count, the converse being the case for "weak bodies." However, (in science as in life), some bodies are far weightier than others: *hook*, for example, has lots of phonological neighbours (*book*, *cook*, *rook*, *took*, etc.), whereas *heard* has none (but one opponent: *beard*). To see whether this factor affected speed of pronunciation in words, we systematically varied the number of orthographic neighbours of the stimulus words in Experiment 2. These word sets not only included cases in which there were vying phonological segments like /ɒk/–/uk/ (*hook-spook*) and /ɜd/–/iəd/ (*heard-beard*), but also cases in which there was only one legitimate pronunciation of the body (e.g. -*eef*→/if/ in *beef* and *reef*). In this way, we could look at the effect of number of neighbours in cases where there is conflicting phonological information *separately* from cases in which there is no conflict.

Method

Subjects

Sixteen people, fulfilling the same criteria as in Experiment 1, took part in this experiment. None had participated in the first experiment.

Materials

Words were selected which fall into three broad groups.

1.   Regular and Consistent Words.   E.g. *seen* and *hunk*, in which there is only one type of pronunciation of the body (and vowel correspondence).

2.   Regular and Inconsistent Words.   E.g. *paid* and *moss*, in which there is more than one type of pronunciation of the body, but the vowel pronunciation is the most common.

3.   Exception Words.   E.g. *kind* and *salt*, in which there is again more than one type of pronunciation of the body and the vowel pronunciation is also not the most frequent.

These groups belong to the conventional classification used by Glushko

(1979), Seidenberg et al. (1984), and others. The results of the previous experiment imply, however, that how the *vowel* is pronounced should have little influence on word-naming speed of regular, inconsistent, and exception words. Moreover, with similar numbers of each type of pronunciation of the body (and with factors such as lexical frequency held constant), these two groups of words should not differ significantly in pronunciation latencies.

Within each of the three groups, further divisions were made. For each group, two subsets of words were selected: one set had *many* orthographic neighbours (with the same pronunciation of the body segment), the other had *few* such neighbours. The number of monosyllabic neighbours in each set was matched as closely as possible across groups (see Table 20.3). The number of orthographic neighbours with competing pronunciations was also controlled for as closely as possible for the regular, inconsistent, and exception words. Half of the words in each set were of high frequency (according to the Kučera and Francis [1967] norms) and half were of low frequency. (Note that for the high-frequency sets, average ratings were higher for the words with few neighbours than for those with many neighbours in all groups. However, this produced a slight bias against the predicted reaction-time advantage for words with many neighbours.) In word selection, it was not possible to control for lexical frequency of neighbours. Words in each of the three groups were matched as closely as possible for positional digram frequencies (Mayzner & Tresselt, 1965).

TABLE 20.3
The Mean Number of Monosyllabic Neighbours of Words Used in Experiment 2 (Mean Numbers of Orthographic Neighbours With Competing Pronunciations Are Shown in Parentheses)

	Regular Consistent		Regular Inconsistent		Exception	
	Many Neighbours	Few	Many Neighbours	Few	Many Neighbours	Few
High Frequency	12	3	9(1)	3(4)	7(1)	1(5)
Low Frequency	10	2	9(1)	2(3)	7(1)	1(3)

Within each of the three groups, there were therefore four separate word sets: high-frequency words with either many or few neighbours and their low-frequency counterparts. To make up our numbers to 9 words in each set within the severe constraints of stimulus selection, we were forced to use 11 words with the same body as others in the groups. Since words with the same body were peppered through the regular-inconsistent and exception word groups, we assumed that any reaction-time cost resulting from the influence of conflicting (or shared) phonology of common segments (cf. Seidenberg et al., 1984) would act against a possible reaction-time difference *within* regular-inconsistent and exception word groups.

Design and Procedure

Two different orders of presentation were prepared. In each one, words from all groups were randomly mixed together, although words with orthographically or phonologically similar vowels were always separated by at least three other words. Words sharing the same body were separated by at least 54 items (and their order of presentation was reversed in the 2 list orders). Eight subjects were given one order of presentation, the remaining eight were given the other. Twelve new words were appended to the beginning of each list and served as practice. The procedure was identical to that used in Experiment 1.

Results

Errors of pronunciation were discarded from the reaction-time analyses. Pronunciation latencies that were more than or less than 2.5 standard deviations from a subject's grand mean were replaced by those values. Subjects' mean naming latencies for each of the conditions are shown in Table 20.4. Numbers of errors are also given in parentheses. Mean latencies for each word in each condition are given in the Appendix. A three-way analysis of variance was carried out on the subjects' reaction-time data, with regularity, type frequency (number of neighbours), and lexical frequency serving as separate within-subjects factors. The analysis showed a significant

TABLE 20.4
Mean Pronunciation Latencies and Numbers of Errors for Words in Each
Condition

	Regular Consistent		Regular Inconsistent		Exception	
	Many Neighbours	Few	Many Neighbours	Few	Many Neighbours	Few
	RT	RT	RT	RT	RT	RT
High-Frequency	515	510	514	510	491	525
Errors	2	1	1	3	0	5
Low-Frequency	525	527	515	559	524	552
Errors	1	0	4	9	9	4

main effect of type frequency (F = 10.43; df = 1,15; $P < 0.01$), a significant main effect of lexical frequency (F = 32.12; df = 1,15; $P < 0.001$), but *no* main effect of regularity (F = 0.95; df = 2,15).

The interaction between regularity and type frequency was significant (F = 12.50; df = 2,30; $P < 0.001$) and that between lexical frequency and type frequency approached significance (F = 4.01; df = 1,15; $P < 0.10 > 0.05$). The interaction between regularity and lexical frequency failed to reach significance (F = 1.01; df = 2,30). There was also a significant three-way interaction between regularity, type frequency, and lexical frequency (F = 8.45; df = 2,30; $P < 0.01$).

A three-way analysis of variance was also carried out on the item means. The main effects of type frequency (F = 4.99; df = 1,8) and lexical frequency (F = 4.90; df = 1,8) just failed to reach significance ($P < 0.10 > 0.05$), as did the three-way interaction (F = 2.33; df = 2,16). None of the other tests approached significance.

Discussion

One of the main findings of Experiment 2 confirms our expectation that the orthographic neighbourhood of a word influences the speed with which it is named. There are a number of important qualifications, however. The data indicate that subjects' responses to *low-frequency* words with few neighbours suffer substantial reaction-time delay when the neighbours have *conflicting* pronunciations (i.e. in regular-inconsistent and exception word groups). In contrast, low-frequency words with few neighbours which have consistent pronunciations (e.g. *reef*, *beef*) are named as fast as their counterparts with many neighbours.

Examination of latency means in Table 20.4 fails to reveal the same pattern of results for high-frequency words. In particular, regular-inconsistent words show *no* effect of number of neighbours and behave like regular-consistent words in this respect. There is also a sign that exception words with few neighbours do take longer to pronounce than regular words (consistent and inconsistent) with few neighbours (525msec vs. 510msec vs. 510msec respectively).

If we take the distinction between words with "many" neighbours and words with "few" neighbours as being isomorphic with "strong" and "weak" bodies, then a comparison of the subject means for the *low-frequency*, regular-inconsistent, and exception words shows a replication of the main finding of Experiment 1: Words with strong bodies are pronounced faster than those with weak bodies. Moreover, weak vowel correspondence had little additional effect in slowing reaction-times to low-frequency exception words. However, the indication that this effect may be found in reaction

APPR-P

times to high-frequency words is worth pursuing in further experimental investigation.

We also observed in the first experiment that, to our surprise, strong-body words with weak vowel (GPC) correspondences were named faster than strong-body, strong-GPC words (a difference found to be significant in the analysis "by subjects." It is worth mentioning a possible echo of that finding in the present experiment: High-frequency exception words with many neighbours (strong-body, weak-GPC words) were pronounced substantially faster than either high-frequency regular-inconsistent or regular-consistent words with many neighbours (strong-body, strong-GPC words) (491msec vs. 514msec and 515msec, respectively). This facilitatory effect was not, however, found for low-frequency exception words with many neighbours.

Finally, we should perhaps briefly highlight the finding that when one simply compares the mean naming latencies for regular-consistent, regular-inconsistent, and exception word groups (without sub-dividing them according to frequency and number of neighbours), no differences can be seen between the groups (519msec vs. 525msec vs. 523msec, respectively).

GENERAL DISCUSSION

A regularity effect in which exception words, with less common or weak *grapheme-phoneme correspondences* (GPCs), take longer to pronounce than regular words with more common or strong GPCs, has frequently been observed in word-naming experiments. The primary significance of Glushko's (1979) work was to demonstrate that regular words themselves could suffer reaction-time delays in naming if the *body* of the word (its vowel and terminal consonant) can be pronounced in more than one way (e.g. -*ave* in *save* and *have*). Thus, Glushko showed that regular but inconsistent words like *save* are slower to be named than regular, consistent words like *sane* (with consistent pronunciations of the body in word neighbours: *mane, pane,* etc.) and as slow to be named as exception words (e.g. *have*). However, in a better-controlled experiment, Seidenberg et al. (1984, Experiment 2) reported that regular-inconsistent words in fact only take longer to name if they are low in frequency. Moreover, their work suggests that such low-frequency inconsistent words are named faster than exception words (see footnote 1). Our experiments were designed to explore further the factors which underpin regularity and consistency effects.

Within the parameters that we have defined in our experiments, we have observed that reaction-time cost in word naming substantially affects low-frequency, regular-inconsistent words which have *weak* representations of the body (i.e. in which there are weightier competing pronunciations of word neighbours). Such words were slower to be named than regular-consistent words (with either many or few neighbours). In contrast, low-frequency regular-inconsistent words which have *strong* bodies (i.e. with few competing neighbours) did *not* suffer a reaction-time penalty. These differences were not observed for corresponding high-frequency words. Thus, our findings suggest that the consistency effect *is* confined to low-frequency regular words, as Seidenberg et al. argue, *but only* to those words with neighbours with stronger, competing pronunciations.

The results of Experiments 1 and 2 indicated that in low-frequency word groups, weak-bodied regular-inconsistent and exception words were penalised to the same extent in speeded naming, compared with corresponding regular-consistent words. Unreliable information about vowel (GPC) correspondences *and* vowel-consonant (body) correspondences did not therefore serve to add an *extra* RT cost to the pronunciation of low-frequency exception words. High-frequency word groups with weak bodies were named faster than corresponding low-frequency groups. Although high-frequency, weak-bodied, regular-consistent, and regular-inconsistent words did not differ, there is an intriguing suggestion that weak-bodied exception words did take longer to name. Seidenberg et al. reported that regular and exception words do not differ in pronunciation latency providing they are high in frequency (Experiment 3). We are almost convinced that they are right! However, our finding suggests that it may be worth looking for effects of regularity in high-frequency exception words in which sub-lexical pronunciations accorded to body and GPCs conflict with that of the whole word.

In sum, our data reveal specific roles played by the body segment in speeded word naming. We would like to consider an account of word naming in which both body and GPC components are the currency of a sub-lexical process and can be separated from mental representations of whole words. Similar proposals have been put forward by Shallice and his colleagues (e.g. Shallice, Warrington, & McCarthy, 1983), Seidenberg et al. (1984), and Patterson and Morton (1985). In common with the first group of authors, we assume that there are specific orthographic and phonological representations for all existing bodies and graphemes and phonemes.[2]

We have proposed that sub-lexical assignment of phonology to an orthographic unit is based on the *strength* of its phonological representation, and the strength of any competing representations, in orthographic word

---

[2]This claim is perhaps too strong. It may be argued, for example, that it is unlikely that lexical hermits, words with unique pronunciations like *waltz* and *yacht*, precipitate the formation of *-altz*→/ɔlts/ and *-acht*→/ɒt/ body correspondences. Such words, often of foreign derivation, unusual orthography, and acquired late in reading development, probably do not lend themselves as easy or useful analogies. However, such bodies may be represented and may possibly be produced in an appropriate context. For example, the /ɔlts/ pronunciation of *-altz* might be elicited when the body is embedded in a series of neologisms which resemble German words. *Osreicher Galtzen Federt.*

neighbours. The "strongest" pronunciation will therefore be the one which is most commonly assigned. However, according to this principle, within individual words, alternative sizes of sub-lexical unit will often specify different pronunciations. Take the word *spook* as an example. "Spook" is a strong-GPC, weak-body (regular-inconsistent) word: The most popular pronunciation of the vowel GPC *-oo-* in words is /u/ (corresponding with how the vowel is actually pronounced), but the most popular pronunciation of the *-ook* body is /ɒk/ (as in *book*, *cook*, *hook*, etc.). A model of phonological assignment procedures must include some way of either resolving or avoiding conflict between different sizes of orthographic-phonological unit. In discussing the findings of our first experiment, we briefly considered the proposal that sub-lexical procedures are *hierarchically ordered*, with information from larger sizes of unit taking priority over that from smaller units. What this means is that, in general, the highest-order unit (smaller than the whole word) will constitute the output of sub-lexical procedures while information from lower levels such as GPCs will be ignored.[3] The product of sub-lexical procedures may, however, conflict with the product of lexical processing. Thus, according to this account, a reaction-time cost in naming *spook* would come about not because of conflict between sub-lexical levels (i.e. between *-ook* and *-oo-* correspondences), but because the dominant correspondence /ɒk/ assigned to the body *-ook* conflicts with the lexically specified pronunciation.

This account suggests that in speeded word naming, specific influences of grapheme-phoneme correspondences over and above those from larger, body segments should not be observed (except perhaps when information from higher-order sources is unavailable). And, indeed, in our tests of low-frequency word naming (in which current research findings suggest effects of irregular phonology should be located), we have shown that strong-GPC information did not compensate for a weak-body correspondence, and neither did weak-GPC information significantly add to the penalty of a weak-body correspondence. However, as we have seen, there are indications that GPCs did have some part to play in naming both high- and low-frequency words. In particular, reaction times were on occasion actually *faster* when words had strong bodies but weak GPCs than when they had strong representations of both components. This finding was present in low-frequency words (Experiment 1) and in high-frequency words (Experiment 2). It was not, however, observed for low-frequency words in Experiment 2.

---

[3] We are not, of course, suggesting that GPC information is never used. It is marshalled when: (1) phonological information about higher-order units is not available (cf. Rosson, 1985); and (2) in deciding how to pronounce nonwords which have no lexically stored phonology (cf. Kay, 1987). In this case, GPC information may be used when a decision process is waiting (in vain) for output from lexical procedures.

Any strong claim for the validity of this effect is further tempered by the fact that analyses of these data were significant "by subjects" but not "by items" (those of a peevish disposition will remark that none of the "by items" tests in Experiment 2 reached significance!). On the other hand, given that the "by items" F-values for the interactions in question were reasonably large, and given that each experiment employed only small numbers of stimuli, it is perhaps unwise to dismiss the effect as simply artifactual. If further investigation demonstrates its reality, then our claim that there is no between-level competition between bodies and GPCs in speeded word naming will have to be changed.

The results of our second experiment suggest that reaction-time delay does not simply result from a word having few neighbours. Thus, we found that regular words with one or two neighbours which are pronounced in the same way (e.g. *reef* has only one -*eef* neighbour, *beef*) were named as quickly as regular words with many, consistently pronounced neighbours (e.g. *weep* has *deep*, *keep*, *peep*, *sleep*, and others as neighbours). Reaction-time delay is observed when a word is pronounced in a way which is shared by only a few of its neighbours (or has a unique type of pronunciation of its body), while an equal or larger number of related words have a different pronunciation (e.g. *shall* is dominated by *wall*, *call*, *tall*, *hall*, etc.). Thus, it appears that conflict can occur *within* an individual sub-lexical level.

In a recent study, Brown (1987) has suggested that body strength is a function of number of word neighbours *and* their combined lexical frequency.[4] He claims that the reason why a weak-bodied word such as *pint* is slower to be named than a word like *pill* (with many consistent neighbours) is not because of competition from alternative correspondences (*mint*, *hint*, *tint*, etc.), but because the correspondence "int→/ɪnt/" occurs only once in English, and in a word that is little used (*pint* has a Kučera and Francis [1967] frequency of 14). In contrast, the correspondence "ill→/ɪl/" occurs in 12 different words which have a cumulative frequency of 2678). In support of this claim, he reports that words like *soap*, with no neighbours (but clearly with no phonological competition), and with similar low-frequency of usage (*soap* has a frequency of 22), take as long to pronounce as words like *pint*, and take significantly longer than words like *pill*. In a post-hoc analysis of our stimulus materials we do not, however, find support for Brown's claims. Consistent words with few neighbours took no longer to pronounce than consistent words with many neighbours (whether they were of high or low individual frequency), even though they had a substantially lower *combined*

---

[4]This view holds that words and nonwords are pronounced by using the same procedures. It is therefore more closely allied to a lexical analogy model than the view we have espoused. We propose that lexical and sub-lexical processes operate under separate principles (lexical frequency and type frequency respectively).

lexical frequency. Further, within the low-frequency groups, regular-consistent words with few neighbours were pronounced faster than regular-inconsistent and exception words with few neighbours, even though their combined lexical frequency was not, on average, higher.

In conclusion, we are drawn to the words of Weiss in the Marat/Sade, which seem to incorporate a fitting description of the phonological process!

> This is a world of bodies
>> each body pushing with a terrible power
>> each body alone racked with its own unrest.

ACKNOWLEDGEMENTS

We are grateful to Johanneke van der Linden for running Experiment 2. We would also like to thank Max Coltheart, George McConkie, Alan Parkin, and an anonymous reviewer for their comments on the paper.

REFERENCES

Baron, J. & Strawson, C. (1976). Use of orthographic and word-specific knowledge in reading words aloud. *Journal of Experimental Psychology: Human Perception and Performance*, 2, 386–393.

Brown, G. D. A. (1987). Resolving inconsistency: A computational model of word naming. *Journal of Memory and Language*, 26, 1–23.

Coltheart, M. (1978). Lexical access in simple reading tasks. In G. Underwood (Ed.), *Strategies of information processing*. London: Academic Press.

Francis, W. N. & Kutera, H. (1982). *Frequency analysis of English usage: Lexicon and grammar*. Boston: Houghton Mifflin.

Glushko, R. J. (1979). The organisation and activation of orthographic knowledge in reading aloud. *Journal of Experimental Psychology: Human Perception and Performance*, 5, 674–691.

Gough, P. B. & Cosky, M. J. (1977). One second of reading again. In N. J. Castellan, D. B. Pisoni, & G. H. Potts (Eds.), *Cognitive theory II*. Hillsdale, N.J.: Lawrence Erlbaum Associates Inc.

Henderson, L. (1982). *Orthography and word recognition in reading*. London: Academic Press.

Hockett, C. F. (1958). *A course of modern linguistics*. New York: Macmillan.

Humphreys, G. W. & Evett, L. J. (1985). Visual word processing: Procedures, representations and routes. *The Behavioral and Brain Sciences*, 8, 728–739.

Kay, J. (1985). Mechanisms of oral reading: A critical appraisal of cognitive models. In A. W. Ellis (Ed.), *Progress in the psychology of language*, *Vol. 2*. London: Lawrence Erlbau.n Associates Ltd.

Kay, J. (1987). Phonological codes in reading: Assignment of sub-word phonology. In D. A. Allport, D. Mackay, W. Prinz, & E. Scheerer (Eds.), *Language perception and production*. London: Academic Press.

Kay, J. & Marcel, A. J. (1981). One process, not two, in reading aloud: Lexical analogies do the work of nonlexical rules. *Quarterly Journal of Experimental Psychology*, *33A*, 397–414.

Kučera, H. & Francis, W. N. (1967). *A computational analysis of present-day American English*. Providence, Rhode Island: Brown University Press.

Marcel, A. J. (1980). Surface dyslexia and beginning reading: A revised hypothesis of the pronunciation of print and its impairments. In M. Coltheart, K. E. Patterson, & J. C. Marshall (Eds.), *Deep dyslexia*. London: Routledge & Kegan Paul.

Mayzner, M. S. & Tresselt, M. E. (1965). Tables of single-letter and digram frequency counts for various word-length and letter position combinations. *Psychonomic Monograph Supplements*, *1*, 13–32.

Patterson, K. E. & Morton, J. (1985). From orthography to phonology: An attempt at an old interpretation. In K. E. Patterson, J. C. Marshall, & M. Coltheart (Eds.), *Surface dyslexia*. London: Lawrence Erlbaum Associates Ltd.

Rosson, M. B. (1985). The interaction of pronunciation rules and lexical representations in reading aloud. *Memory and Cognition*, *13*, 90–99.

Seidenberg, M. S., Waters, G. S., Barnes, M. A., & Tanenhaus, M. K. (1984). When does irregular spelling or pronunciation influence word recognition? *Journal of Verbal Learning and Verbal Behaviour*, *23*, 383–404.

Shallice, T., Warrington, E., & McCarthy, R. (1983). Reading without semantics. *Quarterly Journal of Experimental Psychology*, *35A*, 111–138.

Stanovich, K. E. & Bauer, D. W. (1978). Experiments on the spelling-to-sound regularity effect in word recognition. *Memory and Cognition*, *6*, 410–415.

Venezky, R. L. (1970). *The structure of English orthography*. The Hague: Mouton.

Wijk, A. (1966). *Rules of pronunciation for the English language*. London: Oxford University Press.

APPENDIX

1. Word Stimuli Used in Experiment 1

Strong GPC Strong "Body"	Mean RT (msec)	Weak GPC Strong "Body"	Mean RT (msec)
PROOF	483	BREAD	488
NOSE	445	HASTE	458
TAUGHT	490	SOUGHT	531
STOOL	535	GHOST	446
DARN	485	MILD	471
STREAK	548	BREATH	482
RAID	480	BULL	469
BOUND	465	GRIND	445
GUT	502	EARN	503
CLASH	482	TIGHT	466
PAVE	511	HOOK	454
DIVE	528	PALM	502
LOAD	435	SIGH	480
BLOOM	494	FOLD	502

Strong GPC Weak "Body"	Mean RT (msec)	Weak GPC Weak "Body"	Mean RT (msec)
GROWN	494	GROSS	483
PRONE	499	PROVE	472
PLOUGH	502	HEIGHT	489
SCOUR	567	SWEAT	559
BOWL	514	PINT	534
THRUSH	532	BREAST	495
DOLL	487	DEAF	491
BEARD	514	FLOOD	516
DON	507	SEW	502
CLOTH	470	CLERK	495
BOMB	478	VASE	568
FOUL	497	AUNT	542
GROW	473	SHOE	459
SPEAR	567	PLAIT	614

2. Word Stimuli Used in Experiment 2

Regular Consistent High Frequency Many Neighbours		Regular Inconsistent		Exception	
SEEN	540	PAID	546	KIND	460
WHOLE	519	START	546	CHILD	513
BEST	533	CAMP	464	CALL	443
BLACK	464	SOUND	540	MIGHT	482
BILL	512	MASS	479	FIND	503
WIDE	493	FIVE	534	TOOK	519
BORN	512	EAST	491	TOLD	497
RACE	499	CARE	472	OUGHT	524
SCALE	521	SPEAK	556	LEARN	484

High Frequency Few Neighbours		Regular Inconsistent		Exception	
SEEM	540	HERE	489	HAVE	499
SHORT	475	SHALL	610	BROAD	565
NEXT	465	HOUR	502	WARM	487
THIRD	529	SOUTH	513	TOUCH	527
TURN	517	HOME	478	BOTH	552
WIFE	503	FOOD	527	SAID	582
FIRM	511	COST	486	GIVE	498
NOTE	449	ROOF	490	PUT	515
SCENE	575	EIGHT	535	DEATH	494

Low Frequency Many Neighbours		Regular Inconsistent		Exception	
SEAM	541	FOOL	532	ROLL	486
CRANE	558	CRUSH	448	STALL	555
HUNK	493	MOSS	456	HIND	594
STAIN	605	WHEAT	542	TREAD	523
WEEP	468	SHUT	497	HOWL	519
HUNT	492	HINT	532	COLT	492
DOCK	538	LASH	505	SALT	541
NAIL	513	CHEW	547	SIGH	538
MEEK	495	BOOT	526	WASTE	486

Low Frequency Few Neighbours		Regular Inconsistent		Exception	
HEAP	501	FOUL	549	SHOE	498
TRIBE	504	BOUGH	637	BREAST	573
FERN	507	FONT	637	SIEVE	615
GROAN	545	PLEAD	549	HEARD	510
SOAP	529	GOLF	514	DEAF	513
HELM	538	JERK	505	MOULD	522
DUSK	493	BOMB	508	AUNT	547
LOAF	482	GILD	590	SOUP	516
REEF	537	BEARD	539	VASE	639

21

The Assembly of Phonology in Oral Reading: A New Model

Patrick Brown and Derek Besner
Department of Psychology
University of Waterloo
Ontario, Canada

ABSTRACT

Oral reading of new words requires assembly of phonology from constituent parts. One view of this operation involves lexical analogies between items sharing an orthographic segment, an operation which may be constrained by the size of the shared segment, its position in the string, its frequency of occurrence in English words, and the frequency of occurrence of those words.

Extant "analogy" models are not capable of predicting the outcome of assembly operations for all possible strings. However, using nonwords for which pronunciation options are limited and relevant neighbours specifiable, the analogy view can be forced to predict the probability of each optional pronunciation. Such probabilities can also be estimated empirically.

In four experiments, subjects were asked to read aloud nonwords for which pronunciation variability was confined to two contiguous letters: CC or OU. The dependent variable was the frequency across subjects of each major pronunciation variant for each stimulus type. Approximately 1250 subjects were tested; each pronounced only 1 string. No model based strictly on the *orthographic* parameters mentioned above can account for the data. A model in which rules produce phonological "frames" which guide search through a *phonological* lexicon is more successful in explaining the results.

INTRODUCTION

Oral reading requires the conversion of visual patterns on the printed page into speech information. It is generally agreed that an operation in which phonology is obtained from a mental lexicon mediates this conversion on at least some occasions. Disagreement centres on whether an alternative operation, in which print and sound are related by a system of rules, is ever involved.

All extant models are compatible with the proposition that *words* are read by finding an entry in an orthographic lexicon, a process called "direct orthographic access." Phonology obtained through such access is said to be "addressed," to distinguish it from "assembled" phonology (discussed later). Support for this view of word reading comes from reports that regularity in spelling-sound correspondence has no effect on naming latency for high-frequency words (Seidenberg, 1985; Seidenberg, Waters, Barnes, & Tanenhaus, 1984), and from the observation that the correct pronunciation of low-frequency irregular words is typically produced, even though naming latency effects of spelling-sound regularity are found.

More substantial differences between the views arise in connection with the derivation of phonology for nonwords, as Humphreys and Evett (1985) and Henderson (1982) have recently pointed out. All sides agree that phonology which is not addressed must be computed or "assembled" from constituent parts. There is disagreement, however, as to how those constituents are obtained and on the nature of the computation.

One possibility is that rules provide segment phonology at least in the pronunciation of nonwords and for neuropsychological patients who cannot retrieve phonology lexically (Coltheart, 1980; Patterson & Morton, 1985). An alternative position is that segment phonology is made available by the lexicon, specifically through analogies to lexical items which are orthographically similar to the nonword being read (Glushko, 1979; Henderson, 1982; Kay & Marcel, 1981; Marcel, 1980; Humphreys & Evett, 1985; Seidenberg et al. 1984; Shallice & McCarthy, 1985).

Both types of model have proven remarkably resilient with respect to empirical findings. For example, the acquired dyslexias have been thought to present problems for single-route models, but Marcel (1980) has offered a coherent account of surface dyslexia. Similarly, Patterson and Morton (1985) have shown that dual-route models are, in principle, able to explain the so-called "consistency" effects (Glushko, 1979) which hitherto had been presented in the literature as a serious obstacle for models invoking nonlexical assembly procedures.

The major difficulty in adjudicating between the competing views is that both are seriously underspecified. On one hand, the dual-route approach holds that assembly can be achieved without any consultation of the lexicon because the system has access to a set of rules; but no complete, working set of rules has ever been specified. In the absence of such specification, this class of models is difficult to test.

On the other hand, analogy models propose that assembly requires two steps: activation of lexical units as a function of their orthographic similarity to the input string, and resolution of uncertainty as to which activated units are to control pronunciation. The specification problems are: (1) that no well-specified procedure exists for determining the set of orthographic neighbours relevant to any arbitrary input string; and (2) that no algorithm exists for evaluating the contributions of individual neighbours once they are defined.

One of the reasons for this underspecification is the sheer size of the task of developing an all-purpose model. But models do not have to be elaborate enough to handle all possible strings in order to be tested. It is sufficient for them to make principled predictions with respect to a small number of strings. In the present case, predictions are made about the pronunciations assigned to these particular strings. Focusing on orthographic analogy theory, we shall set it a small task, requiring it first to generate a single testable prediction about pronunciation assignments.

PROCEDURES FOR TESTING AN ANALOGY MODEL
OF ASSEMBLY

There are two reasons why an attempt to make analogy theory generate predictions about pronunciation assignments might fail. The first is that the appropriate set of neighbours cannot be defined. The second is that the appropriate computation, using the information provided by the set of neighbours to generate a pronunciation, cannot be specified. So far, analogy theory has not been strongly tested because of the first of these problems: Lack of consensus as to what might constitute a set of neighbours for a string such as JOOV.

In other words, if one considers "worst-case" strings, for which the set of neighbours is controversial, one never gets around to asking how well orthographic analogy theory might do given the necessary raw material. But there *are* strings for which a set of neighbours could, we think, be agreed upon. With strings of that sort, we can overcome one of the barriers to the testing of analogy theory.

However, given an agreed-upon set of neighbours, we might find that a test of analogy theory is not possible because we cannot agree on how to use the information they contain to predict the pronunciation of new strings. Fortunately, here again there are strings for which the uncertainty is negligible. For such strings, all the weight of evidence from orthographically similar strings predicts a certain pronunciation.

Thus, if we agree upon a set of neighbours, and if this set of neighbours is entirely systematically pronounced with respect to the sub-word element of interest, then even if we cannot say exactly how the system recovers the necessary information from the lexicon, analogy theory must predict the systematic pronunciation for the target string.

This may seem to be trivially true. What we are suggesting is that if all the orthographic neighbours of a new string have the same pronunciation for their common segments, that pronunciation is predicted for the new string. In fact, this is not a trivial prediction. It permits a test of the fundamental proposition of analogy theory, that *all and only the orthographic neighbours of a string determine its pronunciation.*

An interesting example of systematic variability in pronunciation, which we can use to test orthographic analogy theory, is provided by words containing a double C. This is most commonly pronounced as [k] in English, less commonly as [ks]. Example words are ACCOUNT, SUCCUMB, ACCOMMODATE, ACCIDENT, SUCCESS, and ACCELERATE. The systematicity here is easily explained. For example, in terms of the smallest orthographic unit, C is pronounced as [s] before I or E, [k] elsewhere. It is not necessary to posit a rule relating letters to sounds, of course. Larger units can be involved: The regularity can be expressed in terms of CC units or even CCE and CCI vs. all other CC segments.[1] This regularity can quite easily be extracted from comparisons involving all strings which contain the CC unit.

If pronunciations for nonwords are assembled using the information resources of an orthographic lexicon, our prediction is that CC should be pronounced in nonwords in the same systematic way. That is, as [ks] before I or E, [k] elsewhere. Since this holds regardless of the size of the sub-word units activated, and regardless of their position within the string, we do not believe it would be possible for any extant version of analogy theory to make alternative predictions. Our first three experiments tested this prediction.

The Experiments

All of the experiments reported here had a common procedure, which we shall describe briefly at this point. Subjects were approached on the University of Waterloo campus, and selected with the following constraints: (1) only occidentals were approached; (2) responses were not recorded for people judged or self-reported not to be native speakers of English (approximately 2% of subjects questioned, across all experiments); (3) when people approached were in groups, only the first response offered by a group member was recorded.

Subjects were shown a 4″ × 8″ white card containing a single letter-string written in ¾″ black, lower-case letters. Each was asked the question: "If this was a word, how would you pronounce it?" This phrasing was used because in a pilot study subjects had been concerned about not recognising the stimulus strings. Subjects in Experiment 2 also pronounced "priming" words before the critical string.

---

[1] Note that in this discussion, "C" means the letter C; it does not mean "Consonant."

Experiment 1

For the first experiment, we selected the critical strings HACCID and HACCEDE. We expected these to be pronounced on analogy to English -CC- words, with particular reference to ACCIDENT, which has a segment in common with HACCID, and ACCEDE, which is contained in HAC-CEDE. In addition, we tested the word ACCEDE to determine its pronunciation empirically, since it is a less common word than ACCIDENT. Responses were recorded by -CC- reading for 78 subjects, 26 for *each* string. The response categories [ks], [k], and [s] were used.

Results and Discussion.   Results for Experiment 1 are shown as percentages of each pronunciation of CC in Table 21.1. We were surprised by the finding that almost 60% of our subjects pronounced ACCEDE with medial [s], but the finding supports a preliminary account of the response distribution for HACCEDE in terms of orthographic analogies to ACCEDE. Unfortunately, this does not help us account for the very high incidence of [s] responses to HACCID.

TABLE 21.1
Pronunciations (in Percentages) as a Function of
String Type in Experiment 1

	Response Type		
Stimulus	[s]	[k]	[ks]
HACCID	84.6	3.8	11.5
HACCEDE	69.9	19.2	7.6
ACCEDE	57.7	0.0	42.3

To our knowledge, the only word in which CC is ever pronounced [s] (at least in Canadian English) is FLACCID. But why should this rare form dominate the assembly operation, in place of the more frequent ACCIDENT? It might happen because of position markings: That is, the -ACCID segment is final in both HACCID and FLACCID, but initial in ACCIDENT.

In a follow-up to Experiment 1, we tested this idea by asking 20 people to pronounce the string ACCID. 16 said [æsəd]; 2 [ækəd]; and 2 [æksəd]. This replicates our result, but undermines the argument that HACCID is pronounced by analogy to FLACCID in preference to ACCIDENT, since there is no reason for such a preference in the case of ACCID.

An alternative proposition is that the analogy mechanism is rather more complex than one might have previously supposed. In particular, it may be that what could be called "simplification" of double consonants by deletion produces relevant parsings. On this view, among the parsings of HACCID would be ACID, which would explain the [s] reading.

A similar explanation can be devised for HACCEDE, based on the single-C neighbour ACE. If we suppose that ACCEDE was not a lexical item for those subjects who read it with medial [s] (i.e. the [s] reading was not a *learned* pronunciation), the account extends to ACCEDE as well.[2] The virtue of this view is that it accounts for all the results in the same way, rather than requiring separate explanations for each stimulus.[3]

If single-C neighbours constrain pronunciation of stimulus strings in this way, we may be able to over-ride their effect by augmenting the activation of -CC- neighbours. To test this idea, we repeated the experiment, attempting to increase the influence of the more regular CC words on the assembly process, using a "priming" paradigm. This manipulation requires subjects to pronounce a real CC word before the critical string. Kay and Marcel (1981) reported that preceding pseudowords with real words in this way had a biasing effect (towards the real-word pronunciation).

Experiment 2

The critical string in this experiment was HACCEL. There were several reasons for choosing this string. First, its closest orthographic neighbour is the word ACCELERATE, about the pronunciation of which there is no uncertainty: It is definitely a [ks] word. Second, we wanted a string not used in Experiment 1, to see if the [s] reading is general, or a relatively isolated phenomenon.

There were three priming conditions, with 50 subjects in each condition. *Each subject saw only one target string.* The first condition was simply no prime. Subjects in this condition saw only the critical string. The second condition was the orthographic prime SUCCESS. In the third condition the prime was the word AXLE, which is phonologically very close to the segment ACCEL, but orthographically quite distinct.

It might be suggested that SUCCESS is not sufficiently similar to HACCEL to give the biasing mechanism a fair chance. We reject that idea,

---

[2]This view is supported by the observation that the [ks] reading was very much more frequent with ACCEDE than with the other two strings: 42% vs. an average 9%. The argument is that for the 42% who responded [ks], ACCEDE is a lexical item; for the others, it is not.

[3]It must be noted, however, that the alternative view—that medial [s] is a learned (i.e. lexical) pronunciation—cannot be dismissed. But if we find the [s] reading with other CCE nonwords, the impetus to consider it a general phenomenon and reject a special explanation for ACCEDE will be strong.

for two reasons. First, it seems to us that for any mechanism charged with assembling phonology from component parts, a construction such as CC would be a godsend. It identifies a small set of words, and (with the single exception of FLACCID) is pronounced systematically.

Secondly, the argument that SUCCESS is not sufficiently orthographically similar to HACCEL does not fit with our observation that the pronunciation of CC in English words can be specified by reference only to the two Cs and the following vowel, a segment which HACCEL and SUCCESS have in common. Unless confronted with compelling evidence, we are reluctant to accept the idea that the system does not have access to information of this sort.

The predictions are simple. If the [s] dominance of Experiment 1 is an isolated phenomenon, then we should see a high probability for [ks] in this experiment, in both the no-prime and SUCCESS-prime conditions, as originally predicted. However, if the [s] reading in Experiment 1 reflected a more general effect (the influence of single-C neighbours), that effect should also be apparent in our no-prime condition, because of the neighbour ACE. This suggests a high [s] probability in the no-prime condition. In addition, given the evidence of Kay and Marcel's (1981) priming study, we should be able to diminish the single-C influence in the SUCCESS-prime condition, yielding a lower [s]-probability than in the no-prime condition.

Results and Discussion. Pronunciations by prime and category are shown in Table 21.2. Results for the no-prime and the SUCCESS-prime conditions are similar. In spite of orthographic neighbours the majority of subjects responded to HACCEL with the [s] pronunciation. This in itself presents difficulties for analogy theory. Compounding these difficulties is the failure to bias pronunciation with an orthographic prime.

One potential explanation for the failure to bias pronunciation with an orthographic prime is that too long an interval transpired between prime and critical strings. This objection is undermined by two observations. First, although not precisely timed, our intervals are unlikely to have been appreciably longer than Kay and Marcel's, who allowed intervening stimuli between prime and critical string. Secondly, we *did* find what we interpret as a priming effect of the *phonological* prime AXLE.

We can compare the AXLE-prime distribution with expected frequencies generated by collapsing across the no-prime and SUCCESS-prime conditions. A chi-squared test of these distributions yielded a value of 36.1 (df = 2, $P < 0.001$). This suggests that the AXLE-prime distribution is different to the other distributions, and we shall interpret this as evidence of an effect of the phonological prime. As such, it undermines the argument that too long a delay occurred between prime and target in the other conditions.

The findings of this experiment, then, are that [ks] was not a high

TABLE 21.2
Pronunciations (in Percentages) as a Function of String
Type in Experiment 2

	Response Type		
Prime Item	[s]	[k]	[ks]
No-prime baseline	54.0	28.0	14.0
SUCCESS	64.0	22.0	14.0
AXLE	38.0	24.0	34.0

NOTE: The test string was HACCEL for all subjects.

probability reading in any condition, and that there was no orthographic priming effect in the direction of [ks]. These data suggest that the [s]-reading found in Experiments 1 and 2 is not an isolated phenomenon, but a more general one, still to be explained. We suggested above that it could be due to the influence of single-C neighbours. If that is the case, evidently our priming manipulation did not over-ride the single-C influence. The next experiment provides a more direct test of the single-C neighbour proposition.

Experiment 3

In this experiment, we used critical -CC- strings which have unexceptional double-C neighbours, but differ in whether or not they also have single-C neighbours. That is, some of the strings have single-C neighbours which stand in relation to them roughly as ACID stands to HACCID; others have no such neighbours. The prediction is again simple: If these neighbours are efficacious, the corresponding nonwords should be associated with a higher [s] response probability than nonwords without single-C neighbours.

The stimulus strings for this experiment are shown in Table 21.3, with relevant neighbours. Forty subjects saw each stimulus; *each subject saw only one stimulus*. Along with the strings which have obvious single-C neighbours, and the strings which have no obvious neighbours, a set having another kind of neighbours was included: -CK- words. If -CK- words act as neighbours to CC strings, that would suggest that we do not have just a strategy of reducing double consonants here, but rather that neighbours are defined in some more complex way than we had supposed.

Results and Discussion.   Pronunciations by -CC- reading are shown in Table 21.4. The focus of our interest here is the comparison between strings which have obvious single-C neighbours and those which do not. There is a small difference between the two sets (RACCET, PACCET, FACCET,

TABLE 21.3
Stimuli for Experiment 3

	Type of Neighbour	
String	-C-	-CK-
GOCCET		
TOCCET		
ROCCET		rocket
POCCET		pocket
LOCCET		locket
HUCCEL		huckle(berry)
BUCCEL		buckle
RACCET	race/ace	racket
PACCET	pace/ace	packet
FACCET	face/facet/ace	
TICCEL	ice	tickle

TABLE 21.4
Pronunciation (in Percentages) as a Function of String Type in
Experiment 3

	[s]	[k]	[ks]	[č]	χ^2
Set Without Single-C Neighbours					
GOCCET	77.5	2.5	0.0	17.5	10.45[a]
TOCCET	52.5	32.5	2.5	12.5	0.33
ROCCET	35.0	52.5	2.5	2.5	3.99[a]
POCCET	40.0	52.5	2.5	5.0	11.06[a]
LOCCET	77.5	15.0	7.5	0.0	9.68[a]
HUCCEL	50.0	35.0	10.0	0.0	0.86
BUCCEL	55.0	35.0	0.0	10.0	0.49
X̄	55.3	32.1	3.6	6.8	
Set With Single-C Neighbours					
RACCET	57.5	35.0	0.0	5.0	0.43
PACCET	65.0	20.0	10.0	2.5	0.83
FACCET	82.5	10.0	5.0	2.5	7.36[a]
TICCEL	60.0	25.0	2.5	12.5	0.57
X̄	66.2	22.5	4.4	5.6	

[a]$P < 0.05$

TICCEL, vs. all the others). The single-C set produced 66.2% [s] responses, while the other set produced 55.2%.

One might conclude from these data that whole-word single-C neighbours are having some influence on the pronunciations assigned to our stimuli. Compromising this conclusion, however, are two findings. First, some strings with no single-C neighbour produced [s] responses as often as FACCET, and more often than PACCET, RACCET, and TICCEL. GOCCET yielded 80% [s] responses, while LOCCET gave 77%. Secondly, out of the 120 subjects who saw one of FACCET, RACCET, or PACCET, only 6 used the [e] vowel in the first syllable, the vowel of ACE, FACE, RACE, and PACE. In the absence of any arguments as to why the CC in RACCET, but not the A, should be pronounced "on analogy" to RACE, we reject the conclusion that whole-word single-C neighbours account for our findings.

While the existence of whole-word single-C neighbours appears not to influence the probability of an [s] response, there is significant variance across the strings. By chi-squared tests comparing each string individually with the average response distribution of all the strings, five are significantly different from the average. For GOCCET, LOCCET, and FACCET, [k] was a very low probability event, averaging less than 10% of responses. For ROCCET and POCCET, the probability of [k] was over 50%.

The question is, why are these sets of strings so different? It is not because of either double-C or single-C neighbours. It may, therefore, be time for us to consider a model which makes no appeal to *orthographic* neighbours at all. The logic of our argument here is that something is wrong with the idea of assembly of phonology by analogy to orthographic neighbours. Logically, the alternatives are that assembly does not involve an analogy operation, or that the neighbours involved are not orthographic.

If analogies are not used, presumably a rule system handles the *entire* task. We shall leave exploration of this possibility to those who are more enamoured of independent rule systems, and turn to the other alternative: That the neighbours are not orthographic.

The obvious question is, if the neighbours are not orthographically similar, what are they? We propose that it is *phonological* similarity that counts. The proposal turns upon the idea of "flexible rules"—rules which, where necessary, associate orthographic inputs with a small number of phonological outputs. Is there any reason why a rule should have to specify only a single output representation and no other? Our position is that a rule which consistently specifies a very restricted subset of phonological representations is doing what rules should do; reducing uncertainty in predictable ways. Patterson and Morton (1985) have made a similar suggestion (rules with multiple outputs) in connection with the body subsystem to their orthographic-phonological conversion (OPC) system.

We suggested that flexible rules have multiple outputs "where necessary."

As Carr and Pollatsek (1985) have recently pointed out, there are "islands of reliability" in spelling-sound correspondence. That is, correspondences are more reliable for some graphemes than for others. Carr and Pollatsek suggested that the reliable translations might permit partial prelexical specifications of phonology which could influence a lexical consultation.

In fact, if we permit rule-generated forms to be modified *after* lexical access (so that, for example, the softening of G need not be specified by pre-lexical rule), we should be able to develop a system which typically (but not always) specifies single rule outputs for consonants and multiple outputs for vowels. This conception acknowledges that most of the problem with irregularity of spelling-sound correspondence is due to vowels. It is compat-ible with the observation that, while English print-sound associations for vowels have changed dramatically since the invention of printing presses, with little deleterious effect on our ability to read, no such dramatic shift has occurred with consonant associations.

Given historical, informational, and reliability differences between vowels and consonants, we propose a system of rules which generates small sets of values for consonants and larger sets of values for vowels. The consonant "frames" and the vowel options then combine to form a small set of candidate readings of the input string. Selection from among these candi-dates is facilitated by an appeal to the lexicon.

Our answer to the question "assembly by rule or assembly by appeal to the lexicon?," then, is: both. Rules generate a small set of options, and the lexicon guides selection of one among them. One aspect of the data from Experiment 3 supports this conclusion. Table 21.5 shows response distribu-tions for the strings BUCCEL and HUCCEL, by -CC- category and initial vowel subcategory. These data reveal an effect attributable to the phonologi-cal neighbours BUCKLE and HUCKLE(BERRY), which have the vowel [ʌ].

TABLE 21.5
Detailed Results for BUCCEL and HUCCEL

			Response Type	
Stimulus			[s]	[k]
BUCCEL	[ju]	(brew)	35.0	2.5
	[ʌ]	(bud)	12.5	32.5
HUCCEL	[ju]		42.5	10.0
	[ʌ]		12.5	25.0

NOTE: Responses by -CC- category and initial-vowel subcategory, in percentages.

A calculation of chi-squared on the data collapsed across the two strings, to test the independence of vowel and -CC- options, yields a value of 21.60 (df = 1, $P < 0.001$). From this we obtain a phi-coefficient of 0.56. Clearly there is a strong relationship, such that the vowel [Λ] is much more likely to be found when -CC- is read as [k] (or vice versa). This is *prima facie* evidence for the involvement of the lexical items BUCK-LE and HUCKLEBERRY as phonological neighbours which influence selection from among the set of candidate readings. This account by itself cannot be complete because for BUCCEL and HUCCEL read with [ju], neither [s] nor [k] makes a word, whereas with [Λ], both [s] and [k] make words.

This is just one version of a more general point, that sometimes multiple candidate readings will be (phonological) words, and provision must be made for distinguishing between them. A mundane approach to this issue is to propose a post-lexical orthographic check (about which we shall have more to say in the General Discussion). By this we do not mean that orthography made available by access to the lexicon is compared element by element to the stimulus representation. Rather, we envisage a process which answers questions like: "Is such a spelling reasonable for this pronunciation, or such a pronunciation reasonable for this spelling?"

There is admittedly a touch of *Deus ex machina* in this proposal. Our purpose in this paper, however, is simply to outline a model and to suggest in a few important cases how it might deal with potential problems. We are content here to observe that the model makes use of the facts that BUC- is usually pronounced [bΛk]- and that [bΛs]- is never spelled BUC- in English. These facts foster the decision that: "BUCCEL is a lot like BUCKLE and could well be pronounced [bΛkl] but BUCCEL is not very much like BUSTLE and should not be pronounced [bΛsl]." It is important to remember that we are talking about nonwords, for which there is no convention about pronunciation. Something like this probabilistic reasoning appears to be unavoidable.

Although the concept of flexible rules in conjunction with a phonological lexicon has considerable explanatory power, it is to this point entirely post hoc, and therefore in need of direct testing. In order to detect the involvement of such "prelexical" phonological rules, we require a situation in which the putative rule/phonological lexical system and information obtained from orthographic environments make opposing predictions. In Experiment 4, a set of pseudoword strings with this quality was presented to 600 people for pronunciation.

Experiment 4

A common vowel digraph in English is OU. This segment appears in, by rough count, just over 100 ordinary English words of varying frequency. In the majority of these (about 65%), OU is pronounced [au], as in HOUSE, MOUTH, GROUCH, COUNT, LOUNGE, and SHROUD. Minor pronunciations include [u] (LOUP, MOUSSE, SOUP); [ɔ] (OUGHT); [ʌ] (TOUCH); [ə] (FAMOUS); and [oʷ] (DOUGH, THOUGH).

More important for our present purpose, the segment OU preceding N is pronounced [au] in all relevant English words with the single exception of the "injury" sense of WOUND. Consider: HOUND, BOUND, FOUND, OUNCE, FLOUNCE, COUNCIL, LOUNGE, SCROUNGE, MOUNTAIN, NOUN, BOUNTY, and so on. It seems to us, therefore, that OUN shares with CC the potential advantage (for experimenters) of functional unanimity among orthographic neighbours as to how the segment should be pronounced. In the savage world of orthographic irregularities, such an advantage should be extremely important. On that basis, we make the prediction (on behalf of orthographic analogy theory) that the segment OUN should be pronounced [aun] in relevant nonwords. This is not intended as a straw man; we do not see how analogy theory can make an alternative prediction.

However, flexible-rule theory does make alternative predictions, based on changes in the context in which OUN appears. Consider the various readings of the vowel digraph in several consonant contexts; for example, in the pseudowords JOUN, FROUN and GOUN. Notice that for JOUN the reading [u] produces a lexical item (JUNE), but no other reading does. On the other hand, for FROUN, [au] produces a word of English (FROWN), but other vowels do not. Finally, with GOUN, both [u] and [au̯] produce lexical items (GOON, GOWN), items whose orthographic forms are about equally similar to the test string—that is, they differ by one letter.

On the view that flexible rules provide a set of optional readings of input strings, options containing [u] become available. If selection from among the candidates is influenced by their lexical status, we should see different distributions of response category probability as a function of the existence of [u] homophones. If, on the other hand, orthographic similarity is the exclusive or primary influence on pronunciation, all the strings should produce the same pattern of responses, with [au̯] very strongly predominating.

Fifteen strings comprised of various initial consonants plus the segment -OUN, were used. Stimuli fell into one of four categories. The first set (BROUN, FROUN, and CLOUN) had real-word homophones containing the diphthong [au̯], but no [u] homophones. The second set (JOUN, SPOUN, and PROUN) had real word [u] homophones only. The third set (TOUN, GOUN, and DOUN) had both [u] and [au̯] homophones. The fourth group was intended to provide the strongest test yet of orthographic analogy theory. These strings are each the first four letters of actual [au̯] words, but each of the strings makes a word when read with the [u] vowel. This group contained the strings COUN, SOUN, MOUN, LOUN, ROUN, and BOUN.

Our predictions are very simple. It seems likely, given the data reported above, that there are sources of variance influencing the response distributions, of which we are not aware. These create the "noise" in the data. At the same time, there is a hypothetical effect of phonological neighbours. In the present case we focus upon neighbours containing the [u] homophone. On the orthographic analogy theory view, these homophones should have no systematic effect. On the flexible-rule model view, [u] responses should be more common in the second, third, and fourth sets than in the first, or control set (items which have no [u] homophones). That is the only prediction we wish to make given our present knowledge.

Results and Discussion. Results by vowel category for each string are presented in Table 21.6. The null hypothesis holds that the existence of [u] homophones is irrelevant, since -OUN is always pronounced [aun] in English (except in WOUND). Therefore, if there is no "treatment effect," all strings should have the same response distribution. This can be estimated using the "control" set of strings having no [u] homophones: BROUN, CLOUN, and FROUN.

The control set gives the following values for [aṳ] and [u]: [aṳ]—74.0%; [u]—12.5%. These values and the observed scores (both in raw form) were used to calculate the chi-squareds shown in the right-hand column of Table 21.6, testing for each string the predicted incidence of [u] and [aṳ] (under the hypothesis of no [u] homophone effect) against the observed incidence. These data provide compelling evidence of variety in the pronunciation of -OUN segments, variety which simply cannot be explained in terms of orthographic neighbours.

Since subjects viewed large, clear, printed stimuli under no time pressure, arguments that subjects misread certain letters are less convincing than the hypothesis that abstract phonological forms influenced response probability. On the latter view, [u] readings are significantly more likely for JOUN, SPOUN, DOUN, and COUN, among others, because these items have [u] homophones (JUNE, SPOON, DUNE, COON). Some of these are orthographically quite dissimilar to the corresponding stimulus.

The fourth set of target strings was selected to provide as strong a test of analogy theory as possible using this procedure. Although these strings have [u] homophones, they are the initial segments of real [aṳ] words: COUNT, SOUND, BOUND, ROUND, MOUND, and LOUNGE. Yet each string in this set, with the exception of MOUN, shows a significantly higher incidence of [u] responses than the control set (the no–[u] homophone set). We conclude that these data constitute evidence of phonological influences on the assembly of phonology.

TABLE 21.6
Pronunciations (in Percentages) as a Function of String Type in
Experiment 4

	Response Type				
Stimulus	[au] brown	[u] boot	[oʷ] bone	[ɔ] bought	χ^2
BROUN	70.0	10.0	2.5	12.5	
CLOUN	67.5	22.5	10.0	0.0	
FROUN	85.0	5.0	5.0	5.0	
JOUN	22.5	42.5	17.5	15.0	40.19[a]
SPOUN	62.5	37.5	0.0	0.0	18.64[a]
PROUN	80.0	5.0	15.0	0.0	2.34
TOUN	65.0	30.0	2.5	0.0	8.75[a]
GOUN	57.5	25.0	10.0	7.5	5.34[a]
DOUN	45.0	37.5	15.0	0.0	22.27[a]
BOUN	40.0	30.0	20.0	10.0	14.32[a]
COUN	42.5	45.0	7.5	2.5	36.26[a]
LOUN	57.5	24.0	14.0	5.0	4.71[a]
MOUN	70.0	22.5	5.0	2.5	2.50
ROUN	62.5	27.5	7.5	2.5	6.64[a]
SOUN	54.0	40.0	6.3	0.0	24.05[a]

[a] $P < 0.05$.

GENERAL DISCUSSION

We have presented evidence that orthographic analogy theory does a poor job of predicting the pronunciations that will be assigned to novel stimuli, even in situations tailored to make prediction very easy for analogy models. In three experiments, using -CC- nonwords, orthographic analogies demanded the pronunciation [ks] for -CC-. In all three studies, however, [ks] occurred on less than 20% of responses, while the unexpected [s] response dominated, occurring as much as 80% of the time.

Not being able to predict an event which occurs on 80% of trials would seem embarrassing to orthographic analogy–type models, and constitutes strong evidence against their sufficiency as an account of the assembly of phonology in oral reading. The finding of only 20% [ks] responses also presents difficulties for rule theory simply conceived. That is, considering rules to be unequivocal translations of minimal orthographic units into phonological units, we cannot account for the data. However, the more sophisticated rule system we have described has no difficulty explaining the preponderance of [s] readings. Before we outline an explanation, we shall briefly review the model.

In place of a model positing analogies between lexical items judged in terms of their orthographic similarity, we have outlined a model based on phonological neighbours and supported by the finding of "homophone influences" on assembly in a fourth experiment. The key operations in this model are generation of candidate pronunciations for an input string via "flexible rules," and selection from among the candidates using the resources of the lexicon.

Description of the first of these operations, that involving flexible rules, is to some extent an empirical issue. Asking large numbers of subjects to read nonwords yields information interpretable in terms of the order of preference of rule outputs. We should be able, by interviewing some thousands of people, to determine which phonemes are associated with which graphemes, and what their probability is as a translation of a given grapheme.

A number of variables are likely to influence the second type of operation, selection from the candidate set. As suggested earlier, one factor contributing to the decision is the lexical status of the options: The system is looking for *words*. Another factor, which could reflect word frequency, might be a "confidence rating" based on how rapidly evidence accumulates to support a match between input and a particular lexical entry. A third source of useful information in reading actual text may be semantic or associative information stored with the lexical entry.

A fourth factor may be the ordering of the rule-generated outputs, in terms of preference within subjects. By this we mean that where items such as OU have multiple possible readings, these are not all equally likely to be correct. One may conceive of this parameter operating in terms of a threshold of activation. That is, candidate readings might be sent to the lexical matching process simultaneously, but with base levels of activation proportional to their preference ranking. If we suppose that activation levels in the candidates count as well as those of lexical entries, and that these levels are augmented by the matching process, the order of preference follows.

A fifth factor, which has been mentioned in connection with other models, also seems to make sense here: a post-lexical check of orthography. Presumably, access to a lexical entry will make available the orthography associated with that entry. This can then be compared with the stimulus representation to provide more information for the decision system. Such information would be useful in cases such as BEAD, allowing the system to distinguish between the lexical possibilities [bid] and [bɛd).

The view developed here is that the system charged with generating oral reading uses all the information it can get to do so. This means that what we are calling the decision process is a complex one. The advantage gained is in the range of data that can be explained, including the reading of even such traditional challenges to rule-based models as YACHT.

All that is necessary for the system to read YACHT is a rule operating on the segment CHT, such as "CHT→[t]." This is not a completely novel or ad hoc suggestion. A similar rule would be necessary for the slightly more common GHT, as in NIGHT and RIGHT. Such rules are reminiscent of Patterson and Morton's (1985) body subsystem of the OPC system. Given the translation "CHT→[t]," and other relevant rules, such as "C→[s] or [k]" and "CH→[č] or [k]," the flexible rule system would generate a set of candidate readings. These would include, for example, [jæčt], [jækt], [jɔčt], and [jɔt], among others. Of these, the last would be selected because only it has lexical status.

The model also provides a simple (dare we say elegant?) explanation for the dominant [s] reading of CC reported above. The latter result is explained in terms of two strategies for parsing the input string. One strategy is invoked for any string with medial double consonants, whether they be NN, PP, TT, or CC. Since consonant length is no longer phonemic in English, a sensible approach is to reduce these elements to single consonants, and apply rules to the reduced forms.

However, that general strategy, while useful, may not always work. In particular, it won't work for some CC items. Therefore, with CC strings, the system also considers the unreduced form. Each of these strategies—one general and one particular—suggests a different parsing, and since it is the essence of the system that such questions are settled later rather than sooner, both parsings are allowed into the candidate set. Thus, the input to the rule system will include both C and CC, yielding the options [s], [k], and [ks]. In the case of SUCCESS, lexical status will cause the selection of the [ks] option. In the case of TOCCET, with no lexical items to bias selection, the rule "C→[s] before E" prevails—usually.

Part of our point here is that the term "rules" is really just shorthand for "what is likely to be the phonological form of a given orthographic element, given the reader's experience." At the risk of belabouring the point, the term "rules" *describes* important aspects of what the reader knows about written language. We use that term without commitment to a particular view of how that knowledge is actually implemented. Thus, the flexible rule system specifies how experience can be used to reduce the burden of oral reading by narrowing down the possibilities that bear closer examination.

CONCLUSION

The data reported here embarrass the isolationist views that oral reading can be achieved entirely by lexical analogy or entirely by phonological rule. A problem for analogy theory is why reference is apparently not made to some obvious orthographic neighbours. For both analogy and rule theory, the variability between strings is confounding. Indeed, the most profound point to be drawn from the data may be that assembling phonology for oral reading is not a reflex activity determined in its entirety once lexical access is achieved, but a complex computation constrained by sources of variance we have not yet identified.

That is another way of saying that the data raise more questions than they answer. Why does one person read TOCCET with [s] and another with [k]? Would the person who gives [k] for TOCCET also give [k] for LOCCET? Would he or she give the same response on repeated presentations of a string a week apart? Why is [k] more likely for ROCCET and POCCET than for LOCCET?

Even more questions could be raised about the decision process; for example, is it slower when the candidate set is large, or when most of the items in the set are real words? In addition the reader may well wonder whether similar patterns of results will be found with on-line (speeded) naming? That is, are the results an artifact of the methodology—are people more likely to make reference to phonological neighbours when not responding under acute time pressure?

Although this possibility clearly requires empirical testing, in which we are currently engaged, it is not obvious to us why people should respond differently in the on-line test. Our stimuli are not difficult; they do not tax the system. If it were the case that orthographic neighbours were of primary importance for on-line naming, that would imply that information about them became available very early (cf. Seidenberg, 1985). Why, if such information is available early, should our subjects discount it and delay a response until phonological information becomes available? These issues await further investigation. Should on-line naming produce a different pattern of pronunciations from that reported here, we may very well have to reconsider the contribution to the literature made by many studies of patients with acquired dyslexias, since their oral reading, too, is typically tested under conditions without time constraints.

ACKNOWLEDGEMENTS

This work forms part of a doctoral dissertation submitted to the University of Waterloo by the first author, and was supported by Grants U0051 and A0998 from the Natural Sciences and Engineering Research Council of Canada to the second author. We are grateful to Max Coltheart, Karalyn Patterson, and Janice Kay for comments on a previous version of the manuscript. Financial support facilitating the senior author's attendance at the conference was provided by the office of the Dean of Arts at Waterloo.

REFERENCES

Carr, T. H. & Pollatsek, A. (1985). Recognising printed words: A look at current models. In D. Besner, T. G. Waller, & G. E. MacKinnon (Eds.), *Reading research: Advances in theory and practice, Vol. 5*. New York: Academic Press.

Coltheart, M. (1980). Deep dyslexia: A review of the syndrome. In M. Coltheart, K. E. Patterson, & J. C. Marshall (Eds.), *Deep dyslexia*. London: Routledge & Kegan Paul.

Glushko, R. J. (1979). The organization and activation of orthographic knowledge in reading aloud. *Journal of Experimental Psychology: Human Perception and Performance, 5*, 674–691.

Henderson, L. (1982). *Orthography and word recognition in reading*. New York: Academic Press.

Humphreys, G. W. & Evett, L. J. (1985). Are there independent lexical and nonlexical routes in word processing? An evaluation of the dual-route theory of reading. *The Behavioural and Brain Sciences, 8*, 689–740.

Kay, J. & Marcel, A. J. (1981). One process, not two, in reading aloud: Lexical analogies do the work of nonlexical rules. *Quarterly Journal of Experimental Psychology, 33A*, 397–414.

Marcel, A. J. (1980). Surface dyslexia and beginning reading: A revised hypothesis of the pronunciation of print and its impairments. In M. Coltheart, K. E. Patterson, & J. C. Marshall (Eds.), *Deep dyslexia*. London: Routledge & Kegan Paul.

Patterson, K. E. (1982). The relation between reading and phonological coding: Further neuropsychological observations. In A. W. Ellis (Ed.), *Normality and pathology in cognitive functions*. London: Academic Press.

Patterson, K. E. & Morton, J. (1985). From orthography to phonology: An attempt at an old interpretation. In K. E. Patterson, J. C. Marshall, & M. Coltheart (Eds.), *Surface dyslexia*. London: Lawrence Erlbaum Associates Ltd.

Seidenberg, M. S. (1985). The time course of phonological code activation in two writing systems. *Cognition, 19*, 1–30.

Seidenberg, M. S., Waters, G. S., Barnes, M. A., & Tanenhaus, M. K. (1984). When does irregular spelling or pronunciation influence word recognition? *Journal of Verbal Learning and Verbal Behavior, 23*, 383–404.

Shallice, T. & McCarthy, R. (1985). Phonological reading: From patterns of impairment to possible procedures. In K. E. Patterson, J. C. Marshall, & M. Coltheart (Eds.), *Surface dyslexia*. London: Lawrence Erlbaum Associates Ltd.

22 Working Memory and Reading Skill Re-examined

Meredyth Daneman and Twila Tardif
Department of Psychology
University of Toronto
Ontario, Canada

ABSTRACT

In current information-processing models, reading draws heavily on working memory, a system responsible for the processing and temporary storage of information in the performance of complex cognitive tasks. Individual differences in reading are assumed to reflect differences in the processing and storage capacity of working memory. This study investigates two questions concerning the role of working memory in reading comprehension. Is reading limited by the capacity of a general working memory system or a specific language-based system? What is the nature of the trade-off between the processing and storage functions of working memory during reading? The results challenge the usefulness of invoking the construct of a general and central working memory capacity to explain and measure individual differences in reading skill. Implications for Baddeley's (1986) tripartite model of working memory are discussed.

INTRODUCTION

The construct of working memory capacity has been invoked to explain and measure individual differences in reading skill. In this paper we present some research which challenges this position. First, we summarise the current position on working memory and reading, highlighting the important questions raised in the initial work. Then we describe how our attempts to find answers to these questions have impelled us to rethink the usefulness of a general working memory construct, both from the standpoint of the theory and more particularly the measurement of individual differences in reading comprehension.

Like most other complex information-processing tasks, reading seems to depend for its skilful execution on the temporary storage of information while new information is being processed. To calculate the solution to $542 + 364 - 11$, the mathematics problem solver must have access to the results of consecutive stages of processing. The unskilled problem solver may rely on external storage aids such as fingers or pen and paper. The adept problem solver will keep track of preliminary results mentally. To solve the problem of cramming lots of luggage into a car trunk, the would-be traveller must also keep track of intermediate results. The unskilled spatial problem solver may have to lug the baggage in and out as he or she tries out various geometric configurations. The adept problem solver can place and rotate each piece mentally, keeping track of the results of each manipulation in memory. To solve the problem of what successively encountered words, phrases, and sentences in a text mean, readers too must have access to the results of earlier processes. Otherwise, how could they make the crucial inference in the following sentence? *Jake decided not to buy his new girlfriend a turtle for Christmas when he discovered she liked soup* (Mitchell, 1982). Or, how could they resolve the apparent inconsistency in the following passage? *Tim opened the magazine. Then he carefully removed the bullets it contained* (Daneman & Carpenter, 1983). If recently processed information cannot be stored temporarily, the reader would continually be backtracking to reread parts or even whole sentences and passages. In other words, fluent reading, like other forms of problem solving, involves a complex and skilful co-ordination of processing and temporary storage requirements.

According to current theory, a single central system is responsible for the processing and temporary storage of information in the performance of all complex information-processing tasks (Baddeley, 1981; 1983; 1986; Baddeley & Hitch, 1974). To emphasise both its processing and storage capabilities, this system has been called *working memory*.[1] The system is assumed to have a limited capacity that must be shared between the work and the memory, between the processing and the storage demands of the task to which the working memory is being applied (Case, Kurland, & Goldberg, 1982). Moreover, individuals differ in their ability to co-ordinate the processing and storage functions. In particular, those individuals with inefficient processes have a functionally smaller temporary storage capacity because they must allocate more of the pooled resources to the processes themselves (Daneman & Carpenter, 1980; Perfetti & Lesgold, 1977). A functionally smaller temporary storage capacity will lead to deficits in reading comprehension, particularly in the processes that integrate successively encountered words,

---

[1] Baddeley and Hitch subdivide working memory into a central processor which they call the *central executive* and two subsidiary slave systems, the *articulatory loop* and the *visuo-spatial sketchpad*. Our use of the term *working memory* in this paper corresponds rather closely to the central executive component of the Baddeley-Hitch working memory model.

phrases, and sentences into a coherent representation (Daneman, 1982; Daneman & Carpenter, 1980; 1983).

Empirical support for the role of working memory in skilled reading has come from several correlational studies in which working memory capacity was assessed by variants of the reading span test. This is a test devised by Daneman and Carpenter (1980) to tax the processing and storage functions of working memory rather than simply the storage functions, as traditional digit span and word span tests do. In the reading span test, subjects are given increasingly longer sets of unrelated sentences to read aloud and, at the end of each set, they attempt to recall the final word of each sentence in the set. The number of sentence-final words recalled is assumed to reflect the efficiency with which the individual could process and comprehend the sentences. The studies have shown that individuals with smaller reading spans perform more poorly on general tests of reading comprehension and on specific tests of integration requiring them to compute a pronoun's referent, monitor for semantic inconsistencies within and between sentences, decipher the meaning of an unknown word from context, and abstract the main theme (Baddeley, Logie, Nimmo-Smith, & Brereton, 1985; Daneman & Carpenter, 1980; 1983; Daneman & Green, 1986; Masson & Miller, 1983). The correlations have been quite impressive, ranging between 0.42 and 0.90.

Although promising, the initial work has raised many more questions than it has answered. In the present study, we pursue two classes of questions. The first has to do with the nature of the working memory processes, the second with the interaction between the processes and memory for them.

The Processes

The research with reading span raised the question of whether comprehension is limited by the capacity of a general working memory system or by one specialised for the language processes. A legitimate concern about the reading span test is that it is too much like reading comprehension itself. Indeed, we have argued elsewhere that reading span may be a successful predictor of reading comprehension precisely because it captures many of the processing requirements of sentence comprehension and consequently has an excellent probability of tapping those aspects of working memory important to comprehension (Daneman, 1982; 1984). But by the same token, the complexity of the reading span processes makes interpretation of the correlation difficult (Baddeley et al., 1985), and the specificity of the reading span processes may leave us with the rather trivial conclusion that all we have shown is that sentence comprehension (reading span) is correlated with paragraph comprehension (reading and listening comprehension tests).

To go beyond the trivial interpretation and explore further the relationship between working memory capacity and reading comprehension, we

APPR-Q

pitted a verbal working memory span measure against two nonverbal measures; one that tapped mathematical processes and the other spatial processes. Strong evidence for a general working memory system would be a situation in which the nonverbal working memory span measures predicted reading comprehension skill as well as did the verbal working memory span measure. Strong evidence against a general and central processor and in favour of a language-specific one would be a situation in which only the verbal working memory span measure was correlated with reading skill.

The Processes and the Memory

The reading span test did not allow us to examine in a direct fashion the way in which the processing and storage components of working memory interact. Although Daneman and Carpenter (1980, p. 45) talked about a: "trade-off between processing and storage," we had a particular kind of trade-off in mind. As mentioned earlier, we assumed that the processes interfere with the storage rather than vice versa; that processing efficiency not storage is the real locus of individual differences in working memory capacity. Hence, although the reading span test yielded a measure of memory, that is, "number of sentence-final words recalled," it was really an indirect measure of the efficiency with which individuals could execute the sentence comprehension processes. It follows from this that another way of measuring individual differences in working memory would have been simply to measure processing efficiency directly. However, the reading span test did not allow us to measure the efficiency or accuracy of the processes directly.[2] Hence, we could not rule out alternate models such as one in which storage interferes predominantly with processing or one in which interference is bi-directional. For this reason, our theoretical descriptions subsequent to the 1980 paper have been intentionally more vague, referring to reading span as a measure of "the conjoint processing and storage capacity of working memory" (Daneman, 1982; 1984; Daneman, Carpenter, & Just, 1982) or "the ability of individuals to process and store information simultaneously in working memory" (Daneman & Green, 1986).

In order to investigate the dynamic interplay between processing and storage functions and the relative weights of these in predicting individual differences in information-processing abilities, our new measures of working memory were devised in such a way as to allow us to evaluate separately the

---

[2] We could have measured reading times for the sentences. However, like Sternberg (1985), we prefer power to speed measures of skilled performance and, in the case of the reading span test, reading the sentences quickly would not necessarily be the most efficient strategy for performing well on the task.

processes and the memory for these processes. The next section describes three new measures of working memory: verbal span, math span, and spatial span.

METHOD

The Measures of Working Memory

The verbal, math, and spatial span tasks were devised according to the following criteria: (1) they were to have as much surface similarity to one another as possible; (2) each would have a processing and a memory component; and (3) performance on the processing and memory components could be assessed separately. We shall describe each task briefly, highlighting first the processing component and then the memory one.

For *verbal span*, each trial consisted of a card containing a series of four separate words such as *par shot don ate*. We dubbed this the "boxcar" task because in a few cases two of the separate words could be linked together to form a new word, like *box* and *car* form a new word *boxcar*. In fact on each card two boxcar words could be created without changing the order of the four given words. In the above example, they are *pardon* and *donate*. In one of the two, here *pardon*, there is a syllable boundary where the two smaller words are linked (*par-don*). In the other, *donate*, there is no syllable boundary at the link; that is, the word is not *don-ate*, but *do-nate*. The rule in each case was to find the boxcar word that did not have a syllable boundary between the two smaller words; in the above example it would be *donate*. In the example *heat line her age*, the two boxcar words are *heather* and *lineage*. The correct response is *heather* (syllabified as *heath-er*) not *lineage* (syllabified as *lin-e-age*) because the former has no boundary between the *t* of *heat* and the *h* of *her* whereas the latter still has a boundary between the *e* of *line* and the *a* of *age*. Table 22.1 contains additional examples from the verbal span task. Subjects saw one card at a time and their task was to say aloud as quickly and accurately as possible the boxcar word that conformed to the rule. As soon as they made their response, they were presented the next card in the set and so on to the end of the set, at which time they had to recall the correct boxcar word from each card in the set. The correct memory response for the set in Table 22.1 would be *potion, sinewed, betray*. Set size varied from 2 to 4 cards. With 5 examples at each set size, subjects saw 45 cards in all. The task allowed us to obtain a measure of subjects' accuracy at the verbal processes by determining whether or not they responded with the appropriate boxcar word for each of the 45 trials. The task also allowed us to obtain a measure of their memory for the products of the processes by determining how many of the appropriate boxcar words they could recall at the end of each set. And finally, we could eliminate the major memory requirement entirely by having subjects perform the same boxcar verbal processes on a set of 45 new

TABLE 22.1
Sample of a Three-Card Set from the Verbal Span
Test and a Three-Card Set from the Math Span Test

	Verbal Span				
	Card				Correct Response
1.	tea	dot	pot	ion	potion
2.	gang	sine	wed	lock	sinewed
3.	bet	dam	ray	age	betray

	Math Span			
	Card			Correct Response
1.	26	9	72	972
2.	4	69	2	42
3.	23	76	3	2376

exemplars, but this time without the requirement of having to store their responses to each trial and recall them at the end of the set. The number of processes correct out of 45 provided a memory-free verbal process measure to be contrasted with the memory-loaded one.

For *math span*, each card contained a series of three numbers such as *3 7 14*. Again a boxcar process was required. Subjects had to shunt together two of the three numbers (without changing their order, adding, or applying any arithmetical operation) so that the resulting larger number was divisible by 3. The correct response in this case would be *714* (formed by joining *7* and *14*) because 714 is divisible by 3. On each card, only one of the potential larger numbers was divisible by 3. Table 22.1 contains additional examples of math span trials. For each card, subjects had to say as quickly and accurately as possible the number that conformed to the rule, and at the end of the set of two, three, or four cards, they had to recall aloud the correct numbers from each card in the set. The correct memory response for the set in Table 22.1 would be *972, 42, 2376*. As in verbal span, both accuracy of the math processes and memory for the products of them could be measured. Also, a memory-free math process score was obtained by having subjects perform the math processes on a new set of 45 cards without the requirement of recalling their responses at the end of a set.

For *spatial span*, each card depicted a two-dimensional representation of a three-dimensional tic-tac-toe game. The card was divided into a top, middle, and bottom panel, each containing a 3 × 3 cell grid which subjects were to imagine as the top, middle, and bottom platforms on a three-dimensional tic-tac-toe board. Some of the cells were occupied by red and blue tokens representing the pieces of the two players in the game. Embedded in this configuration of tokens was winning sequence, that is, three tokens of the same colour that formed a straight line in conformity with the rules of three-dimensional tic-tac-toe (a line that was horizontal, vertical, or diagonal in a two-dimensional or three-dimensional plane). The subject's task in each case was to locate the winning line. Figure 22.1 illustrates a set of three consecutive cards from the spatial span task, with the red and blue tokens represented as Os and Xs, respectively. On the first card, depicted at the extreme left of Fig. 22.1, the winning line is a two-dimensional vertical row of Xs on the top plane. On the second card, it is a three-dimensional diagonal

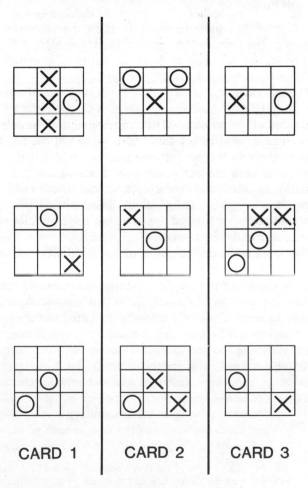

FIG. 22.1.   Sample of a three-card set from the spatial span test.

row of Os, beginning in the top right-hand corner of the top plane and ending in the bottom left-hand corner of the bottom plane. On the third card, the winning line is a three-dimensional horizontal row of Os forming a stairway through the middle row. Subjects saw one card at a time and identified the winning line by touching the three tokens with their index finger. At the end of a set of two, three, or four such cards, subjects had to recall the locations of each winning line in the set by pointing to the correct positions on an actual three-dimensional Plexiglas tic-tac-toe gameboard. For the memory-free version, they did not have to recall the locations from successive trials in a set.

Subjects and Procedure

The subjects were 36 adults recruited during the summer from advertisements posted at the Erindale Campus of the University of Toronto. Most, although not all, subjects were undergraduate students enrolled in summer courses. Subjects were paid for their participation.

Subjects were administered the verbal, math, and spatial working memory span measures at three successive sessions, with the order of presentation counterbalanced across subjects. Within a session, half the subjects received the memory-free version before the memory-loaded version; for the other half, the presentation order was reversed.

Reading comprehension was assessed with a standardised test called the Nelson-Denny. In this test, subjects have to read a series of prose passages and answer 36 multiple-choice questions based on the passages. Subjects were given the speeded version of the test, that is, 15 minutes rather than 20 minutes to complete the 36 questions.

To obtain a more general measure of verbal ability, subjects were also administered a test of vocabulary knowledge. This was the vocabulary portion of the General Aptitude Test Battery. There are 60 test items which subjects must complete in 6 minutes. Each item consists of four words and subjects have to identify two of the four which are most nearly the same or opposite in meaning. For example, for the item: (a) *poison*, (b) *toxin*, (c) *poultice*, (d) *pillory*, the correct answer is *poison* and *toxin* because these two words have the same meaning. For the item (a) *ally*, (b) *villain*, (c) *adversary*, and (d) *conqueror*, the correct answer is *ally* and *adversary* because these two words are opposite in meaning.

Subjects' reading comprehension and vocabulary scores were converted to standard scores and then combined to obtain an overall verbal ability score.[3]

---

[3] One might ask why working memory capacity would be expected to correlate with a test of vocabulary knowledge, since the vocabulary test does not require individuals to integrate successively encountered ideas into a coherent representation and hence does not make the kinds

RESULTS AND DISCUSSION

Table 22.2 contains the means and standard deviations for each task. Table 22.3 shows how the verbal, math, and spatial span measures correlated with reading comprehension, vocabulary knowledge, and overall verbal ability. Table 22.3 is organised into a top and bottom panel, reflecting the order in which the issues will be covered in the two main subsections that follow.

TABLE 22.2
Mean Performance and Standard Deviations for Measures

	Mean	SD
Verbal Ability Measures		
Reading Comprehension (max = 36)	24.0	5.7
Vocabulary Knowledge (max = 60)	28.1	7.5
Working Memory Measures (max = 45)		
Verbal Span		
Processes	35.0	6.5
Memory	31.0	6.8
Math Span		
Processes	36.0	7.9
Mcmory	20.6	6.1
Spatial Span		
Processes	44.0	1.3
Memory	19.6	4.6
Memory-Free Process Measures (max = 45)		
Verbal Processes	35.0	6.5
Math Processes	39.2	5.4
Spatial Processes	43.2	1.8

of demands on working memory that a reading comprehension test does. However, one popular view of why vocabulary is the best single predictor of overall verbal intelligence is that it reflects an individual's ability to infer the meanings of new words from verbal contexts (Jensen, 1980; Sternberg & Powell, 1983), an ability that requires the individual to hold and integrate successively encountered cues to a word's meaning in working memory (Daneman & Green, 1986). And indeed, Daneman and Green (1986) showed that readers with large working memory capacities were more able to infer the meanings of new words from the verbal contexts in which the words were encountered. To the extent that the ability to infer meaning from context is an important component of real-world vocabulary acquisition, the net products of this ability will be measured by the size of an individual's current vocabulary knowledge; consequently, we'd expect our measure of vocabulary knowledge to correlate with a measure of working memory capacity for the same reason that Daneman and Green's measure of vocabulary acquisition did.

TABLE 22.3
Correlations Among Variables

	Reading Comprehension	Vocabulary Knowledge	Verbal Ability
Working Memory			
Verbal Span			
Processes	0.58[c]	0.55[c]	0.62[c]
Memory	0.55[c]	0.56[c]	0.61[c]
Math Span			
Processes	0.26	0.34[a]	0.33[a]
Memory	0.49[b]	0.44[b]	0.51[b]
Spatial Span			
Processes	−0.13	0.12	−0.01
Memory	−0.06	−0.11	−0.09
Memory-Free Processes			
Verbal Processes	0.56[c]	0.56[c]	0.62[c]
Math Processes	0.38[a]	0.35[a]	0.40[a]
Spatial Processes	0.05	0.12	0.09

[a]$P < 0.05$
[b]$P < 0.01$
[c]$P < 0.001$

The Processes

The Issue of a General Versus Language-specific Processor

Strong support for the view that reading depends on a general working memory system would have been a situation in which the math span and spatial span measures predicted reading skill as well as the verbal span measure did. Strong support for the view that reading depends on a language-specific processor would have been a situation in which only the verbal span measure predicted reading skill. Although the actual results fall between the two extremes, we think they still provide considerable support for a language-specific system, or at least one that is specialised for manipulating and representing symbolic information.

As seen in the top panel of Table 22.3, the predictive power of a working memory measure was directly related to the surface similarity between its processing requirements and the processing requirements of the criterion task(s). Because the criterion tasks were verbal, verbal span (either its process or its memory component) was the best predictor. Verbal span was highly correlated with reading comprehension, vocabulary, and overall verbal ability, with correlations ranging from 0.56 to 0.62, all $Ps < 0.001$. Math span, which is likely to share some of the symbol manipulating processes of verbal span, also tended to be significantly correlated with verbal ability. However, given that math span uniquely taps additional quantitative processes, it was not as good a predictor as verbal span. The correlations between math span and the verbal ability tests ranged from 0.26 to 0.51. Because math span was correlated with verbal span ($r = 0.41$, for the process component, $P < 0.05$, and $r = 0.57$, for the memory component, $P < 0.001$), partial correlations were computed. None of the correlations between math span and the verbal ability tests was significant when the effects of verbal span were partialled out first. By contrast, verbal span remained significantly correlated with all verbal ability tests when the effects of math span were removed statistically. And finally, spatial span, which appears to have the least overlap in processes with the verbal and mathematical tasks, did not correlate significantly with verbal span, math span, or any of the verbal ability tests. Indeed, all correlations involving spatial span and the verbal ability tests were virtually zero.

Of course, the finding that verbal span was the best predictor of reading comprehension is open to two interpretations. One is that reading relies on a language-specific system rather than a general working memory system. The second is that math span and spatial span were not good measures of working memory capacity.[4] We would like to argue against the second interpretation on the basis of the findings of a larger study (see Daneman, Note 1) in which the same 36 subjects who participated here were given a wide range of mathematical and spatial ability tests in addition to the reading and vocabulary ability tests reported here. The findings of the larger study showed a high degree of domain specificity; math span was the best predictor of mathematical ability and spatial span was the best predictor of spatial ability. Hence, all three span measures seemed to be equally good at tapping task-specific skills. Having ruled out the second interpretation, we think that the results for the reading portion reported here are consistent with the interpretation that reading is limited by a system specialised for representing and processing verbal or symbolic information only.

The present results are consistent with two recent individual-differences studies showing a high degree of processing specificity in working memory (Baddeley et al., 1985; Daneman & Green, 1986).

Daneman and Green (1986) contrasted the original reading span test with a speaking span variant which required subjects to generate sentences for increasingly longer sets of unrelated words rather than comprehend sentences containing the words. While the two measures of working memory were themselves correlated, speaking span was the better predictor of a contextual vocabulary production task and reading span was the better predictor of a contextual vocabulary comprehension task. Because the two

---

[4]For example, performance on the spatial processing component was close to ceiling.

span tests imposed identical storage requirements, namely storing increasingly longer sets of unrelated words, Daneman and Green argued that their differential predictive power reflected their rather different processing requirements—verbal production processes in the case of speaking span, and verbal comprehension ones in the case of reading span. Daneman and Green argued against a general processor with a unitary capacity, but in keeping with functional notions of working memory, we argued for a general processor whose storage capacity will depend on how efficient the individual is at the specific processes demanded by the task to which it is being applied. Of course the Daneman and Green (1986) study only involved a contrast between two verbal measures of working memory capacity. On the basis of the current study, which extended the analysis to a mathematical and spatial measure of working memory capacity, we believe the concept of a general or central processor needs revision.

Baddeley et al. (1985) pitted reading span against counting span, a nonverbal working memory measure used by Case et al. (1982), in order to determine which was the better predictor of reading comprehension. The two span measures were moderately correlated with one another, and again, reading span, the measure with the processing requirements most resembling the criterion task, was the better predictor of the two, with counting span contributing nothing to the correlation after the effects of reading span were partialled out. Despite this pattern of results, Baddeley et al. (1985) were reluctant to abandon the notion of a single central processor. Their general argument (Baddeley et al., 1985, p. 130) against positing a separate language-specific processor for reading comprehension was that: "other investigations into working memory have not indicated the need for separate central processors." Their specific argument was that the counting span test, a measure designed to tax the processing capacities of children, may not have been sufficiently taxing to provide an appropriate measure of working memory for adults (cf. also Daneman & Carpenter, 1980 for a similar argument). Baddeley et al. (1985, p. 130) chose to defer their decision on the issue of "a general and central limitation in information processing" until "the development of a wider range of measures of working memory capacity."

We think we now have a wider range of measures of working memory capacity and that the picture suggests the need for abandoning the notion of a "general and central limitation on information processing," a "central executive" (Baddeley, 1981; 1983; 1986) if you will. At the very least we may have to posit two separate processors, one for representing and manipulating verbal-symbolic information, and a second for representing and manipulating spatial information. These ideas will be expanded on later in the section on the Baddeley-Hitch model of working memory. It is the verbal-symbolic processor that would be directly involved in reading, the task of interest here.

Our view of a language-specific processor for reading will need further qualification in light of the results discussed in the next section on the interaction between processing and storage functions.

The Processes and the Memory

The Issue of their Relative Importance

In the previous section we hardly differentiated between the process and memory components of the span measures, except to point out that the verbal process and verbal memory components were both highly correlated with reading comprehension. Indeed, the correlations were very similar, $r(34) = 0.58$ for verbal processes, and $r(34) = 0.55$ for verbal memory. The near equivalence of the processing capacity and memory capacity measures of working memory (see also Daneman, Note 1) is entirely compatible with the theory of individual differences in working memory capacity espoused earlier. According to the theory, temporary storage capacity is contingent upon processing efficiency. Consequently, performance on the processing and memory components should be positively correlated and both should be related to the same complex information-processing tasks. However, it was our next manipulation that seriously called into question the necessity for invoking the concept of temporary storage in accounting for individual differences in reading.

One way to investigate how important the memory component is, and in fact whether memory interferes at all with processing, is to eliminate the major memory requirements of the span task altogether. This, you will remember, we did by having subjects perform memory-free versions of our verbal, mathematical, and spatial processes. The bottom panel of Table 22.3 shows how the memory-free process scores correlated with reading and verbal ability. A comparison of the predictive power of the two process measures, the one with the additional memory load (top panel) and the one without the additional memory load (bottom panel) shows an almost identical pattern of results. In other words, presence or absence of a memory component during processing was irrelevant for the predictive power of a measure. The only factor that seemed to be important in determining whether a particular task would or would not predict reading skill was the domain of the processes that task tapped. For the task to predict reading skill, the processes had to be symbolic, that is, involve the manipulation of words (verbal processes) and, to a lesser extent, numbers (math processes). The additional memory requirement during process execution was dispensable. Of course we recognise that there are theoretical problems with making a distinction between process and storage (cf. also Baddeley & Hitch, 1974), and that eliminating the requirement to store the final product of a process does not eliminate all memory requirements from the task because each stage in the execution of that process is likely to generate intermediate products to be stored. However, to the extent that we have shown that elimination of the major memory load did not affect the predictive power of the measure, there seems little reason to use measures of temporary storage for *assessing* individual differences in verbal abilities.

But what about invoking the concept of temporary storage for *understanding* individual differences in verbal comprehension abilities? Here, the answer is not so clear. From a theoretical standpoint, the concept of temporary storage in comprehension is very attractive. As discussed earlier, linguistic analyses of text seem to demand that information be retained temporarily while new information is being processed. Our data do not demand that we relinquish the concept of temporary storage: Indeed, they corroborate earlier arguments that the amount of storage capacity an individual will have is a direct function of how efficient that individual is at the computational aspects of the task. Consequently, like the computational aspects, functional storage capacity will also be related to the skill with which the processor can do its work.

However, because the data now show that for matters of measurement it is not mandatory to tax the memory component, and thereby suggest that memory does not influence processing efficiency in any relevant way, one might argue that working memory as an individual-differences construct is unnecessary theoretical baggage. Of greater concern that this, we think that the individual-differences construct of working memory may stunt theoretical advancement. If the "memory" is simply a by-product of the "processes," it is the processes themselves and what leads to skilled execution of the processes that should be receiving the lion's share of our attention.

Implications for the Baddeley-Hitch Model of Working Memory

So far we have treated working memory as if it were a single monolithic system, as a general working memory (WMG) in Baddeley's (1986) terms. However, ours is not the only conception of working memory. Indeed, this unitary conception can be constrasted with what Baddeley (1986) terms his specific model of working memory (WMS), in which working memory is viewed as an alliance of separate but interacting temporary storage systems; three in its current form (Baddeley, 1981; 1983; 1986). The core of the tripartite system is the central executive component; it is the centre responsible for processing information and temporarily storing the products of its processes. It is assumed to have a limited amount of capacity to be divided between its processing and storage functions (Baddeley & Hitch, 1974). However, the central executive is able to discharge some of its storage responsibilities to the two auxiliary slave systems it controls. These are the articulatory loop, which is specialised for maintaining verbal material by sub-vocal rote rehearsal, and the visuo-spatial sketchpad, which is specialised for maintaining visuo-spatial information in a similar fashion. Although our findings may be inconsistent with the concept of a single monolithic working memory as we have tried to argue here, it remains to be determined whether they are inconsistent with the tripartite Baddeley-Hitch view as well. In this section we will briefly consider the implications of the current findings for the Baddeley-Hitch model.

The Baddeley-Hitch model differs from the unitary model in its assumptions about what our three working memory tasks measure. Within the framework of a single monolithic working memory, we had to assume that the verbal, math, and spatial span tasks all measure the capacity of the central processor; the central executive in the Baddeley-Hitch model. However, within the Baddeley-Hitch framework of a tripartite working memory, the verbal, math, and spatial span tasks could be assumed to involve more than the central executive. Presumably, verbal span and math span would rely on both the central executive and the articulatory loop; spatial span would rely on both the central executive and the visuo-spatial sketchpad. To the extent that reading comprehension relies on the central executive and the articulatory loop (Baddeley, 1986), the Baddeley-Hitch model would predict that our verbal span and math span measures should correlate equally highly with reading comprehension and that spatial span should correlate significantly less. However, this is not quite the pattern of results we found. It was the case that verbal span and math span correlated more highly with reading than did spatial span, a finding consistent with the Baddeley-Hitch articulatory loop/visuo-spatial sketchpad distinction. However, spatial span did not correlate at all with reading, a finding inconsistent with the Baddeley-Hitch view that a common central executive is involved in reading and all information processing.

We believe the present results are compatible with Baddeley and Hitch's distinction between a verbal and a spatial system. However, we think the present results, with their emphasis on process over storage, call for a reconceptualisation of Baddeley and Hitch's verbal and spatial systems—the articulatory loop and the visuo-spatial sketchpad. Rather than the articulatory loop and the visuo-spatial sketchpad acting as temporary storage systems with processing functions limited primarily to rehearsal, they should be the processors themselves. In other words, they would have all the processing and control functions now assigned to the central executive, rendering the concept of a general and central executive, or a central processing capacity, defunct. This concept of two processors need not be seen as a radical departure from the tentative working memory framework set up by Baddeley, because he himself has said (Baddeley, 1983, pp. 315–316): "that it may ultimately prove unnecessary to assume a central executive," and his strategy has been to focus first on the articulatory loop and visuo-spatial sketchpad, presumably with the view to transferring to them more and more of the functions of the central executive. Hence, even though the present results and our two-processors interpretation of them may be inconsistent with details of the current Baddeley-Hitch model of working memory, they are not inconsistent with potential evolutions of the model.

Not only did we challenge the notion of a single central processor for reading, but we also challenged the usefulness of pursuing the whole concept of temporary storage in understanding and measuring individual differences in reading. This second conlusion does not bear directly on structural details of the Baddeley-Hitch working memory model. However, it may have implications for the functional aspect of the model. After all, the Baddeley-Hitch working memory model has been considered an attractive replacement for traditional short-term memory models because of its potential to throw light on a wide range of nonmemory information-processing skills and not simply because of its potential to explain the memory system itself. If working memory does not prove useful for understanding complex cognitive skills and how individuals differ in them, it will have lost much of its appeal.

CONCLUDING REMARKS

The major purpose of this paper was to question the usefulness of a central working memory construct for measuring and understanding *individual differences* in reading comprehension. However, we would like to make a few comments on the implications of this criticism for general models of reading. There are two common and related arguments used against extrapolating from individual-differences models to general models. One is the everybody-has-it argument. A particular system or process may be needed to carry out a complex skill even if it does not account for individual differences in that skill. To use Hunt's (1985) analogy, two legs are needed to run. However "number of legs" will not account for individual differences in speed or skill on the track because virtually everybody has two legs. The second is the argument of nonlinearity. To use another athletic analogy, a certain amount of upper-body strength is needed to do the pole vault, but extraordinary upper-body strength will not guarantee superior pole-vaulting performance. Both of these arguments would apply to situations in which individual differences in a given factor fail to correlate with individual differences in reading. For this reason they are not relevant with respect to the working memory research we have reported here. It was not that working memory capacity did not account for individual differences in verbal skills. It did. But it did not appear to be necessary, at least for measuring skill differences. Moreover, it may, we have argued, be detrimental for theory development.

Our biased bet is that what turns out to be important for individual-differences models will be important for general models too. Individual differences are abundant and not easily eradicated. Those interested in general models of cognition have traditionally resorted to averaging over large numbers of data points or using within-subjects designs as a way of keeping individual differences to a minimum. Let us rather capitalise on the fact that individuals differ, and use systematic sources of individual differences as clues to the important components of reading in particular, and cognition in general.

ACKNOWLEDGEMENTS

This research was supported in part by Grant A2690 from the Natural Sciences and Engineering Research Council of Canada to Meredyth Daneman.

REFERENCES

Baddeley, A. D. (1981). The concept of working memory: A view of its current state and probable future development. *Cognition, 10*, 17–23.

Baddeley, A. D. (1983). Working memory. *Philosophical Transactions of the Royal Society, London, 302*, 311–324.

Baddeley, A. D. (1986). *Working memory*. Oxford: Clarendon Press.

Baddeley, A. D. & Hitch, G. J. (1974). Working memory. In G. A. Bower (Ed.), *The psychology of learning and motivation, Vol. 8*. New York: Academic Press, 47–90.

Baddeley, A. D., Logie, R., Nimmo-Smith, I., & Brereton, N. (1985). Components of fluent reading. *Journal of Memory and Language, 24*, 119–131.

Case, R., Kurland, D. M., & Goldberg, J. (1982). Operational efficiency and the growth of short-term memory span. *Journal of Experimental Child Psychology, 33*, 386–404.

Daneman, M. (1982). The measurement of reading comprehension: How not to trade construct validity for predictive power. *Intelligence, 6*, 331–345.

Daneman, M. (1984). Why some readers are better then others: A process and storage account. In R. J. Sternberg (Ed.), *Advances in the theory of intelligence, Vol. II*. Hillsdale, N.J.: Lawrence Erlbaum Associates Inc.

Daneman, M. & Carpenter, P. A. (1980). Individual differences in working memory and reading. *Journal of Verbal Learning and Verbal Behaviour, 19*, 450–466.

Daneman, M. & Carpenter, P. A. (1983). Individual differences in integrating information between and within sentences. *Journal of Experimental Psychology: Learning, Memory, and Cognition, 9*, 561–583.

Daneman, M., Carpenter, P. A., & Just, M. A. (1982). Cognitive processes and reading skills. In B. Hutson (Ed.), *Advances in reading/language research, Vol. 1*. Greenwich, Conn.: J.A.I. Press, Inc.

Daneman, M. & Green, I. (1986). Individual differences in comprehending and producing words in context. *Journal of Memory and Language, 25*, 1–18.

Hunt, E. (1985). Verbal ability. In R. J. Sternberg (Ed.), *Human abilities: An information processing approach*. New York: W. H. Freeman & Co.

Jensen, A. R. (1980). *Bias in mental testing*. New York: Free Press.

Masson, M. & Miller, J. A. (1983). Working memory and individual differences in comprehension and memory of text. *Journal of Educational Psychology, 75*, 314–318.

Mitchell, D. C. (1982). *The process of reading: A cognitive analysis of fluent reading and learning to read.* New York: Wiley.

Perfetti, C. A. & Lesgold, A. M. (1977). Discourse comprehension and individual differences. In P. Carpenter & M. Just (Eds.), *Processes in comprehension.* Hillsdale, N.J.: Lawrence Erlbaum Associates Inc.

Sternberg, R. J. (1985). *Beyond IQ: A triarchic theory of human intelligence.* Cambridge: Cambridge University Press.

Sternberg, R. J. & Powell, J. S. (1983). Comprehending verbal comprehension. *American Psychologist, 38*, 14–38.

REFERENCE NOTE

1. Daneman, M. (1986). *Taking the memory out of working memory.* Unpublished manuscript, University of Toronto.

23

Sentence Comprehension and Phonological Memory: Some Neuropsychological Evidence

Alan Baddeley
M.R.C. Applied Psychology Unit
Cambridge, U.K.

Giuseppe Vallar
Istituto di Clinica Neurologica
Universitá di Milano
Milano, Italia

Barbara Wilson
Department of Psychology
Charing Cross Hospital
London, U.K.

ABSTRACT

The role of the articulatory loop in comprehension was studied in the case of two patients with severely reduced immediate verbal memory span following brain damage. Both patients were perfect in comprehending individual words and short sentences but showed difficulty in understanding longer and more complex sentences. Evidence is presented to indicate that the effect of sentence length is not attributable to syntactic processing problems. It is suggested that the phonological storage component of the articulatory loop acts as a "mnemonic window" that facilitates comprehension by storing and maintaining the order of the sequences of words comprising the incoming text.

INTRODUCTION

There is abundant evidence that subjects required to retain small amounts of material for short periods of time rely heavily on some form of phonological code. This was initially conceptualised in terms of a short-term memory system with a phonological basis, an approach that has subsequently been elaborated and developed into a multi-component framework typically known as *working memory*. One conceptualisation of working memory assumes it to comprise a controlling central executive system assisted by a number of subsidiary slave systems. One of these, the articulatory loop, is assumed to be responsible for the phonological aspects of working memory (Baddeley, 1986; Baddeley & Hitch, 1974).

The articulatory loop is assumed to comprise two sub-components; a phonological store in which material is encoded by means of a trace that decays over a matter of seconds, and an articulatory control process. Material can be registered in the store either directly through auditory presentation, or indirectly when the articulatory control process is used to convert a visual item into a phonological code. In this respect, our presumed store is quite different from certain other postulated acoustic stores such as the PAS proposed by Crowder and Morton (1969), for which auditory presentation is essential. The articulatory control process is also capable of maintaining items in the phonological store by a process of sub-vocal rehearsal.

Evidence for this model comes from a number of related phenomena. These include:

1. The phonological similarity effect: Sequences of items that are phonologically similar (e.g. a letter sequence such as $B\,C\,T\,G\,V$) are harder to recall then dissimilar items (e.g. $Y\,K\,W\,R\,L$). This is because the similar items have more readily confusable codes within the phonological store.

2. The word length effect: Immediate memory for sequences of long words is poorer than that for short word sequences. This occurs because the process of maintaining the items in a phonological store depends on subvocal rehearsal; long words take longer to say than short words, are rehearsed more slowly, and hence are refreshed in the store less frequently.

3. The unattended speech effect: When sequences of items are presented visually for immediate recall, performance is impaired when they are accompanied by spoken items, even though these items are to be ignored by the subject, and even though the spoken items are in an unknown foreign language. This occurs because the unattanded items gain obligatory access to the phonological store. Since this store is used to help retain the visually presented items, the unattended material impairs performance.

4. Articulatory suppression: When the subject is prevented from subvocal rehearsal by being required to utter a stream of irrelevant verbal material, all three previously described phenomena are affected in ways that are entirely compatible with the simple articulatory loop model outlined earlier.

5. Neuropsychological evidence: Shallice and Warrington (1970) pointed out that certain neuropsychological patients appeared to have a specific deficit of auditory verbal short-term memory. A recent, more detailed analysis of such a patient suggests that her deficit is entirely compatible with

the view that she has impaired capacity of the phonological store component of the articulatory loop (Vallar & Baddeley, 1984b).

WHAT USE IS THE ARTICULATORY LOOP?

Although the concept of an articulatory loop provides a simple account of a rich and complex set of laboratory findings, the question still arises as to what function might be served by such a system. In particular, the patients studied by both Shallice and Warrington and Vallar and Baddeley were both able to return to work and to function with little apparent cognitive impairment. While there is evidence to suggest that impaired functioning of the articulatory loop system may be a major handicap in learning to read (Baddeley, 1976; Campbell & Butterworth, 1985; Jorm, 1983), from an evolutionary point of view, reading is presumably a relatively recent development, suggesting that the articulatory loop system must surely have evolved for some other purpose. One obvious possibility is that it may be an important component of speech perception. Such a view was proposed by Clark and Clark (1977), who suggest that the process of speech comprehension requires the listener to hold each incoming sentence in some form of phonological store until the necessary syntactic and semantic analysis has taken place. This is probably the strongest version of the view that phonological working memory is necessary for comprehension, since it assumes that the unit of storage is a complete sentence. The opposite extreme is represented by the views of Butterworth, Campbell, and Howard (1986), who argue that the phonological short-term store plays no role in sentence comprehension, a position they suggest follows from their analysis of a subject who appears to have grown up with a reduced memory span, but who is none the less capable of performing a range of tests of language comprehension. We will discuss this case in more detail later.

COMPREHENSION IN STM PATIENTS

One way of tackling the question of the role of the articulatory loop in comprehension is to study the speech comprehension of patients who show a deficit in this system following brain damage. A number of studies have shown that such patients have difficulty in performing the Token Test, in which subjects are required to follow instructions increasing in sentence length and complexity; they can comply correctly with short sentences, but break down in handling the longer and syntactically more complex items (see

Vallar & Baddeley, 1984a for a review). These patients also appear remarkably impaired in the case of sentences where word order conveys crucial information, such as semantically reversible items (Caramazza, Basili, Koller, & Berndt, 1981; Saffran & Marin, 1975). While this pattern is consistent with the suggestion that their deficit stems from a problem of storing the sentence, it remains possible, of course, that a primary syntactic deficit underlies the defective performance of these patients.

We propose to explore this issue further by discussing two patients who both show a clear deficit in the functioning of the articulatory loop, but who have no difficulty in perceiving individual words. If the articulatory loop system is essential for comprehension, then we would expect such patients to show comprehension deficits as sentence length increases, deficits that are not attributable to problems of syntactic processing. We shall cite data from two patients, one an Italian patient, PV, who has a very pure STM deficit, and a second English patient, TB, whose deficit is less pure, but more severe.

CASE PV

PV, who suffered damage to the perisylvian region of the left hemisphere following a cerebrovascular attack, had a very pure deficit of auditory-verbal short-term memory and a mild sentence comprehension impairment on the Token Test. Details of this case have been described elsewhere (Basso, Spinnler, Vallar, & Zanobio, 1982; Vallar & Baddeley, 1984b), but briefly she was characterised by above-average intelligence, excellent capacity for long-term verbal learning, coupled with a grossly reduced auditory digit span of only two items. A more detailed examination of her performance on tasks assumed to reflect the articulatory loop showed that her immediate memory performance reflected an influence of phonological similarity with auditory but not visual presentation. This suggests she made some limited use of the phonological store with auditory presentation, but did not recode visually presented items. She showed no evidence of using articulatory rehearsal, and had a memory span that was uninfluenced by either word length or articulatory suppression. Her capacity to articulate, however, appeared to be unimpaired, both in normal speech and in rapid counting or recitation of the alphabet. We interpreted this pattern of results as suggesting that the capacity of her phonological store was substantially reduced, and since it was not sufficient to increase her capacity substantially to remember items using a visual code, she refrained from using the articulatory control process to feed items into the store (Vallar & Baddeley, 1984b).

Two subsequent studies explored PV's comprehension of spoken material (Vallar & Baddeley, 1984a; Note 2). We tested her on a wide range of material, and will summarise our results first by describing those tasks on which her performance is unimpaired, then go on to describe those on which impairment is clear cut, before discussing those cases in which interpretation is less straightforward.

What PV Can Comprehend

Phonological Processing.   We began by testing PV's ability to perceive individual items. She proved entirely capable of making same-different judgements on pairs of consonant-vowel nonwords (e.g. *ba-ba*—yes; *ba-pa*—no). She was quite capable of repeating spoken polysyllabic words, and with spoken and written trisyllabic words was able to indicate which syllable was stressed. She was also able to judge whether the names of pairs of pictured objects rhymed. On the basis of these tests, we concluded that her capacity for phonological discrimination was normal, as was her capacity for making phonological judgements on visually presented items (see Vallar & Baddeley, 1984a).

Syntactic Processing.   This was assessed using a test devised by Parisi and Pizzamiglio (1970), in which she was required to point to one of two pictures that was consistent with a spoken sentence. The sentences ranged from one to nine words and involved the comprehension of many aspects of syntax including grammatical units such as prepositions, bound morphemes, passives, negatives, and word-order errors. With visual presentation her performance on the Parisi and Pizzamiglio sentences was again normal, even when the number of alternatives was increased from two to four per sentence (55/60 correct). As shown by Table 23.1, her performance was well within the normal range (Vallar & Baddeley, 1984a). She also proved virtually perfect in detecting both syntactic anomalies that were created by reversing the order of two words in a spoken sentence and mismatches of number or gender within a short spoken sentence (Vallar & Baddeley, 1986).

Semantic Processing.   PV showed no difficulty in performing tasks that depended primarily on semantic processing. She performed perfectly on the "silly sentences" test in which each *simple* spoken or written sentence comprised a statement about the world that was obviously true or obviously false (e.g. *Slippers are sold in pairs; Popes are made in factories*). She was equally good at verifying "*verbose* sentences," silly sentences that were increased in length by adding verbiage (e.g. *A creature such as the rabbit falls within the category of animals that have four legs*). Finally, and more impressively, she was capable of performing extremely well on a task in which a sequence of four spoken sentences was followed by a statement that she must judge to be either compatible or incompatible with the preceding sentences. In some cases the verification could be made in terms of the literal information, whereas on the other occasions inference was necessary. Slowiaczek and Clifton (1980) have shown that normal subjects have some difficulty with this task under articulatory suppression.

TABLE 23.1
Sentence Comprehension in Case PV

Syntactic Comprehension (Parisi and Pizzamiglio)	78/80 (77.7,sd 1.52)	

	Sentence Verification	
	Auditory	*Visual*
Simple	25/28 (27.6,sd 0.57)	26/28 (28)
Verbose	26/28 (28)	26/28 (26.6,sd 0.57)
Complex	17/28 (26,sd 1)	16/28 (25,sd 1)
Complex Shortened	26/28 (28)	—

NOTE: Control data in brackets.
SOURCE: Vallar and Baddeley, 1984a; Vallar and Baddeley, 1986.

What PV Cannot Comprehend

On one type of spoken and written sentence, PV's verification ability was virtually at chance. In this condition subject and predicate were semantically compatible and false items were created by reversing the relevant items. Here comprehension depends upon mapping the surface characteristics of the sentence, such as the order in which the items are presented, onto the underlying semantics. Examples of such *complex* sentences are *The earth divides the equator into two hemispheres the northern and the southern* and *One could reasonably claim that sailors are often lived on by ships of various kinds* (Vallar & Baddeley, 1984b).

The second area in which PV encountered difficulties was in detecting errors of anaphoric reference in which a mismatch in number or gender occurred between the occurrence of the relevant item, and a subsequent reference to it, separated by one or more intervening spoken sentences (Vallar & Baddeley, 1986).

Areas of Doubt

In one study (Vallar & Baddeley, 1986), we examined PV's capacity to detect anaphoric mismatches of number or gender within a complex spoken sentence. She was able to perform almost perfectly in this study, despite the fact that a phrase containing an average of 11 words was interposed between the initial presentation of an item and its anaphoric reference. We were, however, concerned that the conditions of presentation had involved a relatively high proportion of instances in which the crucial distinction was in the matching of an item and its referent, and were worried that PV might have adopted a strategy of attempting to ensure that it was encoded sufficiently richly to allow the match to be made on semantic or lexical grounds. We therefore opted to re-test on a later occasion where errors of anaphoric reference were mixed in with semantic errors and word-order errors. Under these conditions her error rate increased to 15% compared with a mean rate of 2.4% for 10 matched control subjects. Her capacity to detect errors of anaphoric mismatch was thus reduced, but not completely disrupted, by interposing a lengthy relative clause.

DISCUSSION

PV's comprehension performance appears to deteriorate when two conditions are fulfilled: (1) the material to be processed exceeds the abnormally reduced capacity of her phonological short-term store; and (2) syntactic structure conveys crucial information such as in the complex sentences of Vallar and Baddeley (1984a) or in the short passages of prose with number/gender mismatches (Vallar & Baddeley, 1986). Although PV's immediate memory is impaired, she still has a sentence span of six words. It is conceivable that her relatively good comprehension both in everyday conversation and as assessed by a number of experimental tasks is due to the fact that she retains her capacity to maintain sufficient incoming words to allow her to comprehend much spoken or written material. One way of testing this is to look at the performance of a patient whose sentence span is substantially lower than that shown by PV. We were able to do so in the case of TB who, like PV, is highly intelligent, but whose STM deficit is even more severe, with a sentence span of only three words.

CASE TB

Our second patient, TB, was a 55-year-old professional mathematician with a Ph.D. who had to cease working when a prolonged epileptic seizure left him unable to continue to operate at his previous level. A CT-scan showed some atrophy in the temporal lobes, and psychological testing indicated a high level of general intellectual functioning coupled with somewhat patchy long-term memory and dramatically reduced STM performance. He also complained of comprehension difficulties, saying that he could always understand the beginning of a conversation, but that after the first few phrases, his mind became cluttered "like a noisy television screen." His spoken conversation appeared to be entirely normal, with no obvious signs of aphasia, and no obvious comprehension difficulties, provided one avoided long and convoluted sentences.

Intellectual Performance.   Performance on the WAIS indicated a verbal IQ of 111, performance IQ of 118. This is almost certainly an underestimate of TB's IQ, since he performed very poorly on the digit span, the arithmetic, and the digit symbol subtests, all of which are likely to involve short-term memory. His performance on Raven's Matrices put him in the 98th percentile, while his National Adult Reading Test gave an estimated premorbid IQ of 123. With the exception of the impaired STM tasks that rely heavily on STM, he appears to have a well-preserved intellect. His wife confirms this and reports that he is still able to play a good game of Scrabble and a tolerable game of chess, occasionally beating the computer at its lower level. He complained, however, that he was no longer able to write mathematical papers.

Perceptual and Motor Skills.   He showed no evidence of perceptual difficulties, performing at a normal level on both the usual/unusual views test (Warrington & Taylor, 1973) and on same/different face matching. He did, however, show some evidence of manual tremor, making his writing laborious and somewhat illegible.

Long-term Memory.   TB passed 6 out of 12 components of the Rivermead Behavioural Memory Test (Wilson, Cockburn, & Baddeley, 1985), suggesting some impairment (a normal subject would be expected to score at least 9, and an amnesic patient less than 3). In general, he seemed to perform better on recall than recognition tests, and was in fact normal on delayed recall of the Rey complex figure, and on the Benton Visual Retention Test, while failing the face and object recognition components of the Behavioural Memory Test. He remembered virtually nothing of the prose passage from the Wechsler Memory Scale, either in immediate or delayed recall, possibly because he failed to comprehend it.

Short-term Memory.   TB had a digit span of two items with auditory and two with visual presentation. His performance was similarly impaired when tested using a serial matching procedure, indicating an input or storage deficit rather than an output limitation. In memory for consonant sequences, he showed no phonological similarity effect with either visual or auditory presentation, and no evidence of a word-length effect. Sentence span was three words. Finally, in free recall, his performance was poor though not disastrously so, but showed no evidence of recency.

Articulation. In conversation and in reading aloud from text, his articulation appeared to be entirely normal. However, when asked to repeatedly count from 1–10 or recite the alphabet, he began fluently and then broke down as if losing track. The point of breakdown varied from trial to trial, and did not seem to be due to a lack of knowledge of the sequence, since it occurred even with a sequence such as A,B,C,D if he was required to repeat it often enough. He described the effect as "like playing the piano and hitting a note that does not sound."

Phonological Processing. TB was perfect in making same-different judgements on consonant-vowel and vowel-consonant pairs. He performed at a normal level on a task requiring him to listen to polysyllabic words and detect occasions in which an error was introduced (e.g. *descliption, xylophome*).

He was able to read aloud both the high- and low-frequency words from the set devised by Coltheart (Note 1) and also read Coltheart's three-letter nonwords perfectly. He was able to perform at a normal level on Coltheart's rhyme judgement list which involves detecting rhymes (such as *burn-learn* and *bake-lake*) and rejecting nonrhymes (such as *key-boy* and *couch-touch*). Performance was also normal on Coltheart's category judgement test, in which the subject must decide whether a pair of items come from the same or different categories (e.g. *tennis-golf* vs. *table-lettuce*).

"Phonological Awareness." We tested him on two tasks that were used by Campbell and Butterworth (1985) as a measure of phonological awareness. One of these involved Spoonerisms, whereby the subject is presented with a well-known name, and then required to reverse the initial sounds (e.g. *Margaret Thatcher* becomes *Thargaret Matcher*). A second test involves presenting a three-word sentence, and requiring the subject to take the initial sound of each word and fit them together to produce the solution word. For example "Harriet eats toast" would produce the word *heat*. TB was quite incapable of performing either of these; not, we suspect, because of any lack of phonological awareness, but because he appeared to forget the later items in the process of analysing the earlier ones. We would suggest that it is unwise to draw conclusions about phonological awareness from such tasks in the case of patients with very short memory spans; even if the material itself is within the subject's span, the need to perform even a single complex manipulation may lead to rapid forgetting. Such patients have difficulty holding even a single letter in the Peterson paradigm (Basso et al., 1982).

TB's Capacities and Limitations. To summarise, TB appears still to be functioning at an above-average intellectual level, he has no obvious signs of aphasia, and no apparent perceptual problems. His memory span, however, is grossly impaired, being limited to two digits, and even with sentential material he has a span of only three words. As in the case of our previous patient PV, he shows no evidence of a word-length effect and no phonological similarity effect with visual presentation. He differs from PV, however, in having impaired digit span for visual as well as auditory presentation, and in showing an absence of the phonological similarity effect with auditory as well as visual presentation. Furthermore, unlike PV, he has articulatory problems when required repeatedly to recite a sequence at speed. Whether this latter effect is a consequence of his reduced span or a contributory cause is unclear. Finally, TB has a somewhat patchy long-term memory; while there is no evidence to suggest that comprehension of individual sentences is heavily dependent on LTM, it is clearly desirable to rule out the possibility that LTM is responsible for his comprehension problems by testing an amnesic control subject. Only if the amnesic patient shows normal comprehension can one conclude that TB's comprehension problems are likely to be due to his STM deficiency.

Clearly TB is not a perfect case for asking certain neuro-psychological questions. The aetiology of his memory deficit remains doubtful, as is the location of the brain damage giving rise to his problems. From a functional point of view, however, neither of these factors is crucial, whereas his combination of a high level of intellectual performance coupled with an absence of obvious signs of aphasia and a dramatically impaired sentence span makes him particularly appropriate for investigating the role of the articulatory loop in language comprehension.

The Control Patient, KJ

KJ is a 60-year-old man who became amnesic following an attack of meningitis. This left him densely amnesic but otherwise intellectually remarkably unimpaired (see Wilson, 1984, pp. 89–90). He does not know the month or day or who is the current prime minister. He has great difficulty learning new routes, new names, or acquiring new information. His immediate prose recall was excellent, but he recalled nothing after a delay. He scored 0/12 on the Rivermead Behavioural Memory Test. On the other hand, his semantic memory performance was excellent whether measured in terms of vocabulary, category generation, fluency, or sentence verification speed. He showed normal procedural learning and well-preserved autobiographical memory (see Baddeley & Wilson, 1986).

What Can TB Comprehend?

We began by testing TB on the three types of sentence used in the Vallar and Baddeley (1984a) study. With auditory presentation, he was able to verify all of the short simple sentences, but was totally incapable of coping with either the verbose sentences or the complex sentences. Indeed, he was so distressed after the first few that we had to stop. In contrast, the amnesic patient KJ scored perfectly on all three sets of sentences.

Parisi and Pizzamiglio Picture Verification Test

We used a translation of this test in which the subject must listen to a sentence and use it to choose between one of two alternative pictures. The sentences ranged in length from one word (e.g. *Jumping*) to sentences that were syntactically more complex, comprising up to 11 words (e.g. *The cat which is on the chair jumps on the mouse*). Of 80 items, 24 involved reversible sentences, in which both the correct interpretation and the reversal formed the 2 alternative pictures. The control patient again made no errors.

Table 23.2 shows TB's performance as a function of sentence length and reversibility. Both of these seem to affect comprehension, but unfortunately they tend to be somewhat confounded.

TABLE 23.2
TB's Correct Answers (Probability of a Correct Response in Brackets) on the Parisi and Pizzamiglio (1970) Sentence-picture Matching Test as a Function of Sentence Length and Reversibility

	Length in Words			
	1–6	*7–11*	*Total*	
Nonreversible	43/45	11/11	54/56	(0.96)
	(0.95)	(1.0)		
Reversible	3/6	6/18	9/24	(0.37)
	(0.30)	(0.33)		
Total	46/51	17/29	80	
	(0.90)	(0.58)		

NOTE: KJ scored 80/80.

Fortunately there is a broadly equivalent test of sentence comprehension in which confounding is less marked, namely Bishop's (1982) Test for Reception of Grammar (TROG). This comprises 20 sets of four sentences, with each set testing a different feature of the subject's semantic or syntactic processing. Performance is tested by requiring the subject to point to one of four pictures. Having four alternatives has the advantage of ruling out certain simple strategies that are possible with two-alternative tests, and in addition may allow the nature of errors (e.g. lexical vs. syntactic) to be identified.

Auditory TROG Performance.   Each sentence was read out, and the subject required to point to one of four pictures. The types of sentence are shown in Table 23.3, together with the number of correct responses out of four made by TB. TB performed at a substantially lower level than the amnesic control patient, who made no errors. Figure 23.1 shows the accuracy with which TB responds as a function of sentence length and reversibility. It is clear that errors are associated with length rather than sentence reversibility. However, as will be obvious from Table 23.2, sentence length is typically confounded with syntactic complexity.

TABLE 23.3
TROG Sentence Type and Performance by TB

		No. Correct (Max=4)	
		Auditory	*Silent Reading*
A	Shoe	4	4
B	Eating	4	4
C	Long	4	4
D	The boy is running	4	4
E	The boy is not running	4	4
F	The boy is jumping over the box	3	4
G	They are sitting on the table	2	4
H	The girl is pushing the horse	4	4
I	She is sitting on the chair	3	4
J	The cats look at the ball	3	4
K	The knife is longer than the pencil	3	4
L	The girl is chased by the horse	2	4
M	The cup is in the box	4	4
N	The boy chasing the horse is fat	1	4
O	The box but not the chair is red	3	2
P	The pencil is above the flower	4	4
Q	Not only the bird but also the flower is blue	1	1
R	The pencil is on the book that is yellow	1	4
S	Neither the dog nor the ball is brown	3	3
T	The book the pencil is on is red	1	3
	Total (Max = 80)	58	73

NOTE: KJ performed without error.

How can the effects of memory load and syntactic complexity be separated? Are they indeed necessarily different explanations? A clear and unequivocal separation is likely to require some generally agreed measure of syntactic complexity, and without this any manipulation that impairs performance may, in a post-hoc manner, be described as increasing com-

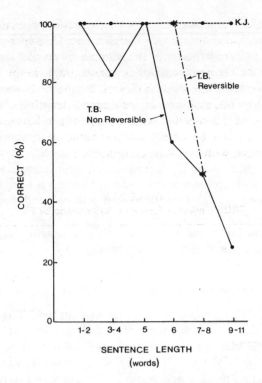

FIG. 23.1. The relationship between sentence length, sentence reversibility and probability of correct comprehension for case TB and for KJ, an amnesic patient who served as a control.

plexity. We know of no generally agreed model of syntax, and will therefore choose to concentrate on the effect of length on behaviour, attempting to increase the potential memory load while keeping to a minimum any changes in syntactic form. We look to our psycholinguistic colleagues to relate our results to models of syntax.

In the present instance, we attempted to test the memory load hypothesis in two ways. First, by taking syntactic forms which we know that TB can comprehend, and testing whether increasing sentence length by adding adjectives and adverbs will impair performance. Secondly, we examine performance when the sentences are written, and the subject allowed as much time as he wishes to comprehend the sentence. Under these circumstances we assumed that the written word will allow some of the memory load to be reduced.

Padded TROG Performance. In this condition, we took six sets of sentences on which TB had shown himself capable of performing at a high level, namely sets *H, I, J, K, M,* and *P.* We took each sentence and extended it from a mean of six to a mean of ten words by adding redundant adverbial and adjectival material. For example *The girl chases the horse* might become *The little girl vigorously chases the poor old horse*. Since all the girls portrayed are identical, all the chasing is equally vigorous, and all the horses are the same, the new information is redundant. Furthermore, we know from earlier work that TB has no difficulty in processing adverbial and adjectival material. On a simple syntactic processing interpretation, therefore, the patient should have little difficulty comprehending the padded material, whereas on the basis of sentence length we might expect substantial impairment. Finally, in order to avoid a regression-to-the-mean artifact, we retested TB on the same sentences in their unpadded form on a later occasion.

The results were straightforward; on the initial and final test of the unpadded sentences, TB was correct on 21/24 and 19/24 respectively. When the sentences were presented in their lengthened version, however, he was correct on 6/24; chance level of performance.

Reading Comprehension

Visual Sentence Comprehension.   As we saw earlier, TB is normal in his oral reading performance, whether of individual words, nonwords, or connected text. He was, for example, able to read a difficult paragraph on Lullism from Frances Yates' *The Art of Memory* without error, and with entirely appropriate phrasing and prosody. We therefore tested his reading comprehension on the simple, verbose, and complex sentences described in our account of PV's comprehension. Each sentence was typed on an index card and was presented under two conditions. In the first of these, TB was allowed to read the sentence silently, and given as much time as he wished to decide whether it was true or false. In the second condition, he was instructed to read out each sentence at a normal reading speed, then look away and decide whether the sentence was true or false.

Mean performance in these two conditions, together with performance under the auditory condition, is shown in Table 23.4. With unpaced silent reading, TB is virtually perfect on the simple and the verbose sentences, and is significantly above chance ($P < 0.05$ Sign Test) on the very complex sentences. He is, however, very slow on both types of long sentence. The task seemed to be more like a problem-solving than a comprehension task. When prevented from scanning to and fro by being required to read the sentence out loud and look away, TB's failure rate on long sentences increased to 50%. It should be noted, however, that all of these failures were "don't know" responses, with all his overt responses being correct. We did not force him to guess, as earlier presentations of the sentences under these instructions had caused him clear distress.

TABLE 23.4
Comprehension as a Function of Sentence Type and Mode of
Presentation

Sentence Type	Auditory		TB			
	TB	KJ	Silent Visual		Reading Aloud	
Simple	16/16	16/16	16/16	(1.69s)	15/16	(2.97s)
Verbose	0/16	16/16	15/16	(16.99s)	10/16	(5.11s)
Complex	0/16	16/16	13/16	(21.55s)	6/16	(5.85s)

NOTE: All TB's failures were "don't know" responses.

Visually Presented TROG Comprehension.   In our final study, TB was given a sheet on which all the TROG sentences were printed, and asked to point to the appropriate picture for each. His time to verify each set of four equivalent sentences was measured by stopwatch. The data from the patient and from the amnesic control patient are shown in Fig. 23.2, which gives latency and reversibility information for each set of sentences.

Our results show an overall improvement in performance from 58 to 73 correct out of 80. The improvement, however, is not uniform across sentence types. For all but 6 of the 20 sentence types, TB's performance with visual presentation is at least as good as that of the control subject, indeed, he responds consistently more rapidly and has a comparable rate of success. On the other hand, his performance on sets *N, O, Q, R, S,* and *T* is dramatically slower than that of the control patient; his error rate also tends to be higher for these sets.

What characterises the atypically difficult sentences? It is not reversibility, since sets *H, K, L, M,* and *P* are reversible but not difficult, while sets *Q* and *S* are difficult though not reversible. Observing TB performing the task suggests that he goes backwards and forwards across the sentence, attempting to assemble the meaning of these complex sentences as if trying to solve a verbal jigsaw puzzle. We would like to suggest that those sentences which produce the greatest difficulty are sentences in which it is necessary to hold *simultaneously* two or three concepts in order to map the syntax onto the semantics. For example, the sentence *The boy chasing the horse is fat* has two noun components, the boy and the horse, and two relationships, chasing and fatness. Correct responding requires the appropriate assignment of the two relationships to the two nouns. It is difficult to achieve this without holding these four components simultaneously in the appropriate order.

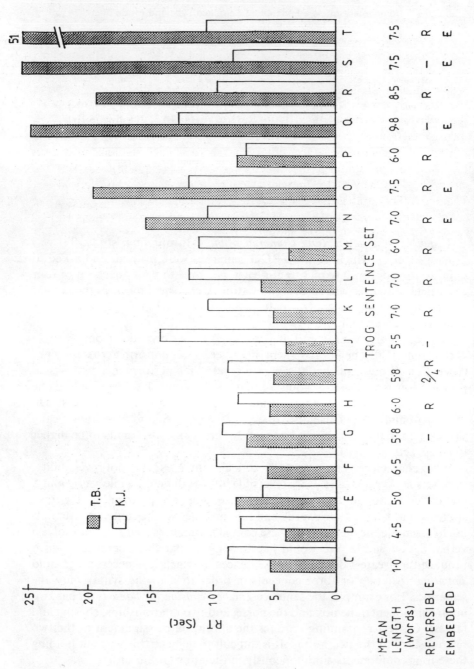

FIG. 23.2.   Sentence type and verification time for visually presented sentences from Bishop's
Test for the Reception of Grammar (TROG). Data for TB and an amnesic control patient, KJ.

GENERAL DISCUSSION

We have observed the comprehension of sentences varying in complexity by two STM patients. The first, PV, has a sentence span of six words, and successfully comprehends short sentences and longer sentences when length is produced by adding verbiage. She does, however, have difficulty in conditions where retention of surface information is important for comprehension. Our second patient, TB, has a much more limited span of three words, and has difficulty with almost all long sentences, except when presentation is visual and he is allowed as much time as he wishes to process the sentence. Before going on to interpret our results, however, we should perhaps consider what might appear to be an inconsistent finding from a study by Butterworth et al. (1986) in which they claim to observe normal comprehension in a subject who has a digit span of 3–4 items.

We do not have space to offer a detailed analysis of the Butterworth et al. study, but would not regard it as crucial to our argument for the following reasons.

1. The case they study is a developmental phonologically dyslexic student, who despite having a reduced digit span nevertheless learnt to read sufficiently well to graduate with a reasonable degree. We regard it as likely that a child who learns to come to terms with a reduced span may well do so by means that are atypical of normal development. These could either be neurological in nature, or reflect the development of novel strategies. Evidence for this view occurs in the subject studied by Butterworth et al. in her performance on the Token Test, where articulatory suppression fails to interfere with performance, leaving her significantly better than the normal controls in this condition.

2. While the span of this subject is somewhat impaired, it remains greater than that shown by most STM patients, including PV, and is substantially more than that of TB. The measure of performance most relevant to comprehension in such cases is probably sentence span; Butterworth et al. do not quote this directly, but one of their tasks would appear to reflect a sentence span somewhere between 10 and 20 words, far greater than that of PV or TB.

3. With a relatively preserved span, detecting a decrement would require demanding tests of comprehension. The tests used by Butterworth et al. tend to be uniformly less demanding that those on which PV has been found to fail. Hence, although such developmental cases are of considerable intrinsic interest, they are not directly relevant to the issue addressed here.

We shall close our discussion by considering two questions. First, could our results be explained in terms of a specific syntactic processing deficit; and secondly, if not, then what do they imply for the role of the articulatory loop in comprehension?

Any syntactic deficit explanation would have to account for the following:

1. Neither patient shows any sign of syntactic difficulty in their spoken discourse, so the deficit would presumably have to be assumed to be an input deficit only.

2. Neither patient shows any difficulty in dealing with the range of syntactic structures that occurred in any of the short sentences.

3. In the case of TB, increasing the length of sentences by adding syntactically simple components such as adjectives and adverbs reduces performance from excellent to chance level.

4. There are sentences which TB cannot comprehend with auditory presentation, but can be understood with unpaced visual presentation.

All these findings are readily explained on the assumption that comprehension depends on the capacity of the articulatory loop system. It is possible that an equally simple syntactic explanation could be offered, but we ourselves are not aware of any such interpretation.

What of those sentences which cannot be comprehended even under unpaced visual presentation? Here, we believe that the syntactic form is relevant, not because we believe that there is an inherent deficit in performing the necessary syntactic operations, but simply because some forms of syntax place higher demands than others on working memory. The case of self-embedded sentences is the most obvious of these. Under such circumstances, explanations in terms of syntax and in terms of limited articulatory loop capacity are not necessarily incompatible. Specifying the syntactic form may be one way of predicting where difficulties will occur; such prediction could be entirely consistent with the articulatory loop hypothesis which offers a processing explanation as to why such syntactic forms should be difficult.

What, then, are the implications of our results for the role of the articulatory loop in comprehension? We believe that our data are inconsistent with both the strong hypotheses outlined earlier. If, as Clark and Clark (1977) suggested, comprehension requires the storage of entire sentences within the phonological input store, then both of our patients should have had substantially more problems than they in fact showed, since both can cope with sentences that are substantially longer than their sentence span. Equally clearly, our results are at variance with the claim by Butterworth et al. (1985), that the phonological input store is not involved in comprehension, since both our patients show obvious deficits in understanding discourse.

We would like to propose an intermediate view whereby the phonological storage component of the articulatory loop acts as a "mnemonic window," holding sequences of incoming discourse, and allowing the components of such sequences to be processed and interrelated. We assume that comprehension occurs on-line, with words, and possibly fragments of words, accessing their phonological and semantic representation as they are heard (Marslen-Wilson, 1984). The comprehension of connected discourse, however, involves more than the understanding of the individual discrete items, with order information typically being very important in performing the necessary syntactic analysis. The size of the chunk necessary to comprehend a sentence, or to detect an error, will depend on the particular material and its structure. Hence an error produced by reversing the order of two adjacent words may be detectable with a window of only two or three words, whereas the analysis of a self-embedded sentence may demand a much wider window.

We assume that items within the window will be stored in a relatively literal form that maintains order information. This will then facilitate the semantic processing of the material, which might perhaps be assumed to involve contructing some form of mental model or representation (cf. Johnson-Laird, 1983). Consider, for example, the sentence *The book the pencil is on is red*, from Set T. Comprehension involves not only understanding the relevant components of the sentence, but mapping them onto the appropriate internal representation. If each item is stored separately, with no representation of word order, then the subject is unable to tell whether his internal model should involve a red pencil or a red book, and whether the pencil should be on the book or vice versa.

Suppose we assume a span of three words; then the subject hearing the sentence would encounter the following triplets: *The book the; book the pencil; the pencil is; pencil is on; is on is; on is red*. None of these is sufficient to allow the correct response. This can be contrasted with sentences of the type that TB can understand, such as: *The girl is pushing the horse*. This yields: *The girl is; girl is pushing; is pushing the; pushing the horse*. Here the second triplet identifies the subject and the fourth triplet the object, quite unambiguously. It should of course be emphasised that the examples given are meant to illustrate the way in which a reduced phonological store might limit comprehension; we are not claiming to offer a model of the rich and complex process of language comprehension.

In conclusion, then, our results suggest that the phonological store does play a role in the comprehension of both spoken and written langauge. Our results are not readily attributable to syntactic processing deficits, although we believe that certain syntactic structures may present particular problems because of the memory load they impose. Bearing this in mind, standard tests of syntactic processing should be interpreted with caution when used to study patients who have reduced memory span.

ACKNOWLEDGEMENTS

This research was supported in part by a European Science Foundation European Training in Brain and Behaviour Research Grant and by a CNR grant. The authors wish to thank Luigi Pizzamiglio and Pierluigi Zoccolotti, who kindly provided the syntactic comprehension test.

REFERENCES

Allport, D. A. (1984). Auditory-verbal short-term memory and conduction aphasia. In H. Bouma & D. G. Bouwhuis (Eds.), *Attention and performance X: Control of language processes*. London: Lawrence Erlbaum Associates Ltd.

Baddeley, A. D. (1976). Working memory and reading. In P. A. Kolers, M. Wrolstad, & H. Bouma (Eds.), *Processing of visible language, Vol. 1*. New York: Plenum Publishing Corp.

Baddeley, A. D. (1986). *Working memory*. Oxford: Oxford University Press.

Baddeley, A. D. & Hitch, G. (1974). Working memory. In G. H. Bower (Ed.), *The psychology of learning and motivation. Advances in research and theory, Vol. 8*. New York: Academic Press.

Baddeley, A. & Wilson, B. (1986). Amnesia, autobiographical memory, and confabulation. In D. Rubin (Ed.), *Autobiographical memory*. New York: Cambridge University Press.

Basso, A., Spinnler, H., Vallar, G., & Zanobio, M. A. (1982). Left hemisphere damage and selective impairment of auditory verbal short-term memory. *Neuropsychologia, 20*, 263 274.

Bishop, D. (1982). *TROG: Test for reception of grammar*. Printed for the Medical Reserach Council by Thomas Leach, Abingdon, Oxon., U.K.

Butterworth, B., Campbell, R., & Howard, D. (1986). The uses of short-term memory: A case study. *Quarterly Journal of Experimental Psychology, 38A*, 705–738.

Campbell, R. & Butterworth, B. (1985). Phonological dyslexia and dysgraphia in a highly literate subject: A developmental case with associated deficits of phonemic processing and awareness. *Quarterly Journal of Experimental Psychology, 37A*, 435–475.

Caramazza, A., Basili, A., Koller, J. J., & Berndt, R. S. (1981). An investigation of repetition and language processing in a case of conduction aphasia. *Brain and Language, 14*, 235–271.

Clark, H. H. & Clark, E. V. (1977). *Psychology and Language*. New York: Harcourt Brace Jovanovic.

Crowder, R. G. & Morton, J. (1969). Precategorical acoustic storage (PAS). *Perception and Psychophysics, 5*, 365–373.

Johnson-Laird, P. N. (1983) *Mental models: Towards a cognitive science of language inference and consciousness*. London: Cambridge University Press.

Jorm, A. F. (1983). Specific reading retardation and working memory: A review. *British Journal of Psychology, 74*, 311–342.

Marslen-Wilson, W. (1984). Function and process in spoken word recognition: A tutorial review. In H. Bouma & D. G. Bouwhuis (Eds.), *Attention and performance X. Control of language processes*. Hillsdale, N.J.: Lawrence Erlbaum Associates Inc., 125–150.

Parisi, D. & Pizzamiglio, L. (1970). Syntactic comprehension in aphasia. *Cortex, 6*, 204–215.

Saffran, E. M. & Marin, O. S. M. (1975). Immediate memory for word lists and sentences in a patient with deficient auditory–verbal short-term memory. *Brain and Language, 2*, 420–433.

Shallice, T. & Warrington, E. K. (1970). Independent functioning of verbal memory stores: A neuropsychological study. *Quarterly Journal of Experimental Psychology, 22*, 261–273.

Slowiaczek, M. & Clifton, C. (1980). Subvocalisation and reading for meaning. *Journal of Verbal Learning and Verbal Behavior, 19*, 573–582.

Vallar, G. & Baddeley, A. D. (1984a). Fractionation of working memory. Neuropsychological evidence for a phonological short-term store. *Journal of Verbal Learning and Verbal Behavior, 23,* 151–161.

Vallar, G. & Baddeley, A D. (1984b). Phonological short-term store, phonological processing and sentence comprehension: A neuropyschological case study. *Cognitive Neuropsychology, 1,* 121–141.

Vallar, G. & Baddeley, A. D. (in press). Phonological short-term store and sentence processing. *Cognitive Neuropsychology.*

Warrington, E. K. & Taylor, A. M. (1973). The contribution of the right parietal lobe to object recognition. *Cortex, 7,* 152–164.

Wilson, B. A. (1984). Memory therapy in practice. In B. A. Wilson & N. Moffat (Eds.), *Clinical management of memory problems.* London: Croom Helm.

Wilson, B. A., Cockburn, J., & Baddeley, A. D. (1985). The Rivermead Behavioural Memory Test. Thames Valley Test Company, 22 Bulmershe Road, Reading, U.K.

REFERENCE NOTE

1. Coltheart, M. (1981). *Analysing acquired disorders of reading.* Unpublished manuscript, Birkbeck College, University of London.

24 Working Memory and Written Sentence Comprehension

Gloria Waters
School of Human Communication Disorders
McGill University
Montreal, Canada

David Caplan and Nancy Hildebrandt
Montreal Neurological Institute
McGill University
Montreal, Canada

ABSTRACT

A series of studies were designed to examine the role of working memory and its subcomponents in written sentence comprehension. In particular, the studies addressed the question of whether working memory plays a role at the syntactic analysis stage and/or at the post-syntactic interpretive stage of sentence comprehension. In four experiments college students performed semantic acceptability judgements about four types of sentences which differed on two dimensions; syntactic complexity and number of propositions. The syntactic complexity variable was assumed to reflect processes occurring at the syntactic analysis stage of sentence comprehension and the number of proposition variable was assumed to reflect post-syntactic interpretive processes. In the first experiment subjects made the acceptability judgements without performing any concurrent task, while in the other three experiments subjects concurrently performed experimental tasks which stressed different components of the working memory system, as a way of determining what parts of the entire system are involved in these two different stages of sentence comprehension.

Results of the first experiment showed that processing time and errors increased as a function of syntactic complexity and of proposition density. The next two experiments showed that when subjects were required to retain a memory load and perform the judgement task concurrently, there was a greater decrement in their performance on syntactically complex than on simple sentences, and on two-proposition than on one-proposition sentences. This result was interpreted as evidence that both of these stages of sentence comprehension draw upon the limited capacity of the central executive component of working memory.

The results of the final experiment showed that a concurrent articulation task, which has been shown to interfere with the articulatory loop component of working memory, resulted in a decrement in subjects' performance on the acceptability judgement task, while a control task (tapping) which was equated with the articulation task for general level of difficulty did not. However, concurrent articulation did not interfere any more with syntactically complex sentences than with simple sentences, although it did interfere more with sentences with two propositions than with sentences with one proposition. This result suggests that the articulatory loop is not involved in the syntactic analysis of a sentence but in post-syntactic interpretive processes involved in the judgement of the acceptability of a sentence.

INTRODUCTION

In the past decade the concept of "working memory" has replaced that of short-term memory as the major theoretical conception of short-duration memory for verbal material (Baddeley, 1976; 1986; Baddeley & Hitch, 1974). Working memory is thought to be responsible for the processing and storage of information in complex cognitive tasks prior to its entry into more permanent memories such as "episodic" (Tulving, 1972) and "semantic" memory (Quillian, 1968). Working memory is comprised of a central executive which has a control function and a limited, general-purpose capacity which is divisible between processing and storage functions, as well as a number of slave systems. The amount of central executive capacity required to perform a given task varies depending upon its complexity, the degree to which it is automatic, and other factors. When the capacity of the central executive is exceeded by the demands of the task at hand, information can be stored temporarily in the slave systems. The slave system which is most relevant to the processing of verbal material is the "articulatory loop." The articulatory loop is comprised of two components—the passive phonological store and an articulatory control/rehearsal process. In this model, material is registered in the phonological store either directly, through auditory presentation, or indirectly when the articulatory control process is used to convert a visual item into a phonological code. Information can be maintained and refreshed in the phonological store by the process of articulation and this in turn can be used to feed the articulatory process. The articulatory loop can account for the wide range of phenomena which indicate that when subjects are required to remember lists of words over a short duration, they remember the items on the basis of their phonological or articulatory characteristics, even when the material to be remembered is presented in print (i.e. phonological intrusion errors, phonological similarity effect, word length effect, effects of concurrent articulation on memory).

An open question regarding this model is how it is related to sentence comprehension. It is clear that sentence comprehension requires that information be stored temporarily while new information is being processed.

Thus, most parsing models postulate a working memory system in which information is held. However, the details of the working memory system in these models are unlike the model of working memory outlined above on two counts: first, parsers are not thought to be general-purpose processors, and second, most parsing models make no mention of the phonological form of lexical items.

Linguistically based sentence comprehension models (e.g. Berwick & Weinberg, 1984; Marcus, 1980) assume that the parser operates upon incoming word strings to produce a syntactic analysis (a parse), assign theta roles, and select antecedents for certain referentially dependent elements such as reflexives. Once a phrase is completed, lexical items are transferred to another part of the parser (the "propositional list" in the Berwick and Weinberg model) at which point semantic processes can interpret thematic roles,[1] select antecedents for pronouns, and accomplish other semantic interpretive functions. The semantic values so assigned determine the propositional content of a sentence, which can be assessed for its truth value, entered into inferential processes, integrated into "semantic" memory structures, etc. Thus, a distinction is made between syntactic processes that occur during the parse, semantic interpretations which are related to the parse, and processes that involve propositional content. For the purposes of this paper, the first two processes can be considered as a single process which yields the literal meaning of a sentence through interpretation of its lexical content and syntactic structure, and this entire process can be contrasted with a second process which is related to operations upon propositional content as a whole.[2]

Phonologically based memory systems (i.e. the phonological store and the articulatory loop) could play roles at several points in sentence comprehension. One suggestion has been that phonologically based memory systems are involved in pre-parsing stages of sentence comprehension. Deterministic parsers (e.g. Berwick & Weinberg, 1984; Marcus, 1980) maintain lexical items along with their syntactic categories in a "look-ahead buffer" prior to

---

[1] Theta roles are the semantically uninterpreted arguments assigned by a verb; thematic roles are semantically interpreted arguments. For instance, in the sentence *The rock broke the window*, theta roles are assigned to the subject and object (the rock, the window) in the syntactic structure because the verb *hit* requires two theta roles to complete its argument structure, and then these theta roles are interpreted as instrument and theme at the level of so-called logical form. For more technical discussion of the differences between theta and thematic roles, see Chomsky (1981), Levin and Rappaport (1986), Williams (1981) and references cited there, and for a discussion of theta and thematic roles in parsers, see Berwick and Weinberg (1984) and Caplan and Hildebrandt (in press).

[2] An important and unresolved question is the temporal relationship between these different processes: Do they operate entirely sequentially, overlap to some degree, or go on simultaneously? This issue is discussed later in this paper.

the construction of phrase markers. The short-duration memory system such as working memory could be important in maintaining lexical items in these buffers. For example, Baddeley, Vallar, and Wilson's (this volume) proposal that working memory is involved in maintaining lexical items in a "window" which is then used to enable "mental models or representations" to be constructed can be understood as suggesting that the phonological memory systems of working memory are equivalent to the look-ahead buffer postulated in many parsing models.

The second possibility that has been advanced regarding the relationship between a phonological short-term memory system and sentence comprehension is that such a memory system is somehow involved in the operations of the parser itself. Caramazza, Basili, Koller, and Berndt (1981), Caramazza and Berndt (1985), and others, maintain positions which suggest this theory. However, these authors do not specify what role phonological representations play in parsing. This role is not immediately obvious. Logically, a sentence interpretation device only needs to maintain a pre-lexical phonological representation of the segmental phonology in an utterance until lexical access is achieved, and can dismiss the phonological form of a lexical item from its memory buffers as soon as the syntactic and semantic features of a word are accessed.

One possibility is that lexical items are maintained in phonological form in (some of) the representations constructed by a parser. For instance, the representations of the lexical items maintained in the phrase markers constructed by the parser may be phonological, or perhaps certain lexical items are maintained in certain phrase markers in phonological form (e.g. lexical items not assigned a theta role on the basis of their grammatical position around a verb). The short-term memory system may be involved in maintaining these lexical representations in these syntactic structures. We term this the "place-holder" theory of the role of short-term phonological memory in parsing.

Finally, phonologically based memory systems might be involved in processes that arise after sentence meaning is determined on the basis of sentence structure. Such processes include checking the meaning derived from the syntactic processing of a sentence against meanings derived pragmatically from individual word meaning and real-world knowledge.

Again, the role that phonologically based memory could play at this post-interpretive stage of sentence processing is not immediately obvious. Referring to the phonological form and the order of the lexical items in a sentence can only re-initiate the parsing process, not yield meaning directly. One of several possible ways that phonological memory may be utilised at this stage of processing is that reference to this form of lexical representation might initiate enough of a parse to establish the first thematic roles and other sentential features which are licensed by the parser, thereby also establishing which are erroneously inferred pragmatically. Such a post-interpretive checking function would presumably only be utilised rarely in actual discourse, where pragmatic and discourse features highly constrain pragmatic inferences.

One way researchers have attempted to study the role of short-duration memory systems in sentence comprehension has been to investigate the sentence comprehension abilities of brain-damaged patients who have good single-word comprehension but severely reduced memory capacity. The memory deficits in the majority of these patients have been studied in the context of short-term memory rather than working memory. Thus, the particular components of the working memory system these patients have difficulty with have not been specified. In addition, most studies have simply investigated auditory, as opposed to written, sentence comprehension abilities. The rationale in these studies is that if short-term memory plays an important role in sentence comprehension, then the sentence comprehension abilities of such patients should be severely impaired. Elsewhere we have argued that the sentence comprehension abilities of the patients that have been studied to date (i.e., Baddeley et al., this volume; Caramazza et al., 1981; Saffran & Marin, 1975; Vallar & Baddeley, 1984; Warrington & Shallice, 1969; 1972) are remarkably good and that these patients do not have difficulty at the syntactic analysis stage of sentence comprehension (Caplan, Vanier, & Baker, 1986; Caplan & Hildebrandt, in press). Furthermore, we have argued that the sentence comprehension problems which these patients do exhibit can all be accounted for by a deficit at the post-syntactic interpretive stage of sentence comprehension (Caplan & Hildebrandt, in press).

The other line of research which bears on the question of the role of working memory and its slave systems in sentence comprehension is that on the use of articulatory codes in reading. Since Huey (1908), researchers have been interested in what role, if any, the inner speech which is often said to accompany silent reading plays in reading comprehension. One suggestion has been that this inner speech reflects the reader's use of articulatory codes for working memory purposes. Following from the work on memory which shows that concurrent articulation (continuously counting or repeating an irrelevant word) interferes with subjects' ability to store information in the articulatory loop, the main research strategy that has been used to test this hypothesis has been to examine the effects of concurrent articulation tasks on reading. Any decrement in reading performance which results when subjects concurrently perform an articulation task is thought to be evidence for the role of the articulatory loop in reading.

In the past decade researchers have examined the effects of concurrent articulation on a wide range of reading tasks: for example, anomaly detection (Baddeley, 1979; Baddeley, Eldridge, & Lewis, 1981), semantic acceptability judgement tasks (Kleiman, 1975), change detection tasks in which subjects must detect a change of wording or meaning from one of a set of previously presented sentences (Levy, 1975; 1977; 1978; Slowiaczek & Clifton, 1980), tasks in which subjects must detect errors in prose (Baddeley et al., 1981) and tasks in which subjects must read and comprehend prose passages (Baddeley, 1979; Waters, Komoda, & Arbuckle, 1985). The results of these studies are inconsistent. In some studies consistent and reliable effects of concurrent articulation have been found, while in others no effect has been found. However, closer inspection of these studies suggests that concurrent articulation tends to have an effect on performance when the stimulus materials consist of longer and/or more "difficult" sentences (e.g. Baddeley, 1979; Levy, 1977), when the task is one which requires memory for the exact wording or order of the words presented (Kleiman, 1975; Levy, 1975; 1977; 1978), and when the task is one in which subjects are required to make judgements about sentences rather than simply read prose (Baddeley, 1979).

There are two plausible interpretations of these findings in terms of the possible roles that phonologically based memory systems may play in sentence comprehension, as outlined earlier. Since articulatory codes seem to play an important role when the stimulus materials are in some way more difficult or complex, it could be that articulatory codes play an integral part in the abstraction of the literal meaning of sentences, particularly when complex syntactic constructions are used. This explanation would also account for the finding that articulatory codes seem to play a role when the task requires memory for word order, since word order is important in the syntactic analysis of a sentence. On the other hand, the finding that concurrent articulation has an effect on tasks in which subjects must make judgements about the meaning or acceptability of sentence, but has little effect on subjects' ability to read prose, suggests that the role that articulatory codes play in reading is post-syntactic and has to do with checking the meaning dervied from the syntactic processing of a sentence against meanings derived pragmatically from individual word meanings and real-world knowledge. Since the pragmatic and discourse features of prose highly constrain pragmatic inferences, post-syntactic interpretive processes would be expected to play a smaller role in prose reading tasks than in sentence judgement tasks in which sentences are anomalous on half the trials.

The studies reported here were designed to determine more directly the role that working memory and its slave systems play in written sentence comprehension. In these studies subjects made semantic acceptability judgements about the four sentence types illustrated in (1)–(4):

1. It was the gangsters that broke into the ware-
   house.   (Cleft Subject: CS)

2. It was the broken clock that the jeweller
   adjusted.   (Cleft Object: CO)
3. The man hit the landlord that requested the
   money.   (Object Subject: OS)
4. The meat that the butcher cut delighted the
   customer.   (Subject Object: SO)

These sentences vary along two dimensions: number of propositions and syntactic complexity. CS and CO sentences have one proposition, while OS and SO sentences have two. Studies of aphasics' error rates on these sentence types show that number of propositions affects ease of interpretation, with two-proposition sentences being more difficult than one-proposition sentences (Caplan, Baker, & Dehaut, 1985). Syntactic complexity also affects ease of interpretation. CO and SO sentences are syntactically more complex than CS and OS sentences, respectively. Evidence for this relationship is found in: (1) studies of aphasic error rates in interpreting semantically reversible sentences with these structures (Caplan et al., 1985); (2) studies of children's error rates in interpreting sentences with these structures (Waters & Caplan, Note 1); (3) for SO and OS sentences, normal subjects' abilities to maintain digit loads during processing of the relative clause (Wanner & Maratsos, 1978); and (4) error rates in sentence verification tasks (Cook, 1975). The additional complexity of CO and SO sentences is presumably due to a memory load imposed during processing of the object relativisation embedded structure (Wanner & Maratsos, 1978; Caplan et al., 1986).

The variables of syntactic complexity and number of propositions can be related to different processes in the sentence comprehension model described above. Assigning thematic roles in syntactically more complex sentences would add to the processing involved in the first and second processes specified in the model, whereas verifying the semantic acceptability of two propositions would add to the processing required in the third process. Given that we can assign these variables to these sentence comprehension processes in this way, the relationship of these variables to experimental conditions which stress different components of the working memory system can indicate what parts of the entire system are involved in these different sentence comprehension processes.

The first experiment was simply designed to determine whether the ordering of sentence difficulty found for aphasics and children would be found with normal adults when a semantic acceptability judgement task rather than an object manipulation task was used, and when the dependent measures were judgement time and errors rather than simply errors. It was expected that sentences which require a complex syntactic analysis (i.e. CO and SO) and sentences with two propositions (i.e. OS and SO) would result in longer judgement times and/or more errors than sentences requiring a simpler syntactic analysis (i.e. CS and OS) and sentences containing one proposition (i.e. CS and CO).

The second experiment explored the hypothesis that sentences with complex syntactic structures and with two propositions require more of the limited capacity of working memory than sentences with simple structures and with one proposition. Subjects were required to make acceptability judgements about the four sentence types while retaining a memory load. If these sentence types differ in terms of the amount of working memory capacity required for comprehension, then there should be differences across the sentence types in the size of the memory load subjects are able to retain or in the ease with which subjects are able to make acceptability judgements when performing the acceptability judgement task and the memory load task concurrently.

The third experiment was designed to investigate the specific role that the articulatory loop plays in sentence comprehension. We hypothesised that if articulatory codes play an important role in the assignment of syntactic structure to a sentence, then tasks such as concurrent articulation should have a greater effect on the comprehension of complex than simple sentences. If articulatory codes play a role in reading, but at a stage subsequent to syntactic analysis (such as in evaluating the plausibility of the propositions), then concurrent articulation may have a greater effect on the comprehension of sentences with two propositions than on sentences with one proposition. Finally, if articulatory codes are not important in the comprehension of sentences, then concurrent articulation should not affect performance.

EXPERIMENT 1

Method

Subjects. The subjects were ten undergraduates who were native speakers of English.

Stimuli. The stimuli consisted of 160 semantically acceptable and 160 semantically unacceptable sentences of the four sentence types: (1) cleft subject; (2) cleft object; (3) object-subject relative; and (4) subject-object relative. Half of the sentences of each type had verbs which require animate subjects and inanimate objects (e.g. "It was the man that clenched the pillow.") and half had verbs which require inanimate subjects and animate objects (e.g. "It was the toy that fascinated the child.") The sentences were all semantically irreversible. Unacceptable sentences were formed by inverting the animacy of the subject and object noun phrases (e.g. "It was the pillow that clenched the man."). This leads to a violation of "selectional restrictions," the inherent restrictions verbs place on semantic features of their arguments. Recognition of the acceptability or unacceptability of a sentence in this task requires a syntactic analysis, assignment of thematic roles to noun phrases, and comparison of these thematic roles with selectional restrictions of the verb. Thus, the task and materials were designed so that they did not require more complex inferencing based on real-world knowledge.

The predictability of the words in the subject and the object positions of the sentences used in the experiment was determined by a cloze procedure. For this task the cleft sentences were presented in their simple active form. For the relative clause sentences the two clauses were separated and each clause was presented as a single sentence. Twenty subjects who had not participated in the experiment were presented with the sentences with the subject noun deleted, and twenty subjects were presented with the sentences with the object noun deleted. They were asked to fill in the blank with the word which best completed the sentence. The percentage of cases in which subjects correctly guessed the word that had appeared in the sentence was calculated. The predictability of the word in the subject and the object position was not found to differ across the four sentence types for either the acceptable or the unacceptable sentences (all F's < 1).

The sentences were all 8 to 11 words in length, with the mean number of words in the CS, CO, OS, and SO acceptable sentences being 8.7, 8.8, 9.6, and 9.6, respectively, and in the unacceptable sentences being 8.1, 8.9, 9.6, and 10.5. Thus, across the four sentence types the length of the acceptable sentences differed by less than one word, while the unacceptable sentences differed somewhat more. In addition to the 320 test sentences, 20 filler sentences which violated world knowledge and which included syntactic structures other than those in the test materials were included so as to lessen the possibility that subjects would be able to anticipate particular types of sentences.

Procedure. Subjects were tested individually in a single session. Testing began with a block of practice trials followed by the 340 test sentences which were randomised and divided into 8 blocks of trials. The sentences were presented on the video monitor of an Apple II computer which was equipped with a real-time clock. On each trial a sentence appeared in the centre of the video screen and the subject's task was to indicate whether or not the sentence made sense by pressing one of two response keys which were interfaced with the computer. Subjects' latencies and errors were recorded. Timing began with the presentation of the sentence and ended when the subject responded.

Results and Discussion

Table 24.1 shows subjects' mean reaction times across the four sentence types and the mean percentage of errors for the acceptable sentences.[3] The reaction time and error data were each analysed in a separate 2 (number of propositions) $\times 2$ (syntactic complexity) analysis of variance with both subject and item data as units.[4] Analysis of the reaction time data showed that there was a main effect of number of propositions: $F^{subj}(1,9) = 143.39$, $P < 0.001$, $F^{item}(1,156) = 51.32$, $P < 0.001$; and an effect of syntactic complexity: $F^{subj}(1,9) = 54.3$, $P < 0.001$, $F^{item}(1,156) = 21.68$, $P < 0.001$. The interaction between number of propositions and syntactic complexity was not significant. In the analysis of the error data there was a significant effect of syntactic complexity: $F^{subj}(1,9) = 51.46$, $P < 0.001$, $F^{item}(1,156) = 24.46$, $P < 0.001$; however, the effect of number of propositions and the interaction between syntactic complexity and number of propositions were not significant.

The results of this study show that, as with aphasics and children, for normal adults, the syntactic complexity of the sentence and the number of propositions influences ease of interpretation. The effect of syntactic complexity is reflected in both the reaction time and the error data, while the effect of number of propositions is seen only in the reaction time data. The two factors of syntactic complexity and number of propositions are additive in their effects and do not interact. Some researchers (e.g. Sternberg, 1969;

---

[3] The reaction-time data from the four types of unacceptable sentences cannot be meaningfully compared, since the implausibility could be detected at very different points across the four sentence types. In particular, the implausibility of SO sentences could be detected much earlier than in the other three sentence types. Inspection of the data suggested that, other than in Experiment 2a where the task required that subjects retain the final word of each sentence, subjects terminated processing at the point the anomaly was detected. For this reason the data for the unacceptable sentences are not reported here.

[4] It has been suggested to us that, although CS and OS sentences are easier than CO and SO sentences, respectively, there is no evidence that CS and OS sentences are equally syntactically simple and that CO and SO sentences are equally syntactically difficult. Accordingly, therefore, it is improper to collapse CS and OS sentences into one level and CO and SO sentences into another level of a single parameter related to syntactic complexity. To take this possibility into account, we also performed analyses on all of the data presented in this paper using a four-valued parameter—sentence type—whose four values consisted of CS, CO, OS, and SO sentences. We undertook planned comparisons between CS and CO, and OS and SO, sentence types in this analysis. In all cases in which there were significant effects of the syntactic complexity parameter in the analyses reported in this paper, there were also significant effects of both the CS vs. CO and OS vs. SO comparisons.

It has also been suggested that the minor differences in length between sentence types may have influenced our results. We therefore also analysed the subset of sentences which were 9 words in length. In this analysis there were 16 CS, 15 CO, 19 OS, and 15 SO sentences. The results for this subset are identical to those reported for the entire set of stimuli.

TABLE 24.1
Mean Reaction Time (Percentage of Errors) for the Four
Sentence Types: Experiment 1

One Proposition		Two Propositions	
Simple (CS)	Complex (CO)	Simple (OS)	Complex (SO)
2178.4	2569.5	2899.9	3282.5
(0.75)	(10.25)	(3.25)	(14.25)

Townsend & Ashby, 1983) have suggested that if two factors in a given task have additive effects and do not interact they do not share a common stage of processing. However, others (e.g. Baddeley, 1986; Broadbent, 1984; Taylor, 1976) have claimed that it is unjustifiable to allocate variables to stages on the basis of additivity or interaction. We will return to this point in the general discussion. The important point is that in Sternberg's view, the failure to find an interaction between syntactic complexity and number of propositions supports the view that these variables affect separate stages of sentence processing.

EXPERIMENTS 2A AND 2B

The first experiment showed that there were differences in the ease with which subjects were able to make acceptability judgements about the four sentence types used. The purpose of the second experiment was to determine whether those sentence types which are more difficult to process place greater demands on working memory. In Experiments 2a and 2b subjects were required to comprehend sentences of the four types which were used in Experiment 1 while performing a concurrent memory task. Our hypothesis was that the concurrent memory task should increase the demands on working memory and so should have a negative effect on the comprehension of sentence structures that normally demand substantial working memory resources. On the basis of the results in Experiment 1, we expected that the decrement in performance due to the memory task should largely occur for more complex syntactic structures and for sentences with two propositions.

The methodology used in Experiment 2a was developed by Daneman and Carpenter (1980) to measure subjects' working memory capacity. Subjects are presented with sentences to be read in increasing set sizes (i.e., first sets of two sentences, then three, four, etc.). They must read each sentence in the set and make a semantic acceptability judgment. Once the subjects have made judgments about all of the sentences in a set they must recall the last word of all of the sentences in that set. Thus, the task has both sentence processing and memory storage requirements.

Method: Experiment 2a

Subjects.   The subjects were 24 undergraduates who had not participated in the previous study. Subjects were tested individually in a single session.

Stimuli.   The stimuli consisted of 200 acceptable and 200 unacceptable sentences, divided equally among the 4 sentence types; CS, CO, OS, and SO. Three hundred and twenty of the sentences were the same sentences that had been used in Experiment 1. The stimuli were blocked by sentence type and the 100 sentences of each sentence type were then divided into 5 sets of sentences. In one set of sentences there were five trials with each trial containing two sentences; in the next set five trials with each trial containing three sentences; and so on up to sets with each trial containing six sentences.

Procedure.   Subjects were tested on this paradigm four times, once with each sentence type. There were four different orders of presentation of the sentence types and an equal number of subjects received each order. Subjects were tested on a block of practice trials and then on five test trials at each of the span sizes two to six with each sentence type. On each trial, an asterisk appeared on the video screen followed 200msec later by the first sentence in the set. The subject read the sentence silently and pushed the right response key if the sentence was acceptable and the left if it was unacceptable. As soon as a decision about one sentence had been made, the next sentence in the set appeared. When the subject had made a decision about the last sentence in the set an asterisk appeared to indicate to the subject that the last word of all the sentences in the set was to be recalled. Subjects were instructed to perform the sentence task very accurately and then to perform as well as they could on the recall task. They were instructed to recall the words in the correct serial order. The number of items out of a total possible of 100 that subjects were able to recall in the correct serial order was calculated for each subject for each of the 4 sentence types. This was then used as an index of the amount of working memory capacity required by each of the 4 sentence types.

Results and Discussion

Table 24.2 shows the mean number of items that subjects were able to recall on the recall task for each of the four sentence types. These data were

TABLE 24.2
Mean Number of Items Recalled for the Four Sentence
Types: Experiment 2a

One Proposition		Two Propositions	
Simple (CS)	Complex (CO)	Simple (OS)	Complex (SO)
76.3	71.8	73.6	66.5

analysed in a 4 (order of presentation) × 2 (number of propositions) × 2 (syntactic complexity) analysis of variance, with order being a between-subjects factor and number of propositions and syntactic complexity being within-subjects factors. There was a significant effect of number of propositions: $F(1,20) = 6.03$, $P < 0.05$; and a significant effect of syntactic complexity: $F(1,20) = 22.79$, $P < 0.001$. The main effect of order and the interactions were not statistically significant. Recall declined for syntactically complex sentences and sentences with two propositions.

Subjects' error rates and reaction times on the acceptability judgment task are shown in Table 24.3. As in Experiment 1 in the analysis of the reaction time data, there was an effect of number of propositions: $F^{subj}(1,20) = 116.8$, $P < 0.001$; $F^{items}(1,197) = 6.71$, $P < 0.001$; and an effect of syntactic complexity: $F^{subj}(1,20) = 49.7$, $P < 0.001$; $F^{items}(1,197) = 12.51$, $P < 0.001$; but no interaction of syntactic complexity and number of propositions. The effect of number of propositions: $F^{subj}(1,20) = 27.5$, $P < 0.001$; $F^{items}(1,197) = 95.44$, $P < 0.001$; and of syntactic complexity: $F^{subj}(1,20) = 26.52$, $P < 0.001$; $F^{items}(1,197) = 30.00$, $P < 0.001$, were also significant in the analysis of the error scores. Table 24.3 shows that subjects did perform the sentence task extremely accurately, since overall the error rate was only 2% higher than in Experiment 1. However, there was some effect of performing the memory task concurrent with the acceptability judgement task, manifest by longer reaction times in this experiment than in Experiment 1.

The pattern of performance on the recall task supports the hypothesis that syntactically complex sentences and sentences with two propositions require more working memory capacity than simple sentences and sentences with one proposition, respectively. On Sternberg's view outlined earlier, the fact that the factors of syntactic complexity and number of propositions do not interact suggests that they affect different components of the working memory system. The two components of the working memory system that might be involved in these effects are the central executive and the articulatory loop/phonological store. We performed two more experiments to investigate the relationship of the syntactic complexity and number of proposition factors to these aspects of working memory.

TABLE 24.3
Mean Reaction Time (Percentage of Errors) for the Four
Sentence Types: Experiment 2a

One Proposition		Two Propositions	
Simple (CS)	Complex (CO)	Simple (OS)	Complex (SO)
3092.4 (3.85)	3547.8 (10.83)	4004.2 (9.54)	4408.7 (15.6)

The first of these experiments was based on the work of Baddeley and Hitch (1974). These authors compared the effect on sentence comprehension of a task which requires articulation but has a minimal memory load (continuously repeating the familiar digit sequence 1,2,3,4,5,6), with that of a task which requires articulation and has a substantial memory load (continuously repeating a different six-digit random sequence on each trial). If interference with sentence comprehension occurs equally with both concurrent tasks, this suggests that the interference arises because the digit task and the sentence task both require an articulatory mechanism. If unfamiliar sequences interfere with sentence comprehension more than familiar sequences, the increase in interference results in part from the increased storage or processing demands of the unfamiliar digit recall task. For our stimuli, if syntactically complex sentences or sentences with two propositions take up more of the limited capacity of the central executive than simple or monopropositional sentences, respectively, then there should be interactions between each of these factors and type of digit load in a dual-task paradigm requiring recall of digits and verification of the semantic acceptability of our stimulus sentences.

Method: Experiment 2b

Subjects.   The subjects were 20 undergraduates who had not participated in either of the previous studies. Subjects were tested in a single session.

Stimuli.   Half of the plausible and half of the implausible sentences from Experiment 1 were used.

Procedure.   The procedure was identical to that in Experiment 1 other than the fact that a sequence of digits appeared on the video screen for two seconds prior to the presentation of each sentence. For half of the sentences of each sentence type the sequence consisted of a familiar six-digit sequence (i.e. the sequence 1,2,3,4,5,6), while for the other half it consisted of an unfamiliar six-digit sequence (i.e. a random sequence of digits taken without replacement from the digits 1 to 9). As soon as the digit sequence appeared on the screen the subject began repeating the digits. The sentence was then presented. The subject stopped repeating the sequence once a judgement had been made about the sentence. In contrast to Experiment 2a, instructions to the subject stressed the importance of performing the digit repetition task accurately. Subjects' performance on the digit repetition task was monitored to ensure that they followed these instructions and that they did in fact perform the digit task accurately.

Results and Discussion

Table 24.4 shows the reaction-time and error data for each sentence type with each digit load. Subjects' mean reaction times and number of errors for true sentences were each analysed in a separate 2 (familiarity of digit load) $\times$ 2 (number of propositions) $\times$ 2 (syntactic complexity) within-subjects analysis of variance with both subject and item data as units. Analysis of the reaction-time data showed that there was a main effect of familiarity of digit load: F^{subj} $(1,19) = 20.73$, $P < 0.001$; F^{item} $(1,72) = 28.79$, $P < 0.001$; a main effect of number of propositions: F^{subj} $(1,19) = 48.66$, $P < 0.001$; F^{item} $(1,72) = 17.41$, $P < 0.001$; and a main effect of syntactic complexity: F^{subj} $(1,19) = 31.93$, $P < 0.001$; F^{item} $(1,72) = 11.22$, $P < 0.001$. In addition, there were significant interactions between familiarity of digit load and number of propositions: F^{subj} $(1,19) = 20.23$, $P < 0.001$; F^{item} $(1,72) = 4.50$, $P < 0.001$; and familiarity of digit load and syntactic complexity, in the subject but not in the item analyses: F^{subj} $(1,19) = 4.38$, $P < 0.001$. There was also a significant three-way interaction between familiarity of digit load, number of propositions, and syntactic complexity: F^{subj} $(1,19) = 10.14$, $P < 0.001$; however, this effect was not significant in the analysis of the data by items.

The results of the analysis of the error data were very similar to those of

TABLE 24.4
Mean Reaction Time (Percentage of Errors) for the Four Sentence Types: Experiment 2b

	One Proposition		Two Propositions	
	Simple (CS)	Complex (CO)	Simple (OS)	Complex (SO)
Familiar Digit Load Condition	3049.8 (9.0)	3650.8 (20.0)	3634.0 (8.0)	3652.7 (12.5)
Unfamiliar Digit Load Condition	3641.4 (6.0)	4091.7 (24.0)	4442.0 (12.0)	5108.9 (36.5)

the reaction-time data. There were main effects of familiarity of digit load: F^{subj} (1,19) = 13.27, $P < 0.001$; F^{item} (1,72) = 4.00; and of syntactic complexity: F^{subj} (1,19) = 34.73, $P < 0.001$; F^{item} (1,72) = 14.21, $P < 0.001$; but not number of propositions. There were also significant two-way interactions between familiarity of digit load and number of propositions: F^{subj} (1,19) = 21.81, $P < 0.001$; F^{item} (1,72) = 3.25, $P < 0.07$; and familiarity of digit load and syntactic complexity: F^{subj} (1,19) − 23.22, $P < 0.001$; F^{item} (1,72) = 3.25, $P < 0.07$. As in the reaction-time data there was a three-way interaction between familiarity of digit load, number of propositions, and syntactic complexity which was significant in the subject but not in the item data: F^{subj} (1,19) = 5.13, $P < 0.05$.

Following the logic of Baddeley and Hitch (1974), the findings of an interaction between familiarity of digit load and syntactic complexity in the error data, and familiarity of digit load and number of propositions in both the reaction-time and the error data, suggest that syntactically complex sentences and sentences with two propositions take up more of the limited capacity of the central executive than simple sentences and sentences with one proposition. If the results of Experiment 2a are taken to indicate that the factors of syntactic complexity and number of propositions involve different parts of the working memory system, this immediately presents a problem for a model which postulates a single, nonmodular central executive. One possible solution to this problem is to subdivide the central executive into different components; in the present case, one dealing with the assignment of the meaning of a sentence on the basis of its syntactic structure and another involved in verifying the truth value of propositions. Digit recall shares processing resources with both these components of the central executive. There are other possible solutions to this problem, which we shall discuss after presenting the results of the last experiment.

EXPERIMENT 3

The results thus far show that more of the limited resources of the central executive are involved in the comprehension of syntactically complex sentences and in the comprehension of sentences with two propositions. In Baddeley's theory, if processing these sentences exceeds the capacity of the central executive, maintenance of information in the articulatory loop would occur. The purpose of the third experiment was to investigate the specific role of the articulatory loop in the comprehension of the four sentence types used in Experiments 1 and 2. In this experiment, subjects made semantic acceptability judgements while concurrently performing an articulation task that has been shown to interfere with the ability to use the articulatory loop component of working memory (Baddeley & Hitch, 1974; Murray, 1968).

A major methodological issue in this type of study concerns the nature of the control tasks that are necessary in order to be able to determine that any single-to-dual task decrement results from specific interference between the two tasks and not from nonspecific interference due to any dual task paradigm. Waters et al. (1985) matched a concurrent articulation (a shadowing task in this case) and a control task on level of difficulty by having subjects perform each of these tasks with another baseline task that required vigilance but which otherwise made minimal demands on encoding, retrieval, and decision processes. Subjects' performance on the baseline task was taken to be an estimate of the level of difficulty or the amount of general processing capacity required by the articulation and the control tasks.

In the present study a tapping task was used as the control task. In order to determine whether the articulation and tapping tasks chosen were of about the same level of overall difficulty, we compared the decrement in performance which resulted when subjects performed the tapping and articulation tasks with a third task (a visual-spatial task) which did not seem to share any specific processes with reading, tapping, or articulation. If the articulatory loop is involved in sentence comprehension, then performance on the sentence verification task should be impaired under conditions of concurrent articulation but not tapping, assuming that articulation and tapping are of about the same level of difficulty. Furthermore, if the articulatory loop is involved in either the process of syntactic analysis or that of proposition verification, there should be an interaction between type of concurrent task (tapping vs. concurrent articulation) and one or both of these factors.

Method

Subjects.   The subjects were 21 undergraduates who had not participated in the previous studies.

Stimuli.   The stimuli consisted of 156 acceptable and 156 unacceptable sentences from Experiment 1. The stimuli were divided into three stimulus sets with each set containing an equal number of sentences from four sentence types, CS, CO, OS, and SO. These three stimulus sets were then each divided into three blocks of trials. Each of the three stimulus sets was seen by one third of the subjects in each of the three conditions.

Procedure.   Subjects performed the semantic acceptability task under three conditions: no interference, concurrent tapping, and concurrent articulation in a single session. The order of conditions and the assignment of the three sets of stimuli was systematically counterbalanced across subjects. In each condition the level of difficulty of the concurrent task was estimated using a technique similar to that used by Waters et al. (1985) both before and after the subject had performed the acceptability task. A pattern mask consisting of 199 randomly placed slashes differing in orientation (e.g. /\) was presented on the screen of a video monitor whose centre was indicated by a dotted vertical line. Asterisks appeared on the screen in different spatial locations at random intervals and the subjects' task was to indicate as quickly as they could (by pressing either the left or right foot-switch) whether the asterisk had appeared on the left or the right side of the screen. A total of 60 asterisks was presented throughout the task. Subjects' latencies and errors were recorded. In the no-interference condition subjects performed the baseline task alone.

The procedure for the semantic acceptability task was the same as that in the previous experiments, other than that in the articulation and tapping conditions subjects performed these tasks concurrently and that subjects indicated whether the sentences were true or false by pushing foot-switches rather than response keys. In the articulation condition, subjects repeated the digits from 1 to 6 continuously throughout the experiment. In the tapping condition subjects repeatedly tapped on the table with each of the fingers on their dominant hand starting with their thumb and ending with their little finger. Subjects were told that it was extremely important to articulate and tap quickly and continuously throughout the experiment. The experimenter recorded the number of times the subject tapped and articulated. Subjects were given a short break between each of the three blocks of trials in a given condition.

Results and Discussion

In order to obtain an estimate of the relative difficulty of the no-interference, concurrent tapping, and articulation tasks, subjects' reaction times on the visual-spatial task in each condition prior to and following the sentence task were averaged. These data were analysed in a one-way analysis of variance with the within-subjects factor being task. There was a significant effect of task: $F(2,40) = 14.99$, $P < 0.001$; which, as can be seen in Table 24.5, resulted from longer reaction times in the articulation and tapping conditions than in the no-interference condition. The error data were analysed in a similar manner; however, there was no significant effect of task in the analysis of these data: $F(2,40) = 1.59$. The reaction-time data show that it was more difficult for subjects to perform the baseline task with a concurrent task than with no interference, but that the two concurrent tasks were well matched in terms of their difficulty.

Table 24.6 shows subjects' reaction times and error rates on the semantic acceptability judgement task in each of the three conditions. The reaction time and error data were each analysed in a 3 (interference condition) × 2 (number of propositions) × 2 (syntactic complexity) within-subjects analysis

TABLE 24.5

Mean Reaction Time (Number of Errors) on the
Processing Capacity Measure for the 3 Conditions in
Experiment 3

No Interference	Tapping	Articulation
414.0	515.0	506.3
(2.0)	(2.9)	(2.7)

of variance with both subject and item data as units. The analysis of the reaction time data showed that there were significant main effects of interference condition: F^{subj} $(2,20) = 20.74$, $P < 0.001$; F^{item} $(2,304) = 58.64$, $P < 0.001$; of number of propositions: F^{subj} $(1,20) = 157.5$, $P < 0.001$; F^{item} $(1,152) = 116.73$, $P < 0.001$; and of syntactic complexity: F^{subj} $(1,20) = 70.7$, $P < 0.001$; F^{item} $(1,152) = 27.45$, $P < 0.001$. The effect of interference condition resulted from longer reaction times in the concurrent articulation condition than in the no-interference and tapping conditions; the effect of propositions reflected longer reaction times on sentences with two propositions than on sentences with one proposition; and the effect of complexity reflected longer reaction times on complex than on simple sentences. Of the possible interactions, only the interaction between interference condition and number of propositions was significant: F^{subj} $(2,40) = 6.56$, $P < 0.001$, F^{item} $(2,304) = 2.71$, $P < 0.06$. Planned comparisons showed that the interaction resulted from the fact that, compared to the no-interference condition, there was a greater decrement in performance for two-proposition than for one-proposition sentences with concurrent articulation.

Analysis of the error data showed that there were significant main effects

TABLE 24.6

Mean Reaction Time (Percentage of Errors) for the Four Sentence Types:
Experiment 3

	One Proposition		Two Propositions	
	Simple (CS)	Complex (CO)	Simple (OS)	Complex (SO)
No-interference Condition	2065.3 (1.5)	2342.7 (8.0)	2629.6 (7.6)	2839.9 (17.6)
Tapping Condition	2049.6 (2.9)	2321.9 (11.5)	2675.8 (4.4)	2912.3 (12.3)
Articulation Condition	2308.8 (3.2)	2655.8 (11.5)	3113.7 (4.4)	3376.8 (14.3)

of number of propositions: F^{subj} $(1,20) = 8.22$, $P < 0.001$; $F^{item}(1,152) = 27.5$, $P < 0.05$; and syntactic complexity: F^{subj} $(1,20) = 41.67$, $P < 0.001$; F^{item} $(1,152) = 27.5$, $P < 0.001$. The interference condition $\times$ number of propositions interaction was also significant: F^{subj} $(2,40) = 6.65$, $P < 0.001$; F^{item} $(2,304) = 5.79$, $P < 0.001$. This interaction resulted from the fact that there was a significantly greater number of errors made on sentences with two than with one proposition in the no-interference condition but not in the tapping or the articulation conditions.

The finding that articulation interfered equally with judgements about syntactically simple and complex sentences indicates that concurrent articulation does not affect the syntactic analysis of sentences. On the assumption made by Baddeley and Hitch (1974), that concurrent articulation interferes with the functioning of the articulatory loop, this suggests that the articulatory loop is not utilised in the assignment and interpretation of syntactic structure. Concurrent articulation did, however, interfere more with judgements about sentences with two propositions than with judgements about sentences with one proposition. This finding suggests that the articulatory loop is recruited at the point where judgement of the semantic acceptability of sentences places higher demands upon the resources of part of the central executive.[5]

GENERAL DISCUSSION

The results of this study showed that there were differences in the ease with which skilled readers made judgements about the acceptability of different types of sentences and that these differences were related to the syntactic

---

[5]We must also consider the possibility that the number-of-propositions variable adds to processing complexity at the first stage of sentence processing (i.e. the stage of interpreting syntactic structure). This is possible, since the presence of two propositions changes the representation of a sentence at the level of syntactic structure and logical form. In this case, the number-of-propositions variable would be related to both the syntactic and post-interpretative stages of sentence processing, while the syntactic complexity variable would only be related to the first of these stages. We might then take the interference with two-proposition sentences by concurrent articulation to represent a role of articulatory rehearsal at the syntactic stage of sentence processing. However, for this analysis to go through, we must account for the absence of an effect of concurrent articulation upon the syntactic complexity variable, which also complicates this stage of processing. To do this, we may hypothesise that the effects of two propositions upon the complexity of processing at this stage are greater than the effects of the syntactic manipulation we used (object- vs. subject-relativisation). However, there is evidence that these two variables are equal in their effects upon the syntactic stage of processing: Caplan et al. (1985) found no differences between CO and OS sentences in aphasics' comprehension of semantically reversible sentences. Thus, it does not appear that the effects of concurrent articulation upon the number-of-propositions variable can be attributed to interference with processing two propositions at the syntactic stage of sentence processing.

complexity and the number of propositions in the sentences. Subjects were faster and more accurate at making judgements about sentences with simple syntactic structures and sentences with one proposition than sentences with complex syntactic structure and two propositions. Sentences whose acceptability was harder to evaluate placed more demands on working memory, as measured by subjects' ability to retain a concurrent memory load when making acceptability judgements.

The factors of syntactic complexity and number of propositions did not interact with each other in any of the experiments we performed, which on Sternberg's (1969) view suggests that they are related to different aspects of sentence processing which occur at different stages. However, both factors interacted with the complexity of the digit load in a dual task paradigm, suggesting that both factors require computational resources in the central executive of the working memory system. These two findings are consistent with the existence of two separate processes occurring at sequential stages in the central executive. This conclusion would require that we abandon the notion of an undifferentiated central executive and replace that notion with the idea that different aspects of sentence processing (and perhaps cognitive functions more generally) have a modular structure (Fodor, 1983). It should be noted that this notion is consistent with mounting evidence against the idea of a general processor with unitary capacity (Daneman & Green, 1986; Daneman & Tardif, this volume; Monsell, 1984). According to this position, the capacity for temporary storage is distributed over diverse cognitive systems specific to and intrinsic to separate processing modules. However, if one does not accept Sternberg's additive factors logic, then this conclusion does not necessarily follow. The results of Experiments 2a and 2b would then simply be taken to indicate that the syntactic analysis of a sentence and the verification of its truth value both require central executive resources.

There was no evidence in this study that subjects used articulatory codes at the syntactic analysis stage of sentence comprehension, since syntactically complex sentences were not interfered with by concurrent articulation any more than were simple sentences. This finding suggests that readers assign the literal meaning of the sentence without the use of articulatory codes. Though many researchers consider some of the sentences used here to be quite complex, it is possible that this result applies only to the specific syntactic structures tested and that other (possibly more complex) structures would produce a different result. This possibility is presently being investigated in our laboratory.

Experiment 3, however, did provide evidence that articulatory codes may be used at the stage of sentence processing that involves verification of the truth value of a proposition, since concurrent articulation interfered more with comprehension of two-proposition than one-proposition sentences. As noted in the introduction to this paper, phonological codes (and articulatory-based rehearsal of representations in these codes) may be used at this stage of processing to initiate enough reanalysis of a sentence to allow a subject to determine which of two readings corresponds to the syntactically licensed sense of a sentence and which is derived from lexico-pragmatic inferences. If this is the mechanism whereby phonological codes and articulatory-based rehearsal of such codes are utilised at the stage of processing related to verification of the truth value of propositional content, we would expect the interaction of concurrent articulation and number of propositions to disappear if all lexico-pragmatically inferred sentence readings were anomalous (that is, if potentially true sentences such as *The boy kissed the girl* and necessarily false sentences such as *The rock kissed the water* were used in experiments similar to those reported here). We are presently carrying out these experiments. Furthermore, since pragmatic and discourse features highly constrain pragmatic inferences in actual discourse, it is perhaps not surprising that few, if any, studies have found that concurrent articulation interferes with subjects' ability to read prose (e.g. Baddeley, 1979; Waters et al. 1985). It is also not surprising that those studies which have found effects of concurrent articulation have used reading tasks which would seem to have heavy post-syntactic interpretive demands (e.g. anomaly detection, change detection, semantic acceptability judgement).[6]

---

[6]Several complex issues arise if we attempt to analyse these results in relation to a theory of which tasks share processing resources, rather than in relation to a theory of which tasks involve functions utilised in other tasks. One possible interpretation of the interference found in Experiment 3 is that the articulation and the sentence verification tasks compete for processing resources of the central executive. This interpretation is ruled out because tapping, a task which was found to require a similar amount of processing resources as articulation, did not interfere with sentence comprehension, if we assume that there is a single general pool of processing resources for which all tasks compete. If, however, there is not one general pool of processing resources but rather multiple pools (Navon & Gopher, 1979), and the sentence verification and visual spatial tasks utilise different pools of processing resources, then the situation becomes much more complicated. On the assumption of multiple pools of processing resources, it is possible for differential effects of articulation and tapping on reading to result from competition for processing resources of one pool between the reading and the articulation task, which the tapping task does not compete for. This may be so even if the articulation and tapping tasks compete for another processing resource pool which is also utilised by the visual spatial task and even if the articulation and tapping tasks are equivalent in terms of difficulty as measured by their interference with this visual spatial task.

The situation is yet more complex. We have some evidence from other work in our laboratory that tapping and concurrent articulation are mutually interfering. This makes it less likely that concurrent articulation and sentence processing compete for central executive resources not used in the tapping task, but does not rule out this possibility, depending upon what constraints are placed upon how resources can be shared by a theory of this aspect of cognition. These considerations illustrate the need for such constraints.

Finally, we note that even if some interpretation of these results in terms of shared processing resources is accepted, the main conclusion of these studies—that articulatory codes do not play an integral role in the syntactic analysis of a sentence—would not change. In fact, the results could be interpreted to show that the syntactic analysis of a sentence does not even share processing resources with the task of articulation.

A possibility that deserves consideration is that the concurrent articulation task used here does not interfere with the functions ascribed to the articulatory loop. Despite the studies by Baddeley and Hitch (1974), some data from studies of patients with severe articulatory problems (dysarthria) suggest that the ability to articulate normally is not required for the functions ascribed to the articulatory loop to be carried out (Baddeley & Wilson, 1986). This suggests that the rehearsal function accomplished by the articulatory loop which serves to maintain a phonological representation in memory can proceed without normal articulation. The fact that concurrent articulation does interfere with certain functions thought to be related to rehearsal, as shown by Murray (1968) and Baddeley and Hitch (1974), would then suggest that rehearsal does make use of articulatory mechanisms in some tasks, though it can proceed reasonably without such mechanisms. If we expand the simple working memory model to include a nonarticulatory rehearsal mechanism as well as an articulatory-based rehearsal mechanism, we may consider another analysis of Experiment 2b. We ascribed the interaction of digit load complexity with both syntactic complexity and number of propositions to the use of the central executive by both the digit load and each of the other factors. However, we could consider that each of these variables makes use of a limited ability to rehearse. Given our failure to find an interaction between syntactic complexity and concurrent articulation in Experiment 3, the rehearsal process common to digit recall and parsing is not articulatory based, while that common to digit recall and truth value verification may be.

In summary, although it has commonly been assumed that articulatory codes may play a role when subjects are required to read syntactically complex material, no support for this notion was found in the present studies. Comprehension of syntactically complex materials required more of the limited processing resources of working memory, but did not result in the use of the articulatory loop. The articulatory loop did, however, play a role in processes involved in the judgement of the semantic plausibility of a sentence. This finding suggests that the role that articulatory codes play in reading complex material is in interpreting the semantic readings extracted from the syntactic structure.

ACKNOWLEDGEMENTS

We would like to thank Max Coltheart and two anonymous reviewers for extremely helpful comments on an earlier version of this manuscript. We are also thankful to Daniel Bub for valuable discussion and comments.

This research was supported by a Natural Sciences and Engineering Research Council of Canada University Research Fellowship and grant (No. U0468) to Gloria Waters and by a Medical Research Council of Canada grant (No. MA8602) to David Caplan.

REFERENCES

Baddeley, A. D. (1966). Short-term memory for word sequences as a function of acoustic, semantic, and formal similarity. *Quarterly Journal of Experimental Psychology, 18*, 362–365.

Baddeley, A. D. (1976). *The psychology of memory.* New York: Basic Books.

Baddeley, A. D. (1979). Working memory and reading. In P. Kolers, E. Wrolstad, & H. Bouma (Eds.), *Processing of visible language.* New York: Plenum Press.

Baddeley, A. D. (1986). *Working memory.* New York: Oxford University Press.

Baddeley, A. D., Eldridge, M., & Lewis, Y. J. (1981). The role of subvocalisation in reading. *Quarterly Journal of Experimental Psychology, 33*, 439–454.

Baddeley, A. D. & Hitch, G. J. (1974). Working memory. In G. Bower (Ed.), *The psychology of learning and motivation, Vol. 8.* New York: Academic Press, 47–90.

Baddeley, A. D. & Wilson, B. (1986). Phonological coding and short-term memory in patients without speech. *Journal of Memory and Language, 24*, 490–502.

Berwick, R. C. & Weinberg, A. (1984). *The grammatical basis of linguistic performance: Language use and acquisition.* Cambridge, Mass: M.I.T. Press.

Broadbent, D. E. (1984). The Maltese Cross: A new simplistic model for memory. *Behavioural and Brain Sciences, 7*, 55–94.

Caplan, D., Baker, C., & Dehaut, F. (1985). Syntactic determinants of sentence comprehension in aphasia. *Cognition, 21*, 117–175.

Caplan, D., Vanier, M., & Baker, C. (1986). A case study of reproduction conduction aphasia II: Sentence comprehension. *Cognitive Neuropsychology, 3*, 129–146.

Caplan, D. & Hildebrandt, N. (in press). *Disorders of syntactic comprehension.* Cambridge, Mass.: Bradford Books.

Caramazza, A., Basili, A., Koller, J. J., & Berndt, R. S. (1981). An investigation of repetition and language processing in a case of conduction aphasia. *Brain and Language, 14*, 234–271.

Caramazza, A. & Berndt, R. S. (1985). A multicomponent view of agrammatic Broca's aphasia. In M. L. Kean (Ed.), *Agrammatism.* New York: Academic Press.

Chomsky, N. (1981). *Lectures on government and binding.* Dordecht: Foris Publications.

Conrad, R. (1964). Acoustic confusion in immediate memory. *British Journal of Psychology, 55*, 75–84.

Cook, V. J. (1975). Strategies in the comprehension of relative clauses. *Language and Speech, 18*, 204–218.

Daneman, M. & Carpenter, P. (1980). Individual differences in working memory and reading. *Journal of Verbal Learning and Verbal Behaviour, 19*, 450–468.

Daneman, M. & Green, I. (1986). Individual differences in comprehending and producing words in context. *Journal of Memory and Language, 25*, 1–18.

Fodor, J. (1983). *Modularity of mind.* Cambridge, Mass.: Bradford Books (M.I.T. Press).

Huey, E. B. (1908). *The psychology and pedagogy of reading.* New York: Macmillan.

Kleiman, G. M. (1975). Speech recoding in reading. *Journal of Verbal Learning and Verbal Behaviour, 14*, 323–329.

Levin, B. & Rappaport, M. (1986). The formation of lexical passives. *Linguistic Inquiry, 17*, 623–661.

Levy, B. A. (1975). Vocalisation and suppression effects in sentence memory. *Journal of Verbal Learning and Verbal Behaviour, 14*, 304–316.

Levy, B. A. (1977). Reading: Speech and meaning processes. *Journal of Verbal Learning and Verbal Behaviour, 16*, 623–628.

Levy, B. A. (1978). Speech processing during reading. In A. M. Lesgold, S. W. Pellergrino, S. W. Fokkema, & R. Glaser (Eds.), *Cognitive psychology and instruction.* New York: Plenum Press.

Marcus, M. P. (1980). *A theory of syntactic recognition for natural language.* Cambridge, Mass.: M.I.T. Press.

Margolin, C. M., Griebel, B., & Wolford, G. (1982). Effect of distraction on reading versus listening. *Journal of Experimental Psychology: Learning, Memory and Cognition, 8,* 613–618.

Monsell, S. (1984). Components of working memory underlying verbal skills: A "distributed capacities" view—A tutorial review. In H. Bouma & D. G. Bouwhuis (Eds.), *Attention and performance X. Control of language processes.* London: Lawrence Earlbaum Associates Ltd.

Murray, D. J. (1968). Articulation and acoustic confusibility in short-term memory. *Journal of Experimental Psychology, 78,* 679–684.

Navon, D. & Gopher, J. (1979). On the economy of the human processing system. *Psychological Review, 86,* 214–255.

Quillian, M. R. (1968). Semantic memory. In M. Minsky (Ed.), *Semantic information processing.* Cambridge, Mass.: M.I.T. Press.

Saffran, E. M. & Marin, O. S. M. (1975). Immediate memory for word lists and sentences in a patient with deficient auditory short-term memory. *Brain and Language, 2,* 420–433.

Salame, P. & Baddeley, A. D. (1982). Disruption of short-term memory by unattended speech: Implications for the structure of working memory. *Journal of Verbal Learning and Verbal Behaviour, 21,* 150–164.

Slowiaczek, M. L. & Clifton, C. (1980). Subvocalisation and reading for meaning. *Journal of Verbal Learning and Verbal Behaviour, 19,* 573–582.

Sternberg, S. (1969). The discovery of processing stages: Extensions of Donders' method. In W. G. Koster (Ed.), *Attention and performance II.* Amsterdam: North-Holland.

Taylor, D. A. (1976). Stage analysis of reaction time. *Psychological Bulletin, 83,* 161–191.

Townsend, J. T. & Ashby, F. G. (1983). *Stochastic modelling of elementary psychological processes.* New York: Cambridge University Press.

Tulving, E. (1972). Episodic and semantic memory. In E. Tulving & W. Donaldson (Eds.), *Organisation of memory.* New York: Academic Press.

Vallar, G. & Baddeley, A. D. (1984). Phonological short-term store, phonological processing, and sentence comprehension: A neuropsychological case study. *Cognitive Neuropsychology, 1,* 121–141.

Wanner, E. & Maratsos, M. (1978). An ATN approach to comprehension. In M. Halle, G. Miller, & J. Bresnan (Eds.), *Linguistic theory and psychological reality.* Cambridge, Mass.: M.I.T. Press, 119–161.

Warrington, E. K. & Shallice, T. (1969). The selective impairment of auditory verbal short-term memory. *Brain, 92,* 885–896.

Warrington, E. K. & Shallice, T. (1972). Neuropsychological evidence of visual storage in short-term memory tasks. *Quarterly Journal of Experimental Psychology, 24,* 30–40.

Waters, G. S., Komoda, M. K., & Arbuckle, T. Y. (1985). The effects of concurrent tasks on reading: Implications for phonological recoding. *Journal of Memory and Language, 24,* 27–45.

Williams, E. S. (1981). Argument structure and morphology. *The Linguistic Review, 1,* 81–114.

REFERENCE NOTE

1. Waters, G. S. & Caplan, D. Unpublished data.

Nancy Hildebrandt is now at the MGH Neurolinguistics Laboratory, Boston, U.S.A.

VI

SENTENCE PROCESSING AND TEXT INTEGRATION

25 Sentence Processing: A Tutorial Review

Lyn Frazier
Linguistics Department
University of Massachusetts
Massachusetts, U.S.A.

ABSTRACT

Considerable empirical evidence indicates that perceivers construct a grammatical representation of sentences during comprehension. The principles underlying constituent structure analysis have been investigated in some detail, and their predictions are beginning to be tested in languages other than English. If the results of these investigations continue to be positive, this will encourage the view that psycholinguistics is indeed making progress in the endeavour to develop a theory of human language processing, not just a theory of processing English. However, even within English, the interaction of structural principles with item-specific lexical preferences and with discourse constraints continues to be debated.

Several relatively neglected areas of research are now receiving attention, including theories of recovery from misanalyses, the role of thematic relations in comprehension, and the processing of various types of long-distance dependencies. Conclusions in these areas remain tenative. However, the hypotheses being explored clearly indicate psycholinguistics has changed considerably. The question is no longer whether the human language comprehension system is structured or whether it uses various broad classes of information (e.g. the grammar of the language): Instead, the focus of attention is on fairly detailed and articulated hypotheses about the nature of that structure and the principles underlying the co-ordination of the myriad information sources implicated in language comprehension.

PRELIMINARIES

An adequate theory of language comprehension must do more than describe the means by which the individual sentences of a text are processed and integrated into a coherent structure representing the meaning of the entire text. It must identify the principles determining the analysis of the input, e.g.

the particular options taken at choice points in the analysis of the string. The theory must also specify how information of distinct types (grammatical vs. nongrammatical, syntactic vs. semantic) is integrated, e.g. whether the scheduling of information is dictated by explicit principles or by intrinsic factors (temporal availability of the information, or structural limitations on the processing device). Further, assuming the goal is a theory of human language comprehension in general, the theory must account for any differences that exist in the processing mechanisms for different specific languages or language types. In short, what we are after goes far beyond a description of the comprehension process. What we seek is an explanatory theory of language comprehension in which the detailed description of comprehension emerges as an automatic consequence of the underlying principles and mechanisms of the comprehension system, together with a specification of the grammar of a particular language.

Ten years ago the central questions in studies of (postlexical) language processing seemed to revolve around one basic issue: Is an essentially complete grammatical description assigned to an input in an orderly fashion during normal language comprehension, or not? The alternatives to systematic grammatical analysis de-emphasised the special or restricted nature of linguistic knowledge. Instead they emphasised the use of a broad collection of facts and hueristics in a fairly unconstrained manner. On this latter view (which was probably most popular among experimental psychologists), systematic linguistic analysis of an input occurred only in special cases (if at all), namely, when all alternative routes to successful comprehension failed.

Though not everyone would agree, today there is in my assessment overwhelming evidence that perceivers do structure a linguistic input grammatically during comprehension (cf. Flores d'Arcais, 1982; Forster, 1979; and references following). Thus, the central questions today concern what principles govern this process and how distinct linguistic and nonlinguistic information types are integrated during comprehension. There are also important questions about the representations implicated in language comprehension as well as unresolved questions about whether processing considerations explain any fundamental properties of natural language grammars (cf. Fodor, Note 5; Frazier, 1985; Weinberg, this volume). In the case of sentence-level representations, there is a fairly broad concensus about the basic nature of the representations—though extremely important differences of detail continue to be debated. In the case of discourse-level representations, not only the details but the basic nature of the representations remain in question.

I do not have the space to discuss the vast literature on text integration here. Let me simply assert without argument that recent advances in formal approaches to discourse representation (see especially Kamp, 1981) and to the control of inferencing (e.g. Grosz, Joshi, & Weinstein, 1983; Joshi &

Weinstein, 1981) are likely to herald the beginning of a new and exciting era of research on the comprehension of connected text (see, for example, the discussion in Clifton & Ferreira, this volume).

Before backing up this assessment with a review of recent psycholinguistic proposals, let me forestall a potential confusion by emphasising one *non*-issue. There is to my knowledge no genuine disagreement in psycholinguistics about what general types of information may contribute to language comprehension. Rather the issue is how the information is used, for what purpose, at what stage of analysis. Even in models which emphasise the role of general conceptual knowledge (e.g. the conceptual dependency model of Riesbeck & Schank, 1978), syntactic knowledge participates in the comprehension process. And, even in models which draw the sharpest boundaries between grammatical processing and other types of cognitive processing (e.g. Forster, 1979), general world knowledge contributes to language comprehension, not just to the grammatical processing system proper. Consequently, empirical studies which only show that some broad type of information (syntactic, lexical, semantic, pragmatic, discourse, general world knowledge) influences some final output of the entire comprehension system are not very informative. They do not allow us to distinguish between different models or theories of language comprehension, and thus they will not be discussed here.

PROCESSING CONSTITUENT STRUCTURE

Structural Principles: The Garden-Path Model

It is convenient for expositional reasons to begin with a model (the "garden-path" model defended by my colleagues and myself) in which an initial syntactic analysis is assigned on the basis of purely structural information. In this model, perceivers incorporate each word of an input into a constituent structure representation of the sentence, roughly as each item is encountered, as illustrated in (1). At each step in this process, the perceiver postulates the minimal number of nodes required by the grammar of the language under analysis, given the structure assigned to preceding items.

1.

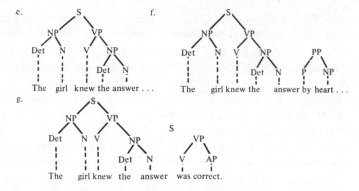

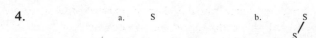

2. Minimal attachment: Do not postulate any potentially unnecessary nodes.
3. Late closure: If grammatically permissible, attach new items into the clause or phrase currently being processed (i.e. the phrase or clause postulated most recently).

This minimal attachment strategy predicts that the transition from (1e) to (1f) should be a smooth one; by contrast, the transition from (1e) to (1g) will require a revision of analysis (addition of the circled "S" node) since the phrase "the answer" will have been taken incorrectly to be the simple direct object of the verb "know." The other strategy implicated in constituent structure analysis is the late closure strategy which adjudicates in cases where two equally minimal attachments exist. It will favour attachments to preceding items (over attachment to subsequent items) and typically will favour attachments to phrases lower in the phrase-structure tree rather than to phrases higher up.

There are several important points to note about this model. The first concerns the generality of the strategies. Many of the construction-specific strategies that had been noted in the psycholinguistic literature follow as a special case of these strategies (see Frazier, 1979, for extensive discussion of this point). For example, Bever's (1970) main clause strategy specifies that perceivers preferentially adopt a main-clause analysis of an input rather than a subordinate-clause analysis. This preference may be viewed as one specific case of minimal attachment. As illustrated in (4), choosing the main clause analysis (4a) over a subordinate clause analysis (4b) follows from choosing the structure with minimal nodes.

4.   a.   S   b.   S
                                                          /
                                                        S

Other examples of minimal attachment include choosing VP attachment over NP attachment of the PP in (5), main clause analysis of the VP in (6), and the

NP-conjunction analysis of (7). Late closure operates to choose the direct object analysis in (8), low attachment of the adverb in (9) (where it modifies *left*), and of the PP in (10) (where *in the library* will modify *reading* rather than *put*). (This list is by no means exhaustive.) These strategies will determine the analysis of ambiguous strings; however, if a string is locally disambiguated (e.g. by punctuation or by clear prosodic effects) then by definition there will be only one permissible analysis of the input and we would expect perceivers to construct that analysis.

5. John hit the girl with a book.
   (cf. Rayner, Carlson & Frazier, 1983)
   (John hit the girl with a book with a bat.)
6. The horse raced past the barn fell.
   (cf. Bever, 1970; Rayner et al., 1983; Ferreira & Clifton, 1986)
7. Ernie kissed Marcie and her sister. . .
   (cf. Frazier, 1979)
   (Ernie kissed Marcie and her sister laughed.)
8. Since Jay always jogs a mile this seems like a short distance to him.
   (cf. Frazier & Rayner, 1982; Kennedy & Murray, 1984)
   (Since Jay always jogs a mile seems like a short distance to him.)
9. Joyce said Tom left yesterday.
   (cf. Frazier, 1979; Kimball, 1973)
10. Jessie put the book Kathy was reading in the library. . .
    (cf. Frazier & Fodor, 1978)

It is presumably no accident that the construction-specific parsing preferences exhibited by the human comprehension mechanism can be unified and viewed as the consequence of just two general strategies. One can easily imagine a system in which there would be absolutely no relation between the ranking of options at one choice point, and the ranking of options at some other choice point; i.e. a system in which it is necessary to add a new strategy each time a new construction is studied. In light of this possible variation, the systematicity exhibited by the sentence comprehension mechanism is really quite impressive. It is unlikely that it is accidental.

This generality in itself argues that language comprehension is not the result of a haphazard collection of whatever clues can be gleaned from superficial analysis of the lexical string, together with whatever general conceptual or world knowledge might influence the plausibility of various analyses. The experimental evidence presented in support of the strategies provides further evidence of the orderly nature of sentence analysis. For example, recording subjects' eye movements as they read sentences like (11), Frazier and Rayner (1982) show that average reading time per character is longer for (11b) than for (11a). There is also a higher probability of making a regressive eye movement in (11b) than in (11a), and, as predicted by minimal attachment, the disruption in (11b) is associated with the disambiguating words (underlined in [11b]). Hence this region takes longer to process in (11b) than in the corresponding region in (11c) which is disambiguated by "that" (cf. Rayner & Frazier, in press). In short, the predictions of immediate minimal analysis are confirmed in detail.[1]

11. a. I suppose the girl knows the answer to the physics problem.

(Minimal attachment)

   b. The girl knows the answer to the physics problem was correct.

(Nonminimal)

   c. The girl knows that the answer to the physics problem was correct.

(Nonminimal-unambiguous)

The fact that the complexity associated with a nonminimal attachment sentence such as (11b) shows up immediately (including on the very first fixation in the disambiguating region) argues strongly for the view that the processor systematically constructs a linguistic analysis of the input as the words of the sentence are encountered. If no analysis had been assigned to preceding items in (11b) there is no reason whatsoever to expect long fixations and regressive eye movements to be associated with the disambiguating region of the sentence.

Before turning to preferences based on nonstructural factors, let me emphasise that the minimal attachment and late closure strategies are not arbitrary; one can understand, for example, why different individuals should each adopt these particular strategies and not, say, their inverses. Both minimal attachment and late closure may be viewed as the result of adopting the first analysis available to the processor. Minimal attachment analyses will be available earlier than nonminimal ones due to the relative number of phrase structure rules that must be accessed for the two analyses, assuming that accessing more rules takes more time (see discussion in Frazier & Fodor, 1978). Late closure analysis permits earlier structuring of new unstructured items than would its opposite (i.e. early closure), since new items may be structured together immediately with already processed material. Hence, the structuring of the current item need not be delayed until subsequent items are received and processed.

Assuming that the need to structure material quickly is related to

---

[1] In Holmes, Kennedy, and Murray (in press), also the first experiment in Holmes (this volume), no difference in the complexity of (11b) and its unambiguous counterpart (11c) is observed, contrary to the predictions of minimal attachment. However, reading times are very long in this study. When subjects simply read for comprehension, significant garden-path effects are observed, cf. Rayner and Frazier, in press.

restrictions on human immediate memory capacity, we might expect all humans to adopt the first available constituent structure analysis. If so, we expect the minimal attachment and late closure strategies to be universal. Ideally we should be able to remove the grammar of English from our theory of sentence processing, plug in the grammar of some other language, and obtain the correct theory of the processing of that language. To the extent that this is so, the theory is in fact a theory of human sentence comprehension, and not merely a theory of the processing of English. And, if it should turn out that language-specific parsing differences do exist, this fact along with the detailed differences will require explanation.

It wouldn't be too surprising if the constituent structure parsing of all head-initial languages (in which the heads of phrases precede their complements) is the same as in English. Indeed, in a head-initial language like Italian, for example, there is at least intuitive evidence supporting the prediction of the above strategies. Marica deVincenzi informs me that there is a preference for noun-phrase conjunction, over sentential conjunction, in cases of temporary ambiguity (e.g. the Italian counterpart to [7]), as predicted by minimal attachment. Frazier (Note 6) investigates Dutch. Dutch is a "verb-second" language exhibiting head-final order in all embedded verb phrases (i.e. the verb follows its objects). Frazier presents both intuitive evidence and initial experimental evidence confirming the predictions of minimal attachment in Dutch. Ueda (Note 13) uses intuitive evidence to argue for the operation of minimal attachment in Japanese, a consistent left-branching (head-final) language (see also discussion in Frazier & Rayner, in press). Clearly more cross-language processing evidence is needed. However, the currently available evidence is encouraging in that it consistently supports the predictions of the strategies, even in languages which are typologically distinct from English.

Viewed from the perspective of this model, the question of how nonstructural information types influence sentence processing is a question concerning the interaction of information types. For example, given the basic model outlined here, one can ask how the processor is influenced by lexical, thematic, or world knowledge which disconfirms the structurally preferred analysis of the sentence. Viewed from the perspective of competing models (e.g. Crain & Steedman, 1985; Ford, Bresnan, & Kaplan, 1983), the question of how nonstructural information types influence processing may be taken to be a question concerning the nature of the decision principles determining the analysis of the input. The evidence which is crucial for distinguishing these two views is whether the information influences the selection of the *initial* syntactic analysis assigned to the string. If so, then the purely structural decision principles discussed above are either wrong altogether or they operate in more restricted circumstances than suggested here. The role of lexical preferences and of discourse constraints will each be taken up directly.

APPR–S*

We shall then turn to questions concerning the revision of an initially computed structure.

Lexical Preferences

Ford et al. (1983) propose a series of principles to guarantee that a sentence is initially analysed in accordance with the strongest or preferred lexical form of the verb (and other heads of phrases). Indeed, they show that the ultimately preferred analysis assigned to the sentences in (12) differ, presumably because "want" occurs more often with just a single argument in its complement whereas "position" typically occurs with both a theme and a locative phrase in its complement.

12. a. The woman positioned [the dress] on that rack.
         (Simple NP preferred)
     b. The woman wanted [the dress on that rack].
         (Complex NP preferred)

Numerous experimental studies show that lexical preferences influence some stage of language comprehension (e.g. Clifton, Frazier, & Connine, 1984; Holmes, this volume; Kurtzman, Note 9; Mitchell & Holmes, 1985).   What these studies do not show is whether lexical preferences are used to guide the initial selection of an analysis or, alternatively, are used only later (e.g. as a filter confirming or disconfirming an analysis identified on other grounds, or contributing to the ease and speed with which a temporary misanalysis is corrected). I shall refer to the former possibility as "lexical proposal" and to the latter as the "lexical filter" view.

Holmes (this volume) discussed a grammaticality-judgement study conducted with Lauri Stowe which she takes to be evidence unambiguously favouring the lexical-proposal view. The basic finding is that a numerically smaller garden-path effect occurs in sentential-complement sentences like (11b) containing verbs, which are biased towards a sentential complement (e.g. *claim*) than in sentences with verbs biased toward a noun-phrase complement (e.g. *hear*). On Holmes' account, perceivers first test a sentential complement analysis for verbs like *claim*, but not for verbs like *hear*. For some reason (I actually don't understand why, since sentential complements usually begin with subject noun phrases) this sentential complement is abandoned when a noun phrase follows the verb. Thus, when the noun phrase is followed by a verb, perceivers must give up their current structural hypothesis and return to their initial (sentential-complement) hypothesis. This reanalysis will be relatively cost-free for a verb like *claim* since it involves re-establishing a hypothesis already considered; for a verb like *hear*, the sentential-complement analysis will not be considered until the disambiguating information is encountered and thus the garden-path effect is larger.[2] Notice, however, that an alternative account of these data is possible. Imagine for a moment that perceivers tend to minimally attach the postverbal noun phrase into the verb phrase following both types of verbs. We must then assume it takes longer to revise a lexically confirmed analysis than to revise an analysis which is inconsistent with the preferred or predominant usage of verbs. In short, this study seems compatible with either a lexical-proposal or a lexical-filter hypothesis (also see footnote 2).

Mitchell (this volume) presents evidence supporting the use of lexical preferences to filter or evaluate the structural analysis of a sentence. In a self-paced reading task, he shows that reading the first display (underlined here) took longer in (13b), containing an obligatorily intransitive verb, than in (13a), containing an optionally intransitive verb. In the second display (not underlined), the a-form takes longer than the b-form.

13. a. After the audience had applauded the actors/sat down for a well-deserved drink.

b. After the audience had departed the actors/ sat down for a well-deserved drink.

According to a lexical-proposal view, we would have expected perceivers to construct the correct intransitive analysis of (13b), whereas in (13a) perceivers would on occasion at least be expected to construct the incorrect analysis. Instead, the pattern of data suggest that a transitive analysis is initially taken in both sentence forms. The incorrect (transitive) analysis is reanalysed during the first display in (13b) but not until the second display in (13a). The lexical-proposal hypothesis does not provide a straightforward account of these data.

---

[2]Holmes (this volume) takes another aspect of her data to support the lexical-proposal hypothesis. She finds reading times for the word *the* (relative to its "unambiguous" control) to be significantly longer following S-bias verbs like *claim*, but not following NP-bias verbs like *hear*. According to Holmes, subjects expect *that* following *claim* and thus are garden-pathed when *the* appears. There are two problems with this argument. First, the appearance of *the* is perfectly consistent with the hypotheses that *claim* takes a sentential complement (i.e. many clauses begin with a subject noun phrase); hence the appearance of *the* does not disconfirm the reader's current structural hypothesis even on the lexical-proposal hypothesis. If anything, the occurrence of the word *the* disconfirms a prediction about the category of the following word, *not* a prediction about the structural type of the verb's complement. Second, if probabilistic predictions about the category of an immediately following word influence the nature or timing of lexical categorisation of ambiguous lexical items (e.g. *that*), then relatively long reading times associated with the word *the* in the control condition, not relatively short times in the reduced complement of NP-bias verbs, might be responsible for the effect. In short, there are several reasons to think the observed effect may not be directly related to the processor's hypothesis about the structural type of the complement.

Two additional types of evidence suggest that lexical proposal of a structural analysis is not correct, at least not in any fully general form. Sentences like (10) ("Jessie put the book Kathy was reading in the library ...") suggest that lexically guided analysis would have to be based on local lexical preferences. Intuitions indicate that the prepositional phrase in (10) is initially interpreted as a sister to "read" despite the fact that "read" does not require a locative phrase but "put" does.

In (10), it might suffice to say that it is only *local* lexical preferences which guide analysis. But in sentences like (14a), one preferentially interprets "to whom" as binding the gap after "say," despite the fact that "say" does not in general seem to occur with an overt goal or any other prepositional phrase. Thus, assuming local lexical preferences guide analysis would not account for this preference.

14. a. To whom did you say that you admitted it?
     b. To whom did you admit that you said it?

Further, since the preferred analysis of (14b) also has "to whom" binding a gap in the matrix clause (the gap following "admit"), the preference in (14a) cannot be attributed to some factor like the relative frequency of say + PP vs. admit + PP. In short, the intuitive evidence in (14) is really not consistent with a lexically guided parsing system, whether lexical guidance is construed as a purely local phenomenon or as a global competition between the lexical preferences of all heads of phrases.[3]

One further bit of evidence weighing against the use of lexical preferences to propose (rather than filter) an initial structural analysis derives from a study of head-final phrases. If the structural analysis of a phrase is initially governed by the lexical preferences of the head, then analysis of verb-final verb phrases should be delayed, i.e. one can't determine the lexical preferences of the verb before the verb is encountered. In other words, the lexical proposal view entails the existence of some language-specific parsing differences. Thus, we may either assume that initial structural analysis is based on

---

[3] Tanenhaus, Stowe, and Carlson (1985) examined word-by-word reading times for sentences like those in (a)

  a. The sheriff wondered which horse/rock the cowboy raced _____ down the hill.

  b. The sheriff wondered which horse/rock the cowboy raced desperately past _____.

They observed a plausibility effect following the verb (e.g. "raced the horse" is more plausible than "raced the rock") only for preferred transitive verbs. This might be taken as evidence in support of the lexical proposal view. For the plausibility relations of only the lexically preferred analysis to be important is entirely expected on the view that only this analysis is computed. However, as Mike Tanenhaus (pers. communication) has pointed out to me, the finding is also consistent with the lexical filter view on the assumption that subcategorisation filtering precedes semantic interpretation and/or pragmatic evaluation.

lexical preferences *only* in head-initial phrases; or we may assume parsing is lexically guided in all languages, but structural analysis occurs immediately, without waiting for the head, only in head-initial languages.

At present there is only extremely limited evidence available concerning the parsing of head-final constructions. However, the evidence does not indicate delays in the analysis of head-final constructions (cf. Frazier, Note 6). This, in turn, favours the view that lexical preferences are used to filter rather than propose structural anlayses since it argues against any universally operative lexical-proposal strategy (which incorrectly predicted delays). Of course, ultimately it may turn out that differences in the parsing mechanisms for distinct languages do exist; but we're not forced to that position yet.

Discourse Constraints

The relation between sentences in a discourse is complex. Sequences of sentences typically maintain not only referential coherence, but temporal and causal coherence. Sentences early in the sequence satisfy the presuppositions of later sentences, determine or constrain the topic/focus structure of subsequent sentences, and provide the context or partial model relevant for the interpretation of later sentences, thereby mediating the operation of Gricean principles. Thus, like lexical preferences, discourse biases are important determinants of the final understanding of a sentence. As with lexical preferences, the question of immediate interest is precisely when and how these biases operate; e.g. do they influence the initial choice of a grammatical analysis of the current input item.

Crain and Steedman (1985) propose various principles intended to guarantee that the structure assigned to the current sentence is whatever structure is maximally compatible with the current discourse model, i.e. whatever analysis requires the fewest revisions or additions to the current discourse model. Specifically, they propose a *principle of a priori plausibility* (choose the most plausible reading in terms of world knowledge and the universe of discourse), a *principle of referential success* (favour readings referring to an entity already established in the perceiver's model), and a *principle of parsimony* (other things being equal, choose a reading that carries fewer unsatisfied but consistent presuppositions).

The observation that plausibility, parsimony, and referential success govern some stage of language processing is widely accepted. What is novel about Crain and Steedman's proposal is the idea that the consequence of applying these principles can be determined immediately, essentially as each word or two is encountered. If true, this would permit the processor to construct basically just a single analysis of an input (except for very short one- or two-word stretches of the sentence), while maximising the chances of computing the correct/intended/contextually appropriate analysis of the sentence.

Having received and analysed an entire sentence, it is certainly possible to identify each of the locally possible analyses of the sentence and determine the presuppositions carried by each, the relative a priori plausibility of each, and the relative referential consistency of each with preceding discourse context. But under what circumstances can this be determined on a word-by-word basis? Traditionally, at least, it seems to have been assumed that one must interpret a structure in order to determine the presuppositions it carries.

With respect to plausibility differences, it is often unclear what would count as a sufficient difference in the plausibility of different readings to permit early resolution of ambiguity. For example, in (15), is the difference in the likelihood of "answer" vs. "duck" as the direct object of "knows" sufficiently great that a simple direct object analysis is selected in (15a) but a sentential complement reading in (15b)? And how could the parser (even in principle) evaluate the relative plausibility of the direct object and sentential complement reading without yet knowing the identity of the embedded verb? Clearly it cannot simply assume, say, that the higher a phrase is on some animacy hierarchy, the more plausible it is as a subject; this might work in (15), but not in general (e.g. consider [16]).

15. a. John knew the answer ...
    b. John knew the duck ...
16. a. John heard the answer ...
    b. John heard the duck ...

Without knowing what constitutes a decisive bias during the left-to-right ongoing analysis of a sentence, we do not know how the above principles apply. We cannot simply appeal to the principles post hoc whenever it is convenient to do so. Further, without some rough idea of the answers to these questions, we do not know when the processor is predicted to assign just a single analysis to an input and when it must compute and maintain several alternative analyses because relative plausibility (referential success or parsimony) differences are not sufficiently great or clear to be decisive.

Despite these questions, there are some circumstances in which clear local plausibility or parsimony differences may be identified. For example, Crain and Steedman note that the local relation between "teacher" and "taught" and between "children" and "taught" will result in clear plausibility differences in (17), i.e. the correct reduced relative-clause analysis will be more plausible in (17b) than in (17a). Indeed, in a grammaticality judgement experiment, Crain and Steedman show that subjects are more likely to call (17b) grammatical than (17a).

17. a. The teachers taught by Berlitz method passed the test.
    b. The children taught by Berlitz method passed the test.

This result (and the others reported by Crain & Steedman, 1985; Kurtzman, Note 9; and Altman, Note 1) might reflect either the initial analysis constructed or, alternatively, the ease of reanalysis. In short, this finding simply cannot choose between the possibility that principles like a priori plausibility govern an initial choice of syntactic analysis and the possibility that plausibility influences the probability and ease of reanalysis.

Ferreira and Clifton (1986) try to distinguish these possibilities by measuring reading times for ambiguous sentence structures such as (18) in disambiguating contexts, e.g. (19) as a context for (18a) and (18b).

18. a. The editor played the tape agreed the story was big.
    b. The editor played the tape and agreed the story was big.
    c. Sam loaded the boxes on the cart onto the van.
    d. Sam loaded the boxes on the cart before his coffee break.
19. John worked as a reporter for a newspaper. He knew a major story was brewing over the mayor scandal. He went to his editors with a tape and some photos because he needed their approval to go ahead with the story. He ran a tape for one of his editors, and he showed some photos to the other. The editor played the tape agreed the story was big. The other editor urged John to be cautious.

Even in a strongly biased context such as (19), there was clear evidence of a temporary misanalysis in the nonminimal attachment sentence forms (18b) and (18d). These results do not argue against the existence of the plausibility, parsimony, or referential success principles as principles which govern some stage of processing; but they do argue strongly against the use of these principles to select an initial syntactic analysis of a sentence in any immediate or nearly word-by-word fashion.

Issues of Reanalysis

In any depth-first model of processing (whether analysis is guided by structural, lexical, or discourse principles) there will be circumstances when it will be necessary to abandon the current analysis of the sentence. The particular circumstances requiring reanalysis will of course depend on the particular principles assumed; but the mere fact that the interpretation of words and phrases may depend not just on a priori context but also on subsequent context entails that every depth-first on-line processing model will need some theory of reanalysis.

Gorrell (1985) proposes one interesting account of reanalysis. In essence, he suggests that syntactic analysis is not completely depth-first or serial. Rather, it is "staggered serial." On this account, more than one analysis of the input is computed. The simplest analysis is initially adopted, but if it proves to be incorrect, the alternative will still be available; e.g. the sentential complement analysis will still be available when "was" is encountered in (20a) (Gorrell, 1985, p. 188).

20. a. John knew the old woman on the train was ill.
    b. They motioned to the man that they couldn't hear.
    c. *John left is surprising.
    d. That apparently healthy sheep die is disturbing.
    e. The horse raced past the barn fell.

The basic claim of the staggered serial account is that "easy" reanalyses—those which do not involve conscious effort—are just those for which the alternative analysis is still available at the point of reanalysis.

Two factors will determine whether an alternative analysis will be available when needed: whether the analysis is computed in the first place and the "distance" between the initially adopted analysis and the alternative, which Gorrell suggests is a function of how long the parser has been committed to the first analysis. According to Gorrell (1985, p. 194): "parallel processing only occurs in the environment of an overt marker which is ambiguous, e.g., an ambiguous verb or lexical item such as 'that'." Thus, reanalysis of (20a) is easy because the alternative to the direct object reading is computed and is still available when the parser encounters the error signal "was." Likewise, in (20b) reanalysis will be simple due to the presence of "that" which permits both analyses to be computed; (20c) is harder, because no overt element is present to mark the alternative analysis. And (20d) is claimed to be hard because of the distance between the error (the analysis of "that" as a demonstrative rather than as a complementiser) and the error signal ("is"). Finally, according to Gorrell, the reason why (20e) involves conscious reanalysis is because no alternative to the simple main-clause analysis is computed in the first place.

Unfortunately, the staggered serial account will not do, even for the limited data in (20) (which provided the basic motivation for this view). Though I cannot go into all the issues in depth here, this approach suffers from several shortcomings. First, counter to Gorrell's discussion, the principles he gives actually predict that (20e) should be *easier* to revise than (20a): Since the verb ("raced") is ambiguous, two anlayses of (20e) should initially be computed; and, the amount of time the parser is committed to the initial analysis is actually less in (20e) (where the misanalysis only spans four words of the input) than in (20a) (where it spans six words of the input). Clearly

Gorrell intends for only a single analysis to be computed in (20e). But it is entirely unclear what principled definition of ambiguous verb would classify an item with multiple subcategorisation frames as ambiguous (e.g. "know") but would not classify verbs with passive participles which are homophonous with their simple past (e.g. "raced") as unambiguous. Thus, it seems the staggered serial model does not really have an account of the circumstances under which an alternative analysis is computed.

Gorrell notes that the failure to find robust reanalysis effects for sentences with very short (one or two word) ambiguous phrases, as in the closure sentences in Frazier and Rayner (1982) and Kennedy and Murray (1984), may indicate that readers may maintain alternative structural descriptions for a small number of words—for two-word phrases, but not four- or five-word phrases in the studies cited. This assumption, however, is itself incompatible with the discussion of the examples in (20); e.g. the statement that reanalysis of (20a) is easy because the alternative is still available after a six-word phrase. I emphasise this point because the apparent impossibility of giving any consistent explicit account of the duration of an alternative structural analysis of a sentence is the major empirical obstacle to every version of parallel processing I've encountered (e.g. consider the parallelism implicit in discourse driven parsing models such as the one discussed earlier). It is of course to Gorrell's credit that he has proposed a sufficiently explicit account of limited parallelism that one may argue against it.

A further empirical difficulty arises for the staggered serial account. The account predicts (see discussion in Gorrell, 1985, p. 195) that processing verbs with multiple subcategorisation frames (e.g. optionally transitive verbs) should be harder than processing verbs with a single frame (e.g. obligatory transitive or obligatory intransitives). This prediction is falsified in Clifton et al. (1984) and in Mitchell (this volume; discussed earlier). Finally, it should be noted that in its present form at least, the staggered serial account of reanalysis is ad hoc. Gorrell (1985, p. 194) correctly notes: "Presumably, there is a cost to constructing parallel representations and the parser will not so do without sufficient reason." But it is not clear why the parser should engage in parallelism just for the particular subset of analyses proposed. Nor is it clear why, if it is bothering to construct parallel analyses at all, it should initially adopt just one analysis, or why it should choose the syntactically simpler one. In short, though the staggered serial account is probably the most extensive, explicit and interesting account of reanalysis to date, it can be faulted on both descriptive and explanatory grounds.

Frazier and Rayner (1982) argued that the complexity of revising an analysis is a function of the "clarity" of the error signal, i.e. whether the signal that the current analysis is ill-formed or inappropriate indicates the location and nature of the error. Like Gorrell, they suggest that the longer the parser is committed to an analysis, the harder it tends to be to revise. In some cases this might be due to the difficulty of locating the original error if the error signal is delayed, as in (20e) and (24). However, in many other cases, minor differences in the length of an ambiguous phrase results in substantial complexity differences. These may be attributed to the greater cost of revising a syntactic error once it has already been semantically interpreted (see discussion in Frazier & Rayner, 1982).

Take (21), for example. The minimal attachment analysis of the words "the men" (shown in [21a]) seems perfectly easy to revise: Indeed, once the preposition is encountered, there is no alternative to the analysis shown in (21b).

21.

The men with guns . . .

a.
```
            S
          /   \
        NP     PP
       /  \   /  \
     Det   N P    NP
      |    | |     |
     the men with guns
```

b.
```
              S
            /   \
          NP     \
         /  \     \
       NP    PP
      /  \   /  \
    Det  N  P    NP
     |   |  |     |
    the men with guns
```

In other words, the revision shown in (21b) will be unambiguously warranted by the occurrence of the prepositional phrase (since the grammar of English will allow no alternative attachment of this phrase). Thus the revision in (21) should be trivial. However, given a discourse context which already contains a potential referent for the simple NP (as in [22] where "the men" in the second sentence might initially be taken to refer to the men introduced in the first sentence), it is possible that the simple NP analysis in (21a) leads to an incorrect semantic interpretation. It is only in this latter case that one is aware of any difficulty in processing the sentence.

22. There were men standing on the corner who were unarmed.
    The men with guns were on the roof.

Sentence (23a) is an interesting case of revision. Intuitively it is more difficult than the closely related sentence in (20a) but less difficult than (20e). In (23a) the error signal "hid" is informative with respect to the nature of the error; "hid" will be missing a subject, assuming *the girl* is initially minimally attached as the direct object of *see*. Further, since the misanalysed NP (the girl) is the immediately preceding phrase, the location of the error (as well as its nature) is flagged by the error signal. Thus, (23) contrasts with (20e) where only the nature of the error ("fell" is again missing a subject) but not its location is marked by the error signal. However, unlike (20a), perception verbs permit a predication analysis (cf. [23b] and [23c]). Hence, the fact that *hid* requires a subject does not by itself require the processor to analyse *the girl* as the subject of a sentential complement. Rather, in this case, it is only the presence of the tense marker which excludes the predication analysis of (23a) (cf. Williams, 1980), requiring the direct object analysis to be revised.

23. a. I saw [[the girl] [hid in the forest]].
    b. I saw [the girl] [hidden in the forest].
    c. I saw [the girl] [hide in the forest].

The idea that it is the informativeness of the error signal which determines the complexity of reanalysis explains another observation about the difficulty of making revisions, namely, that errors at one level of analysis tend to be difficult if they are detected only at some later level, especially if they appear to have been confirmed at this or some other subsequent level of analysis. For example, in (24), due to Marcus (1980), *cotton* is lexically misanalysed (as a derivative adj. or as part of a compound) but the error is only later signalled by the syntactic illformedness which ensues as a result of this lexical analysis.

24. The cotton clothing is made from grows in Mississippi.

Eventually a theory of reanalysis must account explicitly for all differences in the ease of making revisions. It must also account for why and how the processor manages to identify an overlooked analysis of the sentence if the initially chosen analysis does not break down. For example, the first analysis may be completely well formed, but simply not quite as plausible on semantic and pragmatic grounds as some alternative analysis. In response to this problem, Rayner et al. (1983) propose the existence of two independent processing subsystems: a syntactic processor and a thematic processor. The two subsystems operate in parallel, each carrying out its own idiosyncratic task on the basis of its own operating principles and its own characteristic information sources. By hypothesis, the thematic processor evaluates the relative plausibility of all thematic frames associated with the head of a phrase using discourse context and world knowledge. It may thus choose some frame which is not compatible with the initially selected syntactic analysis of the phrase.

We might assume that a thematic frame for a verb will always contain one external argument (i.e. one argument appearing outside the verb phrase) and possibly one or more internal arguments. A thematic role and syntactic category label will be supplied for each argument, as illustrated for "see" in (25). By convention, the external argument (the experiencer in [25]) is underlined; thus, thematic frames permit the external argument to be distinguished from any internal arguments. Assuming all internal arguments must be sisters to the head, a frame like (25a) will be consistent only with a syntactic analysis in which "see" has exactly one sister phrase and it is a noun phrase. Consequently, if the syntactic processor builds the (minimal attachment) structure in (26) for the phrase "saw a cop with a revolver" and the thematic processor selected the frame in (25a), there will be a clear conflict: In (26) "see" has two sisters but (25a) claims it has only one.

25.   see
 a. [Experiencer Theme]
    NP   NP
 b. [Experiencer Theme—Instrument]
    NP   NP   PP
    etc.
26.   The spy saw the cop with a revolver . . .

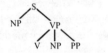

This conflict can act as an error signal, indicating to the syntactic processor that there is a locally more plausible analysis of the sentence. Rayner et al. present eye-movement data in support of this account.

The general idea that thematic structure actively participates in sentence analysis by confirming a syntactic analysis or initiating reanalysis attempts receives further support by a (makes-sense judgement) study conducted by Mike Tanenhaus (personal communication).

27. a. A gambler visited his cousin tonight. (Transitive expectation)
    b. A gambler visited tonight.
28. a. A gambler cheated his cousin tonight. (Intransitive expectation)
    b. A gambler cheated tonight.
29. a. The girl was walking on the grass. (Locative expectation)
    b. The girl was walking.
30. a. The girl was reading on the grass. (No locative expectation)
    b. The girl was reading.

If a sentence contains a direct object noun phrase or a locative prepositional phrase (as in the a-forms above), the processor has no alternative other than to analyse the phrase syntactically and assign a thematic role to it, whether the occurrence of the phrase is lexically predicted or not (i.e. whether the phrase conforms to the most frequent usage of the verb or not). However, in the simple intransitive sentence forms without a locative phrase (the b-forms above), the processor will expect a particular thematic role that won't arrive if the verb is one that usually occurs with two arguments (e.g. *visit* usually occurs with both an agent and a theme, *walk* usually occurs with both an agent and a locative phrase). Thus we might expect the facilitation from a match between the actual sentence form and the preferred verb form to be greater in the "short" b-forms than in the a-forms. This is precisely what Tanenhaus found, i.e. preferred transitives (locatives) took longer than preferred intransitives (nonlocative) sentences, with a crossover interaction—preferred monadic verbs did not take longer in the dyadic (b-) sentence forms. Of course, if thematic predictions governed the selection of an initial analysis (rather than playing a confirmatory role or a role in reanalysis) we would not expect this crossover (see also Carlson & Tanenhaus, Note 3; Stowe, Note 11).

Summary

We have reviewed the evidence supporting the claim that the human sentence processor initially computes just one constituent structure analysis of a sentence. We have also examined the principles which determine the particular analysis the processor tries first, including proposed structural principles, lexical principles and discourse principles. It was emphasised that quite different theories of sentence processing result depending on whether the proposed nonstructural (lexical and discourse) principles guide initial syntactic analysis or alternatively reflect the fast operation of a theoretically distinct (nonsyntactic) processing subsystem. The lexical and discourse principles discussed here may be viewed either way: They may provide an alternative to structural principles and thus guide which particular syntactic analysis the processor tries first, or they may be viewed as principles which guide subsequent analysis, and thus only modulate syntactic preferences, by determining the eventual fate of the initially selected syntactic analysis. Though most experimental evidence is ambiguous and may be interpreted either way, in my (clearly partisan) opinion the current evidence which is not open to either interpretation (see discussion earlier of Mitchell, this volume; Ferreira & Clifton, 1986) favours the view where lexical and especially discourse principles do not directly influence syntactic analysis by determining which analysis the processor will initially construct. Finally it was emphasised that any depth-first theory of sentence processing must ultimately offer a detailed account of reanalysis. At present only the barest outlines of such a theory have been sketched in.

PROCESSING LONG-DISTANCE DEPENDENCIES

The previous section was concerned with the recovery of constituent structure relations. Here we will briefly consider long-distance grammatical dependencies, such as the so-called "filler-gap" dependencies, e.g. the relation between "what" and the empty object following "eat" in (31).

31. What did John eat _____?

We will refer to any empty position in the constituent structure representation as a "gap" and refer to any phase which controls the interpretation of a gap as a "filler" (regardless of the grammatical nature of the relation involved).

Traditionally (Fodor, 1978; 1979; Jackendoff & Culicover, 1971; Wanner & Maratsos, 1978) it has been assumed that gaps are only identified if the processor predicts the occurence of a phrase of a certain type, and then the input lexical string fails to contain an item of that type in the appropriate position. This gap-identification strategy would correctly account for the fact that (32a) is the preferred interpretation of (32), where the gap is taken to correspond to the second of two postverbal noun phrases (though see Woolford, 1986 for an alternative account of these facts and Frazier, Note 6, for a discussion of problems with this gap-identification strategy).

32. Which patient did the nurse bring the doctor?
   a. Which patient did the nurse bring the doctor _____.?
   b. Which patient did the nurse bring _____ the doctor?

It is clear that the postulation of gaps is influenced by lexical preferences (cf. Clifton et al., 1984; Fodor, 1978; Tanenhaus et al., 1985). However, just as in the case of nonempty phrases, there remain questions about whether the expected form or use of a lexical item influences initial-gap hypotheses or just the subsequent evaluation of gap-hypotheses based on nonlexical information (see discussion earlier).

It has usually been assumed that the assignment of a filler to a gap is accomplished immediately, as soon as the gap is postulated. Several indirect sources of evidence support this assumption (e.g. Crain & Fodor, 1985; Frazier et al., 1983; Stowe, 1986; Tanenhaus et al., 1985; Wanner & Maratsos, 1978). Recent evidence from auditory (Clifton & Frazier, in press; Swinney, personal communication) and visual (Clifton & Frazier, in press) priming studies present direct evidence in support of this assumption.

With respect to the assignment of fillers to gaps, it is quite clear that perceivers of English will assign the more recent of two grammatically permissable fillers in cases of ambiguity (cf. Crain & Fodor, 1985; Fodor, 1978; Frazier, Clifton, & Randall, 1983).[4] There is also intuitive evidence that this "recent filler" strategy applies in other languages (see Engdahl, Note 4, for results of an extremely interesting study in Swedish). What is not clear at present is whether the identification of an obligatory filler induces a special mode of processing where the filler, if you will, actively searches for a gap, as suggested by Frazier (Note 6).

The processing classification of gap types is just being worked out now and is far from securely established, even if we restrict our attention to a single language such as English. Most studies of filler-gap processing (e.g. all those cited here) have restricted their attention to gaps of a very limited type (those considered to be wh-trace in Chomsky, 1981, obligatorily controlled null pronominals and most recently NP-trace, cf. Bever & McElree, Note 2). It is quite clear that certain gap types (presumably those which can receive case vs. those which cannot) are distinguished even in very initial stages of processing. For example, Frazier and Clifton (in press) show that "thematically controlled' null pronominals (e.g. the PRO in [33]) are not subject to the recent filler strategy.

33. a. John lent the book to <u>Mary</u> <u>PRO</u> to read _____ on vacation
       (PRO = null pronominal)
    b. <u>John</u> borrowed the book from Mary <u>PRO</u> to read _____ on vacation.

Another gap type which is not well understood is the parasitic gap (cf. Chomsky, 1982; Engdahl, 1983). The processing of parasitic gaps is only beginning to be studied empirically. Unlike ordinary gaps, parasitic gaps may only occur in sentences containing some independent filler-gap relation, as illustrated in (34b), where the parasitic gap is labelled "pg."

34. a. *Which film did you discuss the screenplay without seeing _____?
    b. Which film did you discuss _____ without seeing _____ pg?
    c. Which film did you discuss _____ without seeing it?

Parasitic-gap sentences exhibit a huge range of acceptability, both within and

---

[4]In the case of multiple filler-gap relations, the recent filler strategy automatically results in nested rather than intersecting dependencies, as illustrated

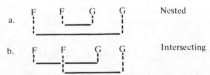

With noun phrase filler-gap relations, nested dependencies do seem to be easier across a variety of languages. However, when it comes to verbal dependencies in "verb raising" structures, it appears that intersecting dependencies are easier than nested ones (cf. Bach, Brown, & Marslen-Wilson, in press). This strongly suggests that perceivers deal differently with structures missing an argument—such as the filler-gap relations discussed in the text—than with structures in which the argument structure is determined by the item that has been displaced.

across speakers. For some speakers (like myself), they range from being completely acceptable to being completely unacceptable, depending on the precise details of the structure, lexical times, length, and meaning of the sentence. For other speakers, even the best examples of parasitic-gap sentences seem to be only marginally acceptable. Nevertheless, in a recent visual grammaticality judgement study by Seely (Note 10), it was found that parasitic gaps in clauses containing null pronominal subjects (e.g. the "without" clause in [34]) were considered just as acceptable as pronouns, as indicated by the error rate, despite the fact that huge acceptability differences between pronoun and parasitic gaps were obtained for sentences containing overt subjects.

In short, though many theoretically crucial questions remain concerning the gap-filling routines employed in English, at least certain basic generalisations seem to have been established. Gaps are recognised and assigned a filler "on-line" (i.e. the processor does not delay such decisions until the ends of clauses or sentences but rather makes them at or immediately following the position of the gap). In cases of temporary ambiguity, the more recent of two potential (grammatically permissible) fillers is assigned to a gap. Certain gap types are distinguished from each other even in initial parsing, i.e. all gaps are not treated equal even in the earliest stages of parsing. Thus, as in the case of constituent structure parsing, the identification and assignment of fillers and gaps appear to occur essentially immediately, following a depth-first (one analysis at a time) strategy. To the extent that the recent filler strategy results because recently encountered phrases may be retrieved from memory more quickly than distant phrases (see Frazier et al., 1983), there may be another similarity between structure building and gap filling. The decision principle of adopting the first available analysis may turn out to guide the analysis of both constituent structure relations and long-distance (filler-gap) relations.

In addition to long-distance relations involving arguments, anaphoric relations involving verbs and verb phrases have recently been investigated. The focus of attention has been on the nature of the antedecent for verbal gaps (see Black, Coltheart, & Byng, this volume) and for various types of verb-phrase anaphors (see Tanenhaus & Carlson, 1986 and references therein).

THE STRUCTURE OF THE PROCESSING MECHANISM

Modularity of the Language Processor

In preceding sections, the emphasis has been on the processing principles implicated in the syntactic processing of sentences. Little has been said about either the structure of the processing mechanism or the principles governing other aspects of language processing. Fodor (1983) has argued for a modular conception of mind, in which the language system, like the various perceptual systems (e.g. the visual system), is viewed as an informationally encapsulated input system, governed by biological principles. On this conception, the early structuring of an input from some natural domain (e.g. language) is accomplished very quickly by mandatory application of specialised routines which deal exclusively with inputs from that domain, producing a "shallow output" which is then open to further interpretation and evaluation by a general cognitive system with full access to general knowledge and beliefs about the world.

The proposals discussed here are consistent in spirit but not in detail with Fodor's modular conception of mind. In particular, the thematic processor (of Rayner et al., 1983, see earlier) implies the existence of an interface system which operates in tandem with the language input system proper. This permits knowledge of the general cognitive variety to influence an input system indirectly, once it has been translated into the specialised vocabulary of the input system. Specifically, in the case at hand, pragmatic plausibility considerations influence thematic assignments, through thematic frame selection. Given our assumption that thematic frames are prestored and contain syntactic category labels, the selection of a thematic frame may influence ongoing syntactic analysis (though not the selection of an initial syntactic analysis).

I have emphasised the thematic processor hypothesis not because there is overwhelming evidence in favour of the hypothesis, nor even a detailed theory of the mechanisms implicated by the hypothesis: Rather, the reason for focusing on this hypothesis is conceptual; anyone favouring more extensive interaction between the language processing system (or more accurately, the grammatical processing system) and nonlinguistic processing system(s) must address the problem of how this interaction could take place. One may not simply assume communication between a nonlinguistic and linguistic system if there is no shared vocabulary. In brief, one must say how any fact I may know about the expected properties of real-world objects or likely events in the world could influence my grammatical decisions (like where to attach a phrase of a particular syntactic category), if one assumes that nongrammatical knowledge influences grammatical processing decisions.

Modularity Within the Language Processor

If the language processing system were one monolithic system, rather than a series of largely independent subsystems, we might expect to be able to identify the information source(s) and decision principles or mode of operation (multiple analysis vs. single analysis, immediate commitment vs.

delay) of the language processor once and for all. In other words, we would be able to make statements like: The language processor operates according to a depth-first strategy, making immediate commitments, after checking all grammatical information sources. But this is not what we find. Instead, it seems that we must restrict such statements, giving one specification for the lexical access subsystem, another for the constituent structure subsystem, and yet another for the thematic subsystem. In short, it appears that the information sources and the decision principles or mode of operation of the processor differs from one subsystem to the next. For example, considerable evidence suggests that lexical access involves multiple analysis (i.e. the processor considers all common representations of an input), using only information about the phonological or orthographic form of an input (i.e. ignoring, at this stage, information about syntactic or semantic compatibility with context) (cf. Seidenberg, Tanenhaus, Leiman, & Bienkowski, 1982; Swinney, 1979; Tanenhaus & Lucas, in press). Clearly this subsystem differs from the constituent structure system and from the gap-filling routines, which clearly do have access to syntactic information but do not follow a multiple analysis strategy.

While it is clear that the lexical-access system differs from the syntactic system, what is not completely clear at present is whether the syntactic processing system responsible for constituent structure analysis also accomplishes all other aspects of syntactic processing, e.g. the identification and assignment of filler-gap dependencies. Several investigators (Berwick & Weinberg, 1984; Clifton & Frazier, in press; Frazier, et al., 1983; Freedman & Forster, 1985) have proposed a distinction between a syntactic subsystem concerned with structure building (i.e. constituent structure) and a subsystem concerned with the identification or evaluation of (the binding and control) relations between phrases in the constituent structure representation. By contrast, working within a generalised phrase structure grammar framework (where filler-gap dependencies are captured by rules cast in the same format as those traditionally assumed for phrase structure dependencies that span only a single "layer" of the tree), Crain and Fodor (1985) propose that there is just a single syntactic processing system responsible for all syntactic decisions.

Whatever the outcome of this particular debate, one thing is reasonably clear. The nature of the debate in psycholinguistics has changed. The issue is no longer whether there is structure in the comprehension system, but rather the precise nature of the structure and the explanation or motivation for its existence.

CONCLUSIONS

At present, we don't have anything like a complete theory of language comprehension, even for a single language such as English. However, there are certain areas where psycholinguists have been able to ask very detailed questions about processing and to develop quite rich theories permitting a large range of disparate facts to be reduced to just one or two general principles. What is striking is how very simple the processing principles are. Once we pay careful attention to the representations involved, to the precise functional decomposition of the overall comprehension task, and to the particular information sources available for accomplishing some subtask, it seems we only need to appeal to rather trivial principles like "don't change current assignments without evidence" (implicit in the discussion in the second section) and "structure the input as soon as possible" (cf. minimal attachment, late closure, recent filler). To my mind, the simplicity of these principles is the most impressive evidence possible for the current modular approach to language and mind. After all, stated in its most general form, a modular theory is simply one which explains some extremely complicated phenomena in terms of the interaction of several simple subsystems.

ACKNOWLEDGEMENTS

I would like to thank Maria Black, Max Coltheart, and one anonymous reviewer for helpful comments on this chapter. The work reported here was supported by NSF Grant BNS 85 10177 to Rayner and Frazier and NIH Grant HD-18788 to Clifton and Frazier.

REFERENCES

Bach, E., Brown, C., & Marslen-Wilson, W. (in press). Crossed and nested dependencies in German and Dutch: A psycholinguistics study. *Language and Cognitive Processes*.

Berwick, R. C., & Weinberg, A. (1984). *The grammatical basis of linguistic performance*. Cambridge, Mass.: M.I.T. Press.

Bever, T. G. (1970). The cognitive basis for linguistic structures. In J. R. Hayes (Ed.), *Cognition and the development of language*. New York: John Wiley & Sons.

Carlson, G. (1983). Logical form: Type of evidence. *Linguistic and Philosophy*, 6, 295–318.

Chomsky, N. (1981). *Lectures on government and binding: The Pisa lectures*. Dordrecht: Foris.

Chomsky, N. (1982). Some concepts and consequences of the theory of government and binding *Linguistic Inquiry Monograph 6*.

Clark, H. & Sengul, C. J. (1979). In search of referents for nouns and pronouns. *Memory and Cognition*, 7, 35–41.

Clifton, C., Frazier, L., & Connine, C. (1984). Lexical expectations in sentence comprehension. *Journal of Verbal Learning and Verbal Behaviour*, 23, 696–708.

Clifton, C. & Frazier, L. (in press). The use of syntactic information in filling gaps. *Journal of Psycholinguistic Research*.

Crain, S. & Fodor, J. D. (1985). How can grammars help parsers? In D. Dowty, L. Kartunnen, & A. Zwicky (Eds.), *Theoretical perspectives on natural language parsing*. Cambridge: Cambridge University Press.

Crain, S. & Steedman, M. (1985). On not being led up the garden-path: The use of context by the psychological parser. In D. Dowty, L. Karttunen, & H. Zwicky (Eds.), *Natural language parsing*. Cambridge: Cambridge University Press.

Dell. G., McKoon, G., & Ratcliff, R. (1983). The activation of antecedent information during the processing of anaphoric reference. *Journal of Verbal Learning and Verbal Behaviour, 22,* 121–133.

Ehrlich, K. & Rayner, K. (1983). Pronoun assignment and semantic integration during reading: Eye movements and immediacy of processing. *Journal of Verbal Learning and Verbal Behaviour, 22,* 75–87.

Engdahl, E. (1983). Parasitic gaps. *Linguistics and Philosophy, 6,* 5–34.

Ferreira, F. & Clifton, C. (1986). The independence of syntactic processing. *Journal of Memory and Language, 25,* 348–368.

Flores d'Arcais, F. B. (1982). Automatic syntactic computation in sentence comprehension. *Psychological Research, 44,* 231–242.

Fodor, J. A. (1983). *Modularity of mind*. Cambridge, Mass.: M.I.T. Press.

Fodor, J. D. (1978). Parsing strategies and constraints on transformations. *Linguistic Inquiry, 9,* 427–474.

Fodor, J. D. (1979). Superstrategy. In W. Cooper & E. C. T. Walker (Eds.), *Sentence processing*. Hillsdale, N.J.: Lawrence Erlbaum Associates Inc.

Ford, M., Bresnan, J., & Kaplan, R. (1983). A competence-based theory of syntactic closure. In J. Bresnan (Ed.), *The mental representation of grammatical relations*. Cambridge, Mass.: M.I.T. Press, 727–796.

Forster, K. (1979). Levels of processing and the structure of the language processor. In W. E. Cooper & E. C. T. Walker (Eds.), *Sentence processing*. Hillsdale, N.J.: Lawrence Erlbaum Associates Inc.

Frazier, L. (1985). Syntactic complexity. In D. Dowty, L. Karttunen, & H. Zwicky (Eds.), *Natural language parsing*. Cambridge: Cambridge University Press.

Frazier, L. & Clifton, C. (in press). Thematic relations in parsing. *University of Massachusetts Occasional Papers in Linguistics*.

Frazier, L., Clifton, C., & Randall, J. (1983). Filling gaps: Decision principles and structure in sentence comprehension. *Cognition, 13,* 187–222.

Frazier, L. & Fodor, J. D. (1978). The sausage machine: A new two-stage parsing model. *Cognition, 6,* 291–325.

Frazier, L. & Rayner, K. (1982). Making and correcting errors during sentence comprehension: Eye movements in analysis of structurally ambiguous sentences. *Cognitive Psychology, 14,* 178–210.

Frazier, L. & Rayner, K. (in press). Parameterising the language processing system: Left- vs. right-branching within and across languages. In J. Hawkins (Ed.), *Explaining linguistic universals*. Oxford: Basil Blackwell Publishing Co.

Freedman, S. & Forster, K. (1985). The psychological status of overgenerated sentences. *Cognition, 19,* 101–132.

Garrod, S. & Stanford, A. J. (1985). On the real-time character of interpretation during reading. *Language and Cognitive Processes, 1,* 43–59.

Gazdar, G. (1981). Unbounded dependencies and co-ordinate structure. *Linguistic Inquiry, 12,* 155–184.

Gorrell, P. (1985). Natural language parsing and reanalysis. *Proceedings of NELS, 16,* 186–196.

Grosz, B. T., Joshi, A., & Weinstein, S. (1983). Providing a unified account of definite noun phrases in discourse. *Proceedings of the ACL, MIT,* 44–50.

Holmes, V. M., Kennedy, A., & Murray, W. (in press). Syntactic structure and the garden path. *Quarterly Journal of Experimental Psychology.*

Jackendoff, R. & Culicover, P. (1971). A reconsideration of dative movement. *Foundations of Language, 7,* 397–412.

Johnson-Laird, P. N. (1983). *Mental models.* Cambridge, Mass.: Harvard University Press.

Joshi, A. & Weinstein, S. (1981). Control of inference: Role of some aspects of discourse centring. *Proceeding of the International Joint Conference on Artificial Intelligence.* August, Vancouver, B.C.

Kamp, H. (1981). A theory of truth and semantic representation. In Groenendijk (Eds.), *Formal methods in the study of language, Vol. I.* Amsterdam: Mathematische Centrum.

Kennedy, A. & Murray, W. S. (1984). Inspection times for words in syntactically ambiguous sentences under three presentation conditions. *Journal of Experimental Psychology: Human Perceptions and Performance, 10,* 833–849.

Kimball, J. (1973). Seven principles of surface structure parsing in natural language. *Cognition, 2,* 15–47.

Kintsch, W. & van Dijk, T. A. (1978). Toward a model of text comprehension and production. *Psychological Review, 85,* 363–394.

Marcus, M. (1980). *A theory of syntactic recognition for natural language.* Cambridge, Mass.: M.I.T. Press.

Mitchell, D. C. & Holmes, V. M. (1985). The role of specific information about the verb in parsing sentences with local structural ambiguity. *Journal of Memory and Language, 24,* 542–559.

Rayner, K., Carlson, M., & Frazier, L. (1983). The interaction of syntax and semantics during sentence processing: Eye movements in the analysis of semantically biased sentences. *Journal of Verbal Learning and Verbal Behaviour, 22,* 358–374.

Rayner, K. & Frazier, L. (in press). Parsing temporarily ambiguous complements. *Quarterly Journal of Experimental Psychology.*

Riesbeck, C. & Schank, R. (1978). Comprehension by computer: Expectation-based analysis of sentences in context. In W. I. M. Levelt & G. B. Flores d'Arcais (Eds.), *Studies in the perception of language.* Chichester: Wiley.

Seidenberg, M. S., Tanenhaus, M. K., Leiman, J. M., & Bienkowski, M. (1982). Automatic access of the meanings of ambiguous words in context: Some limitations of knowledge-based processing. *Cognitive Psychology, 14,* 489–537.

Stowe, L. (1986). Parsing wh-constructions: Evidence for on-line gap location. *Language and Cognitive Processes, 1,* 27–245.

Swinney, D. (1979). Lexical access during sentence comprehension: (Re) Considerations of context effects. *Journal of Verbal Learning and Verbal Behaviour, 18,* 645–659.

Tanenhaus, M., Stowe, L., & Carlson, G. (1985). The interaction of lexical expectation and pragmatic information. *Proceedings of the Seventh Annual Cognitive Science Society Meetings.*

Tanenhaus, M. & Lucas, M. (in press). Context effects in lexical processing. In U. Frauenfelder & L. Tyler (Eds.), special issue of *Cognition.*

Wanner, E. & Maratsos, M. (1978). An ATN approach to comprehension. In M. Halle, J. Bresnan, & G. A. Miller (Eds.), *Linguistic theory and psychological reality.* Cambridge, Mass.: M.I.T. Press.

Williams, E. (1980). Predication. *Linguistics Inquiry, 11,* 203–238.

Woolford, E. (1986). The distribution of empty nodes in Navajo: A mapping approach. *Linguistic Inquiry, 17,* 301–330.

REFERENCE NOTES

1. Altman, G. (1985). *Modularity and interaction in sentence processing.* Paper presented at Cognitive Science Meeting, Amherst, Mass., June 1985.
2. Bever, T. G. & McElree, B. (1986). *Empty categories access their antecedents during comprehension.* University of Rochester manuscript.
3. Carlson, G. & Tanenhaus, M. (1986). *Thematic roles and language comprehension.* University of Iowa manuscript.
4. Engdahl, E. (1981). *Interpreting sentences with multiple filler-gap dependencies.* Max-Planck-Institut for Psycholinguistik, Nijmegen, manuscript.
5. Fodor, J. D. *Freedom of expression.* University of Connecticut manuscript.
6. Frazier, L. Syntactic processing: Evidence from Dutch. Max-Planck Institute, Nijmegen, Holland, manuscript. (To appear in *Natural Language and Linguistic Theory*).
7. Frazier, L. (1979). *On comprehending sentences: Syntactic parsing strategies.* University of Connecticut doctoral dissertation.
8. Hudson, S., Tanenhaus, M. K., & Dell, G. S. (1986). *The effect of the discourse centre on the local coherence of a discourse.* Paper presented at Cognitive Science Society conference, Amherst, August 15–17.
9. Kurtzman, H. (1985). *Studies in syntactic ambiguity resolution.* M.I.T. doctoral dissertation.
10. Seely, T. Daniel. (in preparation). *Processing parasitic gaps: The dependence hypothesis.*
11. Stowe, L. *Thematic structure and sentence comprehension.* Manuscript.
12. Tanenhaus, M. & CArlson, G. (1986). *Processing verb phrase anaphors.* Paper presented at Annual Meeting of Cognitive Science Society, Amherst, Massachusets, August 1986.
13. Ueda, M. (1984). *Notes on parsing in Japanese.* University of Massachusetts manuscript.

26

Syntactic Parsing: In Search of the Garden Path

V. M. Holmes
Department of Psychology
University of Melbourne
Parkville, Victoria, Australia

ABSTRACT

The parsing principle of minimal attachment predicts that a noun phrase occurring after verbs such as "report" or "indicate" will first be assumed by readers to be the direct object of the verb. If this hypothesis turns out to be false, as in clausal-complement sentences such as "The attendant indicated the main exit was blocked," then readers should be led up the garden path. The first experiment found no evidence for "garden-pathing" as a general rule. The second experiment showed that, when verbs were classified according to their dominant usage in direct-object versus clausal-complement constructions, garden-pathing did occur for direct-object expectation verbs. Thus, lexical information about the characteristic usage of a verb directs the parser's initial decisions, rather than a general parsing strategy such as minimal attachment. The third experiment indicated the possibility of individual differences in readers' susceptibility to garden-pathing.

INTRODUCTION

Identifying letters and words is but a small part of the reading process (though of course a critical one). Combining words into phrases, or syntactic parsing, is a further essential step on the way to comprehending written sentences. The active imposition of syntactic structure may be especially important in reading, since printed text lacks the prosodic information which presumably assists listeners to decide on phrasal groupings during spoken language understanding. The aim of the research described here is to shed some light on the use of syntactic knowledge in reading.

Recently, it has been suggested that parsing decisions during reading are guided by a set of general principles that operate when the reader is confronted with particular syntactic configurations (Fodor & Frazier, 1980; Frazier & Fodor, 1978). One of these principles is minimal attachment, according to which readers assign phrasal structure to a word string so that the "simplest" structure results. The best way to illustrate how this strategy might operate is with certain sentences that contain temporary structural ambiguities.

Take the sentence fragment: "A journalist reported the inquest's finding . . ." "The inquest's finding" can be either the direct object of the verb "reported," or the subject of a new clause which is itself the complement of the verb. Thus, there is either a transitive version: "A journalist reported the inquest's finding in today's paper," or a reduced clausal-complement version: "A journalist reported the inquest's finding was very wrong." Minimal attachment predicts that for structures like this readers do not wait to see how the sentence will develop, but instead commit themselves to a direct-object interpretation as soon as they encounter the noun phrase. Accordingly, subjects will be led up the garden path in cases where this interpretation turns out to be wrong, that is, in reduced complements.

In a study by Frazier and Rayner (1982), subjects' eye movements were monitored while they were reading sentences like these. Evidence for "garden-pathing" came from the finding of more regressive eye movements at the area of disambiguation for the reduced complement than the transitive sentences.

EXPERIMENT 1. "TRUE" GARDEN-PATHING?

The first experiment to be considered has already been described in Holmes, Kennedy, and Murray (in press). It was designed to assess a different possible explanation of the added complexity of reduced complement over transitive sentences. We included, as a baseline comparison, clausal-complement sentences containing the complementiser "that," for example: "A journalist reported that the inquest's finding was very wrong." In these cases, once the word "that" is followed by a word that cannot be integrated with it to form a noun phrase, minimal attachment is blocked straight away. However, we wondered whether such "that" complements might also require more processing than transitives, but for a different reason. Perhaps the additional set of sentential relations to be determined in both clausal-complement structures might add to processing complexity. If so, any "garden-pathing" obtained in reduced complement sentences might be more apparent than real.

Subjects in the experiment were 33 Scottish undergraduates, who were presented with 1 of the 3 structural versions from each of a set of 24 sentences constructed with complement verbs. The sentences were mixed in with a large number of fillers in a word-by-word self-paced reading task. Subjects pressed a button to display each word across the screen in a cumulative fashion. Each sentence was followed by a question requiring either a "yes" or a "no" answer. Statistical decisions in the experiment and in the following ones were based on a Type 1 error rate of 0.05.

Viewing times per word were averaged across several critical "zones." The results are shown in Fig. 26.1. An example sentence illustrating the words of each zone has been included in the figure. As would be expected, there were no differences between the three types at the noun phrase. However, at the point of disambiguation, the auxiliary, reduced complements produced longer viewing times than transitives. In a combined analysis of these two zones there was a significant interaction of zone and structural type, with min F' $(2,93) = 3.84$. Individual contrasts showed that readers' viewing times were slowed down in moving from the noun phrase to the disambiguating zone

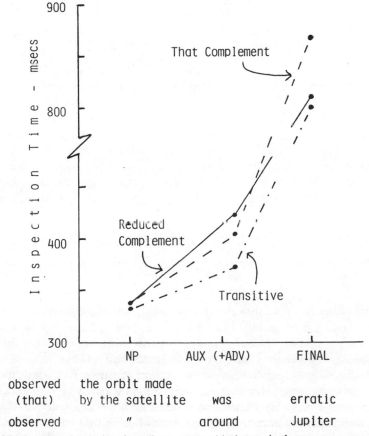

FIG. 26.1.   Mean inspection times (in msec) at critical zones in three sentence types.

APPR-T

more for the reduced complements than for the transitives, with min $F'(1,51) = 7.53$. Can this effect be attributed to garden-pathing as a result of the false application of minimal attachment? If it can, then the fact that the unambiguous "that" complements displayed a similar effect is difficult to understand. Readers were also slowed down in the disambiguating zone relative to the noun phrase for "that" complements compared with transitives, with $minF'(1,50) = 4.64$. In addition, there was no significant difference betwen the interaction pattern across zones for the reduced complements and the "that" complements, with $F_1(1,30) = 1.85$ and $F_2 < 1$.

The structural effects apparent at the final word were significant only by subjects, with $F_1(2,60) = 3.29$, and not by items, with $F_2(2,42) = 1.62$.

On the basis of these results, we attributed the greater complexity of *both* clausal-complement structures compared with the simple direct-object versions to the additional processing required for the handling of two clauses as opposed to just one.

EXPERIMENT 2: STRUCTURAL BIASES

Despite the preceding result, the search for the garden path was not abandoned. Previous work has pointed to the importance of preferences that different verbs have for appearing in particular syntactic environments (Fodor, 1978; Ford, Bresnan, & Kaplan, 1982; Holmes, 1984; Mitchell & Holmes, 1985). If complement verbs have structural biases, and readers make use of these biases in assigning structure to a sentence, then it could be that verbs which are used predominantly in clausal-complement constructions will *not* lead to inappropriate analyses during processing, but those that are used predominantly with a direct object may indeed produce garden-pathing. That is, it may be that not all complements are processed in the same way. Thus, the purpose of Experiment 2 was to examine systematically whether complement verbs have structural biases that determine parsing decisions. Further details about the experiment can be found in Holmes, Stowe, and Cupples (Note 2).

First of all, we pre-tested a large number of complement verbs for their structural biases in a paraphrasing task. Thirty-nine subjects were required to complete sentence fragments beginning "She believed ...," "He noticed ...," "They found ...," and so on. A large number of verbs that did not take clausal complements was included in the list. These continuations showed that some complement verbs were not strongly biased to one structure over the other. However, we were able to select 16 verbs that take as complement a direct object much more often than a clause, such as "hear," "read," and "answer," and 16 verbs that are followed by a clause more often than a direct object, such as "claim," "know," and "believe." The verbs are listed in the Appendix. Using these verbs we constructed pairs of "that" and reduced clausal-complement sentences. An example using a noun-phrase (NP) bias verb is: "The reporter saw (that) her friend was not succeeding"; and an example using a "that" bias verb is: "The candidate doubted (that) his sincerity would be appreciated."

We again presented the subjects with sentences mixed in with a large number of other kinds of constructions in a word-by-word self-paced reading task. Words were presented cumulatively as before, but this time the subject had to decide whether the sentence continued grammatically or not. On half the trials, sequences that contain a grammatical violation or were grammatically incomplete were presented (e.g. "The teapot smashed into," "John brought that the," "I can't remember if the firm that I hired Liz for as an accountant." Subjects were 48 native speakers of Australian English drawn from the general population of University of Melbourne students.

The viewing times in the critical regions after the main verb in the sentences containing NP bias verbs are shown in Fig. 26.2. The times were analysed separately for each zone. First of all, there was no significant difference between the two sentence types at the determiner, with $F_1(1,44) = 2.07$ and $F_2(1,12) = 1.81$. For these verbs, both minimal attachment and the structural expectation hypothesis predict that an NP will occur here, so a determiner is a perfectly acceptable category. There was a small difference at the noun, with the reduced complements taking 55msec longer to process than the unambiguous sentences. However, this was significant only by subjects, with $F_1(1,44) = 6.08$, and not by items, with $F_2(1,12) = 2.85$. More importantly, on reaching the auxiliary in the reduced complement versions, subjects paused for 403msec longer than in the unambiguous versions! This was significant, with $minF'(1,24) = 30.58$. This is, of course, the point of disambiguation for the reduced complements. The enormous magnitude of the effect shows quite clearly how far subjects have been led up the garden path.

There were no significant carry-over effects by the second word of the verb phrase, with $F_1(1,44) = 2.91$ and $F_2(1,12) = 1.06$.

Is the garden-pathing support for minimal attachment or the structural expectation hypothesis? It is performance on the sentences with "that" bias verbs which should critically distinguish the two hypotheses. These data are shown in Fig. 26.3.

Inspection of Fig. 26.3 shows that, in contrast with the NP bias items, there was already a significant difference (61msec) between the two versions at the determiner, with $minF'(1,42) = 5.55$. The most reasonable way to explain this effect is by postulating that subjects were *not* expecting a noun phrase at that stage, but instead were expecting the complementiser "that." Hence, the absence of the complementiser immediately after these verbs resulted in longer processing time. This is a form of garden-pathing too, since

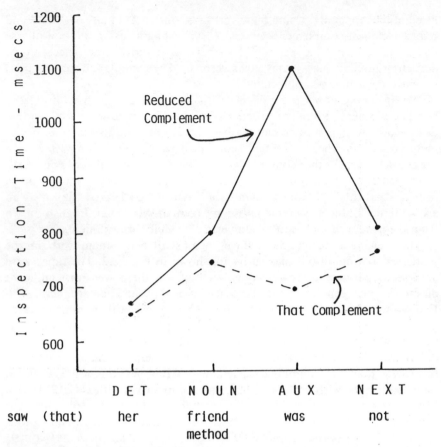

FIG. 26.2.   Mean inspection times (in msec) at critical regions in three sentence types containing NP bias verbs.

a structural expectation has been contradicted. The relatively small magnitude of the difference indicates that the garden-pathing is clearly much less devastating than that resulting when an NP expectation is disconfirmed. This would no doubt be due to the fact that a complementiser is not an essential, but only a likely, introduction to these clausal-complement sentences. Nevertheless, it is a critical result, because it does suggest that the order in which the structural hypotheses are tested is determined by the verb's predominant usage.

At the following noun, the ambiguous sentences were still taking longer to process, by 56msec, than the "that" complements: significant by subjects, with $F_1(1,44) = 4.85$, and by items, with $F_2(1,12) = 5.57$, though not jointly, with $minF'(1,40) = 2.59$. Perhaps this indicates a carry-over effect of the temporary garden-pathing at the determiner.

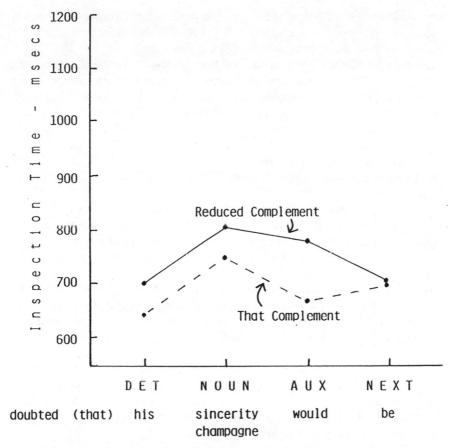

FIG. 26.3.   Mean inspection times (in msec) at critical regions in three sentence types containing "that" bias verbs.

At the point of disambiguation, the auxiliary, the difference increased to 110msec, a difference which was significant, with minF′(1,17)=4.84. How can this difference be explained? The additional time for the reduced complements may represent the extra processing necessary to reject the briefly adopted direct-object hypothesis and re-establish the clausal-complement hypothesis. Notice that this garden-pathing is still only one quarter the size of that obtained for the NP bias verbs. Re-establishing a structural option that has already been tested seems to be much less time-consuming than changing to an entirely new option.

By the next word in the verb phrase, both types were processed with equal ease, with both Fs < 1.

These results demonstrate quite clearly that, in this task, information contained in a verb's lexical entry about its preferred environments *is* used to guide subjects' structural analyses. This type of lexical information has not previously been incorporated in models of parsing.

This raises the question as to whether the same structural biases were operating in the previous experiment, but the effect was masked because a mixture of NP bias and clausal-complement bias verbs was used. Any verbs used in the previous experiment for which norms were not available were included in a new list of sentence fragments, again mixed in with fragments containing noncomplement verbs. A further 39 subjects provided sentence continuations. From the 24 items, 9 with NP bias and 10 with clausal-complement bias verbs were identified. These verbs thus classified are listed in the Appendix.

The viewing times of sentences with the two different types of verb are shown in Table 26.1. Post hoc item analyses were carried out on the data for each zone. There were no significant effects of structure at all at the NP for either sentence type (both $Fs_2 < 1$). However, at the disambiguating zone, reduced complements with NP bias verbs *were* read for significantly longer (80msec per word) than the corresponding "that" complements, with $F_2(1,16) = 12.75$. This is exactly what the structural expectation hypothesis would predict. The effect carried over somewhat into the last word, but owing to the greater variability, the difference there was not significant, with $F_2 < 1$.

For the "that" bias verbs, at the disambiguating zone, "that" complements took 21msec per word *longer* to read than reduced complements. However, being of much smaller magnitude, the difference failed to reach significance, with $F_2(1,18) = 1.34$. Again, the difference between the two types at the final word was not significant ($F_2 < 1$).

TABLE 26.1
Mean Reading Times (in Msec) for Sentence Zones as a Function of Verb Bias in Experiment 1

	NP	Aux (+ Adv)	Final
NP Bias Verbs (n = 9)			
Transitive	324	375	775
"That" Complement	332	389	835
Reduced Complement	347	469	879
"That" Bias Verbs (n = 10)			
Transitive	322	366	779
"That" Complement	333	419	877
Reduced Complement	330	398	841

On the basis of these post hoc tests, it would seem hard to argue that both groups of sentences were acting in a uniform manner. The data are entirely consistent with the idea that structural biases within the verbs *were* determining the performance of our Scottish subjects. Obviously, this effect was obscured when an average was taken across both types of item.

EXPERIMENT 3: INDIVIDUAL DIFFERENCES

The final experiment aimed to see whether there might be individual differences in the way in which syntactic strategies are used by adults when reading. The experiment comes from a study conducted by one of my graduate students, Linda Cupples (Cupples, Note 1).

University of Melbourne undergraduate students were classified as good or average comprehenders on the basis of their accuracy at answering factual questions after reading each of a number of paragraph-length passages. From their passage reading speeds, these groups were further divided into fast and slow readers. There were 18 subjects in each group.

We had examples of all three sentence types that have been discussed: transitives, "that" complements, and reduced complements; and used two reading tasks. For each task, there were four sets of sentences, matched on character length and frequency of content words. Unfortunately, at this stage we were not aware of the importance of the verbs' structural biases, so the sentences did not take this factor into account. Nevertheless, the results are still very informative.

The two tasks we used were as follows. In one, subjects read a series of individual sentences and answered a simple question about each one directly afterwards. They were to do this as quickly and as accurately as possible. In the other, they made a grammaticality judgement about the whole sentence as quickly as possible. Distractors were ungrammatical sequences.

Figure 26.4 shows the mean reading times for the test sentences in the question-answering task for the four groups of readers. It can be seen that enough NP-bias verbs were apparently used in the reduced complement sentences to produce garden-pathing, but it occurred only for some of the groups.

Relative to the amount of variation, the best readers (the fast good) showed little garden-pathing, taking 169msec longer to read reduced than "that" complements. This difference was not significant, with both Fs < 1. This is not to say that a more on-line measure might not detect reliable evidence of complexity for these readers. Nonetheless, the lack of significant structural effects for these readers may mean that they do not use a "predictive" strategy based on probable structures, but instead wait, and make use of *all* the structural information as it comes in, in a rapid, efficient

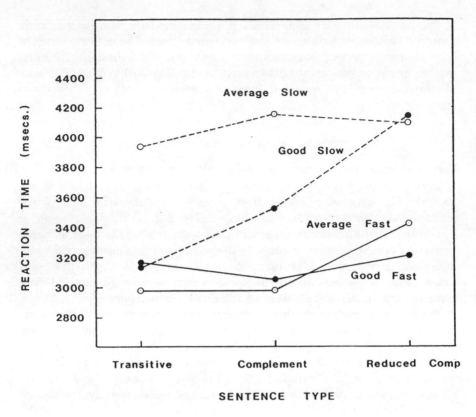

FIG. 26.4.   Mean sentence reading times (in msec) for three sentence types and four reader groups.

manner. The worst readers (the slow average) showed no garden-pathing at all, with a reverse effect of 60msec (both Fs < 1). But this was by no means due to their efficiency as readers. Rather, they read all sentences extremely slowly. Their insensitivity to structure may reflect the fact that they make very little use of syntactic cues, and rely more on word meanings to achieve a representation of the sentence.

Only the two intermediate groups read reduced complements significantly more slowly than their unambiguous counterparts. The slow good readers took 621msec longer to read reduced than "that" complements, with min F′ $(1,29) = 5.55$. The difference for the fast average readers was 449msec, significant by subjects, with $F(1,68) = 6.22$, and by items with $F(1,9) = 5.44$, though not jointly, with minF′$(1,29) = 2.90$. Like the readers in the previous experiments, these two groups often seemed to be using a strategy of committing themselves to an incorrect structure before they had finished reading the sentence.

The same pattern of differences as a function of reader group emerged in the grammaticality classification task, this time in the percentage of errors the subjects made. The values are shown in Fig. 26.5. Not one of the unambiguous "that" complements was misclassified. In addition, the best readers (the fast good) made relatively few errors on the reduced complements; only 6.9%. This difference was not significant, with $F_1(1,68) = 3.63$ and $F_2(1,9) = 2.73$. Similarly, the worst readers (the slow average) made only 4.2% errors on these sentences, with $F_1(1,68) = 1.35$ and $F_2(1,9) = 1.01$. But the slow good and the fast average readers mistakenly classified these sentences as ungrammatical much more often. For the slow good readers, the rate was 14.8%, which was significant, with $minF'(1,26) = 7.16$, and for the fast average readers, the rate was 17.1%, which was also significant, with $min F'(1,26) = 9.56$. These effects would presumably result from readers being so firmly committed to a direct-object analysis that they were not even aware that the succeeding disambiguating information could be used to create an

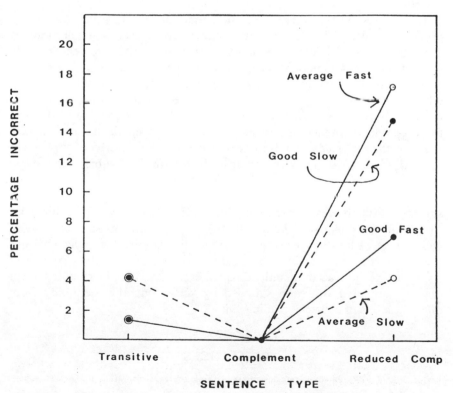

FIG. 26.5.   Mean percent grammaticality classification errors for three sentence types and four reader groups.

APPR–T*

alternative structure. In this task, these readers have not only been led up the garden path, they have got off the beaten track altogether!

CONCLUSION

These experiments have succeeded in clearing away at least some of the shrubbery from the sometimes hidden garden path. The results have shown that the way many people read sentences is influenced by information contained in a verb's lexical entry about its preferred structural environments. Frazier and Rayner's general parsing principle of minimal attachment makes no allowance for the use of this kind of lexical information. Furthermore, the results demonstrate that information about the verb's predominant usage is used *immediately* by the parser to create an initial structural hypothesis, rather than being used at some subsequent checking stage. To argue, for example, that the structural bias information acts to make the initial application of minimal attachment easier or harder seems difficult to sustain.

It is interesting that these conclusions may not apply to all reasonably proficient readers. The slow average readers may be relying much more on semantic than syntactic information to understand written sentences, while the fast good readers may be using syntactic cues, but not in a "predictive" way. Complement structures may not garden-path these readers for very different reasons. How, then, can the absence of garden-pathing in these reader groups be reconciled with the significant garden-pathing in the first two experiments? In fact, the best and worst readers were the hardest subjects to find in the final study, so it is quite possible that the majority of students in the first two experiments were similar to the intermediate subjects in the last experiment, who did actually show garden-pathing.

The results of the final experiment are important because they reveal substantial differences in processing strategies during reading within relatively skilled individuals. The fact that these differences exist in the way in which *syntactic* knowledge is used during reading is something which has not previously been given much consideration. Models of syntactic parsing will have to take into account individual differences, not only resulting from different lexical information supplied by verbs, but also stemming from different levels of subjects' reading skill.

REFERENCES

Fodor, J. D. (1978). Parsing strategies and constraints on transformations. *Linguistic Inquiry*, 9, 427–473.

Fodor, J. D. & Frazier, L. (1980). Is the human sentence parsing mechanism an ATN? *Cognition, 8*, 417–459.

Ford, M., Bresnan, J. W., & Kaplan, R. M. (1982). A competence-based theory of syntactic closure. In J. W. Bresnan (Ed.), *The mental representation of grammatical relations.* Cambridge, Mass.: M.I.T. Press.

Frazier, L. & Fodor, J. D. (1978). The sausage machine: A new two-stage parsing model. *Cognition, 6,* 291–325.

Frazier, L. & Rayner, K. (1982). Making and correcting errors during sentence comprehension: Eye movements in the analysis of structurally ambiguous sentences. *Cognitive Psychology, 14,* 178–210.

Holmes, V. M. (1984). Parsing strategies and discourse context. *Journal of Psycholinguistic Research, 13,* 237–257.

Holmes, V. M., Kennedy, A., & Murray, W. (in press). Syntactic structure and the garden path. *Quarterly Journal of Experimental Psychology.*

Mitchell, D. & Holmes, V. M. (1985). The role of specific information about the verb in parsing sentences with local structural ambiguity. *Journal of Memory and Language, 24,* 542–559.

REFERENCE NOTES

1. Cupples, L. (1986). *Individual differences in reading ability.* Unpublished Ph.D. thesis, University of Melbourne.
2. Holmes, V. M., Stowe, L., & Cupples, L. (in preparation). *Lexical expectations in processing structurally ambiguous sentences.*

APPENDIX

A. Verbs Used in Experiment 2

NP Bias: answer, expect, find, hear, judge, read, recognise, remember, repeat, see, show, teach, understand, urge, warn, write

"That" Bias: argue, believe, claim, confess, decide, deny, discover, doubt, explain, forget, known, learn, prove, realise, say, swear

B. Verbs Used in Experiment 1

NP Bias: accept, check, consider, disclose, hear, observe, observe, propose, understand

"That" Bias: believe, claim, deny, doubt, explain, known, learn, notice, predict, prove

27

Lexical Guidance in Human Parsing: Locus and Processin Characteristics

D. C. Mitchell
Department of Psychology
University of Exeter
Exeter, Devon, U.K.

ABSTRACT

Recent work has shown that parsing processes can be influenced by detailed information recovered from the lexicon (e.g. the subcategorisation class of verbs). However, it is not clear exactly how this effect is mediated. There has been an increasing tendency to distinguish between parsing submechanisms responsible for *proposing* new structures and those that are mainly concerned with *filtering or checking* the structures generated in this way. An experiment was therefore carried out to determine whether lexical effects exert their major influence during the first or second of these phases of parsing. The results indicated that the primary effect occurs at the second (checking) stage. Indeed, the data suggest that the first processor, using "rough and ready" procedures, may sometimes set about its task by proposing (and assembling words into) structures that are actually illegitimate, leaving the second processor to check the details, note the inconsistencies, and trigger the process of revising the structural interpretation of the sentence. The results of the experiment also throw light on the effects of text format or layout and suggest that parafoveal information may play a role in guiding the parsing process. The data are discussed in terms of a general model of parsing.

INTRODUCTION

In order to understand a passage of text, readers must do more than identify the individual words in the sentence. They must compute all the structural relationships between them. Part of the problem is to determine the role of words and word-strings within each sentence (i.e. to parse the sentence syntactically).

Recent work suggests that decisions of this kind are made in a two-phase process (see, for example, Crain & Steedman, 1985; Mitchell, Note 1; in press; Rayner, Carlson & Frazier, 1983). In the first stage, immediate information about words and their order is used to assign a preliminary structure to the phrase or clause under analysis. This is used as a temporary working hypothesis in the early stages of the construction process. In the second phase the initial structure is examined and tested to see whether it is compatible with information subsequently made available from other sources (e.g. structures assigned to word strings appearing earlier and later in the sentence; contextual, semantic, and pragmatic information; etc.). At this point a decision is made as to whether to *retain* the first hypothesis or to *drop* it and set about testing alternative structures. The two phases are represented schematically in Fig. 27.1, which is based on diagrams and descriptions used earlier by Mitchell (Note 1; in press). In this outline the first procedure is dubbed the director (or assembler) and the second is referred to as the monitor. Following conventions introduced previously (see Mitchell, 1982, pp. 141–142), circles represent computational procedures and rectangles temporary forms of storage. A double-headed arrow between a procedure and a store indicates that in performing its function the procedure has access to the source of information specified in the diagrams. Bold arrows identify

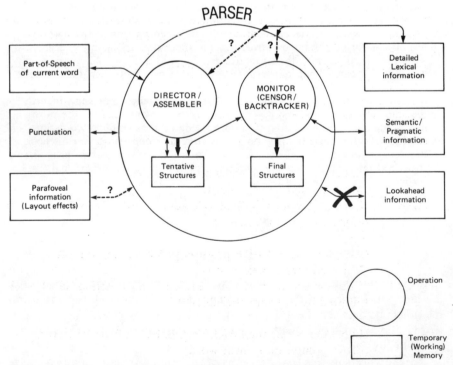

Fig. 27.1   Outline of a two-phase parser. See text for a description of the conventions used.

the stores used to hold the products of given procedures. (Experimental support for each of these links is outlined below. The tentative connections are the ones to be examined in the present study.)

This general framework offers a useful way of expressing many of the current questions and issues in work on parsing. However, it does not throw any light on the nature of the component procedures themselves. One way of doing this is to use the formalisms of production systems to describe the computations that may be carried out within each state. (It should be noted that the observations to follow are of a fairly general kind and could equally well be expressed in terms of ATNs, as used for example by Woods (1970), or in terms of connectionist devices, as formulated for example by Waltz and Pollack (1985). To this extent the elaboration of a single formalism simply serves to illustrate a general approach to the question of parsing.)

A production system consists of a set of primitive condition/action rules together with a protocol for applying those rules. Each production takes the general form PO.

(PO)   Condition (C)
            =>
            Action (A)

where C is a statement about the contents of a database and A is an operation or set of operations carried out on a second (possibly overlapping) database. For example, in the director, particular productions might be something like (DIR1), (DIR2), and (DIR3). (In order to simplify the present discussion, the conditions and actions in these examples are expressed in the form of informal verbal descriptions. A more rigorous presentation may be found in Anderson, Kline & Lewis, 1977.)

(DIR1)   (Current Setting = NP) & (Current Word = "the")
          =>
          (Label current word as definite article) &
          (Move pointer to next word)
(DIR2)   (Current Setting = VP) & (Current Word is a VERB—from information in the lexicon)
          =>
          (Attach word in VERB position in VP parsing tree) &
          (Move pointer to next word)
(DIR3)   (Current Setting = VP) & (Presence of a string labelled V followed by a string labelled NP)
          =>
          (Label the NP as the DIRECT OBJECT of the VERB) &
          (Move pointer on to next word)

In a system of this kind it is clear that the final products of the parsing process can be influenced only by those properties which appear within the condition expressions of one or more of the parsing productions. Thus, if we can establish that parsing is influenced by some property P of a sentence, then, within this framework, it follows that there must be at least one production with an expression containing P in its left-hand side. Conversely, if the structural analysis is entirely *unaffected* by manipulations of P, then it would seem likely that the system contains *no* productions which refer to this property. (In fact, there is an alternative possibility; that there *are* productions of this kind, but that they are not activated because they somehow fail to gain access to the fact that property P has been registered. Clearly, the preceding inference would not be justified in this case.) Using this approach the ultimate goal would be to set out a complete and detailed specification of the productions that are used in the various different stages of processing. At present this is not possible, since there are too many gaps in the data. However, existing empirical evidence *can* be used to tell us something about the kinds of production that would have to be incorporated in such a set. Some of this evidence is outlined in the next few paragraphs.

Factors Influencing Parsing

Punctuation.   There is some evidence that on-line parsing can be influenced by the insertion of commas into the material (e.g. Mitchell & Holmes, 1985; Mitchell, Note 1). These studies used materials which people tend to parse incorrectly on the first pass through the sentence. In such cases the mistakes often come to light within a few words and the readers pause detectably as they reinterpret the material. Psycholinguists often refer to the first part of this sequence of events by saying that the subjects are "led up the garden path."

In the studies mentioned above we were able to show that the normal "garden-path" effects could be eliminated if commas were displayed at appropriate points in the sentence. The most likely reason for this is probably that the subjects were able to use the punctuation marks to make the correct structural decision the first time, thereby avoiding garden-pathing at a later stage. However, alternative accounts based on influences on the monitoring process cannot be ruled out on current evidence.

Pragmatic and Contextual Information.   There is ample evidence that these factors can influence structural decisions in sentence comprehension. Minor changes in the context have been shown to influence the accuracy with which subjects are able to paraphrase sentences with certain kinds of local structural ambiguity (Rayner et al., 1983). Also the pragmatic context in which a sentence appears has been shown to influence the probability with which subjects get led up structurally induced garden paths (see, for example, Mitchell & Zagar, 1986; Tyler & Marslen-Wilson, 1977).

Lexical Information on Current Word.   We need not dwell on this for long since it is self-evident that at least *some* lexical information is used in parsing. If the identity of the words played no role at all in the process, then all N-word sentences would have to be parsed identically and this is obviously not the case.

Lookahead.   In contrast with information about the current word, there is *no* evidence that lexical information about future words has any effect on human parsing decisions. Subjects seem to be led up structural garden paths just as readily when lookahead information is available within the display as when it is not (Frazier & Rayner, 1982; Mitchell, Note 1; in press; Mitchell & Zagar, 1986).

From this evidence we can conclude that in order to parse sentences during reading there must be productions that direct operations by testing for punctuation marks, productions that make use of pragmatic or contextual information, and, perhaps most obviously, productions that work on information recovered from the lexicon for each successive word of the text.

The present paper is concerned largely with the last form of analysis and, in particular, with the use made of different categories of information from this source. Investigators typically distinguish between several different kinds of information which might be recovered from the lexicon. These include (at least) part-of-speech of the word, more detailed syntactic information (e.g. with verbs—whether they can take direct objects, various complement structures, etc.), semantic information, the accepted pronunciation of a word, its normal spelling, etc. It is quite conceivable that the parser only checks and uses one or two features from this rather complex representation. For example, it might only refer to part-of-speech, or perhaps to syntactic information generally, and ignore all other information presented to it.

In fact, the evidence suggests that whatever information is used it is *not* restricted to part-of-speech alone. Several studies using sentences with local structural ambiguity have shown that readers' biases between alternative structural interpretations can often be changed or reversed if a major verb in the sentence is replaced by another. This has been demonstrated when subjects make off-line judgements about their preferences (Ford, Bresnan, & Kaplan, 1982), when a secondary task is used to measure the relative ease of processing associated with alternative continuations of the sentence (Clifton, Frazier, & Connine, 1984), and when garden-path effects are used to highlight choices that people make while interpreting sentences in self-paced reading tasks (Mitchell & Holmes, 1985). Since this establishes that the structural interpretation of a sentence can be altered by changing the verb, it follows that one or other of the phases of parsing must make use of information that is not shared by both verbs (e.g. subcategorisation or semantic information). At the moment it is not entirely clear whether this detailed information is used by the director, by the monitor, or by both sub-processes separately. To date, most investigators have opted for explanations of the first kind, i.e. accounts in which the lexical information is used to guide the initial course of processing. Thus, Ford et al. (1982) proposed that material recovered from the lexicon specifies: (1) what kinds of structural frame the verb can legitimately enter; and (2) the "strength" or "salience" of each alternative. When the word is encountered the most salient structure is set up as a preliminary working hypothesis. The reader then tries to interpret the remainder of the sentence in terms of this framework. If this is feasible, the initial form is taken as the intended structure of the sentence. Otherwise the parser goes on to consider the strongest remaining hypothesis and proceeds either until an acceptable analysis is discovered or until the complete set of hypotheses has been exhausted (in which case the analysis fails). According to this model, then, the detailed lexical information is used to guide the *initial* choice of parsing hypothesis, and not to assess the viability of this choice in the second phase of processing. Similar explanations have been considered, with differing degrees of favour, by Clifton et al. (1984) and by Mitchell and Holmes (1985).

Despite the attention given to this hypothesis there is nothing in the literature to indicate that lexical effects are restricted to the first phase of processing. In fact, in another rather different form of syntactic processing (assigning fillers to gaps), Frazier, Clifton, and Randall (1983) have presented evidence that people use verb control information to *evaluate* preliminary structural hypotheses rather than to direct the course of processing in the first place. Also, a recent study by Mitchell (Note 1) suggests that similar effects might occur in sentence structures similar to those used earlier by Mitchell and Holmes (1985) and several other investigators. The materials were like (1a) and (1b):

1a. After the audience had applauded the actors sat down for a well-earned drink.
1b. After the audience had departed the actors sat down for a well-earned drink.

The effect of verb guidance was shown by the fact that subjects took significantly longer to process the material after the word "actors" in (1a) than in (1b). This was taken as evidence that the readers were garden-pathed in (1a) because they initially took the NP "the actors" to be the direct object of the first verb, rather than as the subject of the main clause. The absence of a comparable effect in (1b) suggests that the alternative verb "departed" (and particularly information about its preferred intransitivity) may have been used to prevent subjects from assigning the wrong role to the potentially ambiguous noun phrase. The suggestion that this guiding effect occurs in the monitor rather than in the director comes from the finding that the reading time for the first part of the sentence (up to and including "the actors") was significantly longer in (1b) than in (1a). This suggests that the subjects may have initially tried to interpret the noun phrase as the direct object of the first verb, even though this interpretation is not compatible with the bias introduced by the verb itself. If this is correct, it implies that the verb has its effect at a relatively late stage of processing—after the preliminary structural choice has been made—and presumably this could be the result of some kind of evaluative process in the monitor.

However, there are grounds for expressing reservations about this conclusion. In particular, the experiment just reported was not designed with the prior intention of making comparisions between the first parts of the two types of sentence. The comparison was made using a *planned* rather than an *unplanned* statistical test, and would not have reached significance if a more appropriate post-hoc technique had been used. Secondly, no attempt was made to match the properties of the alternative words (e.g. frequency, length, etc.) and it is possible that the differences can be attributed to variations at this level rather than to changes in syntactic processing. Finally, not all of the verbs in the "intransitive" condition were words that are invariably intransitive. Instead, in some cases, the intransitive usage was signalled by the fact that the noun phrase following the verb was not compatible with its alternative transitive form (as in the partial sentence "Just as the guards shouted the intruder . . ."). In these cases the increased difficulty in reading the partial sentence could have been attributed, not to a lexical effect in the monitor, but to a *clash* between a preliminary (transitive) choice made by the director and the fact that the following noun phrase turns out to be one that is not a legitimate direct object for the transitive form of the verb. In short, the presence of "optionally" intransitive words in the material makes the interpretation of the data somewhat ambiguous. The present experiment was carried out with a new set of materials so that each of these problems could be avoided.

EXPERIMENT

The main change in the present experiment was that the "intransitive" verbs were genuinely intransitive and that the two alternative verbs were matched for frequency and length. In addition to this, two new manipulations were introduced to investigate some of the nonlexical factors which might guide the process of parsing. The first of these concerns the effect of partitioning the sentence in different ways in the subject-paced reading task. This allows us to ask whether the parsing process is influenced in any way by the segmentation of the material. The alternative segmentation points are indicated by the oblique lines in Table 27.1, which presents a summary of the various sentence types used in the study.

The second change involved inserting a propositional phrase at the end of the preposed clause as in sentence types 3 and 4 in Table 27.1. Since prepositional phrases are not normally interposed between transitive verbs and their direct objects, it was assumed that the presence of such a phrase immediately after an optionally transitive verb would act as a clear signal that the verb was being used intransitively. If so, the prepositional phrase should serve to mark the end of the preposed clause just as a comma does when inserted in the same position. On this hypothesis, prepositional phrases might be used to guide the parsing process and avoid the garden-pathing that tends to occur when the clause boundaries are not marked in any way.

TABLE 27.1
A Sample of the Experimental Materials Used in the Study

Type 1—First Verb Intransitive: No Prepositional Phase
After the child had sneezed / the doctor // prescribed a course of injections.

Type 2—First Verb Optionally Transitive: No Prepositional Phrase
After the child had visited / the doctor // prescribed a course of injections.

Type 3—First Verb Intransitive: Prepositional Phrase Included
After the child had sneezed during surgery / the doctor // prescribed a course of injections.

Type 4—First Verb Optionally Transitive: Prepositional Phrase Included
After the child had visited during surgery / the doctor // prescribed a course of injections.

NOTE: On half of the trials the first display consisted of the words up to the single oblique line (/) while in the remainder the double line (//) marked the division between the two displays.

Method

Materials

The basic materials consisted of 24 sentences between 12 and 15 words long (see Appendix). Each sentence consisted of a preposed subordinate clause followed by a main clause starting with a noun phrase. Given the left context alone this noun phrase was structurally ambiguous: It could either be interpreted as the object of the subordinate clause or as the subject of the main clause. In every case, however, the material *following* the ambiguous phrase established the latter reading as the correct one. The sentences were constructed in such a way that two alternative verbs could be used in the subordinate position and the resulting sentences were fully plausible in both cases. In one condition the verbs were strictly intransitive (according to the classification used by the Concise Oxford Dictionary). In the other case the verb was one that could either be used transitively or intransitively and in every case here the following noun phrase was fully compatible with the transitive form. Overall, the verbs were matched for length and word frequency (mean lengths—7.50 and 7.38 letters for optional and intransitive words respectively: mean frequency—16.58 and 18.54 per million, respectively, using the Kučera and Francis [1967] norms).

In half of the conditions these sentences were presented in this basic form (cf. type 1 and type 2 sentences in Table 27.1). In the rest (types 3 and 4) a temporal prepositional phrase (PP) was added at the end of the subordinate clause.

Each sentence was displayed in two parts. On half of the trials the segmentation point coincided with the clause boundary (marked by the single oblique line in Table 27.1). On the remainder, the first display took in the potentially ambiguous noun phrase as well as the subordinate clause. Apart from the full-stop at the end of the sentence there was no punctuation in any of the conditions.

In addition to these experimental materials there were 36 filler sentences with a variety of syntactic structures. Twelve of these were followed by simple yes/no comprehension questions to encourage subjects to focus on the meanings of the sentence. The order of the experimental sentences and the foils was randomised separately for each session subject to the constraint that each test sentence was followed by either one or two fillers. In addition, the first five trials of each session were always occupied by fillers.

Procedure

The sentences were presented in a subject-paced reading task on a Microvitec CUB display unit controlled by a BBC B microcomputer. Each trial was preceded by the prompt "Press SPACE BAR" which appeared half-way down the screen. When the subject pressed the space bar the prompt was immediately replaced by the first display of the sentence. This and all subsequent displays of materials were left-justified and appeared half-way down the screen. Subjects were instructed to press the space bar again when they had read the first display. On doing this the first segment was immediately replaced by the second display of the sentence. On filler trials with comprehension probes the second part of the sentence was followed by a 1sec display of the word "Question" and this, in turn, was followed by the (unpartitioned) comprehension question itself. Subjects were required to answer this as rapidly as possible by pressing the Y or N keys (for yes or no). When they did this the prompt for the next trial appeared and the cycle continued. The computer recorded the response time to each segment of the sentence, the time taken to answer the question (if there was one), and the key pressed in each case.

Each subject saw all 24 test sentences. For half of these they saw the version in which the subordinate verb could either be transitive or intransitive. Six of these sentences were presented with a PP at the end of the first clause (type 4) and six were presented *without* such phrases (type 2). In the other 12 sentences the intransitive verb was used. Again, half of the sentences included a PP (type 3) and half did not (type 1). In half of each of the four types of sentence, the first display ended at the point marked (/) (i.e. at the end of the subordinate clause). In the rest, the following two words—up to the mark (//)—were also included in the first display. All conditions were counterbalanced over the entire experiment so that each sentence appeared in each of the eight different experimental forms for three different subjects. The main experimental session was preceded by a short practice session which was intended to clarify the procedure for the subjects. The filler sentences at the beginning of the main experimental session provided a further opportunity for practice.

Subjects

These were 13 female and 11 male undergraduates from the University of Exeter pool of volunteers. They had not previously participated in any similar experiments.

Results and Discussion

The results are shown in Table 27.2.

The viewing times for the various displays were submitted to a four-factor repeated measures ANOVA with verb type, segmentation position, sentence structure, and display (first or second) as fixed factors and subjects (or materials) as a random effect. Almost all of the significant effects can be accounted for directly by variations in display size in the different conditions and a more informative analysis, in terms of planned comparisons, is presented under the series of headings below. However, for the record, the significant effects were as follows: (1) *Main Effects*: display (MinF' $(1,46) = 5.26$, $P < 0.05$); segmentation position (MinF' $(1,36) = 6.87$, $P < 0.05$); and structure (MinF' $(1, 46) = 15.52$, $P < 0.001$); (2) *2-Way Interactions*: display × segmentation position (MinF' $(1,42) = 28.2$, $P < 0.001$); display × structure (MinF' $(1,48) = 35.8$, $P < 0.001$); (3) *Higher-Order Interactions*: display × segmentation position × verb (MinF' $(1,46) = 7.91$, $P < 0.05$); and, finally, the interaction of all four factors (MinF' $(1,46) = 4.81$, $P < 0.05$).

TABLE 27.2
Results of the Experiment

Sentences Without Prepositional Phrases

	Display Segmentation Point			
	At Clause Boundary		*After Clause Boundary*	
Verb Type:	*Intransitive*	*Transitive*	*Intransitive*	*Transitive*
Display 1	2249	2146	3449	2740
Display 2	2844	3001	2354	3346
Total	5093	5147	5803	6086

Sentences With Prepositional Phrases

	Display Segmentation Point			
	At Clause Boundary		*After Clause Boundary*	
Verb Type:	*Intransitive*	*Transitive*	*Intransitive*	*Transitive*
Display 1	3182	3326	4037	4890
Display 2	2918	2949	2263	2750
Total	6100	6275	6300	7640

NOTE: Mean viewing times (in msec) for the first and second displays of sentences with transitive or intransitive subordinate verbs. The results are given separately for the partitioning conditions in which the display segmentation coincided with the clause boundary and those in which it came after the noun phrase following the boundary. The top half of the table gives the data for sentences without prepositional phrases at the end of the preposed clauses and the bottom half gives the corresponding data for sentences *with* prepositional phrases.

1. Sentences Without Prepositional Phrases

a. In these sentences, subjects were garden-pathed by displays containing a transitive verb followed by an NP which initially appeared to be its object. The evidence for this is that the mean viewing time for segments *following* such displays (3346msec) was 992msec longer than the reading time for comparable displays following segments with intransitive verbs plus NPs (2354msec). This effect was significant as a planned comparison (MinF' $(1,43) = 6.93$, $P < 0.025$). Following earlier work, this result is taken as evidence that subjects, on reading structures of the form $(..v.i.—NP..)$, correctly interpret the NP as the subject of the main clause and consequently have little difficulty in interpreting the following display when it goes on to confirm this hypothesis. With the pattern $(..v.t.—NP..)$, however, they initially treat the NP as the direct object of the verb and the result is that they have to spend a considerable amount of time reinterpreting the sentence when they come to the second display

b. Displays containing sequences of the form (.. v.i.—NP ..) are harder to read than displays containing strings like (.. v.t.—NP ..). The mean viewing times were 3449 and 2740msec, respectively, and this 709msec difference was significant as a planned comparison (MinF' $(1,43) = 4.10$, $P < 0.05$). This replicates the result reported earlier by Mitchell (Note 1) and confirms that the earlier finding cannot be dismissed simply on the grounds that the "intransitive" verbs used in the previous study were not strictly intransitive.

c. Nor can the result in 1a be attributed entirely to differences in the reading times for the *verbs* themselves, because the effect is significantly reduced when the NP is excluded from the first display. The relevant viewing times were 2249msec (for intransitive verbs) and 2146msec (for transitive verbs)—a difference which does not approach significance (F1, F2 < 1). More important, an interaction contrast showed that the reduction of this verb effect relative to that in 1a was significant—at least by subjects (F1 $(1,22) = 5.06$, $P < 0.05$; F2 = 3.82, $0.05 < P < 0.1$). The implications of these findings will be discussed after the remaining results have been presented.

2. Sentences with Prepositional Phrases (PPs)

a. Previous work has shown that with suitable punctuation it is possible to avoid garden-path effects such as those in 1a. For example, if a comma is placed between the verb and the NP (as in "After the child had visited, the doctor ..."), then the garden-path effect is eliminated (Mitchell, Note 1). Does the same thing happen when a PP is inserted in this position? The quick answer is .. No. A direct comparison (corresponding to the 3346/2354 contrast in 1a) shows that the difference between 2750msec (in the transitive condition) and 2263msec (intransitive) is still statistically reliable (F1 $(1,22) = 4.80$; F2 $(1,22) = 4.79$; $P < 0.05$, in each case) and so it is clear that the PP, unlike a comma, does not entirely rule out garden-pathing.

b. If the PP fails to mark the end of the first clause then the sentences with PPs should produce processing problems similar to those outlined earlier. A new comparison (corresponding, in effect, to the 3449/2740 contrast in 1b) shows that there *was* a verb effect, but in the *opposite* direction to that in 1b (4037msec for intransitive verbs, 4890msec for transitive verbs: MinF' $(1,40) = 4.21$, $P < 0.05$). A speculative interpretation of this result is that the PP *does* cause the reader to close the clause but that this decision is rather tentative and is reversed when an NP (an apparently acceptable direct object) is found at the end of the display in the transitive condition.

c. As before, we can rule out the suggestion that this difference is a purely *lexical* effect resulting from the use of different verbs. A contrast comparable to the 2249/2146 difference in 1c showed that, in sentences with PPs, the viewing time for displays without NPs was slightly (but nonsignificantly) *shorter* for intransitive verbs (3182msec) than for transitive verbs (3326msec): F1, F2 < 1. Overall, it seems that the two sets of verbs were well matched and were not responsible for differences at the level of lexical processing.

This provides further support for the view that explanations of the difference outlined in 1b must be sought primarily at the structural or syntactic level of processing.

3. Segmentation Effects

Several of the basic results were substantially influenced by the manner in which the sentences were partitioned into displays.

a. The garden-path effects in 1a and 2a were specific to the conditions in which the ambiguous NP appeared at the end of the first display. When it was shifted to the beginning of the second display, the garden-path effect disappeared. In contrast with the earlier results, viewing time for display 2 was no greater in the transitive condition than the intransitive condition (3001msec vs. 2844msec for sentences *without* PPs; 2949msec vs. 2918msec for sentences *with* PPs: F1, F2 < 1, in both cases). These results suggest that garden-path effects can be eliminated by suitable segmentation of the material.

b. Other results highlight the role of segmentation in this study. The total time required to read sentences (i.e. viewing time for display 1 plus that for display 2) was markedly affected by whether the sentence was split *before* or *after* the ambiguous NP. For example, after averaging over verb-type, the sentences without PPs were read 825msec faster when the split occurred in the first position rather than the second (5120msec vs. 5945msec: MinF' $(1,44) = 5.85$, $P < 0.025$). Similar effects occurred in sentences *with* PPs, particularly in the transitive verb condition where the corresponding difference was 1365msec in the same direction (6275msec vs. 7640msec: MinF' $(1,33) = 5.37$, $P < 0.05$).

4. Recap and Interpretation

a. The garden-path effect in 1a and in earlier studies is taken as evidence that, in the absence of clear structural cues such as punctuation and display segmentation, subjects tend to interpret a (. . v.t.—NP . .) sequence as a verb plus its direct object. If this interpretation is wrong (as it frequently was in the present experiment) then the reader has to spend time revising this decision in the second display.

b. In 1b it was shown that sequences of the form (. . v.i.—NP . .) are more difficult to process than (. . v.t.—NP . .) sequences and this difference cannot be attributed to the lexical properties of the two different types of verb (1c and 2c). Various alternative interpretations of this effect are possible, but some of the more obvious proposals can be ruled out on the basis of previous evidence. One hypothesis is that the difference occurs because the intransitive condition involves end-of-clause processing whereas the transitive condition does not. However, this explanation is unsatisfactory because there is no comparable effect in transitive material when a comma is used to force clausal processing (see Mitchell, Note 1, for details). Similarly, there is no reason to suspect that the structure involving early closure is somehow more difficult to propose or assemble than the alternative "S-V-O" structure favoured by the transitive verb. As argued in detail earlier (Mitchell, Note 1), the most likely explanation of the effect seems to be that the director is "blind" to detailed lexical information such as that concerning transitivity and that it assigns the tentative structure "S-V-O" to the display irrespective of the properties of the verb. This account is elaborated in the General Discussion.

c. The insertion of a PP after the first verb apparently does *not* cause readers to close the first clause as they do when a comma is used to mark this position (see 2a). However, the PP does have *some* effect (see 2b). A possible interpretation of the data is that the PP acts as a weak signal for closure and that readers respond tentatively to this at first, but then revise the decision when further information arrives.

d. Processing is strongly influenced by the way in which sentences are segmented (see section 3). The overall pattern of results can be explained reasonably well if it is assumed that at choice points the parser makes use of the presence (or absence) of display information which is still to be processed. When the display ends at a potential clause boundary the *absence* of printed material to the right of this point may cause the parser to close the clause *immediately*, with the result that the NP at the beginning of the following display is directly interpreted as the subject of the main clause, avoiding all garden-pathing. Where such information is *present*, the bias appears to be to keep the clause open even for materials in which this leads to considerable processing difficulty (e.g. when an NP follows an intransitive verb or a PP, both of which would ordinarily signal that the clause has ended).

GENERAL DISCUSSION

The results of this experiment allow us to refine the description of parsing put forward in Fig. 27.1. First, the data confirm that at least part of the effect of detailed lexical information must be introduced in the monitor. If the verb information had been used in full by the director, this device would immediately have been able to assign the appropriate structure to the NP in the critical "v.i.—NP" sequences used here. The fact that these materials introduced processing difficulties suggests that this did not happen.

The data therefore suggest that only part of the information from the lexicon is passed on to the director. The indications are that this sub-sample may be restricted to the "part-of-speech" of the word under examination. Other potentially relevant information (e.g. more detailed syntactic information, semantic specification of the word) is apparently either not made available to the director or, alternatively, cannot be used by this device (perhaps because it includes no productions which can be activated by such information). Thus, we are proposing that when the parser comes across a verb, it picks up just the label "V" and uses this to carry out preliminary operations either to look out for a noun phrase to take as its direct object (in a top-down analysis) or to allow such a structure to be attached to it (again as a direct object) once it has been discovered following routine bottom-up analysis. Since the director is apparently "blind" to any other information about the verb, this occurs even when the verb is strictly intransitive and cannot legitimately take a direct object. In other words, by operating in a "short-sighted" fashion, it seems that the director may actually assemble a structure which would never be acceptable in English. It is left to the monitor to detect the mistake. Presumably this device is capable of doing so because it is fed with the additional lexical information required to disqualify the structural candidate offered by the director. However, at this point a structure has already been built and the need to destroy it (and to prompt the director to generate another proposal) takes an appreciable time, which explains the pattern of results obtained in the experiment.

Turning to a second issue considered in this paper, the effects of processing a prepositional phrase were rather uncertain. While the PP is not totally ignored by the parser, it apparently does not act like a comma and provide a clear signal that the preposed clause has ended. At best it seems to act as a weak and tentative cue to segmentation.

In contrast, there was clear evidence that parsing is influenced by the layout or format of the material. The most obvious interpretation of the data seems to be this: At potential clause boundaries, the director has the option of closing the current clause immediately or of testing the following phrase to determine whether that should also be incorporated into the first clause. The data can be explained if we assume that the director adopts the first strategy if the display ends at this point (i.e. if there is no further unprocessed parafoveal information to the right of the potential clause boundary). However, if there *is* such information, we assume that it selects the second option and proceeds to try to include this information in the existing clause. On this hypothesis, parafoveal information to the right of the fixation point would play a role in guiding the parsing process.

CONCLUSIONS

The present study suggests that we have to make two small changes to the model outlined in Fig. 27.1. First, we have to modify the double-headed arrows to indicate that detailed lexical information influences the monitor but not the director (on present evidence). Second, we have to introduce firm connections to show that the director is influenced by parafoveal information (layout effects). With respect to procedural descriptions of the sub-processes in terms of production rules, this implies that the director has no productions which are capable of testing (and using) detailed lexical information other than part-of-speech, but that is *does* have productions to test for the presence of parafoveal information and to use this information to terminate clauses. This takes us a step or two closer to our eventual goal of providing a detailed computational specification of the human parsing process.

ACKNOWLEDGEMENTS

I am grateful to Alan Garnham for useful comments at various stages of this work.

REFERENCES

Anderson, J. R., Kline, P. J., & Lewis, C. H. (1977). A production system model of language processing. In M. A. Just & P. A. Carpenter (Eds.), *Cognitive processes in comprehension*. Hillsdale, N. J. : Lawrence Erlbaum Associates Inc.

Clifton, C., Frazier, L., & Connine, C. (1984). Lexical and syntactic expectations in sentence comprehension. *Journal of Verbal Learning and Verbal Behavior, 23*, 696‑708.

Crain, S. & Steedman, M. (1985). On not being led up the garden path: The use of context by the psychological syntax processor. In D. R. Dowty, L. Karttunen, & A. M. Zwicky (Eds.), *Natural language parsing: Psychological, computational, and theoretical perspectives*. Cambridge: Cambridge University Press.

Ford, M., Bresnan, J. W. & Kaplan, R. M. (1982). A competence based theory of syntactic closure. In J. W. Bresnan (Ed.), *The mental representation of grammatical relations*. Cambridge, Mass.: M.I.T. Press.

Frazier, L., Clifton, C., & Randall, J. (1983). Filling gaps: Decision principles and structure in sentence comprehension. *Cognition, 13*, 187–222.

Frazier, L. & Rayner, K. (1982). Making and correcting errors during sentence comprehension: Eye movements in the analysis of structurally ambiguous sentences. *Cognitive Psychology, 14*, 178–210.

Kučera, H. & Francis, H. A. (1967). *A computational analysis of present-day American English*. Providence, R. I.: Brown University Press.

Mitchell, D. C. (1982). *The process of reading: A cognitive analysis of fluent reading and learning to read*. Chichester: John Wiley & Sons.

Mitchell, D. C. (in press). Reading and syntactic analysis. In J. Beech & A. Colley (Eds.), *Cognitive approaches to reading*. Chichester: John Wiley & Sons.

Mitchell, D. C. & Holmes, V. M. (1985). The role of specific information about the verb in parsing sentences with local structural ambiguity. *Journal of Memory and Language, 24*, 542–559.

Mitchell, D. C. & Zagar, D. (1986). Psycholinguistic work on parsing with lexical functional grammars. In N. E. Sharkey (Ed.), *Advances in cognitive science*. Chichester: Ellis Horwood.

Rayner, K., Carlson, M., & Frazier, L. (1983). The interaction of syntax and semantics during sentence processing: Eye movements in the analysis of semantically biased sentences. *Journal of Verbal Learning and Verbal Behavior*, 22, 358–374.

Tyler, L. K. & Marslen-Wilson, W. D. (1977). The on-line effects of semantic context on syntactic processing. *Journal of Verbal Learning and Verbal Behavior*, 16, 683–692.

Waltz, D. L. & Pollack, J. B. (1985). Massively parallel parsing: A strongly interactive model of natural language interpretation. *Cognitive Science*, 9, 51–74.

Woods, W. A. (1970). Transition network grammars for natural language analysis. *Communications of the ACM*, 13, 591–606.

REFERENCE NOTES

1. Mitchell, D. C. (1986). *On-line parsing of structurally ambiguous sentences: Evidence against the use of lookahead*. Submitted for publication.
2. Zagar, D. & Mitchell, D. C. (1986). *Characteristics of lexical guiding effects in parsing*. Submitted for publication.

APPENDIX

The sentences used in the experiment. The verb mentioned first can either be transitive or intransitive. The second verb (in brackets) is strictly intransitive according to the Concise Oxford Dictionary. The single and double oblique lines represent the alternative segmentation points (see Table 27.1 for details).

1. After the dog had stopped scratching (struggling) (this afternoon) / the vet // took off the muzzle.
2. As soon as the sheep had halted (strayed) (earlier today) / the dog // moved away to herd them in.
3. As soon as he had phoned (arrived) (last night) / his wife // started to prepare for the journey.
4. After the choirboy had practised (prayed) (last Saturday) / the choruses // were repeated to rehearse the changes.
5. After the telephonist had dialled (responded) (yesterday evening) / the caller // promptly hung up the phone.
6. After the small dog woke (yelped) (just now) / his owner // decided to put him outside for a while.
7. While all of the revellers cheered (gaped) (last night) / the girl // playfully removed her clothes.
8. After the dinner guests had eaten (gossiped) (this evening) / the desserts // were taken away by the waiters.
9. To stop the poodle biting (yapping) (last week) / the trainer // had to tug sharply at its lead.
10. Although her baby daughter kept clutching (squirming) (last Tuesday) / the woman // stayed until the end of the programme.
11. Shortly after the chairman rang (died) (last Friday) / his secretary // sent out letters to announce a new election.

12. After the young Londoner had visited (arrived) (on Sunday) / his parents // prepared to celebrate their anniversary.
13. Immediately before he interrupted (appeared) (at teatime) / the conversation // had been taking an interesting turn.
14. After the child had visited (sneezed) (during surgery) / the doctor // prescribed a course of injections.
15. After the bees had attacked (swarmed) (earlier on) / the beekeeper // decided to put on his mask.
16. After the private had saluted (fainted) (during exercises) / the sergeant // decided to end the military drill.
17. While the new employee was reversing (dozing) (during the journey) / the lorry // went out of control and overturned.
18. After the woman had dressed (slimmed) (on her holiday) / her children // behaved as if she was a stranger.
19. As the passenger sat contemplating (daydreaming) (during the flight) / the book // was stolen from her bag.
20. After the cock had woken (crowed) (early this morning) / the farmer // prepared to move the chicken shed.
21. While the prisoners were fighting (fasting) (last month) / the authorities // refused to discuss their grievances.
22. While the pensioner was decorating (gardening) (before lunch) / his kitchen // became more and more untidy.
23. While the bachelor sat smoking (musing) (yesterday evening) / his pipe // fell to the floor and started a fire.
24. After the customer had visited (complained) (last month) / the manager // changed the wording of the advert.

28 Syntactic Processing During Reading for Comprehension

Giovanni B. Flores d'Arcais
Max-Planck-Institut für Psycholinguistik
Nijmegen
and
Department of Psychology
University of Leiden
The Netherlands

ABSTRACT

The paper reports on a series of experiments on the comprehension of written sentences or passages of prose. The main question addressed concerns the amount of syntactic computation performed during reading, and the use of the results of this computation for comprehension of the written material.

The approach taken in the present study assumes that in normal fast reading the reader is likely to rely for comprehension on various heuristics, which allow a first and efficient use of the different cues available in the text. But if this is true, does the reader need to compute a full syntactic representation of the material read? It will be argued that during reading for comprehension the reader normally executes a full syntactic analysis of the material, although the system can rely on other sources of data for the comprehension process.

The position taken here distinguishes computation, that is, full processing of the various sources of information available in the text, from the use of this information for message interpretation. The paper offers some evidence on the notion that the results of the syntactic computation are redundant with respect to the use of this computation made during reading, and that they can be used as a kind of backup device when the text becomes difficult, incoherent, or pragmatically unplausible.

The first experiment provides evidence for the notion of automatic computation of the syntactic structure, which, however, does not seem to be fully exploited for text comprehension. The second experiment offers evidence favouring the hypothesis that the results of syntactic computation become more important with pragmatically unplausible texts. The third experiment shows that readers differ with regard to their sensitivity to the properties of the syntactic structure.

INTRODUCTION

This paper reports a series of experiments on the comprehension of written sentences or passages of prose, and examines how the syntactic properties of the text affect reading behaviour and text comprehension.

In reading a text for comprehension, the reader normally tries to get information as quickly and efficiently as possible. In many situations, such as when looking into a newspaper or browsing a book in order to be informed about the content quickly, readers may extract from the text a few words or phrases which, integrated with each other and related to readers' knowledge and expectations, are often enough to obtain the information wanted. Reading a book, a newspaper, or a journal to get relevant information is a very different activity from reading a sentence word-by-word or letter-by-letter during galley proofs correction.

Even in "normal" reading for comprehension, the reader is likely to shift several times along a continuum, ranging from a very rapid skimming through the text to close examination of a given passage or of a few words. This process is something like a kind of "zooming" in and out of the text. Whereas for a quick search through a page one is very likely to be guided by expectations about critical words and concepts, based on stored knowledge, on awareness of issues of current interest, etc., close examination of a passage might require a very careful and conscious analysis of various details of the passage capable of giving information about properties of the text, subtle intentions of the writer, etc.

It is therefore inappropriate to talk in general about *reading processes* or *reading strategies* tout court, disregarding the situation in which reading takes place, the type of material being read, and, most importantly, the primary purpose of reading. In other words, a theory of reading should take into account at least some ecological aspects of reading behaviour. In order to account for the variety of ways with which skilled readers rapidly explore a text, and at the same time explain how fine details of a text are noticed and interpreted, many of the available general models on reading would have to be modified or at least adjusted.

THE PROCESS OF READING FOR COMPREHENSION

Language comprehension during reading involves a series of complex processes, ranging from recognition of certain patterns in the printed material to the construction of an abstract representation containing most of the contents and the communicative intentions conveyed by the writer. Thus, comprehension of a text requires the construction of an internal representation of the meaning intended by the writer. This internal representation can be described as a set of abstract propositions. The process which eventually will produce this representation can be described and modeled in various ways, basically on two accounts. On the one side the reader would perform a full grammatical computation of the input by use of the rules of the grammar. At the other extreme the reader could get along with various parsing heuristics strategies of the type first proposed by Bever (1970). All models available within psycholinguistics and AI have been or are characterised by emphasis on one or the other of these two accounts, and can be located on a kind of continuum with these two possibilities as the extremes.

Thus, contemporary models on language comprehension include a broad range, from theories assuming exhaustive grammatical processing to models and theories which manage to get along with little or no grammatical computation at all. (See Flores d'Arcais & Schreuder, 1983, for a brief discussion and further references.) The idea of heuristic strategies as the essential devices in language comprehension has been central in various parsers, within cognitive psycholinguistics, linguistics, and AI (see Flores D'Arcais, in press), and has produced a large amount of interesting and "realistic" models of parsing. The heuristic strategies proposed range from the use of superficial properties of words at the surface level to deeper relations and even to heuristics based on rather distant elements of the sentence. Much research on parsing strategies during the last years has even focused on processing dependencies between input elements which may be rather distant.

A related and old question in psycholinguistic research is whether syntactic computation is obligatory or optional, or even whether it takes place at all. Again, the positions with respect to this question vary along a range of possibilities. Forster (1974) and Garrett (1976) argue that the syntactic structure of a sentence is always computed, even when the listener would be able to grasp the meaning of the sentences without it. On the other hand, other positions hold that syntactic computation is not a required stage in sentence processing: Bever (1970) argued that language users will rely on deep syntactic analysis only when sufficient semantic cues are not available; whenever possible, they will extract sentence meaning on the basis of relations directly available from lexical semantic constraints and surface structure. The amount of syntactic analysis required in other models is very small or practically nonexistent. For example, Wilks' (1978) translation program manages to operate without any syntax, all input being directly transformed into meaning structures. Other approaches, such as that of Riesbeck and Schanck (1978), try to reduce the amount of syntactic processing to a minimum.

According to some of these models, such as Riesbeck's (1982) or DeJong's (1979), in understanding a text such as a newspaper's article the readers use stored *scripts*. The processor in these cases looks in the text only at the few items which are needed to fill out some "sketchy scripts." For example, in reading in a paper a report of an earthquake, the understanding system looks for key words capable of giving information about the place, the severity on the Richter's scale, the amount of damage caused, and the number of casualties. Once the system has got this information out of a few words in the text, it constructs a full interpretation without getting involved further in detailed processing of the text.

Earlier work on comprehension of written language carried out with a variety of techniques (Flores d'Arcais, 1974; 1978; 1982; in press), in fact, showed that during language comprehension readers make use of a variety of strategies to get the meaning of a sentence or of a text passage in the most efficient and fastest possible manner. But if it is possible to get meaning out of a text without performing an exhaustive syntactic computation, why should the system not dispense with such computation at all?

THE PROBLEM

The main question addressed by the present study concerns the amount of syntactic computation performed during reading, and the use of the results of this computation for comprehension of the written material. It will be argued that during reading for comprehension the reader normally does compute syntactic analysis of the material, even if the comprehension system can rely on other sources of data for the comprehension process, such as on various heuristic strategies.

The position taken here will distinguish computation, that is, full processing of the graphemic, morphological, lexical, and syntactic information, from the use of this information for message interpretation. Computation is taken to be highly redundant, and normally the reader has available different sources of data for the interpretation of the message. I will offer some evidence on the notion that the results of the syntactic computation are redundant with respect to the use of this computation made during reading, and that they can be used as a backup device when the text becomes more difficult or the information conveyed is pragmatically incoherent.

THE EXPERIMENTS

How can we find out how much syntactic computation is performed during reading? One possibility is to introduce distortions and violations in the syntactic structure of a text, and see how these violations affect reading behaviour. This is the procedure chosen for the experiments reported in the present study.

Thus, a simple paradigm was used throughout. Various types of violations were introduced in sentences and texts, and the effects of the violations on reading behaviour, and the extent to which these violations were detected, were observed. The rationale underlying this procedure is very simple: To the extent to which a violation introduced at a given structural level in a text affects reading behaviour, it can be concluded that the reader dedicates some computational effort to the structural level in question. Thus, for example, if the presence of a semantic violation affects reading behaviour, we can conclude that the reader is busily interpreting the semantic representation of the sentence.

The violations introduced in the material were of the following types:

1. *Spelling errors or "printing" errors* of one of the words in the text, or use of a nonsense word, e.g. "The old lady spifted the white chair."

2. *Syntactic violations.* These were of various types, and consisted of violations of subcategorisation rules, e.g. "The old lady sat the white chair" (in which the appropriate preposition is omitted), other types of omission of a word, using an inappropriate preposition, etc.

3. *Semantic violations*, such as violations of selectional restrictions, e.g. "The old lady drank the white chair." Under this category I classified both violations of pragmatic character and of more semantic character.

The first experiment addressed in the first place the question whether syntactic computation always takes place during normal reading for comprehension. This experiment provided some evidence for the notion of automatic computation of syntactic structure even when this does not seem to be fully and consciously exploited for the comprehension of the text.

The second experiment provided results favouring the hypothesis that the results of syntactic computation become more important when the reader cannot use clues normally provided by texts, namely cohesion of information presented and pragmatic plausibility.

Finally, a third experiment showed that "good" and "poor" readers of texts might differ with regard to their sensitivity to the properties of the syntactic structure.

The material used in the experiments was characterised by the following properties. First, all stimulus material was selected on the basis of ratings of judges on syntactic complexity, on the type and "seriousness" of the violations involved, and on the degree of pragmatic cohesiveness. Second, the critical experimental material was embedded in a variety of fillers of various types. Third, in all experiments the instructions emphasised that the text had to be read for comprehension, and that questions would be asked after each or most sentences/passages. It is likely that these features had direct consequences for the range and the type of results. Emphasis on the goal of reading for comprehension might in fact have reduced the subject's sensitivity to given features of the material, such as the syntactic violations.

DETECTION OF VIOLATIONS AND SYNTACTIC
PROCESSING DURING READING

In this section I will report an experiment which provides some evidence for the notion that syntactic computation is likely to take place automatically during reading, even when the reader does not seem to be consciously dependent on this computation for the understanding of the text. The experimental situation consisted of a word-by-word self-paced reading with sentences which included either a syntactic violation, a semantic one, or a spelling error.

This experiment essentially represented a replication and a validation of a previous experiment in which subjects were presented with sentences and were requested to read them for comprehension and detect errors and violations while the eye movements and eye fixations were recorded (Flores d'Arcais, 1982). The results of that experiment were as follows: spelling errors, nonwords, and semantic violations were detected rather easily, whereas the detection of syntactic violations was poor. The number of eye fixations per word and their total duration indicated that the locus of spelling errors and of the semantic violations were fixated significantly longer than the syntactic violations. The most intriguing result of the study, however, was the following: Whether a syntactic error was reported or not did not affect the number and lengths of the fixations. Even when the readers did not seem to be aware of the presence of syntactic violations, they tended to fixate more often, and for a significantly longer time, at the locus of the syntactic anomaly.

Experiment 1. Word-by-word Presentation of Sentences
and Error Detection

Material, Subjects, and Methods.   The experimental material consisted of 48 Dutch sentences or short prose passages of length 10 to 24 words. These sentences were correct and appropriate, or could contain a nonword string (or a printing/spelling error) or a semantic or a syntactic violation of the type described in the previous section. The material included also a number of filler sentences.

The subjects were 20 volunteer paid students; they were tested individually. The sentences were presented on a CRT display, under the control of a PDP 11/45, one word at a time, in a word-by-word self-paced presentation triggered by the subject's pressing on a button. The latencies between the pressing responses of the subjects were recorded.

Each of the experimental sentences was followed by a question about the content of the sentence, to ensure that the subjects had understood the material read.

Results. The data of the present experiment consisted of the latencies between the pressing responses, which were taken to indicate reading and processing time of the various words of the sentences, and the proportions of errors detected.

The proportions of error detections are presented in Table 28.1, while Table 28.2 displays the average inter-word latencies per word, taken over the three words following the locus of the violation.

TABLE 28.1

Experiment 1: Proportion of Correct Detection of Syntactic and Semantic Violations and of Spelling/Printing Errors

Type of Errors Detected		
Syntactic	*Semantic*	*Nonwords*
0.28	0.67	0.78

The results of Table 28.1 indicate a better error detection performance for spelling errors and semantic violation than the rather poor detection of syntactic violations. An analysis carried out on the arc-sin transformation of the individual proportions of reports of errors showed the difference to be highly significant: $F = 27.31$; 2,19 df; $P < 0.001$.

TABLE 28.2

Experiment 1: Mean Inspection Time per Word (Msec) Averaged Over Three Words Following the Violation or the Corresponding Control Word

Correct	Syntactic Violation	Semantic Violation	Nonword
454	497	691	683

The results of Table 28.2 show an increase in reading time per word in the sentences at the positions immediately following semantic violations and a printing error. As compared to the control sentences, syntactic violations also produced a smaller effect on reading times. The analysis of variance on the latencies showed a significant effect due to the type of violation: $F = 19.23$; 2,19 df; $P < 0.001$).

The latencies for the words following the locus of syntactic violations were divided in two groups; those corresponding to cases in which the reader had reported a violation and those in which he/she had not. The average latencies were 489 and 501msec respectively. This difference is statistically not significant. Thus, the effects of syntactic violation seems approximately the same for the words immediately following the locus of the syntactic violation, whether the readers reported the violation or not.

The results leave a question open: To what extent is comprehension of a text related to the detection of the violations? A 2 × 2 contingency table was generated for each subject, with comprehension response (sentence correctly understood/not understood) and detection of a given type of violation (e.g. syntactic violation detected/not detected) as row and columns respectively, and the frequency of sentences as entries. Collapsing over subjects, 3 2 × 2 contingency tables were thus obtained (one each for syntactic violations, semantic violations, and spelling errors). Coefficients were computed, as indicators of the degree of association between the capacity for detecting violations and the answer to the comprehension questions. The results showed a higher degree of association betwen detection of semantic violations and comprehension ($\varphi = 0.56$, $P < 0.01$) than between comprehension and detection of syntactic violations ($\varphi = 0.19$, $P > 0.05$). Thus, detection of semantic violations is related to comprehension, while reporting a syntactic violation is rather independent of the process of comprehending a text. In other words, comprehension of a text remains relatively unaffected by the presence of syntactic violations.

Discussion.   First, the results of this experiment replicated, with a very different technique, the findings of the Flores d'Arcais (1982) experiment. The effect isolated thus seems reliable. A word of caution is appropriate here: The present experiment required the subjects to report the violations, whenever detected, immediately after the end of the sentences. Thus, a memory component is involved in the task, and this might have affected the responses. On the other hand, in another study (Flores d'Arcais, in press) with serial rapid presentation of sentences and an on-line task requiring the readers to press a button every time they detected a violation, rather similar results were obtained, indicating that the poor performance in the detection of small syntactic violations during rapid reading is probably not exclusively a result of memory-loss.

The results obtained, together with the evidence from the coefficients of association between comprehension scores and error detections, allow the conclusion that the presence of syntactic violations does not disturb comprehension. The simplest interpretation of the results would be that syntactic anomalies tend to remain largely unnoticed during rapid reading, and that they do not interfere with the comprehension process. On the other hand, the present evidence can be taken as a basis for the following conclusions. First, the fact that syntactic violations tend to affect readers' behaviour even when they are not consciously reported could be interpreted as an indication that syntactic computation is always carried out. Second, the fact that readers tend to ignore syntactic violations would allow the conclusion that they "pay little attention" to syntactic structure, and base comprehension more on the results of other computational sources.

The present results can thus be taken as favouring the hypothesis of automatic processing of syntactic information. Readers seem to record syntactic violations in an automatic way, even when they are not capable of reporting such violations. The fact that fewer syntactic violations are reported than semantic ones while text comprehension remains intact, and that reporting syntactic violations is independent of comprehension performance, can be taken as an indication that the results of syntactic computation are not fully or completely exploited for text comprehension. On the other hand, the fact that the processor is sensitive to syntactic violations, even when it cannot report them, could be taken as a basis for the notion that syntactic analysis is always carried out during reading, whether it is necessary for comprehension of the text or not.

LEVELS OF TEXT COHESIVENESS AND USE OF SYNTACTIC INFORMATION

This section reports the results of an experiment on the detection of errors with texts characterised by different levels of internal consistency or pragmatic plausibility. The hypothesis tested here was that the result of syntactic computation might become more important when the reader can rely less on semantic and thematic information of the passage being read.

Experiment 2. Detection of Syntactic Violations in Texts with Different Levels of Cohesiveness

In this experiment, I tried to examine whether subjects would detect syntactic violations in experimental passages which were characterised by different levels of internal coherence and consistency, that is, containing sentences related to the context by different levels of pragmatic cohesiveness.

Material, Subjects, and Method.   The material consisted of 48 passages of narratives, 5 to 7 sentences long. Twenty-four were fillers and 24 critical passages, 12 containing a syntactic violation and 12 a spelling error or a nonword string of letters. The passages were characterised by three different levels of pragmatic cohesiveness, as determined on the basis of rating of a group of eight judges. They classified a large number of passages into three categories, on a scale from low pragmatic cohesiveness to high pragmatic cohesiveness. The experimental passages were chosen from those which displayed significant differences in the cohesiveness judgment scores.

The subjects, 16 Dutch students at Leiden University, were presented with the passages, one sentence at a time, in a self-paced situation. The passages were presented on a CRT display under the control of a PDP 11/45 computer. The subjects were trained to read as fast as they could. Immediately after the end of each passage, they were requested to answer a question about the content of the passage and to report any error or violation observed.

Results.   The dependent variable of interest here was the proportion of correct report of errors. By and large, the subjects were much better at reporting spelling errors than syntactic violations (76.7% spelling errors vs. 39.2% syntactic errors). The analysis of variance on the transformed individual proportions of error detections showed a significant effect of the type of errors: $F = 27.73$; 1,15 df; $P < 0.001$; and of cohesiveness: $F = 18.12$; 2,15 df; $P < 0.01$). The level of pragmatic coherence had a larger effect on the detection of syntactic violations than on the detection of spelling errors, as shown by the significant interaction between type of violations and level of pragmatic coherence: $F = 18.63$; 1,15 df; $P < 0.01$.

The proportions of detection of the syntactic violations are displayed in Fig. 28.1, which shows a clear and significant increase in the proportion of correct detections of syntactic violations with increased level of pragmatic unplausibility: The analysis of variance on the arc-sin transformations of

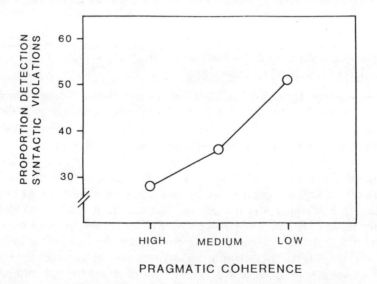

FIG. 28.1.   Experiment 2: Proportion of reports of syntactic violations in texts characterised by three levels of pragmatic coherence.

these proportions yielded $F = 23.91$; 2,15 df; $P < 0.01$. Thus, it seems easier to detect a syntactic violation with sentences characterised by a low pragmatic plausibility than with sentences with high pragmatic consistency with the rest of the text.

Discussion.   Reporting syntactic violations was easier with less coherent texts as compared to pragmatically well-integrated ones. This result might at first look paradoxical, for one would expect better detection of syntactic violations with the simpler passages, presumably the pragmatically coherent ones. The results obtained would seem incompatible with notions such as those of allocation of attention and of processing load, in the sense that pragmatically inconsistent texts should require more processing effort: Therefore the amount of attention or energy available for detecting errors should be smaller, and fewer errors and violations should be reported on this account. On the other hand, a plausible interpretation of the results is at hand: When readers work through an inconsistent text, they should be more "concentrated" on the task and might therefore detect violations more easily. This would be consistent with the idea of allocation of energy in models of attention such as Kahneman's (1973): The reader would demand and be able to allocate more attention to the difficult than to the easy task.

The finding that readers are better at reporting syntactic violations with unplausible material can be interpreted in the two following ways, which are not to be taken as mutually exclusive explanations. The first is that, with incoherent material, readers cannot rely on semantic and pragmatic sources and therefore have to "fall back" on syntax. Since this last source becomes more important for the comprehension process, the readers, now actively using syntactic information, are more likely to detect the syntactic violations. The other explanation is suggested by the notion of allocation of attention introduced in the preceding paragraph. Since readers are allocating more attention to the task, they are also more likely to detect syntactic violations.

At any rate, the experiment suggests that syntactic information becomes more relevant when readers have problems in getting a meaningful representation of the text. While with normal, plausible, and coherent texts readers might rely more on the semantic and pragmatic information available, with semantically and pragmatically implausible texts syntactic information plays a more important role.

Experiment 3. Good and Poor Readers' Ability in Detecting Violations

This experiment required the same error report task as Experiment 2, but in this case the subjects were given reading material presented at a rather rapid rate and under the experimenter's control.

APPR-U*

Material Subjects, and Method. The passages of prose used in this experiment were either well-integrated and coherent, or some sentences were pragmatically incoherent with the text and contained pragmatic inconsistencies. The coherence of the passages was determined on the basis of the ratings of 12 judges on a large number of passages. On the basis of these ratings, two types of passages were selected, characterised respectively by high and low coherence. Eight of each of the high- and low-coherence texts contained a syntactic violation, and eight a spelling error. Thus, 32 experimental passages of narratives, with a length of 3–7 sentences, made up the experimental material. The passages were presented on a CRT display, 1, 2, or 3 words at a time (depending on their length), in a "window" of 11 characters on average, in a rapid serial presentation situation at the presentation rate of some 450 words per minute. This rate is rather high; however, it still allows comprehension of the material.

The subjects were 40 Dutch students. They were requested to answer various questions designed to test their comprehension of the passages, and to signal immediately after the end of a passage any violations or errors they had noticed. Given the very rapid rate of presentation of the material, the performance on error detection was not expected to be very good, and the results confirmed this prediction.

Results. On the basis of the distribution of the comprehension scores, the upper and the lower quartile of subjects was selected for analysis. These two groups were called "good" and "poor" readers respectively, and the proportions of reports of errors were computed for these groups separately. Notice that the definition "poor" reader must be taken only as relative to the best performances in our experiment, and only apply to the performance on the *comprehension* task in this experiment. None of the subjects, in fact, showed any indication of reading problems of any sort.

The proportions of reports of syntactic violations for the two groups are presented in Fig. 28.2. An analysis of variance was carried out on the arc-sin transformations of the individual proportions of error detections for the two types of violations and for the two levels of text coherence. As in the previous experiment, there was a significant difference in the detection of syntactic violations for the different levels of pragmatic coherence: $F = 15.71$; 1,18 df; $P < 0.01$. Good readers were significantly worse in reporting syntactic violations than "poor" readers: $F = 12.21$; 1,18 df; $P < 0.01$. Another interesting result was the significant interaction between error detection and pragmatic consistency in the passages, for good and poor readers: $F = 7.92$; 1,18 df; $P < 0.05$. "Good" readers showed a tendency towards a worse performance in detection of violations with coherent text and towards a "relatively" better capacity in reporting violations with pragmatically inconsistent text.

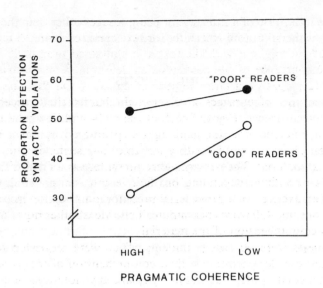

28. 2 Experiment 3: proportions of reports of syntactic violations in texts characterised by two levels of pragmatic coherence, by subjects in the upper ("good" readers) and lower ("poor" readers) quartile of the distribution of the comprehension scores.

Discussion.   The results of this experiment are consistent with those of Experiment 2. There seems to be a kind of trade-off between capacity for fast and efficient processing of passages of text and the capacity for detecting syntactic violations. The fact that readers who seem better at getting the gist out of a text in a rapid reading condition (i.e. the good readers here) are relatively worse in error detection is in agreement with the results of the previous experiment. The data seem to support the notion that what characterises "good" readers is their capacity for relying more on "higher-order" strategies, which decreases the tendency to use the results of syntactic computation for text comprehension.

Is, then, the property which characterises good readers their capacity to make a more rapid and efficient use of the various sources of information from the text? In principle, the answer could be positive. On the other hand, it is not just a general capacity for using the various elements and characteristics of the text which distinguishes the poor and the good reader. For example, recent evidence (e.g. Perfetti, Goldman, & Hogaboam, 1979) indicates that, contrary to previous assumptions, in word recognition poor readers tend to make more use of the context than good readers do: The latter would not need to rely very much on the context, because they would be good at recognising words anyhow. In the present experiment, the relatively poorer detection of syntactic violations by good readers can be taken as an indication of a capacity for using sources other than the syntactic properties of the text more efficiently for text comprehension.

CONCLUSIONS

In the experiments reported in the present study, the critical variable investigated was the capacity of subjects to report syntactic violations during reading. The results of the experiment on the detection of syntactic violations during rapid word-by-word reading indicate that such violations remain largely unnoticed. The fact that syntactic violations attract readers' attention without their conscious awareness has been taken as supporting the hypothesis that syntactic computation is an obligatory, automatic process during text comprehension. The fact that the syntactic violations are not necessarily noticed, while at the same time readers are capable of understanding the text, has been interpreted as supporting the notion that readers rely for text comprehension, at least to some extent, on the results of other computational sources.

The differential ability of detecting syntactic violations with texts of different levels of semantic and pragmatic cohesiveness has been taken as an indication that the use of the output of the syntactic computation depends on textual constraints. Normally a text has a considerable amount of redundancy, its different thematic elements are consistent with each other, and the text is designed in such a way that readers can use their knowledge of the world, and a variety of conceptual sources, to understand what is presented. When the overall thematic structure of the text and the cohesiveness of the various parts become insufficient for comprehension, then readers have to rely, as a kind of backup data, on "lower" level information. This conclusion is consistent with an enormous amount of evidence within cognitive psychology: When top-down sources are impoverished, the reader has to rely more on bottom-up sources.

The results of the last experiment reported have also shown that readers who are good at extracting information from rapidly presented texts seem to be less sensitive to syntactic violations than less efficient readers. Again, this has been interpreted as indicating that what makes good readers good is their ability to deal more efficiently with "higher order" kind of strategies, thus relying less on the results of syntactic computation.

Overall, the results have been taken as favouring the distinction between a computational level and the level of selection and of use of this information for text comprehension. Thus, the notion that computation takes place at various levels in an automatic way, while readers do not use all the results of the computation, seems to receive some support from the results of the present experiment.

The distinction between computation and use of the results of the computation is consistent with various findings in the psycholinguistic literature, including some recent conclusions from aphasia research. This has shown that syntactic processing abilities of so-called agrammatics are much better than what one could suspect on the basis of their behaviour in various traditional grammatical tasks. Agrammatic patients are sensitive to grammatical structure (Linebarger, Schwartz, & Saffran, 1983) and seem to preserve syntactic comprehension even when their performance in ordinary tests of sentence understanding is very poor. Thus, sentence comprehension disturbances do not necessarily reflect a loss of capacity to recover syntactic structure. The capacity for giving correct judgements of grammaticality speaks in favour of a preserved syntactic processing capacity, accompanied by a lack of ability to access the results of the syntactic computation for a given task.

REFERENCES

Bever, T. G. (1970). The cognitive basis for linguistic structures. In J. R. Hayes (Ed.), *Cognition and the development of language*. New York: Wiley.

DeJong, G. (1979). Skimming stories in real time: An experiment in integrated understanding. *Research Report 158, Computer Science Department*. New Haven, Conn.: Yale University.

Flores d'Arcais, G. B. (1974). Is there a memory for sentences? *Acta Psychologica, 38*, 33–58.

Flores d'Arcais, G. B. (1978). The perception of complex sentences. In W. J. M. Levelt & G. B. Flores d'Arcais (Eds.), *Studies in the perception of language*. Chichester: Wiley.

Flores d'Arcais, G. B. (1982). Automatic syntactic computation and use of semantic information during sentence comprehension. *Psychological Research, 44*, 231–242.

Flores d'Arcais, G. B. (in press). Language comprehension. In F. Newmeyer (Ed.), *Cambridge linguistic survey*. Cambridge: Cambridge University Press.

Flores d'Arcais, G. B. & Schreuder, R. (1983). The process of language understanding: A few issues in contemporary psycholinguistics. In G. B. Flores d'Arcais & R. J. Jarvella (Eds.), *The process of language understanding*. Chichester: Wiley.

Forster, K. I. (1974). The role of semantic hypotheses in sentence processing. In F. Bresson (Ed.), *Problems actuels en psycholinguistique*. Paris: Centre Nationale de la Recherche Scientifique.

Garrett, M. F. (1976). Sentence production. In R. J. Wales & E. C. T. Walker (Eds.), *New approaches to language mechanisms*. Amsterdam: North Holland.

Kahnemann, D. (1973). *Attention and effort*. Englewood Cliffs, N. J.: Prentice Hall.

Linebarger, M. C., Schwartz, M. F., & Saffran, E. M. (1983). Sensitivity to grammatical structure in so-called agrammatic aphasics. *Cognition, 13*, 361–392.

Perfetti, C. A., Goldman, S. R., & Hogaboam, T. W. (1979). Reading skill and the identification of words in discourse context. *Memory and Cognition, 7*, 273–282.

Riesbeck, C. K. (1982). Realistic language comprehension. In V. G. Lenhert & M. H. Ringle (Eds.), *Strategies for natural language processing*. Hillsdale, N. J.: Lawrence Erlbaum Associates Inc.

Riesbeck, C. K. & Schank, R. C. (1978). Comprehension by computer: Expectation based analysis of sentences in context. In W. J. M. Levelt & G. B. Flores d'Arcais (Eds.), *Studies in the perception of language*. Chichester: Wiley.

Wilks, Y. (1978). Computational models for language processing. *Cognitive psychology: Language*. Milton Keynes: Open University Press.

29

Discourse Structure and Anaphora: Some Experimental Results

Charles Clifton, Jr. and Fernanda Ferreira
University of Massachusetts at Amherst
Massachusetts, U.S.A.

ABSTRACT

Three self-paced reading experiments investigated the nature of the representation in which pronouns and other NP anaphors find antecedents. The first experiment provided no evidence that the representation consisted of syntactic constituents, and was consistent with the widely-held opinion that antecedents for pronouns are found in a representation that captures referential identity. The second and third experiments examined the effects of topichood and distance between antecedent and pronoun on pronoun reading time. They demonstrated that pronouns with topic antecedents were read quickly, regardless of distance. However, closer analysis of the data indicated that some sentences seemed to have more than one equally quickly accessed antecedent, in line with suggestions that discourse centres, not topics, are preferred antecedents for pronouns.

INTRODUCTION

In the process of comprehending language, people can ultimately bring to bear all their cognitive resources and all their linguistic and nonlinguistic knowledge. Nonetheless, careful examination of how a variety of linguistic devices are used in language comprehension has pointed to the existence of specialised processors that seem to operate very quickly and on the basis of far less than all the relevant information (cf. Frazier, 1985; Frazier, this volume; and Clifton & Frazier, in press, for reviews; cf. Fodor, 1983, for a general theoretical perspective). The present paper begins to examine how pronouns (and, secondarily, NP anaphors) are processed, in an effort to determine whether any interesting linguistic specialisations exist for them.

Most current research on the comprehension of pronouns views the process as an exercise in problem solving, constrained by memory limitations. Readers and listeners are presumed to keep a representation (possibly verbatim, but possibly semantic; cf. van Eckhardt & Potter, 1985) of the most recent clause in an active memory (Caplan, 1972; Jarvella, 1971), together with some propositions of particular importance in the current discourse structure (van Dijk & Kintsch, 1983). They presumably search through these representations for an attractive antecedent when a pronoun or an anaphoric definite NP appears (Clark & Sengul, 1979; Ehrlich & Rayner, 1983). Search takes longer the more clauses back the antecedent of an anaphor. Search may be guided by the gender of the pronoun, so that only appropriate-gender antecedents receive full consideration (Corbett & Chang, 1983; but cf. Caramazza, Grober, Garvey, & Yates, 1977; Ehrlich, 1980), and choice of antecedent is eventually determined by a complex of information including the relative syntactic positions of the antecedent and the pronoun (Grober, Beardsley, & Caramazza, 1978), verb causality (Garvey & Caramazza, 1974), the identity of the current discourse topic (Crawley, Note 2), the existence of and role played by the referent of the antecedent in the current mental model of the discourse (Garrod & Sanford, 1977; Stenning, 1978), etc.

While we acknowledge that all these factors must play a role in the comprehension of pronouns, we want to entertain the possibility that the comprehension process is not the relatively unstructured problem-solving task that the view just described suggests. We will begin in a way that has proven useful in the analysis of other aspects of language comprehension, namely, asking questions about the nature of the mental representation in which antecedent-anaphor relations are initially established. We briefly consider an experiment designed to determine whether antecedents are sometimes constituents in a surface structure representation, as opposed to elements of the mental model (or discourse model, or propositional structure) representation assumed in the generally shared view described earlier. Given that the answer we obtained is a tentative "no," we address the question of what structure exists in the actually used representation. We focus on the possibility, often mentioned but seldom studied experimentally until recently (cf. Blanchard, Note 1; Carroll & Slowiaczek, in press; Fletcher, 1984; Hudson, Tanenhaus, & Dell, Note 3), that a unique NP occupies the role of *sentence topic* in a discourse structure, and is a preferred antecedent for any pronoun. After presenting positive evidence for this possibility, we present preliminary data that bear on the question of what, exactly, constitutes a topic, and conclude by suggesting that "topic" is not quite the right concept.

EXPERIMENT 1

Antedecents for pronouns and definite NP anaphors certainly can be found in a representation that preserves referential identity, such as a mental model of a discourse representation. One can use a pronoun in a deictic fashion to refer to something perceptually salient, even if it has not been mentioned; one can use a pronoun to refer to a set of things whose existence as a set can only be inferred from what was explicitly said. It is an open question whether some coreferential (as opposed to bound anaphoric)[1] pronouns can take surface structure constituents as their antecedents. There is evidence that some VP anaphors may have antecedents in the surface structure of a sentence (or some other representation that maintains information about form and morphology; see Tanenhaus & Carlson, 1985, Note 4, for evidence regarding surface VP anaphors; and see Black, Colthcart, & Byng, this volume, for evidence regarding VP gapping). The first experiment (which was undertaken jointly with Lyn Frazier, Barbara Malt, and Rosemary Stevenson) was designed to assess the possibility that antecedents for pronouns can similarly be found in the surface structure of a sentence.

Method

Thirty-two undergraduates read 48 stories like that in Table 29.1 (mixed in with 40 other stories of a variety of forms), using a self-paced reading procedure. Each story was divided into several segments, indicated by a "/" in Table 29.1. Segments were presented one by one, centred on a video monitor, when the subject pressed a button. Each story was followed by a single yes/no question to ensure comprehension. Accuracy feedback was given for answers to these questions. Each story had four versions, one of which was read by each subject. In two versions, the antecedent for a pronoun was a syntactic constituent (two proper names conjoined as an NP), while in the other two versions, the antecedent consisted of two proper names in different grammatical relations to a single verb. We reasoned that if readers could find an antecedent in surface structure, and if they check surface structure before or simultaneously with discourse structure, their time to process a pronoun would be faster than if the only possible antecedent was in a discourse or mental model structure. The other manipulation in the experiment was whether the antecedent was in the same sentence as the pronoun or in the previous sentence. We reasoned that readers might

---

[1]The distinction can be seen in Reinhart, 1983, who singles out bound anaphora pronouns, such as "John shot himself" or "Every man loves his whiskey" for different treatment. Bound anaphors may at least sometimes obtain their antecedent from surface structure.

TABLE 29.1
Sample Item, Experiment 1

Conjoined Antecedent, Single Sentence
A crowd was starting to gather / even before the ticket booth opened./ JOHN AND MARY
pushed / toward the head of the line,/ but suddenly / they discovered / that all their money
was missing.

Conjoined Antecedent, Two Sentences
A crowd was starting to gather / even before the ticket booth opened./ JOHN AND MARY
pushed / toward the head of the line. / Suddenly / they discovered / that all their money was
missing.

Separated Antecedent, Single Sentence
A crowd was starting to gather / even before the ticket booth opened. JOHN pushed MARY
/ toward the head of the line, but suddenly / they discovered / that all their money was
missing.

Separated Antecedent, Two Sentences
A crowd was starting to gather / even before the ticket booth opened. JOHN pushed MARY
/ toward the head of the line. / Suddenly / they discovered / that all their money was missing.

NOTE: / indicates a division between presentation segments. Antecedents appear in CAPI-
TALS, anaphors are underlined.

be more likely to find a surface structure antecedent when it was in the same
sentence as the pronoun, and thus, that the advantage of the conjoined NP
condition over the separated NP condition would be greater in the same
sentence than in the different sentence condition.

Results

The times taken to read the segment with the pronoun appear in Table 29.2.
There was no effect of conjoined vs. separated NP antecedent: $F(1,31) < 1$;
and the apparent interaction between the factors of conjoined/separated NP
and one/two sentences was also nonsignificant: $F(1,31) < 1$. Two possible
interpretations are apparent. It may be that differences do exist between the
conjoined and separated NP conditions, but the self-paced reading time task
is not sensitive enough to pick them up. We cannot eliminate this possibility,
and in fact are currently conducting an eye-movement recording experiment
using the materials described here to obtain increased sensitivity. Alternatively, it may be that the apparent implication of the results is correct: A pronoun
does not take a surface structure constituent as its antecedent, but instead
must find its antecedent in a constructed representation, e.g. a discourse
representation or a mental model. We turn to an examination of the nature
of such a representation.

TABLE 29.2
Mean Reading Times, Experiment 1

Antecedent	Number of Sentences		
	Single	Two	Mean
Conjoined	777	777	777
Split	792	756	775

EXPERIMENT 2

Some researchers emphasise the possibility that the representation in which NP antecedents are found is simply a list or hierarchy of the recently read or heard propositions which is searched in reverse order when an NP anaphor appears (Clark & Sengul, 1979; Ehrlich & Rayner, 1983). This simple and straightforward claim is sufficient to account for the "distance effect" in pronoun comprehension, in which readers slow down more in the vicinity of a pronoun or an NP anaphor when its antecedent had occurred several clauses back than when it had occurred in the most recent clause or two.

However, examination of the materials used in studies like Clark and Sengul's and Ehrlich and Rayner's indicates that, in the distant antecedent conditions, the text was no longer discussing the antecedent when the anaphor occurred: The text had introduced a new topic by that time. (Cf. Blanchard, Note 1; Carroll & Slowiaczek, in press, for statements of this same point.) An equally good account of the data, then, would suggest that topics are quickly found as antecedents for pronouns, and nontopics only found slowly. Both Clark and Sengul (1979) and Ehrlich and Rayner (1983) acknowledge that the representation which is searched for the antecedent may contain information about the current topic, at the same time pointing out that such an assumption is not needed to account for their data. The suggestion that topics are preferred antecedents for pronouns has much to recommend it. Such an idea has long been advanced by linguists of various functional schools (e.g., Chafe, 1974; Halliday, 1967), and several psycholinguists have presented data that suggest that people use pronouns to maintain continuity of discourse and to make assertions about the current topic (e.g. Fletcher, 1984; Marslen-Wilson, Levy, & Tyler, 1982; van Dijk & Kintsch, 1983). Some results event indicate that pronouns are read more quickly when their antecedent is the global topic of the discourse than when it is not the topic (Crawley, Note 2), and when the referent of their antecedent is still plausibly in the situation being discussed than when the scene has changed in a way likely to eliminate that referent (Garrod & Sandford, 1977).

The first experiment to be reported here on topic effects was designed to contrast conditions very much like those used by Ehrlich and Rayner (1983) with conditions that changed the topic structure but maintained the distance between antecedent and pronoun. The notion of topic used in preparing the materials (a notion to be revised, see later) was that of sentence topic (Reinhart, 1982). The notion is essentially a pragmatic one, "what a sentence is about" (a concept that Reinhart takes some pains to explicate). As Reinhart notes, there is a strong (but not overwhelming) preference to take a sentence's subject as its topic. Experiment 2 used stories that manipulated topichood (via subjecthood) and distance in an essentially orthogonal way, and measured self-paced reading time for them.

Method

Twenty-three stories like the one presented in Table 29.3 were prepared (plus a 24th story that was eliminated after the experiment when a typing error was discovered). The antecedent of the pronoun or NP anaphor is capitalised in Table 29.3, and the anaphor is underlined. Each story began with a lead-in sentence or two, and then established a sentence topic by introducing an NP (NP_1) in subject position, referring to a person. At a later point in the story, another NP, NP_2, was introduced, referring to a different person. In one version of each story, NP_2 was introduced as the subject of the next sentence, and constituted the new sentence topic. In the other version, NP_2 was introduced inside an adjunct sentence (a gerund clause), and did not constitute a new sentence topic. The two NPs were always distinct in gender on pragmatic or semantic grounds, and in all cases, the materials passed the rule-of-thumb test for topichood mentioned by Reinhart (1982): The sentences that introduced NP_2 as a new topic could be paraphrased as "He said about NP_2 that . . .," whereas the sentences that introduced NP_2 as a nontopic could not felicitously be paraphrased in this manner. Each story then continued with a pronoun or a definite NP (a definite description), referring back to either the far antecedent, NP_1, or the near antecedent, NP_2, and continued on to something like a reasonable conclusion.

Each story thus came in eight versions, defined by the factorial combination of NP_1 antecedent (far) vs. NP_2 antecedent (near), topic antecedent (TA) or nontopic antecedent (NTA), and pronoun (P) vs. definite description (DD) anaphor. Each of 64 undergraduates read 1 version of each of 88 stories (including the 23 under discussion here), using a self-paced reading procedure and separate randomisations of the story order for each subject. Each story was read in each form by an equal number of subjects, and each subject read an equal number of stories in each form. A trial began with the presentation of the story on a video terminal, with an underline character replacing each letter. Punctuation marks and spaces were preserved. When the subject pressed a button, each successive segment in the story (indicated by a "/" in Table 29.3) appeared, with its letters replacing the underlines, and the previous segment reverted to underline marks. A single question followed each story to assure comprehension. The times subjects took to read each segment, and question-answering accuracy, were recorded.

Results and Discussion

The results for the segment immediately before the pronoun or DD anaphor (A–1), the pronoun/anaphor segment itself (A), and the remainder of the last sentence (A to end) appear in Fig. 29.1. These times are adjusted for differences in length between segments, so that a negative number indicates faster reading times than expected on the basis of length, and a positive number, slower times.[2]

The most illuminating effect in the data is the interaction between topic vs. nontopic antecedent and segment: $F_1(2,126) = 4.19$; $F_2(2,44) = 5.50$; $P < 0.02$. This interaction can be seen in Fig. 29.1 by noting that the adjusted reading times are consistently less for topic antecedents than for nontopic antecedents at and after the anaphor, but not before. No effect involving far vs. near antecedent was significant, and the mean adjusted reading times for the regions at and after the anaphor were -10 for far antecedents and -7 for near antecedents.

The conclusions to be drawn about the difference between pronouns and definite NPs are less clear. There was no significant interaction between pronoun/DD, topic vs. nontopic antecedent, and segment: $F < 1$. However, the crucial interaction between TA vs. NTA and segment was not statistically significant when the NP anaphor data were considered alone: $F_1(2,126) = 1.48$; $F_2(2,44) = 2.38$; $P > 0.10$). We had expected not to find a topic effect for the definite description NPs, or possibly even to find a reverse effect (faster reading times when a DD had a nontopic as antecedent), given that a felicitous use of a definite NP is to promote a previously mentioned nontopic to topic. The definite description data, which are somewhat disorderly especially in the region before the anaphor, do not permit us to conclude with certainty whether a topic effect was or was not obtained with definite NP anaphors.

We conducted a follow-up study with the materials used in Experiment 2

---

[2]The adjustment procedure is similar to dividing reading times by numbers of characters in a segment, except that it takes into account the fact that self-paced reading time would not go to zero if the number of characters in a segment equalled zero. A linear regression equation, expressing reading time as a function of segment length, was fitted individually to each subject's data. This function was used to predict, subject-by-subject, how fast each segment should be read based on length alone. The reported data are the differences between these predictions and the observed times. In fact, since the segments containing the anaphors were of the same length in each version of our stories, as were the following segments, the adjustment for length had no important influence in the effects we observed. It simply made the times for successive segments of different lengths more comparable to one another.

TABLE 29.3
Sample Item, Experiment 2

Near Topic Antecedent (Topic Change Before Anaphor)
Weddings can be / very emotional experiences for everyone involved. / The cigar smoking caterer / was obviously / on the verge / of tears, / and the others / were pretty upset too. / In fact, / THE ORGANIST, / who was an old maid, / looked across the room / and sighed. / (She, The organist) was / still looking for / a husband.

Far Topic Antecedent (No Topic Change Before Anaphor)
Weddings can be / very emotional experiences for everyone involved. / THE ORGANIST,/ who was an old maid, / was obviously / on the verge / of tears, / having just noticed that / the cigar smoking caterer / was holding hands / with someone else./ (She, The organist) was / still looking for / a husband.

Near Nontopic Antecedent (No Topic Change Before Anaphor)
Weddings can be / very emotional experiences for everyone involved. / The cigar smoking caterer / was obviously / on the verge / of tears, / having just noticed that / THE ORGANIST, / who was an old maid, / was holding hands / with someone else./ (She, The organist) was / still looking for / a husband.

Far Nontopic Antecedent (Topic Change Before Anaphor)
Weddings can be / very emotional experiences for everyone involved. / THE ORGANIST, / who was an old maid, / was obviously / on the verge / of tears, / and the others / were pretty upset too. / In fact, / the cigar smoking caterer / looked across the room / and sighed. / (She, The organist) was / still looking for / a husband.

NOTE: ANTECEDENT of anaphor is capitalised and anaphor is underlined in the table (but not for experimental subjects).

---

in which we asked 23 subjects to rate how well the sentences with anaphors "fitted with" the preceding part of their stories. These subjects uniformly, and significantly, gave higher ratings to the stories whose anaphors had topics as antecedents than stories with nontopic antecedents, regardless of distance. Further, the rated preference for topics as antecedents was just as great for definite NP anaphors as for pronouns. Thus, we are inclined to suggest that the same basic topic preference exists for all nominal anaphors, but violations of it may be more easily overcome when a definite NP provides more information to guide interpretation.

The remaining significant effects in the data from Experiment 2 were not illuminating, primarily reflecting the fact that adjusted reading times were particularly fast for NP anaphors, but slow for pronouns. Precisely the opposite pattern emerged in an analysis of the actual, unadjusted reading times, which otherwise indicated conclusions about the effects of topic changes that were totally congruent with the conclusions made on the basis of the analysis of adjusted scores. We must simply conclude either that the second occurrence of an NP is read rapidly, or that pronouns are read more slowly than their short length would suggest, or both.

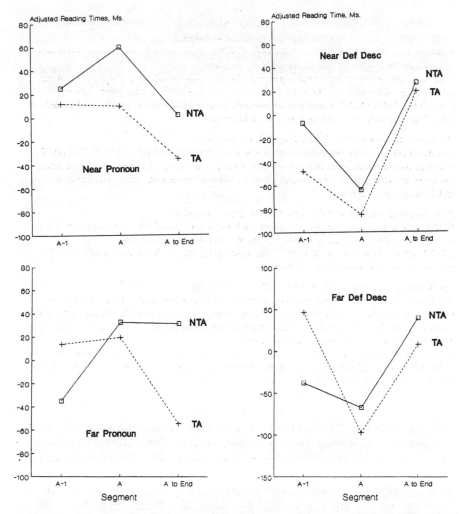

FIG. 29.1. Reading times in msec, adjusted for segment length, Experiment 2. Top panels: Near antecedent conditions. Bottom panels: Far antecedent conditions. Data plotted separately for nontopic antecedents and topic antecedents.

The basic implication of Experiment 2 seems clear: An anaphor is read quickly even when its antecedent is rather far back in the text, so long as the antecedent is still the topic of the sentence. An anaphor with a nontopic antecedent is read slowly, regardless of whether or not its antecedent is far or near. One might wish to qualify this interpretation, however. For one thing, the stories in which the far antecedent was the topic shared one possibly relevant property: Each of them contained one or more gerund clauses (e.g.

"... having just noticed that ...," in Table 29.3), which can be analysed as containing an empty constituent ("PRO"; Chomsky, 1981) as the subject of the gerund "having." This PRO could function as an anaphoric NP whose antecedent is the subject of the main sentence. Under this analysis, stories in which NP_2 was introduced as a new nontopic not only maintain the original topic; they also makes anaphoric reference to the topic before the occurrence of the pronoun, which could increase the availability of the antecedent in the far condition. Experiment 3 was designed to test the importance of this property of the materials.

EXPERIMENT 3

Method

Fourteen stories were made up on the model of the sample in Table 29.4.[3] In each case the first NP, NP_1, was the antecedent of a later pronoun. Each story occurred in four versions: nontopic antecedent (NTA), which was similar to

TABLE 29.4
Sample Item, Experiment 3

Nontopic Antecedent NTA
The housemates / were out grocery shopping. / PETER felt / that they were spending / too much money / on junk food, / but the others / didn't agree. / In fact, / Gail was trying / to get Sharon / to pick up / another bag of chips. / He had / recently gotten into / health foods.

Topic Antecedent 1 TA-1 (Gerunds, No New Proper Name)
The housemates / were out grocery shopping. / PETER felt / that they were spending / too much money / on junk food, / having just decided / that it was important / to try to lose / some weight, / and being concerned / about the food bill./ He had / recently gotten into / health foods.

Topic Antecedent 2 TA-2 (Gerunds, New Nontopics)
The housemates / were out grocery shopping. / PETER felt / that they were spending / too much money / on junk food, / having just decided / that it was important / to try to lose / some weight, / and having told Gail and Sharon that. / He had / recently gotten into / health foods.

Topic Antecedent 3 TA-3 (Nongerund Intervening Material)
The housemates / were out grocery shopping. / PETER felt / that they were spending / too much money / on junk food / that only rots teeth / and makes people / put on lots of weight / that even / the most strenuous exercise / wouldn't help./ He had / recently gotten into / health foods.

---

[3] An additional ten stories like the sample were constructed, but in the topic change conditions, these contained a pronoun referring to the NP_1 topic between NP_1 and the occurrene of the critical pronoun. Since this could artifactually increase the salience of NP_1 and thus affect time to read the critical pronoun, these stories were eliminated from the analysis.

the far–NTA condition of Experiment 2, except that two new proper names were introduced when the topic change occurred; topic antecedent 1 (TA–1), in which the sentence with NP_1 as topic included one or more gerund clauses but no new nontopic NPs; topic antecedent 2 (TA–2), with one or more gerund clauses, similar to the Far–TA condition of Experiment 2 except that the new nontopic NP was a conjoined pair of proper names; and topic antecedent 3 (TA–3), in which the length between NP_1 and the pronoun was filled primarily with a long relative clause. The TA–3 condition did not have any anaphoric reference to NP_1 (e.g. PRO) prior to the critical pronoun, and thus should not receive any benefit that such reference should confer.

Forty-eight undergraduates read the 14 stories, intermixed with 74 other stories of various forms. The procedure used was the same as that described for Experiment 2.

Results and Discussion

Adjusted reading times for the segment before the pronoun, the pronoun itself, and the rest of the sentence appear in Fig. 29.2. Reading times on and after the pronoun were dramatically increased in the NTA condition relative to the other conditions, which did not differ in pattern among themselves. The interaction between NTA vs. the pooled TA conditions and segment (A, A–1, A–cnd) was significant: $F_1(2,94) = 4.56$; $F_2(2,26) = 4.23$; $P < 0.05$; as were the main effects of each factor. Considering the three TA conditions alone, the interaction between conditions and segments was nonsignificant: $F_1(4,188) = 1.18$; but each main effect was significant. In particular, while the TA–1 condition resulted in fast reading rates (perhaps because very little new information was presented in the critical regions), the rates were not especially fast in the region of the pronoun.

Experiment 3 thus indicated that relatively fast reading times for pronouns that refer to a distant topic are characteristic of at least several different ways of filling the interval between antecedent and anaphor, and are not dependent upon repeated implicit reference (via PRO) to the topic. Failure to replace the topic with a new topic seems sufficient.

BUT WHAT COUNTS AS A TOPIC?

So far, we have taken the topic of a sentence to be the NP that a sentence is about. This point of view is not as devoid of content as it might seem. The concept of aboutness (or pragmatic aboutness; Reinhart, 1982) is distinct from other, related concepts that have been discussed in connection with anaphora. It is, for instance, distinct from the pragmatic factors that Garrod and Sanford (1977) demonstrated to affect pronoun comprehension time.

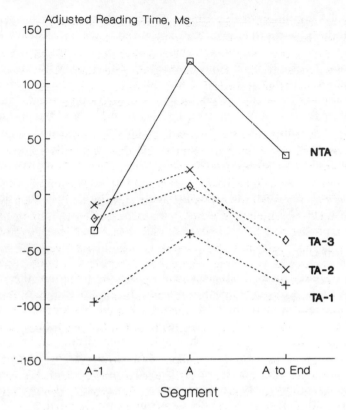

FIG. 29.2.   Reading times in msec, adjusted for segment length, Experiment 3.

They showed that readers had difficulty interpreting (e.g.) a pronoun whose referent probably disappeared from the situation several hours before the time under discussion (when discussing what happened at the end of a party, you can't felicitously use a pronoun to make a first reference to a person who left at the very beginning). The concept of topic Garrod and Sanford used was a referential one. Its appropriateness was determined by the likelihood that the referent of a pronoun was present in the situation being discussed. Reinhart (1982) argues that the concept of sentence topic is not a referential one. As she notes, the topic of a sentence like "Felix praised Max" (in response to the question, "Who did Felix praise?") is "Felix." It is not "Max." "Max" is the focus, and in simple assertions, the topic and the focus are distinct. But similarly, if the answer to the question is, "Felix praised himself," the topic has to be the expression "Felix," not the referent of that expression, because otherwise one and the same thing would serve as both topic and focus of the sentence.

Similarly, the notion of sentence topic is not a syntactic one. It is, for instance, not just "subject of the sentence." A sentence like "Max saw Rosa yesterday" (again from Reinhart, 1982) can have its subject, "Max," as topic, if it answers a question like "What did Max do yesterday?" However, it could just as well have its grammatical object, "Rosa," (or perhaps, its VP, "saw Rosa") as topic, if it was a response to a question like "Who saw Rosa yesterday?"

Further, while "topic" is a pragmatic concept, it is not the same as "old information," as some analysts seem to assume. Reinhart gives examples where the clear topic is only one of several items of old information, showing that oldness is not sufficient for topichood. In one example (Reinhart's example [38]), a grandfather talking about the difficulty of pleasing his grandson utters a sentence in which oatmeal cereal is the topic ("And the cereal, grandma don't like cereal . . .") and then says "He didn't want the cereal," treating "he," not the previously mentioned "cereal," as topic. Reinhart also provides examples where the clear topic is not old information, showing that oldness is not necessary for topichood. In fact, there are distinct devices in the language for introducing new information as topics. Reinhart's example (43) begins "Pat McGee, I don't know if you know him, he—he lives in Palisades . . .." The sentence is clearly about Pat McGee, whose existence is new information.

The concept of topichood thus seems to have enough content that it should be possible to show that it is the wrong concept, if such is in fact the case. There is reason to think that it is. In the first place, a topic is a linguistic expression, not a referent. But this means that in Experiment 1 the antecedent for a pronoun could be a topic only when it was a conjoined NP (a linguistic expression), not when the antecedent was a pair of individuals referred to by the two distinct NPs (which is not a linguistic constituent, at least in any superficial linguistic structure). If topics are preferred as antecedents for pronouns, facilitating reading time, we should have observed faster reading times in the conjoined conditions of Experiment 1 than in the separate conditions. We did not.

Further, a given sentence in a given context can have at most a single phrase as topic (although a sentence need not have any topic at all, and as noted above, a sentence can have different topics in different contexts as when it is used to answer different questions). Reinhart sketches a model in which a sentence has a set of possible topics, at most one of which is selected as topic by the context of the utterance of the sentence.[4] We have spoken as if our materials permitted fast selection of only a single NP antecedent of a

---

[4]More precisely, each sentence has a set of possible pragmatic assertions, each about some NP, and a function maps from the pair < sentence, context > onto 0 or 1 of these assertions, with the effect that the NP the chosen assertion is about is the topic.

pronoun, consistent with the notion of topic we have set forth. However, a post-hoc analysis of our data calls this analysis seriously into question, and suggests that some other way of determining the preferred antecedent(s) of a pronoun may be in order.

An examination of the materials used in Experiment 2 which introduced NP_2 as a nontopic indicated that 12 of the stories introduced it as an argument of a complement sentence, preposition phrase, relative clause, or adverbial phrase embedded within the gerund clause that served as an adjunct to the sentence containing the original topic. We will call these "subordinate" cases. The other 11 introduced NP_2 as an argument of the main predicate of the gerund clause (which we will refer to as the "matrix" cases). An example appears in Table 29.5, where NP_2 is introduced as the object of *promised*, the main verb of the gerund.

Intuitively, the NPs in the matrix cases are introduced as arguments of a predicate that the sentence topic is also an argument of (under the analysis where PRO is the subject of the adjunct gerund clause, and is taken to have the sentence topic as an antecedent). These NPs are on a par, in some sense,

TABLE 29.5
Sample Item, "Matrix" Nontopic, Experiment 2

Near Topic (Topic Change Before Antecedent)
The plane crew / was trying / to calm down / the passengers / during the rough, / tropical storm. / The hairy navigator / was assuring / the passengers / that everything / would be alright, / and the rest / of the crew / was busy as well. / THE YOUNG STEWARDESS / helped answer all/ the requests for / sick bags / which were / suddenly being made. / (She) (The stewardess) hoped / the flight / would soon / be over.

Far Topic (No Topic Change Before Antecedent)
The plane crew / was trying / to calm down / the passengers / during the rough, / tropical storm. / THE YOUNG STEWARDESS / was assuring / the passengers / that everything / would be alright, / knowing how frightening / it could be / for them,/ and having promised / the hairy navigator / to do so. / (She) (The stewardess) hoped / the flight / would soon / be over.

Near Nontopic (No Topic Change Before Antecedent)
The plane crew / was trying / to calm down / the passengers / during the rough, / tropical storm. / The hairy navigator / was assuring / the passengers / that everything / would be alright, / knowing how frightening / it could be / for them,/ and having promised / THE YOUNG STEWARDESS / to do so. / (She) (The stewardess) hoped / the flight / would soon / be over.

Far Nontopic (Topic Change Before Antecedent)
The plane crew / was trying / to calm down / the passengers / during the rough, / tropical storm. / THE YOUNG STEWARDESS / was assuring / the passengers / that everything / would be alright, / and the rest / of the crew / was busy as well. / The hairy navigator / helped answer all/ the request for / sick bags / which were / suddenly being made. / (She) (The stewardess) hoped / the flight / would soon / be over.

---

with the topic expression (although, by the test for topichood mentioned earlier, they clearly do not serve as the topic). In the subordinate cases, on the other hand, NP_2 is introduced in a way that subordinates it to the topic expression. It is an argument of a clause or phrase that is subordinated to the verb that has the topic as subject. One can easily imagine that the matrix and the subordinate cases would function differently as possible antecedents for pronouns. Expressions introduced as arguments at the same "level" as the topic might well be more available than expressions introduced as arguments of a subordinated construction.

Figure 29.3 indicates that this may be the case. The left panel presents the data for cases in which NP_2 was introduced as a new topic, collapsed over the (logically irrelevant) factor of whether new nontopics were introduced as matrix or embedded arguments. The second panel shows adjusted reading times for cases in which a nontopic NP_2 was introduced as an argument of a phrase or clause embedded within the gerund. The third panel shows adjusted reading times for cases in which a nontopic NP_2 was introduced as a matrix argument of the gerund. The leftmost, topic change, panel shows the familiar result: An anaphor whose antecedent is a distant nontopic is read more slowly than one whose antecedent is a recent topic. However, the right two panels show that the results presented earlier hold only for the subordinated cases.[5] Only here do we find faster reading times at the anaphor and thereafter for distant topic antecedents than for recent nontopic antecedents. When the nontopics are introduced as arguments of the gerund matrix, the superiority of topic antecedents disappears. However, note that reading an anaphor with a nontopic antecedent may not be facilitated in an absolute sense when the antecedent is introduced as an argument of a matrix clause. Reading times at and after anaphors with either topic or nontopic antecedents in the nontopic change matrix condition are comparable to, not faster than, reading times for anaphors with nontopic antecedents in the nontopic change subordinate condition. While we cannot tell whether this apparent equality is real or simply an artifact of comparing different stories in the two conditions, all we can claim with certainty is that there is an advantage for topic antecedents over nontopic antecedents only when the nontopic is introduced within a subordinated construction.

While an after-the-fact analysis such as this one must be taken with a grain of salt, it seems proper to doubt that the current sentence topic is the generally preferred antecedent for a pronoun. An attractive alternative is the concept of discourse centres introduced by Joshi and Weinstein (1981; Grosz, Joshi, & Weinstein, 1983). The centres of a sentence are taken to be entities

---

[5]An analysis of variance permitting generalisation to subjects shows that the interaction between type of item (topic change, nontopic change subordinate, and nontopic change matrix), topic vs. nontopic antecedent, and segment was significant: $F(4,252) = 3.32$; $P < 0.02$.

650

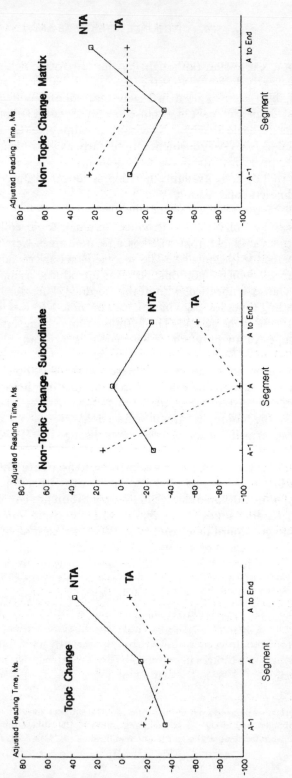

FIG. 29.4. Reading times in msec, adjusted for segment length, Experiment 2 post-hoc analysis, combining pronoun and definite NP anaphors.

mentioned in a sentence that are singled out to play special roles in determining how sentences are linked together in constructing a coherent discourse model. Centres are elements in a model that provide an interpretation of a sentence; they need not be linguistic constituents of a sentence. The forward-looking centres of a sentence i, $C_f(S_i)$, determine "how S_i will get linked up to the succeeding discourse" (Joshi & Weinstein, 1981), and the backward-looking centre of the sentence, $C_b(S_i)$, determines "how S_i is going to be incorporated in the preceding discourse." A sentence can have several forward-looking centres, which can get added to the set of forward-looking centres of the discourse context, and a sentence can have at most one backward-looking centre.[6] For a sentence S_i to be integrated easily into a given discourse context ("appropriate" for the context), its backward-looking centre must be included in the set of forward-looking centres of the preceding discourse, or be a proword for or "functionally dependent upon" a member of this set. Joshi and Weinstein hypothesise that the forward-looking centre(s) of a sentence are chosen from arguments of the main verb of that sentence. Some of their examples suggest that the whole set of arguments of the main verb of a sentence constitute the C_f for that sentence (e.g. when they say that C_f for *John hit Bill* is [*John, Bill*], while C_f for *It was John who hit Bill* is simply [*John*]). They note that the following discourse is awkward: *It was John who hit Bill. He (= Bill) was taken to the hospital.* The awkwardness arises because the backward-looking centre (*Bill*) of the second sentence is not included in the forward-looking centre of the preceding context.

Some workers (Hudson, Tanenhaus, & Dell, 1986) have suggested that the backward-looking centre of sentence i is the preferred antecedent for a pronoun in sentence $i + 1$. They may be correct, in cases where sentence i has a backward-looking centre.[7] However, in cases where no item in sentence i is referentially linked to a centre from earlier in the discourse, and thus no backward-looking centre exists,[8] we would like to suggest that the preferred

---

[6] Joshi and Weinstein suggest that the notion "backward-looking centre" is roughly the same as the notion "topic," and the notion "forward-looking centre" is roughly the same as "focus."

[7] Joshi and Weinstein explicitly deny this, claiming that in a cleft sentence such as "It was John who hit Bill," the forward-looking centre, *John*, not the backward-looking centre, *Bill*, is the preferred antecedent of a following pronoun (e.g. "He was taken to jail/the hospital"). Note further that *Bill* is also the likely topic of the sentence "It was John who hit Bill," indicating that the claim that topics are preferred antecedents may be wrong. However, Experiment 1 of the present paper contained 12 items designed to test this prediction, but found no effect of the cleft construction as compared to a simple declarative construction such as "John hit Bill," in which both *John* and *Bill* are forward-looking centres.

[8] It is debatable whether the materials we used in Experiment 2 had a backward-looking centre in the sentence preceding the pronoun. In some cases, the topic of that sentence was functionally dependent, in some very general sense, upon an element introduced earlier in the story—e.g. the stewardess and the navigator of the story in Table 29.5 are functionally

antecedent for a pronoun is any member of the set of forward-looking centres of sentence *i*. This claim fits with the evidence we have provided. To review: First, a linguistic constituent is not preferred over a nonconstituent as antecedent for a pronoun, consistent with the claim that antecedents are elements in an interpretive model, not linguistic expressions. Second, more than a single element in a sentence's intepretation can be an equally good antecedent for a pronoun. The preferred antecedent need not be a topic or other singleton. (However, as Joshi & Weinstein note, and as our post-hoc analysis of the data suggested, the ease of integrating a new sentence into a discourse model may decrease as the size of the set of forward-looking centres increases.) And third, the set of possible good antecedents may be essentially equivalent to the set of arguments of the verb of the matrix sentence (or verbs of clauses that are co-ordinated with or in an adjunct relation to this sentence). NP interpretations that are introduced as arguments of a subordinated clause, such as a subcategorised complement of the main verb, are not easily available as antecedents of a pronoun.

We must end with a disclaimer. A crucial part of our argument is based on a post-hoc analysis of data, and we cannot adequately assess even in a post-hoc way the role backward-looking centres (as opposed to forward-looking centres) might play in the pronoun comprehension process. Further, we have not disproved the importance of the problem-solving processes we described earlier as the focus of most current theories of pronoun comprehension. All we have done is to restrict the scope of their initial activity to a subset of the possible antecedents of a pronoun. However, we suggest that even this step is of some value. We have some reason to claim that a mental representation that plays a role in theories of inferencing and text comprehension (Grosz, Joshi, & Weinstein, 1983; Joshi & Weinstein, 1981) plays a role in anaphor comprehension. We can further claim that the role it plays permits the activity of general problem-solving processes to be restricted to a subset of the otherwise possible targets, and that this is precisely the function one would expect an efficient, linguistically specialised processor to serve.

ACKNOWLEDGEMENTS

This research was supported by grant HD 18708 from the National Institutes of Health to the first author and Lyn Frazier, and by a Natural Sciences and Engineering Research Council of Canada Postgraduate scholarship to the second author. Barbara Malt and Rosemary Stevenson conceived and conducted Experiment 1 with the first author and Lyn Frazier. We would also like to thank John

---

dependent upon "plane crew"—and thus may constitute backward-looking centres. However, our materials do not permit us to test whether these cases are distinguished in any way from cases where no backward-looking centre exists, so we defer further discussion of the role of backward-looking centres.

Roberts for his help in preparing the materials and conducting Experiment 2, and Lyn Frazier, Marica DeVincenzi, Sandy Pollatsek, and Keith Rayner for their helpful comments on an early draft of this report.

REFERENCES

Caplan, D. (1972). Clause boundaries and recognition latencies for words in sentences. *Perception and Psychophysics, 23*, 506–514.

Caramazza, A., Grober, E., Garvey, C., & Yates, J. (1977). Comprehension of anaphoric pronouns. *Journal of Verbal Learning and Verbal Behaviour, 16*, 601–610.

Carroll, P. & Slowiaczek, M. L. (in press). Modes and modules: Multiple pathways in the language processor. In J. L. Garfield (Ed.), *Modularity in sentence comprehension: Knowledge representation and natural language understanding*. Cambridge, Mass.: M.I.T. Press.

Chafe, W. (1974). Language and consciousness. *Language, 50*, 111–133.

Chomsky, N. (1981). *Lecutres on government and binding: The Pisa Lectures*. Dordrecht: Foris.

Clark, H. H. & Sengul, C. J. (1979). In search of referents for nouns and pronouns. *Memory and Cognition, 7*, 35–41.

Clifton, C. Jr. & Frazier, L. (in press). Processing sentences with long-distance dependencies. In M. Tanenhaus & G. Carlson (Eds.), *Linguistic structure in language processing*. Dordrecht: Reidel.

Corbett, A. & Chang, F. (1983). Pronoun disambiguation: Accessing potential antecedents. *Memory and Cognition, 11*, 383–394.

Ehrlich, K. (1980). Comprehension of pronouns. *Quarterly Journal of Experimental Psychology, 32*, 247–255.

Ehrlich, K. & Rayner, K. (1983). Pronoun assignment and semantic integration during reading: Eye movements and immediacy of processing. *Journal of Verbal Learning and Verbal Behaviour, 22*, 75–87.

Fletcher, C. (1984). Markedness and topic continuity in discourse processing. *Journal of Verbal Learning and Verbal Behaviour, 23*, 487–493.

Fodor, J. A. (1983). *Modularity of mind*. Cambridge, Mass.: M.I.T. Press.

Frazier, L. (1985). Modularity and the representational hypothesis. *NELS 15: Proceedings of the 15th Northeast Linguistics Society*, November, 1984. Amherst, Mass.: G.L.S.A.

Garrod, S. & Sanford, A. J. (1977). Interpreting anaphoric relations: The integration of semantic information while reading. *Journal of Verbal Learning and Verbal Behaviour, 16*, 77–90.

Garvey, C. & Caramazza, A. (1974). Implicit causality in verbs. *Linguistic Inquiry, 5*, 459–464.

Grober, E. H., Beardsley, W., & Caramazza, A. (1978). Parallel function strategy in pronoun assignment. *Cognition, 6*, 117–133.

Grosz, B., Joshi, A., & Weinstein, S. (1983). Providing a unified account of definite noun phrases in discourse. *Proceedings of the Association for Computational Linguistics, M.I.T.* 44–50.

Halliday, M. (1967). Notes on transitivity and theme in English. Part 2. *Journal of Linguistics, 3*, 177–274.

Jarvella, R. J. (1971). Syntactic processing of connected speech. *Journal of Verbal Learning and Verbal Behaviour, 10*, 409–416.

Joshi, A. & Weinstein, S. (1981). Control of inference: Role of some aspects of discourse structure-centring. *Proceedings of the International Joint Conference on Artificial Intelligence*, Vancouver, B.C., August, 1981, 385–387.

Marslen-Wilson, W., Levy, E., & Tyler, L. (1982). Producing interpretable discourse: The establishment and maintenance of reference. In R. J. Jarvella & W. Klein (Eds.), *Speech, place, and action*. Chichester: Wiley.

APPR-V

Reinhart, T. (1982). *Pragmatics and linguistics: An analysis of sentence topics*. Bloomington, Indiana: Indiana University Linguistics Club.

Reinhart, T. (1983). *Anaphora and semantic interpretation*. London: Croom Helm.

Stenning, K. (1978). Anaphora as an approach to pragmatics. In M. Halle, J. Bresnan, & G. A. Miller (Eds.), *Linguistic theory and psychological reality*. Cambridge, Mass.: M.I.T. Press, 162–200.

Tanenhaus, M. K. & Carlson, G. N. (1985). Processing deep and surface anaphors. *Proceedings of NELS 15*, Brown University, November, 1984. Amherst, Mass: G.L.S.A.

van Dijk, T. A. & Kintsch, W. (1983). *Strategies of discourse comprehension*. New York: Academic Press.

van Eckhardt, C. & Potter, M. (1985). Clauses and the semantic representation of words. *Memory and Cognition, 13*, 371–376.

REFERENCE NOTES

1. Blanchard, H. (1985). *The dynamics of perception during fixations in reading*. Unpublished doctoral dissertation, University of Illinois.

2. Crawley, R. (1986). *Some factors influencing the comprehension of pronouns in text*. Paper presented at the Eighth Annual Conference of the Cognitive Science Society, Amherst, Mass., August, 1986.

3. Hudson, S., Tanenhaus, M., & Dell, G. (1986). *The effect of the discourse centre on the local coherence of a discourse*. Paper presented at Eighth Annual Conference of the Cognitive Science Society, Amherst, Mass., August, 1986.

4. Tanenhaus, M. K. & Carlson, G. N. (1986). *Processing verb phrase anaphors*. Paper presented at Cognitive Science Society, University of Massachusetts, August, 1986.

30 Forms of Coding in Sentence Comprehension During Reading

Maria Black
Department of Phonetics and Linguistics
University College London
London, U.K.

Max Coltheart and Sally Byng
Department of Psychology
Birkbeck College, University of London
London, U.K.

ABSTRACT

It is widely believed that the syntactic processor operating upon sentences during reading needs to use a phonological buffer, upon whose contents this processor operates. We provide evidence for this view using verb-gapped sentences such as *Sue polished the table and Frank the shoes*. Subjects were asked to detect semantic anomalies in such sentences, the anomalies being dependent upon the relationship of the verb to the object noun phrase in the second clause (as in *Sue polished the table and Frank the sea*). Anomaly detection was slower or less accurate for those anomalous sentences where a homophone of the verb would yield an acceptable sentence (as in *he rights injustices and she books*), suggesting that when the syntactic processor is dealing with verb gaps, the filling of the gap involves consulting phonological representations from the first clause.

It turned out that processing of these sentences was also impeded when the verb and its gap differed in number, even when past tenses, where singular and plural verbs do not differ in phonology, are used (as in *Your friends mended the car and your brother the bike*). Implications of this result, and of the homophone effect, for modelling sentence processing are considered.

INTRODUCTION

Consider the sentence "Gibson influenced Turvey, and Sternberg Besner." We are not asking you to judge the truth of this sentence. We are inviting you to agree with our assertion that the sentence is perfectly understandable despite the fact that one of its two clauses, viz. "Sternberg Besner," is by itself utterly incomprehensible. How does the reader or listener cope with this potential difficulty in the comprehension of such sentences?

Our psychohistorical sentence embodies the phenomenon known as *verb gapping*.[1] In certain types of two-clause sentences in English, it is permissible, whilst not obligatory, to omit the verb from the second clause. Both (1) and (2) are acceptable English sentences:

1. Sue polishes the furniture and Frank polishes the shoes.
2. Sue polishes the furniture and Frank the shoes.

For (1), each of the two conjoined clauses is complete in itself; each clause is both parsable in isolation and understandable in isolation. When processing sentences like (2), however, the reader/listener has first to recognise that the second clause is missing its verb and to parse the clause as if it contained a verb slot, even though no actual lexical material fills this slot. A suitable antecedent for the missing verb then has to be found, by referring back to the first clause of the sentence, since one of the very many constraints on verb gapping is that a verb can only be omitted from any clause in a sentence if it has occurred in a previous clause.[2] It follows that some representation of some or all of the first clause will have to be available and accessible during the processing of the second clause. Our paper concerns the nature of this representation.

There are a number of different hypotheses that might be advanced here. First of all, one might ask whether any kind of specifically *linguistic* representation is involved at all. It is possible that elliptical sentences of the kind exemplified by (2) are interpreted by referring to some kind of nonlinguistic representation of the first clause. For instance, some conceptual representation or "discourse model" of the action or state expressed by the verb in the first clause might be used as the antecedent of the verb gap. This is what Tanenhaus, Carlson, and Seidenberg (1985, p. 385) have termed the direct reference hypothesis: ". . . an anaphor is assigned the same denotation as its antecedent by being directly linked to some element in the constructed representation. Thus the anaphor does not have to be replaced by a linguistic antecedent in order for it to be assigned a denotation."

---

[1] In this paper we deal only with cases involving one tense-carrying verb and its associated gap. For a discussion of other cases—cases involving auxiliaries, for example—see Fodor (Note 1; 1985).

[2] See Hankamer and Sag (1976), Williams (1977), and Koster (1978) for a detailed discussion of the linguistic constraints on verb gapping. Different psycholinguistic interpretations of some of these constraints can be found in Sag and Hankamer (1984), Berwick and Weinberg (1984) and Fodor (1985).

There is some linguistic and psycholinguistic evidence in favour of this hypothesis for at least some cases of overt anaphoric reference, such as that involved in the use of personal pronouns. For example, Clifton and Ferreira (this volume) provide evidence that antecedents for pronouns are found by consulting a representation that captures referential identity, rather than by consulting a syntactic representation. They go on to argue that the relevant representation is the "discourse centre" (rather than the discourse topic).

However, this form of hypothesis about the nature of the representation consulted appeared much less promising in the case of null anaphors ("gaps"). For example, overt anaphors such as pronouns can be pragmatically controlled, whilst null anaphors such as verb gaps cannot be (see Sag & Hankamer, 1984). Imagine you hear somebody singing: You might say (3) but you would not say (4).

3. I wonder who *she* was   (pronominal anaphora)
4. *I wonder who *was* [Ø]   (verb phrase ellipsis)

A second reason for being dubious about the hypothesis that it is a nonlinguistic representation that is consulted in processing verb gaps is that verb gapping requires parallelism of linguistic structure between the first and the second clauses of sentences like (2), as the following examples illustrate:

5. The furniture is polished by Sue and the shoes by Frank.
6. *The furniture is polished by Sue and Frank the shoes.
7. The furniture is polished by Sue and Frank polishes the shoes.

Thus, in two-clause sentences like these it is permissible for the clauses to differ in voice; but if they do, verb gapping is not permissible. Whether the first clause is active or passive makes no difference to the conceptual information the clause conveys. Therefore, if it were conceptual information from the first clause that was being consulted, the voice of the first clause should not affect the permissibility of verb gapping—yet it does.

These arguments in favour of the view that what is consulted in such cases is some type of linguistic representation derive from consideration of some of the constraints on the occurrence of verb gapping. Tanenhaus et al. (1985, p. 399) derived a similar view from consideration of the results of experimental studies of sentence verification. Their conclusion was that: "... surface anaphors (e.g. verb phrase ellipsis) are understood by going back to a linguistic representation, while deep anaphors (e.g. pronouns) are understood by going back to a non-linguistic representation."[3]

---

[3] Tanenhaus and Carlson (1984) report failures to replicate the results upon which this conclusion was based.

If it is, in fact, the case that verb-gapping is dealt with by referring to linguistic representations of information in the first clause of sentences like (2), what types of linguistic representations are involved? In the case of reading comprehension, which is the case we are concerned with in this paper, these representations might be orthographic, or they might be phonological, or they might be semantic.

ORTHOGRAPHIC FORM

Suppose that what the reader does when confronted with a verb gap is to retrieve from the first clause the *orthographic* form of the verb in this clause, and to "insert" this form in the gap. This would make the second clause complete, and so it could be parsed and understood. Hence the problem of the verb gap would be solved—except for such sentences as:

8. Soldiers wound enemies and watchmakers clocks.

This sentence is semantically anomalous—but the anomaly could not be detected if the verb gap was dealt with by inserting the orthography of the first verb in the gap, since

9. Soldiers wound enemies and watchmakers wound clocks

is semantically acceptable. Thus if subjects are asked to judge the acceptability of sentences, and if sentences like (8) are compared to sentences like (10):

10. *Soldiers wound enemies and watchmakers books

one would observe poorer performance for sentences like (8) than for sentences like (10) if orthographic representations of first-clause verbs are used. If the two sentence types do not yield differences in performance, that would be evidence against the orthographic hypothesis.

PHONOLOGICAL FORM

Using the same reasoning, one can construct sentences like (11) and (12):

11. *He rights injustices and she books.
12. *He rights injustices and she the sugar.

If the reader is inserting the phonological form of the first-clause verb in the second-clause verb gap, then (11) will become the acceptable:

13. He rights injustices and she /raɪts/ books.

and so an error will be made, whilst (12) will still correctly be judged unacceptable, since it becomes:

14. *He rights injustices and she /raɪts/ the sugar.

Thus, poorer performance with sentences like (11) compared to sentences like (12) would suggest that phonological representations are being used, and equivalence of performance would be evidence against this hypothesis.

"LITERAL" FORM VERSUS SEMANTIC REPRESENTATION

The two types of representation we have considered so far—the orthographic and the phonological—are both "literal" in the sense that they represent a particular kind of surface form for words. An alternative possibility for the code used when dealing with verb gaps is the semantic code: Perhaps it is the meaning of the verb, rather than some literal representation of it, that is used?

Consider these two examples:

15. I play the violin and she the drums.
16. Mary plays the violin and her brothers the drums.

These examples show that, despite the stringency of the various constraints on verb gapping that we have discussed, a *little* freedom is allowed. It is not demanded that the antecedent verb and the verb that fits the gap be absolutely identical. They are permitted to differ in number, and also in person.[4]

Is there a processing cost associated with these permissible number and person mismatches? If the reader uses a semantic representation of the verb, which is not likely to specify number or person, then there should be no cost. If, instead, any "literal" representation is used, be it orthographic, phonological, or anything else that specifies number and person, then performance might be impaired when there is a mismatch. This can be investigated by comparing sentences like (16) to sentences like (17):

17. Mary plays the violin and Sue the drums.

---

[4]This is not a general property of filler-gap constructions. In wh- questions, for example, the wh-phrase (the filler) and the gap are required to agree in grammatical gender and number (see, e.g. Engdhal (1985) for more on this).

The experiments we report investigate all these possible effects. Subjects were asked to judge whether or not printed sentences were anomalous. The sentences they saw included sentences like (8) and (10), to explore the orthographic-coding hypothesis; sentences like (11) and (12), to explore the phonological-coding hypothesis; and sentences like (16) and (17), to explore the semantic hypothesis.

The construction of sentences like (8) and (10) depends upon selecting pairs of verbs with identical spellings and different pronunciations. We were able to find only two: *wound* and *bow*. Hence this comparison unfortunately involves only two sentences per condition.

EXPERIMENT 1

Subjects

These were ten female undergraduate or graduate students from the University of London.

Materials

These were 140 sentences from 5 to 11 words long. Half were considered to be semantically anomalous and half were considered to be acceptable. Thirty were filler sentences and the data from these were discarded. The remaining 110 sentences all consisted of 2 clauses with a verb gap in the second clause. All anomalies arose because of a semantic incompatibility between the verb and the object of the second clause.

Let V_1 denote the verb in the first clause and V_G denote its gap in the second clause. These 110 sentences represented the following 12 conditions:

Homophone Sentences and Their Controls (N=26)

Anomalous sentences in which a homophone of V_1 inserted at the gap would yield an acceptable sentence, e.g. "He rights injustices and she books" (N = 13).

Controls derived from the homophone sentences by altering the last noun in each sentence, e.g. "He rights injustices and she water" (N = 13).

Homograph Sentences and Their Controls (N=4)

Anomalous sentences in which a homograph of V_1 inserted at the gap would yield an acceptable sentence, e.g. "Soldiers wound enemies and watchmakers clocks" (N = 2).

Controls derived from the homograph sentences by altering the last noun in each sentence, e.g. "Soldiers wound enemies and watchmakers books" (N = 2).

Number match/mismatch sentences	(N = 80)
YES sentences	(N = 40)
V_1 and V_G same number	(N = 20)
Both singular	(N = 10)
Both plural	(N = 10)
V_1 and V_G different in number	(N = 20)
V_1 plural, V_G singular	(N = 10)
V_1 singular, V_G plural	(N = 10)
NO sentences	(N = 40)
V_1 and V_G same number	(N = 20)
Both singular	(N = 10)
Both plural	(N = 10)
V_1 and V_G different in number	(N = 20)
V_1 plural, V_G singular	(N = 10)
V_1 singular, V_G plural	(N = 10)

Procedure

Subjects were instructed that they would be seeing sentences on a VDU controlled by an APPLE microcomputer, and that their task was to press a YES key when a sentence was well formed and a NO key when it was anomalous. Response accuracy and latency was recorded by the microcomputer. After 4 practice trials, the 140 sentences referred to above were presented, in a different random order for each subjects. The sentence display was terminated by the subject's response, or after five seconds had elapsed (whichever occurred first). Responses with latencies exceeding five seconds were treated as errors. The interval between each response and the following stimulus was two seconds.

Results

The Homophone Effect

Table 30.1 shows the data from the homophone and homophone controls conditions. Significantly more errors were made to the homophone sentences than to their controls (t = 2.753, P = 0.0224). The fact that errors were common in one condition and almost entirely absent in the other makes direct comparison of mean latencies complicated, because the materials in the two conditions would no longer be matched when many items from one

APPR-V*

condition and very few from the other are excluded from consideration, errors having been made to them. This problem was rectified by excluding from calculations those items to which errors were made, *and* the matched items for these pairs in the other condition. The mean correct RTs of Table 30.1 were computed in this way. These means did not differ significantly: $t = 0.243$, $P = 0.41$.

Although the two conditions differed greatly in error rate, four of the ten subjects made no errors at all in either condition. All four yielded slower mean latencies in the homophone condition than in the control condition, the differences being 11, 69, 314 and 335msec. Analysis of the latency data for these four subjects yielded a marginally significant result: $t = 2.193$, one-tailed $P = 0.0579$.

TABLE 30.1
Effect of Homophony on Sentence Acceptability Judgements

	Mean Error Rate	Mean Correct RT (See Text)
Homophone Sentences He rights injustices and she books	13.85%	2466
Control Sentences He rights injustices and she water	1.54%	2447

The Homograph Effect

Table 30.2 shows the data from the homograph and homograph control conditions. Neither error rates nor response latencies differed significantly between conditions (for the latency data, $t = 0.542$, $P = 0.2971$).

TABLE 30.2
Effect of Homography on Sentence Acceptability Judgements

	Mean Error Rate	Mean Correct RT
Homograph Sentences Soldiers wound enemies and watchmakers clocks	1.0%	2452
Control Sentences Soldiers wound enemies and watchmakers books	0.5%	2586

The Number Mismatch Effect

Table 30.3 shows the mean YES/NO judgement rates (error rates) and mean correct latencies for the four relevant conditions. For the YES sentences, error rate was significantly greater when V_1 and V_G were different in number than when they were the same: $t = 3.545$, $P = 0.0062$. Response latency was also greater: $t = 4.803$, $P = 0.001$. For the NO sentences, neither error rate nor response latency differed between conditions.

TABLE 30.3
Effect of Mismatching Verb Number on Sentence Acceptability Judgements

YES Sentences	Mean % NO Responses	Mean Correct RT
Number Match		
John eats bananas and Mary apples		
Cats chase mice and dogs cats	6.5	2506
Number Mismatch		
John feeds the pigs and the workers the cows		
Your aunts see ghosts and Mary apparitions	26.0	2877

NO Sentences	Mean % YES Responses	Mean Correct RT
Number Match		
John eats bananas and Mary cars		
Cats chase mice and dogs dishes	4.0	2420
Number Mismatch		
John feeds the pigs and the workers the tables		
Your aunts see ghosts and Mary noises	6.5	2472

Summary of Results and Their Implications

There was no evidence that subjects were consulting orthographic representations of the early part of the sentences when dealing with the verb gap, although the smallness of the number of sentences in the relevant conditions means that this negative conclusion must be a very tentative one. In contrast, there was clear evidence from both error rates and latencies of the use of phonological representations of the verbs in the first clauses of the sentences. Finally, performance was slowed for the YES sentences when the first-clause verb differed in number from the gap in the second clause.

DISCUSSION

Phonological Recoding and Reading Comprehension

Previous work on the relationship between phonological coding and reading comprehension is reviewed by Patterson and Coltheart (this volume). Various techniques have been used in this work, but all have provided evidence for some role of phonological coding for reading comprehension. For most studies, in any condition where ambiguity or difficulty would be introduced by a use of phonological codes, error rates are increased whilst response latency is unaffected. A few studies have observed effects upon latency as well as upon accuracy. A general conclusion reached by those who have carried out this kind of research, and by Patterson and Coltheart in their review, is that the syntactic processor requires, during reading, the use of a phonological buffer, upon whose contents it operates. Why such a buffer is needed, and what operations are performed upon the contents of the buffer by the syntactic processor, are questions which are not considered much in the previous literature.

The technique we have used differs from those previously used in studies of phonological recoding and sentence comprehension in that it is capable not only of yielding evidence of the use of such recoding, but also of defining one of the ways in which the syntactic processor uses such recoding—namely, to deal with constructions involving verb gapping. Of course, there is much more that needs to be learned about this situation. One point is that, if subjects solely referred to the phonological form of the verb in the first clause, they would be at chance in judging the homophone sentences: One meaning of the homophone is acceptable, the other anomalous. Error rates are high, but do not approach chance levels. Why not? This could reflect a bias towards responding "No" when there is ambiguity, which would lead one to expect very high miss rates with *acceptable* sentences containing homophonic verbs, such as (18).

18. The cowboy chews tobacco and the child gum.

Alternatively, reference to phonology might be common but not invariable: If this were so, what other code is referred to? A second point is that what is consulted is the phonological code *of the verb* in the first clause. Hence the representation accessed must be syntactically labelled in some way. Otherwise the reader would not know which of the phonological forms from the first clause was the verb. Both these issues need to be explored.

The Number Mismatch Effect

We have just noted that it is not only phonology, but also some aspect of syntax, that must be consulted in the first clause in order to deal with verb gapping. One method for investigating this a little further is to consider why it is that performance is impeded when the *number* of the verb in the first clause is inappropriate for the second clause (at least for YES sentences; we consider this in relation to NO sentences later).

This number mismatch effect could in fact be phonological in origin. Perhaps it occurs because the precise phonological form of the verb in the first clause is not an entirely appropriate filler of the gap in the second when the subject NPs in the two clauses differ in number. This (relatively minor) inappropriateness might need to be dealt with, and this might cost processing time.

Alternatively, the effect could be morphosyntactic in origin. It might arise because of a clash between the morphosyntactic features of the verb gap and those of its antecedent in the first clause.

It is possible to adjudicate between these two accounts of the number mismatch effect by using the past tense, rather than the present tense, which was used in Experiment 1. In past-tense sentences, you can have a morphosyntactic clash but no phonological clash, as in sentences like (19a–b).

19. a. Sue polished the shoes and the adults the furniture.
    b. The children polished the shoes and John the furniture.

These sentences can be compared to sentences like (20a–b), where there is no number mismatch.

20. a. Sue polished the shoes and John the furniture.
    b. The children polished the shoes and the adults the furniture.

If the number mismatch effect observed in Experiment 1 is phonological, it will not be present with past-tense materials of this kind. If the effect is morphosyntactic, it will remain even when one switches to the past tense.

EXPERIMENT 2

Subjects

These were ten female undergraduate or graduate students from the University of London or City University, London.

Materials

These were 80 sentences from 8 to 10 words long. All consisted of two clauses with a verb gap in the second clause. The verb in the first clause was always in the past tense. These 80 sentences represented the following 8 conditions:

YES sentences	(N = 40)
V_1 and V_G same number	(N = 10)
Both singular	(N = 10)
Both plural	(N = 10)
V_1 and V_G different in number	(N = 20)
V_1 singular, V_G plural	(N = 10)
V_1 plural, V_G singular	(N = 10)
NO sentences	(N = 40)
V_1 and V_G same number	(N = 20)
Both singular	(N = 10)
Both plural	(N = 10)
V_1 and V_G different in number	(N = 20)
V_1 singular, V_G plural	(N = 10)
V_1 plural, V_G singular	(N = 10)

Examples of these sentences can be found in Table 30.4 below. As in Experiment 1, the anomaly always concerned the object of the second clause.

Procedure

Exactly as for Experiment 1.

Results

Table 30.4 shows the mean YES/NO judgement rates (error rates) and mean correct latencies for the four conditions, collapsing across number. For the YES sentences, error rates were significantly greater when V_1 and V_G differed in number than when they were the same: $z = 2.2032$, $P = 0.0422$.

Response latency was also greater: $t = 6.41$, $P = 0.0002$. For the NO sentences, niether error rate nor response latency differed between conditions.

Discussion

The number mismatch effects observed in Experiment 1 with YES sentences still occur with past tense sentences where there is no clash of phonological forms. This suggests that the effects stem from the use of a morphosyntactic representation of the verb from the first clause.

TABLE 30.4
Effect of Mismatching Verb Number on Sentence Acceptability Judgements: Past-tense
Sentences

YES Sentences	Mean % NO Responses	Mean Correct RT
Number Match		
Sue polished the table and Frank the shoe		
The actors learned the play and the singers the music	0.5	2378
Number Mismatch		
Your friends mended the car and your brother the bike		
John fed the pigs and the workers the cows	6.5	2638

No Sentences	Mean % YES Responses	Mean Correct RT
Number Match		
Sue polished the table and Frank the river		
The actors learned the play and the singers the place	19.0	2626
Number Mismatch		
Your friends mended the car and your brothers the ocean		
John fed the pigs and the workers the tables	13.0	2694

Another way in which the two experiments agreed was that NO sentences yielded no number mismatch effects in either experiment. Why are these effects confined to YES sentences? The semantic incompatibility in our NO sentences is always between the verb and its object NP in the second clause. The number mismatches, when present, are between the verb and its subject NP in the second clause. Perhaps what is happening is that, for NO sentences, processing stops after the verb is linked to its object NP and the phrase interpreted, but before the resulting VP is linked to the subject NP to assemble the entire second clause. Hence a NO decision will be made before the number clash between subject NP and verb can have any effect. For YES sentences, processing continues beyond the point at which the VP is assembled, and so the number clash can have an effect.

There is a simple way to test this: Use sentences where the semantic incompatibility is between the verb and its *subject* NP in the second clause—sentences like (21):

21. *John eats bananas and the car apples.

For these sentences, the anomaly cannot be detected until the subject NP in the second clause is related to the verb. If our explanation of why Experiments 1 and 2 obtained number mismatch effects for only YES sentences is correct, it follows that with subject-anomalous sentences like (21) the number mismatch effects should occur for both YES *and* NO sentences.

EXPERIMENT 3

Subjects

These were ten female undergraduates from London University and the City University, London.

Materials

These were 80 sentences from 6 to 10 words long. All consisted of two clauses with a verb gap in the second clause. Half were anomalous, and this was always because of the relationship of the first-clause verb to the subject NP in the second clause. These 80 sentences represented the following 8 conditions:

YES sentences	(N = 40)
V_1 and V_G same number	(N = 20)
Both singular	(N = 10)
Both plural	(N = 10)
V_1 and V_G different in number	(N = 20)
V_1 singular, V_G plural	(N = 10)
V_1 plural, V_G singular	(N = 10)
NO sentences	(N = 40)
V_1 and V_G same number	(N = 20)
Both singular	(N = 10)
Both plural	(N = 10)
V_1 and V_G different in number	(N = 20)
V_1 singular, V_G plural	(N = 10)
V_1 plural, V_G singular	(N = 10)

Procedure

Exactly as for the previous two experiments.

Results

Table 30.5 shows the mean YES/NO judgement rates (error rates and mean correct latencies for the four conditions, collapsing across number). As in the previous two experiments, for the YES sentences error rates were significantly greater when V_1 and V_G differed in number than when they were the same: $z = 2.392$, $P = 0.0168$. Response latency was also greater: $t = 5.389$, $P = 0.0004$.

In contrast to the previous two experiments, however, a number mismatch effect occurred with NO sentences. The effect on error rate was not significant, but the effect on response latency was: $t = 3.222$, $P = 0.0104$.

GENERAL DISCUSSION

All the results of Experiment 1 can be given a single explanation if the phonological form of the antecedent verb serves as "the filler" for the gap in

TABLE 30.5

Effect of Mismatching Verb Number on Sentence Acceptability Judgements: Subject-NP Anomalies

YES Sentences	Mean % NO Responses	Mean Correct RT
Number Match		
Sue polishes the table and Frank the shoe		
The actors learn the play and the singers the music	1.5	2445
Number Mismatch		
Your friends mend the car and your brother the bike		
John feeds the pigs and the workers the cows	24.0	2731
NO Sentences	Mean % YES Responses	Mean Correct RT
Number Match		
Sue polishes the table and the river the shoe		
The actors learn the play and the plates the music	8.0	2439
Number Mismatch		
Your friends mend the car and the ocean the bike		
John feeds the pigs and the table the cows	8.5	2539

the second clause. But the number, and perhaps person, of the antecedent verb must also be available and "carried over" with the phonological form. What is recovered cannot be a simple ummarked phonological form because of the results of Experiment 2. Since the past form of verbs does not vary with the number and person of the subject noun phrase, the unmarked phonological form of the antecedent should always be an appropriate filler for the gap. Yet the mismatch effect does not disappear when past tenses are used. If we want to maintain a unitary explanation for both the homophone effect and the mismatch effect, we have to add some morphosyntactic features to the simple phonological form we started with.

Alternatively, one could claim that the homophone effect and the mismatch effect have little to do with one another: They could be said to involve different types of representations at different stages of processing. The homophone effect could still be explained in terms of the involvement of phonological forms in the initial filling of the gap. But the mismatch effect would have to be seen as resulting from the lack of parallelism between the subject noun phrases in the two clauses at the logico-semantic and/or conceptual level, as there is little reason to assume that the semantic representation of the verb itself carries number and person specifications. In this case, the mismatch effect tells us something about another kind of parallelism that must exist between clauses in verb gapping structures, though it throws little light on the type of representation involved in filling the verb gap itself.

As we have argued, the number mismatch effect cannot be entirely phonological in origin. However, nor can it be the case that it has nothing to do with phonology. If the effect arises solely because the first clause and its gap differ in number, the effect should be independent of tense. However, this is not so. Subjects' rates of responding NO to YES sentences with number mismatch were much higher in Experiments 1 and 3 (which used present tenses) than in Experiment 2 (which used past tenses). These differences were significant: Kruskal–Wallis Test, $P = 0.05$. Planned comparisons showed that the rates of NO response were significantly lower in Experiment 2 than in the other two experiments ($P = 0.0343$), whilst the difference between Experiment 1 and Experiment 3 was not significant. Thus, in Experiments 1 and 3 there are two contributions to the number mismatch effect: a phonological clash, and an effect due to morphosyntactic, logico-semantic or conceptual differences between the two clauses. Only the second of these effects could (and indeed does) arise in Experiment 2.

The various interpretations of this second effect influence how we understand the absence of a mismatch effect for the NO sentences of Experiments 1 and 2, and the appearance of the effect in Experiment 3. We have argued that the anomaly, or implausibility, of the verb phrase in the second clause must be detected before the mismatch is perceived, since subjects' judgements are not slowed down by number mismatches in the NO sentences of the first two experiments. Speed of judgement is only affected when the *subject* and the verb of the second clause are incompatible. This means that the verb phrase is semantically interpreted before assembly of the whole clause is completed. We then have to decide whether semantic interpretation at a phrasal level takes place before the syntactic representation of the whole clause is assembled, or before some kind of logico-semantic, or even conceptual, representation of the clause is constructed. The two interpretations of the mismatch effect suggest different answers to this question. If by mismatch we mean a clash of morphosyntactic features, it is more plausible that such a clash should be detected at an "earlier" stage of processing when the syntactic structure is being assembled. On the other hand, if the mismatch arises from lack of semantic/conceptual parallelism, a semantic/conceptual level of representation would be implied.

The questions raised by this consideration of our results are, clearly, numerous, but at least a few questions have been answered. We have obtained evidence that one of the uses made of the phonological buffer by the syntactic processor during sentence reading is as a source of information when verb gaps are being dealt with; and we have also shown that morphosyntactic information from the first clause may be accessed when such constructions need to be analysed.

ACKNOWLEDGEMENTS

We thank Chuck Clifton and John Duncan for their comments on an earlier draft. This work was supported by a grant from the Medical Research Council of Great Britain.

REFERENCES

Berwick, R. C. & Weinberg, A. S. (1984). *The grammatical basis of linguistic performance: Language use and acquisition.* Cambridge, Mass.: M.I.T. Press.

Engdhal, E. (1985). Interpreting questions. In D. R. Dowty, L. Karttunen, & A. M. Zwicky (Eds.), *Natural language parsing: Psychological, computational, and theoretical perspectives.* Cambridge: Cambridge University Press.

Fodor, J. (1985). Deterministic parsing and subjacency. *Language and Cognitive Processes, 1,* 3–42.

Hankamer, J. & Sag, I. (1976). Deep and surface anaphors. *Linguistic Inquiry, 7,* 391–426.

Koster, J. (1978). *Locality principles in syntax.* Dordrecht: Foris Publications.

Sag, I. & Hankamer, J. (1984). Toward a theory of anaphoric processing. *Linguistics and Philosophy, 7,* 325–345.

Tanenhaus, M. K. & Carlson, G. N. (1984). Processing deep and surface anaphors. In S. Berman, J-W. Choe, & J. McDonough (Eds.), *Proceedings of NELS 15.* Amherst: North Eastern Linguistic Society.

Tanenhaus, M. K., Carlson, G. N., & Seidenberg, M. S. (1985). Do listeners compute linguistic representations? In D. R. Dowty, L. Karttunen, & A. M. Zwicky (Eds.), *Natural language parsing: Psychological, computational, and theoretical perspectives*. Cambridge: Cambridge University Press.

Williams, E. S. (1977). Discourse and logical form. *Linguistic Inquiry, 8*, 101–113.

REFERENCE NOTE

1. Fodor, J. (1975). *Gapping gapped*. Unpublished manuscript, University of Connecticut.

31 Language Processing and Linguistic Explanation

Amy Weinberg
Linguistics Program
University of Maryland at College Park
Maryland, U.S.A.

ABSTRACT

Recent experimental work in psycholinguistics has led to rather contradictory results, with different experimental paradigms pointing to mutually incompatible parsing algorithms and even contradictory parsing architectures. This chapter tries to provide supplementary criteria using evidence from linguistic and computation theory that can help us to narrow the range of possible human language comprehension systems that can be submitted to more effective experimental test. The paper discusses three algorithms and two general parsing architectures (ATN and LR(k) parsers) that are compatible with results from reading comprehension and recall studies first discussed by Wanner and Maratsos (1978). We show that only the LR(k) parser using an analogue of the successive cyclic movement analysis can both predict Wanner and Maratsos' data and explain why natural languages are universally governed by a linguistic restriction known as the subjacency constraint. Along the way, we provide general criteria for distinguishing when a mechanism explains a body of experimental data from those cases where the mechanism is merely compatible with a class of empirical results.

INTRODUCTION

In this paper I will discuss a somewhat novel way of uncovering the properties of the human language comprehension system. Other work in this volume (see the chapters by Clifton, Holmes, Mitchell, and the studies reviewed in the chapter by Frazier) explore this question using a variety of experimental paradigms. This work is surely crucial, but a review of even the papers in this volume reveals that, at the moment, it is somewhat equivocal. In fact different experimental paradigms seem to favour mutually incompatible processing mechanisms. Another problem is that a large class of experimental data seems to be consistent with a wide variety of processing algorithms and even with a wide variety of mutually incompatible parsing architectures. In fact, I would argue that the main task facing the theory of human sentence processing today is to provide criteria to constrain the class of possible natural language comprehension systems and provide a much smaller range of possible parsing systems that can be subjected to experimental test. In this paper I will argue that paying attention to the constraints on syntactic representations proposed by linguists is essential to achieving this goal. The search for an algorithm that can retrieve previously encountered material in a way that is embeddable in those parsers can explain an important constraint on the form of grammars; the subjacency constraint on Chomsky (1973).

Before proceeding, it is important to distinguish what we mean by *explanation of a constraint*.

In developing a theory of human sentence comprehension, it is important to differentiate cases where a particular parsing algorithm or general proposal for parser design actually allows us to *explain* some feature of linguistic behaviour or linguistic structure from those cases where the algorithm or device is merely compatible with these phenomena. As a minimal condition on explanation, we would like the observed properties to fall out as a *necessary* consequence of the processor or algorithm's design. That is, these properties are not explained if we can show that the parser or algorithm would run equally well on data not characterised by the property in question.

I will proceed with this investigation by considering the interpretation of questions. I will first briefly recapitulate some experiments by Wanner and Maratsos (1978) on memory constraints during reading. Then I will describe three algorithms that claim to model the experimental findings; the augmented transition network (ATN) of Wanner and Maratsos (1978), Harman's "generative encoding procedure," and a procedure modelled after the successive cyclic theory of movement of Chomsky (1973). I will show that *all* three algorithms are compatible with a body of relevant psycholinguistic data.

ON THE INTERPRETATION OF QUESTIONS: WANNER AND MARATSOS' MODEL

Wanner and Maratsos (1978) provided evidence from a reading comprehension task to show that the interpretation of questions is performed by linking a quasi quantifier (question word) from a syntactic position in which it appears in the surface string to a position elsewhere in the structure that allows it to be associated with an appropriate semantic role. Their experiments suggested that the quasi quantifier in a structure like (1) had to be held in a memory store until the position associated with its logical role was located as shown in (2). We can see that the element "e_i" is in the position associated with the logical role of the quantifier by noticing that the quantifier has the same logical role, *subject* of the embedded sentence as the underlined phrase in (3) and that this phrase appears in the same position as the element e_i in (2).

1. Who did John think ate the cake?
2. Who$_i$ did John think e$_i$ ate the cake?
3. John thought that <u>Mary</u> ate the cake.

Wanner and Maratsos assumed that holding a semantically uninterpreted element (an element not associated with a logical role) would place a burden on the memory system which predicted that memory load would increase in the region between the quantifier and the gap. They presented subjects with sentences involving the linking of a WH quantifier to a gap position in a sentence. The sentence was interrupted at various points by an unrelated word list of proper names. Subjects were asked to both recall and comprehend the sentence *and* to recall the associated list of names. Recall of this list was significantly retarded if it was presented in the region between the position of the quantifier and its gap. The retardation was attributed to the fact that since the parser was holding an unintegrated item in its linguistic memory (an item with no assigned logical role in the sentence), memory capacity was being used up and what remained was simply insufficient to accomplish the recall task successfully. Wanner and Maratsos proposed to model this prediction in their parser by claiming that this device was augmented with a special storage bin (called a HOLD store) that retained semantically uninterpreted question words until the position indicating the quantifier's logical role was encountered.[1] The algorithm works by having the processor place a copy of the WH element in the HOLD store as soon as it is encountered in the syntactic string. The parser also has access both to syntactic and lexical information about sentence structure that tells it when to access the HOLD mechanism. For example, it is a fact that English sentences must have lexical subjects. However the surface string (1) contains no overt element that can act as the subject of the embedded sentence "ate the cake." Before marking the structure as unacceptable, however, the processor consults the HOLD store to see if it contains any elements that can fill this position. If there is such an element, the parser removes it from the HOLD store and inserts it in the appropriate position. A successful parse involves associating all elements in the surface string with a syntactic position

---

[1] Wanner and Maratsos' model is an Augmented Transition Network based on a design proposed in Woods (1970) and Kaplan (1973).

and having no elements left in the HOLD store. Having semantically uninterpreted items in the HOLD store is what triggers the memory overload.

HARMAN'S METHOD OF GENERATIVE ENCODING

Wanner and Maratsos are quite careful to point out that these results, while compatible with an ATN augmented with a HOLD store, are not decisive evidence either for an ATN or for the HOLD hypothesis.[2]

This caution seems to be well motivated because in fact there are many algorithms that will make exactly the same predictions about the burden placed on memory by carrying along a semantically uninterpreted element over a stretch of lexical material.

For example, Harman (1963) proposed an algorithm that has been widely adopted within the Generalised Phrase Structure Theory of Grammar. As in many traditional theories, this approach assumes that sentence comprehension involves the construction of a syntactic phrase structure tree. In this system, one chooses a different set of rules depending on whether or not a lexical item can receive a semantic interpretation from its position in the acoustic or printed signal. A sentence like (4), where all items can be interpreted in place, would require the phrase structure rules in (5) and produce the syntactic representation in (6).

4. John saw Mary.
5. S(entence)→N(oun) P(hrase) V(erb) P(hrase)
   NP→N
   VP→V NP

6.

However, in a sentence like (7) the semantic role of the question word is not known until we reach the underscored position. In order to keep track of the presence of the question word in the syntactic string, we choose a different set of phrase structure rules that represents the presence of the question word at all points in the parse. The rules are given in (8).

---

[2]Wanner and Maratsos (1978, p. 157): "This localised effect ... (the fact that transient memory load increases in the region between the quantifier and its position of interpretation [ASW]) is consistent with the HOLD hypothesis ... Thus our results provided initial support for the HOLD hypothesis and demonstrate the feasibility of using ATN notation to construct psychological models of syntactic processing."

7. Who did you see?
8. S/NP→NP VP/NP
   VP/NP→V NP/NP (intepreted as a gap)
   NP/NP→e

The presence of an element to the right of the slash ("/") in (8) means that the parser has detected an uninterpreted noun phrase (the initial question word) in (7). We preserve this information (and the fact that the question word awaits semantic interpretation) by encoding the "/NP" notation as part of each successive phrase structure rule until we reach the point where the category can be intepreted. As in the first algorithm, the parser does not retrieve the presence of the question word by reaccessing the position where it appears in the written string directly. Rather, this algorithm creates a representation that allows the parser to retrieve the presence of the question word while retracing its steps *only* to the category that immediately dominates the point from which semantic interpretation takes place. The syntactic tree structure for (7) is given in (9).

9.

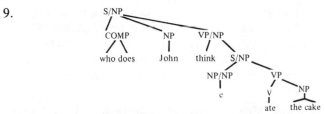

Assuming this algorithm, the memory complexity comes from storing the additional semantically uninterpreted members (the elements to the right of a slash in a slashed category) of the phrase structure rules in the structure intervening between the quantifier and the gap position. Similarly, under the HOLD hypothesis, the parser can access the HOLD store without retracing its steps through the syntactic structure that it has already constructed because it can locally access a copy of the question word that was previously encountered in the HOLD store.[3]

---

[3] These two algorithms are similar in that they allow for the local encoding of an element that can be potentially unboundedly far away in the string from its position of semantic interpretation, as is shown in a case like (a).

  a. Who_i do you think John said that Fred believed that Alice thought e_i ate the cake?

A parser would have to backtrack over a potentially unbounded amount of material if it had to look back from the position of the "gap" to the position where the quantifier actually occurs in the phonetic string associated with (5). Wanner and Maratsos presumed that this backtracking would take quite a bit of time, but this does not correlate with our intuition that sentences like (a) are not particularly difficult to comprehend; nor does it seem possible to guarantee that these sentences could be processed efficently, if such backtracking were necessary.

CHOMSKY'S SUCCESSIVE CYCLIC THEORY OF MOVEMENT

A third algorithm stores the presence of the question word in the actual phrase structure without recourse to HOLD stores or augmented phrase structure components. This algorithm corresponds to the *successive cyclic theory of movement* proposed in Chomsky (1973). This theory assumes that sentences are introduced by the following rule:

10. S' → COMP S

The COMP is the category that holds the sentence introducing categories; "that" as in (11a) or "what," the question word in indirect questions like (11b).

11. a. I know that John is a nice guy.
    b. I wonder who ate the cake.

Chomsky assumes that this complementiser can also hold a copy of the question word that will eventually be linked with the position from which the category will be semantically interpreted. Thus the structure of (7) would be (12). The question word "who" is linked to its semantic position by landing successively in the complementiser position of every intervening sentence.

12. $[_{COMP}$ Who$_i$ do $[_S$ you think $[_{COMP}$ e$_i$ $[_S$ John said $[_{COMP}$ e$_i$ $[_S$ Fred believed $[_{COMP}$ e$_i$ $[_S$ Alice thought $[_{COMP}$ e$_i$ $[_S$ e$_i$ ate the cake]]]]]]]]]]

Put in terms of a parsing algorithm, we assume that the parser builds each clause with an initial complementiser. A question word (or its copy) in the complementiser position of the immediately dominating clause triggers the creation of an empty category (e$_i$) in the complementiser position under construction. This process continues until the parser comes to a position in the string where the question word can be associated with an appropriate logical role. The ability to encode locally the presence of a question word that is potentially unboundedly far away from this logical position is guaranteed; the parser does not have to access this question word directly, but rather can access the copy of the question word that occurs in the COMP of the sentence that immediately dominates the position of semantic interpretation to recover this category's presence. This algorithm also stores semantically uninterpreted elements (traces in COMP) and so it also predicts that memory is subject to overload from the time that the question word is detected until the time when the parser reaches the position which associates the question word with a logical role.

ON CHOOSING BETWEEN ALGORITHMS AND PARSERS

The previous discussion shows that the HOLD store mechanism is only one of three algorithms compatible withthe psycholinguistic data. Obviously we will need to find other criteria to tell us which algorithm is actually used by the human sentence processing mechanism. Let us assume that we could find such criteria and that it turned out that the HOLD store mechanism was in fact used by the comprehension system. We could than ask two deeper questions. First, we could ask whether the psycholinguistic data were *explained* by assuming that the human language processor was an ATN. We could also ask whether the choice of the HOLD store algorithm *followed* from the design of the ATN system. This comes down to asking two questions:

a. If the psycholinguistic data had been different, i.e. if the interpretation of questions placed no greater transient burden on memory than did the interpretation of constructions that do not involve relating a category to a potentially different syntactic position, could this state of affairs also be modelled using an ATN? IN other words, is the HOLD store or some other mechanism that locally encodes previously examined material a necessary part of the ATN?

b. Is the HOLD mechanism the only algorithm that can locally encode the presence of previously encountered context in a way that is compatible with properties of the ATN system or are all three algorithms discussed earlier compatible with this type of processor?

Using these criteria, it is easy to see that neither the HOLD mechanism nor the psycholinguistic data it was designed to model is explained by assuming that the human sentence processing mechanism is an ATN.

We have already discussed the fact that Wanner and Maratsos admit that the HOLD hypothesis is only one of the algorithms compatible with both the psycholinguistic results and an ATN, and so the answer to the second question is certainly "NO".

If the relevant memory effects were not observed, then we would simply assume that the ATN was not supplemented with any of the mechanisms to locally store previously processed text. These mechanisms are certainly not a *necessary* feature of the ATN. In fact these mechanisms are independently justified only by the fact that examples like the questions in (13) are easily interpretable:

13. a. What did John believe Fred said that Bill ate?
    b. Did John believe Fred said that Bill ate?

In order to associate these two sentences with the correct interpretations, the parser must recognise that "ate" in the first case is transitive and thus should be associated with the structure (14a) while in (13b) it is intransitive and should thus be associated with the structure (14b).

14. a. What$_i$ did John believe Fred said that Bill ate e$_i$
    b. Did John believe Fred said that Bill ate

It is only the presence of the question word that tells the parser the correct analysis for each sentence. Since there is a question word at the beginning of the sentence that needs to be interpreted from another syntactic position, "eat" in this sentence is a transitive verb. If we also assume that it takes time for the parser to rescan all the material that it previously processed before it reaches the verb "eat," we make two predictions. Either people should take a long time to process these sentences correctly because they would have to backtrack over a rather long string in order to provide the right analysis for these cases, or they should have trouble interpreting these sentences correctly. Neither of these predictions comports with our intuitions or with psycholinguistic data, because both sentences are perfectly easy to understand.

This is Wanner and Maratsos' initial justification for adding a local encoding subroutine to the ATN. However, since Wanner and Maratsos assume ATN that is *nondeterministic* we can model these intuitions without local encoding techniques. Nondeterminism is a property of a processing system that is defined with respect to how that system handles cases of ambiguity like the ones discussed in (10). If a system is allowed either to hypothesise and then retract a particular structure or to hypothesise all possible structures compatible with the information that is locally available to it, then the parser is called *nondeterministic*. In a case like (10) this means that we can supplement the limited backtracking procedures with a process that allows the parser to pursue all analyses compatible with locally available information in parallel. The parser would pursue both the transitive and intransitive analyses of an ambiguously transitive/intransitive verb like "eat," eventually discarding the incorrect structure. Alternatively, by producing a model where backtracking was not associated with an increase in parse time, we could disallow parallel processing in all cases.[4]

---

[4]That is, we could permit the parser to backtrack in order to determine whether a question word actually appears in the string, but claim that backtracking is associated with parsing complexity only in those cases where we must restructure previously analysed material in order to integrate currently unintegrated material. This would correctly distinguish cases like (14) which are not associated with any parsing complexity from cases like (a) where, in order to integrate the final verb into a coherent phrase marker, the parser must change its initial analysis of the sentence from (b) to (c).

Thus, as long as we assume that the system is nondeterministic, in the sense of either allowing parallel computation or unlimited backtracking, we cannot force the system to include any special mechanisms to locally encode previous context. Since the prediction of transient memory effects only follows from the parser's encoding of an uninterpreted element in *local* memory, the prediction is not explained by assuming an ATN, although an ATN can be supplemented with devices that make the system compatible with this result.

In order to *force* the system to locally encode the presence of the quantifier and thus predict the transient memory effects, we must make two assumptions. We must assume that the parser computes *only* the correct analysis for a given structure (i.e. we must disallow parallel processing) and we must assume that backtracking (or at least unlimited backtracking) is disallowed. The ATN architecture thus does not *predict* the observed memory load because it is compatible with both local and nonlocal algorithms. In the next section we will discuss an alternative parsing architecture that does force local encoding, provide some independent evidence for this architecture, and show that, coupled with evidence from linguistic theory, we can pick out which of the local encoding mechanisms discussed earlier is actually used by people when they understand questions.

LR(k) PARSING

Both parallel processing and backtracking are necessarily disallowed by a class of parsers proposed by Knuth (1965) under the name of LR(k) parsers.

Interestingly, Knuth proved that such a parser could process sentences *even in the worst case* in linear time.[5] This has important psycholinguistic implications because a major property of the human sentence comprehension process is that we can understand sentences in basically *just* the time it takes us to *hear* the words of the sentence that we are trying to understand. While this appears to be an obvious fact about the comprehension process, most of the basic architectures currently proposed as natural language processors

---

a. The boat floated sank.
b. [s The boat [vp floated . . .
c. [s [np The boat, [s PRO floated e,]] [vp sank]

[5] By *linear time* we mean the time it takes simply to represent the tokens of the input string (the time it takes to encode the words mentally in the written or spoken text) plus some constant amount of time (for example, the additional time that it takes to bundle material into sentential packages as proposed in Fodor, Bever, and Garrett's (1974) theory of sentential closure. The term also corresponds to the looser definition of "real time" found in the psychological literature.

cannot provably duplicate this ability.[6] The fact that LR(k) systems can model this major fact about language comprehension thus counts as important independent evidence that the human language comprehension system has LR(k) properties.

In previous work (Berwick & Weinberg, 1984), we showed that transformational grammar could be parsed in an LR(k) framework and provided some other arguments for the psychological plausibility of the LR(k) approach. We will see later that the properties of such a system are crucial to the explanation for subjacency provided.

The main properties that guarantee LR(k) parsing efficiency are:

a. These parsers are deterministic. A deterministic parser cannot by definition compute possible analyses of a given structure in parallel.[7]

b. Previously analysed material must be representable in a finite control table that uses a literal representation of this material. That is, any previously encountered information needed to make a parsing decision must be stored without the use of an essential variable. We provide an example to show what this means. Consider the structure (15):

15. Who did you believe Bill liked?

As discussed earlier, we assume that the processor recovers the standard syntactic analysis of this sentence and links the quasi-WH-quantifier to the position from which it receives its semantic role, yielding a structure like (16):

16. Who$_i$ did you believe [Bill liked e$_i$].

Thus the interpretation of this sentence involves creating a variable (e$_i$) in the postverbal position and linking it to its quasi-quantifier. We might store the quasi-quantifier in the finite control table of an LR(k) device as follows:

17. WH . . . X . . . (where X stands for a potentially unbounded stretch of material).

Unfortunately, this kind of representation of previously analysed material is prohibited in the LR(k) framework. All the nonterminal symbols intervening betwen the WH and the variable position must be literally encoded in this

---

[6] We cannot *guarantee* for example, that ATNs, chart parsers (see Kay, 1967), context free parsers employing the Earley algorithm (see Earley, 1970), or a variety of other *fast* parsing schemes can parse in linear time.

[7] For a full discussion of the concept of determinism, see Marcus (1981) and Berwick and Weinberg (1984).

representation. Furthermore, we must be able to ensure that there will be only a finite number of these symbols. This rules out the option of unlimited backtracking, because if the parser can backtrack over a potentially unbounded string, it must store potentially unboundedly many symbols (all the symbols that could possibly intervene between the question word and the position where the question word receives its logical role in a case like [14]). Thus an LR(k) system *necessarily* includes some method of locally encoding the presence of a question word. This is the only way that we can explain why cases with ambiguous verbs like (13) cause no trouble for such a device. The only way that the parser can correctly tell whether a verb like "eat" is being used transitively or intransitively is by recovering the presence or absence of the question word from previous context in the sentence, but it cannot backtrack indefinitely to retrieve this information, so the information must be locally encoded. This is enough to allow this device to *explain* why transient memory effects of type discussed by Wanner and Maratsos were observed. The LR(k) parsing device *forces* us to locally encode the semantically uninterpreted question word until its position of semantic interpretation is found. Therefore we predict that this item will impose the type of burden on memory that Wanner and Maratsos observed.

ON CHOOSING BETWEEN ALGORITHMS IN THE LR(k) FRAMEWORK

The discussion here suggests that an *explanation* of the memory effects previously discussed is available if we assume that the human language processing device has the properties of an LR(k) parser. While this assumption constrains the class of possible human language parsers considerably, it is not strong enough to tell us which of the three algorithms discussed is used to comprehend questions. This is because all three algorithms are compatible with the LR(k) framework. None of these algorithms involves parallel computation and all of them can retrieve the presence of the question word while storing only a finite stretch of previous context. The HOLD store mechanism eliminates backtracking entirely because we can retrieve the presence of the question word from the special HOLD cell. The generative encoding method signals the presence of a question word by using special "slashed category" phrase structure rules. Recall that the "slashed categories" get passed down through the phrase structure and so in a case like (13) the parser need only look back as far as the phrase dominating the ambiguous verb "eat" to see whether this verb is used transitively or intransitively. If a question word was previously encountered in the structure, indicating that the verb is transitive, the verb phrase will contain a slashed category. If the verb phrase is intransitive, the dominating phrase will be a simple unslashed VP.

The successive cyclic theory encodes the presence of a question word by putting an empty category in the complementiser position of each clause between the overt question and the position in which the question receives its semantic interpretation. Therefore in a case like (7) the parser will only have to look as far back as the complementiser position of the clause dominating a potential gap position to see whether an empty category should be put in this position. Again the parser can deterministically decide the correct analysis of questions while using only *bounded* search procedures and so it need only store a *bounded* number of symbols from the string that it has already scanned in order to make its parsing decisions.

Consideration of the linguistic constraints that are imposed on question formation can tell us which of these three algorithms we actually use. We will see that only the successive cyclic theory of movement algorithm can explain why question formation is governed by the subjacency condition.

Subjacency

Consider the following contrasts:

18. a. I believe the claim that Bill thought Mary would eat ice cream.
    b. *What$_i$ do you believe the claim that Bill thought that Mary would eat e$_i$.
19. a. I wonder who John likes.
    b. What$_i$ do you wonder who$_j$ e$_j$ likes e$_i$

Chomsky (1973) proposes to rule out the ungrammatical structures by the following condition:

20. No rule may relate X and Y in the configuration:
    Y...[$_a$...[$_b$...X...] Y where a and b are the bounding nodes NP or S.

Assuming the structures (21) and (22) for these sentences, we see that binding the question word *or its copy* to the position in which this category receives a semantic role violates subjacency.

21. [$_{COMP}$ What$_i$ do [you believe [$_{NP}$ the claim [$_S$ that Bill thought [$_{COMP}$ e$_i$ Mary would eat e$_i$]]]]]
22. [$_{COMP}$ what$_i$ do you wonder [$_{COMP}$ who$_j$ [$_S$ e$_j$ saw e$_i$]]]

Successive cyclic movement will not save the derivations in (21) and (22). In (21), even assuming that the first move of the WH phrase is to the complementiser of the relative clause, the next move will violate subjacency because this category must move out of a noun phrase, thus crossing one bounding node and going over the S node of the clause that dominates the relative clause. Thus subjacency is violated and the sentence is ruled out. Similar remarks serve to rule out (22). Assuming that we cannot allow two nodes to fill the complementiser slot, the "what" phrase must cross the S bounding nodes of both the matrix and embedded sentences, again violating subjacency.[8]

Returning to our three algorithms for handling question formation in the LR(k) framework, we see that the successive cyclic analysis of WH movement *forces* us to adopt a condition like subjacency. The successive cyclic theory of movement forces us to retrieve the presence of the question word by literally backtracking over the phrase marker that the parser has created. In order to be able to do this without the need for storing a potentially infinite amount of previously analysed material (which the parser's finite control table cannot do), we must be sure that the WH element (or the trace that it leaves successive cyclically in COMP) is only *boundedly* far away from the "gap" position in the string. The subjacency condition enforces just such a restriction. The subjacency condition guarantees *for all cases* that the parser will be able to retrieve the presence of the question word without having to store any more symbols than can be contained in the adjacent NP of S; this is because all acceptable questions will contain a clue to the presence of a previously encountered question word in the adjacent NP or S.[9]

Obviously, the effects of subjacency follow under this interpretation. In a structure like (21) or (23), the parser can only interpret the question word inside the relative clause. Assuming a subjacency constraint on the parsing algorithm, this means that the parser will place a copy of the question word in the complementiser or other position only if there is another copy of the question word in the adjacent clause or NP. However, the NP in the relative clause contains no complementiser position and thus the chain of subjacent copies of the question word is broken as soon as we get to the complex noun phrase. Therefore there will be no trace or WH phrase in the subjacent domain from the postverbal position of the most embedded clause and so the parser has no evidence to allow it to create a postverbal empty category. Thus these sentences, with the intended interpretations, become unparsable. The relevant structure is given in (23).

23. What$_i$ do [you believe [$_{NP}$ the claim [$_{COMP}$ Mary said [$_{COMP}$ [John would eat . . .]]]]].

---

[8] This assumption is justified in Chomsky (1973).

[9] See Berwick and Weinberg (1984) for reasons limiting the search domain to the adjacent (as opposed to trijacent or quadracent) clause.

Returning now to the other two algorithms that are compatible with the LR(k) approach, we see that neither of them provides an explanation for the subjacency constraint. If we put things in a HOLD store, then we never need to access the left context of the parse tree directly and so the restrictions on left context become irrelevant. Of course we could always model subjacency by claiming that the HOLD store is emptied before the parser begins a relative clause, thus deriving the ungrammaticality of (21b). The problem is, though, that this restriction is entirely ad hoc. We could retrieve elements from a HOLD store that didn't encode subjacency using only a finite amount of left context because the whole point of the HOLD store is to allow us to retrieve the question word without having to access any of the previously constructed phrase marker at all.

The same remarks can be made with respect to the proposal to generatively encode the presence of the quantifier by annotating the phrase structure with slashed categories. Since the presence of the question word is passed through the phrase marker we could retrieve the presence of a question word locally, by looking at the phrase immediately dominating the potential gap position, even if that gap position were in a relative clause. Again, we could say that we cannot pass a slash into a relative clause, but again this assumption is only motivated to get the subjacency facts and is ad hoc.

Let us review what we have done:

a. We motivated an LR(k) parsing device as an efficient language processor. On the assumption that previously stored material must be accessed directly from its phrase structure position in the tree, we could provide a functional explanation for the subjacency condition. This assumption, which is crucial to our functional derivation of subjacency, rules out any algorithm that allows the parser to locally encode the presence of previously encountered material by any means other than rescanning the actual phrase marker. This rules out both the HOLD store and generative encoding algorithm. This explanation crucially involved two features of this type of parser (see b).

b. The fact that the parser is deterministic and could not perform parallel computation insured that it would have to access previously analysed structure in order to correctly analyse questions formed from verbs with multiple argument structures. The fact that left context had to be stored in a finite control table meant that the grammar had to insure that the question word was finitely far away from the variable.

CONCLUSION

In this paper, I have tried to argue that experimental data alone will not suffice to reveal the structure of the human natural language comprehension system. Experimental evidence is most useful when it can be employed to distinguish between a narrowly constrained class of alternatives. I have argued that using evidence from linguistic theory, in this case about the constraints that govern question formation in natural language, and evidence from computation theory about how to guarantee efficient parsing, provides exactly the preliminary constraint that can make experimental studies more meaningful. An additional problem in constructing a theory of language comprehension, or in constructing a computational model of *any* psychological ability, comes from failure to distinguish cases where a particular computational model is merely consistent with a set of experimental data from those cases where the data is actually predicted by the model. In this discussion I have contrasted the LR(k) and ATN systems with a view to highlighting this distinction. I have argued that there is independent evidence for believing that human natural language processors have LR(k) properties and that these devices use an analogue of the successive cyclic movement algorithm to interpret questions. The general LR(k) architecture also has the virtue of *predicting* rather than simply modelling the transient memory effects discovered by Wanner and Maratsos. Assuming that this architecture uses a successive cyclic movement algorithm *entails* that natural languages must be governed by a locality constraint (subjacency) and thus provides a functional explanation for why natural languages always conform to this condition. Under this interpretation, grammars for natural languages must contain such a condition in order to guarantee that the structures they output can be processed by the language processing system during the course of language understanding.

REFERENCES

Berwick, R. & Weinberg, A. (1984). *The grammatical basis of linguistic performance*. Cambridge, Mass.: M.I.T. Press.

Chomsky, N. (1973). Conditions on transformations. In S. Anderson & P. Kiparsky (Eds.), *A Festschrift for Morris Halle*. New York: Holt Rinehart.

Earley, J. (1970). An efficient context-free parsing algorithm. *Communications for the Association of Computing Machinery, 14*, 453–460.

Fodor, J., Bever, T., & Garrett, M. (1974). *The psychology of language*. New York: McGraw-Hill.

Harman, G. (1963). Generative grammar without transformation rules: A defence of phrase structure. *Language, 39*, 597–616.

Kaplan, R. (1973). A general syntactic processor. In R. Rustin (Ed.), *Natural language processing*. Englewood Cliffs, N.J.: Prentice-Hall.

Kay, M. (1967). *Experiments with a powerful parser*. Santa Monica: Rand.

Knuth, D. (1965). On the translation of languages from left to right. *Information and Control, 8*, 607–639.

Marcus, M. (1981). *A theory of syntactic recognition for natural language*. Cambridge, Mass.: M.I.T. Press.

Wanner, E. & Maratsos, M. (1978). An ATN comprehension system. In M. Halle, J. Bresnan, & G. Miller (Eds.), *Linguistic theory and psychological reality*. Cambridge, Mass.: M.I.T. Press.

Woods, W. (1970). Transition network grammars for natural language analysis. *Communications of the Association for Computing Machinery, 13*, 591–606.

ATTENTION AND PERFORMANCE SYMPOSIA: MODUS OPERANDI

The International Association for the Study of Attention and Performance, under whose aegis the Attention and Performance symposia are held, is an association without members, whose activities are nonetheless quite public. It is, therefore, reasonable that over the years there has been an increasing interest in the mechanics of these symposia: how are they organised? who decides on the topics? how are participants selected? etc. The following brief description of the steps leading up to a symposium has been prepared to answer some of these questions.

The Association is run by an Executive Committee and an Advisory Council, some of whose functions will become apparent from the descriptions that follow. Members of the advisory council are chosen by the executive committee on the basis of the consistent excellence of their work in the area of attention and performance. At this time the advisory council is at its full complement of 50 members representing scientists from over 20 different countries. The conduct of the Association is governed by a constitution and a set of by-laws. The aims of the Association are: (1) to increase and to disseminate scientific knowledge in the area of human attention, performance, and information processing; (2) to foster international communication in this area; (3) to provide an international forum for the established as well as the young and promising scientists to present their best work. The two principal means of attaining these objectives are the series of international symposia, and the publication of the volumes of proceedings following each symposium.

The ultimate responsibility for each symposium and volume of proceedings rests with the organiser. In choosing an organiser, therefore, the Association's executive committee weighs the candidates' scientific qualifications above all others. Organisers automatically become members of the executive committee. Therefore, expertise in a narrow field is not, by itself, a sufficient condition for selection. Candidates must be broadly knowledgeable and have good judgment in many areas of psychology.

The selection of a symposium organiser is the first step where some of the Association's multiple objectives are first dealt with. Here, scientific excellence and international diversity are carefully examined and must accommodate each other because of the constitution's provisions: (1) no more than two symposia may be convened in the same country in succession, and (2) no person may be elected to the executive committee if his/her election increases the number of committee members with permanent residence in the same country above three.

Once an organiser is selected, how does he or she proceed?

First, he or she prepares a rough outline to be discussed at the meeting of the executive committee that is simultaneously held with the symposium preceeding his or hers. Early during the following year the organiser circulates a tentative list of topics and subtopics to members of the executive committee and the advisory council with a request for suggestions for additional topics but, more importantly, for nominations of potential invitees.

This is the most critical step for obtaining the widest possible geographical diversity among the symposium participants. One of the advisory council's principal responsibilities is to nominate as potential contributors either well-established scientists, or lesser known but nevertheless good or promising scientists who might otherwise be overlooked. This is particularly important for countries who are not in the mainstream of the scientific world. If persons are nominated whose work is not appropriate for this particular symposium but who would nevertheless profit from and contribute to it, they are often invited as non-presenting participants.

The organiser, armed with a list of potential topics and participants, now proceeds to put together the first draft of the program, listing prospective speakers with the tentative title of their contributions, and the topic heading under which it is scheduled to appear on the programme. This is distributed to the executive committee who send their comments and suggestions back to the organiser with this cycle repeating until a consensus is reached.

These iterations mark the third stage at which provisions designed to maximise the Association's objectives come into play. Even though excellence is the single most important criterion at every step in the selection process, it is occasionally constrained by other concerns such as geographical breadth, the encouragement of promising younger and lesser known scientists, and the desire to avoid the circus atmosphere of large conferences where it is difficult to have meaningful discussions. Some of the specific constraints are listed below.

Symposia can have no parallel sessions, are limited to eight papers per day, can have no more than 36 papers and no more than 65 participants. These provisions are intended to increase the opportunities for leisurely discussions while at the same time limit the size, hence the cost, of the volume of proceedings. A serious attempt must also be made to avoid having a single country present more than two-thirds, and preferably less than half, of the papers at any one symposium. No person may be a contributor in more than two out of three consecutive symposia, and each symposium must contain at least four papers by someone who has *never* been to an Association symposium. These provisions are aimed at spreading the opportunity for participation as widely as possible and appropriate. It is interesting to note that of the 420 authors and co-authors of papers since Attention and Performance VI in 1975, only 34 have been authors of more than one paper. Whatever other concerns there may be, however, quality is the dominant criterion throughout these procedures.

The last check on quality is made in the preparation of the volume of proceedings. Not every paper presented is necessarily published, and all papers are reviewed by at least two referees. One is a participant who has heard the paper and the discussion at the symposium, the other is usually a member of the advisory council or executive committee.

Finally, since one of the Association's principal objectives is to disseminate scientific knowledge, we have been profoundly concerned by the extent to which the generally escalating cost of books has put these volumes out of reach of those into whose hands we would most like to place them. Thus, we have been actively fighting the rising price of these volumes for many years and, together with the publisher, are presently engaged in an experiment which we hope will bring, and keep, prices down.

This is a brief thumbnail sketch of the principal steps involved in the transformation of a symposium from an abstract idea, to a live meeting, and finally into an archival record. Readers with any suggestions for improving or expanding the Association's activities are invited to send us their comments.

Sylvan Kornblum
Secretary-Treasurer
I.A.S.A.P.

Author Index

Aaronson, D., 356
Abrol, S., 166
Adams, M. J., 106, 179, 186, 187, 248, 249
Ahmar, H., 166
Alcott, D., 176, 179, 202, 204, 211, 212
Alford, J. A., 162
Allmeyer, D. H., 98
Allport, D. A., 40, 43, 45, 58, 59, 84, 97, 98, 99, 107, 175, 177, 202, 301, 306, 307, 442
Altman, G., 571
Ambler, B., 46, 47
Anderson, J. R., 603
Andrews, S., 158
Anstis, S. M., 363
Arbuckle, T. Y., 536, 547, 552
Arnold, D., 331
Asanuma, C., 90
Ashby, F. G., 541

Baddeley, A. D., 306, 317, 441, 442, 443, 491, 492, 493, 501, 502, 503, 504, 505, 506, 510, 511, 512, 513, 514, 515, 516, 518, 532, 534, 535, 536, 541, 544, 546, 550, 552, 553
Badgio, P. C., 66, 67, 70, 75, 76, 78, 99, 101
Baker, C., 535, 537
Balota, D. A., 123, 134, 202, 211, 213,

221, 229, 230, 231, 232, 233, 234, 236, 249, 333, 335, 336, 337, 338, 339, 340, 341, 342, 343, 344, 350, 351, 354, 357
Banich, M., 305, 307, 309
Barnard, P., 441, 442
Barnes, M. A., 212, 225, 228, 229, 232, 234, 426, 430, 433, 451, 453, 455, 456, 459, 460, 462, 463, 472
Baron, J., 185, 296, 422, 437, 438, 440, 450
Barresi, J., 166
Bartlett, F. C., 184
Basili, A., 512, 534, 535
Basso, A., 512, 517
Batcholder, W. H., 166, 167
Bates, E., 22
Bauer, D. W., 450
Beal, A. L., 404
Beardsley, W., 636
Beck, J., 46, 47
Becker, C. A., 176, 193, 202, 203, 205, 214, 215, 221, 223, 224
Becker, W., 347
Bednall, E. S., 135
Bellugi, U., 166, 167
Bentin, S., 233
Bergen, J. R., 47, 52
Berger, D. E., 167
Bergman, M. W., 232
Berndt, R. S., 512, 534, 535

McDonald, J. E., 175, 176, 190, 191, 193, 202, 203, 205, 215, 221, 222, 223, 224, 225, 235, 341
McElree, B., 579
McGill, J., 98, 107, 177
MacKay, D. G., 282
MacKinnon, G. E., 84
MacLeod, C. M., 166
McLeod, P., 321
McMullen, M., 427
McNew, S., 22
MacWhinney, B., 22

Madigan, S., 166, 167
Malt, B., 637
Manelis, L., 191, 266
Mann, V. A., 30
Manso de Zuniga, C., 123
Maratsos, M., 442, 537, 578, 673, 674, 675, 676, 677, 680, 683, 687
Marcel, A. J., 106, 107, 117, 296, 396, 423, 428, 432, 450, 457, 472, 476, 477
Marchetti, F. M., 177
Marcus, M. P., 29, 533, 575, 682
Marcus, S. M., 178
Marin, O. S. M., 535
Marshall, J. C., 306
Marslen-Wilson, W. D., 13, 404, 527, 605, 639
Martin, D. S. M., 512
Martin, R. C., 437, 442
Mason, M., 177
Massaro, D. W., 14, 193
Masson, M. E. J., 162, 493
Masterson, J., 316
Mattingly, I. G., 193
Mayzner, M. S., 272, 453, 459
Mehler, J., 353
Merikle, P. M., 106, 107
Messmer, O., 173
Mewhort, D. J. K., 43, 177, 404
Meyer, D. E., 223, 224, 236, 246, 351
Michaels, C. F., 106, 118
Milech, D., 159, 160, 163, 166
Miller, G. A., 183
Miller, J., 67

Miller, J. A., 493
Millis-Wright, M., 191, 250
Minsky, M., 90
Mitchell, D. C., 492, 566, 567, 573, 577, 590, 601, 602, 604, 605, 606, 612, 614, 673
Miyake, S., 90
Monk, A. F., 180, 415
Monsell, S., 166, 194, 246, 302, 304, 305, 306, 307, 309, 320, 551
Morris, D., 434
Morris, R. K., 343
Morrison, I. R., 43
Morrison, R. E., 329, 333, 338, 342, 345, 346, 347, 348, 403
Morton, J., 85, 127, 137, 147, 162, 166, 194, 195, 203, 204, 209, 215, 276, 283, 296, 302, 320, 422, 428, 431, 433, 436, 442, 450, 463, 472, 480, 487, 510
Mozer,, M. C., 43, 80, 86, 96, 97, 98, 99, 100, 107, 114, 177, 178, 195, 202
Muise, J. G., 234
Murray, D. J., 546, 553
Murray, W. S., 353, 563, 573, 564, 573, 588
Murrell, G. A., 162
Myers, J. L., 355, 357

Navon, D., 176, 552
Neiser, J. J., 162
Neisser, U., 1, 39, 84, 162, 171, 172, 174, 176, 184, 185, 186, 187, 188, 189, 190, 191, 192, 193
Newcombe, F., 306
Newsome, S. L., 175, 176, 190, 193, 202, 203, 204, 205, 208, 211, 215, 221, 235, 341
Niemi, P., 366
Nimmo-Smith, I., 493, 501, 502
Nissen, M. J., 79
Noel, R. W., 175, 190, 191, 202, 203, 204, 208, 211, 215
Norman, D. A., 101, 148
Norris, D., 136, 143, 201, 203, 204, 224, 433
Novik, N., 139

Subject Index